ORGANIZATIONAL BEHAVIOR AND INDUSTRIAL PSYCHOLOGY

ORGANIZATIONAL BEHAVIOR AND INDUSTRIAL PSYCHOLOGY

readings with commentary

edited by

KENNETH N. WEXLEY and GARY A. YUKL
UNIVERSITY OF AKRON BARUCH COLLEGE

New York • OXFORD UNIVERSITY PRESS • London Toronto 1975

for/Max and Martha Karol

Copyright © 1975 by Oxford University Press, Inc.
Library of Congress Catalogue Card Number: 74-22887
Printed in the United States of America

Preface

This book presents an up-to-date collection of readings in organizational behavior and industrial psychology. It is designed to supplement regular texts used in undergraduate and graduate courses in industrial psychology, management, organizational behavior, and personnel administration. We also believe, however, that the book can be used as the sole text in a course with sufficient lectures to supplement the readings.

The content of the book has been strongly influenced by feedback we obtained about our previous book of readings. From comments by undergraduates who were using the earlier volume, we concluded that many of the research articles were not fully comprehended. The lack of strong statistical background for these students is probably the source of the problem. We suspect that this problem prevails in most universities, and it cannot be assumed away by the editors of readings books. From responses to a survey conducted by Oxford University Press of more than a hundred professors in psychology and management departments, we concluded that the professors preferred more articles that integrate many studies, as opposed to research articles describing a single study. Since undergraduates and professors were basically in agreement, we have adjusted our mix of readings so that there is a much larger proportion of review and discussion articles. In making this change, however, we kept in mind undergraduate complaints about review articles that are too detailed and technical to be understood by a person without extensive prior familiarity with the topic. Consequently, we attempted to select articles that not only dealt with the major issues, trends, and theories, but also were written in a clear and concise fashion. We were also concerned to find the most up-to-date articles available, as is shown by the fact that nearly 75 per cent of the readings were published in the 1970s.

Comments and suggestions by professors also led to some changes in coverage of topics. The section on Consumer Psychology was deleted because a large proportion of professors believed that it was not "in the mainstream of industrial-organizational psychology." The section on Working Conditions, Accidents, and Fatigue and the section on Human Factors Engineering were merged, since respondents suggested that these areas were less important relative to the others and should be given less coverage. Many professors also expressed a preference for more coverage of job enrichment, organization development, management by objectives, behavior

v

modification, and equal employment opportunity. Therefore, we have included articles on these and other currently popular topics. The final result is a collection of 52 readings divided into the following eight sections: (1) Job Satisfaction and Motivation to Work, (2) Leadership and Decision-Making, (3) Organization Structure, Technology, and Environment, (4) Organization Development and Conflict Management, (5) Performance Appraisal and Management by Objectives, (6) Personnel Selection and Equal Employment Opportunity, (7) Training and Behavior Modification, and (8) Human Factors Engineering, Working Conditions, Safety, and Fatigue.

Each section is prefaced by an introduction that provides the reader with background information about the subject area and discusses the significance of the readings in that section. In the introduction we attempted also to explain how the articles are related to each other. Finally, the interested student is referred to other relevant articles and books. Some of the many fine sources that could not be used in the book by reason of extensive length, overlapping content, or overly difficult content are listed in the References and Suggested Readings.

We are grateful to the publishers and authors who gave us permission to use their material in this book. We are also grateful to the many persons who responded to the survey of reactions to our previous volume. We should also like to thank Michael Malone and Michael Spendolini for their help in preparing the manuscript.

East Windsor, New Jersey   K. N. W.
March 1975   G. A. Y.

Contents

1 JOB SATISFACTION AND MOTIVATION TO WORK

2 LEADERSHIP AND DECISION-MAKING

3 ORGANIZATION STRUCTURE, TECHNOLOGY, AND ENVIRONMENT

4 ORGANIZATION DEVELOPMENT AND CONFLICT MANAGEMENT

5 PERFORMANCE APPRAISAL AND MANAGEMENT BY OBJECTIVES

6 PERSONNEL SELECTION AND EQUAL EMPLOYMENT OPPORTUNITY

7 TRAINING AND BEHAVIOR MODIFICATION

8 HUMAN FACTORS ENGINEERING, WORKING CONDITIONS, SAFETY, AND FATIGUE

1

JOB SATISFACTION
AND WORK MOTIVATION

Introduction

The term "job satisfaction" refers to an employee's general attitude toward his job. To the extent that a person's job fulfills his dominant needs and is consistent with his expectations and values, the job will be satisfying. A number of characteristics of the job may be relevant to a person's need fulfillment and can therefore influence his job satisfaction. These characteristics include pay and benefits, supervision, working conditions, the nature of the work itself, co-workers, and company policies. The term "motivation" refers to the way in which a person's needs determine his behavior. Although a person's job satisfaction and his work motivation are two distinct variables, they are bound together in a complex network of relationships.

Although there is little agreement among industrial-organizational psychologists about ways of classifying human needs, a number of proposed need categories appear to be useful for explaining behavior in industrial organizations. Subsistence needs (e.g., food, housing) may be satisfied indirectly by means of job income, or in some cases, directly by the organization, as part of the employment contract. Need for security may be satisfied by various features of the job that protect an employee from physical harm, loss of income (e.g., disability insurance), unusual medical expenses (e.g., health insurance), or arbitrary dismissal (e.g., tenure, seniority, grievance, and appeal procedures). A person's social-affiliation need may be satisfied by friendly interaction with co-workers. Need for esteem may be satisfied by recognition from the organization, supervisor praise, status symbols, and co-worker respect. A person who has strong needs for competence and achievement will be satisfied most with a job that is moderately difficult and provides frequent performance feedback. A person with a strong need for self-actualization will be satisfied most by a job in which he creates a product or performs a service that he believes is meaningful and that provides him with a sense of self-fulfillment.

The universality of any particular need category and the manner in which a person's needs interact to determine behavior have been the subject of considerable speculation. The possibility that an employee's need priorities change over time and that employees differ in their focal needs has considerable practical significance for designing jobs and incentive systems to satisfy and motivate employees. The most widely known theory relevant to these issues is Maslow's Need Hierarchy Theory. The article by Wahba and Bridwell briefly describes Maslow's theory and reviews research attempting to test it.

In addition to needs, a person's job satisfaction is believed to be determined by expectations based on social comparisons. According to equity theory, an employee compares his pay and other job outcomes to those of other employees with a similar job or with similar qualifications. Comparisons with subordinates or with employees in different organizations can also occur. An employee will perceive his job outcomes to be equitable only if they are in the same ratio to his job inputs (e.g., experience, effort, education, seniority) as the ratio of outcomes and inputs for the comparison person(s). For example, an employee's pay will usually be perceived as inequitably low if people with fewer qualifications are receiving the same pay or if people with equal qualifications are receiving more pay. Such inequity will reduce a person's satisfaction with his job, and if not corrected, may result in the person's quitting or reducing his level of effort. The article by Goodman and Friedman reviews a substantial number of studies that have been conducted to test the motivational and behavioral implications of underpay and overpay inequity.

It was once a popular assumption that employees who are satisfied with their jobs will be motivated to perform effectively, presumably, out of gratitude to the organization. This assumption has generally not been supported by research. In the article by Lawler and Porter, a more sophisticated model of the relationship between job satisfaction and job performance is proposed. According to Lawler and Porter, job satisfaction will be correlated with performance only when intrinsic and extrinsic rewards are contingent upon performance. The implications of the model are discussed, and some data in support of the model are presented.

The Lawler and Porter model is based on an expectancy theory of employee motivation. A number of different versions of expectancy theory have been proposed during recent years. A common feature of these theories is that employees make a conscious choice among the available behavior alternatives or task goals. The attractiveness of each alternative depends on the perceived probability that it will lead to valued and satisfying outcomes. For example, an employee is more likely to select a difficult performance goal if he believes that his effort will result in attainment of the goal and goal attainment will result in satisfaction of his needs. Heneman and Schwab discuss two versions of expectancy theory and review the evidence from studies designed to test one or more aspects of the theory. A number of problems and deficiencies of expectancy theory are also noted in this article, and in other recent reviews by Lawler (1971), Wahba and House (1974), and Mitchell and Biglan (1971).

Another cognitive theory has been proposed by Locke (1968). According to Locke, employees will perform at a higher level if they set specific hard goals than if they set easy goals or do not consciously set specific goals. Locke hypothesized also that incentives, performance feedback, and participation in decision-making will increase employee performance only if they cause the employee to set harder goals. Most of the evidence supporting Locke's theory is derived from laboratory research with college students. The article by Latham and Kinne describes one of the few field experiments ever conducted to test the theory. The results support Locke's claim that giving employees specific hard goals to strive for will result in better performance than asking employees to "do your best."

Theories of motivation generally imply using one of two basic approaches for increasing employee performance. The first approach is to increase the "extrinsic" motivation of employees by means of an incentive program. A number of different types of extrinsic rewards can be used, including supervisor praise, company awards, and promotion, but the most common incentive is pay. The next selection, by Lawler, describes how an organization can establish an effective program of pay incentives. Various methods of relating pay to performance are described, including individual, group, and company-wide programs. Different types of incentives plans are evaluated, and the conditions under which pay incentives are most effective are enumerated.

The second approach for increasing employee motivation is commonly referred to as job enrichment. An employee who attempts to do a good job because the work is interesting, challenging, and fulfilling is said to be "intrinsically" motivated. Job enrichment is an approach toward increasing an employee's intrinsic motivation rather than his extrinsic motivation. Jobs are enriched by providing more challenging and interesting tasks, more responsibility and self-direction, and the opportunity for achievement, advancement, and psychological growth. The article by Paul, Robertson, and Herzberg describes five field studies on the effects of job enrichment. The manner in which the jobs were enriched is explained, and the effects on employee performance and job satisfaction are summarized. A number of general questions about the feasibility of job enrichment in different situations and the implications of job enrichment for management are also discussed in this article.

The article by Ford provides further elaboration of job enrichment principles and describes the application of these principles to clerical workers at AT&T. The key element in the job enrichment at AT&T has been the design of jobs so that each employee can identify with some meaningful unit of production or can service a specific set of clients or customers. Knowledge of results was supplied to the employees in order to facilitate self-monitoring, and they were gradually allowed to assume full control and responsibility for handling their work "module." Ford describes also an attempt to go beyond the enrichment of individual jobs by "nesting" several enriched jobs. This approach appears to be a promising one for reducing training cost as well as for increasing productivity and job satisfaction.

REFERENCES AND SUGGESTED READINGS

Alderfer, C. P. A new theory of human needs. *Organizational Behavior and Human Performance*, 1969, 4, 142-75.

Hackman, J. R., and Lawler, E. E. Employee reactions of job characteristics. *Journal of Applied Psychology*, 1971, 55, 259-86.

Herzberg, F. One more time: How do you motivate employees? *Harvard Business Review*, 1968, 46 (1), 53-62.

King, N. A clarification and evaluation of the two-factor theory of job satisfaction. *Psychological Bulletin*, 1970, 74, 18-31.

Lawler, E. E. *Pay and organizational effectiveness*. New York: McGraw-Hill, 1971.

Locke, E. Toward a theory of task motivation and incentives. *Organizational Behavior and Human Performance*, 1968, 3, 157-89.

Mitchell, T. R., and Biglan, A. Instrumentality theories: Current uses in psychology. *Psychological Bulletin*, 1971, 76, 432-54.

Opshal, R. L., and Dunnette, M. D. The role of financial compensation in industrial motivation. *Psychological Bulletin*, 1966, 66, 94-118.

Pritchard, R. D. Equity theory: A review and critique. *Organizational behavior and human performance*. 1969, 4, 176-211.

Schwab, D. P., and Cummings, L. L. Theories of performance and satisfaction: A review. *Industrial Relations*, 1970, 9, 408-30.

Wahba, M. A., and House, R. J. Expectancy theory in work and motivation: Some logical and methodological issues. *Human Relations*, 1974, 27, 121-47.

Wanous, J. P., and Lawler, E. E. Measurement and meaning of job satisfaction. *Journal of Applied Psychology*, 1972, 56, 95-105.

Maslow Reconsidered:

A Review of Research on the Need Hierarchy Theory

MAHMOUD A. WAHBA AND LAWRENCE G. BRIDWELL

PURPOSE AND BACKGROUND

Maslow's Need Hierarchy Theory [references 21; 22; 24] presents the student of work motivation with an interesting paradox: the theory is widely accepted, but there is little research evidence to support it. Since Maslow first published his theory thirty years ago, it has become one of the most popular theories of motivation in the management and organizational behavior literature. Furthermore, the theory has provided an a priori conceptual framework to explain diverse research findings. [26] Such widespread acceptance of the Need Hierarchy Theory is rather surprising in light of the fact that until the mid-sixties (1; 7; 14] little empirical evidence existed that tested predictions of the theory. It has become a tradition for writers to point out the discrepancy between the popularity of the theory and the lack of clear and consistent empirical evidence to support it. [6; 9; 10; 30]

Recently, the interest in Maslow's Need Hierarchy Theory has been revived, due to the publication of a number of empirical studies testing some predictions of the theory. As yet, however, no known review

of the literature compares and integrates the findings of these studies. The purpose of this paper is to review and evaluate the empirical research related to Maslow's Need Hierarchy Theory, thereby assessing the empirical validity of the theory itself.

Several constraints were imposed on this review. First, the review will deal only with the test of Maslow's theory in the work situation. [For a review of the empirical evidence in other situations, see footnote 10.] Second, this review will include only studies that used statistical rather than clinical methodology. [25] Third, this review will deal only with what is considered to be the core or the main elements of Maslow's theory as it relates to work motivation.

MASLOW'S NEED HIERARCHY THEORY: A BRIEF DESCRIPTION

Part of the appeal of Maslow's Need Hierarchy Theory is that it provides both a theory of human *motives* by classifying basic human needs in a hierarchy, and a theory of *human motivation* that relates these needs to general behavior. As a theory of motives or needs, Maslow proposed that basic needs are structured in a hierarchy of prepotency and

Reprinted from *Proceedings of the Thirty-third Annual Meeting of the Academy of Management*, 1973, 514-20, by permission of the Academy of Management and the authors.

probability of appearance. The hierarchy of needs is as follows (in ascending order of prepotency): the physiological needs, the safety needs, the belongingness or love needs, the esteem needs, and the need for self-actualization.

As a theory of motivation, Maslow utilized the two concepts of deprivation and gratification to provide the dynamic forces that linked needs to general behavior. He used the deprivation concept to establish "dominance" within his hierarchy of needs. He postulated that deprivation or dissatisfaction of a need of high prepotency will lead to the domination of this need over the organism's personality.

Following the satisfaction of a dominating need, the second element of the dynamic force in Maslow's Theory will then take place. Relative gratification of a given need submerges it and "activates" the next higher need in the hierarchy. The activated need then dominates and organizes the individual's personality and capacities so that instead of the individual's being hunger obsessed, he now becomes safety obsessed.

This process of deprivation → domination → gratification → activation continues until the physiological, safety, affiliation and esteem needs have all been gratified and the self-actualization need has been activated. In a later work [23], Maslow modified the gratification/activation idea by proposing that gratification of the self-actualization need causes an increase in its importance rather than a decrease. Maslow also acknowledged numerous exceptions to his theory. Notably, he pointed out that long deprivation of a given need may create a fixation for that need. Also, higher needs may emerge not after gratification, but rather after long deprivation, renunciation, or suppression of lower needs. Maslow emphasized again and again that behavior is multi-determined and mult-motivated. From this general approach Maslow dealt with a wide range of consequences to his theory.

The present paper will review the research literature that attempted to test Maslow's theory or parts of it. The review will be divided into three related sections, each section dealing with one main element of Maslow's Need Hierarchy Theory. These elements are:

1. Maslow's Need Classification scheme;
2. The Deprivation/Domination proposition;
3. The Gratification/Activation proposition.

Maslow's Need Classification Scheme

Most of the research dealing with Maslow's need classification scheme has utilized factor analytic techniques. In the literature, eight factor analytic studies attempted explicitly to test Maslow's need classification scheme. These studies raised three related questions:

1. Does the factor analysis yield five factors that can be interpreted conceptually in terms of Maslow's five need categories?

2. Are Maslow's need categories independent from each other or do they overlap? What is the pattern of overlapping? Is the overlapping between adjacent or non-adjacent categories?

3. Are Maslow's need categories independent from supposedly unrelated items or factors?

The samples in these studies were composed of various groups (professionals, non-professionals, students, managers, males, and females) and four different measuring scales were used. A modified Porter [27] Need Satisfaction Questionnaire (NSQ) was the research instrument in four studies. Although it was designed basically to reflect Maslow's need classification scheme, the NSQ appears to suffer from a number of methodological problems particularly due to response bias. Subjects filling out the instrument give the fulfillment and importance ratings almost simultaneously. This produces a high correlation between fulfillment and importance. [3] Also, Lawler and Suttle [19] pointed out that the correlations among the

NSQ items in the same category were not high and that all items correlated with each other. As a result the NSQ may not accurately reflect Maslow's need classification scheme.

Three researchers [3; 5; 17] used three different scales. Huizinga's 24-item questionnaire appears to be the best designed scale for several reasons. One, it reflects all of Maslow's categories including the physiological needs. Two, the questionnaire is oriented to work motivation in general rather than being specific to the employee's present job. The questions were placed in the context of how important each of the items would be in the respondent's evaluation of *any* job. Unlike the NSQ, this minimizes the situational aspects of the current job affecting the answers of respondents. Three, it contains both positive and negative items to reflect the concepts of gratification and deprivation. Fourth, the scale was well validated by various methods. However, the scale did have one weakness; no reliability figures were reported.

The following conclusions can be drawn from the results of the factor analytic studies testing Maslow's need classification scheme.

1. None of the studies has shown *all* of Maslow's five need categories as independent factors. Only Beer's study showed four independent factors reflecting four needs; the fifth need overlapped with an unrelated factor.

2. In some studies, lower-order needs and higher-order needs clustered together independently from each other.

3. Self-actualization needs emerged as an independent factor in some studies, and in other studies, they overlapped with other need categories.

4. Two studies using two samples each showed no support for Maslow's need categories.

Another type of evidence related to the test of Maslow's need classification scheme comes from studies that attempted to classify human needs empirically by factor analysis techniques without an a priori theoretical framework. [8; 12; 28] These studies do not show need categories similar to those proposed by Maslow.

Taken together, the empirical results of the factor analytic studies provide no consistent support for Maslow's need classification as a whole. There is no clear evidence that human needs are classified into five distinct categories, or that these categories are structured in a special hierarchy. Some evidence exists for possibly two types of needs, higher- and lower-order needs, even though this categorization is not always operative. Self-actualization needs may emerge as an independent category. However, it is not possible to assess from the studies reviewed whether self-actualization is, in fact, a need or simply a social desirability response resulting from certain cultural values. [6] There is some empirical evidence to substantiate this latter conclusion. [17]

The Deprivation/Domination Proposition

The deprivation/domination proposition is closely related to the gratification/activation proposition. Consequently, some studies have provided a test of both propositions at the same time. However, to allow for careful examination of both propositions, it was decided to review each proposition independently.

The deprivation/domination proposition can be interpreted as follows: the higher the deprivation or deficiency of a given need, the higher its importance, strength, or desirability. Deficiency is usually measured as the difference between what is expected and what is attained. The evidence to test this proposition is derived from two groups of studies. The first group of studies utilizes the Porter NSQ in the measurement of job satisfaction, and the second group of studies investigates the relationship between satisfaction and the judged importance of environmental and job characteristics.

The samples for the first group of studies consisted mostly of managers. These studies utilized the Porter NSQ or a modified variation of it. Although these studies were not originally designed to test Maslow's ideas, they provide the necessary data to test the deprivation/domination proposition. In particular, these studies present a measure of need deficiency and a measure of need importance. According to Maslow's theory, the most deficient need should be the most dominant or important need. Consequently, the rank in order of both need deficiency and need importance should correspond to each other. In particular, the most deficient need should be ranked as the most important need. The results generally showed that the deprivation/domination proposition is partially supported with regard to self-actualization and autonomy needs; but the results do not support the proposition with regard to security, social and esteem needs. Findings of other studies utilizing different scales or methodologies are generally consistent with the Porter type studies. [1; 2; 3; 14; 17; 19; 29] These studies show directly or indirectly that the proposition of deprivation/domination is not always supported.

It is difficult to assess whether the higher order needs (autonomy and self-actualization) are ranked more important in the Porter type studies because they are deficient, or reported deficient because they are important. Some evidence for the latter conclusion comes from another group of studies dealing with satisfaction and the judged importance of environmental and job characteristics. Two studies [13; 20] showed a V-curve relationship between satisfaction and judged importance. That is, the higher the satisfaction *or* the dissatisfaction, the higher the ranked importance. Another study [11] showed that this relationship is limited to cases where a Likert-type scale is used. Under an alternative scale of measurement (e.g., Job Descriptive Index) only high satisfaction is correlated to importance which is the opposite of Maslow's hypoth-

esis. These studies indicate that the issue of need deprivation and the domination of behavior may not be as simple as suggested by Maslow.

The Gratification/Activation Proposition

The gratification/activation proposition has been mostly operationalized in two ways:

1. Need satisfaction should be generally decreasing going up in the Maslow need hierarchy;

2. The higher the satisfaction with a given need:

   a. the lower the importance of the need, *and*

   b. the higher the importance of the need at the next level of the hierarchy.

Several studies that used the original or modified version of the NSQ provide a test of the idea that need satisfaction should decrease going up in Maslow's need hierarchy. The samples consisted mostly of managers and also included professionals and workers. The results indicate that either self-actualization or security are the least satisfied needs, and social needs are the most satisfied. The degree of satisfaction of other needs varies widely; it is difficult to determine their general pattern. These trends are not in agreement with those proposed by Maslow.

Four cross-sectional studies explicitly tested the proposition, the higher the satisfaction with a given need, the lower the importance of this need *and* the higher the importance of the need at the next level in the hierarchy. Two studies [29; 32] produced findings opposite to Maslow's proposition. Two others [2; 3] showed limited support for individual needs of the hierarchy, and no support for other needs.

Two longitudinal studies [14; 19] also tested the gratification/activation proposition. The longitudinal studies are based on the assumption that changes in need satisfaction and need strength or importance can only be studied over time using longitudinal data. The proposition tested is that the satisfaction of needs in one category should correlate negatively with the importance of these same needs and positively with the importance of needs in the next higher level of the hierarchy. The longitudinal studies used a cross-lagged correlational analysis in addition to static correlational analysis. The former technique makes it possible to test with some confidence the strength and direction of casual relationships by using longitudinal data and correlational analysis. The two longitudinal studies indicate no support for Maslow's propositions. The two studies, however, provide the most appropriate methodology to test Maslow's theory in general and its dynamic aspects in particular.

General Evaluation and Conclusion

This literature review shows that Maslow's Need Hierarchy Theory has received little clear or consistent support from the available research findings. Some of Maslow's propositions are totally rejected, while others receive mixed and questionable support at best. The descriptive validity of Maslow's Need Classification scheme is not established, although there are some indications that low-order and high-order needs may form some kind of hierarchy. However, this two-level hierarchy is not always operative, nor is it based upon the domination or gratification concepts. No strong evidence supports the deprivation/domination proposition except with regard to self-actualization. Self-actualization, however, may not be a basic need, but rather a romantic throwback to the eighteenth century notion of the "noble savage." [6] That is, it may be based more on wishes of what man should be than on what he actually is. Furthermore, a number of competing theories explain self-actualization with more rigor than does Maslow's theory. [10] Longitudinal data does not support Maslow's gratification/activation proposition, and the limited support received from cross-sectional

studies is questionable because of numerous measurement and control problems.

Do these findings invalidate Maslow's Need Hierarchy Theory? The answer to this question is rather difficult, partly because of the nature of the theory which defies empirical testing, and partly because of the conceptual, methodological and measurement problems of the research reviewed. Maslow's Need Hierarchy Theory is almost a non-testable theory. This is evident by the relatively limited research that has sought to test it, and the difficulty of interpreting and operationalizing its concepts. For example, what behavior should or should not be included in each need category? How can a need be gratified out of existence? What does dominance of a given need mean? What are the conditions under which the theory is operative? How does the shift from one need to another take place? Do people also go down the hierarchy as they go up in it? Is there an independent hierarchy for each situation or do people develop a general hierarchy for all situations? What is the time span for the unfolding of the hierarchy? These and similar questions are not answered by Maslow and are open for many interpretations.

The most problematic aspect of Maslow's theory, however, is that dealing with the concept of need itself. There is ample evidence that people seek objects and engage in behavior that are in no way related to the satisfaction of needs. [15; 31] Cofer and Appley [10] concluded that this is probably true also for animals. Vroom [30] does not use the concept of needs in his discussion of motivation. Lawler [18] limits the use of the term to certain stimuli (or outcomes) that can be grouped together because they are sought by people. Even if we accept such a limited view of needs, the remaining question should be, Why should needs be structured in a fixed hierarchy? Does this hierarchy vary for different people? What happens to the hierarchy over time? How can we have a fixed hierarchy when behavior is multi-determinate? These and other logical arguments have been raised about Maslow's theory by many writers [e.g., 6] and have resulted in some attempts to reformulate the theory which have shown some validity. [e.g., 1; 2; 3; 4; 16]

The research reviewed in this paper is not free from weakness. In particular, there are two drawbacks in most of the research reviewed; the interpretation and operationalization of the theory, and the measurement problems. The variations in interpretations are evident by the hypotheses and the operational definitions attached to Maslow's main concepts by different authors. Methodologically, Maslow's theory is a clinically derived theory and its unit of analysis is the individual. Most of the research used the group as the unit of analysis. The theory is a dynamic theory, while most of the research, except the two longitudinal studies, dealt with the theory as a static theory. Maslow's theory is based upon a causal logic, while most of the studies were correlational (again except for the dynamic correlations used by the two longitudinal studies). The dependent variables in most of the research varied and were measured usually by self-reporting techniques, but none of the studies included observable behavior. Although there are six different scales designed especially to reflect Maslow's ideas, there are many measurement problems associated with these scales. Some of the scales do not show acceptable reliability coefficients and their construct validity is questionable.

Future research dealing with Maslow's theory should concentrate upon the areas that show some promise and ignore those areas that received little support. It is possible to develop further some of the ideas that received some support from the empiric research and improve its predictive validity, e.g., two-level hierarchy, gratification concept, and self-actualization needs. These areas should be clarified and operationalized to facilitate the formulation of testable hypotheses. The dynamic aspects of the theory should be subjected to further tests, and scales of measurements should be more refined to allow more reliable and valid tests of the theory.

REFERENCES

1. Alderfer, C. P. Differential importance of human needs as a function of satisfaction obtained in the organization. Ph.D. diss., Yale University, 1966.
2. Alderfer, C. P. An empirical test of a new theory of human needs. *Organizational Behavior and Human Performance*, 1969, 4, 142-75.
3. Alderfer, C. P. *Existence, relatedness, and growth.* New York: Free Press, 1972.
4. Barnes, L. B. *Organizational systems and engineering groups.* Boston: Harvard Graduate School of Business, 1960.
5. Beer, M. *Leadership, employee needs and motivation.* Columbus: Bureau of Business Research, Ohio State University, 1966.
6. Berkowitz, L. Social motivation. In Lindzey, G., and Aronson, E. (Eds.), *Handbook of social psychology*, 2nd ed., vol. 3. Reading, Mass.: Addison-Wesley, 1969.
7. Blai, B., Jr. An occupational study of job satisfaction and need satisfaction. *Journal of Experimental Education*, 1964, 32, 383-88.
8. Centers, R. Motivational aspects of occupational stratification. *Journal of Social Psychology*, 1948, 28, 187-217.
9. Clark, J. B. Motivation on work groups: A tentative view. *Human Organization*, 1960-61, 13, 198-208.
10. Cofer, C. N., and Appley, M. H. *Motivation: Theory and research.* New York: Wiley 1964.
11. Dachler, H. P., and Hulin, C. L. A reconsideration of the relationship between satisfaction and judged importance of environmental and job characteristics. *Organizational Behavior and Human Performance*, 1969, 4, 252-66.
12. Friedlander, F. Underlying sources of job satisfaction. *Journal of Applied Psychology*, 1963, 47, 246-50.
13. Friedlander, F. Comparative work value

systems. *Personnel Psychology*, 1965, 18, 1-20.

14. Hall, D. T., and Nougaim, K. E. An examination of Maslow's need hierarchy in an organizational setting. *Organizational Behavior and Human Performance*, 1968, 3, 12-35.

15. Harlow, H. F., Mice, monkeys, men, and motives. *Psychological Review*, 1953, 60, 23-32.

16. Harrison, R. *A Conceptual framework for laboratory training.* Unpublished manuscript, 1966.

17. Huizinga, G. *Maslow's need hierarchy in the work situation.* The Netherlands: Wolters-Noordhoff nv Groningen, 1970.

18. Lawler, E. E. *Pay and organizational effectiveness: A psychological review.* New York: McGraw-Hill, 1971.

19. Lawler, E. E., and Suttle, J. L. A casual correlation test of the need hierarchy concept. *Organizational Behavior and Human Performance.* 1972, 7, 265-87.

20. Locke, E. A. Importance and satisfaction in several job areas. Paper delivered at American Psychological Association convention, New York, 1961.

21. Maslow, A. H. A theory of human motivation. *Psychological Review*, 1943, 50, 370-96.

22. Maslow, A. H. *Motivation and personality.* New York: Harper, 1954.

23. Maslow, A. H. *Eupsychian management.* Homewood, Ill.: Irwin-Dorsey, 1965.

24. Maslow, A. H. *Motivation and personality*, 2nd ed. New York: Harper and row, 1970.

25. Meehl, P. E. *Clinical vs. statistical prediction.* Minneapolis: University of Minnesota Press, 1954.

26. Miner, J. B., and Dachler, H. P. Personnel attitudes and motivation. *Annual Review of Psychology* (in press).

27. Porter, L. W. Job attitudes in management: I. Perceived deficiences in need fulfillment as a function of job level. *Journal of Applied Psychology*, 1962, 46, 375-84.

28. Schaffer, R. H. Job satisfaction as related to need satisfaction in work, *Psychological Monographs*, 1953, 47, Whole no. 364.

29. Trexler, J. T., and A. J. Schuh. Longitudinal verification of Maslow's motivation heirarchy in a military environment. *Experimental Publication System.* Washington, D. C.: American Psychological Association, 1969, Manuscript no. 020A.

30. Vroom, V. H. *Work and motivation.* New York: Wiley, 1964.

31. White, R. W. Motivation reconsidered: The concept of competence. *Psychological Review*, 1959, 66, 297-333.

32. Wofford, J. C. The motivational basis of job satisfaction and job performance. *Personnel Psychology*, 1971, 24, 501-18.

2

An Examination of Adams' Theory of Inequity

PAUL S. GOODMAN and ABRAHAM FRIEDMAN[1]

This paper examines the empirical evidence directly testing Adams' (1963a, 1965) theory of inequity. Adams' theoretical statement and initial experimental design have stimulated considerable interest among researchers interested in motivation, organizational performance, and compensation systems. Although others (Homans, 1961; Jaques, 1961) have presented similar concepts of inequity, Adams' formulation has generated more systematic empirical evidence. Given this growing body of data, it is useful to assess critically the validity of the theory in order to determine possible directions for future research and possible implications of the theory for practice. This type of review is particularly important now because a number of researchers have recently questioned the utility of the theory (Lawler, 1968a; Pritchard, 1969; Wiener, 1970).

ADAMS' THEORY OF INEQUITY

Adams (1965: 280) defined inequity as follows: Inequity exists for Person whenever he perceives that the ratio of his outcomes

1. This paper was supported in part by Grant USPHS 5-ROI MH-18 512−02 to the senior author and Dr. L. Richard Hoffman.

Reprinted from *Administrative Science Quarterly*, 1971, 16, 271-88, by permission of the authors and the publisher.

to inputs and the ratio of Other's outcomes to Other's inputs are unequal. This may happen either (a) when Person and Other are in a direct exchange relationship or (b) when both are in an exchange relationship with a third party and Person compares himself to Other. Outcomes refer to rewards such as pay or job status which Person receives for performing his job. Inputs represent the contributions Person brings to the job, such as age, education, and physical effort. Outputs, a term not used in the definition, refer to products of Person's work, such as the number of interviews completed or pages proofed.

The basic assumptions, propositions, and derivations of the theory (Adams, 1965: 280-96) can be divided into two general classes: those dealing with the conditions of inequity and those dealing with the resolution of inequity. Propositions concerning conditions of inequity include: inequity is a source of tension; the greater the feeling of inequity, the greater drive to reduce this tension; inequity results from input-outcome discrepancies relative to Other versus absolute input-outcome discrepancies; the threshold for underpayment is lower than for overpayment; inputs and outcomes are additive. Sample propositions dealing with resolution of inequity include: Person will allocate rewards in a dyad proportionate to each member's contributions; Person will resist changing input-outcome cognitions about self more than about Other; Person who is overpaid in an hourly pay system will produce more than an equitably paid Other; Person who is overpaid in a piece-rate system will produce higher quality but fewer units than an equitably paid Other.

Listing these propositions serves two functions. (1) It indicates the range of the theory requiring empirical assessment. Previous reviewers (Lawler, 1968a; Pritchard, 1969) have considered propositions dealing mainly with the effect of inequity on performance. (2) It provides a logical basis for organizing the paper. The evidence relevant to propositions concerning resolution of inequity are analyzed first, because there are more studies in this area, and because the evidence for these propositions bears on propositions concerning conditions of inequity. Empirical evidence about conditions of inequity are analyzed second.

RESOLUTION OF INEQUITY AND PERFORMANCE

Inequity-Performance

These studies examine how resolution of inequity affects job performance. The basic design is as follows: The experimenter, posing as an employer, advertises for individuals interested in part-time work – for example, interviewing for attitude survey. A contact is made, and the subject comes to the prospective employer. The experimenter creates the inequity induction by paying the subject more or less than the going rate, or by paying more or less than the going rate and also telling the subject that his qualifications for the job are lower than a comparison Other receiving the same pay. The pay is on either an hourly or a piece-rate basis. After some initial job training, the subject performs the task over a stated period of

time, returns to the employer, completes a postjob experimental questionnaire, and is paid. The number of units – for example, interviews – completed, quality of work, and attitudinal responses from the questionnaire represent the major dependent variables.

There are four types of studies in this area: overpaid-hourly, overpaid-piece rate, underpaid-hourly, and underpaid-piece rate.

Overpaid-hourly. The basic hypotheses is that overpaid subjects will raise their inputs by producing more as a means of reducing inequity. Four studies (Adams and Rosenbaum, 1962; Arrowood, 1961; Goodman and Friedman, 1969; Pritchard et al., 1970) have generally supported this hypothesis. Kalt (1969) provided nominal support for the hypothesis, but the induction in this study was not particularly effective. Studies by Valenzi and Andrews (1969), Evan and Simmons (1969), and Anderson and Shelly (1970) indicated no differences in productivity between over and equitably paid groups. Three studies (Friedman and Goodman, 1967; Lawler, 1968b; Wiener, 1970) have obtained findings which support and some which reject the hypothesis.

The studies which did not support the hypothesis had two distinguishing characteristics: their hourly rate of pay was lower and their induction of overpayment differed from the supporting studies. The lower rate of pay was a limitation because it undermined the notion of overpayment. The supporting studies, on the other hand, paid an hourly rate higher than the modal rate for most of the subjects and, therefore, produced a more powerful induction.

The second distinguishing characteristic of the nonsupporting studies was the use of an induction which overpays by circumstances. Subjects were told their pay exceeded the modal rate for the job because of a special circumstance – for example, a private foundation was subsidizing the work, or there was a mistake in the advertisement for the job. If subjects in these studies selected the most similar comparison Others — those working on the same job — their outcomes would be high relative to their inputs, but the same as their comparison Others and, therefore, although they may have reported their pay as high, they should not have experienced inequity. In Evan and Simmons' (1969: 234) study, using an overpaid-by-circumstnace design, only 53 per cent of their overpaid subjects reported they were overpaid. Also, in their second experiment they (1969: 234) concluded: "Although acknowledging the discrepancy between their authority and salary (it was higher) the overpaid subjects did not translate this awareness into a psychological feeling of being inequitably paid." Therefore, this evidence indicates that the overpaid-by-circumstance induction is not very successful in creating feelings of inequity, and studies using this induction, and the lower hourly rate are not suitable tests of the overpaid hypothesis (Adams, 1968). A similar induction is used in selected experimental groups in Lawler (1968b) and Pritchard et al. (1970); the results also do not support the hypothesis.

The main criticism against the supporting studies is that the results are attributed to devalued self-esteem rather than to feelings of inequity (Lawler, 1968a; Pritchard, 1969). The inductions in these studies (Adams and Rosenbaum, 1962; Arrowood, 1961) provided similar pay to equitably and overpaid subjects, but told the overpaid subject his qualifications were lower—devalued—and thus he was overpaid relative to the equitably paid Other. If the subject's increased productivity was an attempt to demonstrate valued abilities that had been devalued by the induction, then the results cannot be interpreted in equity terms even though the data appear in the predicted direction.

A number of studies (Friedman and Goodman, 1967; Andrews and Valenzi, 1970; Wiener, 1970) demonstrated that feelings of self-qualification can affect performance

variation in equity experiments. However, it is difficult to extrapolate from these studies to those supporting the main hypothesis. For example, Wiener (1970) showed that overpaid subjects—those whose inputs were devalued—produced significantly more than equitably paid subjects in an ego-involved task, but not more in a less ego-involved task. Since these subjects only produced more in a condition where task abilities were central to one's self-concept, Wiener argued that their behavior represented a reaction to devalued self-esteem rather than to feelings of overpayment. Even if this interpretation is accepted, it is difficult to extrapolate from this study to those supporting the equity hourly hypothesis for two reasons. First, the induced ego orientation in this study far exceeded that in any other equity study. Second, subjects in the overpaid-unqualified group did not report significantly greater feelings of overpayment than those in the equitably paid group; a relationship which does appear in the supporting studies. Empirically we know that reaction to devalued self-esteem can affect performance in inequity experiments. What has not been empirically demonstrated is that reaction to devalued self-esteem accounts for more production variance than feelings of inequity in studies supporting the hypothesis.

An analysis of supporting studies indicates that the inequity explanation is more tenable than the devalued self-esteem explanation. Some studies have minimized conditions likely to evoke feelings of devalued self-esteem by: (1) not hiring qualified subjects (Adams and Rosenbaum, 1962); (2) distinguishing in the analysis between qualified subjects and those who felt overpaid (Arrowood, 1961); (3) using a pseudotest to pretend to validate the subjects' lower qualifications (Goodman and Friedman, 1968); (4) not selecting an ego-involved task; and (5) using a reduced dissonance control group. In these studies inputs were devalued and pay was also reduced, commensurate with the lower qualifications. Since subjects in both the overpaid and reduced dissonance groups were devalued, then no differences should have appeared between these groups if reaction to devalued self-esteem was more salient than to wage inequity; however, the differences did appear (Goodman and Friedman, 1968).

A study by Pritchard et al. (1970) employed an induction which did not rely on devaluation of self or on overpaid-by-circumstance, and successfully supported the hourly hypothesis. In their induction the payment system was changed after several days' work so that subjects were getting more or less money for the same amount of work; that is, the relationship between past and present input and outcome rations was modified to create feelings of inequity. Since their design used a relatively unambiguous method to create feelings of inequity, did not rely on devaluation of self nor on overpaid-by-circumstance (Wiener, 1970), and it embraced a longer experimental time period—greater than 30 hours—than in most experiments (for example, Valenzi and Andrews, 1969—2 hours), its supporting data provides one of the most powerful tests of the hourly hypothesis.

Another major criticism (Lawler, 1968a) of the supporting studies is that feelings of job insecurity evoked by the experimental induction reduce the efficacy of the equity explanation. That is, if the subject feels that subsequent employment is based on initial high job performance, and if this feeling is more salient in the overpaid-unqualified condition, then differential performance represents a way of buying job security rather than reducing inequity.

In a study on the possible effects of job insecurity, Arrowood (1961) found overpaid subjects produced more than control subjects in both high and low job-security conditions. Perhaps more important, however, is the likelihood of job-insecurity feelings being evoked by the inductions of the studies under consideration. Only the Adams and Rosenbaum (1962) study leaves the

length of future employment ambiguous, and therefore, likely to evoke feelings of insecurity. The other stuides seem quite clear in stating the employment period, and the employment period is relatively short—2 hours to part-time for 7 days. The authors' own experience indicates that presenting a clear, short work period with a statement that no future work is available substantially reduces the contamination from feelings of job insecurity.

Summary. There is some evidence to support the hypothesis that overpaid subjects increase their productivity as a way of bringing their inputs and outcomes in balance and thus of reducing feelings of inequity. Studies which used the overpay-by-circumstance induction and paid a lower rate were not considered adequate tests of the hypothesis. Although the effects of devalued self-esteem and job insecurity can affect performance variation in the equity studies, there is no compelling evidence that they represent the major source of production variance in the supporting studies. The Pritchard et al. (1970) study, which supports the hypothesis, offers a more useful way to test the hypothesis.

Overpaid piece-rate. The basic hypothesis is that overpaid subjects will produce higher quality and lower quantity than equitably paid subjects. The assumption for this hypothesis is: Overpaid subjects will increase their inputs as a means of achieving equity. These inputs can lead to greater quantity or quality. However, increases in quantity can only increase inequity because every unit is overpaid. Therefore, inputs are invested in increased quality and inputs and outcomes per unit achieve a balanced relationship.

The design for the piece-rate studies is the same as that described for the hourly system except that the job is advertised and paid by the piece.

The empirical support for this hypothesis seems relatively straightforward. Adams and Rosenbaum (1962), Adams (1963b), Adams and Jacobsen (1964), and Goodman and

Friedman (1969) reported lower quantity and higher quality for the overpaid group. Lawler *et al.* (1968) supported this relationship for the initial work session but not over subsequent experimental sessions. Wood and Lawler (1970) reported lower quantity for the overpaid piece-rate subjects. Andrews (1967) reported lower quantity and higher quality for the overpaid subjects as compared to equitably paid subjects, but the differences were not statistically significant. Moore (1968) presented data contrary to the equity prediction; however, she used the overpaid-by-circumstance induction, which is not particularly effective. Moore (1968: 101) indicated that the connection between inputs and outcomes was not successfully created, hence the divergence between this and other piece-rate studies.

Although there seems to be support for the piece-rate hypothesis, alternative explanations should be considered. First, the piece-rate system probably does not initially evoke feelings of overpayment. Most of the subjects had never worked piece-rate and no referent in these studies was available to translate the piece-rate into some effective wage. Therefore, at the time of employment the subjects probably did not feel overpaid, which is in contrast to a basic assumption of the piece-rate hypothesis.

A second dimension of the induction is whether it evokes perception of pay on a global or unit basis. The hypothesis assumes perception of pay on a unit basis; that is, to reduce inequity one can not increase production since each unit is overpaid. Therefore, by increasing quality, balance per unit can be achieved. However, it is not clear that subjects perceived pay on a unit basis. Most of the subjects were unfamiliar with a piece-rate system. Their work time was limited and specified in hours. Also, the fact that overpaid subjects reduced the number of units produced, and thus their pay over time (Andrews, 1967), suggests that they evaluated in a global sense the amount earned, the amount they could earn in the

next time period, and how much they thought they should earn as a function of the induction or past wages. This conclusion does not mean the subject did not feel overpaid. The process of overpayment could have worked as follows: The subject was hired and told his qualifications were low in comparison to some Other who received the same rate. At that time, feelings of inequity would not have been salient because the 30-cent rate was not translatable into a common referent. After a period of work, a global or dollar amount would have been calculated and compared to some minimal acceptable rate. If the amount earned seemed reasonable, the induction should have taken effect. That is, the subject knew he could earn an acceptable wage and he knew that his qualifications were less than those of Other receiving the same potential wage, therefore, it was congruent to reduce quantity and to invest more time in improving the quality of his inputs. Andrews (1967) reported overpaid piece-rate workers did produce fewer pieces in their second hour of production than in the first hour.

The implication of asserting that the individual adopts a global versus unit assessment is that this assertion rejects the assumption that differential in quality and quantity from the overpaid group are a function of intrinsic characteristics of the payment scheme, as Adams has hypothesized. The differential emphasis between quality and quantity can be traced to the nature of the induction and characteristics of the task. Most of the overpaid inductions (Adams and Jacobsen, 1964; Lawler, 1968b) emphasized the importance of quality, and thus focused on one salient way to achieve equity; that is, the induction provided the subjects with an instrumental way to reduce inequity. The task became an added dimension in this explanation for two reasons. First, in both proofreading and interviewing tasks quality is an important component; it is difficult for someone proofreading not to recognize quality as an intrinsic part of task performance. Second, in both tasks quality and quantity are inversely related; and if the induction and task focus on quality, it is not surprising that while quality increases as a means of dissonance reduction for the overpaid subjects, quantity decreases. Goodman and Friedman (1969) examined the effect of differential emphasis on quantity or quality in a piece-rate induction, indicating that the perceived instrumentality of quantity or quality in resolving overpayment led to the amount of quantity or quality produced. That is, overpaid subjects increased quality or quantity if it was perceived as instrumental to reducing inequity, not because of some characteristic of the payment scheme.

There are two other studies relevant to the quantity-quality issue. A study by Andrews (1967) used a task similar to most of the other studies but omitted statements emphasizing quality over quantity. Inequity was induced by varying the level of pay. The results seemed to suggest that overpaid piece-rate workers produce better quality and lower quantity. However, the quantity and quality differences between the experimental and control subjects were not statistically examined and were not very substantial. Therefore, this study does not provide strong support for Adams' basic hypothesis.

The second study, by Wood and Lawler (1970), also focused on whether subjects in an overpaid situation first reduce their outcomes to avoid inequity and as a consequence increase quality or first increase quality and as a consequence reduce quantity and their outcomes. A task was designed in which quantity was not dependent on quality. Wood and Lawler (1970) reported that overpaid subjects produced less than equitably paid subjects and that low productivity was not dependent on striving for increased quality. This study is not in conflict with the present paper's interpretation of the quality-quantity issue. It merely stated that given a task where quantity was not dependent on quality, and quantity

was the focal output measure, then lower quantity in the overpaid situation was selected as a means of avoiding increased dissonance.

A third dimension of the induction which may reduce the internal validity of the piece-rate studies is the problem of devalued self-esteem. That is, as with the hourly studies, production differences may be a reaction to devalued self-esteem rather than to feelings of inequity. There are several studies which provide additional information on this problem. Lawler *et al.* (1968) used the unqualified induction in a piece-rate study but designed the study to cover several work periods rather than the single two-hour session found in most inequity experiments. He (1968) reported the modal finding — lower quantity-higher quality for overpaid subjects — in the initial session but no differences between overpay and controls in subsequent sessions, and also that feelings of self-qualification to perform the job increased over the three work sessions for the overpaid subjects. One interpretation of these findings is that subjects reduced productivity in the initial session as a reaction to devalued self-qualification, learned that they could perform the task, and then increased their feelings of confidence and produced more. Another interpretation, consistent with inequity theory, is that increasing quality and lowering the quantity in the initial work situation followed the hypothesized resolution strategy, but that the piece-rate system, which rewarded for increasing rather than reducing outputs, and the failure to repeat the inequity induction, caused the hypothesized differences not to reappear in the latter work sessions. The increase in feelings of self-qualification could reflect both a desire to increase inputs and a successful work experience. Therefore, either interpretation is tenable, and additional information is necessary to indicate a preferred choice.

On the self-qualification issue, Andrews (1967) used the same task and procedures as the other studies, but varied pay to induce inequity rather than to devaluate qualifications. His data supported Adams' hypothesis but the differences were not strong and did not provide definitive support to the inequity versus self-qualification argument. Because neither of these two studies demonstrated the importance of devalued self-esteem in explaining production variance in inequity studies, and because the supporting piece-rate studies tried to minimize the effect of reactions to devalued self-esteem, this alternative explanation of the piece-rate findings is not accepted.

Job security represents the last dimension which can affect internal validity of the piece-rate studies. The problem is exactly the same as in the hourly studies. The unqualified induction can increase feelings of job insecurity which can lead to higher quality productivity as a way of protecting the job. Adams and Jacobsen (1964) designed a study to deal with the job security issue by creating high and low job security conditions as well as the inequity experimental conditions. Because the high and low prospect condition did not contribute significantly to production variation, nor did it interact with the inequity conditions, job security was not considered a major confounding variable. Evans and Molinari (1970), employing a similar design, reported that for quality of work produced there was a weak inequity main effect ($p > .10$) and no significant inequity-security interaction effect; for quantity of work produced there was a significant inequity-security interaction. They (1970) suggested that in their secure condition the inequity effect paralleled Adams' hypothesis, but did not hold in the insecure condition. Although the present experiment indicated that feelings of insecurity could affect performance in inequity experiments, it did not indicate that this dimension is important in evaluating the internal validity of the supporting piece-rate studies. First, the insecurity induction was quite strong in the Evans and Molinari

(1970) study and it had no parallel in the studies supporting the hypothesis. Second, the secure condition in their experiment paralleled the studies under consideration and provided data supporting the piece-rate hypothesis. Also, most researchers in the piece-rate studies had been quite clear in advertising that the job was for a limited time to minimize any insecurity effect.

Summary. The data from the overpaid piece-rate studies supported Adams' hypothesis more consistently than that from the hourly studies. However, it is less clear that the data supported some of the assumptions underlying the hypothesis. It is unlikely that piece-rate subjects initially felt overpaid or conceptualized overpayment on a unit basis — two assumptions necessary to explain the differential emphasis on quantity versus quality for overpaid subjects.

Although the data did not support some of the mechanisms underlying the piece-rate hypothesis, the findings could be interpreted in the inequity framework. That is, overpaid subjects did experience inequity after an initial performance period and differentially emphasized quantity or quality outputs — whichever seemed more successful in resolving inequity. The problem with most piece-rate studies is that the perceived instrumentality of quantity or quality outputs was a function of artifacts in the induction and task rather than intrinsic characteristics of the payment system as suggested by Adams.

Underpaid-hourly. The basic hypothesis is that underpaid subjects decrease their inputs to achieve an input-outcome balance. Masters (1968) showed that increasing outcomes is also a relevant resolution strategy in the underpaid hourly condition. Since his population — young children — and design differ greatly from the studies under consideration, Masters' study is not included.

The change in inputs can affect the quantity or quality of outputs; Adams does not specify which output dimension would change. The emphasis on quality or quantity seems a function of the instrumental task characteristics and the relationship between quantity and quality. If quality is an instrumental task requirement, as in proofreading, then decreased inputs will lead to lower quality. If quality and quantity are inversely related, then quantity will increase as quality decreases. On the other hand, if quantity and quality are positively related, decreased inputs will decrease quantity.

Four underpaid-hourly studies, using the same general design of the other studies, tested Adams' hypothesis. An experiment by Evan and Simmons (1969) and one by Pritchard et al. (1970) supported the underpaid hourly hypothesis. Another experiment by Evan and Simmons (1969) and one by Valenzi and Andrews (1969) did not support the underpaid hypothesis.

In the Evan and Simmons (1969: 234) experiment which did not support the hypothesis, the induction probably did not create strong feelings of inequity. It was thus not an effective test of the hypothesis. The differences in results between the Valenzi and Andrews (1969) and the supporting studies are more difficult to reconcile because many factors — populations, rates of pay, tasks, length of employment — were different.

While it is difficult to delineate why there were no differences among underpaid and equitably paid groups in the Valenzi and Andrews (1969) study, the following factors seem relativly clear for the Evan and Simmons (1969) and Pritchard et al. (1970) studies. First, underpaid subjects did express feelings of underpayment. Second, the time periods for both studies were short and clearly stated, thus minimizing feelings of insecurity. In the Valenzi and Andrews (1969) study subjects were to work for at least six weeks, a more ambiguous recruitment procedure. Third, the Pritchard et al. (1970) study used an unambiguous referent for creating feelings of underpayment — past work and wages to present work and wages. Thus it created a powerful induction. From these three factors it seemed reasonable to conclude that the Evan and Simmons (1969) and Pritchard et al. (1970) studies did provide some positive evidence for the underpaid-hourly hypothesis.

Summary. There were not enough studies to adequately test the validity of the hourly underpaid hypothesis, but from the few existing studies there appears to be some preliminary support for the hypothesis.

Underpaid-piece rate. The basic hypothesis is that underpaid subjects will produce a large number of low quality outputs because the production of low quality outputs permits increasing outcomes without substantially increasing inputs.

Two studies (Andrews, 1967; Lawler and O'Gara, 1967) successfully tested this hypothesis. Both reported greater quantity and lower quality from the underpaid subjects. Lawler and O'Gara (1967) also reported that the underpaid subjects perceived the job as interesting — an outcome — and at the same time simpler and less challenging — inputs — than the equitably paid subjects. The attitudinal differences were congruent with Adams' hypothesis that inequity resolution would occur by increasing outcomes and decreasing inputs. Although Moore (1968) examined the underpaid condition, the induction in that study did not provide a satisfactory test of the hypothesis.

Many problems in interpreting the other inequity-performance studies have been avoided in this payment condition. In addition, by introducing new measures to capture additional forms of the resolution process these studies tested the hypothesis better. Because these studies specifically demonstrated that underpaid subjects cognitively devalued their inputs and raised their outcomes, one is more certain that the underpaid subjects were attempting to resolve inequity.

Summary. The data from these studies supported Adams' hypothesis. Although more studies are needed to provide full confirmation of the hypothesis, the two cited studies were probably freer of alternative explanations than the other inequity-performance studies.

Other Inequity Resolution Studies

The majority of studies testing Adams' theory focused on the effect of inequity on performance. Recently other studies have been designed to test resolution strategies unrelated to job performance. These studies were distinguished from the inequity-performance studies in one or more of the following ways: (1) The inequity resolution process between Person and Other was examined. Inequity-performance studies have focused on the employer-Person relationship, with Other's identity generally ambiguous. (2) The dependent variable in these studies concerned the allocation of rewards rather than changes in performance to achieve equity. (3) The studies occurred in either a laboratory setting or in an on-going organization. The inequity-performance studies were experiments in a simulated work situation in the field.

Leventhal and his associates (see Leventhal et al., 1969a) have conducted most of the laboratory experiments in this area. Typically, subjects participated in an experiment to fulfill a class requirement. The subject was led to believe he was performing with a partner on a task for monetary rewards. The experimenter varied the inputs contributed by each member, and Other initially allocated the rewards after the task performance on an overpaid, equitably paid or underpaid basis. The subject could then reallocate the rewards, thus providing a test of inequity theory.

Findings from these studies supported the general proposition from Adams' model that Person will allocate rewards earned by the dyad in accordance with each members' contributions. Each study by Leventhal attempted to test some theoretical elaboration of this general proposition; for example, Leventhal et al. (1969a) showed that when Person could not change his inputs he was likely to reduce inequity by reallocating available rewards. Overpaid subjects reduced their share of outcomes; underpaid subjects increased their share. Leventhal et al. (1969b) indicated that alternative theoretical explanations were not as useful as the inequity model in explaining this reallocation behavior. Leventhal and Bergman (1969) examined conditions in which the general proposition did not hold, and found that under extreme conditions of underpayment, Person would reduce rather than try to increase his outcomes. Leventhal and Lane (1970) and Leventhal and Anderson (1970), using a different strategy to refine the hypothesis, indicated that sex was a moderator of the inequity resolution process.

Lane and Messé (1969), using a similar design, reported some parallel findings. Given a task where inputs were equal, outcomes were most frequently allocated on an equal basis. Other variables which related to the selection of equal distribution of outcomes included: (1) the sex composition of the dyad — heterogeneity was associated with role symmetric choices, or, equal allocation of outcomes; (2) sex of chooser — females made more role symmetric choices; (3) whether choices were made publicly or privately — the former was more associated with the role symmetric choices; and (4) personality — the greater the concern for others the more role symmetric choices. In a second experiment Lane and Messé (1969) varied the inputs of the chooser and receiver in the dyad and analyzed the allocation of rewards. The inputs of the receiver — high or low — seemed more important in affecting allocation of rewards than those of the chooser. That is, when the receiver's inputs were low the chooser allocated in his own favor, regardless of whether his own inputs were high or low. Also, there was some evidence that the chooser would distort the levels of his inputs as a way of alleviating feelings of dissonance. When choosers worked one-third as long as receivers, about 40 percent said they worked about the same as receivers and preferred a more equal distribution of outcomes.

These findings are directed to hypotheses not previously tested, and deal with critical dimensions in the theory. For example, the definition of relevant inputs affects the resolution of inequity. Leventhal extended theoretically and empirically some aspects of this definition process, arguing that the locus of control for Other's behavior affects Person's assessment of Other's inputs. If Person believes Other operates under involuntary constraints, Person is more likely to attribute higher inputs to him. This hypothesis is based on the assumptions that Person's perception of inputs is affected by the difference between actual and expected performance and that Person expects lower performance when constraints on Other are high. Leventhal and Michaels (1970) varied the external constraints by telling Person that Other had useful or nonuseful training for a particular task. As predicted, with performance held constant, individuals with nonuseful training were considered more deserving of rewards than those with useful training.

These laboratory studies do represent a new direction in inequity research, but they have several limitations which should be noted. First, pay, the main outcome in the experiments, does not seem very relevant (Leventhal and Michaels, 1969). Subjects were recruited to participate in the study and course credits were the initial payments. At the conclusion of the experiment subjects returned the money they subsequently received. These conditions are not conducive to making pay a relevant outcome.

Second, the mechanisms for reallocating rewards, a critical dimension in testing for inequity resolution strategies, lack credibility. For example, in Leventhal *et al.* (1969b), subjects were told that the high-scoring member of their dyad would divide the money after the task was finished, but that the low-scoring member could modify the initial allocation. The subjects were then told that the two members of the dyad tied in their scores and a coin was flipped to determine who would allocate the money. The other member of the dyad, who really was nonexistent, won and then the subject was told that the winner had decided on the allocation himself or randomly selected the basis of allocation. Allocation occurred and then the subject reallocated. The low relevance of the pay, and the low credibility of this reallocation induction as further evidenced by the fact that some subjects recognized the deception (Leventhal and Michaels, 1969) increased the salience of experimental demand characteristics and thus chances for experimental error.

A third problem concerns how well the induction creates perceptions that one's inputs are related to outcomes. This relationship is basic to testing Adams' hypotheses. Because the subject had little time in these studies to test how his inputs were related to outcomes and because prior to task performance the subject knew that the other member of the dyad could determine his rewards, it was likely that his outcomes would not be perceived as directly dependent on his inputs (Leventhal *et al.*, 1969b).

Weick and Nesset (1968) in using a different design to examine the inequity resolution process, developed a force choice format which contains 20 pairs of hypothetical work situations, the situations varying in degrees of inequity. Subjects have to select the professed work situation and then to indicate preferred resolution strategies to make the least preferred choice in the pair more comfortable. Analysis of the resolution strategies indicated subjects were more likely to change individual circumstances by increasing effort than interpersonal circumstances by finding a new comparison Other. This was consistent with Adams' (1965: 294) hypothesis. Seeking higher wages was the most preferred strategy for underpaid subjects. It is interesting that this alternative had not been examined in the inequity resolution studies. Subjects did select quitting as an alternative, which seems contrary to Adams' hypothesis that leaving the field would occur only when other strategies were blocked. However, because the instrument permitted responding to more than one resolution strategy, it is not surprising to see that leaving the field was selected as an option, and therefore, Adams' hypothesis about withdrawal was not adequately tested.

Weick and Nesset's (1968) force choice instrument represents a new approach in testing inequity theory hypotheses. Refinements of this methodology would be important for assessing the validity of inequity theory because the use of different methods to test similar hypotheses is a very powerful validation strategy. Some of the limitations of this force choice instrument were discussed by Weick and Nesset (1968: 414). Other additions, such as assessing the instrument's reliability and using an independent criterion, would improve the instrument's validity.

In a correlational study in an organization, Penner (1967), directly testing dimensions of Adams' hypothesis, indicated that propensity to leave the company was twice as likely for those individuals who perceived their salary as inequitable. Although there has been other research on the satisfaction, absenteeism, and turnover relationships (Hulin, 1968), these studies were not direct tests of Adams' theory. Therefore more work is needed to test preferences for alternative resolution strategies in the field.

Summary. Studies in this section focused on inequity resolution between Person and Other, considered resolution strategies other than changing performance, and used designs different from the inequity-performance studies. The basic proposition tested is that Person allocates outcomes to himself and Other proportional to their respective inputs. The effects of the source of inequity, of how much control Other had over his inputs, and of Person's sex on the distribution of outcomes between Person and Other were investigated. Redefinition of Other's

inputs and anticipation of future behavior from Other were other processes mediating the distribution of outcomes. These findings seemed congruent with Adams' theory, and in some cases (Weick and Nesset, 1968; Leventhal and Michaels, 1970) offered extensions to the theory. Additional studies are needed, however, to provide a more critical analysis.

CONDITIONS OF INEQUITY

Other studies which bear on Adams' theory concern determinants of feelings of inequity and the psychological state of inquity. The role of the comparison Other as a determinant of inequity has received surprisingly little attention. There have been field studies which indicated that an imbalance between Person and Other led to feelings of inequity (Penner, 1967; Lawler, 1965); these provided a confirmation of a basic assumption in the theory. An experiment by Wicker and Bushweiler (1970) indicated that the degree of liking between Person and Other could moderate perceptions of inequity during an exchange in this dyad. However, the complex processes leading to the selection of a comparison Other had not been pursued. Weick and Nesset (1968) made the most significant advance in this area, distinguishing between three comparison conditions of equity: own equity – Person had a balanced input-outcome ratio (L/L, low inputs-low outcomes) but it is unbalanced in regard to Other (H/L, high inputs-low outcomes); comparison equity – Person had an equal input-outcome ratio with Other but both were unbalanced (H/L, H/L); own comparison equity – Person had a balanced input-outcome ratio which equaled Other's (L/L, H/H). Weick and Nesset's (1968) findings indicated that subjects chose equitable conditions in terms of Other's input-outcome ratio (H/L, H/L) rather than in terms of their own input-outcome ratio. Subjects also chose situations where their own input-outcome ratio was in balance and equal to

Fairness

Other's ratio rather than a situation of own equity (L/L, H/L). Other analyses indicated that overpayment relative to one's own inputs (L/H, L/H) was preferred to overpayment in terms of Other's inputs (L/L, H/L). This study was especially important as the first that empirically examined some of the alternative comparison models, and focused on Person's input-outcome ratio as a source of inequity without reference to Other.

There are some very preliminary findings on the effect of past and future input-outcome ratios on the evaluation of present feelings of inequity, for example, Pritchard et al. (1970) indicated that past input-outcome ratio could induce present feelings of inequity. Although there is some data indicating that optimism about future outcomes is associated with present feelings of satisfaction (Goodman, 1966), the evidence supporting the effect of future input-outcome ratios on inducing present feelings of inequity is not yet clear (Lawler, 1970).

Other factors, such as characteristics of the individual and the organization providing the outcomes, can affect feelings of inequity. Penner (1967) indicated that high performers were more likely to feel dissatisfied with their pay; high inputs were more likely to lead to feelings of inequity. Klein and Maher (1966), using education as an input, indicated that college educated respondents were more likely to feel dissatisfied with their pay than noncollege respondents.

Organizational factors also seem to affect feelings of inequity. Penner (1967) reported that when pay and performance were not perceived as related, feelings of dissatisfaction with pay would more likely occur. In equity terms this reward system did not reward increased inputs for performance, and therefore, inequity resulted. A corollary finding was that when pay was determined by budgetary constraints rather than by inputs, dissatisfaction with pay resulted. Probably the most provocative finding from Penner's study was that increasing one organizational reward, like amount of freedom, could affect feelings of inequity about other rewards, like pay. Implicit in this finding was a hypothesis from Adams' theory which asserts tha outcomes are additive. Although Penner's (1967) study represented an important test in the field of Adams' work, it lacked some important control procedures. For example, variables such as amount of pay, organizational level, and type of job should have been controlled in an analysis of the relationship between amount of freedom and feelings about pay. Since these controls were absent in Penner's (1967) analysis, the findings must be considered tentative.

The last set of studies to be reviewed concerns the psychological state of inequity. Adams argued that inequity is a source of tension which an individual is motivated to reduce. To some extent, all the studies confirming any inequity hypotheses are testing this assumption. Some studies, however, directly measured the affective state associated with inequity, and confirmed Adams' basic contention (Leventhal et al., 1969a; Pritchard et al., 1970). Pritchard et al.'s (1970) research went beyond confirming the inequity and dissatisfaction relationship to indicate that inequity with one input-outcome ratio may generalize to other outcomes. For example, their data indicated that subjects in a condition of pay inequity exhibited lower job satisfaction than equitably paid subjects.

Another hypothesis in inequity theory — that the threshold for underpayment is lower than for overpayment — received fairly consistent support from different investigators (Andrews, 1967; Weick and Nesset, 1968).

Summary. Studies in this section extended our understanding of inequity theory by examining how the comparison process affected feelings of inequity, individual and organizational factors which affected feelings of inequity, as well as some aspects of the state of inequity. Although none of the findings presented seriously challenged Adams' theory, more, better controlled studies are needed to adequately test the validity of the hypotheses discussed in this section.

METHODOLOGICAL ISSUES

Recruitment-Selection

There are a number of important moderators — ability (Bass, 1968; Moore, 1968); past work experience (Friedman and Goodman, 1967); past wages (Andrews, 1967); need preferences (Lawler and O'Gara, 1967) — which can affect interpretation of inequity studies. Some moderators, like need for money represent an alternative explanation for variation in the dependent variables, and therefore must be controlled to assess the role of the inequity explanation. For example, individuals high in need for money may work hard in a piece-rate experiment not as a means of reducing inequity but to satisfy a need for more money. Although it can be argued that these moderators should be equally distributed across experimental conditions, given the relatively small sample size in most studies and the fact that despite random assignment the moderators often are not equally distributed (Goodman and Friedman, 1968), it seems desirable to measure and analyze the effects of the relevant moderators. The fact that few investigations (Lawler *et al.,* 1968 is an exception) have done this casts doubt on the internal validity of the studies we have examined.

A recruitment-selection bias is also relevant for interpreting the external validity or generalizability of some inequity studies. For example, since the method of payment is often advertised during recruitment, there is probably a differential selection process for hourly and piece-rate studies, with the latter selecting out more subjects because of the ambiguity of how much they can make (Evans and Molinari, 1970). Although this differential selection does not limit the internal validity of a particular study, it does

limit one's ability to compare hourly and piece-rate studies (Adams, 1963b). One solution to this problem would be to examine the differences between people who respond and do not respond to the simulated advertisements about either hourly or piece-rate jobs.

Induction

The induction is an important experimental event for explaining differences among studies. Inequity theory postulates an imbalance between Person's outcomes and inputs in comparison to Other as a condition of inequity. To successfully operationalize this concept, however, one must deal with the following cognitions (Vroom, 1964):

1. Person's evaluation of his inputs;
2. Person's perception of the relevance of his inputs for task performance;
3. Person's perception of E's perception of his inputs;
4. Person's perception of Other's outcome-input ratio;
5. Person's perception of future outcomes.
6. Person's perception of the outcomes relative to alternative outcomes — his past outcomes — the outcomes for this class of tasks, and so forth;
7. The relative importance Person attaches to using 4, 5, and 6 as comparison points.

These conditions are basic to assessing the internal validity of any inequity experiment. If, for example, the subject selects comparison Others different from those intended by the experimenter, then the substantive interpretation of an experiment is limited, and since the comparison Other in most experiments is ambiguously specified, this particular problem is likely to occur. Or subjects could define relevant outcomes differently from the experimenter. Because many of the studies are advertised as part of some research and because helping in research has been identified as an additional outcome which affects performance differences in inequity studies (Heslin and Blake, 1969), failure to control on definition of outcomes introduces a source of experimental error.

None of the studies reviewed recognized most of these conditions in specifying their experimental design; therefore, another source of error has not been controlled. These conditions could be controlled either by directly building them into the induction of measuring these cognitions and including them in the analysis.

Developing an adequate control group, a problem relevant to inequity resolution studies, is another aspect of the induction which deserves attention. The equitable condition, characterized by an absence of tension, has been the modal control group. At issue is the source and degree of motivation exhibited by subjects in this group. One equity study (Friedman and Goodman, 1967) showed that equitably paid control subjects, as a way of confirming their valued abilities, were actually highly motivated to produce. Although this problem has been identified by others (Weick, 1967b), it has not captured the attention of researchers concerned with inequity. The Pritchard *et al.* (1970) study illustrated how the subject's own performance could provide a baseline for assessing subsequent feelings of inequity. Also, by introducing various levels of inequity – high, medium, and low overpayment – more refined contrasts could be made and assumptions about the similarity between an overpaid and equitable induction could be avoided.

Task

The experimental task represents another source of error which should be controlled. The design of future studies, especially when performance is a major dependent variable, must reflect the following problems found in past inequity studies. First, if the hypothesis indicates a differential emphasis on quality or quantity, tasks in which these two are relatively independent should be developed.

This issue is particularly important in studies where one wants to know if the subject is reducing quantity or increasing quality. Some recent studies (Wood and Lawler, 1970; Wiener, 1970) have reported tasks where quantity and quality are independent.

Second, if the subject modifies the task in a way unintended by the experimenter (Weick, 1967a), internal validity can be reduced. Although there are no data available to assess the effect of task modifiability in these studies, it does represent a problem in interpreting inequity studies. For example, it is possible for the subject to modify some of the scoring procedures in the questionnaire or proofreading tasks used in inequity-performance studies. The problem is how to evaluate the modification. On one hand, it might represent a new input and it should then be measured. However, it would be difficult to add this input to other measures of outputs such as the number of units produced and form some common index of contributions to the job. On the other hand, if this modification increases productivity, counting this additional productivity may not reflect an increase in inputs; the subject may merely have found a more efficient way to increase outputs without additional effort.

A third and related problem concerns the need for an independent assessment of the relationship between inputs and outputs for different tasks. Basic to the inequity-resolution studies is the strategy of modifying inputs to reduce inequity. Outputs are taken to be measures of inputs. The problem is to what extent do the number of outputs – questionnaires for example – reflect the amount of inputs – effort – expended. If the amount of effort per unit varies with the level of performance and type of task, then evaluation of inputs from outputs becomes a less desirable measure. Unfortunately, there is no evidence on this particular point, and therefore, the issue can only be raised for consideration in future studies.

The fourth task-related problem concerns

the amount of time allocated for task performance. There has been considerable variation in the studies reviewed; some took less than 10 minutes (Leventhal *et al.*, 1969b), others took more than 30 hours (Pritchard *et al.*, 1970). Although there do not seem to be any clear differences between studies which support or do not support the inequity hypotheses on the time dimension, there is evidence that the time dimension is relevant in assessing the validity of inequity studies. For example, change over time in subject behavior within an experimental session (Andrews, 1967) was important in assessing whether subjects were overpaid in piece-rate studies. The fact that some studies (Lawler *et al.*, 1968; Pritchard *et al.*, 1970) have not supported the inequity hypotheses over several experimental sessions raises questions about the effectiveness of the theory or the induction over time. In any case, it would seem desirable to use multiple sessions over time in future studies — most studies have been single sessions — and to systematically assess behavior over time both within and between sessions and to identify factors like differential task success which affect performance over time.

Measurement and Data Analysis

There are a number of problems of measurement and analysis which confound the interpretation of the reviewed studies and should be eliminated in future studies. First, measures of the effectiveness of the induction must be introduced immediately after the induction. This would require one experimental group that would be tested after the induction but would not complete the experimental session. In many of the reviewed studies this measurement was taken after the experiment and thus was contaminated by the experimental experience. Second, and most important, inequity theory focuses on the complex interrelationship among multiple cognitions. Most of the research reviewed has dealt with only a few cognitions.

One contribution to research would be to develop additional measures using different methods to capture the multiple cognitions used to define inequity (Zedeck and Smith, 1968) and to resolve it.

Problems in working with a small sample size, with subject mortality, and with weak statistical techniques which characterized some of the earlier studies (Arrowood, 1961; Goodman and Friedman, 1968), seem to have been avoided in the most recent studies (Pritchard *et al.*, 1970; Wiener, 1970). Thus it seems that data analysis issues have been recognized and probably will receive continued attention in future studies.

THEORETICAL OVERVIEW

The purpose of this paper is to examine the empirical evidence testing Adams' theory of inequity. It is important in making this assessment to review all the varied propositions in the theory, not just inequity-performance; for this alone does not permit an adequate evaluation of the theory.

Three general conclusions about the relative validity can be offered. First, some assumptions and hypotheses derived from the theory have relatively clear empirical support; they are: inequity is a source of tension (Pritchard *et al.*, 1970); the greater the inequity the greater the drive to reduce it — all supporting studies; input-outcome discrepancies relative to Other are a source of inequity (Weick and Nesset, 1968); the threshold for underpayment is lower than for overpayment (Leventhal *et al.*, 1969b); Person maximizes positive outcomes in inequity resolution (Leventhal and Michaels, 1970); Person allocates rewards in a dyad in proportion to each member's contributions (Leventhal *et al.*, 1969a); underpaid piece-rate subjects produce more than equitably paid subjects (Lawler and O'Gara, 1967).

Second, there are a set of assumptions and hypotheses which have tentative empirical support. The tentative label is applied to these hypotheses either because there have not been enough tests of the hypothesis or because the evidence is mixed. In this latter category, we have argued that the supporting evidence is greater than the nonsupporting evidence. Hypotheses in this second set include: Person will resist changing input-outcome cognitions central to his self-concept (Leventhal and Lane, 1970); Person will resist changing his comparison Other once Other has become a referent (Weick and Nesset, 1968); overpaid-hourly subjects produce more than equitably paid subjects (Pritchard *et al.*, 1970); overpaid piece-rate subjects produce less quantity and higher quality than equitably paid subjects (Adams and Jacobsen, 1964); underpaid-hourly subjects will invest lower inputs than equitably paid subjects (Evan and Simmons, 1969).

Third, the following are a set of hypotheses which either have not been tested, or have been tested in a single study with poor controls: if input-outcome discrepancies are the same for Person and Other no inequity results; inequity is greater when both inputs and outcomes are discrepant for Other; inputs and outcomes are additive; within certain limits of inequity Person manipulates inputs and outcomes to reduce inequity; Person will resist changing cognitions about his own inputs and outcomes more than about Other's inputs and outcomes; Person will leave the field when inequity is high and other reduction strategies are unavailable.

The evidence seems to provide initial support for some of Adams' propositions, but the critical test of the theory will depend on: (*1*) empirical support for the propositions listed above that are not fully tested; (*2*) elaboration of conceptual areas not fully specified by Adams to generate new propositions for testing; and (*3*) contrasting of inequity theory with other theories to evaluate its comparative advantages in prediction.

Although the general concept of inequity has been well stated by Adams, the components of perceived inequity have not been theoretically specified in sufficient detail.

One important problem concerns the process by which inputs and outcomes are defined as relevant. Advancing our knowledge in this area would permit identification of determinants of inequity and prediction of inequity. Weick (1966) and Leventhal and Michaels (1970) have provided some provocative thinking about the input-outcome specification problem which should stimulate further theorizing and research.

A related problem concerns how information is combined when Person evaluates his input-outcome ratio. Person must deal with information not only about his own multiple inputs and outcomes, but also about input-outcome ratios of Others. How is this information combined? Einhorn (1970a, 1970b) has developed a conceptual and operational procedure for testing whether people use linear or nonlinear models when combining information. This type of research could be applied to inequity studies to provide a better understanding of how different methods of combining information lead to feelings of inequity.

Another problem subsumed in the inequity concept is the selection and use of a referent in evaluating one's inputs and outcomes. The major theoretical focus has been derived from social comparison theory and Other has been critical in the determination of inequity. There are, however, other relevant referents in inequity evaluation such as Person's concept of his own self-worth, past input-outcome ratios, and future input-outcome ratios. The critical issue, then, is specifying a theoretical framework to permit the identification and weighting of multiple referents used in evaluating the input-outcome ratio.

The inequity resolution process requires further elaboration and testing before the utility of the theory can be assessed. The basic issues for both cognitive and behavioral resolution modes are how are salient resolution strategies defined and which strategies are most likely to be evoked. Expectancy theory (Lawler, 1970) might provide a general framework for predicting resolution processes. The expectancy and valence components could be defined for each resolution strategy and the expected force associated with each strategy assessed.

Testing competing hypotheses from inequity theory and other theoretical perspectives provides another way to assess its comparative validity. For example, expectancy theory (Porter and Lawler, 1968), which focuses primarily on the perceived relationship between behavior and valued rewards, would not predict increased performance for overpaid subjects in the hourly condition since performance is not related to pay; inequity theory does predict increased performance. Lawler (1968a) has argued that the reported performance differences in the hourly study are attributed to the characteristics of the induction, and that expectancy theory represents a preferred theoretical perspective. We would argue that there is an inequity effect in those studies, although expectancy theory probably is a more powerful long-run predictor. Pritchard et al.'s (1970) study suggests a future model for comparing both theories; it examines different levels of inequity in payment systems with different expectancies that pay and performance are related.

The concept of insufficient rewards (Weick, 1967b) represents another theoretical position which contrasts with inequity theory predictions. Inequity theory predicts no increase in effort from underpaid subjects in the hourly condition; the insufficient rewards concept predicts increased effort. A design incorporating different levels of underpayment would permit a test of these contrasting hypotheses. We would expect inequity theory predictions to be supported at moderate levels of underpayment, and insufficient reward predictions at greater levels.

Research on the norm of reciprocity (Pruit, 1968), the norm of social responsibility (Goranson and Berkowitz, 1966; Berscheid et al., 1968; Greenglass, 1969), or the belief in a just world (Simmons and Lerner, 1968) poses an interesting challenge to the development of inequity theory. To what extent, for example, is there a norm of equity? How would such a norm differ from the reciprocity or social responsibility norms? Levanthal et al. (1969b) have made some preliminary attempts to empirically separate these concepts; however, there seems to be little interchange in the development of these three perspectives. Messé et al. (1970) examined the effect of inequity in the resolution of interpersonal conflict; another potentially useful area to expand inequity theory.

Until research in the above areas is well developed, it will be difficult to delimit with certainty the relevance of Adams' theory for organizational processes. However, there are some indications of directions in which the theory may contribute. First, and its most general contribution, inequity theory offers a relatively simple model to explain and to predict an individual's feelings about various organizational rewards. Although the experimental studies have focused primarily on feelings of inequity about pay, the model seems generalizable to other types of rewards such as promotion, supervisor support, status (Stephenson and White, 1968), and to other types of relationships such as that of buyer-seller (Leventhal et al., 1970). The primary contribution of the model will certainly not be in explaining performance. The data at the present time only indicate a very short term effect of inequity on performance. Also, it is important to remember that variations in performance represent only one inequity resolution mode. Neither the theory nor present research indicates it is the dominant resolution strategy. Unfortunately, the large number of studies in the inequity-performance area have led some people to think of Adams' theory as primarily a motivation-performance model.

Second, the delineation of the comparison model an individual uses in evaluating his input-outcome ratio should be relevant for organizational decision makers involved in determining appropriate levels of rewards. For example, identifying Others Person considers in evaluating his pay should indicate what groups of individuals should be included in a salary survey, one mechanism for setting levels of pay.

Another contribution of the inequity model to administration may be in the area of the interchangeability of rewards. A topic that needs further empirical analysis concerns how an individual combines his outcomes and inputs. This type of research should aid organizational decision makers by identifying what kind of rewards like freedom have an additive effect on other rewards like pay, and which rewards can be substituted for others (Penner, 1967).

Finally, research on allocation of rewards suggests that achieving balance between input and outcome is an important decision rule. However, there may be alternative forces or competing decision rules in organizations that conflict with an equitable allocation. For example, an experiment by Rothbart (1968) indicated supervisors consider competing models of inequity and of the relative effectiveness of different reward-punishment schedules in allocation of possible outcomes. Identifying individual or structural factors which evoke these competing decision rules and their consequences would represent another contribution of the theory.

REFERENCES

Adams, J. Stacy. Toward an understanding of inequity. *Journal of Abnormal and Social Psychology*, 1963a, 67, 422-36.

Adams, J. Stacy. Wage inequities, productivity and work quality. *Industrial Relations*, 1963b, 3, 9-16.

Adams, J. Stacy. Inequity in social exchange. In L. Berkowitz (Ed.), *Advances in Experimental Social Psychology*, 2, 267-300. New York: Academic Press, 1965.

Adams, J. Stacy. Effects of overpayment: two comments on Lawler's paper. *Journal of Personality and Social Psychology*, 1968, 10, 315-16.

Adams, J. Stacy, and Jacobsen, Patricia R. Effects of wage inequities on work quality. *Journal of Abnormal and Social Psychology*, 1964, 69, 19-25.

Adams, J. Stacy, and Rosenbaum, William B. The relationship of worker productivity to cognitive dissonance about wage inequities. *Journal of Applied Psychology*, 1962, 46, 161-64.

Anderson, Bo, and Shelly, Robert. A replication of Adams' experiment and a theoretical formulation. *Acta Sociologica*, 1970, 13, 1-10.

Andrews, I. R. Wage inequity and job performance: an experimental study. *Journal of Applied Psychology*, 1967, 51, 39-45.

Andrews, I. R., and Valenzi, E. Overpay inequity or self-image as a worker: a critical examination of an experimental induction procedure. *Organizational Behavior and Human Performance*, 1970, 53, 22-27.

Arrowood, Arthur J. Some effects on productivity of justified an;unjustified levels of reward under public and private conditions. Ph.D. diss., University of Minnesota, 1961.

Bass, Bernard M. Ability, values, and concepts of equitable salary increases in exercise compensation. *Journal of Applied Psychology*, 1968, 52, 299-303.

Berscheid, Ellen, Boye, David, and Walster, Elaine. Retaliation as a means of restoring equity. *Journal of Personality and Social Psychology*, 1968, 10, 370-76.

Einhorn, Hillel J. The use of nonlinear, noncompensatory models in decision making. *Psychological Bulletin*, 1970a, 73, 221-30.

Einhorn, Hillel J. Use of nonlinear, noncompensatory models as a function of task and amount of information. *Organizational Behavior and Human Performance*, 1970b, 6, 1-27.

Evan, William M., and Simmons, Roberta G. Organizational effects of inequitable rewards: two experiments in status inconsistency. *Administrative Science Quarterly*, 1969, 14, 224-37.

Evans, Martin G., and Molinari, Larry. Equity, piece-rate overpayment, and job-security: Some effects on performance. *Journal of Applied Psychology*, 1970, 54, 105-14.

Friedman, Abraham, and Goodman, Paul S. Wage inequity, self-qualifications, and productivity. *Organizational Behavior and Human Performance*, 1967, 2, 406-17.

Goodman, Paul S. A study of time perspective: Measurement and correlates. Ph.D. diss., Cornell University, 1966.

Goodman, Paul S., and Friedman, Abraham. An examination of the effect of wage inequity in the hourly condition. *Organizational Behavior and Human Performance*, 1968, 3, 340-52.

Goodman, Paul S., and Friedman, Abraham. An examination of quantity and quality of performance under conditions of overpayment in piece rate. *Organizational Behavior and Human Performance*, 1969, 4, 365-74.

Goranson, Richard E., and Berkowitz, Leonard. Reciprocity and responsibility reactions to prior help. *Journal of Personality and Social Psychology*, 1966, 3, 227-32.

Greenglass, Esther R. Effects of prior help and hindrance on willingness to help another: reciprocity or social responsibility. *Journal of Personality and Social Psychology*, 1969, 11, 224-31.

Heslin, Richard, and Blake, Brian. Performance as a function of payment, commitment and task interest. *Psychonomic Science*, 1969, 15, 323-24.

Homans, George. *Social Behavior*. New York: Harcourt, Brace & World, 1961.

Hulin, Charles L. Effects of changes in job-satisfaction levels on employee turnover. *Journal of Applied Psychology*, 1968, 52, 122-26.

Jacques, E. *Equitable Payment*. New York: Wiley, 1961.

Kalt, Neil C. Temporal resolution of inequity: An exploratory investigation. Ph.D. diss., University of Illinois, 1969.

Klein, S. M., and Maher, J. R. Education level and satisfaction with pay. *Personnel Psychology*, 1966, 19, 195-208.

Lane, Irving M., and Messé, Lawrence A. Equity and distribution of rewards. Working paper, Michigan State University, 1969.

Lawler, Edward E. Manager's perceptions of their subordinates' pay and their superiors' pay. *Personnel Psychology*, 1965, 18, 413-22.

Lawler, Edward E. Equity theory as a predictor of productivity and work quality. *Psychological Bulletin*, 1968a, 70, 596-610.

Lawler, Edward E. Effects of hourly overpayment on productivity and work quality. *Journal of Personality and Social Psychology*, 1968b, 10, 306-13.

Lawler, Edward E. *The psychology of pay*. New York: McGraw-Hill, 1970.

Lawler, Edward E., and O'Gara, Paul W. Effects of inequity produced by underpayment on work output, work quality, and attitudes toward work. *Journal of Applied Psychology*, 1967, 51, 403-10.

Lawler, Edward E., Koplin, Cary A., Young, Terence F., and Fadem, Joel A. Inequity reduction over time in an induced overpayment situation. *Organizational Behavior and Human Performance*, 1968, 3, 253-68.

Leventhal, Gerald S., and Anderson, David. Self-interest and the maintenance of equity. *Journal of Personality and Social Psychology*, 1970, 15, 57-62.

Leventhal, Gerald S., and Bergman, James T. Self-depriving behavior as a response to unprofitable inequity. *Journal of Experimental and Social Psychology*, 1969, 5, 153-71.

Leventhal, Gerald S., and Lane, Douglas W. Sex, age, and equity behavior. *Journal of Personality and Social Psychology*, 1970, 15, 312-16.

Leventhal, Gerald S., and Michaels, James W. Extending the equity model: perception of inputs and allocation of reward as a function of duration and quantity of performance. *Journal of Personality and Social Psychology*, 1969, 12, 303-9.

Leventhal, Gerald S., and Michaels, James W. Locus of cause and equity motivation as determinants of reward allocation. Working paper, North Carolina State University, 1970.

Leventhal, Gerald S., Allen, John, and Kemelgor, Bruce. Reducing inequity by reallocating rewards. *Psychonomic Science*, 1969a, 14, 295-96.

Leventhal, Gerald S., Weiss, Thomas, and Long, Gary. Equity, reciprocity, and reallocating rewards in the dyad. *Journal of*

Personality and Social Psychology, 1969b, 13, 300-5.

Leventhal, Gerald S., Younts, Charles M., and Lund, Adrian K. Tolerance for inequity in buyer-seller relationships. Working paper, North Carolina State University, 1970.

Masters, John C. Effects of social comparison upon subsequent self-reinforcement behavior in children. *Journal of Personality and Social Psychology*, 1968, 10, 391-401.

Messé, Lawrence, Dawson, Jack, and Lane, Irving. Equity as a mediator of the effect of reward level on behavior in the prisoner's dilemma game. Working paper, Michigan State University, 1970.

Moore, Loretta M. Effects of wage inequities on work attitudes and performance. M.A. thesis, Wayne State University, 1968.

Penner, Donald. A study of causes and consequences of salary satisfaction. Crotonville, N.Y.: General Electric Behavioral Research Service, 1967.

Porter, Lyman, and Lawler, Edward E. *Managerial attitudes and performance.* Homewood, Ill.; Irwin, 1968.

Pritchard, Robert D. Equity theory: a review and critique. *Organizational Behavior and Human Performance*, 1969, 4, 176-211.

Pritchard, Robert D., Jorgenson, Dale O., and Dunnette, Marvin D. The effects of perceptions of equity and inequity on worker performance and satisfaction. Working paper, Purdue University, 1970.

Pruit, Dean. Reciprocity and credit building in a laboratory dyad. *Journal of Personality and Social Psychology*, 1968, 8, 143-47.

Rothbart, Myron. Effects of motivation, equity and compliance on the use of reward and punishment. *Journal of Personality and Social Psychology*, 1968, 9, 353-62.

Simmons, Carolyn, and Lerner, Melvin. Altruism as a search for justice. *Journal of Personality and Social Psychology*, 1968, 9, 216-25.

Stephenson, G. M., and White, J. H. An experimental study of some effects of injustice on children's moral behavior. *Journal of Experimental Social Psychology*, 1968, 4, 367-83.

Valenzi, E. R., and Andrews, I. R. Effect of underpay and overpay inequity when tested with a new induction procedure. In *Proceedings, 77th Annual Convention,* American Psychological Association, 1969, pp. 593-94.

Vroom, Victor. *Work and motivation.* New York: Wiley, 1964.

Weick, Karl E. The concept of equity in the perception of pay. *Administrative Science Quarterly*, 1966, 11, 414-39.

Weick, Karl E. Organizations in the laboratory. In Victor Vroom (Ed.), *Methods of Organization Research*, 1-56. Pittsburgh: University of Pittsburgh Press, 1967a.

Weick, Karl E. Dissonance and task enhancement: a problem for compensation theory. *Organizational Behavior and Human Performance*, 1967b, 2, 189-207.

Weick, Karl E., and Nesset, Bonna. Preferences among forms of equity. *Organizational Behavior and Human Performance*, 1968, 3, 400-16.

Wicker, Allan W., and Bushweiler, Gary. Perceived fairness and pleasantness of social exchange situations: Two factorial studies of inequity. *Journal of Personality and Social Psychology*, 1970, 15, 63-75.

Wiener, J. The effect of task and ego oriented performance on two kinds of overcompensation inequity. *Organizational Behavior and Human Performance*, 1970, 5, 191-208.

Wood, Ian, and Lawler, Edward E. Effects of piece-rate overpayment on productivity. *Journal of Applied Psychology*, 1970, 54, 234-38.

Zedeck, Sheldon, and Smith, Patricia Cain. A psychophysical determination of equitable payment: a methodological study. *Journal of Applied Psychology*, 1968, 52, 343-47.

3

The Effect of Performance on Job Satisfaction

EDWARD E. LAWLER III and LYMAN W. PORTER

The human relations movement with its emphasis on good interpersonal relations, job satisfaction, and the importance of informal groups provided an important initial stimulant for the study of job attitudes and their relationship to human behavior in organizations. Through the thirties and forties, many studies were carried out to determine the correlates of high and low job satisfaction. Such studies related job satisfaction to seniority, age, sex, education, occupation, and income, to mention a few. Why this great interest in job satisfaction? Undoubtedly some of it stemmed from a simple desire on the part of scientists to learn more about job satisfaction, but much of the interest in job satisfaction seems to have come about because of its presumed relationship to job performance. As Brayfield and Crockett have pointed out, a common assumption that employee satisfaction directly affects performance permeates most of the writings about the topic that appeared during this period of two decades.[1] Statements such as the following characterized the literature: "Morale is not an abstraction; rather it is concrete in the sense that it directly affects the quality and quantity of an individual's output," and "Employee morale — reduces turnover — cuts down absenteeism and tardiness; lifts production."[2]

It is not hard to see how the assumption that high job satisfaction leads to high performance came to be popularly accepted. Not only did it fit into the value system of the human relations movement but there also appeared to be some research data to support this point. In the Western Electric studies, the evidence from the Relay Assembly Test Room showed a dramatic tendency for increased employee productivity to be associated with an increase in job satisfaction. Also, who could deny that in the Bank Wiring Room there was both production restriction and mediocre employee morale. With this background it is easy to see why both social scientists and managers believed that if job dissatisfaction could be reduced, the human brake on production could be removed and turned into a force that would increase performance.

1. Arthur H. Brayfield and Walter H. Crockett, Employee attitudes and employee performance, *Psychological Bulletin.* 42 (September 1955). 396-424.

2. Ibid.

Reprinted from *Industrial Relations,* October 1967, 7, 20-28, by permission of the authors and the Institute of Industrial Relations, University of California.

PREVIOUS RESEARCH

But does the available evidence support the belief that high satisfaction will lead to high performance? Since an initial study, in 1932, by Kornhauser and Sharp, more than thirty studies have considered the relationship between these two variables.[3] Many of the earlier studies seemed to have assumed implicitly that a positive relationship existed and that it was important to demonstrate that it in fact did exist. Little attention was given to trying to understand *why* job satisfaction should lead to higher performance; instead, researchers contented themselves with routinely studying the relationship between satisfaction and performance in a number of industrial situations.

The typical reader of the literature in the early fifties was probably aware of the fact that some studies had failed to find a significant satisfaction-performance relationship. Indeed, the very first study of the problem obtained an insignificant relationship.[4] However, judging from the impact of the first review of the literature on the topic, by Brayfield and Crockett, many social scientists, let alone practicing managers, were unaware that the evidence indicated how little relationship exists between satisfaction and performance.[5] The key conclusion that emerged from the review was that "there is little evidence in the available literature that employee attitudes bear any simple—or, for that matter, appreciable —relationship to performance on the job." (The review, however, pointed out that job satisfaction did seem to be positively related, as expected, to two other kinds of employee behavior, absenteeism and turnover.)

The review had a major impact on the field of industrial psychology and helped shatter the kind of naive thinking that characterized the earlier years of the Human Relations movement. Perhaps it also discouraged additional research, since few post-1955 studies of the relationship between satisfaction and performance have been reported in scientific journals.

Another review, covering much of the same literature, was completed about the same time.[6] This review took a more optimistic view of the evidence: ". . . there is frequent evidence for the often suggested opinion that positive job attitudes are favorable to increased productivity. The relationship is not absolute, but there are enough data to justify attention to attitudes as a factor in improving the worker's output. However, the correlations obtained in many of the positive studies were low."[7] This review also pointed out, as did Brayfield and Crockett, that there was a definite trend for attitudes to be related to absenteeism and turnover. Perhaps the chief reasons for the somewhat divergent conclusions reached by the two reviews were that they did not cover exactly the same literature and that Brayfield and Crockett were less influenced by suggestive findings that did not reach statistical significance. In any event, the one conclusion that was obvious from both reviews was that there was not the *strong, pervasive* relationship between job satisfaction and productivity that had been suggested by many of the early proponents of the Human Relations movement and so casually accepted by personnel specialists.

A more recent review of the literature by Vroom has received less attention than did the two earlier reviews,[8] perhaps because it is now rather generally accepted that satisfaction is not related to performance. However, before we too glibly accept the view that satisfaction and performance are unrelated, let us look carefully at the data from

3. Arthur Kornhauser and A. Sharp, Employee attitudes: Suggestions from a study in a factory, *Personnel Journal,* 10 (1932), 393-401.
4. Ibid.
5. Brayfield and Crockett, op. cit.
6. Frederick Herzberg, Bernard Mausner, R. O. Peterson, and Dora F. Capwell, *Job attitudes: Review of research and opinion* (Pittsburgh: Psychological Service, 1957).
7. Ibid., p. 103.
8. Victor H. Vroom, *Work and motivation* (New York: Wiley, 1964).

studies reviewed by Vroom. These studies show a median correlation of +.14 between satisfaction and performance. Although this correlation is not large, the consistency of the direction of the correlation is quite impressive. Twenty of the 23 correlations cited by Vroom are positive. By a statistical test such consistency would occur by chance less than once in a hundred times.

In summary, the evidence indicates that a low but consistent relationship exists between satisfaction and performance, but it is not at all clear *why* this relationship exists. The questions that need to be answered at this time, therefore, concern the place of job satisfaction both in theories of employee motivation and in everyday organizational practice. For example, should an organization systematically measure the level of employee satisfaction? Is it important for an organization to try to improve employee job satisfaction? Is there theoretical reason for believing that job satisfaction should be related to job behavior and if so, can it explain why this relationship exists?

WHY STUDY JOB SATISFACTION?

There are really two bases upon which to argue that job satisfaction is important. Interestingly, both are different from the original reason for studying job satisfaction, that is, the assumed ability of satisfaction to influence performance. The first, and undoubtedly the most straightforward reason, rests on the fact that strong correlations between absenteeism and satisfaction, as well as between turnover and satisfaction, appear in the previous studies. Accordingly, job satisfaction would seem to be an important focus of organizations which wish to reduce absenteeism and turnover.

Perhaps the best explanation of the fact that satisfaction is related to absenteeism and turnover comes from the kind of path-goal theory of motivation that has been stated by Georgopoulos, Mahoney and Jones; Vroom; and Lawler and Porter.[9]

According to this view, people are motivated to do things which they feel have a high probability of leading to rewards which they value. When a worker says he is satisfied with his job, he is in effect saying that his needs are satisfied as a result of having his job. Thus, path-goal theory would predict that high satisfaction will lead to low turnover and absenteeism because the satisfied individual is motivated to go to work where his important needs are satisfied.

A second reason for interest in job satisfaction stems from its low but consistent *association* with job performance. Let us speculate for a moment on why this association exists. One possibility is that, as assumed by many, the satisfaction *caused* the performance. However, there is little theoretical reason for believing that satisfaction can cause performance. Vroom, using a path-goal theory of motivation, has pointed out that job satisfaction and job performance are caused by quite different things: "... job satisfaction is closely affected by the amounts of rewards that people derive from their jobs and . . . level of performance is closely affected by the basis of attainment of rewards. Individuals are satisfied with their jobs to the extent to which their jobs provide them with what they desire, and they perform effectively in them to the extent that effective performance leads to the attainment of what they desire."[10]

RELATION BETWEEN SATISFACTION AND PERFORMANCE

Vroom's statement contains a hint of why, despite the fact that satisfaction and perfor-

9. Basil S. Georgopoulos, G. M. Mahoney, and N. W. Jones, A path-goal approach to productivity, *Journal of Applied Psychology*, 41 (1957), 345-53; Vroom, op. cit.; Edward E. Lawler and Lyman W. Porter, Antecedent attitudes of effective managerial performance, *Organizational Behavior and Human Performance*, 2 (1967), 122-43. See also Lyman W. Porter and Edward E. Lawler, *Managerial attitudes and performance* (Homewood, Ill.: Irwin-Dorsey, 1968).

10. Vroom, op. cit., p. 246.

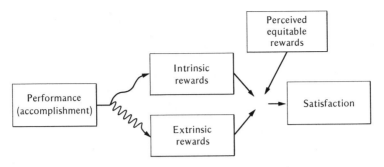

Fig. 3-1. The Theoretical Model

mance are caused by different things, they do bear some relationship to each other. If we assume, as seems to be reasonable in terms of motivation theory, that rewards cause satisfaction, and that in some cases performance produces rewards, then it is possible that the relationship found between satisfaction and performance comes about through the action of a third variable— rewards. Briefly stated, good performance may lead to rewards, which in turn lead to satisfaction; this formulation then would say that satisfaction, rather than causing performance, as was previously assumed, is caused by it. Figure 3-1 presents this thinking in a diagrammatic form.

This model first shows that performance leads to rewards, and it distinguishes between two kinds of rewards and their connection to performance. A wavy line between performance and extrinsic rewards indicates that such rewards are likely to be imperfectly related to performance. By extrinsic rewards is meant such organizationally controlled rewards as pay, promotion, status, and security—rewards that are often referred to as satisfying mainly lower level needs.[11] The connection is relatively weak because of the difficulty of tying extrinsic

rewards directly to performance. Even though an organization may have a policy of rewarding merit, performance is difficult to measure, and in dispensing rewards like pay, many other factors are frequently taken into consideration. Lawler, for example, found a low correlation between amount of salary and superiors' evaluation for a number of middle and lower level managers.[12]

Quite the opposite is likely to be true for intrinsic rewards, however, since they are given to the individual by himself for good performance. Intrinsic or internally mediated rewards are subject to fewer disturbing influences and thus are likely to be more directly related to good performance. This connection is indicated in the model by a semiwavy line. Probably the best example of an intrinsic reward is the feeling of having accomplished something worthwhile. For that matter, any of the rewards that satisfy self-actualization needs or higher order growth needs are good examples of intrinsic rewards.

The model also shows that intrinsic and extrinsic rewards are not directly related to job satisfaction since the relationship is moderated by expected equitable rewards. This variable refers to the level or amount of rewards that an individual feels he *should* receive as the result of his job performance.

11. Abraham H. Maslow, *Motivation and personality* (New York: Harper, 1954). According to Maslow, needs are arranged in a hierarchy, physiological and security needs being the lowest-level needs, social and esteem needs next, and autonomy and self-actualization needs the highest level.

12. Edward E. Lawler, Managers' attitudes toward how their pay is and should be determined, *Journal of Applied Psychology,* 50 (1966), 273-79.

Thus, an individual's satisfaction is a function both of the number and amount of the rewards he receives as well as what he considers to be a fair level of reward. An individual can be satisfied with a small amount of reward if he feels that it is a fair amount of reward for his job.[13]

This model would seem to predict that because of the imperfect relationship between performance and rewards and the importance of expected equitable rewards there would be a low but positive relationship between job satisfaction and job performance. The model also leads to a number of other predictions about the relationship between satisfaction and performance. If it turns out that, as this model predicts, satisfaction is dependent on performance, then it can be argued that satisfaction is an important variable from both a theoretical and a practical point of view despite its low relationship to performance. However, when satisfaction is viewed in this way, the reasons for considering it to be important are quite different from those that are proposed when satisfaction is considered to cause performance. But first, let us look at some of the predictions that are derivable from the model and at some data that were collected in order to test the predictions.

RESEARCH DATA

Usable data were collected from 148 middle and lower level managers in five organizations. One of the organizations was a large manufacturing company; the others were small social service and welfare agencies. As determined from the demographic data collected from each manager, the sample was typical of other samples of middle and lower level managers, with one exception—31 of the managers were female.

Two kinds of data were collected for each manager. Superior and peer rankings were obtained on two factors: (1) how hard the manager worked, and (2) how well the manager performed his job. Since a number of peers ranked each manager, the average peer's rankings were used for data analysis purposes. The rankings by the superiors and peers were in general agreement with each other, so the rankings met the requirements for convergent and discriminant validity. In addition to the superior and peer rankings each manager filled out an attitude questionnaire designed to measure his degree of satisfaction in five need areas. This part of the questionnaire was identical to the one used in earlier studies by Porter.[14] It consists of 13 items in the following form:

The opportunity for independent thought and action in my management position:

(a) How much is there now?
      (min) 1 2 3 4 5 6 7 (max)
(b) How much should there be?
      (min) 1 2 3 4 5 6 7 (max)

The answers to the first of these questions (a) for each of the 13 items was taken as the measure of need fulfillment or rewards received. The answer to the second of the questions (b) was taken as a measure of the individual's expected equitable level of rewards. The difference in answers between the second and first of these questions was taken as the operational measure of need satisfaction. That is, the larger the difference between "should" and "is now" in our findings, the greater the *dis*satisfaction.[15]

The 13 items, though presented in random order in the questionnaire, had been preclassified into five types of needs that have been described by Maslow: security, social, esteem, autonomy, and self-actualization.

13. Lyman W. Porter, A study of perceived need satisfactions in bottom and middle management jobs, *Journal of Applied Psychology*, 45 (1961), 1-10.

14. Ibid.
15. A third question about the importance of the various types of needs was also included, but the results based on it are not reported in the findings presented in this article.

PREDICTIONS AND RESEARCH RESULTS

Let us now consider two specific predictions that our model suggests. The first is that an individual's degree of need satisfaction is related to his job performance as rated by his peers and by his superior. A second prediction is that this relationship is stronger for managers than for nonmanagers.

The basis for this second prediction can be found in the assumed connection between rewards and performance. It seems apparent that most organizations have considerably more freedom to reward their managers differentially than they do their often unionized rank-and-file employees (unless the latter are on incentive pay plans). Even in a nonunionized organization (such as a governmental unit), management jobs generally offer the possibility of greater flexibility in differential rewards, especially in terms of prestige and autonomy in decision-making. Management jobs also typically provide greater opportunities to satisfy higher order intrinsic needs. As the model shows, satisfaction of these higher order needs is more closely tied to performance.

Satisfaction and Performance

Data collected from our sample of managers generally support the first two predictions. Job satisfaction (the sum of the difference scores for all 13 items) correlates significantly with both the superiors' rankings ($r = .32$, $p < .01$) and peers' rankings ($r = .30$, $p < .01$) of performance. Although the correlations are not large, they are substantially larger than the median correlation between satisfaction and performance at the level of rank-and-file workers ($r = .14$ as given in Vroom's review). It is possible that this higher relationship came about because we used a different measure of need satisfaction than has been typically used before or because we used a better performance mea-

sure. However, our belief is that it came about because the study was done at the management level in contrast to the previous studies which mainly involved nonmanagement employees. Neither our measure of job performance nor our measure of satisfaction would seem to be so unique that either could account for the higher relationship found between satisfaction and performance. However, future studies that use the same measure for both managers and nonmanagers are needed if this point is to be firmly established.

Satisfaction and Effort

An additional prediction from the model is that satisfaction should be more closely related to the rankings obtained on performance than to the rankings obtained on effort. The prediction is an important one for the model and stems from the fact that satisfaction is seen as a variable that is more directly dependent on performance than on effort. Others have pointed out that effort is only one of the factors that determines how effective an individual's performance will be. Ability factors and situational constraints are other obviously relevant determinants. It is also important to note that if we assume, as many previous writers have, that satisfaction causes performance then it would seem logical that satisfaction should be more closely related to effort than to performance. Satisfaction should influence an individual's performance by affecting his motivation to perform effectively, and this presumably is better reflected by effort than by job performance.

The results of the present study show, in fact, a stronger relationship between the superiors' rankings of performance and satisfaction ($r = .32$), than between the superiors' rankings of effort and satisfaction ($r = .23$). Similarly, for the peer rankings there is a stronger relationship between performance and satisfaction ($r = .30$), than between effort and satisfaction ($r = .20$).

Intrinsic and Extrinsic Rewards

The model suggests that intrinsic rewards that satisfy needs such as self-actualization are more likely to be related to performance than are extrinsic rewards, which have to be given by someone else and therefore have a weaker relationship between their reception and performance. Thus, the satisfaction should be more closely related to performance for higher than for lower order needs. Table 3-1 presents the data relevant to this point. There is a slight tendency for satisfaction of the higher order needs to show higher correlations with performance than does satisfaction with lower order needs. In particular, the highest correlations appear for self-actualization which is, of course, the highest order need, in the Maslow need hierarchy.

Table 3-1. Pearson Correlations Between Performance and Satisfaction in Five Need Areas

Needs	Rankings by	
	Superiors	Peers
Security	.21[a]	.17[b]
Social	.23[a]	.26[a]
Esteem	.24[a]	.16[b]
Autonomy	.18[b]	.23[a]
Self-actualization	.31[a]	.28[a]

a. $p < .01$
b. $p < .05$

Over-all, the data from the present study are in general agreement with the predictions based on the model. Significant relationships did appear between performance and job satisfaction. Perhaps even more important for our point of view, the relationship between satisfaction and performance was stronger than that typically found among blue-collar employees. Also in agreement with our model was the finding that satisfaction was more closely related to performance than to effort. The final prediction,

which was supported by the data, was that the satisfaction of higher order needs would be the most closely related to performance. Taken together then, the data offer encouraging support for our model and in particular for the assertion of the model that satisfaction can best be thought of as depending on performance rather than causing it.

IMPLICATIONS OF THE FINDINGS

At this point we can ask the following question: what does the strength of the satisfaction-performance relationship tell us about an organization? For example, if a strong positive relationship exists we would assume that the organization is effectively distributing differential extrinsic rewards based on performance. In addition, it is providing jobs that allow for the satisfaction of higher order needs. Finally, the poorer performers rather than the better ones are quitting and showing high absenteeism, since, as we know, satisfaction, turnover, and absenteeism are closely related.

Now let us consider an organization where no relationship exists between satisfaction and performance. In this organization, presumably, rewards are not being effectively related to performance, and absenteeism and turnover in the organization are likely to be equally distributed among both the good and poor performers. Finally, let us consider the organization where satisfaction and performance bear a negative relationship to each other. Here absenteeism and turnover will be greatest among the best performers. Furthermore, the poor performers would be getting more rewards than the good performers.

Clearly, most organization theorists would feel that organizational effectiveness is encouraged by rewarding good performers and by restricting turnover to poorer performers. Thus, it may be desirable for organizations to develop a strong relationship between satisfaction and performance. In effect, the argument is that the less positive relationship between satisfaction and performance in an organization, the less effective the organization will be (*ceteris paribus*). If this hypothesis were shown to be true, it would mean that a measure of the relationship between satisfaction and performance would be a helpful diagnostic tool for examining organizations. It is hardly necessary to note that this approach is quite different from the usual human relations one of trying to maximize satisfaction, since here we are suggesting trying to maximize the relationship between satisfaction and performance, rather than satisfaction itself.

One further implication of the model appears to warrant comment. It may well be that a high general level of satisfaction of needs like self-actualization may be a sign of organization effectiveness. Such a level of satisfaction would indicate, for instance, that most employees have interesting and involving jobs and that they probably are performing them well. One of the obvious advantages of providing employees with intrinsically interesting jobs is that good performance is rewarding in and of itself. Furthermore, being rewarded for good performance is likely to encourage further good performance. Thus, measures of higher order need satisfaction may provide good evidence of how effective organizations have been in creating interesting and rewarding jobs and, therefore, indirect evidence of how motivating the jobs themselves are. This discussion of the role of intrinsic rewards and satisfaction serves to highlight the importance of including measures of higher order need satisfaction in attitude surveys. Too often attitude surveys have focused only on satisfaction with extrinsic rewards, such as pay and promotion, and on the social relations which were originally stressed by the human relations movement.

In summary, we have argued that it is important to consider the satisfaction level that exists in organizations. For one thing, satisfaction is important because it has the power to influence both absenteeism and turnover. In addition, in the area of job performance we have emphasized that rather than being a cause of performance, satisfaction is caused by it. If this is true, and we have presented some evidence to support the view that it is, then it becomes appropriate to be more concerned about which people and what kind of needs are satisfied in the organization, rather than about how to maximize satisfaction generally. In short, we suggest new ways of interpreting job satisfaction data.

the route to high satis isn't the only route so high satis doesn't necessarily mean hiperf in interesting jobs

4
Evaluation of Research on Expectancy Theory Predictions of Employee Performance

HERBERT G. HENEMAN III and DONALD P. SCHWAB[1]

A central concern of industrial relations is the identification and measurement of factors associated with individual differences in employee job performance, since efficient utilization of manpower resources is dependent upon our ability to account for such differences. Recently, two statements of a theory of employee job performance, usually referred to as expectancy theory, have been advanced by Vroom (1964) and Porter and Lawler (1968). These formulations have stimulated considerable thought and research. Unfortunately, it appears that there is substantial confusion in interpretation of, and conduct of research on, the theory. Our purposes are thus to attempt to resolve this state of confusion and make suggestions for improvement in future research on expectancy theory.

In subsequent sections, Vroom's (1964) and Porter and Lawler's (1968) descriptions of the theory are summarized and shown to be quite similar. Nine field studies that have tested hypotheses of expectancy theory are the summarized. Finally, these studies are critically evaluated and recommendations are made for needed additional research.

1. The authors thank R. J. Adams, L. L. Cummings, and W. E. Scott, Jr., for their critical comments on an earlier draft of this paper.

THE THEORY

Vroom (1964) hypothesized that employee job performance P is a function of the interaction between force to perform F, or motivation, and ability A.

$$P = f(F \times A). \qquad [1]$$

Porter and Lawler (1968), alternatively, hypothesized that performance is a function of the three-way interaction among exerted effort *(E)*, or motivation, ability, and role perceptions *(R)*.

$$P = f(E \times A \times R). \qquad [2]$$

Conceptualizations of motivation, ability, and role perceptions are described below. While terminological differences exist between the two theories, the only substantive difference between them is the inclusion of role perceptions as an additional performance determinant by Porter and Lawler. For this reason, and for purposes of clarification, the theories are combined into one comprehensive framework, shown in Figure 4-1.

Force or Effort

In Vroom's formulation, force to exert effort level i is a function of the sum of the

Reprinted from *Psychological Bulletin*, 1972, 78, 1—9, by permission of the authors and the publisher.

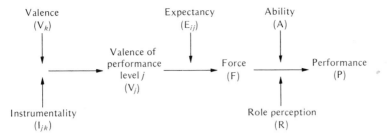

Fig. 4-1. Expectancy Theory Predictions of Job Performance, Based upon Vroom (1964) and Porter and Lawler (1968).

interactions between (a) the valence of each performance level (V_i) and (b) the perceived probability that an ith amount of effort will result in the achievement of each performance level; this perception is termed expectancy (E_{ij}).

$$F_i = f[\sum_{j=1}^{n}(V_j \times E_{ij})] \qquad [3]$$

It is hypothesized that the individual chooses the effort level exerting the strongest positive or weakest negative force.

A performance level (first-level outcome), in turn, acquires valence if it is perceived as leading to the attainment of valent second-level outcomes (V_k), such as pay and recognition. The perception that performance level j will result in the attainment of second-level outcome k is termed the instrumentality of the performance level (I_{jk}). The valence of performance level j is hypothesized to be a function of the sum of the interactions between (a) the valence of second-level outcomes and (b) the instrumentalities of the performance level.

$$V_j = f[\sum_{k=1}^{n}(V_k \times I_{jk})]. \qquad [4]$$

Porter and Lawler (1968) presented a theoretical treatment of motivation to perform, further refined by Lawler (1970), which is similar to Vroom's except for differences in terminology. Vroom's terminology, and the corresponding terminology by Porter and Lawler, is as follows: force (effort), valence of second-level outcomes (value of rewards), instrumentality

(performance-reward probability), and expectancy (effort-performance probability). The latter two form what Porter and Lawler term the effort-reward probability.[2] For expository convenience the terminology of Vroom is employed throughout the rest of this discussion.

Ability

Both Vroom (1964) and Porter and Lawler (1968) hypothesized that the individual's actual performance is additionally dependent upon his ability to perform. Vroom defined ability as characteristics of the individual that represent "a potential for performing some task which may or may not be utilized" (p. 198). Similarly, Porter and Lawler (1968) defined ability as "relatively stable, long-term individual characteristics (e.g., personality traits, intelligence, manual skills, etc.) that represent the individual's currently developed power to perform" (p.

2. Another apparent discrepancy between Vroom (1964) and Porter and Lawler (1968) is that the latter first multiply the effort-performance and performance-reward probabilities, and then multiply this product and value of rewards to form their definition of effort. In the case of only one second-level outcome, this procedure results in a definition of effort identical to Vroom's (1964) definition of force. With more than one second-level outcome, however, this procedure leads to a definitional discrepancy between Vroom and Porter and Lawler. Consistency with Vroom requires that the value of reward and performance-reward probabilities be multiplied and summed accross second-level outcomes, and that this total product be multiplied by the effort-performance probability. In his latest statement of expectancy theory, Lawler (1970) did combine the variables in this manner, and thus is consistent with Vroom.

22). In both models emphasis is placed on the individual's capacity, as opposed to his willingness, to perform at a task.

Role Perceptions

Porter and Lawler (1968) additionally included role perceptions as a determinant of performance. Role perceptions are defined as "the direction of effort—the kinds of activities and behaviors the individual believes he should engage in to perform his job successfully" (p. 24). Evaluation of these behaviors by his supervisor, however, is dependent upon the supervisor's role perceptions for the job. This suggests that accuracy of role perceptions may be a more important performance determinant than the individual's role perception per se.

THE EVIDENCE

Nine published field studies were found that investigated one or more hypotheses of expectancy theory using various measures of employee performance as the dependent variable. In reviewing these studies the terminology previously developed is employed. Reference to significant results indicates statistical significance at or beyond the .05 level. Critical evaluation of the studies is reserved for the following section since a number of the comments apply to more than one study.

Georgopolous, Mahoney, and Jones (1956) preceded Vroom's (1964) and Porter and Lawler's (1968) formulations by testing a portion of expectancy theory on 621 manufacturing operatives. Productivity was hypothesized to be a function of path-goal perceptions (i.e., instrumentality), level of need (i.e., valence), and freedom to alter one's performance behavior. Instrumentality and valence perceptions were obtained for three second-level outcomes. Freedom consisted of self-reported freedom, age, and length of service. Productivity was measured by subjects' reports of their productivity relative to established standards. A contingency problem format (Blalock, 1960) was

employed to compute main and "interaction" effects of the three independent variables. Generally, significant differences and "interactions" were obtained for the outcome "making more money in the long run." For example, the percentage of high producers was significantly greater for the high money need—positive path-goal perception group than the high money need—negative path-goal perception group.

Lawler (1966) investigated the effects of instrumentality and ability on the performance of 211 state government managers. Subjects were asked to indicate the instrumentality[3] of three factors (quality, productivity, and effort) for the determination of their pay. Responses to these items were summed to form a composite instrumentality index. Ability was measured by supervisor rankings of managerial qualifications. Supervisor rankings and self-ratings of performance served as dependent variables. The independent variables were dichotomized and a two-way analysis of variance was performed for each dependent variable. The main instrumentality effect was significant for both dependent variables; ability and interaction effects were each significant for one dependent variable.

Galbraith and Cummings (1967) obtained ratings of the valence of seven second-level outcomes, and the instrumentality of performance for their attainment, from 32 operatives in a manufacturing organization. Ability was measured by length of time on the job, and performance was measured by daily output as a percentage of standard averaged over a 1-month interval. The independent variables were dichotomized,

---

3. In this and several other studies (Gavin, 1970; Hackman and Porter, 1968; Lawler, 1968a; Lawler and Porter, 1967; Porter and Lawler, 1968), individuals were asked to indicate the relationship between "working hard" or "effort" and second-level outcomes. Their responses presumably represent the perceived effort-reward probability. As such, they confound the effort-performance (expectancy) and performance-reward (instrumentality) probabilities. For purposes of simplicity, however, such perceptions are referred to as instrumentality perceptions in this review.

coded in dummy variable format (including interaction variables), and subjected to stepwise multiple regression analysis. No valence, instrumentality, or ability variables entered any of the regression equations significantly, and only 6 of 54 possible interaction variables entered the equations significantly.

Lawler and Porter (1967) examined the effects of valence, instrumentality, role perceptions, and their interactions on the performance of 154 managers. Subjects were asked to indicate how instrumental three factors (effort, high productivity, and good job performance) were for the attainment of seven second-level outcomes and the valence of these outcomes. Responses to the instrumentality items were summed to form a composite instrumentality index. Role perceptions were obtained from 55 of the managers by having them rank 10 inner- and outer-directed traits (Riesman, 1950; Whyte, 1956) first on the basis of self-description and second on the basis of importance for success. Six criteria (three ratings of effort and three of performance) were obtained.

The median correlation between instrumentality and (a) performance was .11 and (b) effort was .18. Correlations between valence and the criteria were not reported. Out of 42 possible correlations between valence times instrumentality scores and the criteria, 29 were larger than the correlations between instrumentality and the criteria alone, 5 were the same, and 8 were smaller. Finally, high and low valence times instrumentality groups were formed, and correlations between role perceptions and performance were computed. Some of the correlations within groups were significant, but the correlations between groups were not significantly different. The results thus offer some support for the effects of role perceptions, but no support for the interaction of valence instrumentality and role perceptions.

Hackman and Porter (1968) obtained ratings of the instrumentality of working hard for the attainment of 18 second-level outcomes, and the valence of each outcome, from 82 female service representatives of a telephone company. Four summated scores were computed for each subject: valence, instrumentality, valence plus instrumentality, and valence times instrumentality. The scores were correlated with 10 subcriteria of job performance and a composite performance criterion. The median correlation between the 10 subcriteria and (1) valence was .16; (b) instrumentality was .11; (c) valence plus instrumentality was .17; (d) valence times instrumentality was .27. The correlation between valence times instrumentality and the composite criterion was a significant .40. Since the valence-instrumentality scores yielded greater correlations with performance than the other sets of scores, Hackman and Porter argued that the results tend to confirm the hypothesized valence-instrumentality interaction effect.

Lawler (1968a) used cross-lagged (Campbell and Stanley, 1963) and dynamic (Vroom, 1966) correlations analyses to test for casuality between valence-instrumentality perceptions and performance. Data were collected from 55 public service managers twice, with a 1-year interval between collections. Subjects indicated how instrumental two factors (working hard and quality of job performance) were for attaining six second-level outcomes and the valence of each outcome. Six composite valence-instrumentality scores were computed for each subject. Three measures of job performance were obtained. The cross-lagged correlation analysis suggested that valence instrumentality was more likely the cause, rather than the result, of job performance. The dynamic correlation analysis, however, generally did not preclude the possibility that some third variable was responsible for the results obtained from the cross-lagged analysis.

Porter and Lawler (1968) investigated the effects of valence of pay, instrumentality, and role perceptions on the performance of 635 managers. These variables were measured as in the Lawler and Porter (1967) study. Dependent measures were self-ratings and supervisory rankings of effort and performance. Hypotheses were tested by the significance of difference between mean performance and effort of managers giving the highest and lowest third of responses to the independent variable(s) in question. In general, the results offered some support for the main effects of instrumentality and role perceptions. Less support was obtained for hypothesized interaction effects.

Gavin (1970) investigated the impact of valence, instrumentality, ability; and role perceptions on the performance of 192 male and 175 female managerial candidates of an insurance company. Each subject was asked to indicate the instrumentality of two factors (good job performance and working hard) for attaining 21 second-level outcomes, and the valence of each outcome. A total composite valence-instrumentality score was computed for each subject. Based upon the work of Barrett (1966), two measures of role perceptions were obtained by the correlations between (a) the subject's and his supervisor's rating of the importance of 22 work behaviors for the subject's performance and (b) the subject's importance and self-descriptiveness ratings of the same behaviors. Ability was measured by a general "in-house" mental aptitude test. Performance was measured by supervisory ratings. Of the independent variables, only ability did not correlate significantly with performance. Multiple regression procedures suggested by Cohen (1968) also were used. Additive regression models generally yielded significant multiple correlations on the order of .30. Interaction variables generally did not significantly "contribute to" these multiple correlations, thus indicating little support for hypothesized interaction effects.

Goodman, Rose, and Furcon (1970) interviewed 66 employees of a government research organization to obtain indications of the three most valent second-level outcomes, the instrumentality of seven factors for attaining these outcomes, and the amount of job control (in order to infer expectancy). A measure of force (see Formula 3) was derived for each of the seven factors. Actual measures of success on four of these seven factors were obtained and correlated with the appropriate force measure. Significant correlations were obtained in each instance.

Summary

Nine field studies that tested hypotheses derived from expectancy theory were reviewed. Generally, valence, instrumentality, and role perceptions were significantly related to performance, while ability was not. Little support was obtained for hypothesized interactions among these variables.

DISCUSSION OF THE EVIDENCE

The review suggests that limitations of existing research pertain primarily to the variables investigated and their measurement and to the analytical procedures employed. Measurement criticisms are aimed at each major independent[4] variable in the theory (force, ability, and role perceptions). In the analysis section, research objectives are specified, and the analyses performed in several of the studies are criticized in light of these objectives.

Force To Perform

Expectancy theory clearly places greatest emphasis on the role of motivation or force to perform as a determinant of job performance. It is disconcerting to observe, therefore, that force has consistently been measured incorrectly in the studies reviewed. Either instrumentality (performance-reward probability) and expectancy (effort-performance probability) has not been clearly delineated, or only instrumentality has been measured directly. For example, Hackman and Porter (1968) confounded instrumentality and expectancy perceptions by asking respondents to specify the probable linkage

4. Discussion of the dependent measure, performance, is omitted because the problem permeates a variety of research problems in organizational settings and because excellent treatments are presented by Campbell, Dunnette, Lawler, and Weick (1970), Dunnette (1966), Guion (1965), Nagle (1953), and Ronan and Prien (1966).

between effort and second-level outcomes. Gavin (1970), Lawler (1966, 1968a), Lawler and Porter (1967), and Porter and Lawler (1968) obtained over-all perceived effort-reward and performance-reward probabilities. In each study the two probabilities were combined, again resulting in confounding. In the remaining three studies (Galbraith and Cummings, 1967; Georgopolous et al., 1957; Goodman *et al.*, 1970) only instrumentality perceptions were measured directly. Attempts were made to infer expectancy by considering the nature of the job on such dimensions as autonomy and self-control, but subjects were never asked to indicate directly their expectancy perceptions.

Additionally, in five of the studies (Gavin, 1970; Lawler, 1966, 1968a; Lawler and Porter, 1967; Porter and Lawler, 1968) instrumentality alone has been confounded. According to the theory, the perceived instrumentality of each first-level outcome should be related separately to measured success on that outcome (e.g., as done by Goodman *et al.*, 1970). For example, if "quality of job performance" is the first-level outcome, instrumentality perceptions of "quality of job performance" should be related empirically to actual "quality of job performance." Such a procedure was not followed in the five studies identified. Rather, managers rated the instrumentality of more than one first-level outcome, the ratings were combined to form a composite instrumentality index, and the composite index was related to actual success on various first-level outcomes.

Turning to valence, the number and type of second-level outcomes used in most of the studies may be questioned. Research on job satisfaction (e.g., Herzberg, Mausner, and Snyderman, 1959; Smith, Kendall, and Hulin, 1969; Vroom, 1964; Weiss, Dawis, England, and Lofquist, 1967) suggests that individuals experience a wide variety of satisfactions in work environments. These may be sorted (either conceptually or empirically) into a number of categories or factors, each of which may be viewed as a second-level outcome derived from participation in the organization and/or performance in a work role. A meaningful measure of force thus should tap valence and instrumentality perceptions for all relevant outcomes. The relevance of outcomes to the individuals under investigation, however, is difficult to determine a priori. This suggests that many outcomes should be included in the measure developed, or that preliminary investigation be conducted to determine the relevant second-level outcomes for the group studied. Unfortunately, the trend has been to include a few second-level outcomes without preliminary investigation.

Finally, the problem of stability of responses appears to be serious, although only two studies have investigated this type of reliability. Galbraith and Cummings (1967) obtained a test-retest reliability of .80 for instrumentality, but only .50 for valence over a one-month interval. Lawler (1968a) reported a test-retest reliability of .48 for valence-instrumentality responses over a one-year interval.

Ability

In only three studies has ability even been considered as an explanatory variable. Lawler (1966) measured ability by having supervisors rank subordinates on overall qualifications. This ranking correlated significantly with the supervisor's ranking of his subordinates on over-all job performance. Criterion contamination in some degree is likely, however, since both rankings were obtained from the same supervisor at the same time. Galbraith and Cummings (1967) defined ability as length of time on the job. The extent to which length of time on the job serves as a proxy for ability as defined, however, is at best unclear. Gavin (1970) used a psychometric ability measure. It did not correlate significantly with performance, nor did its interactions with force and role perceptions generally contribute significantly to the multiple correlations. In part, this was probably due to restriction of range since the measure was employed as a selection instrument by the organization. Gavin also argued that the measure may not tap the relevant intellectual capacities.

Future research requires experimentation with numerous psychometric ability measures. Use of these measures should be guided by the validity evidence of various aptitude and achievement tests used for predicting employee performance in a selection context (e.g., Ghiselli, 1966; Guion, 1965). In addition, given the broad definition of ability presented by Vroom (1964) and Porter and Lawler (1968), measures of interest, temperament, and personality also might be considered. Their use requires caution, however, for they generally have not correlated significantly with performance (Dunnette, 1966; Guion and Gottier, 1965; Nash, 1965), and they may tap motivational characteristics of individuals (Guion, 1965).

Role Perceptions

The effects of role perceptions have also been investigated in only three instances. Lawler and Porter (1967) and Porter and Lawler (1968) asked managers to rank a number of psychological traits in the order of perceived importance for determining success in their present position. By defining the traits with one word it is doubtful that even approximately equal meanings were triggered for all respondents (Stryker, 1958). Moreover, no attempt was made to tap role perception accuracy as defined by Porter and Lawler (1968).

Gavin's (1970) role perception measures appear to represent an improvement over Porter and Lawler's since Gavin employed more behaviorally descriptive items and included accuracy. Nevertheless, because the items that formed the basis of the measures were not developed with specific reference to the managerial positions investigated by Gavin, their relevance and completeness of description are open to question.

More attention should be devoted to accuracy of role perceptions in future research. Additionally, it seems that more

meaningful measures would concentrate on the inclusion of the job duties and objectives derived from detailed analysis of the specific job under consideration. It is these duties and requirements that ultimately define the individual's job and form the basis of his performance evaluation.

Statistical Analysis

Expectancy theory hypothesizes that performance is a function of several independent variables operating in an interactive fashion. Thus, it is reasonable to assume that analytical procedures performed in tests of the theory would indicate (a) the amount of performance variance explained by additive and interactive variables and (b) the extent to which hypothesized interactions among variables made independent, significant contributions to explained performance variance beyond their additive (main) effects (i.e., the "usefulness" of interaction variables, Darlington, 1968).

The procedures employed by Gavin (1970) is the best to date in terms of these analytical objectives. He regressed performance on the additive variables, and then the additive and interactive variables, to obtain estimates of performance variance explained and the usefulness of the interactions investigated. This procedure thus has much to commend it in future research on expectancy theory.

Lawler (1966) also obtained interpretable indications of interaction effects by performing a two-way analysis of variance. Dichotomization of independent variables, however, may have led to an understatement of effects. Moreover, computation of omega squared (Hays, 1963) would have been desirable to indicate the strength of main and interaction effects.

Lawler and Porter (1967), and Hackman and Porter (1968), correlated valence, instrumentality, or both with performance. Valence and instrumentality scores were than multiplied, and the product score was correlated with performance. Generally, the latter correlations exceeded the former. The significance of the increase was not reported, however, and the usefulness of the valence-instrumentality interaction is thus indeterminant. Goodman *et al.* (1970) and Lawler (1968a) merely correlated valence-instrumentality scores with performance, and thus there is no indication of the usefulness of those interactions.

Galbraith and Cummings (1967) stepwise regressed performance against all independent variables, which were dichotomized. Two problems may be noted with this approach. First, the reduction of continuous variables to dichotomous ones may have lowered possible predictability. Second, such a procedure does not necessarily indicate the usefulness of interaction variables. If an interaction variable enters a stepwise regression before one or more of its component variables, it is impossible to demonstrate that the interaction variable made a unique contribution to the multiple correlation beyond the additive effects of its component variables.

In the remaining studies (Georgopolous *et al.*, 1957; Porter and Lawler, 1968) significance of difference tests were performed on groups created by dichotomizing independent variable scores. Interactions, in turn, were assessed by performing significance of difference tests on the dependent variables between levels of one independent variable, within levels of one or more other independent variables. Such techniques are suboptimal for several reasons. First, dichotomization may result in an underestimate of possible effects. Second, no direct indications about the strengths of relationships are given. Third, it is difficult to precisely determine and convey interaction effects. Finally, a substantial number of significance tests are required, resulting in possible nonindependence of significance tests and an underestimate of the number of Type I errors.

CONCLUSIONS

Expectancy theory differs in several promising respects from much previous theorizing about the determinants of employee per-

formance. Campbell *et al.* (1970), for example, pointed out that the concept of force to perform focuses on the major classes of variables (valence, instrumentality, and expectancy) that determine motivated behavior. This is in direct contrast to other industrial motivation theories (e.g., Herzberg *et al.*, 1959; Maslow, 1965) that tend to emphasize only identification of second-level outcomes. Expectancy theory additionally includes ability and role perceptions as potential performance determinants. This multivariate approach seemingly has potential for increasing the proportion of explained variance in employee performance. Finally, interactions among independent variables are explicitly hypothesized, and presumably these interactions will account for significantly greater performance variance than additive formulations alone.

Unfortunately, these potential theoretical improvements have not been adequately reflected in the research. First, in only one study was a measure of force to perform developed according to its theoretical definition. Second, in only one study were measures of all three independent variables (force, ability, and role perceptions) included. The predictive power of the total theory is thus essentially unknown. Finally, while various interactions were supposedly computed in all of the studies, in only two was the contribution of the interactions to explained performance variance, beyond additive effects, appropriately computed. A minimum requirement for future research is thus that it avoid replication of these three general inadequacies in past research.

At the level of specific measurement issues, the review and discussion of the evidence warrants the following conclusions and suggestions for future research. First, in terms of force to perform, efforts should be made to incorporate an adequate number and type of second-level outcomes, and to develop measures of both instrumentality and expectancy that are more reflective of their corresponding constructs as defined by Vroom (1964) and Porter and Lawler (1968). Second, psychometrically sound ability measures should be employed. Finally, the development and use of behaviorally descriptive role-perception measures, and assessment of the impact of role perception accuracy, are required.

A noteworthy aspect of research on expectancy theory is the emphasis on investigating employees in their natural work environments, thus providing a high degree of external validity. In the case of motivation, this is in direct contrast to research on equity theory (Adams, 1965) and goal-setting theory (Locke, 1968), which has usually entailed student subjects working on laboratory tasks in experimental situations. The "cost" of external validity has been, of course, a general inability to make casual inferences. Lawler's (1968a) design exemplifies one potential compromise between the needs to study employees in their natural work environments and to obtain evidence that permits causal inferences. A variety of such designs are suggested by Campbell and Stanley (1963), and hopefully they will be used more fully in future research.

While there is an obvious need for substantial additional research on the validity of expectancy theory as formulated, work should also be performed on the determinants of valence, instrumentality, and expectancy perceptions. It has been hypothesized, for example, that the valence of second-level outcomes is a function of the satisfaction derived from their past attainment (Porter and Lawler, 1968) and their perceived equity (Lawler, 1968b). A number of specific variables have been hypothesized to influence instrumentality. In general, they all pertain to the nature of the actual relationships between performance and second-level outcomes, on the assumption that these "objective" relationships will influence instrumentality perceptions. This approach has been most noticeable in the discussions of compensation systems (Opsahl and Dunnette, 1966; Schneider and Olson, 1970). Recently it has been extended to considerations of job design as a means of more directly relating performance and intrinsic second-level outcomes (Lawler, 1969), and to considerations of the supervisor as a motivational agent to the extent that he can differentially reward the performance of his subordinates (Evans, 1970). In terms of expectancy determinants, Lawler (1970) hypothesized that past expectancy experiences and self-esteem influence expectancy. In addition, the nature of the task on such dimensions as difficulty, control over work pace, and length of job cycle may be important determinants. Considerably more theoretical and empirical work of this nature is necessary for the development of an expanded model of force to perform.

REFERENCES

Adams, J. S. Inequity in social exchange. In L. Berkowitz (Ed.), *Advances in experimental social psychology*. Vol. 2. New York: Academic Press, 1965.

Barrett, R. S. The influence of supervisor's requirements on ratings. *Personnel Psychology*, 1966, 19, 375-87.

Blalock, H. M. *Social statistics*. New York: McGraw-Hill, 1960.

Campbell, D. T., and Stanley, J. C. *Experimental and quasi-experimental designs for research*. Chicago: Rand-McNally, 1963.

Campbell, J. P., Dunnette, M. D., Lawler, E. E., and Weick, K. E. *Managerial behavior, performance, and effectiveness*. New York: McGraw-Hill, 1970.

Cohen, J. Multiple regression as a general data-analytic system. *Psychological Bulletin*, 1968, 70, 426-43.

Darlington, R. B. Multiple regression in psychological research and practice. *Psychological Bulletin*, 1968, 69, 161-82.

Dunnette, M. D. *Personnel selection and placement*. Belmont, Calif.: Wadsworth, 1966.

Evans, M. G. The effects of supervisory behavior on the path-goal relationship. *Organizational Behavior and Human Performance*, 1970, 5, 277-98.

Galbraith, J., and Cummings, L. L. An empirical investigation of the motivational determinants of task performance: Interactive effects between valence-instrumentality and motivation-ability. *Organizational Behavior and Human Performance*, 1967, 2, 237-57.

Gavin, J. F. Ability, effort, and role perception as antecedents of job performance. (Experimental publication system, manuscript number 190A) Washington, D.C.: American Psychological Association, 1970.

Georgopolous, B. S., Mahoney, G. M., and Jones, N.W. A path-goal approach to productivity. *Journal of Applied Psychology*, 1957, 41, 345-53.

Ghiselli, E. E. *The validity of occupational aptitude tests*. New York: Wiley, 1966.

Goodman, P. S., Rose, J. H., and Furcon, J. E. Comparison of motivational antecedents of the work performance of scientists and engineers. *Journal of Applied Psychology*, 1970, 54, 491-95.

Guion, R. M. *Personnel testing*. New York: McGraw-Hill, 1965.

Guion, R. M., and Gottier, R. F. Validity of personality measures in personnel selection. *Personnel Psychology*, 1965, 18, 135-64.

Hackman, J. R., and Porter, L. W. Expectancy theory predictions of work effectiveness. *Organizational Behavior and Human Performance*, 1968, 3, 417-26.

Hays, W. L. *Statistics for psychologists*. New York: Holt, Rinehart & Winston, 1963.

Herzberg, F., Mausner, B., and Snyderman, B. *The motivation to work*. New York: Wiley, 1959.

Lawler, E. E. Ability as a moderator of the relationship between job attitudes and job performance. *Personnel Psychology*, 1966, 19, 153-64.

Lawler, E. E. A correlational–causal analysis of the relationship between expectancy attitudes and job performance. *Journal of Applied Psychology*, 1968, 52, 462-68.(a)

Lawler, E. E. Equity theory as a predictor of productivity and work quality. *Psychological Bulletin*, 1968, 70, 596-610.(b)

Lawler, E. E. Job design and employee motivation. *Personnel Psychology*, 1969, 22, 426-35.

Lawler, E. E. Job attitudes and employee motivation: Theory, research, and practice. *Personnel Psychology*, 1970, 23, 223-38.

Lawler, E. E., and Porter, L. W. Antecedent attitudes of effective managerial job performance. *Organizational Behavior and Human Performance*, 1967, 2, 122-42.

Locke, E. A. Toward a theory of task motivation and incentives. *Organizational Behavior and Human Performance*, 1968, 3, 157-89.

Maslow, A. *Eupsychian management*. Homewood, Ill.: Irwin-Dorsey, 1965.

Nagle, B. F. Criterion development. *Personnel Psychology*, 1953, 6, 271-89.

Nash, A. N. Vocational interests of effective managers: A review of the literature. *Personnel Psychology*, 1965, 18, 21-37.

Opsahl, R. L., and Dunnette, M. D. The role of financial compensation in industrial motivation. *Psychological Bulletin*, 1966, 66, 94-118.

Porter, L. W., and Lawler, E. E. *Managerial attitudes and performance*. Homewood, Ill.: Irwin-Dorsey, 1968.

Riesman, D. *The lonely crowd*. New Haven: Yale University Press, 1950.

Ronan, W. W., and Prien, E. P. *Toward a criterion theory*. Greensboro, N. C.: Richardson Foundation, Creativity Research Institute, 1966.

Schneider, B., and Olson, L. K. Effort as a correlate of organizational reward system and individual values. *Personnel Psychology*, 1970, 23, 313-26.

Smith, P. E., Kendall, L. M., and Hulin, C. L. *The measurement of satisfaction in work and retirement*. Chicago: Rand-McNally, 1969.

Stryker, P. On the meaning of executive qualities. *Fortune*, 1958, 57, 116-19.

Vroom, V. H. *Work and motivation*. New York: Wiley, 1964.

Vroom, V. H. A comparison of static and dynamic correlation methods in the study of organizations. *Organizational Behavior and Human Performance*, 1966, 1, 55-70.

Weiss, D. J., Dawis, R. V., England, G. W., and Lofquist, L.H. *Manual for the Minnesota Satisfaction Questionnaire*. Minneapolis: Industrial Relations Center, University of Minnesota, 1967.

Whyte, W. H. *The organization man*. New York: Simon and Schuster, 1956.

5

Improving Job Performance
Through Training in Goal Setting

GARY P. LATHAM and SYDNEY B. KINNE III[1]

Research on goal-setting theory (Locke, 1968) has been criticized for its lack of emphasis on investigating employee behavior in a natural work environment (Heneman and Schwab, 1972). Data supporting the theory are based largely on laboratory experiments in which the dependent variable is typically a task requiring simple addition. As Campbell, Dunnette, Lawler, and Weick (1970) have stated, the differences between college students solving addition problems and the behavior of workers in industrial settings must be considered.

Criticism on the theory's lack of external validity is not completely justified. Latham and Ronan (1970) factor analyzed data obtained from a random sample of 292 pulpwood producers. The results showed that goal setting and supervision loaded on the same factor as two measures of production (positive) and one measure of injuries

(negative). Goal setting without supervision loaded on the only factor containing measures of turnover (positive). Supervision that did not include goal setting loaded on a third factor that did not include any criterion variables. No relationship was found between goal setting or supervision and absenteeism.

Although zero-order correlations between the previously mentioned independent and dependent variables were generally significant at the .05 level, the values were quite low. In order to corroborate these results, Latham and Kinne (1971) collected data on 892 additional producers and conducted an analysis of variance on the man-hour production. The results indicated that producers who supervise their employees and set production goals have higher productivity than producers who supervise their men but do not set production goals. In summarizing the results of these two studies, Ronan, Latham, and Kinne (1973) interpreted their findings as supporting Locke's (1966) contention that supervision leads to superior performance only insofar as it results in the establishment of specific performance goals. However, supervision, as defined by staying on the job with the crew, is required to

1. This study is based in part on a technical report written by the authors for the American Pulpwood Association, Harvesting Research Project. The opinions expressed herein are those of the authors and do not necessarily reflect the position of the American Pulpwood Association or the Georgia Kraft Company. The authors are grateful to Edwin A. Locke and Gary A. Yukl for reading and commenting on an earlier draft of this manuscript.

insure that the worker accepts these goals. Goal setting without the presence of supervision may lead to an increase in labor turnover.

A limitation of the above studies is that both were correlational in nature. In no instance was the independent variable manipulated by the authors. The purpose of the present study was to determine the effects of a one-day training program in goal setting on the job performance of pulpwood workers. The primary criteria for measuring the effectiveness of the program were cords-per-sawhand-hour and cords-per-crew-hour production. Additional criteria included measures of turnover, absenteeism, and injuries.

METHOD

Sample

Twenty-six producers and their crews were selected and matched on the following variables: (a) crew size, (b) cords-per-man-hour production, (c) geographic location, (d) logging system, (e) delivery point, (f) sawhand function, (g) delivery system, (h) number of hours the producer spent on the job site with the crew, and (i) "did not previously set a daily, weekly, or monthly production goal." One crew from each pair was randomly assigned to the training group; the remaining subjects constituted a control group. The method of payment for both groups was their normal piece-rate system. No monetary or nonmonetary bonus other than verbal praise was tied to goal attainment.

Procedure

Seven company foresters who were aware of the aims and objectives of the producer's job, who frequently observed the producer on the job site and who were well-known by the producers, were given instruction in training. A three-hour program was conducted in which the purpose of the experiment and the assumptions underlying it were explained. This program was followed by an intensive discussion period.

Each forester contacted the selected producers and requested their participation in the study. The explanation given to the experimental and control groups was similar: Each was told that they would be participating in a research program, that the study would last three months, that they were under no obligation to enter the program, and that they could leave the program at any time. The essential difference in the instructions to the two groups was that the experimental subjects were told that the purpose of the study was to give them a one-day training program in learning to set production goals and to determine its effects on performance. The control subjects were told that the study was designed to determine the effects of injuries, absenteeism, and turnover on production.

Three producers assigned to the experimental group expressed an unwillingness to participate in the study. This nonparticipation necessitated the removal of the 3 control producers who had been paired with them. Thus, the results of this study are based on 20 producers.

Training in goal setting was based on the premise that increasing the performance of the sawhand results in an increase in the productivity of the crew. This premise was based on the fact that the felling of a tree is vital to achieving the remaining tasks in pulpwood harvesting. By using regression equations that had been developed from actual field measurements to predict cords per man-hour and number of trees cut per sawhand-hour, production tables were constructed to systematically establish production goals.[2] These tables took into account

2. These equations were developed by Georgia Kraft Company prior to this study. Time studies were made of more than 300 logging operations on varying harvesting conditions. The resulting production goal may be characterized as moderate in difficulty in that average to above average production is necessary in order to achieve the goal. Information concerning these tables can be obtained from the second author.

factors that could affect production due to differences in harvesting stand conditions.

On the first working day of each week, the trainer visited the experimental and control producers on the job site. The average diameter breast height based on 30 to 40 trees to the nearest inch was determined for the harvesting area. By using the table which represented the sawhand function and stand condition, a production goal in trees per sawhand hour was determined for the existing day and/or week. This goal was explained to the producers in the experimental group who in turn explained it to their sawyers. This goal was stressed as a minimum standard of acceptable performance; however, no penalties were provided for failure to attain the goal. The production goal was not made known to producers in the control group.

Tally meters were provided for the sawyers in the experimental group so that they could constantly monitor or evaluate their performance. The assumption at this point was that each number accumulated on the tally meter provides information feedback to the employee and thus is reinforcing for the individual. The possible confounding effects of goal feedback with goal setting were considered minimal, since previous research has shown that knowledge of score alone does not lead to higher performance unless it is used to set goals (Locke, Cartledge, and Kneer, 1970; Locke, Cartledge, and Koeppel, 1968).

Producers in both the experimental and control groups were given a form similar to that used by Latham (1971) to record production, turnover, absenteeism, and injuries. The only difference between the form given to the experimental group and that given to the control group was that the former contained an item requesting information concerning the production goal. The trainer had a questionnaire on which the production goal for the control group was recorded. These forms served the same purpose as the tally meter for the sawyer, namely, knowledge of results to the producer.

Data were collected for 14 consecutive weeks. The three-month study period was employed in order to determine the effects of the one-day training program over a considerable length of time. The results of only 12 weeks were retained, inasmuch as mill shutdowns occurred in 2 of these weeks, and hence the majority of the sample were unable to deliver timber.

RESULTS

The results of this study were based on six performance scores. The two primary criteria, cords per sawhand-hour and cords per crew-hour, were based on the arithmetic difference between actual production and expected (goal) production for the sawhand and the crew. Expected production was the assigned performance goal determined from the production tables.

The four remaining criteria included measures of turnover, absenteeism, and injuries. Turnover was defined by two measures, namely, the number of men who quit and the number of men who were fired. Each of these variables was divided by the total number of men in the producer's work force. Injury rate was defined as the number of men hurt on the job who missed eight or more hours of work. Absenteeism was defined as the number of men off the job eight or more hours for reasons other than an injury. Both of these variables were divided by the number of men in the crew. These definitions are identical to those used in a previous study by Latham (1971).

An analysis of variance was conducted to determine the significance of goal setting and weeks on the production of the individual sawhands. The difference in production between the group of sawyers who received training in goal setting and the control group was in the expected direction but the difference was only marginally significant ($F = 3.43$, $df = 1/9$, $p < .10$). The performance means and standard deviations of the individual sawyers in the experimental and control group are shown in Table 5-1. The effect of weeks and the Weeks × Treatment interaction (goal training) was not significant.

A similar analysis was performed on the cords-per-man-hour production for the entire crew. First, this analysis provided a test of a key assumption in this study, namely, that increasing the productivity of the sawyer results in an increase in the productivity of the crew. In general, there is only one sawyer in a crew ranging in size from two to eight men. Second, the analysis provided a test of the balance of the producer's operation in terms of the number of his employees and his equipment. The results showed that the performance of the experimental crews was significantly higher than that of the control group ($F = 7.44$, $df = 1/9$, $p < .05$), thus supporting the assumption that the sawyer has a key position in the producer's work force. Again, the effects of weeks and the Weeks × Goal Setting interaction were not significant. Thus, it may be concluded that goal setting leads to a significant increase in the productivity of the group as well as the individual. Table 5-2 shows the means and standard deviations for each crew.

The finding that the difference between the experimental and control crews was at a higher level of significance than that between experimental and control sawyers is noteworthy. This result underscores the importance of a well-balanced harvesting system in terms of manpower and equipment. Any improvement in performance in one function in harvesting, even if only slight, can have an appreciable effect on the total performance of the operation when its effects are distributed (and hence magnified) over a well-balanced operation. Conversely, if performance in one function is greatly improved, its effects on the entire system are nullified to the extent that the operation is unbalanced.

Table 5-1. Summary of Differences Between Goal and Actual Performance for Sawhand in Cords per Sawhand-hour

Pro- ducer pair	Treated		Control	
	$\bar{X}$	SD	$\bar{X}$	SD
1	2.05	.43	.58	.83
2	−.25	.58	−.11	.69
3	.20	.56	−.17	.48
4	.02	.79	−.13	.73
5	.20	.45	.05	.61
6	.64	.97	−.09	.43
7	.36	.58	−.45	.59
8	1.26	.63	1.68	.68
9	.69	.88	−.21	.93
10	.44	.35	.86	.57

Table 5-2. Summary of Differences Between Goal and Actual Performance for Crews in Cords per Man-hour

Pro- ducer pair	Treated		Control	
	$\bar{X}$	SD	$\bar{X}$	SD
1	.23	.04	.09	.15
2	−.09	.21	−.09	.29
3	.05	.20	−.08	.17
4	.05	.20	−.07	.20
5	.04	.09	.01	.11
6	.13	.20	−.02	.12
7	.08	−.14	−.16	.22
8	.22	.11	.24	.10
9	.08	.12	−.07	.29
10	.11	.07	.13	.12

Two-way analyses of variance (tables are not shown) were conducted to determine the effects of a month (four weeks) and goal setting on turnover, absenteeism, and injuries. No significant differences were found between months. Moreover, goal setting had no significant effect on the two measures of turnover or injuries. The number of people who quit or were fired or injured was very low in both groups. Absenteeism, however, was significantly higher ($p < .05$) in the control group than in the experimental group.

DISCUSSION

The present study has shown that training in goal setting can lead to an increase in production and a decrease in absenteeism. The theoretical advantage of approaching the problem of worker motivation through goal setting is that it is not dependent on the use of mythological terms such as id, ego, and superego; nor does goal setting postulate personality mechanisms, or drive states, or separate and distinct factors independent of each other that contribute differentially to short-term and long-term performance. However, goal setting, as a theory of motivation, does focus on variables intrinsic to the job, namely, the job task(s) itself. It is based on a learning model in that the worker must be taught to set a task objective and he should be given information feedback concerning his performance. Knowledge of results provides meaning to a task. It is probable that tree counting in the present study enabled the sawyer to obtain a sense of achievement. The number of trees cut assumed meaning in that the worker was able to determine the extent to which his performance was above average. It may have been this "meaningful" dimension that contributed to the lower absenteeism in the goal-training group, that is, goal setting led to effective performance, effective performance led to job satisfaction, and job satisfaction led to a reduction in absenteeism.

The use of the production tables as a systematic method for setting production goals is of theoretical importance. Work on levels of aspiration has shown that if the individual sets a performance goal before carrying out a task, he tends to raise the goal if he is successful, since he increases his expectations of himself (Lewin, 1951). Thus, to improve one's performance one must first aspire but to aspire one must see

that success is possible, that is, clear evidence must be available that others under similar conditions are succeeding. The production tables were based on data collected from a large number of sawyers and hence provided this evidence. The sawyer knows that the goal is attainable and that it is not based on the whim of a demanding supervisor or on the unrealistic expectations that he himself has.

While there is an obvious need for additional research on the validity of goal-setting theory, the situation is by no means as serious as previous researchers have led us to believe. As a theory of motivation, goal setting appears to be effective in an industrial setting, and its effects appear to hold over time. A possible limitation of training in goal setting is that it is too simplistic for a complex situation, that is, it leads to a significant improvment in the performance of the average or above average worker, but it does little for the worker who is badly in need of a comprehensive training program. Nevertheless, even in such instances the supervisor who sets a specific task goal for his subordinates is in effect making it clear what it is they are supposed to do (Campbell et al., 1970). Thus, in the process of discussing with the worker the nature of these goals, the worker may acquire specific knowledge concerning his job tasks, their priorities, and the most effective methods that lead to their attainment.

REFERENCES

Campbell, J. P., Dunnette, M. D., Lawler, E. E., and Weick, K. E. *Managerial behavior, performance, and effectiveness.* New York: McGraw-Hill, 1970.

Heneman, H. G., III, and Schwab, D. P. Evaluation of research on expectancy theory predictions of employee performance. *Psychological Bulletin*, 1972, 78, 1-9.

Latham, G. P. *Indicators of productivity, turnover, absenteeism, and injuries.* Atlanta: American Pulpwood Association, Harvesting Research Project, 1971.

Latham, G. P., and Kinne, S. B., III. *Goal setting as a means of increasing the performance of the pulpwood harvester.* Atlanta: American Pulpwood Association, Harvesting Research Project, 1971.

Latham, G. P., and Ronan, W. W. *The effects of goal setting and supervision on the motivation of pulpwood workers.* Atlanta: American Pulpwood Association, Harvesting Research Project, 1970.

Lewin, K. *Field theory in social science: Selected theoretical paper.* New York: Harper, 1951.

Locke, E. A. The relationship of intentions to level of performance. *Journal of Applied Psychology,* 1966, 50, 60-66.

Locke, E. A. Toward a theory of task motivation and incentives. *Organizational Behavior and Human Performance,* 1968, 3, 157-89.

Locke, E. A., Cartledge, N., and Knerr, C. S. Studies of the relationship between satisfaction, goal setting, and performance. *Organizational Behavior and Human Performance,* 1970, 5, 135-58.

Locke, E. A., Cartledge, N., and Koeppel, J. Motivational effects of knowledge of results: A goal-setting phenomenon? *Psychological Bulletin,* 1968, 70, 474-85.

Ronan, W. W., Latham, G. P., and Kinne, S. B., III. The effects of goal setting and supervision on worker behavior in an industrial situation. *Journal of Applied Psychology,* 1973, 58, 302-7.

6

Using Pay To Motivate Job Performance

EDWARD E. LAWLER III

The research evidence reviewed so far and the Motivation Model clearly indicate that under certain conditions pay can be used to motivate good performance. The required conditions are deceptively simple and obvious when they are drawn from the model. They are deceptively simple in the sense that establishing the conditions is easier said than done. Theory and research suggest that for a pay plan to motivate people, it must (1) create a belief among employees that good performance will lead to high pay, (2) contribute to the importance of pay, (3) minimize the perceived negative consequences of performing well, and (4) create conditions such that positive outcomes other than pay will be seen to be related to good performance. In this chapter, we shall consider some of the problems an organization confronts when it tries to set up a pay system that will satisfy these four conditions. We shall not, however, go into the second condition—the importance of pay—in detail. Of the other three conditions, the first is the most basic; it is the central issue around which any discussion of pay and motivation must revolve. We shall approach this issue by asking the following questions: To what degree is pay actually tied to performance in organizations? Do employees feel that pay should be tied to performance? Which of the various ways of tying pay to performance lead most directly to the establishment of the conditions that must exist if pay is to motivate job performance?

TYING PAY TO PERFORMANCE

One obvious means of creating the perception that pay is tied to performance is actually to relate pay closely to job performance and to make the relationship as visible as possible. Several studies have attempted to determine the degree to which this is done in organizations and have come up with some unexpected results. Their evidence indicates that pay is not very closely related to performance in many organizations that claim to have merit increase salary systems. Lawler and Porter (1966) show that pay is related to job level, seniority, and other non-performance factors. Svetlik, Prien, and Barrett (1964) show that there is a negative relationship between amount of salary and performance as evaluated by superiors. Lawler (1964) shows that managers' pay is relatively unrelated to superiors' performance evaluations. Meyer,

Kay, and French (1965) show that managers' raises are not closely related to what occurs in their performance appraisal sessions.

Studies by Haire, Ghiselli, and Gordon (1967) and by Brenner and Lockwood (1965) also indicate that at the managerial level, pay is not always related to performance. The evidence in both these studies consists of salary history data; they point up some interesting tendencies. Haire *et al.,* for example, have established that the raises managers get from one year to another often show no correlation with each other. If the companies were tying pay to performance, the lack of correlation would mean that a manager's performance in one year was quite different from his performance in another year. This assumption simply does not fit with what is known about performance: A manager who is a good performer one year is very likely to be a good performer the next. Thus, we must conclude that the companies studied were not tying pay to performance. Apparently, pay raises were distributed on a random basis, or the criteria for awarding raises were frequently changed. As a result, recent raises were often not related to past raises or to performance.

Over-all, therefore, the studies suggest that many business organizations do not do a very good job of tying pay to performance. This conclusion is rather surprising in light of many companies' very frequent claims that their pay systems are based on merit. It is particularly surprising that pay does not seem to be related to performance at the managerial level. Here there are no unions to contend with, and one would think that if organizations were effectively relating pay to performance for any group of employees, it would be at the managerial level. Admittedly this conclusion is based on sketchy evidence, and future research may prove it to be wrong. It may be, for instance, that pay is indirectly tied to performance and that the tie is obscured by promotion policies. All the studies reviewed here looked at the relationship between pay and performance within one management level. Even though there is no relationship between pay and performance within a level, there may actually be a relationship if the better performing managers are promoted and because of this receive higher pay. There is little evidence, however, to suggest that this is true.

Failure to tie pay closely to performance in many companies could mean that pay is not motivating job performance. In order for pay to motivate performance, it must appear to be related to performance; and employees are not likely to believe that pay is related to performance if it actually is not. Lawler (1967b) has shown that in one instance where pay was not related to performance, mangers were aware of this fact and, consequently, were not motivated by pay. This study also showed that in a group of organizations where measurements indicated that pay was only marginally tied to performance, managers had a fairly high belief that pay was related to performance. Thus, the data suggest that, given some positive indicators, employees are willing to believe that pay is based upon performance. Often, however, the positive indicators are missing, and as a result, pay does not motivate the employees to perform effectively.

DO EMPLOYEES WANT PAY TO BE BASED UPON PERFORMANCE?

One reason pay is not closely related to performance in many organizations may simply be that employees object to this way of handling pay. If employees object to seeing their pay tied to their performance, there can be real problems in trying to implement any kind of merit pay system, since it could be and, in fact, would probably be undermined by the employees themselves. One of the clearest findings that comes out of the research on incentive systems like the Scanlon Plan is that these plans work best when the employees want the plan and when they trust management (Whyte, 1955). Thus, the issue of whether employees in general are favorably inclined toward incentive plans is a crucial one when consideration is given to using pay as a motivator.

Two studies have measured managers' attitudes toward how their pay should be determined, and both show that managers prefer to have their pay based upon performance. Lawler (1967b), for example, found that managers believe that performance should be the most important determinant of their pay, but feel that in fact it is not. There was a consistent tendency across all companies for there to be a large gap between how important managers felt performance was in determining pay and how important they felt it should be. This gap between what should be and what was reflects the inability of the companies to develop pay plans that fit the needs of employees. It also indicates that pay could be a much stronger source of motivation in these organizations. In one sense this gap represents a challenge to management to develop a more motivating pay system.

Andrews and Henry (1963) have also presented data to show that managers prefer to have their pay based upon performance. Perhaps the most interesting finding they reported was a tendency for educational level to be related to preferences. Less-educated managers were less in favor of having their pay based upon performance than more highly educated managers. This finding also is congruent with evidence that blue-collar employees are somewhat less enthusiastic about having their pay based upon performance than are managers. But before the studies concerned with blue-collar employees are discussed in detail, a study of salesmen should be mentioned. It shows that they, like the managers, prefer to have their pay based upon general performance and merit rather than upon such factors as seniority and market competition (Research Institute of America, 1965).

Studies done among blue-collar workers to determine their preferences with respect to pay plans, do not show overwhelming acceptance of merit-based plans. The studies are a little difficult to interpret, however, since many of them asked for reactions to specific pay plans, such as piece-rate plans, rather than to the general idea of merit-based pay. Workers might, for example, object to piece-rate plans but still favor other kinds of merit-based systems. Thus, it is hard to tell if the workers studied objected to the principle of merit pay or to the specific plans queried.

Two studies provide strong evidence that often workers are not favorably inclined toward incentive pay schemes. A large-scale study by the Opinion Research Corporation (1949) found that, although workers felt that incentive plans got the highest output per man, 65 per cent of the respondents preferred hourly pay plans. Similarly, a study in Great Britain by Davis (1948) found that 60 per cent of the workers sampled were opposed to a system of payment based on results. There is evidence that opposition to incentive plans is lower among workers who have been working on such plans. In the Opinion Research Corporation study (1949), for example, 59 per cent of the workers who had been on incentive plans opposed them while 74 per cent of the workers who had been on hourly wages opposed incentive plans. Other studies show that incentive plans are usually endorsed by workers already on them, and suggest that in some instances the majority of workers favor them. A study reported by *Factory* (1947), for example, reports that 59 per cent of the workers sampled who were not paid on an incentive basis said "they would like to work under such a system if it were fairly run." This finding suggests that employees in general are not against pay based upon performance, although they might be against certain merit pay systems. The results of another study by the Opinion Research Corporation (1946) are presented in Table 6-1. They show the same pattern: Workers on merit plans prefer such plans, and workers on hourly rates prefer them. The

Table 6-1.   Replies to Question: "On a job which could be paid by either piece rate or hourly rate, which would you rather work on?" (Opinion Research Corporation, 1946)

	No. of Mfg. Manual Workers	Percentage Who Prefer		
		piece rate	hourly rate	do not know
Total	919	36	61	3
Paid by:				
Hourly rate	658	24	73	3
Incentive plan	131	57	39	4
Piece rate	130	75	22	3
Union status:				
No union where work	220	43	53	4
Have union	699	34	63	3
Members	597	33	65	2
Nonmembers	102	35	54	11

data show, however, that overall only 36 per cent of the workers studied prefer piece-rate plans. It is possible that a far larger proportion would be in favor of merit pay in principle, but would not prefer the piece-rate plan to an hourly pay rate.

Beer and Gery (undated) have carefully analyzed what determines whether an employee will prefer merit-based pay. Their data suggest that individual preferences are influenced by a person's needs and by the situation in which he finds himself. Employees high in advancement and responsibility needs seemed to prefer merit systems; those with strong security needs did not. The more competent the individual, the better his past experience with the system, and the better his relationship with his boss, the more he preferred merit-based pay. Jones and Jeffrey (1964) have found that in one plant workers strongly preferred incentive pay schemes, while in another they strongly rejected the idea of incentive pay. Considered together, this evidence suggests that workers are not necessarily opposed to incentive schemes, but that the situation in which they work and their work history may lead them to oppose them. Presumably in many situations opposition to incentive pay comes about because the employees feel

they cannot trust the company to administer incentive shemes properly.

Over-all, the studies indicate that workers are less favorably disposed toward merit pay plans than are managers; in fact, the majority of the work force in many organizations may be against them. This conclusion has important practical implications for management. Clearly, to install an incentive plan successfully at the worker level will be difficult. A lot of effort may have to be devoted to building up a relationship of trust between management and workers, and to explaining the particular plan to be instituted as well as the whole concept of incentive pay. To install an incentive plan at the management level may be much easier, since the value system of managers appears to be more congruent with the idea of merit pay.

No incentive pay plan will ever work at any level in an organization unless superiors are committed to the plan and are willing to see their subordinates paid different amounts of money based upon their performance. Superiors must provide a large part of the performance information upon which pay decisions are based. If superiors reject systems that reward people according to their performance, then they are unlikely to provide valid performance evaluations and it will be impossible to base pay upon performance. The evidence indicates, however, that, in general, at least in the United States, managers in business organizations are willing to base pay upon performance. There is some evidence to suggest that good managers are much more amenable to the idea than poor managers, but still, the generalization holds (Gruenfeld and Weissenberg, 1966). It is, of course, consistent with the research that shows managers generally in favor of basing pay on merit.

Some preliminary evidence indicates that there may be cross-cultural differences among managers in their attitudes and values concerning pay. My own research shows that English managers are less willing to distribute pay on the basis of performance than American managers. In making pay-raise decisions, the English respondents seem to give much greater weight to nonperformance factors, such as seniority and family situation. Similar findings for other European countries have been reported by Bass (1968). If these preliminary findings are confirmed by future studies, the possibility of using pay to motivate people may be more limited than is frequently suggested. To base pay on performance in many countries, an organization would probably have to undertake a tremendous educational program among managers as well as workers. Even then they might find it ineffective because it conflicts with the basic values of the people.

METHODS OF RELATING PAY TO PERFORMANCE

There are virtually as many methods of relating pay to performance as there are organizations, and at times it seems that every organization is in the process of changing its approach. The R.I.A. (1965) study found, for example, that one out of every three companies has "recently" changed its method of paying salesmen.

Campbell, Dunnette, Lawler, and Weick (1970) report that their survey of company personnel practices showed widespread dissatisfaction with current pay systems. Such dissatisfaction is hardly surprising in light of the previously reported finding that pay is not closely related to performance in many companies. It is doubtful, however, that the problems and the dissatisfaction can be corrected simply by changing the mechanics of the plan already in use. Many plans seem to fail not because they are mechanically defective, but because they were ineffectually introduced, there is a lack of trust between superiors and subordinates, or the quality of supervision is too low. No plan can succeed in the face of low trust and poor supervision, no matter how valid it may be from the point of view of mechanics.

Still, some types of plans clearly are more capable than others of creating the four conditions mentioned at the beginning of the chapter. Some plans certainly do a better job of relating pay to performance than others, and some are better able to minimize the perceived negative consequences of good performance and to maximize the perceived positive consequences. One of the reasons pay often is not actually related to performance is that many organizations simply do not have pay plans that are correctly set up in order to accomplish this. Often this comes about because the particular conditions in the organization itself may not have been taken into account when the plan was developed. No plan is applicable to all situations. In a sense, one may say that a pay plan should be custom-tailored. Companies often try to follow the latest fads and fashion in salary administration, not recognizing that some plans simply do not fit their situation (Dunnette and Bass, 1963). Let us stress again, however, that mechanical faults are by no means the only reason that pay plans fail to relate pay to performance. Many of those which fail are not only well designed mechanically but also appropriate to the situation where they are used.

In looking at the mechanics of various types of pay programs, we shall group them together according to the way they differ on three dimensions. First, pay plans distribute rewards on different bases: individual, group, or organizationwide. Second, they measure performance differently: The measures typically vary from admittedly subjective (i.e., based on superiors' judgments or ratings) to somewhat objective (i.e., based on costs, sales, or profits). Third, plans differ in what they offer as rewards for successful performance: salary increases, bonuses, piece rates, or—in rare cases—fringe benefits. Table 6-2 presents a breakdown of the various plans, following this classification system. This classification yields some eighteen different types of incentive plans. A more detailed classification system would, of course, yield more. The table shows where the better-known plans fit in. It also shows a number of plans that are seldom used, and thus do not have a commonly known name. For example, companies do not typically base salary increases to individuals on the cost effectiveness of their work group. This does not mean that such a plan is a bad approach to distributing pay; it just means that it is not used very often.

EVALUATING THE DIFFERENT APPROACHES TO MERIT-BASED PAY

It is possible to make some general statements about the success of the different merit pay plans. We shall evaluate the plans in terms of how capable they have proved to be in establishing three of the conditions that are necessary if pay is to motivate performance. Such an evaluation must, of course, reflect actual experience with the different approaches in a number of situations. Here we are ignoring for the moment the effect of situational factors on the effectiveness of the plans in order to develop general ratings of the plans.

Table 6-3 lists the different types of incentive plans and provides a general effectiveness rating for each plan on three separate criteria. First, each plan is evaluated in terms of how effective it is in creating the perception that pay is tied to performance. In general, this indicates the degree to which the approach actually ties pay closely to performance, chronologically speaking, and the degree to which employees believe that higher pay will follow good performance. Second, each plan is evaluated in terms of how well it minimizes the perceived negative

Table 6-2. A Classification of Pay-incentive Plans

	Performance measure	Reward Offered	
		Salary increase	Cash bonus
Individual plans	productivity cost effectiveness superiors' ratings	merit rating plan	sales commission piece rate
Group plans	productivity cost effectiveness superiors' rating		group incentive
Organizationwide plans	productivity cost effectiveness profit	productivity bargaining	Kaiser, Scanlon Profit sharing (e.g., American Motors)

Table 6-3. Ratings of Various Pay-Incentive Plans

Type of plan	Performance measure	Tie pay to per- formance	Minimize negative side effects	Tie other rewards to per- formance
SALARY REWARD Individual plan	productivity	+2	0	0
	cost effectiveness	+1	0	0
	superiors' rating	+1	0	+1
Group	productivity	+1	0	+1
	cost effectiveness	+1	0	+1
	superiors' rating	+1	0	+1
Organizationwide	productivity	+1	0	+1
	cost effectiveness	+1	0	+1
	profits	0	0	+1
BONUS Individual plan	productivity	+3	−2	0
	cost effectiveness	+2	−1	0
	superiors' rating	+2	−1	+1
Group	productivity	+2	0	+1
	cost effectiveness	+2	0	+1
	superiors' rating	+2	0	+1
Organizationwide	productivity	+2	0	+1
	cost effectiveness	+2	0	+1
	profit	+1	0	+1

consequences of good performance. This criterion refers to the extent to which the approach eliminates situations where social ostracism and other negative consequences become associated with good performance. Third, each plan is evaluated in terms of whether it contributes to the perception that important rewards other than pay (e.g., recognition and acceptance) stem from good performance. The ratings range from +3 to −3, with +3 indicating that the plan has generally worked very well in terms of the criterion, while −3 indicates that the plan has not worked well. A 0 rating indicates that the plan has generally been neutral or average.

A number of trends appear in the ratings presented in Table 6-3. Looking just at the criterion of tying pay to performance, we see that individual plans tend to be rated highest, while group plans are rated next, and organizationwide plans are rated lowest. This reflects the fact that in group plans to some extent and in organizationwide plans to a great extent, an individual's pay is not directly a function of his *own* behavior. The pay of an individual in these situations is influenced by the behavior of others with whom he works and also, if the payment is based on profits, by external market conditions.

Bonus plans are generally rated higher than pay raise and salary increase plans. Under bonus plans, a person's pay may vary sharply from year to year in accordance with his most recent performance. This does not usually happen with salary increase programs, since organizations seldom cut anyone's salary; as a result, pay under the salary increase plan reflects not recent performance but performance over a number of years. Consequently, pay is not seen to be closely related to present behavior. Bonuses, on the other hand, typically depend on recent behavior, so that if someone performs poorly, it will show up immediately in his pay. Thus, a person under the bonus plan cannot coast for a year and still be highly paid, as he can be under the typical salary merit pay program.

Finally, note that approaches which use objective measures of performance are rated higher than those which use subjective measures. In general, objective measures enjoy higher credibility; that is, employees will often grant the validity of an objective measure, such as sales or units produced, when they will not accept a superior's rating. Thus, when pay is tied to objective measures, it is usually clear to employees that pay is determined by their performance. Objective measures such as sales volume and units produced are also often publicly measurable, and when pay is tied to them, the relationship is often much more visible than when it is tied to a subjective, nonverifiable measure, such as superior's rating. Over-all, then, the suggestion is that individually based bonus plans which rely on objective measures produce the strongest perceived connection between pay and performance.

The ratings with respect to the ability of pay programs to minimize the perceived negative consequences of good performance reveal that most plans are regarded as neutral. That is, they neither contribute to the appearance of negative consequences nor help to eliminate any which might be present. The individual bonus plans receive a negative rating on this criterion, however. This negative rating reflects the fact that piece-rate plans often lead to situations in which social rejection, firing, and running out of work are perceived by individuals to result from good performance. Under a piece-rate system, the perceived negative consequences of good performance may cancel out the positive motivational force that piece-rate plans typically generate by tying pay closely to performance.

With respect to the final criterion for pay plans, tying nonpay rewards to performance, the ratings are generally higher for group and organizationwide plans than for individual plans. Under group and organizationwide plans, it is generally to the advantage of everyone for an individual to work effectively. Thus, good performance is much more likely to be seen to result in esteem, respect, and social acceptance, than it is under individual plans. In short, if a person feels he can benefit from another's good performance, he is much more likely to encourage his fellow worker to perform well than if he will not benefit, and might even be harmed.

It should be clear from this short review that no one pay plan presents a panacea for a company's job motivation problems. Unfortunately, no one type of pay program is strong in all areas. Thus, no organization probably ever will be satisfied with its approach, since it will have problems associated with it. It is therefore not surprising to find that companies are usually dissatisfied with their pay programs and are constantly considering changing them. Still, the situation is not completely hopeless. Clearly, some approaches are generally better than others. We know, for example, that many of the approaches not mentioned in the table, such as stock-option plans, across-the-board raises, and seniority increases, have no real effect on the performance motivation of most employees. In addition, the evidence indicates that bonus-type plans are generally superior to wage increase plans and that individually based plans are generally superior to group and organizationwide plans. This suggests that one widely applicable model for an incentive plan might take the following form.

Each person's pay would be divided into three components. One part would be for the job the employee is doing, and everyone who holds a similar job would get the same amount. A second part of the pay package would be determined by seniority and cost-of-living factors; everyone in the company would get this, and the amount would be automatically adjusted each year. The third part of the package, however, would not be automatic; it would be individualized so that the amount paid would be based upon each person's performance during the immediately preceding period. The poor performer in the organization should find that this part of his or her pay package is minimal, while the good performer should find that this part of his or her pay is at least as great as the other two parts combined. This would not be a raise, however, since it could vary from year to year, depending on the individual's performance during the last performance period. Salary increases or raises would come only with changes in responsibility, cost of living, or seniority. The merit portion of the pay package would be highly variable, so that if a person's performance fell off, his or her pay would also be decreased by a cut in the size of the merit pay. The purpose of this kind of system is, of course, to make a large proportion of an individual's pay depend upon performance during the current period. Thus, performance is chronologically closely tied to large changes in pay.

The really difficult problem in any merit pay system, including this one, is how to measure performance. A valid measure of performance must meet several requirements. Not only must it be valid from the point of view of top management, but it must lead to promotion and pay decisions that are accepted by people throughout the organization: supervisors, subordinates, and peers must all accept the results of the system. Without this wide acceptance, pay raises will not be seen to reflect merit. Employees gain much of their knowledge about how pay systems operate by watching what happens to other people in the organization. If people whom they feel are doing good work get raises, then they accept the fact that a merit pay system exists. On the other hand, if workers they do not respect get raises, their belief in the system breaks down. Obviously the more the appraisal system yields decisions that are congruent with employee consensus about performance, the more the employees will believe that a merit system exists. The performance measure should also be such that employees feel that their contributions to the organization show up in it very directly. They must feel that they have control over it, rather than feeling that it reflects so many other things that what they do has little weight.

This point relates to the first part of our Motivation Model (E→P). Finally, the performance measure or measures should be influenced by all the behaviors that are important for the job holder to perform. People perform those behaviors that are measured, and thus it is important that the measure be sufficiently inclusive.

The performance appraisal systems that are actually used by organizations range all the way from superiors' subjective judgments to the complicated "objective" accounting-based systems that are used to measure managers' effectiveness. The problems with the simple, subjective, superiors' judgments are obvious—the subordinates often see them as arbitrary, based upon inadequate information, and simply unfair. The more objective systems are appealing in many ways. Where they can be installed, they are the best, but even they often fail to reflect individual efforts. Stock option plans are a good example. With these plans, pay is tied to the price of the stock on the market, and this presumably motivates managers to work so that the price of the stock will go up. The problem with this approach is that for most managers the connection between their effort and the price of the stock is very weak.

Plans that base bonuses or pay increases on profit centers or on the effectiveness of certain parts of the business may work, but all too often much of the profitability of óne part of the organization is controlled more by outside than by inside forces. Another problem with this kind of system is illustrated by the fate of most piece-rate incentive plans used at the worker level. They give the false illusion that objective, highly measurable rates can be "scientifically" set and that trust between superiors and subordinates is not necessary, since the system is objective. Experience has shown that effective piece rate systems simply cannot be established where foremen and workers do not trust each other and have a participative relationship. No completely "objective" system has ever been designed, nor will one ever be. Unexpected contingencies will always come up and have to be worked out between superiors and subordinates. Such events can be successfully resolved only when trust based upon mutual influence exists. Where poor relationships exist, workers strive to get rates set low and then they restrict their production, because they do not believe that good performance will in fact lead to higher pay in the long run.

Thus the answer in many organizations must rest in a reasonable combination of the simple, superior-based rating system and a system which uses more objective measures. First, we must accept the fact that no system can ever be 100 per cent objective and that subjective judgments will always be important. Second, we must realize that the key to general acceptance of the decisions that the appraisal system yields lies in having as broad as possible participation in the system.

What would such a system look like? It would be based upon superior-subordinate appraisal sessions where subordinates feel that they have a real opportunity to influence their boss. Obviously, such a system cannot operate, nor can any other for that matter, unless superior-subordinate relations are such that mutual influence is possible. In the first appraisal session the superior and subordinate would jointly decide on three things. First, they would decide on the objectives the subordinate should try to achieve during the ensuing time period. This period might last from three months to several years, depending on the level of the job. Second, they would decide on how the subordinate's progress toward these objectives will be measured. Objective measures might be used as well as subjective ratings by peers and others. Third, they would decide what level of reward the subordinate should receive if he accomplishes his objectives. A second meeting would be held at the end of the specified time period in order for the superior and subordinate to jointly assess the progress of the subordinate and decide upon

any pay actions. Finally, a few weeks later the whole process would begin again with another objectives-setting session. The advantages of this kind of system extend far beyond pay administration. It can create a sisuation where superiors and subordinates jointly become much more certain of what the subordinate's actual job duties and responsibilities are. Some recent studies suggest that there is often greater than 70 per cent disagreement between superior and subordinate about what constitutes the subordinate's job, so agreement on his score would not be an insignificant step forward.

The fact that the subordinate has a chance to set goals and that he commits himself to a certain level of performance may have an impact on his motivation that is independent of rewards like pay. There is evidence that when people commit themselves to challenging goals, needs like esteem and self-realization can come into play and motivate them to achieve the goals. This system also offers the subordinate a chance to become involved in important decisions about his own future and thereby encourages a kind of give-and-take that seldom exists between superiors and subordinates.

Despite the fact that it is possible to state some general conclusions about the effectiveness of different pay plans, perhaps the most important conclusion arising from the discussion so far is that it is vital to fit the pay plan to the organization. What might be a wonderful plan for one organization may for a whole series of reasons be a bad plan for another. Thus, although it is tempting to say that X approach is always best, it is wiser to turn now to a consideration of the factors that determine which kind of plan is likely to be best in a given situation.

FACTORS INFLUENCING THE EFFECTIVENESS OF DIFFERENT PAY PLANS

In selecting a plan for a particular organization, what situational factors must be considered? One factor that must be considered when an organization is deciding what type of pay plan to use is the degree of cooperation that is needed among the individuals who are under the plan. When the jobs involved are basically independent from one another, it is perfectly reasonable to use an individual-based plan. Independent jobs are quite common; examples are outside sales jobs and certain kinds of production jobs. In these jobs, employees contribute relatively independently to the effectiveness of the total group or organization, and thus it is appropriate to place them on an incentive scheme that motivates them to perform at their maximum and to pay little attention to cooperative activities.

As organizations become more complex, however, more and more jobs demand that work be done either successively (i.e., work passes from one person to another) or coordinately (i.e., work is a function of the joint effort of all employees) (Ghiselli and Brown, 1955). With successive jobs and especially with coordinate jobs, it is doubtful that individual incentive plans are appropriate. For one thing, on these jobs it is often difficult to measure the contribution of a given individual, and therefore difficult to reward individuals differentially. The organization is almost forced to reward on the basis of group performance. Another problem with individual plans is that they typically do not reward cooperation, since it is difficult to measure and to visibly relate to pay. Cooperation is essential on successive and coordinate jobs, and it is vital that the pay plan reward it. Thus, the strong suggestion is that group and organizationwide plans may be best in situations where jobs are coordinate or successive.

A related issue has to do with the degree to which appropriate inclusive subgoals or criteria can be created for individuals. An example was cited earlier of an individual pay plan that motivated salesmen to sell but did not motivate them to carry out other necessary job activities such as stocking shelves. The problem was that pay was tied to the most obvious and most measurable goal in the job, and some of the less measurable activities were overlooked and unrewarded. This situation occurs frequently; for many jobs, it is quite difficult to establish criteria that are both measurable quantitatively and inclusive of all the important job behaviors. The solution to the problem with the salesmen was to establish a group incentive plan. Indeed, inclusive criteria may often be possible at the group and organizational level but not at the individual level. It is quite easy to think of jobs for which a criterion like productivity might not be inclusive enough when individuals are looked at, but might be inclusive enough when a number of jobs or employees are grouped together. The point, of course, is that in choosing an incentive plan an organization must consider whether the performance measures that are related to pay include all the important job activities. One thing is certain: If an employee is not evaluated in terms of an activity, he will not be motivated to perform it.

The point has often been made that, wherever possible, objective performance measures should be used. There are, however, many situations where objective measures do not exist for individual or even group performance. One way of dealing with such situations is to measure performance on the basis of larger and larger groups until some objective measures can be found. Another approach is to measure performance on the individual or small group level and to use admittedly subjective measures. This is possible in some situations but not in others. The key factor in determining whether this approach is feasible is the degree of superior-subordinate trust. The more subjective the measure, the higher the degree of trust needed, because without high trust there is little chance that the subordinate will believe that his pay is really fairly based upon performance. Figure 6-1 illustrates the relationship between trust and the objectivity of the performance criteria. Note

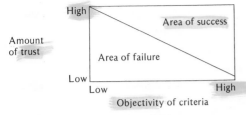

Fig. 6-1. Relationship of Trust and the Objectivity of Performance Criteria to Success of the Program

that it indicates that, even with the most objective system, some trust is still required if the individual is going to believe in the system. It also shows that unless a high degree of trust exist, pay plans based on subjective criteria have little chance of success.

One further issue must be considered when an organization is installing a pay plan: Will the individuals under the plan actually be able to control the criteria on which they will be evaluated? All too often the criteria are unrelated to the individual worker's efforts. A good example of this is the American Motors Corporation profit-sharing plan: the individual worker is not in a position to influence the profits of the company, yet this is a criterion upon which part of his pay is based. If a pay system is going to motivate employees, the criteria must be such that the employees can directly influence them. The criteria must, in short, be within the employees' control. This point, of course, argues for the use of individual criteria where possible, since they best reflect an individual's efforts.

Pay systems may also be results- or process-oriented; that is, they may reward employees chiefly for results (e.g. actual production) or for the way the task or job is carried out. There are usually problems with any system that rewards process only, just as there are problems with systems that reward results only. Perhaps the ultimate example of what can happen in the process-oriented system can be seen in the large bureaucracies that grow up in many civil service and other large organizations. In these bureaucracies people seem motivated to follow the rules, and not to accomplish the objectives for which the organization was established. On the other hand, a salesman may be motivated only by a short-term desire to maximize results. His behavior may lead to a sale, but it may be such that his organization never makes another sale to that buyer. A pay system must be designed to reward both process and results. This may be difficult in many situations; process is particularly difficult to measure objectively, and thus subjective measures may have to be used. As has already been pointed out, subjective measures can only be used effectively where a high degree of trust exists.

SHOULD PAY BE USED TO MOTIVATE?

Although we have not said so explicitly, it is clear that there are many situations in which pay should not be used to motivate job performance. In many jobs, it is impossible to develop adequate criteria for relating pay to performance. There may be no objective measures of performance, so that very subjective measures are needed but cannot be used because of the low level of trust between superiors and subordinates. On the other hand, the problem may be that objective measures are available but the level of trust is not even sufficient to allow their use. As was illustrated in Figure 6-1, there are situations where it simply may not be wise to measure performance for the purpose of relating it to pay. As has already been pointed out, it may be possible to measure some but not all of the relevant aspects of performance. A number of new problems can be created if pay is tied only to those aspects of performance that are measurable: the measurable aspects may receive all the employee's attention, while the others are neglected. In this situation it may well be better not to try to use pay to motivate performance.

Often, profit-sharing plans are used where

individual performance measures are not appropriate, and the organization desires to use pay to motivate performance. There is some doubt whether this is worthwhile in large organizations. The larger the organization, the less likely it is that a companywide profit-sharing or cost-effectiveness plan will work. The reason for this is simple: The larger the organization, the less influence any one individual has over companywide results, and the less an individual feels that his pay is related to performance. Thus, where individual-based pay plans are not possible, it is not always advisable to use an organizationwide plan. It may in fact be better to have no incentive pay plan at all. Often when organizationwide plans are installed in large organizations, they produce no extra motivation but do produce quite a few extra costs for the company: thus, the suggestion that the cost effectiveness of each plan should be considered.

Finally, motivating people with financial rewards is not a piker's game. Large amounts of money must be given to the good performers if employees are to place a high value on good performance and the raises to which it leads. A company must be willing and able to give certain employees very large raises and/or bonuses if pay is to motivate performance. If a company cannot afford to do this or is not willing to, it should probably forget about using pay to motivate performance. Even if they are willing to spend large amounts of money it may be that pay is not important to the employees and because of this not a possible source of motivation. In this case some other reward may be more appropriate. For example, in one factory that employed large numbers of unmarried women, time off the job was more important than money; so when the women were told they could go home after a certain amount of work was done, productivity increased dramatically. Several earlier attempts to use pay to motivate high productivity had failed.

In summary, serious thought should be given to *not* using pay as an incentive in organizations where:

1. The trust level is low;
2. Individual performance is difficult to measure;
3. Performance must be measured subjectively;
4. Inclusive measures of performance cannot be developed;
5. Large pay rewards cannot be given to the best performers.

PAY SECRECY

Secrecy about pay rates seems to be an accepted practice in organizations, regardless of whether they use individual or group plans, bonus or salary increases, objective or subjective performance measures. Secrecy seems to be particularly prevalent with respect to management pay (Lawler, 1972). Some research suggests that one of the effects of secrecy may be to reduce the ability of pay to motivate (Lawler, 1965a; Lawler, 1967c). The argument that has been presented against secrecy is that it makes accurate social comparisons impossible (Festinger, 1954). Secrecy thus makes it difficult to conclusively and visibly establish that pay is tied to performance. Further, it is argued that because social comparisons are difficult, employees often get incorrect feedback about their own performance.

One of the findings that has consistently appeared in the research on pay secrecy is that managers tend to have incorrect information about the pay of other managers in the organization. Specifically, there is a general tendency for them to overestimate the pay of managers around them. For example, in one organization the average raise given was 6 per cent, yet the managers believed that it was 8 per cent, and the larger their raise was, the larger they believed other people's raises were (Lawler, 1972). This had the effect of wiping out much of the motivational force of the differential reward system that was actually operating in the company. Almost regardless of how well the individual manager was performing, he felt that he was getting less than the average raise. This problem was particularly severe among the high performers, since they believed that they were doing well yet receiving a minimal reward. They did not believe that pay was in fact based upon merit. This was ironical, since their pay *did* reflect their performance. What actually existed did not matter as far as the motivation of the managers was concerned; they responded to what they thought existed. Thus, even though pay was tied to performance, these managers were not motivated because they could not see the connection.

There is another way in which pay secrecy may affect motivation. Several studies have shown that accurate feedback about quality of work is a strong stimulus to good performance (Vroom, 1964). People work better when they know how well they are doing in relation to some meaningful standard. For a manager, pay is one of the most meaningful pieces of feedback information. High pay means good performance. Low pay is a signal that he is not doing well and had better improve. The research shows that when managers do not really know what other managers earn, they cannot correctly evaluate their own pay and the feedback implications of it for their own performance. Since they tend to overestimate the pay of subordinates and peers and since they overestimate the raises others get, the majority of them consider their pay low; in effect, they receive negative feedback. Moreover, although this feedback suggests that they should change their work behavior, it does not tell them what type of change to make. When managers are not doing their jobs well, negative feedback is undoubtedly what they need. But it is doubtful that it is what managers who are working effectively need.

Note that one recommendation that appears in the discussion of factors affecting the importance of pay as well as in the discussion of factors affecting the belief that pay depends upon performance is that pay information should be more public. Unless this condition exists, pay is not likely to motivate performance, because it will be seen neither as an important satisfier of higher-order needs nor as something that is obtainable from good performance. Making pay information public will not itself establish the belief that pay is based upon merit or ensure that people will get accurate performance feedback. All it can do is clarify those situations where pay actually *is* based upon merit but where it is not obvious because relative salaries are not accurately known. This point is apparent in some unpublished data collected by the author. An organization was studied that had a merit-based plan and pay secrecy. At the beginning of the study, the data collected showed that the employees saw only a moderate relationship between pay and performance. Data collected after the company became more open about pay showed a significant increase in the employees' perceptions of the degree to which pay and performance were related. The crucial factor in making this change to openness successful was that pay was actually tied to performance. Making pay rates public where pay is not tied to performance will only serve to emphasize more dramatically that it is not, thereby further reducing the power of pay to motivate.

MAKING MEN RICH

Gellerman (1968) has argued that if pay is to motivate performance, very large amount of pay must be involved. He also quite correctly points out that these large amounts of pay must be perceived to be dependent upon performance. This argument is basically in agreement with the emphasis of this book—i.e., that increasing the value of the rewards that are tied to performance should increase motivation, since it will lead to an increase in the size of the second factor in the Motivation Model (the attractiveness of the performance). It is possible, however, to offer rewards that are too large and, as a result, depress the motivation to perform. This can come about in two ways.

First, because of the operation of a concept of equity in many people, a very large amount of additional pay might be seen as unfairly large and thus not as attractive as a smaller amount. Jaques (1961) has stressed the point that amounts of pay that are unfairly large can produce anxiety on the part of the employee; therefore, employees often do not seek very large amounts. Jaques, in fact, implies that people will actually go out of their way to avoid making amounts of money that they feel are unfairly large. All this strongly suggests that, when very large raises are considered, it is important to determine what the employees feel a fair raise would be. This estimate will probably be conservative, since as the equity theory research suggests, people can quickly raise their perceptions of what a fair pay rate is. But seriously violating people's perceptions of what a fair raise or pay rate is can have harmful effects on motivation because of its effects on the importance of pay. Thus, pay raises can be both too high and too low.

A second reason that very high pay raises or salaries can be harmful is that the accumulation of large amounts of money will affect the way a person views a given amount of pay. Because the needs upon which pay depends are satiable, it seems likely that once a certain amount of money is acquired, money will begin to have a lower valence. Once it loses its value, it ceases to motivate behavior. Thus, one of the effects of "making men rich" may be to make them disinterested in pay. When this happens, pay cannot motivate them. Very few people ever reach a level where pay ceases to be important. Nevertheless, the issue does present a potential problem for the type of pay administration strategy that emphasizes very large raises and pay based upon performance. It is quite possible that this strategy

could, paradoxically, destroy the extrinsic motivation of the good performer because of the great amounts of money he can acquire over time. This rarely happens, since it requires that a person be operating almost wholly on the self-fulfillment need level, and as Maslow and others have pointed out, few people ever reach this level.

SELECTION

The Motivation Model indicates that there are some relatively fixed individual difference factors that determine how employees will see the relationship between pay and performance. Specifically, it suggests that people vary in the degree to which they believe in external versus internal control of the events that affect them. People high in external control essentially feel that they have little control over what happens to them and that they have little ability to influence their environment. People high in internal control feel that they can influence their own destiny. It has been suggested that high external-control people are not likely to feel that they can influence their pay, regardless of what they do and regardless of the kind of pay system an organization uses. On the other hand, people high in internal control are likely to believe that they can influence their pay—if the pay system gives them any reason to hold this belief.

It is quite likely that a person's position on the continuum from high internal control to high external control is rather fixed; thus, selection decisions may play an important role in determining the success of pay programs. If an organization is populated entirely by people who are high in external control, a merit pay system may be doomed to failure almost from the beginning. On the other hand, if it is populated by people who believe in internal control, then it is an excellent position to use pay as an incentive. This suggests two points. First, before organizations decide what kind of pay system they are going to use, they might wish to determine what kind of employees they have. Second, in selecting people for jobs where pay is supposed to be an incentive, organizations should look for high internal-control people. Rotter (1966) has developed a test to measure the degree to which people believe in internal control, and it is likely that in the near future more such measures will appear. This raises the possibility that people can be tested and selected initially on the basis of the degree to which they are likely to accept a merit pay system. Or, to state the issue more broadly, it might be possible to identify, at the time of hiring, those people who can be motivated by extrinsic rewards.

REFERENCES

Andrews, I. R., and Henry, M. M. Management attitudes toward pay. *Industrial Relations*, 1963, 3, 29-39.

Bass, B. M. Ability, values, and concepts of equitable salary increases in exercise compensation. *Journal of Applied Psychology*, 1965, 49, 295-98.

Beer, M., and Gery, G. J. Individual and organizational correlates of pay system preferences: Implications for planned change of a pay system and for the effects of pay systems on motivation and satisfaction. Mimeographed paper, Corning, New York, undated.

Brenner, M. H., and Lockwood, H. C. Salary as a predictor of salary: A 20-year study. *Journal of Applied Psychology*, 1965, 49, 295-98.

Campbell, J. P., Dunnette, M. D., Lawler, E. E., and Weick, K. E. *Managerial behavior, performance and effectiveness*. New York: McGraw-Hill, 1970.

Davis, N. M. Attitudes toward work among building operatives. *Occupational Psychology*, 1948, 22, 56-62.

Dunnette, M. D., and Bass, B. M. Behavioral scientists and personnel management. *Industrial Relations*, 1963, 2 (3), 115-30.

Factory. What the factory worker really thinks about his job, unemployment, and industry's profit. *Factory Management and Maintenance*, 1947, 105 (12), 86-92.

Festinger, L. A theory of social comparison processes. *Human Relations*, 1954, 7, 117-40.

Gellerman, S. W. *Management by motivation.* New York: American Management Association, 1968.

Ghiselli, E. E., and Brown, C. W. *Personnel and industrial psychology.* New York: McGraw-Hill, 1955.

Gruenfeld, L. W., and Weissenberg, P. Supervisory characteristics and attitudes toward performance appraisals. *Personnel Psychology*, 1966, 19, 143-52.

Haire, M., Ghiselli, E. E., and Gordon, M. E. A psychological study of pay. *Journal of Applied Psychology Monograph*, 1967, 51 (4), Whole No. 636.

Jaques, E. *Equitable payment.* New York: Wiley, 1961.

Jones, L. V., and Jeffrey, T. E. A quantitative analysis of expressed preferences for compensation plans. *Journal of Applied Psychology*, 1964, 48, 201-10.

Lawler, E. E. Manager's job performance and their attitudes toward their pay. Ph.D. diss., University of California, Berkeley, 1964.

Lawler, E. E. Managers' perceptions of their subordinates' pay and of their superiors' pay. *Personnel Psychology*, 1965, 18, 413-22(a).

Lawler, E. E. The multitrait-multirater approach to measuring managerial job performance. *Journal of Applied Psychology*, 1967, 51, 369-81(b).

Lawler, E. E. Secrecy and the need to know. In Tosi, H. L., House, R. J., and Dunnette, M.D. (Eds.), *Managerial motivation and compensation. A selection of readings.* East Lansing, Mich.: Division of Research, Graduate School of Business Administration, Michigan State University, 1972.

Lawler, E. E., and Porter, L. W. Predicting manager's pay and their satisfaction with their pay. *Personnel Psychology*, 1966, 19, 363-73.

Meyer, H.H., Kay, E., and French, J. R. P. Split roles in performance appraisal. *Harvard Business Review*, 1965, 43 (1), 123-29.

Opinion Research Corporation. *Wage incentives.* Princeton, N.J., 1946.

Opinion Research Corporation. *"Productivity" from the worker's standpoint.* Princeton, N.J., 1949.

R.I.A. *Sales compensation practices, an RIA survey.* New York: Research Institute of America, File No. 32, 1965.

Svetlik, B., Prien, E., and Barrett, G. Relationships between job difficulty, employee's attitudes toward his job, and supervisory ratings of the employee effectiveness. *Journal of Applied Psychology,* 1964, 48, 320-24.

Vroom, V. H. *Work and motivation.* New York: Wiley, 1964.

Whyte, W. F. (Ed.), *Money and motivation: An analysis of incentives in industry.* New York: Harper, 1955.

7

Job Enrichment Pays Off

WILLIAM J. PAUL, JR., KEITH B. ROBERTSON,
and FREDERICK HERZBERG

In his pioneering article, "One More Time: How Do You Motivate Employees?"[1] Frederick Herzberg put forward some principles of scientific job enrichment and reported a successful application of them involving the stockholder correspondents employed by a large corporation. According to him, job enrichment seeks to improve both task efficiency and human satisfaction by means of building into people's jobs, quite specifically, greater scope for personal achievement and its recognition, more challenging and responsible work and more opportunity for individual advancement and growth. It is concerned only incidentally with matters such as pay and working conditions, organizational structure, communications, and training, important and necessary though these may be in their own right.

But like a lot of pioneering work, Herzberg's study raised more questions than it answered. Some seemed to us to merit further consideration, particularly those in regard to the (1) generality of the findings, (2) feasibility of making changes, and (3) consequences to be expected. Consider:

1. *Generality*—Can similarly positive results

1. HBR January-February 1968, p. 53.

be obtained elsewhere with other people doing different jobs? How widespread is the scope or need for equivalent change in other jobs? Can meaningful results be obtained only in jobs with large numbers of people all doing the same work and where performance measures are easily available?

2. *Feasibility*—Are there not situations where the operational risk is so high that it would be foolhardy to attempt to pass responsibility and scope for achievement down the line? Because people's ability and sense of responsibility vary so much, is it not necessary to make changes selectively? Do all employees welcome having their jobs enriched, or are there not some who prefer things to be left as they are? Can one enrich jobs without inevitably facing demands for higher pay or better conditions to match the new responsibilities? And, in any case, is not the best route to motivational change through participation?

3. *Consequences*—In view of so many possible difficulties in the way, are the gains to be expected from job enrichment significant or only marginal? Do they relate primarily to job satisfaction or to performance? What are the consequences for supervision if jobs are loaded with new tasks taken from above—i.e., does one man's enrichment be-

come another's impoverishment? Finally, what are the consequences for management if motivational change becomes a reality? Is the manager's role affected? If so, how? And what are the implications for management development?

There are undoubtedly more questions that could be raised and investigated. But these seem particularly important from a corporate point of view if job enrichment is to take place on a widespread basis, as part of management practice rather than as a research activity. Accordingly, the purpose of this article is to probe into the complexities of job enrichment in an attempt to shed light on these questions and to determine how the concept may be most effectively applied in furthering the attainment of corporate business objectives.

In order to do this, we shall report in Part I on five studies carried out in Imperial Chemical Industries Limited and other British companies. Two of the studies—covering laboratory technicians in an R & D department and sales representatives in three companies—will be examined in some detail. The other three—encompassing design engineers, production foremen on shift work, and engineering foremen on day work—will be summarized. In Part II, the main conclusions emerging from the studies will be presented in the form of answers to the questions raised at the beginning of this article.

Each study was initiated in response to a particular problem posed by managment, and the conclusions drawn from any one can be only tentative. Among them, however, they cover not only widely different business areas and company functions, but also many types and levels of jobs. Collectively, they provide material which adds to our understanding of both theory and practice.

Part I: The Job Enrichment Studies

As in all studies on job satisfaction and performance, the need to measure results introduced certain constraints which do not exist in normal managerial situations. Consequently, three main features were common to the studies we are reporting in this discussion:

First, the "hygiene" was held constant. This means that no deliberate changes were made as part of the investigation, in matters such as pay, security, or working conditions. The studies were specifically trying to measure the extent of those gains which could be attributed solely to change in job content.

Second, recognition of the normal hygiene changes led to the need to have an "experimental group" for whom the specific changes in job content were made, and a "control group" whose job content remained the same.

Third, the studies had to be kept confidential to avoid the well-known tendency of people to behave in an artificial way when they know they are the subject of a controlled study. Naturally, there was no secret about the changes themselves, only about the fact that performance was being measured.

All studies set out to measure job satisfaction and performance for both the experimental and control groups over a trial period following the implementation of the changes. The trial period itself generally lasted a year and was never less than six months. The performance measures always were specific to the group concerned and were determined by local management of the subject company. To measure job satisfaction, we relied throughout on a job reaction survey which measures the degree of people's satisfaction with the motivators in their job as they themselves perceive them.

LABORATORY TECHNICIANS

Managers in an industrial research department were concerned about the morale of laboratory technicians, or "experimental officers" (EOs). This group's job was to implement experimental programs devised by scientists. The EOs set up the appropriate apparatus, recorded data, and supervised laboratory assistants, who carried out the simpler operations. The EOs were professionally qualified people, but lacked the honors or doctorate degrees possessed by the scientists.

The average age of the experimental officers was increasing. A quarter of them had reached their salary maximums, and fewer now had the chance to move out of the department. Their normal promotion route into plant management had become blocked as manufacturing processes grew more complex and more highly qualified people filled the available jobs. Management's view of the situation was confirmed by the initial job reaction survey. Not only were the EOs' scores low, but many wrote of their frustration. They felt their technical ability and experience was being wasted by the scientists' refusal to delegate anything but routine work.

Against this background, the research manager's specific objective was to develop the EOs into "better scientists." If job enrichment was to be useful, it would have to contribute to the attainment of that goal.

Changes and Experimental Design

Here is the specific program of action devised and implemented for the experimental officers.

Technical: EOs were encouraged to write the final report, or "minute," on any research project for which they had been responsible. Such minutes carried the author's name and were issued along with those of the scientists. It was up to each EO to decide for himself whether he wanted the minute checked by his supervisor before issue, but in any case he was fully responsible for answering any query arising from it.

EOs were involved in planning projects and experiments, and were given more chance to assist in work planning and target setting.

They were given time, on request, to follow up their own ideas, even if these went beyond the planned framework of research. Written reports had to be submitted on all such work.

Financial: EOs were authorized to requisition materials and equipment, to request analysis, and to order services such as maintenance, all on their own signature.

Managerial: Senior EOs were made responsible for devising and implementing a training program for their junior staff. In doing so, they could call on facilities and advice available within the company.

Senior EOs were involved in interviewing candidates for laboratory assistant jobs, and they also acted as first assessor in any staff assessment of their own laboratory assistants.

These changes drew on all the motivators. Each one gave important chances for achievement; together, they were designed to make the work more challenging. Recognition of achievement came in the authorship of reports. Authority to order supplies and services was a responsibility applying to all the EOs involved. The new managerial responsibilities reserved to senior EOs opened up room for advancement within the job, while the technical changes, particularly the opportunity for self-initiated work, gave scope for professional growth.

Some 40 EOs in all were involved in the study. Two sections of the department acted as experimental groups ($N = 15$) and two as control groups ($N = 29$). One experimental and one control group worked closely together on the same type of research, and it was anticipated that there would be some interaction between them. The other two groups were separate geographically and engaged on quite different research.

The changes were implemented for the experimental groups during October and November 1966, and the trial period ran for the next twelve months. After six month, the same changes were introduced into one of the control groups, thus converting it into an experimental group (*N* = 14). This was done to see whether a similar pattern of performance revealed itself, thereby safeguarding against any remote possibility of coincidence in the choice of the original groups.

Research work is notoriously difficult to measure, but as the aim was to encourage more scientific contribution from EOs, this was what had to be judged in as objective a way as possible. All EOs were asked to write monthly progress reports of work done. Those written by experimental and control group EOs were assessed by a panel of three managers, not members of the department, who were familiar with the research work concerned.

Reports were scored against eight specifically defined criteria thought to reflect the kind of growth being sought: *knowledge,*

comprehension, synthesis, evaluation, original thought, practical initiative, industry, and *skill in report writing.* Whenever the assessor found particular evidence of one of these qualities in a report, he would award it one mark, the total score for a report being simply the sum of these marks.

In order to establish a baseline for clarifying standards and testing the assessors' consistency of marking, reports were collected for three months prior to the introduction of any job enrichment changes. The very high consistency found between the marking of the three assessors encouraged confidence in the system. The assessors, naturally, were never told which were the experimental and control groups, though it became easy for them to guess as the trial period went on.

The other main measure was to use the same system to assess research minutes

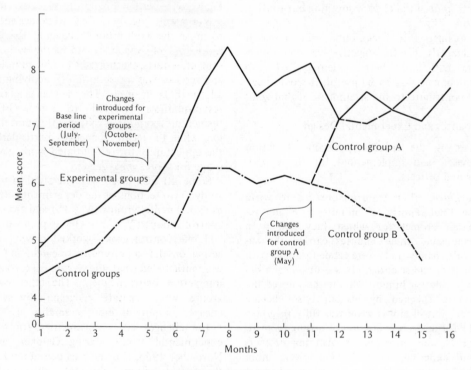

Fig. 7-1. Assessment of EO's Monthly Reports

written by the EOs. These were compared against an equivalent sample of minutes written by scientists over the same period, which were submitted to the panel for assessment, again without identification.

Motivational Results

The assessment of monthly reports written by the experimental officers is given in Figure 7-1, which compares the mean score achieved by all experimental group EOs each month with that achieved by all control group EOs. On occasions when a monthly report had obviously suffered because of the attention devoted to writing a research minute covering much the same ground, a marginal weighting factor was added to the score depending on the quality of the minute concerned. Both experimental and control groups improved their monthly report scores at about the same rate during the first five months. There is no doubt that with practice all were getting better at report writing, and it may be that the mere fact of being asked to write monthly reports itself acted as a motivator for both groups.

Once the changes had been fully implemented in the experimental groups, however, performance began to diverge. Although the reports of the control groups continued to improve for a time, they were far outpaced by those of the experimental groups. With some fluctuations, this performance differential was maintained throughout the rest of the trial period. When, after six months, the motivators were fed into one of the two control groups, its performance improved dramatically, following the pattern achieved by the original experimental groups. Meanwhile, the performance of the other control group, unaffected by what was happening elsewhere, began to slip back toward its original starting point.

During the twelve months of the trial period, a total of 34 research minutes were written by EOs, all from the experimental groups, compared with two from the department as a whole during the previous twelve-month period. There were also a number of minutes jointly authored by scientists and EOs, which are excluded from this analysis. Of the 34 being considered, nine were written by EOs in the control group which was converted into an experimental group, but all came from the time after the changes had been introduced.

It is one thing for laboratory technicians to write research minutes, but whether the minutes they write are any good or not is a different matter. Figure 7-2 shows the quality of the EOs' minutes compared with that of the scientists.' The EOs' mean score was 8.7; the scientists,' 9.8. All EO scores except three fell within the range of scores obtained by the scientists; the three exceptions were written by one man. Three of the EOs' minutes, one in fact written by a laboratory assistant with guidance from an EO, were judged to be as good as the best of the scientists' minutes.

Encouraged by the success of a training scheme designed for laboratory assistants, the EOs initiated one for themselves. It aimed to give them the opportunity to come to terms with the ideas and terminology of chemical engineering. Managers judged it to have been of considerable value, ane one EO summed it up by saying, "A couple of pages of chemical engineering calculations and formulas won't frighten us off now."

One original idea followed up, as the changes now permitted, by an EO from an experimental group resulted in an important discovery with possible applications in certain kinds of national emergency. The idea was investigated further by a government department, which described it as the most promising of some two hundred ideas submitted on that topic.

Three staff assessments on EOs were carried out—at the beginning, middle, and end of the trial period. Each followed the normal company procedure. The only group which showed a consistent improvement was one of the experimental groups.

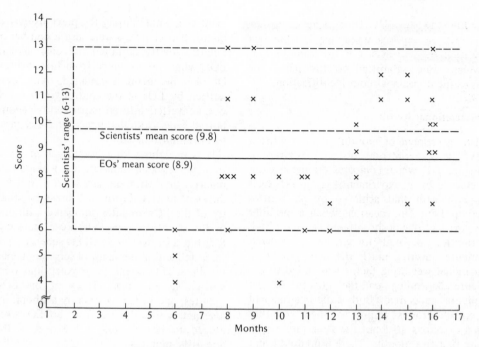

Fig. 7-2. Assessment of EO's Research Minutes

The job reaction survey was given both before and after the trial period. In the initial survey, experimental and control group EOs could not be specifically identified, and so an exact comparison of the before and after scores of each group cannot be made. The over-all mean score attained by all EOs in the department was no higher at the end of the trial period than it had been at the beginning. Although managers believed there had been a positive change in job satisfaction, that is not a conclusion which can be supported with data.

An internal company report, written by the personnel officer who managed and coordinated the study throughout, concluded that there had been definite evidence of growth among the EOs, particularly in one group, and that much useful work had been accomplished during the exercise. One of the experimental groups had been able to keep abreast of its commitments even though it lost the services of two of its six

scientists during the trial period and functioned without a manager for the last five months of the study. There can be little doubt that job enrichment in this case helped to further the research manager's objective of tackling a morale problem by getting at the root of the matter and developing experimental officers as scientists in their own right.

SALES REPRESENTATIVES

To investigate the potential of job enrichment in the sales field, work has been done in three British companies dealing with quite different products and markets, both wholesale and retail. In only one study, however, were experimental conditions strictly observed.

The company concerned had long enjoyed a healthy share of the domestic market in one particular product range, but its position was threatened by competition. A decline in the market share had been stabilized before the study began, but 1967 sales still showed no improvement over those of 1966. So far as could be judged, the company's products were fully competitive in both price and quality. The critical factor in the situation appeared to be sales representatives' effort.

The representatives' salaries—they were not paid a commission—and conditions of employment were known to compare well with the average for the industry. Their mean score in the job reaction survey, like that of other groups of salesmen, was higher than most employees of equivalent seniority, which suggested that they enjoyed considerable job satisfaction.

The problem in this case, therefore, was that for the vital business objective of regaining the initiative in an important market, sustained extra effort was needed from a group of people already comparatively well treated and reasonably satisfied with their jobs. Here, job enrichment would stand or fall by the sales figures achieved.

Changes and Experimental Design

Here is the specific program of action devised and implemented for the sales representatives.

Technical: Sales representatives were no longer obliged to write reports on every customer call. They were asked simply to pass on information when they thought it appropriate or request action, as they thought it was required.

Responsibility for determining calling frequencies was put wholly with the representatives themselves, who kept the only records for purposes such as staff reviews.

The technical service department agreed to provide service "on demand" from the representatives; nominated technicians regarded such calls as their first priority. Communication was by direct contact, paperwork being cleared after the event.

Financial: In cases of customer complaint about product performance, representatives were authorized to make immediate settlements of up to $250 if they were satisfied that consequential liability would not be prejudiced.

If faulty material had been delivered or if the customer was holding material for which he had no further use, the representative now had complete authority, with no upper limit in sales value, to decide how best to deal with the matter. He could buy back unwanted stock even if it was no longer on the company's selling range.

Representatives were given a discretionary range of about 10 per cent on the prices of most products, especially those considered to be critical from the point of view of market potential. The lower limit given was often below any price previously quoted by the company. All quotations other than at list price had to be reported by the representative.

The theme of all the changes was to build the sales representative's job so that it became more complete in its own right. Instead of always having to refer back to headquarters, the representative now had the authority to make decisions on his own—he was someone the customer could really do business with. Every change implied a greater responsibility; together they gave the freedom and challenge necessary for self-development.

The company sold to many different industries, or "trades." In view of the initial effort needed to determine limit prices and to make the technical service arrangements, it was decided that the study should concentrate on three trades chosen to be typical of the business as a whole. These three trades gave a good geographical spread and covered many types of customers; each had an annual sales turnover of about $1 million.

The experimental group ($N = 15$) was selected to be representative of the sales force as a whole in age range, experience, and ability. An important part of each member's selling responsibility lay within the nominated trades. The rest of the sales force (N = 23) acted as the control group. The changes were introduced during December 1967, and the trial period ran from January 1 to September 30, 1968.

The background of static sales and the objective of recapturing the market initiative dictated that sales turnover would be the critical measure, checked by gross margin. The difficulties of comparing unequal sales values and allowing for monthly fluctuations and seasonal trends were overcome by making all comparisons on a cumulative basis in terms of the percentage gain or loss for each group against the equivalent period of the previous year.

Since they were selling in the same trades in the same parts of the country, the performance of all the representatives was presumably influenced by the same broad economic and commercial factors. In two of the trades, the experimental group had the bigger share of the business and tended to sell to the larger customers. In these cases it may be surmised that prevailing market conditions affected the experimental group's performance, favorably or unfavorably, more than the control group's. As it happened, in one of these trades commercial trends were favorable, while in the other they were distinctly unfavorable. In the third trade, the experimental and control groups were evenly matched. Taken together, then, the three trades give as fair a comparison as can be obtained between the performances of sales representatives under those two sets of conditions.

Motivational Results

During the trial period the experimental group increased its sales by almost 19 per cent over the same period of the previous year, a gain of over $300,000 in sales value. The control group's sales in the meantime declined by 5 per cent. The equivalent change for both groups the previous year had been a decline of 3 per cent. The difference in performance between the two

groups is statistically significant at the 0.01 level of confidence.

Figure 7-3 shows the month-to-month performance of the two groups, plotted cumulatively. It can be seen that the control group in fact started the year extremely well, with January/February sales in the region of 30 per cent above the equivalent 1967 figures. This improvement was not sustained, however, and by May cumulative sales had dropped below their 1967 level. By the last five months of the trial period, performance was running true to the previous year's form, showing a decline of about 3 per cent.

The experimental group, on the other hand, started more modestly, not exceeding a 20 per cent improvement during the first quarter. During the second quarter, outstanding results in May compensated for poorer figures in April and June. The third quarter showed a steady, if slight, rise in the rate of improvement over 1967. This sustained increase of just under 20 per cent was in marked contrast to the previously declining performance of the trades as a whole.

Comparisons with other trades suffer from the disadvantage that different economic and commercial factors affect the various parts of the business. Nevertheless, the experimental group's performance was consistently between 6 per cent and 7 per cent better than that for the rest of the business. Figure 7-3 shows the month-to-month picture. It can be seen not only that the experimental group maintained a higher rate of improvement than the rest of the business throughout the trial period, but that the gap widened if anything as time went on. At the 1967 rates of turnover, this performance differential in all trades would be worth $1.5 million in sales value in a full year.

In view of the greater negotiating authority granted to the experimental group representatives, it is important to check whether their substantial increase in turnover was achieved at the expense of profit. As all quotations other than at list price

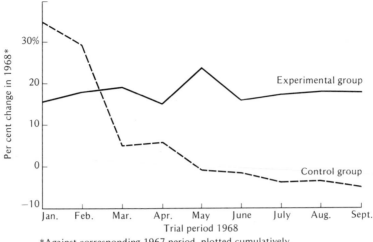

*Against corresponding 1967 period, plotted cumulatively.

Fig. 7-3. Sales Turnover within Trades Chosen as Typical of the Business

were reported by the representatives, it was possible to analyze the gross margin achieved by both groups. The analysis showed without doubt that the gross margin of the experimental group's sales was proportionally as high, if not higher, than that of the control group's sales.

Managers had the impression that representatives actually used their price discretion less often than they had previously asked for special prices to be quoted by the sales office. Also, in the sales manager's view, once the representatives were given real negotiating authority they discovered that price was not the obstacle to sales which they had always imagined it to be. Under the new arrangements they were able to assess more completely what the true obstacles to sales were in each individual case.

Over the trial period the control group's mean score in the job reaction survey remained static. In contrast, the experimental group's score rose by 11 per cent.

DESIGN ENGINEERS

The engineering director of one of the divisions of ICI wanted to see whether the job of design engineer might lend itself to motivational change. His design department faced an increasing work load as more design work for the division's plants was being done internally. The situation was exacerbated by difficulties in recruiting qualified design engineers. People at all levels in the department were being overloaded and development work was suffering.

Changes and Experimental Design

Here is the specific program of action devised and implemented for the design engineers.

Technical: Experienced engineers were given a completely independent role in running their projects; the less experienced technical men were given as much independence as possible. Occasions on which reference to supervision remained obligatory were reduced to an absolute minimum. The aim was that each engineer should judge for himself when and to what extent he should seek advice.

Group managers sponsored occasional in-

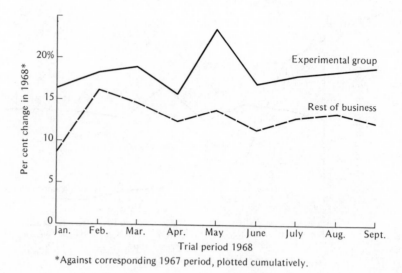

Fig. 7-4. Sales Turnover: Experimental Group and Rest of Business

vestigatory jobs, and engineers were encouraged to become departmental experts in particular fields. They were expected to follow up completed projects as they thought appropriate.

When authority to allocate work to outside consultants was given, the engineers were to have the responsibility for making the choice of consultants.

Financial: Within a sanctioned project with a budget already agreed on, all arbitrary limits on engineers' authority to spend money were removed. They themselves had to ensure that each "physical intent" was adequately defined and that an appropriate sum was allocated for it in the project budget. That done, no financial ceiling limited their authority to place orders.

Managerial: Engineers were involved in the selection and placing of designers (drawing office staff). They manned selection panels, and a recruit would only be allocated to a particular engineer if the latter agreed to accept him.

Experienced engineers were asked to make the initial salary recommendations for all their junior staff members.

Engineers were allowed to authorize overtime, cash advances, and traveling expenses for staff.

Motivational Results

In summary fashion, these are the deductions that can be drawn from this study:

Senior managers saw a change in both the amount and the kind of consultation between experimental group design engineers and their immediate supervisors. The supervisors' routine involvement in projects was much reduced, and they were able to give more emphasis in their work to technical development. Some engineers still needed frequent guidance; others operated independently with confidence. The point is that not all were restricted for the benefit of some; those who could were allowed to find their own feet.

The encouragement of specialist expertise among design engineers was a long-term proposition, but progress was made during the trial period.

The removal of any financial ceiling on engineers' authority to place orders within an approved project with an agreed budget proved entirely effective. Whereas before the design engineers had to seek approval from as many as three higher levels of management for any expenditure over $5,000—a time-consuming process for all concerned— now they could, and did, place orders for as much as $500,000 worth of equipment on their own authority.

There is no evidence of any poor decision having been taken as a result of the new arrangements. In fact, at the end of the trial period, none of the senior managers concerned wanted to revert to the old system.

The changes involving the engineers in supervisory roles were thought by the senior managers to be at least as important as the other changes, possibly more so in the long term.

There was no doubt about the design engineers' greater involvement in the selection process, which they fully accepted and appreciated. Significantly, they began to show a greater feel for the constraints involved in selection.

The responsibility for overtime and travel claims was fully effective and taken in people's stride. There was no adverse effect from a budgetary control point of view.

The involvement of design engineers in making salary recommendations for their staff was considered by the senior managers to have been a major improvement. If anything, engineers tended to be "tighter" in their salary recommendations than more senior management. There was general agreement that the effectiveness of this change would increase over time.

Senior managers felt that none of the changes of its own accord had had an overriding effect, nor had all problems been solved. But there was no doubt that the cumulative effect of the changes had been significant and that the direction of solutions to some important problems had been indicated.

The changes may have been effective, but in this particular study the important question was whether they had a significant impact on job satisfaction. Some of the motivators introduced into the experimental groups had been in operation in the control group for some time; others—because of the specialist nature of the control group's work —were not as important to it as to the experimental groups. The control group had scored high in the initial job reaction survey, while the experimental groups had both achieved very low scores. If the experimental groups' scores did not improve, doubt would inevitably be cast on the relationship between job content and job satisfaction. As it turned out, comparison results of the before and after job reaction surveys revealed that the mean scores of the two experimental groups had increased by 21 percent and 16 per cent, while those of the control group and all other design engineers in the department had remained static.

FACTORY SUPERVISORS

The final two studies, one in ICI and one in another British company, concerned factory supervisors: production foremen on shift work fabricating nonferrous metals, and engineering foremen on day work providing maintenance services. As the two studies seem to be complementary, they are considered jointly.

In both cases management was concerned about the degree to which the traditional role of the foreman had been eroded in recent years. The increasing complexity of organizational structures, plant and equipment, and industrial relations had left the foreman isolated. Decisions in the areas of planning, technical control, and discipline— originally in his province—were now passed up the line or turned over to a specialist staff. Many managers believed that as a consequence small problems too often escalated unnecessarily, managers were being overloaded, and day-to-day relationships between the foreman and his men had been weakened.

Changes and Experimental Design

Here is the specific program of action devised and implemented for the production and engineering foremen.

Technical: Foremen were involved more in planning. Production foremen were authorized to modify schedules for loading and sequencing; engineering foremen were consulted more about organizational developments, given more responsibility for preventive maintenance, and encouraged to comment on design.

All were assigned projects on specific problems such as quality control, and could draw on the necessary resources for their implementation.

Other changes included giving foremen more "on the spot" responsibility, official deputizing for engineers, the writing of monthly reports, and more recognition of formen's achievement of plans.

Financial: Engineering foremen were given complete control of certain "on cost" budgets. Production foremen were encouraged to make all decisions on nonstandard payments.

Managerial: Production foremen were given the authority to hire labor against agreed manning targets. They interviewed candidates for jobs and made the decision on their selection.

All the foremen were given complete disciplinary authority, except for dismissal. They decided what disciplinary action to take, consulted the personnel department if they thought it necessary, conducted the interviews, and kept the records.

All were given formal responsibility for the assessment, training, and development of their subordinates, and in some cases for the appointment of their own deputies. On the production side, a newly appointed training officer acted as a resource person for the foremen. Engineering foremen were involved more in the application of a job appraise-

ment scheme and in joint consultation and negotiation with union officials.

The objective of integrating the foreman more fully into the managerial team dictated that responsibility should be the motivator chiefly concerned in these changes. Control of his own labor force, backed up by more technical and financial responsibility, was designed to give the foreman more opportunities for achievement and personal growth in the job. The main issue in these studies was whether foremen would prove themselves capable of carrying the increased responsibility. Thus, in monitoring the effectiveness of the changes, the aim was primarily to detect any instability or shortcomings in performance.

Motivational Results

In summary fashion, these are the deductions that can be drawn from this study:

In six months the production foremen recruited nearly 100 men, and were judged by the personnel officer to be "hiring a better caliber of man at an improved rate." Their immediate supervisors were categorical in their approval and noted that the foremen were taking special care to "design their own shifts." Recruitment interviews were said to have improved the foremen's ability to handle encounters with existing staff and shop stewards.

Training was handled equally successfully by the production foremen. For each job it was specified that there should be a certain number of men trained to take over in an emergency. During the trial period, the margin by which the target number was missed was reduced from 94 to 55; the number of operators unable to do another's job fell by 12 per cent, and the number of assistants unable to do the job of the man they assisted fell by 37 per cent. No comparable improvement was achieved in the control group.

It became clear from both studies that foremen were fully capable of carrying disciplinary responsibility. An analysis of all cases arising during the trial year showed that there had been a reduction in the number of "repeat offenses" among employees with poor disciplinary records and a substantial reduction in short-term work stoppages. The analysis concluded that foremen were not prone to take one kind of action rather than another, they had developed a purposeful approach to such problems, and there had been no adverse union reaction.

About 50 per cent of the engineering foremen's monthly reports during the trial year referred to consultation and negotiation with union officials—this on a site not noted for its harmonious industrial relations. Topics included demarcation, special payments, and the easing of bans imposed on "call outs." The incidence of such reports was spread evenly throughout the experimental group; their frequency increased during the trial period as the foremen became more confident of their abilities. All such matters appear to have been handled capably.

From both studies came evidence, confirming what has long been demonstrated in training courses, that special investigatory projects give foremen much needed opportunity to contribute their experience and expertise to the solution of long-standing technical and organizational problems. In only three cases where financial evaluation was possible, the estimated annual savings totaled more than $125,000.

Regarding the engineering foremen's control of budgets, in some cases the aim was to meet the target exactly; in others it was to reduce costs as much as possible. Both aims were achieved by the foremen at least as well as they had been by the managers. There is no evidence that plant efficiency or work effectiveness suffered in any way as a result of cost savings achieved by the foremen.

In the case of the engineering foremen, the experimental group's staff assessments at the end of the trial year were markedly better than those of the control groups. Despite the attempt made in the initial selection of experimental and control groups to achieve as good a balance as possible in ability and experience, there can be little doubt that the experimental group did in any case contain some more able men. But no one anticipated that such a large difference would show itself at the end of the trial period. As evidence of development, 45 per cent of the experimental group's assessments referred to significant improvements in performance during the year, and 36 per cent made particular mention of how effectively the foremen had dealt with increased responsibility received during the year. These assessments were written by managers who were not party to the study.

In the production foremen's study, superintendents reported that the new conditions were "separating the wheat from the chaff"; some of those who had previously been thought to be among the best of the foremen had not lived up to their reputations in a situation which placed little value on compliance, while others had improved enormously.

The production foremen's job reaction survey scores showed no particular improvement over the trial period. In the case of the engineering foremen, the experimental group's mean score showed a 12 per cent increase, while the control group's had only risen by 3 per cent.

Part II: The Main Conclusions

What has been described in the first part of this article is the consistent application of theory in an area where custom and practice are normally only challenged by individual hunch or intuition. As we have seen, each study posed a separate problem concerning a different group of employees; the only common element among them was the conceptual framework brought to bear on the problem, enabling a specific program of action to be devised and implemented. Much was learned in the process, by ourselves and managers alike.

Now in Part II, the main conclusions which emerged from the job enrichment studies are presented in the form of answers to the questions raised at the beginning of this article.

GENERALITY OF FINDINGS

Can similarly positive results be obtained elsewhere with other people doing different jobs?

Yes. The studies reflect a diversity of type and level of job in several company functions in more than one industry. From the evidence now available, it is clear that results are not dependent on any particular set of circumstances at the place of study. Our investigation has highlighted one important aspect of the process of management and has shown that disciplined attention to it brings results. The findings are relevant wherever people are being managed.

How widespread is the scope or need for equivalent change in other jobs?

The scope seems enormous. In brainstorming sessions held to generate ideas for change in the jobs covered by the studies, it was not uncommon for over a hundred suggestions to be entertained. The process of change in these particular jobs has started, not finished. In many places it has not even started. Though there probably are jobs which do not lend themselves to enrichment, we have never encountered a level or a function where some change has not seemed possible. It is difficult to say in advance what jobs are going to offer the most scope; the most unlikely sometimes turn out to have important possibilities. We have certainly not been able to conclude that any area of work can safely be left out of consideration.

The need is deep as the scope is wide. The responsiveness of so many people to changes with a common theme suggests that an important and widespread human need has indeed been identified in the motivators. Moreover, it would seem to be a need which manifests itself in a variety of ways. If, from a company point of view, a gain once demonstrated to be possible is accepted as a need, then the performance improvements registered in these studies would seem to betray an organizational need which is far from fully recognized as yet.

Can meaningful results be obtained only in jobs with large numbers of people all doing the same work, and where performance measures are easily available?

No. Meaningful results can be obtained in situations very far from the experimental ideal. Indeed, the very awkwardness of many "real-life" situations leads to perceptions which could not come from a laboratory experiment.

Organizational changes are made, work loads fluctuate, people fall sick, managers are moved, emergencies have to be dealt with. The amount of attention which can be given to managing changes designed to enrich people's jobs is often slight. When a man's immediate supervisor does not even know that a study is taking place, there is no vested interest in its success. In circumstances such as these, whatever is done stands or falls by its own merits.

In few of the studies could members of the experimental groups be said to be doing exactly the same work. Changes sometimes had to be tailor-made to suit specific individual jobs. Yet from the diversity of application came an understanding of the commonality of the process. Although laboratory technicians were engaged in quite different kinds of research, they were all doing research work; although foremen were looking after radically different operations, they were all supervising.

The changes that seemed to have the most impact were precisely those which related to the common heart and substance of the role played by people whose jobs differed in many important details. More than this, it became clear that all of them—the laboratory technician following up an original idea, the design engineer buying equipment, the foreman taking disciplinary action, the sales representative negotiating in the customer's office—are essentially in the same situation, the crux of which is the private encounter between an individual and his task. Only a change which impacts on this central relationship, we believe, can be truly effective in a motivational sense.

Real-life conditions not only give an investigation authenticity; they highlight the problem of measurement. What is most meaningful to a manager, of course—a foreman's proprietary attitude toward his shift, for example—is not always quantifiable. An important discovery, however, was that the better the motivator, the more likely it was to provide its own measure. Employees' "sense of responsibility," judged in a vacuum, is a matter of speculation; but the exercise of a specific responsibility, once given, is usually capable of meaningful analysis. Laboratory technicians may or may not be thought to have innate potential; the number and quality of their research minutes can be measured. Several times managers commented that job enrichment had opened up measurement opportunities which not only allowed a more accurate assessment of individual performance, but often led to a better diagnosis of technical problems as well.

FEASIBILITY OF CHANGE

Are there not situations where the operational risk is so high that it would be foolhardy to attempt to pass responsibility and scope for achievement down the line?

Probably there are, but we have not encountered one. The risks attached to some of the changes in the sales representatives' study seemed frightening at tht time. Few managers who have not tried it can accept with equanimity the thought of their subordinates placing orders for $500,000 worth of equipment on their own authority, even with a sanctioned project. The research manager in the laboratory technicians' study concluded that a change was only likely to be motivational for his subordinates if it made him lose sleep at nights.

Yet in no case did disaster result. In reviewing the results of the studies with the managers concerned, it was difficult in fact for us as outsiders not to have a sense of anticlimax. By the end of the trial period, the nerve-racking gambles of a few months before were hardly worth a mention. The new conditions seemed perfectly ordinary. Managers had completely revised their probability judgments in the light of experience.

Theory provides an explanation for the remarkable absence of disaster experienced in practice. Bad hygiene, such as oppressive supervision and ineffectual control systems, constrains and limits performance, and may even lead to sabotage. Administrative procedures that guard against hypothetical errors and imaginary irresponsibility breed the very carelessness and apathy which result in inefficiency. With too many controls, responsibility becomes so divided that it gets lost. Hygiene improvements at best lift the constraints.

The motivators, on the other hand, make it possible for the individual to advance the base line of his performance. The road is open for improvement, while present standards remain available as a reference point and guide. When a man is given the chance to achieve more, he may not take that chance, but he has no reason to achieve less. The message of both theory and practice is that people respond cautiously to new responsibility; they feel their way and seek advice. When responsibility is put squarely with the person doing a job, he is the one who wants and needs feedback in order to do his job. His use of the motivators, not our use of hygiene, is what really controls performance standards.

As managers, we start having positive control of the job only when we stop concentrating on trying to control people. Mistakes are less likely, not more likely, than before; those which do occur are more likely to be turned to account, learned from, and prevented in the future, for they are seen to matter. Monitoring continues, but its purpose has changed. Now it provides the jobholder with necessary information and enables management to see how much more can be added to a job rather than how much should be subtracted from it. That way, continual improvement, while not being guaranteed, at least becomes possible as the scope for the motivators is extended. It is the nearest thing to a performance insurance policy that management can have.

Such is the theory, and from the evidence of the studies, practice bears it out. If the studies show anything, they show that it pays to experiment. No one is being asked to accept anything on faith; what is required is the courage to put old assumptions and old fears to the test. For the manager, the process is like learning to swim: it may not be necessary to jump in at the deep end, but it surely is necessary to leave the shallow end. Only those who have done so are able to conquer the fear which perverts our whole diagnosis of the problem of managing people.

Because people's ability and sense of responsibility vary so much, is it not necessary to make changes selectively?

No. To make changes selectively is never to leave the shallow end of the pool. We are in no position to decide, before the event, who deserves to have his job enriched and who does not. In almost every study managers were surprised by the response of

individuals, which varied certainly, but not always in the way that would have been forecast. As the job changed, so did the criteria of successful performance change. Some people who had been thought to be sound and responsible under the old conditions turned out merely to have been yes-men once those conditions were changed; their performance was the same as it had always been, but now compliance was no longer valued so highly. At the other extreme was one classic example of an awkward employee, about to be sacked, who turned out to unusually inventive and responsible when he has given the opportunity to be so.

In one study, not reported, a promising set of changes brought relatively disappointing results—the changes had been implemented selectively. When pressed to explain the grounds on which people had been chosen, the manager quoted as an example someone who had already carried similar responsibility in a previous job. It is exactly this kind of vicious circle that job enrichment seeks to break.

When changes are made unselectively, the genuinely good performers get better. Some poor performers remain poor, but nothing is lost. Because the changes are opportunities and not demands, all that happens is that the less able ignore them and go on as before. Some people, however, develop as they never could under the old conditions, and do better than others originally rated much higher. This is the bonus from job enrichment. Not only is over-all performance improved, but a clearer picture emerges of individual differences and potential.

So long as a foundation of new job opportunities available to all is firmly established, there is no harm in restricting certain changes to the more senior of the jobholders. Such changes can be seen in both the laboratory technicians' and the design engineers' studies. This is a very different matter from introducing changes selectively in the first place. It is a way of providing scope for personal advancement within the job and recognizing the achievements of those who build well on the foundation of opportunity already provided.

Do all employees welcome having their jobs enriched, or are there not some who prefer things to be left as they are?

Individual reaction to job enrichment is as difficult to forecast in terms of attitudes as it is in terms of performance. Those already genuinely interested in their work develop real enthusiasm. Not all people welcome having their jobs enriched, certainly, but so long as the changes are opportunities rather than demands, there is no reason to fear an adverse reaction. If someone prefers things the way they are, he merely keeps them the way they are, by continuing to refer matters to his supervisor, for example. Again, there is nothing lost.

On the other hand, some of the very people whom one might expect to duck their chance seize it with both hands, developing a keenness one would never have anticipated. In attitudes as well as in performance, the existence of individual differences is no bar to investigating the possibilities of job enrichment.

Can you enrich jobs without inevitably facing demands for higher pay or better conditions to match the new responsibilities?

Yes. In no instance did management face a demand of this kind as a result of changes made in the studies. It would seem that changes in working practice can be made without always having a price tag attached.

Here, as in the matter of operational risk, what is surprising in practice is easily explicable in terms of theory. The motivators and the hygiene factors may not be separate dimensions in a manager's analysis of a situation, but they are in people's experience. It is time that our diagnosis of problems took more account of people's experience. The studies demonstrate again that,

when presented with an opportunity for achievement, people either achieve something or they do not; when allowed to develop, they either respond or stay as they are. Whatever the result, it is a self-contained experience, a private encounter between a person and his task.

It is something quite separate when the same person becomes annoyed by his poor working conditions, worries about his status or security, or sees his neighbors enjoying a higher standard of living. The cause-effect relationship between hygiene and motivation scarcely exists. Motivation is not the product of good hygiene, even if bad hygiene sometimes leads to sabotage. Higher pay may temporarily buy more work, but it does not buy commitment. Nor does commitment to a task, by itself, bring demand for better hygiene.

Managers often complain of their lack of room for maneuver. In doing so, they are generalizing from the rules of the hygiene game to the total management situation. There is little evidence that the workforce in fact prostitutes its commitment to a task, although incentive bonus schemes, productivity bargaining, and the like assiduously encourage such prostitution. Before the process goes too far, it seems worth exploring more fully the room for maneuver freely available on the motivator dimension.

This is not to say, however, that the motivators should be used as an alibi for the neglect of hygiene. If people genuinely are achieving more, taking more responsibility, and developing greater competence, that is no reason to take advantage of them for a short-term profit. Any tendency to exploitation on management's part could destroy the whole process.

Is not the best route to motivational change through participation?

Yes and no. We have to define our terms. So far as the process of job enrichment itself is concerned, experimental constraints in the studies dictated that there could be no participation by jobholders themselves in deciding what changes were to be made in their jobs. The changes nevertheless seemed to be effective. On the other hand, when people were invited to participate—not in any of the reported studies—results were disappointing. In one case, for example, a group of personnel specialists suggested fewer than thirty fairly minor changes in their jobs, whereas their managers had compiled a list of over a hundred much more substantial possibilities.

It seems that employees themselves are not in a good position to test out the validity of the boundaries of their jobs. So long as the aim is not to measure experimentally the effects of job enrichment alone, there is undoubtedly benefit in the sharing of ideas. Our experience merely suggests that it would be unwise to pin too many hopes to it—or the wrong hopes.

Participation is sometimes held, consciously or unconsciously, to be an alternative to job enrichment. Instead of passing responsibility down the line and possibly losing control, the manager can consult his subordinates before making a decision, involve them, make them feel part of the team. It all seems to be a matter of degree, after all. Participation, in this sense of consultation, is seen as a safe halfway house to job enrichment, productive and satisfying to all concerned.

A multitude of techniques are available to help the manager be more effective in consultation: he can be trained to be more sensitive to interpersonal conflict, more sophisticated in his handling of groups, more ready to listen, more oriented toward valuing others' contributions. Better decisions result, especially in problem-solving meetings that bring together colleagues or opponents in different roles or functions.

But in the specific context of the management of subordinates, it is worth asking who is motivated in this kind of participation. The answer would seem to be the person who needs a second opinion to make sure he comes to the right decision—the manager in fact. The subordinate does not have the same professional or work-inspired need for the encounter, for he is not the one who has to live with responsibility for the decision. It is doubtful whether his "sense of involvement" even makes him feel good for long, for an appeal to personal vanity wears thin without more substance. However well-intentioned, this halfway-house kind of participative management smacks of conscience money; and receivers of charity are notoriously ungrateful. In the case of professional staff it is downright patronizing, for the subordinate is paid to offer his opinion anyway.

Theory clarifies the position. It is not a matter of degree at all. The difference between consultation and enrichment is a difference in kind. Consultation does not give a subordinate the chance for personal achievement which he can recognize; through involvement, it subtly denies him the exercise of responsibility which would lead to his development, however humbly, as an executive in his own right. Far from being the best route to motivational change, this kind of participation is a red herring. It is hygiene masquerading as a motivator, diverting attention from the real problem. It may help to prevent dissatisfaction, but it does not motivate.

The laboratory technicians, sales representatives, design engineers, and foremen did indeed participate, but not in a consultative exercise designed to keep them happy or to help their managers reach better decisions. Nor was it participation in ambiguity—an all too common occurrence in which, although no one quite knows where he stands or what may happen, the mere fact of participation is supposed to bring success. The participation of employees involved in the studies consisted of doing things which had always previously been done by more senior people. In all cases consultation continued, but now it was consultation upward. In consultation upward there is no ambiguity; tasks and roles are clear. Both parties are motivated, the subordinate by the need to make the best decision, to satisfy himself, to justify the trust placed in him, to enhance his professional reputation; the manager by the need to develop his staff.

When design engineers consulted their more senior colleagues, it was on questions of technical difficulty, commercial delicacy, or professional integrity—all more to the point than the mere price of a piece of equipment. Foremen consulted their managers on unusual budgetary worries, or the personnel department on tricky disciplinary problems. Sales representatives consulted headquarters on matters such as the stock position on a certain product before negotiating special terms with a customer.

Participation is indeed the best route to motivational change, but only when it is participation in the act of management, no matter at what level it takes place. And the test of the genuineness of that participation is simple—it must be left to the subordinate to be the prime mover in consultation on those topics where he carries personal responsibility. For the manager, as for the subordinate, the right to be consulted must be earned by competence in giving help. Therein lies the only authority worth having.

EXPECTED CONSEQUENCES

In view of so many possible difficulties in the way, are the gains to be expected from job enrichment significant or only marginal?

We believe the gains are significant, but the evidence must speak for itself. In all, 100 people were in the experimental groups in the studies described. A conservative reckoning of the financial benefit achieved, arrived at by halving all estimated annual gains or savings, would still be over $200,000 per year. Cost was measurable in a few days of managers' time at each place.

Do the gains relate primarily to job satisfaction or to performance?

Contrary to expectation, the gains, initially at least, seem to relate primarily to performance. Wherever a direct measure of performance was possible, an immediate gain was registered. In one or two instances, performance seemed to peak and then drop back somewhat, though it stayed well above its starting point and well above the control group's performance. Elsewhere there seemed to be a more gradual improvement; if anything it gained momentum through the trial period. We have no evidence to suggest that performance gains, once firmly established, are not capable of being sustained.

In the short term, gains in job satisfaction would seem to be less spectacular. Attitudes do not change overnight. Satisfaction is the result of performance, nor vice versa, and there is a long history of frustration to be overcome. When direct measurement of job satisfaction was possible, the most significant gains seemed to come when the trial period was longest. There is every reason to think that in the long term attitudes catch up with performance and that job enrichment initiates a steady prolonged improvement in both.

What are the consequences for supervision if jobs are loaded with new tasks taken from above—i.e., does one man's enrichment become another's impoverishment?

The more subordinates' jobs are enriched, the more superfluous does supervision, in its old sense, become. Several of the studies showed that short-term absences of the experimental groups' supervisors could be coped with more easily as day-to-day concern for operational problems shifted downward. The need for the supervisor to be always "on the job" diminished; greater organizational flexibility was gained.

But though supervision may become redundant, supervisors do not. Fears of loss of authority or prestige were never realized. Far from their jobs being impoverished, supervisors now found that they had time available to do more important work. Design engineers' supervisors were able to devote more effort to technical development; production foremen's supervisors found themselves playing a fuller managerial role.

The enrichment of lower-level jobs seems to set up a chain reaction resulting in the enrichment of supervisors' jobs as well. Fears that the supervisor may somehow miss out are based on the premise that there is a finite pool or responsibility in the organization which is shared among its members. In practice new higher-order responsibilities are born.

Even when subordinates are given responsibilities not previously held by their own supervisors, as happened in the sales representatives' study and to a lesser extent in some of the others, there is no evidence that supervisors feel bypassed or deprived, except perhaps very temporarily. It soon becomes apparent to all concerned that to supervise people with authority of their own is a more demanding, rewarding, and enjoyable task than to rule over a bunch of automatons, checking their every move.

Finally, what are the consequences for management if motivational change becomes a reality? Is the manager's role affected? If so, how? And what are the implications for management development?

The main consequence is that management becomes a service, its purpose to enable, encourage, assist, and reinforce achievement by employees. Task organization and task support are the central features of the manager's new role. In task *organization* two complementary criteria emerge: (1) tasks have to be authentic—i.e., the more opportunity they give employees to contribute to business objectives, the more effective they are likely to be motivationally; (2) tasks have to be motivational—i.e., the more they draw upon the motivators, the more likely they are to produce an effective contribution to business objectives. In task *support*, factors such as company policy and administration, technical supervision, interpersonal relations, and working conditions all have to be pressed into the service of the motivators. Control of the job is achieved by providing people with the tools of their trade, with the information they require, with training as appropriate, and with advice when sought.

The job itself becomes the prime vehicle of all individual development, of which management development is only one kind. In aiding the process of development, our starting point, as always, is problem diagnosis—in this case, assessment of individual abilities, potentials, and needs. When people are underemployed, we have no way of distinguishing between those who are near the limit of their abilities and those who have a great deal more to contribute. All too often, potential has to be inferred from risky and subjective judgments about personality. Such judgments, once made, tend to be static; people become categorized. The studies show that when tasks are organized to be as authentic and motivational as possible, management receives a more accurate and a continuing feedback on individual strengths and weaknesses, ability, and potential. Task support becomes a flexible instrument of management, responsive to feedback.

If the job itself is the prime vehicle of individual development, task support is the means by which management can influence it. We still think of individual development, especially management development, far too much as something which can be imposed from outside. We pay lip service to on-the-job training but go on running courses as a refuge. We speak of self-development, but we are at a loss to know how to encourage it. Now, however, we can postulate a criterion: self-development is likely to be most effective when the task a person is engaged in is authentic and motivational and when in doing it he receives understanding, imaginative, and capable support. When these conditions are met, the job itself becomes a true learning situation, its ingredients the motivators.

Though only one study set out specifically

to measure individual development, the most pervasive impression from all was one of development and personal growth achieved. The latent inspirational value of jobs appeared to have been released. People were able to demonstrate and utilize skills they already possessed, and go on to learn new ones. Each new facet of the task required a response in terms of individual development, and results suggest that the response was seldom lacking.

The best evidence of development came, however, not from the experimental groups in the studies, but from the managers who put the studies into effect. It is sometimes said that attitude change is the key to success. But in seeking to improve the performance of our business, perhaps we rely too much on efforts to change managers' attitudes. These studies went ahead without waiting for miracles of conversion first. Just as the experimental groups in the studies represented a cross section of employees engaged on those jobs, so the managers who put the studies into effect represented a cross section of managers. Enthusiasts and skeptics alike agreed to judge the studies by their results. They did, and the effect was clear for the observer to see. Success proved to be the key to attitude change. In retrospect, who would want it otherwise?

8

Job Enrichment Lessons from A T & T

ROBERT N. FORD[1]

There is a mounting problem in the land, the concern of employed persons with their work life. Blue-collar workers are increasingly expressing unhappiness over the monotony of the production line. White-collar workers want to barter less of their life for bread. More professional groups are unionizing to fight back at somebody.

The annual reports of many companies frequently proclaim, "Our employees are our most important resource." Is this a statement of conviction or is it mere rhetoric? If it represents conviction, then I think it is only fair to conclude that many business organizations are unwittingly squandering their resources.

The enormous economic gains that sprang from the thinking of the scientific management school of the early 1900s—the time-and-motion study analysts, the creators of production lines—may have ended insofar as they depend on utilizing human beings more efficiently. Without discarding these older insights, we need to consider more recent

evidence showing that the tasks themselves can be changed to give workers a feeling of accomplishment.

The growing pressure for a four-day work-week is not necessarily evidence that people do not care about their work; they may be rejecting their work in the form that confronts them. To ask employees to repeat one small task all day, at higher and higher rates of speed, is no way to reduce the pressure for a shorter work-week, nor is it any longer a key to rising productivity in America. Work need not be so frequently a betrayal of one's education and ability.

From 1965 to 1968 a group of researchers at AT&T conducted 19 formal field experiments in job enrichment. The success of these studies has led to many company projects since then. From this work and the studies of others, we have learned that the "lifesaving" portion of many jobs can be expanded. Conversely, the boring and unchallenging aspects can be reduced—not to say eliminated.

Furthermore, the "nesting" of related, already enriched jobs—a new concept—may constitute another big step toward better utilization of "our most important resource."

1. The author wishes to acknowledge the collaboration of Malcolm B. Gillette of AT&T and Bruce H. Duffany of Drake-Beam & Associates in the formulation of the job enrichment strategy discussed in this article.

First in this article I shall break down the job enrichment strategy into three steps. Then I shall demonstrate what we at AT&T have been doing for seven years in organizing the work beyond enrichment of individual jobs. In the course of my discussion, I shall use no illustrations that were not clearly successful from the viewpoint of both employees and the company.

While obviously the functions described in the illustrations differ superficially from those in most other companies, they are still similar enough to production and service tasks in other organizations to permit meaningful comparison. It is important to examine the nature of the work itself, rather than the external aspects of the functions.

Moreover, in considering ways to enrich jobs, I am not talking about those elements that serve only to "maintain" employees: wages, fringe benefits, clean restrooms, a pleasant atmosphere, and so on. Any organization must meet the market in these respects or its employees will go elsewhere.

No, employees are saying more than "treat me well." They are also saying "use me well." The former is the maintenance side of the coin; the latter is the work motivation side.

ANATOMY OF ENRICHMENT

In talking about job enrichment, it is necessary to go beyond such high-level concepts as "self-actualization," "need for achievement," and "psychological growth." It is necessary to specify the steps to be taken. The strategy can be broken down into these aspects—improving work through systematic changes in (a) the module of work, (b) control of the module, and (c) the feedback signaling whether something has been accomplished. I shall discuss each of these aspects in turn.

Work Module

Through changing the work modules, Indiana Bell Telephone Company scored a striking success in job enrichment within the space of two years. In Indianapolis, 33 employees, most of them at the lowest clerical wage level, compiled all telephone directories for the state. The processing from clerk to clerk was laid out in 21 steps, many of which were merely for verification. The steps included manuscript reception, manuscript verification, keypunch, keypunch verification, ad copy reception, ad copy verification, and so on—a production line as real as any in Detroit. Each book is issued yearly to the customers named in it, and the printing schedule calls for the appearance of about one different directory per week.

In 1968, the year previous to the start of our study, 28 new hires were required to keep the clerical force at the 33-employee level. Obviously, such turnover had bad consequences. From every operating angle, management was dissatisfied.

In a workshop, the supervisors concluded that the lengthly verification routine, calling for confirmation of one's work by other clerks, was not solving the basic problem, which was employee indifference toward the tasks. Traditional "solutions" were ineffective. They included retraining, supervisor complaints to the employees, and "communicating" with them on the importance to customers of error-free listing of their names and places of business in the directories. As any employee smart enough to be hired knows, an incorrect listing will remain monumentally wrong for a whole year.

The supervisors came up with many ideas for enriching the job. The first step was to identify the most competent employees, and then ask them, one by one, if they felt they could do error-free work, so that having others check the work would be pointless. Would they check their own work if no one else did it?

Yes, they said they could do error-free work. With this simple step the module dropped from 21 slices of clerical work to 14.

Next the supervisory family decided to

take a really big step. In the case of the thinner books, they asked certain employees whether they would like to "own" their own books and perform all 14 remaining steps with no verification unless they themselves arranged it with other clerks—as good stenographers do when in doubt about a difficult piece of paperwork. Now the module included every step (except keytape, a minor one).

Then the supervisors turned their attention to a thick book, the Indianapolis directory, which requires many hands and heads. They simple assigned letters of the alphabet to individuals and let them complete all 14 steps for each block of letters.

In the past, new entries to all directories had moved from clerk to clerk; now all paperwork connected with an entry belonging to a clerk stayed with that clerk. For example, the clerk prepared the daily addenda and issued them to the information or directory assistance operators. The system became so efficient that most of the clerks who handled the smaller directories had charge of more than one.

Delimiting the module: In an interview one of the clerks said, "It's a book of my own." That is the way they felt about the books. Although not all modules are physically so distinct, the idea for a good module is usually there. Ideally, it is a slice of work that gives an employee a "thing of my own." At AT&T I have heard good modules described with pride in various ways:

. . . "a piece of turf" (especially a geographic responsibility);

. . . "my real estate" (by engineers responsible for a group of central offices);

. . . "our cradle-to-grave modem line" (a vastly improved Western Electric switching-device production line);

. . . "our mission impossible team" (a framemen's team, Long Lines Department).

The trouble with so much work processing is that no one is clearly responsible for a total unit that fails. In Indianapolis, by contrast, when a name in a directory is misspelled or omitted, the clerk knows where the responsibility lies.

Delimiting the module is not usually difficult when the tasks are in production, or at least physically defined. It is more difficult in service tasks, such as handling a telephone call. But modules make sense here, too, if the employee has been prepared for the work so that nobody else need be involved— in other words, when it is not necessary to say to the caller, "Let me connect you with my supervisor about that, please" or "May I give you our billing department, please?"

It is not always true that any one employee can handle a complete service. But our studies show that we consistently erred in forming the module; we tended to "underwhelm" employees. Eventually we learned that the worker can do more, especially as his or her experience builds. We do not have even one example from our business where job enrichment resulted in a *smaller* slice of work.

In defining modules that give each employee a natural area of responsibility, we try to accumulate horizontal slices of work until we have created (or recreated) one of these three entities for him or her:

1. A customer (usually someone outside the business);
2. A client (usually someone inside the business, helping the employee serve the customer);
3. A task (in the manufacturing end of the business, for example, where, ideally, individual employees produce complete items).

Any one of these three can make a meaningful slice of work. (In actuality, they are not separated; obviously, an employee can be working on a task for a *customer*.) Modules more difficult to differentiate are those in which the "wholeness" of the job is less clear—that is, control is not complete. They include cases where—

... the employee is merely one of many engaged in providing the ultimate service or item;

... the employee's customer is really the boss (or, worse yet, the boss's boss) who tells him what to do;

... the job is to help someone who tells the employee what is to be done.

While jobs like these are harder to enrich, it is worth trying.

Control of the Module

As an employee gains experience, the supervisor should continue to turn over responsibility until the employee is handling the work completely. The reader may infer that supervisors are treating employees unequally. But it is not so; ultimately, they may all have the complete job if they can handle it. In the directory-compilation case cited—which was a typical assembly-line procedure, although the capital investment was low—the supervisors found that they could safely permit the employee to say when sales of advertisements in the yellow pages must stop if the ads were to reach the printer on time.

Employees of South Central Bell Telephone Company, who set their own cut-off dates for the New Orleans, Monroeville, and Shreveport phone books, consistently gave themselves less time than management had previously allowed. As a result, the sale of space in the yellow pages one year continued for three additional weeks, producing more than $100,000 in extra revenue.

But that was only one element in the total module and its control. The directory clerks talked *directly* to salesmen, to the printer, to supervisors in other departments about production problems, to service representatives, and to each other as the books moved through the production stages.

There are obvious risks on the supervisors' side as they give their jobs away, piece by piece, to selected employees. We have been through it enough to advise, "Don't worry."

Be assured that supervisors who try it will say, as many in the Bell System have said, "Now, at last, I feel like a manager. Before I was merely chief clerk around here."

In other studies we have made, control has been handed by the supervisor to a person when the employee is given the authority to perform such tasks as these:

Set credit ratings for customers;

Ask for, and determine the size of, a deposit;

Cut off service for nonpayment;

Make his or her own budget, subject to negotiation;

Perform work other than that on the order sheet after negotiating it with the customers;

Reject a run or supply of material because of poor quality;

Make free use of small tools or supplies within a budget negotiated with the supervisor;

Talk to anyone at any organizational level when the employee's work is concerned;

Call directly and negotiate for outside repairmen or suppliers (within the budget) to remedy a condition handicapping the employee's performance.

Feedback

Definition of the module and control of it are futile unless the results of the employee's effort are discernible. Moreover, knowledge of the results should go directly to where it will nurture motivation—that is, to the employee. People have a great capacity for mid-flight correction when they know where they stand.

One control responsibility given to excellent employees in AT&T studies is self-monitoring; it lets them record their own "qualities and quantities." For example, one employee who had only a grade-school education was taught to keep a quality control chart in which the two identical parts of a dry-reed switch were not to vary more than .005 from an ideal dimension. She found that for some reason too many switches were failing.

She proved that the trouble occurred when one reed that was off by .005 met another reed that was off by .005. The sum, .010, was too much in the combined component and it failed. On her own initiative, she recommended and saw to it that the machine dies were changed when the reeds being stamped out started to vary by .003 from the ideal. A total variance of .006 would not be too much, she reasoned. Thus the feedback she got showed her she was doing well at her job.

This example shows all three factors at work—the module, its control, and feedback. She and two men, a die maker and a machine operator, had the complete responsibility for producing each day more than 100,000 of these tiny parts, which are not unlike two paper matches, but much smaller. How can one make a life out of this? Well, they did. The six stamping machines and expensive photometric test equipment were "theirs." A forklift truck had been dedicated to them (no waiting for someone else to bring or remove supplies). They ordered rolls of wire for stamping machines when they estimated they would need it. They would ship a roll back when they had difficulty controlling it.

Compared with workers at a plant organized along traditional lines, with batches of the reeds moving from shop to shop, these three employees were producing at a fourfold rate. Such a minigroup, where each person plays a complementary part, is radically different psychologically from the traditional group of workers, where each is doing what the others do.

(In the future, when now undreamed-of computer capacities have been reached, management must improve its techniques of feeding performance results directly to the employee responsible. And preferably it should be done *before* the boss knows about it.)

IMPROVING THE SYSTEM

When a certain job in the Bell System is being enriched, we ask the supervisory family, "Who or what is the customer/client/ task in this job?" Also, "How often can the module be improved?" And then, "How often can control or feedback be improved? Can we improve all three at once?"

These are good questions to ask in general. My comments at this stage of our knowledge must be impressionistic.

The modules of most jobs can be improved, we have concluded. Responsibilities or tasks that exist elsewhere in the shop or in some other shop or department need to be combined with the job under review. This horizontal loading is necessary until the base of the job is right. However, I have not yet seen a job whose base was too broad.

At levels higher than entrance grade, and especially in management positions, many responsibilities can be moved to lower grade levels, usually to the advantage of every job involved. This vertical loading is especially important in mature organizations.

In the Indianapolis directory office, 21 piecemeal tasks were combined into a single, meaningful, natural task. There are counterparts in other industries, such as the assembly of an entire dashboard of an automobile by two workers.

We have evidence that two jobs—such as the telephone installer's job and the telephone repairman's job—often can make one excellent "combinationman's" job. But there are some jobs in which the work module is already a good one. One of these is the service representative, the highly trained clerk to whom a customer speaks when he wants to have a telephone installed, moved, or disconnected, or when he questions his telephone bill. This is sometimes a high-turnover job, and when a service representative quits because of work or task dissatisfaction, there goes $3,450 in training. In fact, much of the impetus for job enrichment came through efforts to reduce these costs.

In this instance the slice of work was well enough conceived; nevertheless, we obtained excellent results from the procedures of job enrichment. Improvements in the turnover

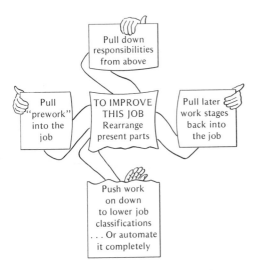

Fig. 8-1. Steps in Improving a Job

situation were as great as 50 per cent. Why? Because we would improve the control and feedback.

It should be recognized that moving the work module to a lower level is not the same as moving the control down. If the supervisor decides that a customer's account is too long overdue and tells the service representative what to do, then both the module and the control rest with the supervisor. When, under job enrichment procedures, the service representative makes the decision that a customer must be contacted, but checks it first with the supervisor, control remains in the supervisor's hands. Under full job enrichment, however, the service representative has control.

Figure 8-1 shows in schematic form the steps to be taken when improving a job. To increase control, responsibility must be obtained from higher levels; I have yet to see an instance where control is moved upward to enrich a job. It must be acknowledged, however, that not every employee is ready to handle more control. That is especially true of new employees.

Moreover, changing the control of a job is more threatening to supervisors than is changing the module. In rejecting a job

enrichment proposal, one depàrtment head said to us, "When you have this thing proved 100 per cent, let me know and we'll try it."

As far as feedback is concerned, it is usually improvable, but not until the module and control of it are in top condition. If the supervisory family cannot come up with good ways for telling the employee how he or she is doing, the problem lies almost surely in a bad module. That is, the employee's work is submerged in a total unit and he or she has no distinct customer/client/task.

When the module is right, you get feedback "for free"; it comes directly from the customer/client/task. During the learning period, however, the supervisor or teacher should provide the feedback.

When supervisors use the performance of all employees as a goal to individual employees, they thwart the internalization of motivation that job enrichment strives for. An exception is the small group of mutually supporting, complementary workers, but even in this case each individual needs knowledge of his or her own results.

These generalizations cannot be said to be based on an unbiased sample of all jobs in all locations. Usually, the study or project locations were not in deep trouble, nor were they the best operating units. The units in deep trouble cannot stand still long enough to figure out what is wrong, and the top performers need no help. Therefore, the hard-nosed, scientifically trained manager can rightfully say that the jury is still out as to whether job enrichment can help in all work situations. But is has helped repeatedly and consistently on many jobs in the Bell System.

JOB 'NESTING'

Having established to its satisfaction that job enrichment works, management at AT&T is studying ways to go beyond the enriching of individual jobs. A technique that offers great promise is that of "nesting" several jobs to improve morale and upgrade performance.

By way of illustration I shall describe how a family of supervisors of service representa-

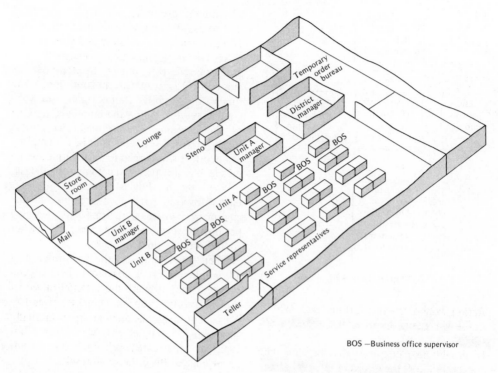

Fig. 8-2. Ferguson District Service Representatives' Office Layout Before Job Enrichment

tives in a unit of Southwestern Bell Telephone Company improved its service indexes, productivity, collection of overdue bills, and virtually every other index of performance. In two years they moved their Ferguson District (adjacent to St. Louis) from near the bottom to near the top in results among all districts in the St. Louis area.

Before the job enrichment effort started, the service representatives' office was laid out as it appears in Figure 8-2. The exhibit shows their desks in the standard, in-line arrangement fronted by the desks of their supervisors, who exercised close control of the employees.

As part of the total job enrichment effort, each service rep group was given a geographical locality of its own, with a set of customers to take care of, rather than just "the next customer who calls in" from

anywhere in the district. Some service reps—most of them more experienced—were detached to form a unit handling only the businesses in the district.

Then the service representatives and their business office supervisors (BOS) were moved to form a "wagon train" layout. As Figure 8-3 shows, they were gathered into a more-or-less circular shape and were no longer directly facing the desks of the business office supervisors and unit managers. (The office of the district manager was further removed too.)

Now all was going well with the service representatives' job, but another function in the room was in trouble. This was the entry-level job of service-order typist. These typists transmit the orders to the telephone installers and the billing and other departments. They and the service order reviewers —a higher-classification job—had been

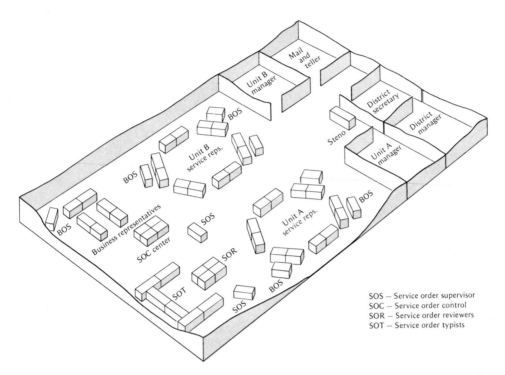

SOS — Service order supervisor
SOC — Service order control
SOR — Service order reviewers
SOT — Service order typists

Fig. 8-3. Service Representatives' Office Layout After Job Enrichment Program Was Implemented

located previously in a separate room that was soundproofed and air-conditioned because the TWX machines they used were noisy and hot. When its equipment was converted to the silent, computer-operated cathode ray tubes (CRTs), the unit was moved to a corner of the service reps' room (see Figure 8-3).

But six of the eight typists quit in a matter of months after the move. Meanwhile, the percentage of service orders typed "on time" fell below 50 per cent, then below 40 per cent.

The reasons given by the six typists who quit were varied, but all appeared to be rationalizations. The managers who looked at the situation, and at the $25,000 investment in the layout, could see that the feeling of physical isolation and the feeling of having no "thing" of their own were doubtless the real prime factors. As the arrange-

ment existed, any service order typist could be called on to type an order for any service representative. On its face, this seems logical; but we have learned that an employee who belongs to everybody belongs to nobody.

An instantly acceptable idea was broached: assign certain typists to each service rep team serving a locality. "And while we're at it," someone said, "why not move the CRTs right into the group? Let's have a wagon train with the women and kids in the middle." This was done (over the protest of the budget control officer, I should add).

The new layout appears in Figure 8-4. Three persons are located in the station in the middle of each unit. The distinction between service order typist and service order reviewer has been abolished, with the former upgraded to the scale of the latter. (Lack of space has precluded arranging the

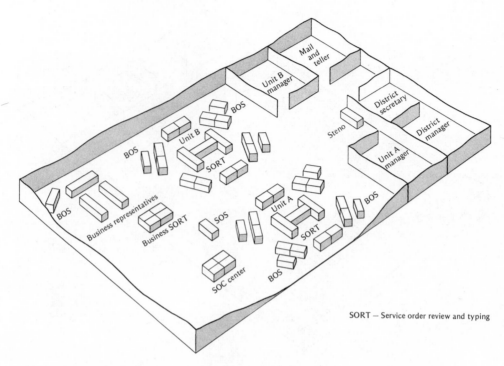

SORT — Service order review and typing

Fig. 8-4.   Office Layout After Service Order Typists Were "Nested"

business customer unit in the same wagon-train fashion. But that unit's service order review and typing desks are close to the representatives' desks.)

Before the changes were started, processing a service request involved ten steps—and sometimes as many persons—not counting implementation of the order in the Plant Department. Now the procedure is thought of in terms of people, and only three touch a service order on its way through the office. (See Figure 8-5.) At this writing, the Ferguson managers hope to eliminate even the service order completion clerk as a specialized position.

Has the new arrangement worked? Just before the typists moved into the wagon train, they were issuing only 27 per cent of the orders on time. Within 30 days after the switch to assigned responsibility, 90 per cent of the orders were going out on time. Half a

year later, in one particular month, the figure even reached 100 per cent.

These results were obtained with a 21 per cent jump in work load—comparing a typical quarter after "nesting" with one before—being performed with a net drop of 22 worker-weeks during the quarter. On a yearly basis it is entirely reasonable to expect the elimination of 88 weeks of unnecessary work (conservatively, 1½ full-time employees). Unneeded messenger service has been dispensed with, and one of two service order supervisor positions has been eliminated. The entire cost has been recovered already.

The service order accuracy measurement, so important in computerization, has already attained the stringent objectives set by the employees themselves, which exceeded the level supervisors would have set. Why are there fewer errors? Because now employees

OLD PROCEDURE

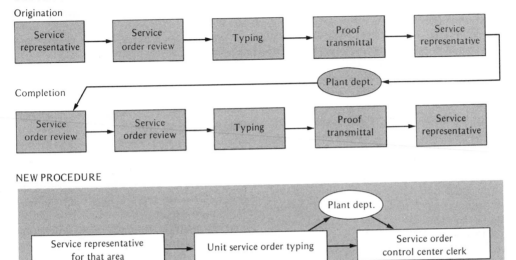

Fig. 8-5. Old and New Processing in Request-for-Service Department

can lean across the area and talk to each other about a service order with a problem or handwriting that is unclear. During the course of a year this will probably eliminate the hand preparation of a thousand "query" slips, with a thousand written replies, in this one district.

And what of the human situation? When on-time order issuance was at its ebb, a supervisor suggested having a picnic for the service representatives and the typists. They did, but not a single typist showed up. Later, when the on-time order rate had climbed over 90 per cent, I remarked, "Now's the time for another picnic." To which the supervisor replied facetiously, "Now we don't need a picnic!"

The turnover among typists for job reasons has virtually ceased. Some are asking now for the job of service representative, which is more demanding, more skilled, and better paid. Now, when the CRTs or the computer is shut down for some reason, or if the service order typist runs out of work,

supervisors report that typists voluntarily help the service reps with filing and other matters. They are soaking up information about the higher-rated jobs. These occurrences did not happen when the typists were 100 feet away; then they just sat doing nothing when the work flow ceased. (Because of this two-way flow of information, incidentally, training time for the job of service representative may drop as much as 50 per cent.)

As the state general manager remarked when the results were first reported, "This is a fantastic performance. It's not enough to enrich just one job in a situation. We must learn how to put them together."

DIFFERENT CONFIGURATION

While the Ferguson District supervisory family was making a minigroup out of the service reps and their CRT typists, a strikingly different minigroup was in formation in the Northern Virginia Area of the Chesapeake and Potomac Telephone Company. There the family hit on the idea of funneling to selected order typists only those orders connected with a given central office, such as the Lewinsville frame. Soon the typists and the framemen—those who actually make the changes as a result of service orders—became acquainted. The typists even visited "their" framerooms. Now some questions could be quickly resolved that previously called for formal interdepartmental interrogations through supervisors.

At the end of the first eight months of 1972, these nine CRT typists were producing service order pages at a rate one-third higher than the 51 service order typists in the comparison group. The absence rate in the experimental unit was 0.6 per cent, compared with 2.5 per cent for the others, and the errors per 100 orders amounted to 2.9 as against 4.6 in the comparison group.

The flow of service orders is from (a) service rep to (b) service order typist to (c) the frameroom. The Ferguson District enjoyed success when it linked (a) and (b), while productivity for the Lewinsville frame improved when (b) and (c) were linked. Obviously, the next step is to link (a), (b), and (c). We are now selecting trial locations to test this larger nesting approach.

Lessons Learned

In summary fashion, at the end of seven years of effort to improve the work itself, it is fair to say that:

Enriching existing jobs pays off. To give an extreme example, consider the fact that Illinois Bell Telephone Company's directory compilation effort reduced the work force from 120 persons to 74. Enriching the job started a series of moves; it was not the only ingredient, but it was the precipitating one.

Job enrichment requires a big change in managerial style. It calls for increasing modules, moving control downward, and dreaming up new feedback ideas. There is

nothing easy about a successful job enrichment effort.

The nesting or configuring of related tasks—we call it "work organization"—may be the next big step forward after the enrichment of single jobs in the proper utilization of human beings.

It seems to produce a multiplier effect rather than merely a simple sum. In the Ferguson District case the job modules were not changed; the service representatives were not asked to type their own orders on the cathole ray tubes, nor were the typists asked to take over the duties of the service representatives. The results came from enriching other aspects (control and feedback) and, more important, from laying out the work area differently to facilitate interaction among responsible people.

While continuing job enrichment efforts, it is important not to neglect "maintenance" factors. In extending our work with job nesting, for example, we plan to experiment with "office landscaping," so called. The furniture, dividers, planters, and acoustical treatment, all must add to the feeling of work dedication. By this I mean we will dedicate site, equipment, and jobs to the employees, with the expectation that they will find it easier to dedicate themselves to customer/client/task. Especially in new installations, this total work environmental approach seems a good idea for experimentation. We will not be doing it merely to offset pain or boredom in work. The aim is to facilitate work.

A "pool" of employees with one job (typing pool, reproduction pool, calculating pool, and so on) is at the opposite extreme from the team or "minigroup" which I have described. A minigroup is a set of mutually supporting employees, each of whom has a meaningful module or part in meeting the needs of customer/client/task. What is "meaningful" is, like a love affair, in the eye of the beholder; at this stage, we have difficulty in describing it further.

A minigroup can have several service representatives or typists; one of each is not basic to the idea. The purpose is to set up a group of employees so that a natural, mutual dependence can grow in providing a service or finishing a task. It marks the end of processing from person to person or group to group, in separate locations or departments and with many different supervisors.

The minigroup concept, however, still leaves room for specialists. In certain Scandinavian auto plants, for example, one or two specialists fabricate the entire assembly of the exhaust pollution control system or the electrical system. Eventually, a group of workers may turn out a whole engine. In the United States, Chrysler has given similar trial efforts a high priority. The idea is to fix authority at the lowest level possible.

Experience to date indicates that unions welcome the kind of effort described in our studies. Trouble can be expected, of course, if the economics of increases in productivity are not shared equitably. In the majority of cases, the economics can be handled even under existing contracts, since they usually permit establishment of new jobs and appropriate wage grades between dates of contract negotiation.

An employee who takes the entire responsibility for preparing a whole telephone directory, for example, ought to be paid more, although a new clerical rating must be established. Job enrichment is not in lieu of cash; good jobs and good maintenance are two sides of the same coin.

New technology, such as the cathode ray tube, should enable us to break free of old work arrangements. When the Ferguson District service order typists were using the TWX machines, nesting their jobs was impractical because the equipment would have driven everybody to distraction. Installation of the high-technology CRTs gave the planners the opportunity to move together those employees whose modules of work were naturally related. This opportunity was at first overlooked.

Everyone accepts the obvious notion that new technology can and must eliminate the dumb-dumb jobs. However, it probably creates more, rather than fewer, fragments of work. Managers should observe the new module and the work organization of the modules. This effort calls for new knowledge and skills, such as laying out work so attractively that the average employee will stay longer and work more effectively than under the previous arrangement.

Moreover, technology tends to make human beings adjuncts of machines. As we move toward computerized production of all listings in the white pages of the phone books, for example, the risk of an employee's losing "his" or "her" own directories is very great indeed. (Two AT&T companies, South Central Bell and Pacific Northwest Bell, are at this stage, and we must be certain the planned changes do not undermine jobs.) Making sure that machines remain the adjunct of human beings is a frontier problem which few managers have yet grappled with.

Managers in mature organizations are likely to have difficulty convincing another department to make pilot runs of any new kind of work organization, especially one that will cause the department to lose people, budget, or size. Individual job enrichment does not often get into interdepartmental tangles, but the nesting of jobs will almost surely create problems of autonomy. This will call for real leadership.

When the work is right, employee attitudes are right. That is the job enrichment strategy—get the work right.

2

*LEADERSHIP
AND DECISION-MAKING*

Leadership is a vital process in organizations. Leadership has been defined in various ways, but the definition usually includes the concept of influence. The source of a leader's influence over his subordinates is his "position power" and his "personal power." Position power includes the leader's legitimate authority and his control over organizational rewards and punishments. Personal power is derived from the affection and loyalty of subordinates ("referent power") and their respect for the leader's expertise ("expert power"). Position power is primarily determined by the organization, while personal power depends upon the personality and behavior of the leader.

The leader's influence aids him in achieving and maintaining a high level of subordinate task motivation and willingness to implement decisions. In addition to motivating subordinates, leaders in organizations usually perform a number of other important functions. These functions include such things as insuring that the group is efficiently organized to perform its tasks, insuring that subordinates receive essential information and instruction, managing conflict among subordinates and maintaining group cohesiveness, and representing the group or coordinating its activities in relation to other organizational subunits and higher-level management.

During the last few decades hundreds of laboratory and field studies have been conducted to learn about the nature of leadership in organizations. Most of the early studies of leadership were attempts to identify unique traits that are characteristic of successful leaders but not of unsuccessful leaders or non-leaders. Failure to find measures of personality and aptitudes consistently associated with successful leadership led to a shift of attention from leader traits to leadership behavior. A series of studies carried out at Ohio State University during the 1950s attempted to identify meaningful and relatively independent categories of leadership behavior by analyzing the relationship among hundreds of specific acts performed by a variety of leaders. Factor analyses of leader-behavior description questionnaires filled out by subordinates indicated that leadership acts could be classified into a few categories or dimensions. The two most important dimensions were labeled "Consideration" and "Initiating Structure." The article by Fleishman and Harris defines these leadership dimensions and examines their relation to subordinate turnover and grievances.

Another important leadership dimension that was investigated extensively during this period is the degree of subordinate participation and influence in decision-making. A sizeable number of studies tested the hypothesis that leaders who allow extensive participation have more satisfied and productive subordinates. This hypothesis was supported in some leadership situations but not in others. Studies on the relation of Consideration and Initiating Structure to group performance also failed to yield consistent results across leadership situations.

These discrepancies led to an increased awareness of the importance of situational variables such as the nature of the task, the characteristics and expectations of subordinates, and the organizational environment of the work group. It was evident that the leadership behavior required for group effectiveness in one type of situation is not necessarily appropriate for all other types of situations. Tannenbaum and Schmidt were among the earliest writers who attempted to explain how the situation determines what leader behavior is practical and desirable. In this updated version of their original article, they differentiate between several styles of decision-making ranging from boss-centered leadership (autocratic) to subordinate-centered leadership (participative), and explain how a manager's choice among alternative decision styles is influenced by various characteristics of the subordinates, the situation, and the manager himself.

The article by Vroom and Yetton provides further elaboration and refinement of the interaction approach to leadership decision-making. Vroom and Yetton propose a normative model of the appropriate styles of decision-making for different situations. The core of their model is Maier's distinction between decision quality and subordinate acceptance of the decision. The situation is analyzed in terms of the importance of quality and acceptance for a particular type of decision and the factors moderating the effect of various decision making styles on decision quality and acceptance.

An interaction model of leadership has also been proposed by Fiedler. His model is based on extensive research on the relationship between leader attitudes toward co-workers (leader LPC scores) and group performance. Since the behavioral correlates of high and low LPC scores have not yet been completely determined, Fiedler's approach is best described as a model of the interaction between a leader trait (LPC) and situational favorableness. Favorableness is determined by such aspects of the situation as the leader's position power, his relations with subordinates, and the extent to which the task is structured. The model has implications for the selection and training of leaders, and Fiedler has suggested that a leader's effectiveness can also be improved by modifying the situation to match the leader's LPC score.

Another interaction model of leadership has been derived from expectancy theory (see the article by Heneman and Schwab in Section I). This approach is usually referred to as the "path-goal theory of leadership." The core of the path-goal model is the effect of leader behavior on subordinate motivation, defined in terms of subordinate expectancies and valences. Leader behavior that results in high subordinate expectation that effort will lead to valued outcomes will increase subordinate motivation, which in turn will usually lead to higher group performance. The effects of leader behavior on subordinate expectancies and valences is hypothesized to vary somewhat depending upon the situation. The article by House and Mitchell reviews different versions of path-goal leadership theory and research conducted to test the theory.

REFERENCES AND SUGGESTED READINGS

Ashour, A. S. The contingency model of leadership effectiveness: An evaluation. *Organizational Behavior and Human Performance*, 1973, 9, 339-55.

Bowers, D. G., and Seashore, S. E. Predicting organizational effectiveness with a four-factor theory of leadership. *Administrative Science Quarterly*, 1966, 11, 238-63.

Carter, E. E. The behavioral theory of the firm and top level corporate decisions. *Administrative Science Quarterly*, 1971, 16, 413-29.

Delbecq, A. L. The management of decision-making within the firm: Three strategies for three types of decision-making. *Academy of Management Journal*, 1967, 10, 239-39.

Gibb, C. A. Leadership. In G. Lindzey and E. Aronson (Eds), *The handbook of social psychology*. Menlo Park: Addison-Wesley, 1969.

Korman, A. On the development of contingency theories of leadership: Some methodological considerations and a possible alternative. *Journal of Applied Psychology*, 1973, 58, 384-87.

Patchen, M. The locus and basis of influence on organizational decisions. *Organizational Behavior and Human Performance*, 1974, 11, 195-221.

Wofford, J. C. Managerial behavior, situational factors, and productivity and morale. *Administrative Science Quarterly*, 1971, 16, 10-17.

Yukl, G. A. Toward a behavioral theory of leadership. *Organizational Behavior and Human Performance*, 1971, 6, 414-440.

9

Patterns of Leadership Behavior
Related to Employee Grievances and Turnover

EDWIN A. FLEISHMAN and EDWIN F. HARRIS

This study investigates some relationships between the leader behavior of industrial supervisors and the behavior of their group members. It represents an extension of earlier studies carried out at the International Harvester Company, while the authors were with the Ohio State University Leadership Studies.

Briefly, these previous studies involved three primary phases which have been described elsewhere (Fleishman, 1951, 1953a, 1953b, 1953c; Fleishman, Harris, and Burtt, 1955; Harris and Fleishman, 1955). In the initial phase, independent leadership patterns were defined and a variety of behavioral and attitude instruments were developed to measure them. This phase confirmed the usefulness of the constructs "Consideration" and "Structure" for describing leader behavior in industry.

Since the present study, as well as the previous work, focused on these two leadership patterns, it may be well to redefine them here:

Consideration includes behavior indicating mutual trust, respect, and a certain warmth and rapport between the supervisor and his group. This does not mean that this dimen-sion reflects a superficial "pat-on-the-back," "first name calling" kind of human relations behavior. This dimension appears to emphasize a deeper concern for group members' needs and includes such behavior as allowing subordinates more participation in decision making and encouraging more two-way communication.

Structure includes behavior in which the supervisor organizes and defines group activities and his relation to the group. Thus, he defines the role he expects each member to assume, assigns tasks, plans ahead, establishes ways of getting things done, and pushes for production. This dimension seems to emphasize overt attempts to achieve organizational goals.

Since the dimensions are independent, a supervisor may score high on both dimensions, low on both, or high on one and low on the other.

The second phase of the original Harvester research utilized measures of these patterns to evaluate changes in foreman leadership attitudes and behavior resulting from a management training program. The amount of change was evaluated at three different times—once while the foremen were still in

Reprinted from *Personnel Psychology*, 1962, 15, 43—56, by permission of the authors and Personnel Psychology, Inc.

the training setting, again after they had returned to the plant environment, and still later in a "refresher" training course. The results showed that while still in the training situation there was a distinct increase in Consideration and an unexpected decrease in Structure attitudes. It was also found that leadership attitudes became more *dissimilar* rather than similar, despite the fact that all foremen had received the same training. Furthermore, when behavior and attitudes were evaluated back in the plant, the effects of the training largely disappeared. This pointed to the main finding, i.e., the overriding importance of the interaction of the training effects with certain aspects of the social setting in which the foremen had to operate in the plant. Most critical was the "leadership climate" supplied by the behavior and attitudes of the foreman's own boss. This was more related to the foreman's own Consideration and Structure behavior than was the fact that he had or had not received the leadership training.

The third phase may be termed the "criterion phase," in which the relationships between Consideration and Structure and indices of foremen proficiency were examined. One finding was that production supervisors rated high in "proficiency" by plant management turned out to have leadership patterns high in Structure and low in Consideration. (This relationship was accentuated in departments scoring high on a third variable, "perceived pressure of deadlines.") On the other hand, this same pattern of high Structure and low Consideration was found to be related to high labor turnover, union grievances, worker absences and accidents, and low worker satisfaction. There was some indication that these relationships might differ in "nonproduction" departments. An interesting sidelight was that foremen with low Consideration *and* low Structure were more often bypassed by subordinates in the informal organizational structure. In any case, it was evident that "what is an effective supervisor" is a complex question, depending on the proficiency criterion emphasized, management values, type of work, and other situational variables.

The present study examines some of the questions left unanswered by this previous work.

PURPOSE

The present study focused on two main questions. First, what is the *form* of the relationship between leader behavior and indices of group behavior? Is it linear or curvilinear? As far as we know, no one has really examined this question. Rephrased, this question asks if there are critical levels of Consideration and/or Structure beyond which it does or does not make a difference in group behavior? Is an "average" amount of Structure better than a great deal or no Structure at all? Similarly, is there an optimum level of Consideration above and below which worker grievances and/or turnover rise sharply?

The second question concerns the interaction effects of different combinations of Consideration and Structure. Significant correlations have been found between each of these patterns and such indices as rated proficiency, grievances, turnover, departmental reputation, subordinate satisfactions, etc. (e.g., Fleishman, Harris, and Burtt, 1955; Halpin, 1954; Hemphill, 1955; Stogdill and Coons, 1957). These studies present some evidence that scoring low on both dimensions is not desirable. They also indicate that some balance of Consideration and Structure may be optimal for satisfying both proficiency and morale criteria. The present study is a more intensive examination of possible optimum combinations of Consideration and Structure.

The present study investigates the relationships between foreman behavior and two primary indices of group behavior: labor grievances and employee turnover. Both of these may be considered a partial criteria of group effectiveness.

PROCEDURE

Leader Behavior Measures

The study was conducted in a motor truck manufacturing plant. Fifty-seven production foremen and their work groups took part in the study. They represented such work operations as stamping, assembly, body assembly, body paint, machinery, and export. At least three workers, drawn randomly from each foreman's department, described the leader behavior of their foreman by means of the *Supervisory Behavior Description Questionnaire* (described elsewhere, Fleishman, 1953, 1957). Each questionnaire was scored on Consideration and Structure; a mean Consideration score and a mean Structure score were computed for each foreman. The correlation between Consideration and Structure among foremen in this plant was found to be − .33. The correlation between these scales is usually around zero (Fleishman, 1957), but in this plant foremen who are high in Structure are somewhat more likely to be seen as lower in Consideratio and vice versa. However, the relationship is not high.

Grievance Measures

Grievances were defined in terms of the number presented in writing and placed in company files. No data on grievances which were settled at lower levels (hence, without their becoming matters of company record) were considered. The frequency of grievances was equated for each foreman's work group by dividing the record for that group by the number of workers in that group. The reliability of these records, computed by correlating the records for odd and even weeks over an 11-month period and correcting by the Spearman-Brown formula, was .73. The entire 11-month record (for each foreman's work group) was used in the present analyais.

Turnover Measures

Turnover was figured as the number of workers who voluntarily left the employ of the company within the 11-month period. Again, the records for each foreman's group were equated by dividing the number who resigned by the number of workers in his group. The nature of the records did not permit an analysis of the reasons which each worker gave for leaving, and so all such terminations are included. The corrected odd-even weeks reliability for this period was .59.

The reliability for the grievance and turnover measures are for the foremen's work groups and not for the individual worker. In the case of turnover, this reliability is quite high when one considers that different workers are involved in each time period. (Once a worker leaves, of course, he cannot contribute to turnover again.) The findings of stable grievance and turnover rates among groups under the same foremen is an important finding in its own right. The correlation between grievances and turnover is .37. This indicates that, while high grievance work groups tend to have higher turnover, the relationship is not very high. Each index is worth considering as an independent aspect of group behavior.

RESULTS

Leader Behavior and Grievances

Figure 9-1 plots the average employee griev-

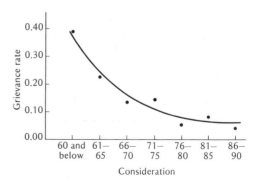

Fig. 9-1. Relation Between Consideration and Grievance Rates

ance rates for departments under foremen scoring at different levels of Consideration. From the curve fitted to these points it can be seen clearly that the relationship between the foremen's behavior and grievances from their work groups is negative and curvilinear. For most of the range, increased Consideration goes with reduced grievances rates. However, increased Consideration above a certain critical level (approximately 76 out of a possible 112) is not related to further decreases in grievances. Furthermore, the curve appears to be negatively accelerated. A given decrease in Consideration just below the critical point (76) is related to a small increase in grievances, but, as Consideration continues to drop, grievance rates rise sharply. Thus, a five-point drop on the Consideration scale, just below a score of 76, is related to a small grievance increase, but a five-point drop below 61 is related to a large rise in grievances. The correlation ratio (eta) represented by this curve is − .51.

Figure 9-2 plots grievances against the foremen's Structure scores. Here a similar curvilinear relationship is observed. In this case the correlation is positive (eta = .71). Below a certain level (approximately 36 out of a possible 80 on our scale) Structure is unrelated to grievances, but above this point increased Structure goes with increased grievances. Again we see that a given increase in Structure just above this critical level is accompanied by a small increase in grievances, but continued increases in Structure are associated with increasingly disproportionately large increases in grievance rates.

Both curves are hyperbolic rather than parabolic in form. Thus, it appears that for neither Consideration nor Structure is there an "optimum" point in the middle of the range below and above which grievances rise. Rather there seems to be a range within which increased Consideration or decreased Structure makes no difference. Of course, when one reaches these levels, grievances are already at a very low level and not much improvement can be expected. However, the important point is that this low grievance level is reached before one gets to the extremely high end of the Consideration scale or to the extremely low end of the Structure scale. It is also clear that extremely high Structure and extremely low Consideration are most related to high grievances.

Different Combinations of Consideration and Structure Related to Grievances

The curves described establish that a general relationship exists between each of these leadership patterns and the frequency of employee grievances. But how do *different combinations* of Consideration and Structure relate to grievances? Some foremen score high on both dimensions, some score low on both, etc.

Figure 9-3 plots the relation between Structure (low, medium, and high) and grievances for groups of foremen who were either low, medium, or high on Consideration. The curves show that grievances occur most frequently among groups whose foremen are low in Consideration, regardless of the amount of emphasis on Structure. The most interesting finding relates to the curve for the high Consideration foremen. This curve suggests that, for the high Consider-

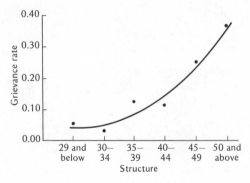

Fig. 9-2. Relation Between Structure and Grievance Rates

ation foreman, Structure could be increased without any appreciable increase in grievances. However, the reverse is not true; that is, foremen who were low in Consideration could not reduce grievances by easing up on Structure. For foremen average on Consideration, grievances were lowest where Structure was lowest and increased in an almost linear fashion as Structure increased. These data show a definite interaction between Consideration and Structure. Apparently, high Consideration can compensate for high Structure. But low Structure will not offset low Consideration.

Before we speculate further about these relationships, let us examine the results with employee turnover.

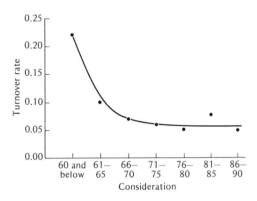

Fig. 9-4. Relation Between Consideration and Turnover Rates

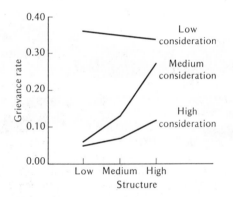

Fig. 9-3. Combinations of Consideration and Structure Related to Grievances

Leader Behavior and Turnover

Figures 9-4 and 9-5 plot the curves for the *Supervisory Behavior Description* scores of these foremen against the turnover criteria. Again, we see the curvilinear relationships. The correlation (eta) of Consideration and turnover is $-$ .69; Structure and turnover correlate .63. As in the case with grievances, below a certain critical level of Consideration and above a certain level of Structure, turnover goes up. There is, however, an interesting difference in that the critical levels differ from those related to grievances. The flat portions of each of these curves are

more extended and the rise in turnover beyond the point of inflection is steeper. The implication of this is quite sensible and indicates that "they gripe before they leave." In other words, a given increase in Structure (to approximately 39) or decrease in Consideration (to 66) may result in increased grievances, but not turnover. It takes higher Structure and lower Consideration before turnover occurs.

Different Combinations of Consideration and Structure Related to Turnover

Figure 9-6 plots the relation between Struc-

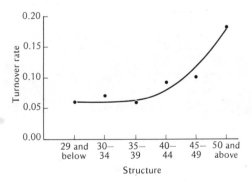

Fig. 9-5. Relation Between Structure and Turnover Rates

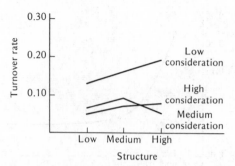

Fig. 9-6. Combinations of Consideration and Structure Related to Turnover

ture (low, medium, and high) and turnover for groups of foremen who were also either low, medium, or high in Consideration. As with grievances, the curves show that turnover is highest for the work groups whose foremen combine low Consideration with high Structure; however, the amount of Consideration is the dominant factor. The curves show that turnover is highest among those work groups whose foremen are low in Consideration, regardless of the amount of emphasis these same foremen show on Structure. There is little distinction between the work groups of foremen who show medium and high Consideration since both of these groups have low turnover among their workers. Furthermore, increased Structure does not seem related to increased turnover in these two groups.[1]

CONCLUSIONS

1. This study indicates that there are significant relationships between the leader behavior of foremen and the labor grievances and employee turnover in their work groups. In general, low Consideration and high Structure go with high grievances and turnover.

1. This, of course, is consistent with our earlier finding that for increased turnover it takes a bigger drop in Consideration and a bigger increase in Structure to make a difference. Thus, our high and medium Consideration groups separate for grievances, but overlap for turnover.

2. There appear to be certain critical levels beyond which increased Consideration or decreased Structure have no effect on grievance or turnover rates. Similarly, grievances and turnover are shown to increase most markedly at the extreme ends of the Consideration (low end) and Structure (high end) scales. Thus, the relationship is curvilinear, not linear, and hyperbolic, not parabolic.

3. The critical points at which increased Structure and decreased Consideration begin to relate to group behavior is not the same for grievances and turnover. Increases in turnover do not occur until lower on the Consideration scale and higher on the Structure scale, as compared with increases in grievances. For example, if Consideration is steadily reduced, higher grievances appear before increased turnover occurs. It appears that there may be different "threshold levels" of Consideration and Structure related to grievances and turnover.

4. Other principal findings concern the interaction effects found between different combinations of Consideration and Structure. Taken in combination, Consideration is the dominant factor. For example, both grievances and turnover were highest in groups having low Consideration foremen, regardless of the degree of Structuring behavior shown by these same foremen.

5. Grievances and turnover were lowest for groups with foremen showing medium to high Consideration together with low Structure. However, one of the most important results is the finding that high Consideration foremen could increase Structure with very little increase in grievances and no increase in turnover. High Consideration foremen had relatively low grievances and turnover, regardless of the amount of Structure engaged in.

Thus, with regard to grievances and turnover, leader behavior characterized by low Consideration is more critical than behavior characterized by high Structure. Apparently, foremen can compensate for high Structure by increased Consideration, but low Consideration foremen cannot compensate by decreasing their Structuring behavior.

One interpretation is that workers under foremen who establish a climate of mutual trust, rapport, and tolerance for two-way communication with their work groups are more likely to accept higher levels of Structure. This might be because they perceive this Structure differently from employees in "low Consideration" climates. Thus, under "low Consideration" climates, high Structure is seen as threatening and restrictive, but under "high Consideration" climates this same Structure is seen as supportive and helpful. A related interpretation is that foremen who establish such an atmosphere can more easily solve the problems resulting from high Structure. Thus, *grievances* may be solved at this level before they get into the official records. Similarly, *turnover* may reflect escape from a problem situation which cannot be resolved in the absence of mutual trust and two-way communication. In support of this interpretation, we do have evidence that leaders high in Consideration are also better at predicting subordinates' responses to problems (Fleishman and Salter, 1961).

One has to be careful in making cause-and-effect inferences here. A possible limitation is that our descriptions of foremen behavior came from the workers themselves. Those workers with many grievances may view their foremen as low in Consideration simply because they have a lot of grievances. However, the descriptions of foremen behavior were obtained from workers drawn randomly from each foreman's group; the odds are against our receiving descriptions from very many workers contributing a disproportionate share of grievances. In the case of turnover, of course, our descriptions could not have been obtained from people who had left during the previous eleven months. Yet substantial correlations were obtained between foremen descriptions, supplied by currently employed workers, with the turnover rates of their work groups. Furthermore, we do have evidence that leader

behavior over a year period tends to be quite stable. Test-retest correlations for Consideration, as well as for Structure, tend to be high even when different workers do the describing on the retest (Harris and Fleishman, 1955). Our present preference is to favor the interpretation that high turnover and grievances result, at least in part, from the leader behavior patterns described.

The nonlinear relations between leader behavior and our criteria of effectiveness have more general implications for leadership research. For one thing, it points up the need for a more careful examination of the *form* of such relationships before computing correlation coefficients. Some previously obtained correlations with leadership variables may be underestimates because of linearity assumptions. Similarly, some previous negative or contradictory results may be "explained" by the fact that (a) inappropriate coefficients were used, or (b) these studies were dealing with only the flat portions of these curves. If, for example, all the foremen in our study had scored over 76 on Consideration and under 36 on Structure, we would have concluded that there was no relation between these leadership patterns and grievances and turnover. Perhaps in comparing one study with another, we need to specify the range of leader behavior involved in each study.

There is, of course, a need to explore similar relationships with other criteria. There is no assurance that similar curvilinear patterns and interaction effects will hold for other indices (e.g., group productivity). Even the direction of these relationships may vary with the criterion used. We have evidence (Fleishman, Harris, and Burtt, 1955), for example, that Consideration and Structure may relate quite differently to another effectiveness criterion: management's perceptions of foremen proficiency. However, research along these lines may make it possible to specify the particular leadership patterns which most nearly "optimize" these various effectiveness criteria in industrial organizations.

REFERENCES

Fleishman, E. A. "Leadership climate" and supervisory behavior. Columbus: Personnel Research Board, Ohio State University, 1951.

Fleishman, E. A. Leadership climate, human relations training, and supervisory behavior. *Personnel Psychology*, 1953, 6, 205-22. (a)

Fleishman, E. A. The description of supervisory behavior. *Journal of Applied Psychology*, 1953, 37, 1-6. (b)

Fleishman, E. A. The measurement of leadership attitudes in industry. *Journal of Applied Psychology*, 1953, 37, 153-58. (c)

Fleishman, E. A. A leader behavior description for industry. In Stogdill, R. M., and Coons, A. E. (Eds.) *Leader behavior: Its description and measurement.* Columbus: Bureau of Business Research, 1957.

Fleishman, E. A., Harris, E. F., and Burtt, H. E. *Leadership and supervision in industry.* Columbus: Bureau of Educational Research, Ohio State University, 1955.

Fleishman, E. A., and Salter, J. A. The relation between the leader's behavior and his empathy toward subordinates. *Advanced Management,* 1961 (March), 18-20.

Halpin, A. W. The leadership behavior and combat performance of airplane commanders. *Journal of Abnormal and Social Psychology*, 1954, 49, 19-22.

Harris, E. F., and Fleishman, E. A. Human relations training and the stability of leadership patterns. *Journal of Applied Psychology*, 1955, 39, 20-25.

Hemphill, J. K. Leadership behavior associated with the administrative reputation of college departments. *Journal of Educational Psychology*, 1955, 46, 385-401.

Stogdill, R. M., and Coons, A. E. (Eds.). *Leader behavior: Its description and measurement.* Columbus: Bureau of Business Research, Ohio State University, 1957.

10

How To Choose a Leadership Pattern

ROBERT TANNENBAUM and WARREN H. SCHMIDT

"I put most problems into my group's hands and leave it to them to carry the ball from there. I serve merely as a catalyst, mirroring back the people's thoughts and feelings so that they can better understand them. . . ."

"It's foolish to make decisions oneself on matters that affect people. I always talk things over with my subordinates, but I make it clear to them that I'm the one who has to have the final say. . . ."

"Once I have decided on a course of action, I do my best to sell my ideas to my employees. . . ."

"I'm being paid to lead. If I let a lot of other people make the decisions I should be making, then I'm not worth my salt. . . ."

"I believe in gettings things done. I can't waste time calling meetings. Someone has to call the shots around here, and I think it should be me. . . ."

Each of these statements represents a point of view about "good leadership." Considerable experience, factual data, and theoretical principles could be cited to support each statement, even though they seem to be inconsistent when placed together. Such contradictions point up the dilemma in which the modern manager frequently finds himself.

NEW PROBLEM

The problem of how the modern manager can be "democratic" in his relations with subordinates and at the same time maintain the necessary authority and control in the organization for which he is responsible has come into focus increasingly in recent years.

Earlier in the century this problem was not so acutely felt. The successful executive was generally pictured as possessing intelligence, imagination, initiative, the capacity to make rapid (and generally wise) decisions, and the ability to inspire subordinates. People tended to think of the world as being divided into "leaders" and "followers."

New focus: Gradually, however, from the social sciences emerged the concept of "group dynamics" with its focus on *members* of the group rather than solely on the leader. Research efforts of social scientists underscored the importance of employee involvement and participation in decision-making. Evidence began to challenge the efficiency of highly directive leadership, and increasing

Reprinted from *Harvard Business Review*, 1973 (May-June), 162-180, by permission of the publisher.

119

attention was paid to problems of motivation and human relations.

Through training laboratories in group development that sprang up across the country, many of the newer notions of leadership began to exert an impact. These training laboratories were carefully designed to give people a first-hand experience in full participation and decision-making. The designated "leaders" deliberately attempted to reduce their own power and to make group members as responsible as possible for setting their own goals and methods within the laboratory experience.

It was perhaps inevitable that some of the people who attended the training laboratories regarded this kind of leadership as being truly "democratic" and went home with the determination to build fully participative decision making into their own organizations. Whenever their bosses made a decision without convening a staff meeting, they tended to perceive this as authoritarian behavior. The true symbol of democratic leadership to some was the meeting—and the less directed from the top, the more democratic it was.

Some of the more enthusiastic alumni of these training laboratories began to get the habit of categorizing leader behavior as "democratic" *or* "authoritarian." The boss who made too many decisions himself was thought of as an authoritarian, and his directive behavior was often attributed solely to his personality.

New need: The net result of the research findings and of the human relations training based upon them has been to call into question the stereotype of an effective leader. Consequently, the modern manager often finds himself in an uncomfortable state of mind.

Often he is not quite sure how to behave; there are times when he is torn between exerting "strong" leadership and "permissive" leadership. Sometimes new knowledge pushes him in one direction ("I should really get the group to help make this decision"), but at the same time his experience pushes him in another direction ("I really understand the problem better than the group and therefore I should make the decision"). He is not sure when a group decision is really appropriate or when holding a staff meeting serves merely as a device for avoiding his own decision-making responsibility.

The purpose of our article is to suggest a framework which managers may find useful in grappling with this dilemma. First, we shall look at the different patterns of leadership behavior that the manager can choose from in relating himself to his subordinates. Then, we shall turn to some of the questions suggested by this range of patterns. For instance, how important is it for a manager's subordinates to know what type of leadership he is using in a situation? What factors should he consider in deciding on a leadership pattern? What difference do his long-run objectives make as compared to his immediate objectives?

RANGE OF BEHAVIOR

Figure 10-1 presents the continuum or range of possible leadership behavior available to a manager. Each type of action is related to the degree of authority used by the boss and to the amount of freedom available to his subordinates in reaching decisions. The actions seen on the extreme left characterize the manager who maintains a high degree of control while those seen on the extreme right characterize the manager who releases a high degree of control. Neither extreme is absolute; authority and freedom are never without their limitations.

Now let us look more closely at each of the behavior points occurring along this continuum.

The manager makes the decision and announces it.

In this case the boss identifies a problem, considers alternative solutions, chooses one of them, and then reports this decision to his

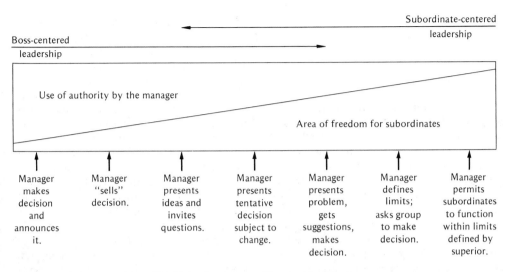

Fig. 10-1. Continuum of Leadership Behavior

subordinates for implementation. He may or may not give consideration to what he believes his subordinates will think or feel about his decision; in any case, he provides no opportunity for them to participate directly in the decision-making process. Coercion may or may not be used or implied.

The manager "sells" his decision.

Here the manager, as before, takes responsibility for identifying the problem and arriving at a decision. However, rather than simply announcing it, he takes the additional step of persuading his subordinates to accept it. In doing so, he recognizes the possibility of some resistance among those who will be faced with the decision, and seeks to reduce this resistance by indicating, for example, what the employees have to gain from his decision.

The manager presents his ideas, invites questions.

Here the boss who has arrived at a decision and who seeks acceptance of his ideas provides an opportunity for his subordinates to get a fuller explanation of his thinking and his intentions. After presenting the ideas, he invites questions so that his associates can better understand what he is trying to accomplish. This "give and take" also enables the manager and the subordinates to explore more fully the implications of the decision.

The manager presents a tentative decision subject to change.

This kind of behavior permits the subordinates to exert some influence on the decision. The initiative for identifying and diagnosing the problem remains with the boss. Before meeting with his staff, he has thought the problem through and arrived at a decision—but only a tentative one. Before finalizing it, he presents his proposed solution for the reaction of those who will be affected by it. He says in effect, "I'd like to hear what you have to say about this plan that I have developed. I'll appreciate your frank reactions, but will reserve for myself the final decision."

The manager presents the problem, gets suggestions, and then makes his decision.

Up to this point the boss has come before the group with a solution of his own. Not so in this case. The subordinates now get the first chance to suggest solutions. The manager's initial role involves identifying the problem. He might, for example, say something of this sort: "We are faced with a number of complaints from newspapers and the general public on our service policy. What is wrong here? What ideas do you have for coming to grips with this problem?"

The function of the group becomes one of increasing the manager's repertory of possible solutions to the problem. The purpose is to capitalize on the knowledge and experience of those who are on the "firing line." From the expanded list of alternatives developed by the manager and his subordinates, the manager then selects the solution that he regards as most promising.[1]

The manager defines the limits and requests the group to make a decision.

At this point the manager passes to the group (possibly including himself as a member) the right to make decisions. Before doing so, however, he defines the problem to be solved and the boundaries within which the decision must be made.

An example might be the handling of a parking problem at a plant. The boss decides that this is something that should be worked on by the people involved, so he calls them together and points up the existence of the problem. Then he tells them:

"There is the open field just north of the main plant which has been designated for additional employee parking. We can build underground or surface multilevel facilities as long as the cost does not exceed $100,000. Within these limits we are free to work out whatever solution makes sense to us. After we decide on a specific plan, the company will spend the available money in whatever way we indicate."

1. For a fuller explanation of this approach see Leo Moore, Too much management, too little change, *Harvard Business Review*, 1956 (January-February), 41.

The manager permits the group to make decisions within prescribed limits.

This represents an extreme degree of group freedom only occasionally encountered in formal organizations, as, for instance, in many research groups. Here the team of managers or engineers undertakes the identification and diagnosis of the problem, develops alternative procedures for solving it, and decides on one or more of these alternative solutions. The only limits directly imposed on the group by the organization are those specified by the superior of the team's boss. If the boss participates in the decision-making process, he attempts to do so with no more authority than any other member of the group. He commits himself in advance to assist in implementing whatever decision the group makes.

KEY QUESTIONS

As the continuum in Figure 10-1 demonstrates, there are a number of alternative ways in which a manager can relate himself to the group or individuals he is supervising. At the extreme left of the range, the emphasis is on the manager—on what *he* is interested in, how *he* sees things, how *he* feels about them. As we move toward the subordinate-centered end of the continuum, however, the focus is increasingly on the subordinates—on what *they* are interested in, how *they* look at things, how *they* feel about them.

When business leadership is regarded in this way, a number of questions arise. Let us take four of especial importance:

Can a boss ever relinquish his responsibility by delegating it to someone else?

Our view is that the manager must expect to be held responsible by his superior for the quality of the decisions made, even though operationally these decisions may have been made on a group basis. He should, therefore, be ready to accept whatever risk is involved whenever he delegates decision-making power to his subordinates. Delegation is not a way of "passing the buck." Also, it should be emphasized that the amount of freedom the boss gives to his subordinates cannot be greater than the freedom which he himself has been given by his own superior.

Should the manager participate with his subordinates once he has delegated responsibility to them?

The manager should carefully think over this question and decide on his role prior to involving the subordinate group. He should ask if his presence will inhibit or facilitate the problem-solving process. There may be some instances when he should leave the group to let it solve the problem for itself. Typically, however, the boss has useful ideas to contribute, and should function as an additional member of the group. In the latter instance, it is important that he indicate clearly to the group that he sees himself in a *member* role rather than in an authority role.

How important is it for the group to recognize what kind of leadership behavior the boss is using?

It makes a great deal of difference. Many relationship problems between boss and subordinate occur because the boss fails to make clear how he plans to use his authority. If, for example, he actually intends to make a certain decision himself, but the subordinate group gets the impression that he has delegated this authority, considerable confusion and resentment are likely to follow. Problems may also occur when the boss uses a "democratic" façade to conceal the fact that he has already made a decision which he hopes the group will accept as its own. The attempt to "make them think it was their idea in the first place" is a risky one. We believe that it is highly important for the manager to be honest and clear in describing what authority he is keeping and what role he is asking his subordinates to assume in solving a particular problem.

Can you tell how "democratic" a manager is by the number of decisions his subordinates make?

The sheer *number* of decisions is not an accurate index of the amount of freedom that a subordinate group enjoys. More important is the *significance* of the decisions which the boss entrusts to his subordinates. Obviously a decision on how to arrange desks is of an entirely different order from a decision involving the introduction of new electronic data-processing equipment. Even though the widest possible limits are given in dealing with the first issue, the group will sense no particular degree of responsibility. For a boss to permit the group to decide equipment policy, even within rather narrow limits, would reflect a greater degree of confidence in them on his part.

DECIDING HOW TO LEAD

Now let us turn from the types of leadership which are possible in a company situation to the question of what types are *practical* and *desirable*. What factors or forces should a manager consider in deciding how to manage? Three are of particular importance:

Forces in the manager;
Forces in the subordinates;
Forces in the situation.

We should like briefly to describe these elements and indicate how they might influence a manager's action in a decision-making situation.[2] The strength of each of them will, of course, vary from instance to instance, but the manager who is sensitive to them can better assess the problems which face him and determine which mode of leadership behavior is most appropriate for him.

2. See also Robert Tannenbaum and Fred Massarik, Participation by subordinates in the managerial decision-making process, *Canadian Journal of Economics and Political Science*, 1950 (August), 413.

Forces in the Manager

The manager's behavior in any given instance will be influenced greatly by the many forces operating within his own personality. He will, of course, perceive his leadership problems in a unique way on the basis of his background, knowledge, and experience. Among the important internal forces affecting him will be the following:

1. *His value system.* How strongly does he feel that individuals should have a share in making the decisions which affect them? Or, how convinced is he that the official who is paid to assume responsibility should personally carry the burden of decision-making? The strength of his convictions on questions like those will tend to move the manager to one end or the other of the continuum shown in Figure 10-1. His behavior will also be influenced by the relative importance that he attaches to organizational efficiency, personal growth of subordinates, and company profits.[3]

2. *His confidence in his subordinates.* Managers differ greatly in the amount of trust they have in other people generally, and this carries over to the particular employees they supervise at a given time. In viewing his particular group of subordinates, the manager is likely to consider their knowledge and competence with respect to the problem. A central question he might ask himself is: "Who is best qualified to deal with this problem?" Often he may, justifiably or not, have more confidence in his own capabilities than in those of his subordinates.

3. *His own leadership inclinations.* There are some managers who seem to function more comfortably and naturally as highly directive leaders. Resolving problems and issuing orders come easily to them. Other managers seem to operate more comfortably in a team role, where they are continually sharing many of their functions with their subordinates.

4. *His feelings of security in an uncertain situation.* The manager who releases control over the decision-making process thereby reduces the predictability of the outcome. Some managers have a greater need than others for predictability and stability in their environment. This "tolerance for ambiguity" is being viewed increasingly by psychologists as a key variable in a person's manner of dealing with problems.

The manager brings these and other highly personal variables to each situation he faces. If he can see them as forces which, consciously or unconsciously, influence his behavior, he can better understand what makes him prefer to act in a given way. And understanding this, he can often make himself more effective.

Forces in the Subordinate

Before deciding how to lead a certain group, the manager will also want to consider a number of forces affecting his subordinates' behavior. He will want to remember that each employee, like himself, is influenced by many personality variables. In addition, each subordinate has a set of expectations about how the boss should act in relation to him (the phrase "expected behavior" is one we hear more and more often these days at discussions of leadership and teaching). The better the manager understands these factors, the more accurately he can determine what kind of behavior on his part will enable his subordinates to act most effectively.

Generally speaking, the manager can permit his subordinates greater freedom if the following essential conditions exist:

If the subordinates have relatively high needs for independence. (As we all know, people differ greatly in the amount of direction that they desire.)

If the subordinates have a readiness to

---

3. See Chris Argyris, Top management dilemma: company needs vs. individual development, *Personnel* 1955 (September), 123-24.

assume responsibility for decision-making. (Some see additional responsibility as a tribute to their ability; others see it as "passing the buck.")

If they have a relatively high tolerance for ambiguity. (Some employees prefer to have clear-cut directives given to them; others prefer a wider area of freedom.)

If they are interested in the problem and feel that it is important.

If they understand and identify with the goals of the organization.

If they have the necessary knowledge and experience to deal with the problem.

If they have learned to expect to share in decision-making. (Persons who have come to expect strong leadership and are then suddenly confronted with the request to share more fully in decision-making are often upset by this new experience. On the other hand, persons who have enjoyed a considerable amount of freedom resent the boss who begins to make all the decisions himself.)

The manager will probably tend to make fuller use of his own authority if the above conditions do *not* exist; at times there may be no realistic alternative to running a "one-man show."

The restrictive effect of many of the forces will, of course, be greatly modified by the general feeling of confidence which subordinates have in the boss. Where they have learned to respect and trust him, he is free to vary his behavior. He will feel certain that he will not be perceived as an authoritarian boss on those occasions when he makes decisions by himself. Similarly, he will not be seen as using staff meetings to avoid his decision-making responsibility. In a climate of mutual confidence and respect, people tend to feel less threatened by deviations from normal practice, which in turn makes possible a higher degree of flexibility in the whole relationship.

Forces in the Situation

In addition to the forces which exist in the manager himself and in his subordinates, certain characteristics of the general situation will also affect the manager's behavior. Among the more critical environmental pressures that surround him are those which stem from the organization, the work group, the nature of the problem, and the pressures of time. Let us look briefly at each of these:

Type of organization. Like individuals, organizations have values and traditions which inevitably influence the behavior of the people who work in them. The manager who is a newcomer to a company quickly discovers that certain kinds of behavior are approved while others are not. He also discovers that to deviate radically from what is generally accepted is likely to create problems for him.

These values and traditions are communicated in numerous ways—through job descriptions, policy pronouncements, and public statements by top executives. Some organizations, for example, hold to the notion that the desirable executive is one who is dynamic, imaginative, decisive, and persuasive. Other organizations put more emphasis upon the importance of the executive's ability to work effectively with people —his human relations skills. The fact that his superiors have a defined concept of what the good executive should be will very likely push the manager toward one end or the other of the behavioral range.

In addition to the above, the amount of employee participation is influenced by such variables as the size of the working units, their geographical distribution, and degree of inter- and intra-organizational security required to attain company goals. For example, the wide geographical dispersion of an organization may preclude a practical system of participative decision-making, even though this would otherwise be desirable. Similarly, the size of the working units or the need for keeping plans confidential may make it necessary for the boss to exercise more control than would otherwise be the case. Factors like these may limit considerably the manager's ability to function flexibly on the continuum.

Group effectiveness. Before turning decision-making responsibility over to a subordinate group, the boss should consider how effectively its members work together as a unit.

One of the relevant factors here is the experience the group has had in working together. It can generally be expected that a group which has functioned for some time will have developed habits of cooperation and thus be able to tackle a problem more effectively than a new group. It can also be expected that a group of people with similar backgrounds and interests will work more quickly and easily than people with dissimilar backgrounds, because the communication problems are likely to be less complex.

The degree of confidence that the members have in their ability to solve problems as a group is also a key consideration. Finally, such group variables as cohesiveness, permissiveness, mutual acceptance, and commonality of purpose will exert subtle but powerful influence on the group's functioning.

The problem itself. The nature of the problem may determine what degree of authority should be delegated by the manager to his subordinates. Obviously he will ask himself whether they have the kind of knowledge which is needed. It is possible to do them a real disservice by assigning a problem that their experience does not equip them to handle.

Since the problems faced in large or growing industries increasingly require knowledge of specialists from many different fields, it might be inferred that the more complex a problem, the more anxious a manager will be to get some assistance in solving it. However, this is not always the case. There will be times when the very complexity of the problem calls for one person to work it out. For example, if the manager has most of the background and factual data relevant to a given issue, it may be easier for him to think it through himself

than to take the time to fill in his staff on all the pertinent background information.

The key question to ask, of course, is: "Have I heard the ideas of everyone who has the necessary knowledge to make a significant contribution to the solution of this problem?"

The pressure of time. This is perhaps the most clearly felt pressure on the manager (in spite of the fact that it may sometimes be imagined). The more that he feels the need for an immediate decision, the more difficult it is to involve other people. In organizations which are in a constant state of "crisis" and "crash programming" one is likely to find managers personally using a high degree of authority with relatively little delegation to subordinates. When the time pressure is less intense, however, it becomes much more possible to bring subordinates in on the decision-making process.

These, then, are the principal forces that impinge on the manager in any given instance and that tend to determine his tactical behavior in relation to his subordinates. In each case his behavior ideally will be that which makes possible the most effective attainment of his immediate goal within the limits facing him.

LONG-RUN STRATEGY

As the manager works with his organization on the problems that come up day by day, his choice of a leadership pattern is usually limited. He must take account of the forces just described and, within the restrictions they impose on him, do the best that he can. But as he looks ahead months or even years, he can shift his thinking from tactics to large-scale strategy. No longer need he be fettered by all of the forces mentioned, for he can view many of them as variables over which he has some control. He can, for example, gain new insights or skills for himself, supply training for individual subordinates, and provide participative experiences for his employee group.

In trying to bring about a change in these variables, however, he is faced with a challenging question: At which point along the continuum *should* he act?

Attaining Objectives

The answer depends largely on what he wants to accomplish. Let us suppose that he is interested in the same objectives that most modern managers seek to attain when they can shift their attention from the pressure of immediate assignments:

1. To raise the level of employee motivation;
2. To increase the readiness of subordinates to accept change;

3. To improve the quality of all managerial decisions;
4. To develop teamwork and morale;
5. To further the individual development of employees.

In recent years the manager has been deluged with a flow of advice on how best to achieve these longer-run objectives. It is little wonder that he is often both bewildered and annoyed. However, there are some guidelines which he can usefully follow in making a decision.

Most research and much of the experience of recent years give a strong factual basis to the theory that a fairly high degree of subordinate-centered behavior is associated

Fig. 10-2. Continuum of Manager–Nonmanager Behavior

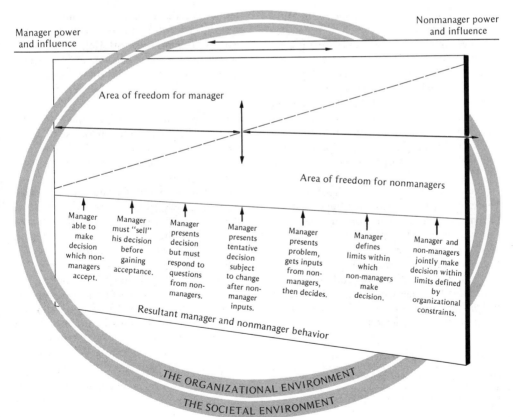

with the accomplishment of the five purposes mentioned.[4] This does not mean that a manager should always leave all decisions to his assistants. To provide the individual or the group with greater freedom than they are ready for at any given time may very well tend to generate anxieties and therefore inhibit rather than facilitate the attainment of desired objectives. But this should not keep the manager from making a continuing effort to confront his subordinates with the challenge of freedom.

CONCLUSION

In summary, there are two implications in the basic thesis that we have been developing. The first is that the successful leader is one who is keenly aware of those forces which are most relevant to his behavior at any given time. He accurately understands himself, the individuals and group he is dealing with, and the company and broader social environment in which he operates. And certainly he is able to assess the present readiness for growth of his subordinates.

But this sensitivity or understanding is not enough, which brings us to the second implication. The successful leader is one who is able to behave appropriately in the light of these perceptions. If direction is in order, he is able to direct; if considerable participative freedom is called for, he is able to provide such freedom.

Thus, the successful manager of men can be primarily characterized neither as a strong leader nor as a permissive one. Rather, he is one who maintains a high batting average in accurately assessing the forces that determine what his most appropriate behavior at any given time should be and in actually being able to behave accordingly. Being both insightful and flexible, he is less likely to see the problems of leadership as a dilemma.

4. For example, see Warren H. Schmidt and Paul C. Buchanan, *Techniques that produce teamwork* (New London, Arthur C. Croft Publications, 1954); and Morris S. Viteles, *Motivation and morale in industry* (New York, W. W. Norton, 1953).

RETROSPECTIVE COMMENTARY

Since this HBR Classic was first published in 1958, there have been many changes in organizations and in the world that have affected leadership patterns. While the article's continued popularity attests to its essential validity, we believe it can be reconsidered and updated to reflect subsequent societal changes and new management concepts.

The reasons for the article's continued relevance can be summarized briefly:

The article contains insights and perspectives which mesh well with, and help clarify, the experiences of managers, other leaders, and students of leadership. Thus it is useful to individuals in a wide variety of organizations—industrial, governmental, educational, religious, and community.

The concept of leadership the article defines is reflected in a continuum of leadership behavior (see Figure 10-1 in original article). Rather than offering a choice between two styles of leadership, democratic or authoritarian, it sanctions a range of behavior.

The concept does not dictate to managers but helps them to analyze their own behavior. The continuum permits them to review their behavior within a context of other alternatives, without any style being labeled right or wrong.

(We have sometimes wondered if we have, perhaps, made it too easy for anyone to justify his or her style of leadership. It may be a small step between being nonjudgmental and giving the impression that all behavior is equally valid and useful. The latter was not our intention. Indeed, the thrust of our endorsement was for the manager who is insightful in assessing relevant forces within himself, others, and the situation, and who can be flexible in responding to these forces.)

In recognizing that our article can be updated, we are acknowledging that organizations do not exist in a vacuum but are affected by changes that occur in society. Consider, for example, the implications for organizations of these recent social developments:

The youth revolution that expresses distrust and even contempt for organizations identified with the establishment.

The civil rights movement that demands all minority groups be given a greater opportunity for participation and influence in the organizational processes.

The ecology and consumer movements that challenge the right of managers to make decisions without considering the interest of people outside the organization.

The increasing national concern with the quality of working life and its relationship to worker productivity, participation, and satisfaction.

These and other societal changes make effective leadership in this decade a more challenging task, requiring even greater sensitivity and flexibility than was needed in the 1950s. Today's manager is more likely to deal with employees who resent being treated as subordinates, who may be highly critical of any organizational system, who expect to be consulted and to exert influence, and who often stand on the edge of alienation from the institution that needs their loyalty and commitment. In addition, he is frequently confronted by a highly turbulent, unpredictable environment.

In response to these social pressures, new concepts of management have emerged in organizations. Open-system theory, with its emphasis on subsystems' interdependency *and* on the interaction of an organization with its environment, has made a powerful impact on managers' approach to problems. Organization development has emerged as a new behavioral science approach to the improvement of individual, group, organizational, and interorganizational performance. New research has added to our understanding of motivation in the work situation. More and more executives have become concerned with social responsibility and have explored the feasibility of social audits. And a growing number of organizations, in Europe and in the United States, have conducted experiments in industrial democracy.

In light of these developments, we submit the following thoughts on how we would rewrite certain points in our original article.

The article described forces in the manager, subordinates, and the situation as givens, with the leadership pattern a resultant of these forces. We would now give more attention to the *interdependency* of these forces. For example, such interdependency occurs in: (a) the interplay between the manager's confidence in his subordinates, their readiness to assume responsibility, and the level of group effectiveness; and (b) the impact of the behavior of the manager on that of his subordinates, and vice versa.

In discussing the forces in the situation, we primarily identified organizational phenomena. We would now include forces lying outside the organization, and would explore the relevant interdependencies between the organization and its environment.

In the original article we presented the size of the rectangle in Figure 10-1 as a given, with its boundaries already determined by external forces—in effect, a closed system. We would now recognize the possibility of the manager and/or his subordinates taking the initiative to change those boundaries through interaction with relevant external forces—both within their own organization and in the larger society.

The article portrayed the manager as the principal and almost unilateral actor. He initiated and determined group functions, assumed responsibility, and exercised control. Subordinates made inputs and assumed power only at the will of the manager. Although the manager might have taken into account forces outside himself, it was *he* who decided where to operate on the continuum—that is, whether to announce a decision instead of trying to sell his idea to his subordinates, whether to invite questions, to let subordinates decide an issue, and so on. While the manager has retained this clear prerogative in many organizations, it has been challenged in others. Even in situations where he has retained it, however, the balance in the relationship between manager and subordinates at any given time is arrived at by interaction—direct or indirect—between the two parties.

Although power and its use by the manager played a role in our article, we now realize that our concern with cooperation and collaboration, common goals, commitment, trust, and mutual caring limited our vision with respect to the realities of power. We did not attempt to deal with unions, other forms of joint worker action, or with individual workers' expressions of resistance. Today, we would recognize much more clearly the power available to *all* parties, and the factors that underlie the interrelated decisions on whether to use it.

In the original article, we used the terms "manager" and "subordinate." We are now uncomfortable with "subordinate" because of its demeaning, dependency-laden connotations and prefer "nonmanager." The titles "manager" and "nonmanager" make the terminological difference functional rather than hierarchical.

We assumed fairly traditional organizational structures in our original article. Now we would alter our formulation to reflect newer organizational modes which are slowly emerging, such as industrial democracy, intentional communities, and "phe-nomenarchy."[5] These new modes are based on observations such as the following:

Both manager and nonmanagers may be governing forces in their group's environment, contributing to the definition of the total area of freedom.

A group can function without a manager, with managerial functions being shared by group members.

A group, as a unit, can be delegated authority and can assume responsibility within a larger organizational context.

Our thoughts on the question of leadership have prompted us to design a new behavior continuum (see Figure 10-2) in which the total area of freedom shared by manager and nonmanagers is constantly redefined by interactions between them and the forces in the environment.

The arrows in the exhibit indicate the continual flow of interdependent influence among systems and people. The points on the continuum designate the types of manager and nonmanager behavior that become possible with any given amount of freedom available to each. The new continuum is both more complex and more dynamic than the 1958 version, reflecting the organizational and societal realities of the 1970s.

5. For a description of phenomenarchy, see Will McWhinney, Phenomenarchy: A suggestion for social redesign, *Journal of Applied Behavioral Science*, May 1973.

11

A Normative Model of Leadership Styles

VICTOR H. VROOM and PHILIP W. YETTON

One of the most persistent and controversial issues in the study of management is that of participation in decision-making by subordinates. Traditional models of the managerial process have been autocratic in nature. The manager makes decisions on matters within his area of freedom, issues orders or directives to his subordinates, and monitors their performance to ensure conformity with these directives. Scientific management, from its early developments in time and motion study to its contemporary manifestations in mathematical programming, has contributed to this centralization of decision-making in organizations by focusing on the development of methods by which managers can make more rational decisions, substituting objective measurements and empirically validated methods for casual judgments.

In contrast, social psychologists and other behavioral scientists who have turned their attention toward the implications of psychological and social processes for the practice of management have called for greater participation by subordinates in the problem-solving and decision-making processes. The empirical evidence provides some, but not overwhelming, support for beliefs in the efficacy of participative management. Field experiments on rank-and-file workers by Coch and French (1948), Bavelas (reported in French, 1950), and Strauss (reported in Whyte, 1955) indicate that impressive increases in productivity can be brought about by giving workers an opportunity to participate in decision-making and goal-setting. In addition, several correlational field studies (Katz, Maccoby, and Morse, 1950; Vroom, 1960) indicate positive relationships between the amount of influence supervisors afford their subordinates in decisions that affect them and individual or group performance.

On the other hand, in an experiment conducted in a Norwegian factory, French, Israel, and Ås (1960) found no significant differences in production between workers who did and those who did not participate in decisions regarding the introduction of changes in work methods. To complicate the picture further, Morse and Reimer (1956) compared the effects of two programs of change, each of which was introduced in two divisions of the clerical operations of a large insurance company. One of the programs involved increased participation in decision-making by rank-and-file workers, while the other involved increased hierarchical control. The results show a significant increase in productivity under both programs, with the hierarchically controlled program producing the greater increase.

The investigations cited constitute only a small portion of those which are relevant to the effects of participation. The reader interested in a more comprehensive review of that evidence should consult Lowin (1968), Vroom (1970), and Wood (1974). We conclude, as have other scholars who have examined the evidence, that participation in decision-making has consequences that vary from one situation to another. Given the potential importance of this conclusion for the study of leadership and its significance to the process of management, social scientists should begin to develop some definitions of the circumstances under which participation in decision-making may contribute to or hinder organizational effectiveness. These could then be translated into guidelines to help leaders choose leadership styles to fit the demands of the situations they encounter.

In this and the following chapter, one approach to dealing with this important problem will be described. A normative model is developed which is consistent with existing empirical evidence concerning the consequences of participation and which purports to specify a set of rules that *should* be used in determining the form and amount of participation in decision-making by subordinates in different classes of situations. This chapter presents the basic assumptions that have guided the development of the normative model and the situational attributes that are contained within it.

BASIC ASSUMPTIONS

1. The normative model should be constructed in such a way as to be of potential value to managers or leaders in determining

which leadership methods they should use in each of the various situations that they encounter in carrying out their formal leadership roles. Consequently, it should be operational in that the behaviors required of the leader should be specified unambiguously.

To be operational, a prescriptive statement must permit the person to determine whether or not he is acting in accordance with the statement. The statement "In case of headache, take one aspirin tablet at intervals of four hours" is quite operational in this sense. It specifies the activities to be performed and the conditions under which they are to be performed. On the other hand, the statement "To maintain one's health, one should lead a clean life" is not operational. The activities subsumed by "leading a clean life" are subject to many differences in interpretation, and there is no clear indication in the statement of the conditions under which the activities are to be carried out.

Many of the prescriptions of behavioral scientists are far closer in operationality to the second statement than to the first. Leaders are told to exhibit maximum concern for people and for production or to develop relationships with subordinates that are supportive. Such prescriptions have some informational value but fall short of the degree of operationality that we believe could be achieved.

2. There are a number of discrete social processes by which organizational problems can be translated into solutions, and these processes vary in terms of the potential amount of participation by subordinates in the problem-solving process.

The term "participation" has been used in a number of different ways. Perhaps the most influential definitions have been those of French, Israel, and Ås (1960) and Vroom (1960), who define participation as a process of joint decision-making by two or more parties. The amount of participation of any individual is the amount of influence he has on the decisions and plans agreed upon. Given the existence of a property such as participation that varies from high to low, it should be possible to define leader behaviors representing clear alternative processes for making decisions that can be related to the amount of participation each process affords the managers' subordinates.

A taxonomy of decision processes created for normative purposes should distinguish among methods that are likely to have different outcomes but should not be so elaborate that leaders are unable to determine which method they are employing in any given instance. The taxonomy to be used in the normative model is shown in Table 11-1.

The table contains a detailed specification of several alternative processes by which problems can be solved or decisions made.

Table 11-1. Decision Methods for Groups and Individual Problems

Group Problems	Individual Problems
AI. You solve the problem or make the decision yourself, using information available to you at the time.	AI. You solve the problem or make the decision by yourself, using information available to you at the time.
AII. You obtain the necessary information from your subordinates, then decide the solution to the problem yourself. You may or may not tell your subordinates what the problem is in getting the information from them. The role played by your subordinates in making the decision is clearly one of providing the necessary information to you, rather than generating or evaluating alternative solutions.	AII. You obtain the necessary information from your subordinate, then decide on the solution to the problem yourself. You may or may not tell the subordinate what the problem is in getting the information from him. His role in making the decision is clearly one of providing the necessary information to you, rather than generating or evaluating alternative solutions.
CI. You share the problem with the relevant subordinates individually, getting their ideas and suggestions without bringing them together as a group. Then *you* make the decision, which may or may not reflect your subordinates' influence.	CI. You share the problem with your subordinate, getting his ideas and suggestions. Then you make a decision, which may or may not reflect his influence.
CII. You share the problem with your subordinates as a group, obtaining their collective ideas and suggestions. Then you make the decision, which may or may not reflect your subordinates' influence.	GI. You share the problem with your subordinate, and together you analyze the problem and arrive at a mutually agreeable solution.
GII. You share the problem with your subordinates as a group. Together you generate and evaluate alternatives and attempt to reach agreement (consensus) on a solution. Your role is much like that of chairman. You do not try to influence the group to adopt "your" solution, and you are willing to accept and implement any solution which has the support of the entire group.	DI. You delegate the problem to your subordinate, providing him with any relevant information that you possess, but giving him responsibility for solving the problem by himself. You may or may not request him to tell you what solution he has reached.

Each process is represented by a symbol (AI, CI, GII, DI) which will be used throughout this book as a convenient method of referring to each process. The letters in this code signify the basic properties of the process (*A* stands for autocratic; *C*, for consultative; *G*, for group; and *D*, for delegated). The roman numerals that follow the letters constitute variants on that process. Thus AI represents the first variant on an autocratic process; AII, the second variant; and so on.

It should be noted that the methods are arranged in two columns corresponding to their applicability to problems which involve the entire group or some subset of it (hereafter called group problems) or a single subordinate (hereafter called individual problems). If a problem or decision clearly affects only one subordinate, the leader would choose among the methods shown in the right-hand column; if it has potential effects on the entire group (or subset of it) he would choose among the methods shown in the left-hand column. Those in both columns are arranged from top to bottom in terms of the opportunity for subordinates to influence the solution to the problem. The distinction between group and individual problems can be illustrated with the following examples.

Group Problems

A. Sharply decreasing profits for the firm has resulted in a directive from top management that makes it impossible to take on any new personnel even to replace those who leave. Shortly after this directive is issued, one of your five subordinates resigns to take a job with another firm. Your problem is how to rearrange the work assignments among the remaining four subordinates without reducing the total productivity of the group.

B. You have been chosen by your firm to attend a nine-week senior executive program at a famous university. Your problem is to choose one of your subordinates to take your place during your absence.

C. You have two main projects under your direction with three subordinates assigned to each. One of these projects is three months behind schedule with only six months remaining before the work *must* be completed. Your problem is to get the project back on schedule to meet the completion date.

Individual Problems

D. As principal of an elementary school, you often handle disciplinary cases. Over the last six months, one of your fifteen teachers has referred an inordinately large number of cases to your attention. This fact, combined with other information you have received, leads you to believe that there is a serious breakdown of discipline within that teacher's classroom.

E. The cost figures for section *B* have risen faster than those of the other three similar sections under your direction. The manager of section *B* is your immediate subordinate.

F. You have the opportunity to bid on a multi-million-dollar government contract. While the decision will be made by top management, you have to formulate a recommendation that has a high probability of being accepted. You have only one subordinate who is a specialist in the area in which the contract is to be granted, and you will have to rely heavily on him to present and defend the recommendation to top management. As you see it, there are at least three options: to bid as prime contractor; to bid as subcontractor for another firm planning to bid as prime contractor; or to do nothing.

The person in the leadership position could presumably employ any one of the alternatives on the left-hand side of Table 11-1 (AI, AII, CI, CII, GII) for problems *A*, *B*, and *C* and could employ any one of the alternatives on the right-hand side of Table 11-1 (AI, AII, CI, GI, DI) for problems *D, E,* and *F.* Since the two sets of alternatives have three common decision processes (AI, AII, CI), this categorization effectively eliminates from consideration *GI* and *DI* as relevant decision processes for group problems (like *A, B,* and *C*) and eliminates CII and GII for individual problems (like *D, E,* and *F*). The reader can verify for himself the appropriateness of these exclusions.

Table 11-2 shows the relationship between the methods shown in Table 11-2 and those described in prior taxonomies. Our methods appear as row headings, and the names of other authors or researches appear as column headings. If there seems to be correspondence between the definition of one of our methods and that used by a given author, his term appears in the intersection of row and column. A vacant cell, defined by the intersection of a column and row, indicates that the investigator whose name heads the column does not recognize any style corresponding to that in the row heading. If a column is partitioned within a row, it means that the investigator uses a finer breakdown than that employed in the model. Similarly, if a column entry cuts across two or more rows, it indicates that the model employs a finer breakdown than that made by the investigator. The relationships presented in Table 11-2 are matters of judgment and are merely intended to suggest the correspondence or lack of correspondence existing between the taxonomy that is used here and those which were previously employed.

3. No one leadership method is applicable to all situations; the function of a normative model should be to provide a framework for the analysis of situational requirements that can be translated into prescriptions of leadership styles.

The fact that the most effective leadership method or style is dependent on the situation is becoming widely recognized by behavioral scientists interested in problems of leadership and administration. A decision-making process that is optimal for a quarter-back on a football team making decisions under severe time constraints is likely to be far from optimal when used by a dean introducing a new curriculum to be implemented by his faculty. Even the advocates of participative management have noted this "situational relativity" of leadership styles. Thus, Argyris (1962) writes:

No one leadership style is the most effective. Each is probably effective under a given set of conditions. Consequently, I suggest that effective leaders are those who are capable of behaving in many different leadership styles, depending on the requirements of reality as they and others perceive it. I call this "reality-centered" leadership. (1962, p. 81)

We must go beyond noting the importance of situational factors and begin to move toward a road map or normative models that attempt to prescribe the most appropriate leadership style for different kinds of situations. The most comprehensive treatment of situational factors as determinants of the effectiveness and efficiency of participation in decision-making is found in the work of Tannenbaum and Schmidt (1958). They discuss a large number of variables, including attributes of the manager, his subordinates, and the situation, which ought to enter into the manager's decision about the degree to which he should share his power with his subordinates. But they stop at this inventory of variables, and do not show how these might be combined and translated into different forms of action.

4. The most appropriate unit for the analysis of the situation is the particular problem to be solved and the context in which the problem occurs.

While it is becoming widely recognized that different situations require different leadership methods, there is less agreement concerning the appropriate units for the

Table 11-2. Correspondence Between Decision Processes Employed in the Model and Those of Previous Investigators

	Lewin, Lippitt, and White (1939)	Maier (1955)	Tannenbaum and Schmidt (1958)	Heller (1971)	Likert (1967)
AI	Autocratic leadership	Autocratic management	Manager makes decision and announces it	Own decision without detailed explanation	Exploitive authoritative (system 1)
AII			Manager sells decision / Manager presents ideas and invites questions	Own decision with detailed explanation	Benevolent authoritative (system 2)
CI		Consultative management	Manager presents tentative decision, subject to change	Prior consultation with subordinate(s)	Consultative (system 3)
CII			Manager presents problem, gets suggestions, makes decision		
GI				Joint decision-making with subordinate(s)	
GII	Democratic leadership	Group decision	Manager defines limits, asks group to make decision / Manager permits group to make decisions within prescribed limits		Participative group (system 4)
DI	Laissez-faire leadership			Delegation of decision to subordinate(s)	

analysis of the situation. One approach is to assume that the situations that determine the effectiveness of different leadership styles correspond to the environment of the system. Thus, Bennis (1966) argues that egalitarian leadership styles work better when the environment of the organization is rapidly changing and the problems with which it has to deal are continually being altered. If this position were extended to provide the basis for a comprehensive normative model, one would prescribe different leadership styles for different systems but make identical prescriptions for all leadership roles within a system.

Alternatively, one might assume that the critical features of the situation concern the role of the leader, including his relations with his subordinates. Examples would include Fiedler's (1967) three dimensions of task structure, leadership position power, and leader-member relations. Implicit is the assumption that all problems or decisions made within a single role require a similar leadership style. Normatively, one might prescribe different amounts or forms of participation for two different leaders but prescribe identical amounts or forms of participation for all problems or decisions made by a single leader within a single role.

The approach taken here is to select the properties of the problem to be solved as the critical situational dimensions for determining the appropriate form or amount of participation. Different prescriptions would be made for a given leader for different problems within a given role. It should be noted that constructing a normative model with the problem rather than the role or any organizational differences as the unit of analysis does not rule out the possibility that different roles and organizations may involve different distributions of problem types that, in aggregate, may require different modal styles or levels of participation.

5. *The leadership method used in response to one situation should not constrain the method or style used in other situations.*

Implicit in the use of the attributes of the particular problem to be solved or decision to be made as the unit of analysis is the assumption that problems can be classified such that the relative usefulness of each alternative decision process is identical for all problems in a particular classification. A corollary to this assumption is that the process or method used on problems of one type does not constrain that used on problems of a different type. It is only in this way that prescriptions could be made for a given problem without knowing the other problems encountered by a leader or his methods for dealing with them.

This assumption is necessary to the construction of a normative model founded on problem differences. It may seem inconsistent with the view, first proposed by McGregor (1944), that consistency in leadership style is desirable because it enables subordinates to predict their superiors' behavior and to adapt to it. However, predictability does not preclude variability. There are many variable phenomena which can be predicted quite well because the rules or processes that govern them are understood. The antithesis of predictability is randomness, and, if McGregor is correct, a normative model to regulate choices among alternative leadership styles should be deterministic rather than stochastic. The model to be developed here is deterministic; the normatively prescribed method for a given problem type is a constant.

CONCEPTUAL AND EMPIRICAL BASIS OF THE MODEL

A model designed to regulate, in some rational way, choices among the decision methods shown in Table 11-1 should be based on sound empirical evidence concerning their likely consequences. The more complete the empirical base of knowledge, the greater the certainty with which one can develop the model and the greater will be its usefulness. In this section we will restrict ourselves to the development of a model concerned only with group problems and, hence, will use only the methods shown in the left-hand column of Table 11-1.

We will now consider the empirical evidence that can at present be brought to bear on such a normative model. You will note that much of the evidence is incomplete, and future research should prove helpful in providing a firmer foundation for a model. In this analysis it is important to distinguish three classes of outcomes that influence the ultimate effectiveness of decisions. These are:

1. the quality or rationality of the decision;

2. the acceptance of the decision by subordinates and their commitment to execute it effectively;

3. the amount of time required to make the decision.

The evidence regarding the effects of participation on each of these outcomes or consequences has been reviewed elsewhere (Vroom 1970). He concluded that

the results suggest that allocating problem solving and decision-making tasks to entire groups as compared with the leader or manager in charge of the groups, requires a greater investment of man hours but produces higher acceptance of decisions and a higher probability that the decisions will be executed efficiently. Differences between these two methods in quality of decisions and in elapsed time are inconclusive and probably highly variable. . . . It would be naive to think that group decision-making is always more "effective" than autocratic decision-making, or vice versa; the relative effectiveness of these two extreme methods depends both on the weights attached to quality, acceptance and time variables and on differences in amounts of these outcomes resulting from these methods, neither of which is invariant from one situation to another. The critics and proponents of participative management would do well to direct their efforts toward identifying the properties of situations in which different decision-making approaches are effective rather than wholesale condemnation or deification of one approach. (Vroom, 1970, pp. 239-40)

Stemming from this review, an attempt has been made to identify these properties of the situation, which will be the basic elements in the model. These problem attributes are of two types: (1) those which specify the importance for a particular problem of quality and acceptance (see *A* and *E* below), and (2) those which, on the basis of available evidence, have a high probability of moderating the effects of participation on each of these outcomes (see *B, C, D, G,* and *H* below). The following are the problem attributes used in the present form of the model.

A. The importance of the quality of the decision. According to Maier (1955, 1963), decision quality refers to the "objective or impersonal" aspects of the decision. For groups embedded within formal organizations with specifiable goals, the relative quality of a set of alternative decisions can be expressed in terms of their effects, if implemented with equal expenditure of energy, on the attainment of those goals.

The first attribute refers to what Maier (1963) has termed the quality requirement for the decision. There are some problems for which the nature of the solution reached within identifiable constraints is not at all critical. The leader is (or should be) indifferent among the possible solutions since their expected value is equal, provided that those who have to carry them out are committed to them. Typically, the number of solutions that meet the constraints is finite, and the alternatives are obvious or do not require substantial search. In such instances, there is no technical, rational, or analytic method of choosing among the alternatives.

In Maier's new-truck problem (Maier, 1955), the issue of which of the five truck drivers should get the new truck has no quality requirement. The foreman is (or should be) indifferent among the various possible alternatives provided they are accepted by the men. On the other hand, the problem of which truck should be discarded to make way for the new one does have a quality requirement. The five present trucks vary in age and condition, and a decision to discard other than the poorest truck in the set would be irrational.

While on a consulting assignment, the senior author encountered another problem which may help to illustrate the meaning of the term "quality requirement." A plant manager and his staff were about to move into a new plant. On inspecting the plans, he discovered that there were insufficient reserved parking places (directly in front of the building) to accommodate all six of his department heads. The design of the building permitted only four such parking places with all other cars having to park across the street in a large parking lot. There was no possible way to increase the number of parking spaces without modifying the design of the structure, and the costs would be prohibitive. Any solution to the parking-space allocation problem would have satisfied the plant manager provided it had the support of his department heads, each of whom, incidentally, expected to receive a reserved parking place. The problem had no quality requirement since he was indifferent among all possible solutions which met the constraints.

In both of the examples given, the constraints were imposed on the leader by forces outside him. The foreman had only one new truck to allocate among his drivers, and the plant manager could do nothing to increase the size of the reserved parking lot. In other instances, the quality requirement can be eliminated from the problem if the leader *imposes* constraints on the possible solutions. By attaching suitable constraints, quality requirements can be eliminated from such problems as the choice of personnel to be assigned to work on each shift, the design of a vacation schedule showing when each person should take his vacation, and the selection of a time at which to hold a meeting.

At the other end of the dimension specified by this attribute are so-called strategic decisions (Ansoff, 1965), which involve the allocation of scarce resources and are not easily reversible. At what level should we price our products? What new businesses should we acquire? Where should we locate our plants? What is the most effective advertising policy? These are just a few of the problems and decisions which have marked consequences for the effectiveness of the organization. No leader should be indifferent among possible alternative courses of action. Even though the relative consequences of the alternatives may not be known at any given point in time, the specific course chosen is going to make a difference in the degree to which the system attains its goals. In such instances, the variance in contribution to organizational objectives of alternative courses of action is large, and the rational quality of the decision is of central importance.

The function of this attribute in the model is to determine the relevance to the choice of decision process of such considerations as the nature and location of information or expertise necessary to generate and evaluate alternatives. If the quality of the decision is unimportant, then attributes *B, C, D,* and *G* below can be shown to be irrelevant to the prescription of that process.

B. The extent to which the leader possesses sufficient information/expertise to make a high-quality decision by himself.
The quality of the decisions reached by any decision-making process is dependent on the resources the leader is able to utilize. One of the most critical of these resources is information. If a rational solution to the problem is to be obtained, alternatives must be generated and evaluated in terms of their organizational consequences. Any such activities require the use of the relevant information and expertise by participants in the decision process.

It is possible to distinguish two different kinds of information that are potentially relevant to problem-solving in an organizational setting. One is information necessary to the task of evaluating the relative quality or rationality of different alternatives. The other is information concerning the preferences of subordinates and their feelings about the alternatives.

These two kinds of information and associated expertise need not be correlated. One leader may be extremely knowledgeable about the terrain to be traversed and its possible pitfalls, and he may have worked out an elegant means of attaining the external objective. However, he may be completely unaware of the preferences of his men. Another may be uninformed about the external environment but highly sensitive to the attitudes and feelings of his subordinates. A low correlation between these two components of information is suggested by research on role differentiation in problem-solving groups. Task facilitative leadership tends to be carried out by different persons than socio-emotional leadership (Bales and Slater, 1955).

The information referred to in attribute *B* deals with the external goals and the consequences of actions on the part of the system for their attainment. In other words, we are interested only in the degree to which the leader possesses facts and skills relevant to the quality of the decision. Thus, in evaluating the level of this attribute in the case of a head dietitian in a hospital faced with the task of preparing the week's menus, one would be concerned with such things as her knowledge of the components of a balanced diet, the availability and cost of different food products, and the existence of special dietary requirements among the patient load. One would not be concerned with the kinds of foods that her staff liked to consume, prepare, or deliver. Similarly, in evaluating the information possessed by a university department chairman faced with the problem of selecting a text to be used by members of his department in teaching the introductory course, the relevant questions would concern his knowledge of the alterna-

tives as they relate to the goal of education and not his information regarding the preferences of those assigned to teach the course.

In defining this attribute solely in terms of information or expertise in matters relating to the quality of the decision, we intend not to render unimportant the task of having decisions accepted by subordinates, but rather to recognize the conceptual and empirical independence of the two kinds of information. As will be seen later in the description of other problem attributes, acceptance requirements are an integral part of the framework being developed.

The decision-making processes shown in Table 11-1 differ in terms of the amount of information and expertise that can be brought to bear on the problem. For example, in AI, only information available to the leader may be utilized in problem-solving, whereas in GII the information base extends to all group members including the leader.

There has been little research on the determinants of whether the leader's information is adequate to deal with the problems he encounters. Since he has been selected by somewhat different criteria, may have received special training, and has access to different information, there is strong *a priori* reason to believe that his information base will be different from (and in most cases superior to) that of the average group member. However, its absolute level must be assumed to be variable with the nature of the problem. There are undoubtedly some situations in which the leader possesses all of the necessary information and others for which his information is critically deficient. In the model, this attribute determines the importance of choosing a decision-making process that augments the information base of the decision.

Kelley and Thibaut (1969) have reviewed the literature on group and individual problem-solving and have advanced a set of hypotheses concerning the conditions in which a group solution is likely to be higher than, equal to, or lower in quality than that of the best member of the group. The studies were conducted principally on ad hoc leaderless groups in laboratory settings, so it is not clear that the best member would always have been a formal leader. However, their hypotheses may ultimately prove fruitful in relating variation on the attribute defined above to problem differences.

Kelley and Thibaut suggest that: (1) group decisions are likely to be above the level of the most proficient member when the problem has multiple parts and when group members have uncorrelated (complementary) deficiencies and talents; (2) groups are likely to perform at the level of the most proficient member when the problem is simple (very few steps are required for its solution) and the solution is highly verifiable by all persons in possession of the original facts; and (3) groups are likely to do less well than the best member when the solution requires thinking through a series of interrelated steps or stages, applying a number of rules at each point, and always keeping in mind conclusions reached at earlier points.

C. The extent to which subordinates, taken collectively, have the necessary information to generate a high-quality decision. This attribute is similar to *B* above except that it deals with the resources of subordinates rather than the leader. There are some situations in which these resources may in fact be very small. For example, the problem may be a highly technical one, and the subordinates may lack any knowledge needed to deal with it. On the other hand, in problems with multiple parts and where the level of information needed to deal with these parts is uncorrelated, the potential contribution of subordinates may be very high. This attribute is relevant to the choice of a decision process only when the information available to the leader is deficient. It determines whether the information search activities can be conducted within the group as part of the decision-making activity or

whether, in order to obtain a high-quality decision, it will be necessary to go outside the group for the necessary information.

D. The extent to which the problem is structured. A distinction is frequently made between problems or decisions that are structured or programmed, and those which are unstructured or nonprogrammed (Simon, 1960). Structured problems are those for which the alternative solutions or methods for generating them and the parameters for their evaluation are known. There are typically specific procedures within the organization for handling them. Under these circumstances, the decision is made once all the necessary information has reached a central source, in this case the leader. The process is essentially that of the "wheel" in communication net experiments, which has been found to be more efficient for the solution of simple problems than less centralized networks (Shaw, 1964).

However, if the problem is unstructured and the relevant information widely dispersed among persons, the organizational task is somewhat different. Under these circumstances it is less clear what information is relevant, and empirical evidence appears to favor a less centralized network which permits those with potentially relevant information to interact with one another in the course of solving the problem. This process is more akin to that in the circle networks, which have been found to be more effective in solving complex problems (Shaw, 1964). Within the model, this attribute bears on the relative efficiency of information collection activities that involve interaction among subordinates (that is, CII and GII) and those which do not involve such interaction (AII and CI).

E. The extent to which acceptance or commitment on the part of subordinates is critical to the effective implementation of the decision. In most situations, the effectiveness of an organizational decision is influenced both by its quality or rationality and by the extent to which it is accepted by subordinates. A decision can be ineffective because it did not utilize all of the available information concerning the external environment or because it was resisted and opposed by those who had to implement it.

The distinction between quality and acceptance is reminiscent of Bales's (1949) distinction between problems of the group involving goal achievement and adaptation to external demands and problems involving internal integration and expression of emotional tensions. Bales divides problems into two groups, adaptive-instrumental problems and integrative-expressive problems. In the framework being developed, quality and acceptance requirements are seen not as discrete types or even as opposite ends of a single continuum but rather as two separable dimensions. Just as the quality of the decision varies in importance from one problem to another, so also does the acceptance of the decision by subordinates, and there is no necessary correlation between these two dimensions.

There are two classes of situations in which acceptance of the decision by subordinates may be regarded as irrelevant to its effective implementation. One of these is what Maier (1970) has termed "outsider problems." In an "outsider problem," the subordinates are not involved in the execution of the decision. One may still desire their participation in order to enhance the quality of the solution, but the decision will be implemented by the leader or some other group. Acceptance by this particular set of persons is not critical to the ultimate success or failure of the decision.

The second type of situation in which acceptance or commitment to the decision by subordinates is not critical is that in which subordinates will be required to execute the decision but its nature is such that compliance on their part, rather than acceptance or commitment, is sufficient. Typically in such situations, subordinates' actions necessary for implementation of the decision are specific; the leader is able to monitor or

observe these actions, and he controls rewards and punishments, which he is able to mete out accordingly. Both in the larger society and in organizations, people carry out directives to which they feel no personal commitment and, in fact, may be strongly opposed. The forces operating on them are "induced" forces rather than "own" forces (Lewin, 1935), and the conditions necessary for the successful induction of a force must be present. The actions must be observable by others who wish to see the directive carried out, and these others must control rewards and/or penalties, which are meted our in accordance with the degree of compliance observed.

Acceptance becomes more critical as the effective execution of the decision requires initiative, judgment, or creativity on the part of subordinates or when one or more of the conditions necessary for obtaining compliance breaks down; for example, the leader is unable to monitor subordinates' behavior and reward or punish deviations. Within the model, the interaction of this attribute with the following one determines the importance of attempting to develop subordinates' commitment to the final solution by employing a participative decision-making process.

F. The prior probability that the leader's autocratic decision will receive acceptance by subordinates. The relationship between participation in decision-making and the acceptance of decisions by subordinates is marked but probably not invariant with the nature of the problem and the context within which it occurs. Thus, Vroom (1960) found that the effects of participation varied with the subordinate's need for independence and authoritarianism. Similarly, in a field experiment in a Norwegian factory, French, Israel, and Ås (1960) discovered that the effects varied with subordinates' perceptions of the legitimacy of their participation, and Marrow (1964) has provided a brief account of some of the problems that occurred when the Harwood Manufacturing Company attempted to increase participation in decision-making, which had proved highly successful in their plants in the United States, in their newly acquired subsidiary in Puerto Rico.

It appears that participation is not a necessary condition for the acceptance of decisions. There are some circumstances in which the leader's decision has high prior probability of being accepted by subordinates. These circumstances are predictable from a knowledge of the relationship between the leader and his subordinates. French and Raven (1959) distinguish among five bases of power all of which are defined in terms of the relationship between the source and object of influence. Three of these bases (legitimate power, expert power, and referent power) are hypothesized to produce "own" forces on the object of influence to engage in the indicated action, thereby conforming to our definition of acceptance. Thus, the subordinates may accept the leader's decision because they believe that it is his legitimate right to make that decision by virtue of the position he occupies (legitimate power), because he is the acknowledged expert and the only one capable of taking all the necessary factors into consideration (expert power), or because he is strongly admired by them (referent power). In such situations, it is not at all difficult for the leader to "sell" his decision to his subordinates, thereby gaining the necessary acceptance.

There are many situations in which the prior probability of acceptance of a decision by subordinates will vary with the nature of the solution adopted. Some alternatives may be acceptable to subordinates and some may not. In effect, the prior probability of acceptance becomes a property of a solution rather than a property of the problem. To deal with the potential complexities introduced by this state of affairs, the following guidelines are suggested. For problems with a quality requirement (attribute A), the relevant prior probability of acceptance is that of the highest quality alternative known

to the leader. Thus, if the leader has worked out a solution to a complex production-scheduling problem using critical path analysis and were convinced that it would work nad would be superior to the present method and other alternatives known to him, one would be interested in the prior probability that this new method would be accepted by his subordinates.

For problems without a quality requirement, the relevant prior probability of acceptance is the highest value for any of the solutions meeting the constraints specified. In a case described earlier in this chapter—that of the plant manager assigning four reserved parking places among his six department heads—the level specified for prior probability would be that of the most palatable alternative to his subordinates.

This attribute is relevant to the choice of method only where acceptance is required in order for the decision to be effectively implemented (attribute E). It, in turn, determines whether participation in decision-making is necessary in order to attain that acceptance.

G. The extent to which subordinates are motivated to attain the organizational goals as represented in the objectives explicit in the statement of the problem. In all problems, there are one or more goals to be achieved. Ultimately, it is the attainment of those goals that determines whether the problem is actually solved. In effect, the general goal of organizational effectiveness is replaced by surrogate and more operational goals such as improving the safety record, reducing costs by 30 per cent, or reorganizing to adapt to a cut in manpower while maintaining volume.

It is assumed that the quality of the decision reached is dependent not only on the information or expertise of those participating in it, but also on their disposition to use their information in the service of the goals stated in the problem. This phenomenon has seldom been examined in laboratory experiments on group problem-solving, where participants are motivated to solve the problem as accurately and as quickly as possible. But in formal organizations, there are many situations in which the goals of the group members may be in conflict with those stated in the problem. For example, decisions concerning the wage levels or the work loads of the participants may be among those which personal rather than organizational goals might dominate the search for and the evaluation of alternatives.

This problem attribute is similar to what Maier (1963) terms "mutual interest," and to the potential amount of trust that the leader can place in his subordinates to solve the problem in the best interest of the organization. It determines the potential risk to the quality of the decision of methods like GII in which the leader relinquishes his final control over the decision.

H. The extent to which subordinates are likely to be in disagreement over preferred solutions. Conflicts or disagreements among group members over the appropriate solution are quite common features of decision-making in organizations. It is possible for group members to agree on a common goal but disagree over the best means of attaining it. Such disagreements can result from access to different information or from the fact that personal gains or losses from different solutions are negatively correlated.

There is substantial evidence from the literature in social psychology (see Brown, 1965) to indicate that interaction among people tends to increase their similarity in attitudes and opinions. Members of a group with initially wide variance in individual judgments will tend to converge on a common position. This process seems to be enhanced when the issue is relevant to their interaction and when the problem is of mutual interest. Thus, Kelley and Thibaut (1969) note in their review of the literature on group problem-solving that "group problem discussion generates pressures toward uniformity" (p. 71). This attribute determines the importance of choosing a decision-making process (CII and GII) in which subordinates interact in the process of solving the problem, as opposed to those (AII and CI) in which no such interaction takes place.

Table 11-3 shows the same eight problem attributes expressed in the form of questions which might be used by a leader in diagnosing a particular problem before choosing his leadership method. In phrasing the questions, technical language has been held to a minimum. Furthermore, the questions have been phrased in yes-no form, translating the continuous variables defined above into dichotomous variables. For example, instead of attempting to determine how important

Table 11-3. Problem Attributes

A. If decision were accepted, would it make a difference which course of action were adopted?

B. Do I have sufficient information to make a high-quality decision?

C. Do subordinates have sufficient additional information to result in a high-quality decision?

D. Do I know exactly what information is needed, who possesses it, and how to collect it?

E. Is acceptance of decision by subordinates critical to effective implementation?

F. If I were to make the decision by myself, is it certain that it would be accepted by my subordinates?

G. Can subordinates be trusted to base solutions on organizational considerations?

H. Is conflict among subordinates likely in preferred solutions?

---

the decision quality is to the effectiveness of the decision (attribute A), the leader is asked in the first question to judge whether there is any quality component to the problem. Similarly, the difficult task of specifying exactly how much information the leader possesses that is relevant to the decision (attribute B) is reduced to a simple judgment by the leader concerning whether he has sufficient information to make a high quality decision.

Expressing what are obviously continuous variables in dichotomous form greatly simplifies the problem of incorporating these attributes into a model that can be used by leaders. It sidesteps the problem of scaling each problem attribute and reduces the complexity of the judgments required of leaders.

It has been found that managers can diagnose a situation quickly and accurately by answering a set of eight questions. But how can such responses generate a prescription for the most effective leadership method or decision process? What kind of normative model of participation in decision-making can be built from this set of problem attributes. These questions and our mode of resolving them will be taken up next.

A NORMATIVE MODEL

Let us assume that you are a manager faced with a concrete problem to be solved. We will also assume that you have judged that this problem could potentially affect more than one of your subordinates. Hence, it is what we have defined as a group problem, and you have to choose among the five decision processes (AI, AII, CI, CII, GII) shown at the left side of Table 11-1.

On *a priori* grounds any of these five decision processes could be called for. The judgments you have made concerning the status of each problem's attributes can be used to define a set of feasible alternatives. This occurs through a set of rules that

eliminate decision processes from the feasible set under certain specifiable conditions.

The rules are intended to protect both the quality and the acceptance of the decision. In the present form of the model, there are three rules that protect decision quality and four that protect acceptance. The seven rules are presented here both as verbal statements and in the more formal language of set theory. In the set theoretic formulation, the letters refer to the problem attributes as stated in question form in Table 11-3. The letter A signifies that the answer to question A for a particular problem is *yes*; $\bar{A}$ signifies that the answer to that question is *no*; $\cap$ signifies intersection; $\Rightarrow$ signifies "implies"; and $\overline{AI}$ signifies not AI. Thus $A \cap B \Rightarrow \overline{AI}$ may be read as follows: when both the answer to question A is yes and the answer to question B is no, AI is eliminated from the feasible set.

1. The information rule. If the quality of the decision is important and if the leader does not possess enough information or expertise to solve the problem by himself, AI is eliminated from the feasible set. (Its use risks a low-quality decision.)

$$(A \cap \bar{B} \Rightarrow \overline{AI})$$

2. The trust rule. If the quality of the decision is important and if the subordinates cannot be trusted to base their efforts to solve the problem on organizational goals, GII is eliminated from the feasible set. (Alternatives that eliminate the leader's final control over the decision may jeopardize its quality.)

$$(A \cap \bar{G} \Rightarrow \overline{GII})$$

3. The unstructured problem rule. When the quality of the decision in important, if the leader lacks the necessary information or expertise to solve the problem by himself, and if the problem is unstructured, that is, he does not know exactly what information is needed and where it is located, the method used must provide not only for him to collect the information but to do so in an efficient manner. Methods which involve interaction among all subordinates with full knowledge of the problem are likely to be both more efficient and more likely to generate a high-quality solution to the problem. Under these conditions, AI, AII, and CI are eliminated from the feasible set. (AI does not provide for him to collect the necessary information, and AII and CI represent more cumbersome, less effective, and less efficient means of bringing the necessary information to bear on the solution of the problem than methods that do permit those with the necessary information to interact.)

$$(A \cap \bar{B} \cap \bar{D} \Rightarrow \overline{AI}, \overline{AII}, \overline{CI})$$

4. The acceptance rule. If the acceptance of the decision by subordinates is critical to effective implementation, and if it is not certain that an autocratic decision made by the leader would receive that acceptance, AI and AII are eliminated from the feasible set. (Neither provides an opportunity for subordinates to participate in the decision, and both risk the necessary acceptance.)

$$(\bar{E} \cap \bar{F} \Rightarrow \overline{AI}, \overline{AII})$$

5. The conflict rule. If the acceptance of the decision is critical, an autocratic decision is not certain to be accepted, and subordinates are likely to be in conflict or disagreement over the appropriate solution, AI, AII, and CI are eliminated from the feasible set. (The method used in solving the problem should enable those in disagreement to resolve their differences with full knowledge of the problem. Accordingly, under these conditions, AI, AII, and CI, which involve no interaction or only "one-to-one" relationships and therefore provide no opportunity for those in conflict to resolve their differences, are eliminated from the feasible set. Their use runs the risk of leaving some of the subordinates with less than the necessary commitment to the final decision.)

$$(E \cap \bar{F} \cap H \Rightarrow \overline{AI}, \overline{AII}, \overline{CI})$$

6. The fairness rule. If the quality of decision is unimportant, and if acceptance is critical and not certain to result from an autocratic decision, AI, AII, CI, and CII are eliminated from the feasible set. (The method used should maximize the probability of acceptance as this is the only relevant consideration in determining the effectiveness of the decision. Under these circumstances AI, AII, CI, and CII, which create less acceptance or commitment than GII, are eliminated from the feasible set. To use them will run the risk of getting less than the required acceptance of the decision.)

$$(\bar{A} \cap E \cap \bar{F} \Rightarrow \overline{AI}, \overline{AII}, \overline{CI}, \overline{CII})$$

7. The acceptance priority rule. If acceptance is critical, not assured by an autocratic decision, and if subordinates can be trusted, AI, AII, CI, and CII are eliminated from the feasible set. (Methods which provide equal partnership in the decision-making process can provide greater acceptance without risking decision quality. Use of any method other than GII results in an unnecessary risk that the decision will not be fully accepted or receive the necessary commitment on the part of subordinates.)

$$(E \cap \bar{F} \cap G \Rightarrow \overline{AI}, \overline{AII}, \overline{CI}, \overline{CII})$$

It should be noted that some rules are nested within other rules such that violating one rule is a special case of violating another. Consider an unstructured problem in which the leader does not have sufficient information on which to make a high quality decision. Rule 1 excludes the use of AI (no opportunity to collect data), and rule 3 excludes AI, AII, and CI (no opportunity for group problem-solving). If rule 1 is violated in a problem for which rule 3 is applicable, then rule 3 is also violated. Since the applicability of rule 1 to the problem is a necessary but not sufficient condition for the applicability of rule 3, one can view rule 3 as "nested within" rule 1. Similarly, rules 5, 6, and 7 are nested within rule 4. Rule 4 is the basic acceptance rule which excludes AI

A. If decision were accepted, would it make a difference which course of action were adopted?
B. Do I have sufficient info to make a high-quality decision?
C. Do subordinates have sufficient additional info to result in high-quality decision?
D. Do I know exactly what info is needed, who possesses it, and how to collect it?
E. Is acceptance of decision by subordinates critical to effective implementation?
F. If I were to make the decision by myself, is it certain that it would be accepted by my subordinates?
G. Can subordinates be trusted to base solutions on organizational considerations?
H. Is conflict among subordinates likely in preferred solutions?

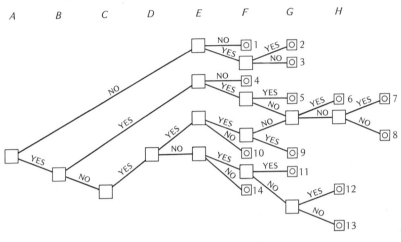

Fig. 11-1. Problem Types

and AII when acceptance is necessary and unlikely to exist for an autocratic decision. Rules 5, 6, and 7 further limit the feasible set as a function of additional properties of the problem. Thus, in the same way as the applicability of rule 1 is a necessary but not sufficient condition for the applicability of rule 3, rule 4 is necessary but not sufficient for rules 5, 6, and 7.

In applying these rules to a problem, you will find that it helps to represent them pictorially in the form of a decision tree. Figure 11-1 shows a simple decision tree that serves this purpose. The problem attributes are arranged along the top of the figure. To apply the rules to a particular problem, one starts at the left-hand side and works toward the right, asking onself the question immediately above any box that is encountered. When a terminal node is reached, the number designates the problem type which in turn designates a set of methods that remain feasible after the rules have been applied.[1] It

can be seen that this method of representing the decision tree generates fourteen problem types. Problem type is a nominal variable designating classes of problems generated by the paths that lead to the terminal nodes. Thus, all problems that have no quality requirement and in which acceptance is not critical are defined as type 1; all problems that have no quality requirement, in which acceptance is critical, but the prior probability of acceptance of the leader's decision is high, are defined as type 2, and so on.[2]

1. Rule 2 has not been applied to problem types 4, 9, 10, 11, and 14. This rule eliminates GII from the feasible set when the answer to question G is no. Thus, we can distinguish two variants of each of these types.

2. An inspection of the structure of the flow diagram reveals that three problem types (6, 7, and 8) can be further subdivided. To each of these three terminal nodes, there are two alternative paths, which diverge at attribute B (leader's information). Thus, one could broaden the classification of problem types, differentiating those of types 6, 7, and 8 into subcategories.

Table 11-4. Problem Types and the Feasible Set of Decision Methods

Problem Type	Acceptable Methods
1	AI, AII, CI, CII, GII
2	AI, AII, CI, CII, GII
3	GII
4	AI, AII, CI, CII, GII*
5	AI, AII, CI, CII, GII*
6	GII
7	CII
8	CI, CII
9	AII, CI, CII, GII*
10	AII, CI, CII, GII*

*Within the feasible set only when the answer to question G is yes

The feasible set for each of the fourteen problem types is shown in Table 11-4. It can be seen that there are some problem types for which only one method remains in the feasible set, others for which two methods remain feasible, and still others for which five methods remain feasible. It should be recalled that the feasible set is defined as the methods that remain after all those which violate rules designated to protect the quality and acceptance of the decision have been excluded.

Choosing Among Alternatives in the Feasible Set

When more than one method remains in the feasible set, there are a number of alternative decision rules which might dictate the choice among them. One, which will be examined in greater depth, utilizes the number of man-hours required to solve the problem as the basis for choice. Given a set of methods with equal likelihood of meeting both quality and acceptance requirements for the decision, it selects the method that requires the least investment in man-hours. This is deemed to be the method furthest to the left within the feasible set. Thus, if AI, AII, CI, CII, and GII are all feasible, as in problem types 1 and 2, AI would be the method chosen. This decision rule acts to minimize man-hours, subject to quality and acceptance constraints.

Figure 11-2 shows the decision tree with methods prescribed for each of the problem types. In addition, two other attributes have been added to cover cases in which the group does not have sufficient information to make a decision. The attributes regulate predecisional activities such as problem identification and prior information collection. They do not affect choice of method except insofar as the net result of these activities is to affect the status of the situational attributes for that problem.

This decision rule for choosing among alternatives in the feasible set results in the prescription of each of the five decision processes in some situations. Method AI is prescribed for four problem types (1, 2, 4, and 5); AII is prescribed for two problem types (9 and 10); CI is prescribed for only one problem type (8); CII is prescribed for four problem types (7, 11, 13, and 14); and GII is prescribed for three problem types (3, 6, and 12). The relative frequency with which the five decision processes would be prescribed for any leader would, of course, be dependent on the distribution of problem types in his role.

It should be noted that the order of problem attributes is irrelevant to the final specification of the decision-making process. The order shown in Figure 11-2 was selected because it minimizes the number of branches and terminal nodes necessary to determine

A. If decision were accepted, would it make a difference which course of action were adopted?
B. Do I have sufficient info to make a high-quality decision?
C. Do subordinates have sufficient additional info to result in high-quality decision?
D. Do I know exactly what info is needed, who possesses it, and how to collect it?
 * Is necessary additional info to be found within my entire set of subordinates?
 † Is it feasible to collect additional info outside group prior to making decisions?
E. Is acceptance of decision by subordinates critical to effective implementation?
F. If I were to make the decision by myself, is it certain that it would be accepted by my subordinates?
G. Can subordinates be trusted to base solutions on organizational considerations?
H. Is conflict among subordinates likely in preferred solutions?

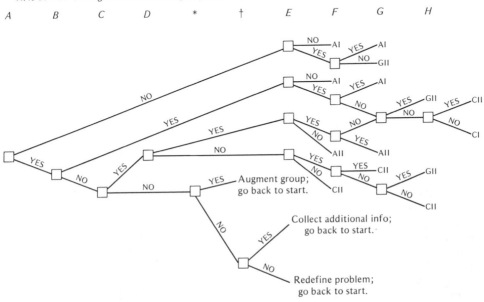

Fig. 11-2. Decision–Process Flow Chart

the process in accordance with the rules given. Any other order would increase the complexity of the decision tree and increase the number of terminal nodes. For example, if conflict were switched from position *H* to position *A* and each other attribute advanced by one position, the number of terminal nodes would be increased. from fourteen to twenty-six.

The Composition of the Group

In phrasing the attributes in the model for group problems, the term subordinates has been used frequently. Attribute *C* deals with

the information possessed by subordinates, attribute *F* with the prior probability of acceptance of the leader's decision by subordinates, and so on. The choice of the term subordinate to refer to other potential participants in the decision-making process should not be taken to mean that the members of the group are necessarily those defined by the organization chart as reporting to the leader. Many problems cut across organizational boundaries, and the groups, task forces, or committees set up to solve them are made up of persons from many different parts of the organization. Such problem-solving units typically have a leader, chairman, or head, and we consider the attributes as being equally relevant for this leader's choice of decision-making process as in the more traditional case of a formal organization unit. Thus, the subordinates referred to in the problem attributes can be taken more broadly to mean members of the group formally established to deal with that problem.

But what of the case in which the group of potential participants is ambiguous and not defined by any existing organizational unit, even one with temporary membership? Does the model have any implications for the composition of the group where none has existed in the past? These questions are potentially separable from the model, which deals primarily with the choice of decision-making process given a specified leader, problem, and group. The following mechanisms are, however, consistent with the basic framework and may be useful as a point of departure for future thinking and research on the subject. Let us begin by defining as the group that set of persons or their representatives who are potentially affected by the decision. This set of persons may be the entire set of subordinates reporting to the leader; they may be a subset of those subordinates; or they may be persons from different parts of the formal organization. In the event that this group, including the leader, does not have the necessary information and expertise, the model shown in Figure 11-2 provides a means of augmenting the size of the group (see pre-decisional mechanism) until such time as the necessary information is represented within the group. It is only at that time when the decision-making process can be determined through the use of the model.

REFERENCES

Ansoff, H. I. *Corporate strategy.* New York: McGraw-Hill, 1965.

Argyris, C. *Interpersonal competence and organizational effectiveness.* Homewood, Ill.: Irwin, 1962.

Bales, R. F., and Slater, P. E. Role differentiation in small groups. In *Family, socialization and interaction process,* by T. Parsons, R. F. Bales, *et al.* Glencoe, Ill.: Free Press, 1955.

Bennis, W. G. *Changing organizations.* New York: McGraw-Hill, 1966.

Brown, R. *Social psychology.* New York: Free Press, 1965.

Coch, L., and French, J. R. P., Jr. Overcoming resistance to change. *Human Relations,* 1948, 1, 512-32.

Fiedler, F. E. *A theory of leadership effectiveness.* New York: McGraw-Hill, 1967.

French, J. R. P., Jr. Field experiments: changing group productivity. In *Experiments in social process: a symposium on social psychology,* ed. J. G. Miller. New York: McGraw-Hill, 1950.

French, J. R. P., Jr., Israel, J., and Ås, D. An experiment on participation in a Norwegian factory. *Human Relations,* 1960, 13, 3-19.

French, J. R. P., Jr., and Raven, B. The bases of social power. In *Studies in social power,* ed. D. Cartwright. Ann Arbor, Mich.: Institute for Social Research, 1959.

Heller, F. A. *Managerial decision making.* London: Tavistock, 1971.

Katz, D., Maccoby, N., and Morse, N. C. Productivity, supervision, and morale in an office situation. Ann Arbor: University of Michigan, Institute for Social Research, 1950.

Kelley, H., and Thibaut, J. Group problem solving. In *Handbook of social psychology,* edited by G. Lindzey and E. Aronson, vol. 4, pp. 1-101. Reading, Mass.: Addison-Wesley, 1969.

Lewin, K. *A dynamic theory of personality.* New York: McGraw-Hill, 1935.

Lewin, K., Lippitt, R., and White, R. K. Patterns of aggressive behavior in experimentally created social climates. *Journal of Social Psychology,* 1939, 10, 271-99.

Likert, R. *The human organization.* New York: McGraw-Hill, 1967.

Lowin, A. Participative decision making: a model, literature critique, and prescriptions for research. *Organizational Behavior and Human Performance,* 1968, 3, 68-106.

McGregor, D. Getting effective leadership in the industrial organization. *Advanced Management,* 1944, 9, 148-53.

Maier, N. R. F. *Psychology in industry.* 2nd ed. Boston: Houghton Mifflin, 1955.

Maier, N. R. F. *Problem-solving discussions and conferences: leadership methods and skills.* New York: McGraw-Hill, 1963.

Maier, N. R. F. *Problem solving and creativity in individuals and groups.* Belmont, Calif.: Brooks-Cole, 1970.

Marrow, A. J. Risk and uncertainties in action research. *Journal of Social Issues,* 1964, 20, 5-20.

Shaw, M. E. Communication networks. In *Advances in experimental psychology,* edited by L. Berkowitz, vol. 1, pp. 111-47. New York: Academic Press, 1964.

Simon, H. A. *The new science of management decision.* New York: Harper, 1960.

Tannenbaum, R., and Schmidt, W. How to choose a leadership pattern. *Harvard Business Review,* 1958, 36, 95-101.

Vroom, V. H. *Some personality determinants of the effects of participation.* Englewood Cliffs. N.J.: Prentice-Hall, 1960.

Vroom, V. H. Industrial social psychology. In *Handbook of social psychology,* edited by G. Lindzey and E. Aronson, vol. 5, pp. 196-268. Reading, Mass.: Addison-Wesley, 1970.

Whyte, W. F. *Money and motivation: an analysis of incentives in industry.* New York: Harper, 1955.

Wood, M. J. Power relationships and group decision making in organizations. *Psychological Bulletin,* 1974 (in press).

12

Validation and Extension of the Contingency Model of Leadership Effectiveness:

A Review of Empirical Findings

FRED E. FIEDLER[1]

A contingency model of leadership effectiveness, described in a theoretical paper seven years ago (Fiedler, 1964), has stimulated numerous studies in the area testing the model as well as attacking it (Graen, Alvares, Orris, and Martella, 1970). The present paper reviews 25 investigations purporting to test or extend the model.

The contingency model postulates that the performance of interacting groups is contingent upon the interaction of leadership style and situational favorableness. It has been suspected for some time that group effectiveness depends on attributes of the leader as well as the situation (e.g., Tannenbaum and Schmidt, 1958; Terman, 1904). The question in leadership theory has been: What kind of leadership style for what kind

of situation? The contingency model specifies that the so-called "task-oriented" leaders perform more effectively in very favorable and very unfavorable situations, while "relationship-oriented" leaders perform more effectively in situations intermediate in favorableness. The theory operationalizes leadership style as well as situational favorableness and, therefore, lends itself to empirical testing.

This study first defines the main terms of the theory, and briefly reviews the findings on which the model is based. It then presents (a) validation evidence relevant to the model's prediction of group performance in real-life studies and laboratory experiments; (b) extensions of the model to a more broadly defined hypothesis; and (c) an analysis of results bearing upon the reclassification and prediction of performance of coacting groups.

DEFINITIONS

The main terms of the theory—*leadership style, situational favorableness,* and *leadership* or *group effectiveness*—are briefly described below, as are the definitions of *interacting* and *coacting* groups.

Interacting groups. These are groups in

1. This review was prepared under Contract N00014-67-A-0103-0012 with the Office of Naval Research and the University of Washington, Seattle (Fred E. Fiedler, Principal Investigator). Research was supported in part by Contract N00014-67-A-0103-0013 with the Advanced Research Projects Agency of the Office of Naval Research. I am indebted to my colleagues, Anthony Biglan, Uriel Foa, Terence R. Mitchell, and Gerald Oncken for their invaluable criticisms and suggestions for the successive manuscripts.

Reprinted from *Psychological Bulletin*, 1971, 76, 128-48, by permission of the author and the publisher. ©1971 by the American Psychological Association.

which the members work cooperatively and interdependently on a common task. The contributions of individual members of these groups cannot, therefore, readily be isolated, and the members, for this reason, are typically rewarded or penalized as a group. In contrast, in *coacting* groups members perform their tasks in relative independence of one another, as for example, members of bowling teams, men in piecework production or in training situations in which each participant typically receives an individual score or evaluation at the end of training.

tiated or stereotyped manner as "all bad." The high LPC person's description has a considerably greater item variance (a standard deviation of 1.43 for the high versus .43 for the low LPC person).

The score has been difficult to interpret. While labels of relationship-oriented versus task-oriented have been given to high versus low LPC persons, the terms are somewhat misleading. First, only in situations which are unfavorable (that is, stressful, anxiety arousing, giving the leader little control) do we find leader behaviors which correspond

Friendly   : —— : —— : —— : —— : —— : —— : —— : —— : Unfriendly
              8   7   6   5   4   3   2   1

Cooperative : —— : —— : —— : —— : —— : —— : —— : —— : Uncooperative
              8   7   6   5   4   3   2   1

Leadership style. The predictor measure used in studies of the contingency model is the least preferred co-worker (LPC) score. This score is obtained by first asking an individual to think of all co-workers he has ever had. He is then asked to describe the one person with whom he has been least able to work well, that is, the person he least prefers as a co-worker. This need not be someone with whom he works at the time. The description is made on 8-point, bipolar adjective scales, for instance.

As a rule, 16 to 24 items have been used in LPC scales. The LPC score is obtained by summing the item values, giving a value of 8 to the favorable pole of each scale. Thus, a high score indicates that the subject has described his least preferred co-worker in relatively favorable terms, that is, with an average item value in the neighborhood of 5 on the 8-point scale. A low score means that the least preferred co-worker is described in a very negative, rejecting manner, that is, an LPC score of about 2 (Fiedler, 1967a, p. 43). It should also be noted that the low LPC person describes his least preferred co-worker in a uniformly, hence undifferen-

to these terms (Fiedler, 1967a). Second, Mitchell (1970) has found evidence that high LPC leaders tend to give more stereotyped cognitively simple responses. Similar results (i.e., a correlation of .35) have been reported by Schroder and his co-workers (H. Schroder, personal communication, 1969).

Thus, the LPC score must be seen as a measure which at least in part reflects the cognitive complexity of the individual and which in part reflects the cognitive complexity of the individual and which in part reflects the motivational system that evokes relationship-oriented and task-oriented behaviors from high versus low LPC persons in situations which are unfavorable for them as leaders.

Situational favorableness. The variable that moderates the relationship between LPC and group performance is the situational favorableness dimension. It is conceptually defined as the degree to which the situation itself provides the leader with potential power and influence over the group's behavior. Situational favorableness appears to be quite important in affecting a wide range of group phenomena, as well as interpersonal behaviors. It seems likely that this dimension may have far-reaching significance in other personality research, as well as in social psychological investigations.

Situational favorableness has been operationalized in a number of ways which are discussed later. The original work on the contingency model presented one method based on three component dimensions that affect the degree to which the situation provides the leader with potential power and influence. These are leader-member rela-

tions, task structure, and position power. The hypothesis was that (a) it is "easier" to be a leader of a group that respects and accepts its leader, or in which the leader feels accepted, than in a group that distrusts and rejects its leader. Likewise (b), it is considered easier to be a leader of a group that has a highly structured, clearly outlined task than of a group that has a vague, unstructured, nebulous task; (c) it is easier to be a leader when the position is vested with power (when the leader has the power

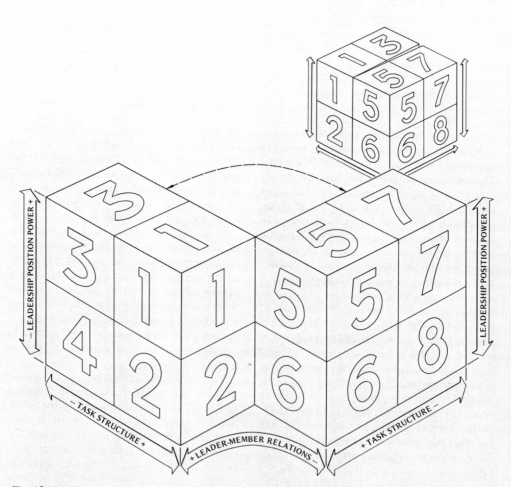

Fig. 12-1. A Model for the Classification of Group Task Situations. (Reproduced with permission from *The Harvard Business Review*, (September-October) 1965, p. 117).

to hire and fire, promote and transfer, give raises or lower salaries) than it is to be a leader who enjoys little or no power over his members: it is easier to be a general manager than the chairman of a volunteer group.

Leader-member relations were considered to be the most important of these situational factors, and subsequent studies have supported this supposition (Fishbein, Landy, and Hatch, 1969; Mitchell, 1969). Detailed instructions for obtaining measures of leader-member relations, task structure, and position power have been described. Leader-member relations can be measured by means of sociometric preference ratings or by a group atmosphere scale which is similar in form and content to LPC, but asks the subject to rate his group as a whole. Scales for rating task structure and position power are described in Fiedler (1967a, pp. 24, 28, 269, 281-91).

We could then classify group situations by means of the three dimensions. For this purpose, all groups were classified as falling above or below the median on each dimension. This led to an eight-celled classification system which can be depicted as an eight-celled cube (Figure 12-1). Each of the eight cells or "octants" can be scaled in terms of how much power and influence a leader might have in such a situation. Obviously, a liked and accepted leader who has a clear-cut task as well as power over the fate of his members (Octant I) will have a very favorable situation. Conversely, a distrusted chairman of a volunteer group with a vague problem-solving or policy-making task (Octant VIII) will be in a very unfavorable situation to exert power. Other octants fall between these two extremes.

Leadership effectiveness. The performance of the leader is here defined in terms of the major assignment of the group; that is, the leader's effectiveness is measured on the basis of the group's performance of its major assigned task. While such other aspects of group behavior as morale, member satisfaction, or personal growth might be important

concomitants of group effectiveness, they are here not considered to be the primary criterion, but rather contributors to performance. In other words, we evaluate the performance of an orchestra conductor not by his ability as a musicologist or the happiness of his musicians, but by how well his orchestra plays. Whether happy musicians play better than unhappy musicians, or whether the man who is a great musicologist is a better conductor is an important research question in its own right. The major question asked here is the relationship of leadership style (specifically LPC) and group or organizational effectiveness.

PREVIOUS RESULTS

Interacting groups from fifteen studies, antedating 1963, were classified according to their situational favorableness, and the correlation between leader LPC and performance was then computed for each set of groups. The correlations between the leader's LPC score and the group's effectiveness measures, when plotted against situational favorableness, generated a bow-shaped distribution indicating that the low LPC leaders performed more effectively than high LPC leaders in very favorable and very unfavorable situations; high LPC leaders performed more effectively in situations intermediate in favorableness (see Figure 12-2).

We here review the validation evidence that has accumulated since publication of the model in 1964. Before specifically reporting any of the studies, it should be stressed that the group classification system was viewed "as a very convenient starting point for presenting the empirical results which we have obtained in our research on interacting groups" (Fiedler, 1967a, p. 34). Improved methods for measuring situational favorableness were expected to be developed in time. The three component dimensions did, however, turn out to be a very convenient method for testing the model since operationalized measures were available.

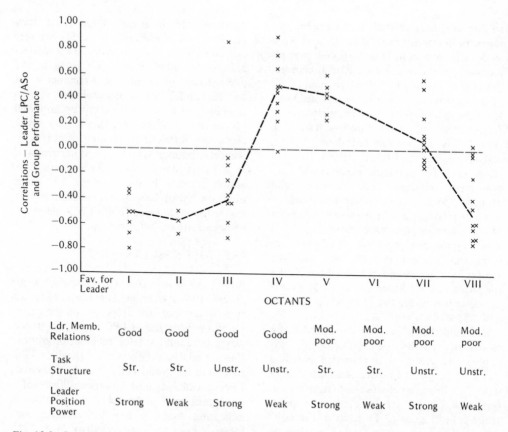

Fig. 12-2. Correlations Between Leadership, LPC Scales, and Group Effectiveness Plotted for Each Cell or Octant of the Situational Favorableness Dimension for Studies of Interacting Groups Conducted Prior to 1963

VALIDATION EVIDENCE OF THE CONTINGENCY MODEL

Classification of Studies

A number of studies designed to test the model have been conducted by various independent investigators as well as by the writer and his associates. Some of these investigators, by design, and others, by oversight, have not followed the methodology originally described. Different operationalizations of situational favorableness were used in some studies, while others extended the model to coacting groups (e.g., Hill, 1969; Hunt, 1967), and some used

leadership style measures unrelated to LPC (Shaw and Blum, 1966). These differences in methodology and divergencies from the model are, of course, quite appropriate and desirable. However, studies that do not conform to the explicit methodology of the earlier work cannot be used as exact tests of the model.

This divergence in method presents difficulties only where the investigator and this reviewer disagree on the appropriateness of a study for testing the contingency model, or where the methodology is inadequate to test the model. This problem has here been handled as follows:

1. Four independent judges carefully read the definition of interacting and co-acting groups, and the definitions of the various subdimensions of the situational favorableness dimension presented by Fiedler (1967a).

2. The judges were then given all studies that purported to test the contingency model. They were asked to read the entire methodology section in the case of shorter investigations, and relevant sections of very extensive studies. They were not asked to read the results. Using the scales described by Fiedler (1967a), the judges classified each study in terms of the group situation into which it should be classified.

3. Groups were included among the validation studies of interacting groups if three of the four judges could agree that the groups were interacting, and if at least three of the judges agreed into which octant the groups should be classified.

Because of the nature of the pre-1963 research on which the original analysis was based, all groups in Octant I, II, and V were from field studies of natural groups and organizations, and all but one set of groups in Octants III, IV, VII, and VIII were from laboratory experiments using ad hoc groups. It is very difficult to reproduce certain effects commonly found in natural groups under experimental conditions. These include, for example, high leader position power, high stress, and very poor leader-member relations. For this reason, the model can be more meaningfully evaluated as a predictor if natural groups and ad hoc groups in laboratory experiments are considered separately, as well as together.

Field Studies

The Hunt studies. The first field study to test the contingency model was conducted by Hunt (1967) in three different organizations, namely, a large physical science research laboratory, a chain of supermarkets, and a heavy machinery plant. In each case

Hunt obtained group atmosphere scores from managers and foremen, and ratings of position power and task structure from management personnel at higher levels in the hierarchy. Higher management of the research laboratory and in the manufacturing plant also provided performance ratings, while objective criteria based on an index of sales per employee manhour was derived for managers of meat markets.

The position power of all managers and foremen was judged to be high. Task structure was rated to be high for developmental research and for meat market managers, and low for managers of basic research groups and for general foremen of the heavy machinery plant. The correlations obtained for each of these groups, by octant, are presented in Table 12-1. (Hunt's results on coacting groups are presented in a later section.)

Electronics firm. A second set of real-life groups was investigated by Hill (1969). The research was conducted in a large electronics firm. The study dealt with supervisors of engineering teams and with instructors of assembly groups. Assembly-line instructors were rated by Hill's judges as having structured tasks and low position power, while supervisors of engineering groups were rated as having unstructured tasks and high position power. Leader-member relations were measured by supervisors' group atmosphere scores, trichotomized, with the upper third considered to have good leader-member relations, and the lower third considered to have poor leader-member relations.

The correlation for nine assembly instructors' teams with high group atmosphere (Octant II) was −.10, and for the nine teams with low group atmosphere (Octant IV), −.24. The correlation between eight engineering supervisors' LPC and performance for high group atmosphere (Octant III) was −.29, and for eight supervisors with low group atmosphere groups (Octant VII), it was .62.

Public Health teams: I. Fiedler, O'Brien,

Table 12-1. Test of the Contingency Model in Hunt's Studies

Sample	Octants			
	I	III	V	VII
Research chemists: basic research		.60 (6)		.30 (5)
Research chemists: development	−.67 (7)			
Meat markets	−.51 (10)		.21 (11)	
General foremen: heavy manufacturing		−.80 (5)		−.30 (5)

Note.—Numbers in parentheses indicate number of cases.

and Ilgen (1969) conducted a study of public health volunteers in Honduras during the summer of 1966. The sample consisted of 225 teenagers who were assigned to teams in Honduras to operate public health clinics and to perform community development work in outlying towns and villages. Formal leaders were not assigned. The teams' informal leaders were identified at the end of the volunteer period on the basis of sociometric questionnaire responses. The task of these groups, namely, to run a public health clinic and, time permitting, to perform some community development work, was fairly well-specified by the sponsoring organization. Problems arose when the villagers and the town officials failed to cooperate and when the population was unsupportive or hostile. Under these conditions the volunteers experienced considerable stress, often verbalized as "feeling at a loss about what to do." Under these stressful conditions, the team members were more or less on their own in trying to cope with the problems they encountered. All judges who evaluated the study agreed that the position power of the leader was low, and three of four judges considered the task to be relatively struc-

tured in the stress-free condition, but unstructured in the situation in which village support was absent.

The informal leader's group atmosphere scores were used to measure the leader-member relations. Groups operating in cooperative or favorable villages could then be classified as falling into Octants II or VI, depending on the leader's group atmosphere score; groups in uncooperative, unfavorable villages could be classified as falling into Octants IV or VIII, again depending on the leader's group atmosphere scores.

Public Health teams. II. A second study, practically identical in procedure, was conducted in the same organization (but with different volunteers) two years later by O'Brien, Fiedler, and Hewett.[2] One major difference in training was that most volunteers had received a culture training program developed for use of the project. This program made the situation somewhat more favorable since it provided some information

2. O'Brien, G. E., Fiedler, F. E., and Hewett, T. The effects of programmed culture training upon the performance of volunteer medical teams in Central America. Urbana: Group Effectiveness Research Laboratory, University of Illinois, 1969.

Table 12-2. Correlations Between Leader LPC Scores and Rates: Team Performance in Two Studies (1966, 1968) of Public Health Volunteer Teams

Situation				1966		1968		
Group atmosphere	Task structure	Position power	Octant	Correlation	n	Correlation	n	Median
High	High	Low	II	−.21	13	−.46	7	−.33
High	Low	Low	IV	.00	15	.47	9	.23
Low	High	Low	VI	.67*	9	−.45	8	.11
Low	Low	Low	VIII	−.51	12	−.14	7	−.32

*$p < .05$.

that enabled the volunteers to understand and to communicate more effectively with their host nationals. A study of the effects of this program on adjustment and performance, conducted in 1967, provided evidence that individuals who had received "culture assimilator" training had adjusted and performed more effectively abroad than those who had not.

The correlations between leader LPC and performance ratings of the headquarters staffs are presented in Table 12-2 for both studies. The median correlations for these groups support the model (correlations for Octant VI were not predicted).

The patterns of the 1966 and 1968 correlations both form a bow-shaped pattern, but the positive correlation was found in Octant VI in the 1966 group, but in Octant IV in the 1968 group.

Unclassifiable Field Studies

A number of other studies designed to test the contingency model cannot be included in the present analysis because the judges rating the published research could not agree on the classification of the groups. Thus, a major study by Butterfield (1968) attempted to compare five theories of leadership, namely, four theories developed at the University of Michigan and the contingency model. The study was conducted in an administrative unit of a federal agency. The sample of groups was not clearly described.

References to groups indicated, however, that "the various work units were engaged in rather different functions ranging from delivering mail to performing financial audits . . ." (p. 61), and measures of effectiveness such as "typed papers, delivered mail, dispatched automobiles, coding systems . . ." (Appendix B). These descriptions led all four judges to the conclusion that a number of groups must have been coacting (e.g., messenger services, typing pools, motor pool dispatchers, etc.). Equally important, however, Butterfield's measure of leader-member relations consisted of only two questionnaire items, one of which dealt with how much annoyance an employee feels with the manager. The important leader-member relations dimension was, therefore, not adequately represented in Butterfield's study.

A field study by Kretzschmar and Lueck (1969) dealt with 67 managers in business administrations of four industrial companies in Germany. In contrast to other studies, all measures of task structure, leader-member relations, and position power were based on supervisors' own ratings. In addition, supervisors also rated their own effectiveness. Our studies have shown that leaders' evaluations of their own performance typically do not correlate with objective measures, and these methodological differences made it impossible to compare this study with others in the group.

The field studies which can be used to test

Table 12-3. Correlations between Leader LPC Scores and Group Performance Scores Obtained in Structured and Unstructured Tasks of the Belgian Navy Study

Homogeneous groups					Heterocultural groups				
Octant	GA	TS	PP	Correlation[a]		Octant	GA	TS	PP	Correlation[a]	
I	+	+	+	−.72	−.77	IX	+	+	+	.03	.77
II	+	+	−	.37	.50	X	+	+	−	.77	−.53
III	+	−	+	−.16	−.54	XI	+	−	+	.20	−.26
IV	+	−	−	.08	.13	XII	+	−	−	−.89	.70
V	−	+	+	.16	.03	XIII	−	+	+	.08	−.19
VI	−	+	−	.07	.14	XIV	−	+	−	.53	−.90
VII	−	−	+	.26	−.27	XV	−	−	+	−.37	.08
VIII	−	−	−	−.37	.60	XVI	−	−	−	−.36	−.60

GA = group atmosphere, TS = task structure, PP = position power.
[a] Two correlations were obtained per cell corresponding to the order of presentation (n = 6).

the contingency model are, then, those by Hunt (1967), by Hill (1969), by Fiedler *et al.* (1969), and by O'Brien *et al.* (see Footnote 2). These results are now discussed, along with those obtained in laboratory studies.

Laboratory and Field Experiments

The contingency model was based on field studies in Octants I, II, and V, and on controlled experiments in Octants III, IV, VII, and VIII. Since that time a number of field and laboratory experiments have attempted to test the predictions of the model in all octants.

The Belgian Navy study. This was a large field experiment conducted in cooperation with the Belgian naval forces. The study involved 96 three-man teams which were experimentally assembled so that 48 teams would be culturally homogeneous (all French or all Dutch speaking) and 48 teams were heterogeneous (the leader from one language sector and the members from the other). In 48 teams the leader was a petty officer who had high position power, while the other 48 teams were headed by a recruit who had low position power. The groups were given four different tasks, one of which was coacting (teaching men to assemble an automatic pistol). The coacting task and one of the two structured tasks could not be

reliably scored, and only one structured and one unstructured task were, therefore, suitable for more intensive analysis.[3] Leader-member relations were assessed on the basis of group climate scores obtained from leaders after each of the task sessions.

Since the contingency model, presented in 1964, was based on culturally homogeneous groups, that is, groups in which all members had the same mother tongue, only these will be used for validation purposes at this time. Table 12-3 presents the correlations between leader LPC scores and group performance scores. Two correlation coefficients, each with n = 6, were computed since the tasks were presented in counterbalanced order. As can be seen, the findings do not support the contingency model which postulates a curvilinear relationship.

A post-facto analysis of the data suggested that the laboratory manipulations had not been adequate for the purpose of creating a sufficiently unfavorable situation for the

3. The Graen *et al.* review (1970) included all three interacting tasks in the analysis of evidential results of the contingency model. However, it was clearly pointed out by the present writer (1967a, p. 161) that the first structured task was methodologically inadequate: 9 groups obtained perfect scores and 62 groups made a total of 189 errors by not following instructions. The first task was, therefore, quite unsatisfactory and could not very well have yielded anything but random results.

leader. The homogeneous groups probably did not develop really poor leader-member relations, and there was also a question whether the supposedly structured task (requiring the group to find the shortest route for a ship which had to cover twelve ports) was sufficiently structured. The task, basically a topological puzzle, requires problem solving, and subsequent studies have shown this type task to be intermediate in structure. A bow-shaped relationship similar to that of the contingency model did emerge when heterocultural groups were included in the analysis to intensify the situational difficulty for the leader. Heterocultural groups are, of course, much more difficult to handle, and leaders reported significantly higher anxiety and greater tension in heterogeneous groups than in homogeneous groups. This effect was, however, not predicted.

The Japanese student study. Shima (1968) tested the contingency model in Japan, using two Guilford[4] tests, namely, the Unusual Uses Test considered to be moderately structured, and an "integration" task which required groups to invent a story using ten unrelated words. All subjects were high-school students, and these were assembled into 32 groups. The leaders were elected by the group members, and the group's relations with the leader were, therefore, assumed to be good. However, the judges rating this study disagreed with Shima's classification of position power. Since the leader was elected and, therefore, had obtained his position from his fellow students, and since the groups were ad hoc, the judges rated position power in this study as being low. Based on the assumption that leader position power was low, the groups would be classified as falling into Octants II and IV. The corresponding correlations were −.26 (*n*

= 16) and .71 (*n* = 16, *p* < .05), thus supporting the model.

Church leadership groups. Mitchell (1969) conducted a small study of group performance as a part of a leadership training workshop to determine the relationship between cognitive complexity and LPC. The participants were members of Unitarian churches who attended a leadership workshop. Each of the groups performed two of four tasks, one structured, and one unstructured. The tasks consisted of finding the shortest route for (a) a school bus and (b) a cross-country road race. The two unstructured tasks were to write a position paper on the church's stand on (c) legalizing abortion and (d) a "Black Caucus" within the Unitarian-Universalist church. Leader position power was low.

Mitchell (1969) originally computed correlations for groups with poor as well as with good leader-member relations, and these correlations were included in the Graen *et al.* (1970) critique. The Mitchell study was not, however, designed as a test of the model, and an analysis of the data showed that only 2 of the 64 group sessions in this study had group atmosphere scores below 55, a score which is roughly at the median of group atmosphere scores for similar studies. As pointed out before, a finding of this type is neither unusual nor unexpected in ad hoc groups. Most researchers, testing the model, have, therefore, tried to increase the difference between groups with high and low group atmosphere scores by using only the upper and lower thirds of the distribution, whenever this was possible. In light of the high group atmosphere scores in the Mitchell study, all groups were classified as falling into Octants II and IV depending upon task structure. The resulting rank-order correlations for Octant II were .24 and .17 (*n* = 16), and for Octant IV, .43 and .38 (*n* = 16).

Executive development workshop. An almost identical study was conducted by Fiedler as part of an executive development program. Here again, all but one of the

4. Guilford, J. P., Berger, R. M., and Christiansen, P. R. A factor analytic study of planning I: Hypothesis and description of tests. Los Angeles, California: Psychological Laboratory, University of Southern California, 1954.

group atmosphere scores was above the usual cutting score, and all groups were classified as having high group atmosphere. The groups were given a relatively structured task and an unstructured task (i.e., routing a truck convoy and writing a recruiting statement inviting college students to become junior executives). All leaders were rated as having low position power, and thus all groups fell into Octants II and IV. The correlations were .34 and .51 for the structured and unstructured tasks, respectively (ns = 11). (See also the section reviewing results on groups in training which might apply to the church leadership and the executive development workshop studies.)

West Point Cadets. Skrzypek[5] recently completed a study of 32 four-man groups composed of cadets at West Point. Leaders were chosen from among a pool of 400 men whose LPC scores fell either one standard deviation above or below the mean. Members were assigned at random. Unlike other laboratory studies, which used postsession questionnaires, leader-member relations in this study were determined a priori on the basis of previously obtained sociometric ratings that identified well-accepted and not-accepted leaders among the cadets. Position power was varied by informing the group that the leader in the high position power would be evaluating each of his group members at the conclusion of the tasks and that these evaluations would become part of the individual's leadership score (a very important aspect of West Point's system). The leaders in the low position power were instructed to act as chairmen, and the group was told that the members as a group would be evaluated on their performance.

Each group performed one structured task and one unstructured task in counterbalanced order. The structured task consisted of drawing a plan for barracks and a military-post area to scale. The unstructured task required the groups to design a program which would educate enlisted men in overseas assignments on world politics and maintain their interest throughout their tour.

The results were as follows for each of the eight octants: Octant I, −.43; Octant II, −.32; Octant III, .10; Octant IV, .35; Octant V, .28; Octant VI, .13; Octant VII, .08; Octant VII, −.33. Thus, while none of the correlations reached the .05 level of significance, all but the correlation for Octant III were in the predicted direction.

Nonclassifiable Studies

Student nurses. A study by Reilly[6] was excluded because the judges could not agree with one another or with the investigator on the position power of the leaders. Reilly studied groups composed of nurses who were given successively structured and unstructured discussion problems. Whether the leader actually had high position power was questioned because the leader was a fellow student, and her additional responsibilities were limited: they consisted of making certain arrangements for the groups as well as assigning 20 per cent of the grade each student would obtain. This study is discussed in a later section, since it may also be classified as a training study.

Experimental change of position power. A second nonclassifiable study was conducted by Nealey and Shiflett (S. Nealey, personal communication, 1969) who attempted experimentally to induce a change of situational favorableness from Octant III to Octant IV and vice versa. The groups were assembled on the basis of LPC and intelligence scores. The experimental manipulation, changing the groups, did not succeed although the study prior to the experimental

5. Skrzypek, G. J. The relationship of leadership style to task structure, position power, and leader-member relations. West Point, N.Y.: United States Military Academy, 1969.

6. Reilly, A. J. The effects of different leadership styles on group performance: A field experiment. Ames: Industrial Relations Center, Iowa State University, 1968.

manipulation yielded relations between LPC and group performance.

Here again, the judges did not agree on whether the leader's position was, in fact, strong, since in the appropriate experimental condition the leader's position power was established basically by instructing the leader to role play a person with a powerful or weak position power.

Graen, Orris, and Alvares (1971) described two laboratory experiments which were specifically designed to test the contingency model. These studies also constituted the main basis for a recent article by Graen et al. (1970), which questioned the adequacy of the model.

Graen et al. (1971) used 78 and 96 male college students randomly assembled into 52 and 64 three-man groups, respectively. Each group worked on two tasks. The students were paid for their participation, and one person in each three-man group was chosen at random to serve as the leader during the first task. Another member of the same group served as leader during the second task.

Each of the groups was given one structured and one unstructured task in counterbalanced order. Using an 8-point scale for assessing task structure (Fiedler, 1967a, p. 25ff.), Graen et al. (1971) chose two structured and two unstructured tasks. Position power was varied by giving the leaders of one set of groups

superior formal status relative to the members . . . special information about the task,

and . . . the highest decision-making authority and responsibility. In the weak leader condition, the leader role was one of discussion leader without special information and with decision-making authority and responsibility close to that of the members. Each group worked on both tasks under only one of the two power conditions. The task sequence was randomized within power conditions. (Graen et al., 1971, p. 198)

Group atmosphere scores were obtained after each task session, and the groups were divided into those whose group atmosphere scores had fallen above and below the median for the entire set. Groups were then assigned to the appropriate cell of the contingency model by dichotomizing the three situational variables of position power, task structure, and group atmosphere. The results of the two experiments are given in Table 12-4.

Graen and his associates claim that their two studies followed as closely as possible the prescriptions of the contingency model and research methodology used in its development. Because their results were nonsignificant, the authors concluded that their studies, therefore, "cast doubt on the plausibility of the contingency model" (Graen et al., 1971, p. 201).

Nonsignificant results obviously can occur for any number of reasons, including inadequate experimental design. A study that attacks a theory, therefore, must not only be methodologically sound (especially if it does not support an alternative hypothesis), but it must also guard against the possibility of

Table 12-4. Correlations Between Leader LPC and Performance in the Graen et al. Studies

Experiment	Octant							
	I	II	III	IV	V	VI	VII	VIII
1	.47[a]	-.41	.46[a]	.33	.25	-.39	.43	-.33
2	-.13	.18[a]	.02[a]	-.08[a]	-.52[a]	-.43	.45	.44[a]

[a]Correlations in a direction counter to the hypothesis of the model

obtaining nonsignificant and randomly distributed data because of inappropriate or marginal experimental manipulations.

A methodological critique in the *Journal of Applied Psychology* (Fiedler, 1971) pointed to various weaknesses in the manipulation of three independent variables in the Graen *et al.* (1971) experimental design. The manipulations were inadequate and make the studies inappropriate for inclusion in the present analysis. A summary of the inadequacies is presented below. The discussion is based on data in the original Graen *et al.* (1971) paper as well as subsequent data included in a rejoinder to the methodological critique of their studies.

1. Task structure. Task structure was assessed by means of a rating scale with scores ranging from a maximum of 8.0 to a minimum of 1.0 (Fiedler, 1967a). The average task structure scores of the studies on which the original contingency model paper was based averaged 7.39 for the structured and 3.15 for the unstructured tasks. In contrast, the scores in the Graen *et al.* (1971) studies were 5.85 and 5.45 for the two structured tasks, and 3.69 and 3.60 for the two unstructured tasks. The scores for the structured task were, therefore, less than 1 scale point above the cutting score of 5.0, and the differences between structured and unstructured tasks were only 2.17 and 1.85 scale points. This clearly represents a very weak manipulation as compared with the differences of 4.24 in the original tasks.

While it may be argued that the task structure scores in some of the original studies were similar to those in the Graen *et al.* studies, an experiment which seeks to disconfirm a theory should not use marginal manipulations in testing the null hypothesis.

2. Position power. Graen *et al.* (1971) manipulated this variable by giving the randomly chosen leader "superior formal status" and "special information about the task," and delegating to him "the highest decision-making authority and responsibility." This was done here by talking directly to the leader in the presence of the members, presenting written task instructions to the leader only, "maintaining body orientation and eye contact with the leader," and giving an official timing device to the leader. In the weak position power condition, the formal status of the leader was not reinforced, verbal instructions were given to no one in particular, and the timing device was placed in the center of the table.

A number of reasons suggest that this power manipulation is inadequate. First of all, it is difficult to believe that the particular experimenter behaviors—like looking the leader in the eye, and giving the leader of an ad hoc group a timing device and written instructions—are sufficiently powerful manipulations to do all the things the authors expected to accomplish. Position power is conceptualized as providing the leader with some real power to give rewards and sanctions. In other words, the leader must have some fate control over his members. It is very difficult to give high position power to a leader in any laboratory situation. Where this was done successfully, it was usually accomplished by using individuals who had some formal position power outside the laboratory. Thus, the Belgian Navy study (Fiedler, 1966) compared petty officers with recruit leaders; a study of ROTC cadets by Meuwese and Fiedler (Fiedler, 1967a) and a study of West Point cadets by Skrzypek (see Footnote 5) used cadet officers who held higher rank than their members. Moreover, Graen *et al.* (1971) demoted the leader appointed for the first task session to member status in the second session and made another member of the same group the leader in the second session. This procedure is likely to dilute the formal leadership power.

Graen *et al.* (1971) subsequently reported data on perceived leader influence in support of their claim that the position power manipulation actually had been effective. Cell means of perceived influence ratings are reported in Table 12-5.

Table 12-5. Cell Means of Perceived Influence Ratings in Graen *et al.* Study

Condition	Octant				$\bar{X}$
Experiment 1					
Strong position power	5.83	6.17	5.14	5.14	5.57
Weak position power	4.33	4.83	3.24	4.86	4.32
M_{diff}					1.25
Experiment 2					
Strong position power	5.75	5.63	6.13	3.50	5.29
Weak position power	5.38	5.00	5.38	4.75	5.13
M_{diff}					.16

Thus, the difference in means over octants in Experiment 2 was only .16. A *t* test comparing the perceived influence ratings in the strong and weak position power conditions was 1.746, which is not significant. As can be seen, some of the weak position power octants had means which were higher than some of the supposedly high position power octants. Specifically, two of the "weak" octants had mean scores of 5.38, while two of the "strong" octants in the first experiment had mean scores of only 5.14. The position power manipulation in Experiment 2 appears, therefore, not to have been effective.

3. Distribution of LPC scores. Leaders were assigned at random and LPC scores were obtained after the three-man groups had been assembled. This procedure does not properly assure that leader LPC scores within each octant will have similar means and distributions. It is obvious that a meaningful test of the contingency model cannot be obtained if, for example, all groups within one octant have leaders with high LPC scores, while all groups in another octant have leaders with very low scores. An appropriate test is an analysis of variance to determine whether the means of various octants are reasonably similar; if so, the *F* test will be nonsignificant.

Data provided by Graen *et al.* (1971) show that the means of LPC scores within the various octants ranged from 84.7 to 42.7 in the first experiment and from 77.3 to 52.9 in the second experiment. A one-way analysis of variance was performed for each study with the eight octants as cells in the design. The *F* ratio for the second study was not significant (1.17), indicating that the various octants did not differ in mean LPC. The *F* ratio for the first study was, however, 3.10, which is significant at the .01 level and indicates that the distribution of leader LPC scores differed markedly from octant to octant. In other words, some octants, (e.g., Octant IV) contained few, if any, low LPC leaders, while others (e.g., Octant V) contained few, if any, high LPC leaders.

Since the position power manipulation in addition to the weak task structure manipulations in Experiment 2 and the LPC score distributions in Experiment 1 were inadequate for testing the contingency model, neither experiment was included in the validation analysis.

SUMMARY OF RESULTS

Table 12-6, which summarizes all correlations from acceptable studies, shows that the median correlations for six of the seven octants are in the predicted direction (Octant VI was not predicted). Of these, the

Table 12-6. Summary of Field and Laboratory Studies Testing the Contingency Model

Study	Octants							
	I	II	III	IV	V	VI	VII	VIII
Field Studies								
Hunt (1967)	−.64		−.80		.21		.30	
	−.51		.60				−.30	
Hill (1969)[a]		−.10	−.29			−.24	.62	
Fiedler et al. (1969)		−.21		.00		.67*		−.51
O'Brien et al. (1969)		−.46		.47		−.45		.14
Laboratory Experiments								
Belgian Navy	−.72	.37	−.16	.08	.16	.07	.26	−.37
	−.77	.50	−.54	.13	.03	.14	−.27	.60
Shima (1968)[a]		−.26		.71*				
Mitchell (1969)		.24		.43				
		.17		.38				
Fiedler exec.		.34		.51				
Skrzypek[a]	−.43	−.32	.10	.35	.28	.13	.08	−.33
Median								
All studies	−.64	.17	−.22	.38	.22	.10	.26	−.35
Field studies	−.57	−.21	−.29	.23	.21	−.24	.30	−.35
Laboratory experiments	−.72	.24	−.16	.38	.16	.13	.08	−.33
Median correlations of Fiedler's original studies (1964)	−.52	−.58	−.33	.47	.42		.05	−.43

Note.—Number of correlations in the expected direction (exclusive of Octant VI, for which no prediction had been made) = 34; number of correlations opposite to expected direction = 11; p by binomial test = .01.
[a] Studies not conducted by the writer or his associates.
* $p < .05$.

joint probabilities of the correlations in Octants I, III, and IV are significant below the .05 level. Also, 34 of the 45 correlations are in the predicted direction, a finding significant at the .01 level by binomial test. It should be noted that the number of correlations in the predicted direction would be significant at the .01 level by binomial test even if we included the two Graen et al. (1970, 1971) experiments. These results permit the conclusion that we are not dealing with random effects: group performance appears to be contingent upon leadership style and situational favorableness.

On the other hand, 5 of the 10 correlations obtained in Octant II are in the positive rather than in the negative direction. These counter-expectational positive correlations, although found only in this octant, throw considerable doubt on the overall generality of the relationship predicted in the Fiedler 1964 paper. It is, therefore, essential that we examine the relations in greater detail.

It will be recalled that in the 1964 study, data for Octants I, II, and V came from field studies, while the data for Octants III, IV, VII and VIII came, with but one exception, from laboratory studies. Field and laboratory results should, therefore, be examined separately.

Field studies. The median correlations for field studies are quite similar to those predicted in the Fiedler 1964 paper. All of the medians are in the predicted direction, and 13 of the 15 predicted correlations are in the expected direction, which is significant at the .05 level. The curve, based on relatively few studies, is not as regular as that obtained in 1964. Octant VI was not predicted. The predicted median correlation of .05 in Octant VII which we based on 12 correlations in the 1964 study, now is shown with a median correlation of .30 based on three correlation coefficients. Over-all, considering the small number of studies and the small number of cases within each of these studies, the results seem rather remarkably consistent with the 1964 data, suggesting that the model is valid for the prediction of leadership performance under field conditions.

Experiments and laboratory studies. Only the Belgian Navy, the West Point, and Graen *et al.* (1971) studies provided data for all predicted octants. It is, therefore, hazardous to draw more than tentative conclusions for any octants but II and IV for which sufficient data are available. Data for Octants I and IV tended to support the prediction of the contingency model, while they did so only directionally in Octants III, V, VII, and VIII. The data clearly indicate that the model does not adequately predict leadership performance in Octant II of laboratory studies. On the other hand, 22 of the 29 predicted correlation coefficients were in the expected direction, which is significant at the .01 level for binomial tests.

A number of possible explanations for the nonpredicted results suggest themselves. The most parsimonious and obvious of these might simply be that it is difficult to manipulate leadership variables in laboratory experiments, and some important aspects of real-life situations do not permit themselves to be readily built into the laboratory.

EXTENSIONS OF THE CONTINGENCY MODEL

A number of studies have tested the more general hypothesis that the situational favorableness affects the relationship between leadership style and performance. Some of these studies tested groups in situations ranging from the very favorable to the very unfavorable; other studies considered groups falling on only two points on the situational favorableness continuum. The various group situations were categorized as being favorable, intermediate, or unfavorable situations by two or more judges. However, since the degree of situational favorableness in some of these investigations was not operationally specified in advance, the rejection of the null hypotheses becomes correspondingly more hazardous in these cases. This is especially so in studies in which the statistical relations do not reach the commonly accepted level of significance. On the other hand, it is difficult to obtain a large sample of groups or organizations in any one study; and it is essential, therefore, that we consider the cumulative evidence from different investigations.

Experimental variation in leadership behavior. Shaw and Blum (1966) instructed nine leaders to act in a highly controlling and directive manner, while a second set of nine leaders was told to be permissive and passive. The groups were given three tasks in counterbalanced order, and the tasks varied in degree of structure. Permissive, passive leaders performed more effectively in the two relatively unstructured tasks (roughly Octant IV); the directive leaders, as predicted by the investigators, performed more effectively in the highly structured tasks (roughly Octant II). These results conform to the general expectations of the model.

Objectification of situational favorableness by structural role theory. O'Brien (1969) measured situational favorableness objectively by applying methods of structural role theory (Oeser and Harary, 1962, 1964). O'Brien assumed that a situation would be more favorable to the leader the greater the number of paths he had to the task structure. The more readily and directly the leader could influence task performance, the greater his influence and control of task-relevant group behavior.

The structural role theory deals with relations among three elements, namely, persons, positions, and tasks, Relations among the first indicate the interpersonal relationships, relations among the positions indicate authority relations, and relations among the tasks indicate allocations and task sequences. O'Brien assembled groups on the basis of personal compatibility depending upon the members' similarity or dissimilarity in scores on Schutz's FIRO scale (1958). The group task consisted of constructing models from spheres and sticks according to a given pattern. Position and task allocation were manipulated by determining the means by which the leader could interact in the task performance. A coefficient of situational favorableness could then be computed which, in oversimplified form, expressed the leader's paths to the task structure as a ratio of all possible paths. The higher the ratio, the more favorable the leader's position power.

The results of O'Brien's study, based on the correlation between leader LPC and the number of models produced, showed the predicted relationships. For 16 groups with high situational favorableness the correlations was −.08; for 16 groups with intermediate favorableness it was .77 (significant at .01); and for 32 groups with low situational favorableness the correlation was −.13.

Heterocultural American and Indian groups. Anderson (1966) conducted a laboratory experiment which used graduate students from India as well as from the United States. These groups consisted of one American leader, one American group member, and one Indian group member. The tasks required the groups to negotiate an agreement on hiring practices between an Indian village and an American company,

and to compose two different stories based on the same TAT card. Half the leaders had high LPC, and half had low LPC scores. Of these, half were instructed to be as considerate as possible in their leadership behavior, while the other half were told to structure the situation as firmly as possible.

Anderson performed a post hoc analysis that scaled the situations on the basis of favorableness. This scaling suggested that the TAT tasks were more favorable than the hiring problem (which required negotiation) and that the considerate condition would be more favorable than the structuring condition. This ordering of situations was supported by leader responses to questions about their anxiety and tension in each of these conditions.

The correlations for the four tasks in order of favorableness (TAT-considerate, TAT-structuring, negotiation-considerate, negotiation-structuring) were −.50, .21, −.22, and −.12, thus suggesting a curvilinear relationship between LPC-performance correlations and situational favorableness ($ns = 8$).

Chemical-processing companies. Lawrence and Lorsch (1967) compared the performance of six chemical processing companies, each of which had four subsystems: production, sales, applied research, and basic research. Each subsystem was under the direction of a senior management official, either at the vice-presidential level or immediately below. The structure of these subsystem tasks was rated by a number of judges. Fundamental research was rated as lowest in structure, while production was rated as highest. This reviewer correlated the manager's LPC and rated performance from the Lawrence and Lorsch data. The results follow the expectation that a low LPC manager would perform better on structured tasks, while a high LPC manager would perform better in unstructured situations. The correlations, in order of rated structure, were for production, −.50; sales, −.31; applied research, −.10; and fundamental research, .66 ($ns = 6$).

Since these results were obtained without

reference to leader-member relations, they suggest that the leader-member relations dimension might be relatively less important at higher levels of the organization. This seems reasonable since the manager at the third and higher levels usually has very few direct contacts with production workers at the non-supervisory levels, and relatively few contacts with first-line supervisors.

Psychiatric nursing organization. Nealey and Blood (1968) investigated the psychiatric nursing service of a large Veterans Administration hospital. LPC scores were obtained from supervisors at the first and second levels of the organization, namely, head nurses in charge of a ward, and "unit supervisors" in charge of one of the hospital's six large units, which are both quite comparable as to structure and function. Performance of wards and of units was judged by management personnel at the level above the head nurse and the unit supervisor, respectively.

The most important difference between the job of the head nurse and that of the unit supervisor for purposes of the present analysis appears to be the structure of her subordinates' tasks. The work of the psychiatric aide is relatively structured since there are fairly specific guidelines available on the management of psychiatric patients and ward personnel. The job of the unit supervisor, or more precisely, the work of the head nurses she supervises, requires considerably more policy and decision-making, and it is correspondingly less structured. Nealey and Blood correlated the LPC scores of these nursing supervisors with rated performance. In a very similar study, Nealey and Owen (1970) about 18 months later recomputed these correlations on 25 head nurses, 15 of whom had participated in the first study. The correlations between head-nurse LPC and performance for the first and second studies were $-.22$ ($n = 21$) and $-.50$ ($n = 25$, $p < .05$), and for unit supervisors tested in the first study, .79 ($n = 8$, $p < .01$). Thus, as in the Lawrence and Lorsch study, the structure of the supervisory task strongly moderates the direction of the relationship between LPC and organizational performance.

Stress as an index of situational favorableness. A study by Fiedler and Barron (cited in Fiedler, 1967a) investigated the relationship between leader LPC and creative group performance under varying conditions of stress. Fifty-four three-man teams composed of ROTC cadets participated in this study under relatively stress-free conditions, intra-

Table 12-7. Summary of LPC-Group Performance Correlations of Studies Extending the Contingency Hypothesis

Study and date	Favorable			Intermediate			Unfavorable		
O'Brien (1969)	$-.08$			$.77^a$			$-.13$		
Anderson (1966)	$-.50$		$.21$		$-.22$			$.12$	
Lawrence & Lorsch (1967)[a]	$-.50$	$-.10$	$-.13$	$.66$					
Nealey & Blood (1968)	$-.22$			$.79^a$					
Nealey & Owen (1970)	$-.50^a$								
Fiedler & Barron[b]									
Task I	$-.42$	$-.56$	$-.32$	$.67$	$-.08$	$-.01$	$-.53$	$-.72$	$.18$
Task II	$-.71$	$-.59$	$.69$	$.41$	$-.15$	$-.20$	$-.47$	$-.61$	$-.14$
Median		$-.37$			$.20$			$-.30$	

Note.—The location of the correlation coefficient in the table degree of judged favorableness of the leadership situation. The farther to the left, the more favorable the situation.
[a] Study not conducted by writer or his associates.
[b] In Fiedler (1967a).

group conflict, and relatively severe external stress. Within each of these stress conditions the groups were divided into those with high, medium, and low leader group-atmosphere scores. The resulting LPC-performance relations were then plotted against stressfulness of the situation and resulted in a bow-shaped curve with low LPC leaders performing better than high LPC leaders in relatively stress-free and stressful conditions, and high LPC leaders performing better in situations of intermediate stress.

Summary of Studies Testing the Contingency Theory

The results presented in this section are, in one respect, quite weak, and in another, quite strong. The investigations do not permit an exact test of a theory since the methodology, the criteria, and the subject populations vary from study to study. At the same time, these studies provide consistent cumulative evidence that the correlation between leadership style and group performance is moderated by the situational favorableness dimension even though this dimension is operationalized in a wide variety of ways. Thus, the Shaw and Blum experiment, the Lawrence and Lorsch investigation, as well as the Nealey and Blood and the Nealey and Owen studies show that the structure of the task is important in determining the direction of the correlation between LPC and group performance. The Fiedler and Barron (Fiedler, 1967a) study used stress as an index of situational favorableness. The O'Brien experiment presented an ingenious new metric of situational favorableness based on structural role theory, and the results of his study yielded relations in the expected direction with one of the correlations highly significant. Finally, the Anderson (1966) experiment, based on post hoc analysis of the data, also yielded data that tended to show an interaction of task and leadership style. Thus, notwithstanding the diversity of the studies,

there is clear evidence that identified situational components determine, in part, the type of leadership style that a particular group requires for effective performance.

EXTENSION OF THE MODEL TO COACTING GROUPS

A number of field studies have attempted to investigate the relation of leader LPC scores to the performance of coacting groups and organizations (Fiedler, 1967b). The number of studies reported is now sufficient so that a review of the findings appears appropriate.

Task Groups and Organizations

Craft shops and grocery markets. Two organizations studied by Hunt (1967) were coacting. These were craft shops in the physical science laboratory and grocery departments of chain stores. Both of these types of organizations performed coacting tasks that were highly structured. In both organizations the leader's position power was high. Performance of craft shops was assessed by ratings, while grocery departments were evaluated on the basis of an objective measure of number of man-hours over total sales volume.

The correlations for six workshops with high, and five with low group atmosphere scores (comparable to Octants I and V), were, respectively, $-.48$ and $.90$ ($p < .05$), those for 13 supermarkets with high group atmosphere, $-.06$, and those with low group atmosphere, $.49$.

Hospital departments. Hill's (1969) study included various departments in a hospital, including the nursing service, the controller's department, dietetics, housekeeping, stores, central supply, and maintenance. All were rated to be coacting, and all supervisory personnel were rated as having high position power. The nursing service was rated by Hill as having an unstructured task, while other departments were rated as having structured tasks. Classifying the groups on the basis of the contingency model classification would make the nursing service fall into Octants III and VII and other departments into Octants I and V, depending on the leader's group atmosphere score. The correlations for the Octant I and V groups were $-.21$ ($n = 8$) and .52 ($n = 8$) and for the Octant III and VII groups (nursing) $-.32$ ($n = 7$) and .87 ($n = 7$, $p < .05$).

Telephone offices. Bates (1967) conducted a study of telephone supervisors in two offices of the Bell Telephone Company. The total sample consisted of 112 operators working in 13 groups. Of these employees, 21 were first-line supervisors who provided LPC and group atmosphere scores. The task was rated as highly structured, and the position power as high. These groups would then fall into Octants I and V.

Bates obtained two criterion scores, a "quality index" reflecting the accuracy and courtesy with which the operators handle calls as well as the accuracy in billing calls. A second index, called the "load factor," reflects the average number of calls handled by an office. Three telephone executives who were independently interviewed agreed that the quality index is the more important and that offices rarely performed below the minimum load factor. Since the quality and load indexes were negatively correlated ($-.43$), only the quality index was here considered. Bates divided his groups into six with relatively high group atmosphere and seven with low group atmosphere scores. The corresponding correlations between supervisors' LPC scores and quality indexes were $-.77$ and .75.

School principals. McNamara (1967) investigated the effectiveness of elementary school principals in 32 elementary schools of the Edmonton, Alberta, school system. The schools were relatively small in size, some containing as few as six teachers. Although McNamara spoke of his schools as interacting, all four judges classified the schools as coacting. Their reason was that there is relatively little interaction among teachers in

the performance of their instructional duties, nor is it likely that the principal's job demands that he share his administrative duties with his staff or teachers. The principal's position power was rated as being high.

The effectiveness of schools was judged by five members of the school system's administrative staff. Leader-member relations were indexed by group atmosphere scores, with the upper third of the schools and the lower third of the schools used, and the middle third deleted from the sample.

The correlation between principal's LPC and performance in high group atmosphere schools (Octant I) was $-.48$ ($n = 11$), while that in low group atmosphere schools (Octant V) was .31 ($n = 12$).

Training Situations

Naval aviation cadets. Fiedler and Hutchins (Fiedler, 1967a) conducted a study of aviation cadets (including some commissioned officers in flight training) and their instructors. The student pilots were in the advanced course which concentrated on formation flying, a rather anxiety-arousing phase of training. The cadets were assigned to "flights" of eight men, and each flight was under the direction of an instructor team. The performance of the men in each flight was evaluated by instructors regularly assigned to another squadron of the training base.

Two samples of 16 instructors were tested, using their groups' performance scores as a criterion of leadership (Octants I and V). The correlation of head instructors' LPC scores and performance of their flights was .45 and .17. Fiedler (1967a) also obtained correlations between the sociometrically chosen men, that is, informal leaders with very little position power. Since all were sociometrically chosen, all had good leader-member relations. The correlation between the LPC scores of 22 leaders and performance ratings was .55 ($p < .02$) and .28 for ns of 22 and 15. The lower correlations in the second set of teams may be due to the smaller range and standard deviation of performance scores in the second sample of teams.

Management trainees. A study by Seifert (1969) used 14 management training groups in Germany. These groups, each consisting of 25 to 30 participants, remained together for almost one year. Similar to the naval aviation cadet study, each group had a team of instructors and a head instructor. Each group also had an informal leader, designated as spokesman of the group, but having very little position power. Similar to the naval aviation cadets, Seifert reported that the men were under considerable pressure and anxiety lest they fail. (Although Seifert treated these groups as interacting, all four judges considered the Seifert study one of coacting groups.) Effectiveness was rated by instructors and was based on several scales of motivational and performance characteristics of the men.

Correlations between the LPC of head instructors and performance was .56 for those with high group atmosphere and −.20 for those with low group atmosphere scores. The correlation between spokesmen's LPC and performance scores was .45, regardless of group atmosphere.

Student nurses. A study by Reilly, mentioned above (see Footnote 6), was designed to test the contingency model. However, the judges rating Reilly's method were divided on the leader's position power. The study involved the assembly of 14 groups of student nurses with each group required to complete 10 sets of discussion problems and examination questions posed by the faculty of the school over the course of the year. Some of these problems were highly structured; that is, there was an answer or a solution available. Other problems were highly unstructured; that is, the group had to discuss a case or an ethical issue for which no definite answer was available. Reilly reported a correlation of .63 between leader

LPC and group performance, irrespective of leader-group atmosphere scores.

The leader had responsibility for arranging the sessions and seeing that the group's solutions were typed and handed in to the faculty. She also had the responsibility to assign 20 per cent of each of her fellow students' grades. Leaving aside for the moment the question of position power on which our judges disagreed, or that these groups may well have been interacting in most tasks, the more important point might well be that the Reilly study, as well as the naval aviation cadet study by Fiedler and Hutchins (Fiedler, 1967a) and the Seifert study of German management trainees, is distinguished by having as its purpose the training of the group members rather than the performance of some task that results in an output beneficial to the organization.[7] In all of the studies, the exercise was designed to be beneficial to the individual group member. There might well be a psychological difference in leading a group for the purpose of benefiting the members and leading a group for the purpose of benefiting the organization. Our data suggest that this may be the case.[8]

Summary of Results from Coacting Groups

As we suggested in the discussion of the Reilly (see Footnote 6) study, the results obtained from studies of coacting groups can best be discussed by separating results from task groups and results from training groups (Table 12-8).

7. An earlier unpublished study of classroom performance by Marse (1958) showed negative correlations of −.70 ($n = 6$) and −.36 ($n = 12$) for physics and rhetoric section instructors at the University of Illinois where rated student performance was the criterion. In that study, however, the class members never interacted in groups as part of their training. Whether this is an important determining factor remains to be seen.
8. Note, however, that a school principal's group membership consists primarily of teachers and clerical staff, not of students.

Table 12-8. Correlational Summary of Studies Extending the Contingency Model to Coaching Task and Training Groups

Group	Octants							
	I	II	III	IV	V	VI	VII	VIII
Task groups								
Craft shops	−.48				.90[a]			
Groceries	−.06				.49			
Hospital departments[a]	−.21		−.32		.52		.87	
Telephone offices	−.77				.75			
School principals[a]	−.48				.31			
Median	−.48		−.32		.52		.87	
Training groups								
Naval aviation								
Chief instructors	.45							
	.17							
Informal leaders			.55					
			.28					
Management trainees[a]								
Head instructors	.56					−.20		
Informal leaders	.45		.45					
Student nurses[a]			.63					
Medians	.45		.50			−.20		

[a]Studies not conducted by writer or his associates.

The results from task groups are highly consistent in showing that groups or organizations with structured tasks and high leader position power perform more effectively under low LPC leaders when the group climate is rated as favorable, and more effectively under high LPC leaders when the group climate is unfavorable. Classifying coacting groups in the same manner as interacting groups indicates that the correlations are quite similar in the two octants for which data are available, namely, Octants I and V.

Hill, in his study of a hospital, classified the supervising nurses' job as unstructured. The correlation for Octant III is in the predicted direction, and the correlation for Octant VII, while much higher than would be expected for this octant, is not incompatible with data from interacting groups.

The data on coacting *task* groups suggest that the distinction between interacting and coacting task groups might be unnecessary, while the distinction between *task* groups and *training* groups might be essential. The latter appear to follow quite dissimilar rules.

The Seifert (1969), the Fiedler and Hutchins (Fiedler, 1967a), and Reilly (see Footnote 6) studies suggest that groups in training might constitute a valid subclassification for leadership studies, a classification that needs to be intensively examined further. The possibility should be considered that this set of studies might also include those by Mitchell (1969) and Fiedler which used participants in leadership workshops.

Empirical Findings from Research on Leadership Training

Despite intensive efforts, research has failed to show that leadership experience or leadership training systematically improve organizational performance (Campbell *et al.*, 1970). These disappointing results can be deduced from the contingency model. Specifically, we can interpret leadership experience and training as improving situational favorableness (e.g., human relations training is supposed to improve leader-member relations; technical training would make the task appear more structured). Training and experience should then differentially affect the performance of high and low LPC leaders. The contingency model would then predict that training for intermediate situations will improve the performance of high LPC leaders—but *decrease* that of low LPC leaders. Likewise, training and experience for favorable and unfavorable situations will improve performance of low LPC leaders—but *decrease* performance of high LPC leaders. These results have now been obtained in several studies and further support the contingency model (Fiedler, 1971).

SUMMARY

A review of studies testing and extending the contingency model evaluated the model's predictive power in field and laboratory situations and in coacting task and training groups.

The model seems to predict leadership performance in field situations, but not completely in laboratory situations. The major discrepancy between the model and the field studies on the one hand, and the laboratory studies on the other, was in Octant II, where the model predicted negative correlations, while the laboratory studies showed predominantly positive correlations between LPC and group performance. This discrepancy, if it is not due to chance, may well bring to light important aspects of leadership interactions that are not usually reproduced in laboratory situations.

A series of studies, extending the theory, was reviewed. Taken as a group, these studies provide strong evidence that the situational favorableness dimension does indeed moderate the relationship between leadership style and group performance, and that it therefore provides an important clue to our understanding of leadership phenomena.

Finally, studies of coacting groups and organizations suggested that we differentiate between groups that exist primarily for the benefit of the organization—that is, the typical task groups—and groups that exist for the benefit of the individual—groups of trainees. Coacting task groups appear to follow the predictions of the contingency model, at least for Octants I and V. Data from groups-in-training showed consistently positive relations between leader LPC and group performance measures in Octants I and III, and only one small negative correlation in Octant VI. These findings suggest a new approach to the classification of coacting groups and training groups which might lead to a better understanding of managerial performance in task and training organizations.

REFERENCES

Anderson, L. R. Leader behavior, member attitudes, and task performance of intercultural discussion groups, *Journal of Social Psychology*, 1966, 69, 305-19.

Bates, P. A. Leadership performance at two managerial levels in the telephone company. Bachelor's thesis, University of Illinois, 1967.

Butterfield, D. A. An integrative approach to the study of leadership effectiveness in organizations. Ph.D. diss., University of Michigan, 1968.

Campbell, J. P., Dunnette, M. D., Lawler, E. E., and Weick, K. E. *Managerial behavior, performance, and effectiveness.* New York: McGraw-Hill, 1970.

Fiedler, F. E. A contingency model of leadership effectiveness. In L. Berkowitz (Ed.),

Advances in experimental social psychology. New York: Academic Press, 1964.

Fiedler, F. E. The effect of leadership and cultural heterogeneity on group performance: A test of the Contingency Model. *Journal of Experimental Social Psychology*, 1966, 2, 237-64.

Fiedler, F. E. *A Theory of leadership effectiveness*. New York: McGraw-Hill, 1967. (a)

Fiedler, F. E. Führungsstil and Leistung koagierender Gruppen. *Zeitschrift für experimentelle und angewandte Psychologie*, 1967, 14, 200-217. (b)

Fiedler, F. E. Note on the methodology of the Graen, Orris and Alvares studies testing the contingency model. *Journal of Applied Psychology*, 1971, 55, 202-4.

Fiedler, F. E. *Leadership*. A module for the General Learning Press, 1971.

Fiedler, F. E., O'Brien, G. E., and Ilgen, D.R. The effect of leadership style upon the performance and adjustment of volunteer teams operating in a stressful foreign environment. *Human Relations*, 1969, 22, 503-14.

Fishbein, M., Landy, E., and Hatch, G. Consideration of two assumptions underlying Fiedler's Contingency Model for the prediction of leadership effectiveness. *American Journal of Psychology*, 1969, 4, 457-73.

Graen, G., Alvares, K. M., Orris, J. B., and Martella, J.A. Contingency model of leadership effectiveness: Antecedent and evidential results. *Psychological Bulletin*, 1970, 74, 285-96.

Graen, G., Orris, J. B., and Alvares, K. M. Contingency model of leadership effectiveness: Some experimental results. *Journal of Applied Psychology*, 1971, 55, 196-201.

Hill, W. The validation and extension of Fiedler's theory of leadership effectiveness. *Academy of Management Journal*, 1969 (March), 33-47.

Hunt, J. G. Fiedler's leadership contingency model: An empirical test in three organizations. *Organizational Behavior and Human Performance*, 1967, 2, 290-308.

Kretzschmar, V., and Luecke, H. E. Zum Fiedlerschen Kontingenzmodell Effektiver Führung. *Arbeit und Leistung*, 1969, 23, 53-55.

Lawrence, P., and Lorsch, J. Differentiation and integration in complex organizations. *Administrative Science Quarterly*, June 1967, 12, 1-47.

Marse, J. E. Assumed similarity between opposites and the performance of leadership functions. M.A. thesis, University of Illinois, 1958.

McNamara, V. D. A descriptive-analytic study of directive-permissive variation in the leader behavior of elementary school principals. M.A. thesis, University of Alberta, 1967.

Mitchell, T. R. Leader complexity, leadership style, and group performance. Ph.D. diss., University of Illinois, 1969.

Mitchell, T. R. Leader complexity and leadership style. *Journal of Personality and Social Psychology*, 1970, 16, 166-74.

Nealey, S. M., and Blood, M. Leadership performance of nursing supervisors at two organizational levels. *Journal of Applied Psychology*, 1968, 52, 414-22.

Nealey, S. M., and Owen, T. M. A multitrait-multimethod analysis of predictors and criteria of nursing performance. *Organizational Behavior and Human Performance*, 1970, 5, 348-65.

O'Brien, G. E. Group structure and the measurement of potential leader influence. *Australian Journal of Psychology*, 1969, 21, 277-89.

Oeser, O. A., and Harary, F. A mathematical model for structural role theory II. *Human Relations*, 1962, 15, 89-109.

Oeser, O. A., and Harary, F. A mathematical model for structural role theory II. *Human Relations*, 1964, 17, 3-17.

Schutz, W. C. *FIRO: A Three-dimensional theory of interpersonal behavior*. New York: Holt, Rinehart & Winston, 1958.

Seifert, K. H. Untersuchungen zur Frage der Führungseffektivität. *Psychologie und Praxis*, 1969, 13, 49-64.

Shaw, M. E., and Blum, J. M. Effects of leadership style upon group performance as a function of task structure. *Journal of*

Personality and Social Psychology, 1966, 3, 238-42.

Shima, H. The relationship between the leader's modes of interpersonal cognition and the performance of the group. *Japanese Psychological Research*, 1968, 10, 13-30.

Tannenbaum, R., and Schmidt, W. H. How to choose a leadership pattern. *Harvard Business Review*, 1958, 36, 95-101.

Terman, L.M. A preliminary study of the psychology and pedagogy of leadership. *Pedagogical Seminary*, 1904, 11, 413-51.

13

Path - Goal Theory of Leadership

ROBERT J. HOUSE and TERENCE R. MITCHELL

There is currently emerging an integrated body of conjecture by students of leadership that is referred to as the "path-goal theory of leadership." According to this theory, a leader is effective because of his impact on subordinate's motivation, ability to perform effectively, and satisfactions. It is called "path-goal theory" because its main concern is how the leader influences the subordinate's perceptions of his work goals, personal goals, and paths to goal attainment. The theory suggests that a leader's behavior is motivating or satisfying to the degree that the behavior increases subordinate goal attainment and clarifies the paths to these goals.

HISTORICAL FOUNDATIONS

The path-goal approach has its roots in a more general motivational theory called expectancy theory (Mitchell, 1974). Briefly, this approach states that an individual's attitudes (e.g., satisfaction with supervision, or job satisfaction) or behavior (e.g., leader behavior or job effort) can be predicted from (1) the degree to which the job, or behavior, is seen as leading to various out-comes (called "expectancy"); and (2) the evaluation of these outcomes (called "valences"). Thus, one is satisfied with his job if he thinks that it leads to things that are highly valued, and he works hard if he believes that effort will lead to things that are highly valued. This type of theoretical rationale can be used to predict a variety of phenomena related to leadership. It could be used to predict why leaders behave the way they do (Nebeker and Mitchell, 1974), or it can help us to understand how leader behavior influences subordinate motivation. This latter approach is the central concern of this paper. The implication for leadership is that subordinates are motivated by leader behavior to the extent that this behavior influences expectancies (e.g., goal paths) and valences (e.g., goal attractiveness).

Several writers have advanced specific hypotheses concerning how the leader effects the paths and the goals of subordinates (Evans, 1970; Hammer and Dachler, 1973; Dansereau *et al.*, 1973; House, 1971; Mitchell, 1973; Graen *et al.*, 1972; House and Dessler, 1974). These writers have focused on two issues: (1) how the leader effects subordinate's expectations that effort

Reprinted from *Contemporary Business*, 1974 (Fall), by permission of the authors and the publisher, the Business School of the University of Washington, Seattle.

will lead to effective performance and valued rewards, and (2) how this expectation effects motivation to work hard and perform well.

While the state of theorizing about leadership in terms of subordinate's paths and goals is in its infancy, we believe that it is promising—for two reasons. First, it suggests effects of leader behavior that have not yet been investigated but appear to be fruitful areas of inquiry. Second, it suggests with some precision the situational factors on which the effects of leader behavior are contingent.

The initial theoretical work by Evans (1970, 1974) asserts that leaders will be effective by making rewards available to subordinates and by making these rewards contingent on the subordinate's accomplishment of specific goals. Evans argued that one of the strategic functions of the leader is to clarify for subordinate's the kind of behavior that will lead to goal accomplishment and valued rewards. This function might be referred to as path clarification. Evans argued also that the leader increases the rewards available to subordinates by being supportive toward subordinates, i.e., by being concerned with their status, welfare, and comfort. Leader supportiveness is in itself a reward that the leader has at his disposal, and the judicious use of this reward increases the motivation of subordinates.

Evans studied the relations between the behavior of leaders, and subordinates' expectations that effort leads to rewards, and the resulting impact on ratings of the subordinates' performance. He found that when leaders were viewed by subordinates as being supportive (considerate of their needs) and when superiors provided directions and guidance to subordinates, these kinds of leader behavior were positively related to the performance ratings of subordinates. However, leader behavior was related to subordinate's performance only when the leader's behavior was related also to the subordinate's expectations that his effort would

result in desired rewards. Thus Evans's findings suggest that the major impact of a leader on the performance of subordinates is in clarifying the path to desired rewards and making such rewards contingent on effective performance.

Stimulated by this line of reasoning, House (1971) and House and Dessler (1974) advanced a more complex theory of the effects of leader behavior on the motivation of subordinates. The theory is intended to explain the effects of four specific kinds of leader behavior on the following three subordinate attitudes or expectations:

1. the satisfaction of subordinates;
2. their acceptance of the leader; and
3. their expectations that effort will result in effective performance and that effective performance is the path to rewards.

The four kinds of leader behavior included in the theory are supportive leadership, directive leadership, participative leadership, and achievement-oriented leadership.

Directive leadership is characterized by a leader who lets subordinates know what is expected of them, gives specific guidance as to what should be done and how it should be done, makes his part in the group understood, schedules work to be done, maintains definite standards of performance, and asks that group members follow standard rules and regulations. *Supportive leadership* is characterized by a friendly and approachable leader who shows concern for the status, well-being, and needs of subordinates. Such a leader does little things to make the work more pleasant, treats members as his equals, and is friendly and approachable. *Participative leadership* is characterized by a leader who consults with his subordinates, solicits their suggestions, and takes them seriously into consideration before making a decision. *Achievement-oriented leadership* is characterized by a leader who sets challenging goals, expects subordinates to perform at their highest level, continuously seeks improvement in performance, *and* shows a high degree of confidence that the subordinates will assume responsibility, put forth effort, and accomplish challenging goals. Thus this kind of leader constantly emphasizes excellence in performance while simultaneously displaying confidence that subordinates will meet high standards of excellence.

We now have a number of studies which suggest that these different leadership styles can be shown by the same leader in various situations (House and Dessler, 1974; Stogdill, 1965; House, Velancy, and Van der Krabben, unpublished). For example, a leader may show directiveness toward subordinates in some instances and be participative or supportive in other instances (Hill, 1974). Thus the traditional method of characterizing a leader as either highly participative and supportive *or* highly directive is invalid. Rather, it can be concluded from the above studies that leaders vary in the particular fashion employed for supervising their subordinates. Moreover, the theory, in its present stage, is a tentative explanation of the effects of leader behavior. It is incomplete in that it does not explain other kinds of leader behavior or the effects of the leader on factors other than subordinate acceptance, satisfaction, and expectations. However, the theory is stated in such a way that additional variables may be included in it as new knowledge is made available.

THE THEORY

General Propositions

The first proposition is that leader behavior is acceptable and satisfying to subordinates to the extent that the subordinates see such behavior as either an immediate source of satisfaction or as instrumental to future satisfaction.

The second proposition is that the leader's behavior will be motivational (e.g., will increase effort) to the extent that (1) such behavior makes satisfaction of subordinate's needs contingent on effective performance, and (2) such behavior complements the

environment of subordinates by providing the coaching, guidance, support, and rewards necessary for effective performance that may otherwise be lacking in the environment or within the subordinates.

These two propositions suggest that the leader's strategic functions are to enhance subordinates' motivation to perform, satisfaction with the job, and acceptance of the leader. From previous research on the expectancy theory of motivation (House, Shapiro, and Wahba, 1974) it can be inferred that the strategic functions of the leader consist of:

1. recognizing and/or arousing subordinate's needs for outcomes over which the leader has some control;

2. increasing personal payoffs to subordinates for work-goal attainment;

3. making the path to those payoffs easier to travel by coaching and direction;

4. helping subordinates clarify expectancies;

5. reducing frustrating barriers; and

6. increasing the opportunities for personal satisfaction contingent on effective performance.

Because the above motivational functions of the leader are stated in terms of paths, needs, and goals, the theory presented here is referred to as the *path-goal theory of leadership*.

Stated less formally, the motivational functions of the leader consist of increasing the number and kind of personal payoffs to subordinates for work-goal attainment, and making the paths to these payoffs easier to travel by clarifying the paths, reducing road blocks and pitfalls, and increasing the opportunities for personal satisfaction en route.

Contingency Factors

Two classes of situational variables are asserted to be contingency factors. A contingency factor is a variable that moderates the relations between two other variables such as leader behavior and subordinate satisfaction. For example, we might suggest

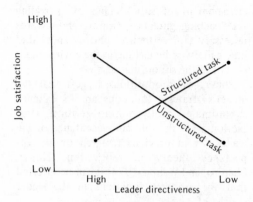

Fig. 13-1. Hypothetical Relationship Between Directive Leadership and Subordinate Satisfaction with Task Structure as a Contingency Factor

characteristics are hypothesized to partially determine this perception. For example, Runyon (1973) and Mitchell *et al.* (1974) show that the subordinates' score on a measure called Locus of Control moderates the relation between participative leadership style and subordinate satisfaction. The Locus of Control measure reflects the degree to which an individual sees the environment as systematically responding to his behavior. People who believe that what happens to them occurs because of their behavior are called internals. People who believe that what happens to them occurs because of luck or chance are called externals. The Mitchell *et al.* (1974) findings suggest that internals are more satisfied with a participative leadership style, while externals are more satisfied with a directive style.

that the degree of structure in the task moderates the relation between the leaders' directive behavior and subordinates' satisfaction with their job. Figure 13-1 shows an example of how such a relationship might look. Thus, subordinates are satisfied with directive behavior in an unstructured task and are satisfied with nondirective behavior in a structured task. Therefore we say that the relationship between leader directiveness and subordinate satisfaction is contingent upon the structure of the task.

The two contingency variables are (a) personal characteristics of the subordinates and (b) the environmental pressures and demands with which the subordinate must cope in order to accomplish his work goals and to satisfy his needs. While other situational factors may also operate to determine the effects of leader behavior, they are not presently known.

With respect to the first class of contingency factors—namely, the characteristics of subordinates—the theory asserts that leader behavior will be viewed as acceptable to subordinates to the extent that the subordinates see such behavior as either an immediate source of satisfaction or as instrumental to future satisfaction. Subordinates'

A second characteristic of subordinates on which the effects of leader behavior are contingent is the subordinates' perception of their own ability with respect to their assigned tasks. The higher the degree of perceived ability relative to task demands, the less the subordinate will view leader directiveness and coaching behavior as acceptable. Where the subordinate's perceived ability is high, such behavior is likely to have little positive effect on the motivation of the subordinate and to be perceived as excessively close control. The acceptability of the leader's behavior is thus determined in part by the characteristics of his subordinates.

The second aspect of the situation—namely, the environment of the subordinate—consists of those factors that are not within the control of the subordinate but are important to his need satisfaction or to his ability to perform effectively. The theory asserts that effects of the leader's behavior on the psychological state of subordinates will be contingent on other parts of the subordinates' environment that are relevant to subordinate motivation. Three broad classifications of contingency factors in the environment are:

1. The subordinates' tasks;

2. The formal authority system of the organization;

3. The primary work group.

Assessment of the environmental conditions makes it possible to predict the kind and amount of influence that specific leader behaviors will have on the motivation of subordinates. Each of the above three environmental factors could act upon the subordinate in any of three ways. First, they may serve as stimuli that motivate and direct the subordinate to perform necessary task operations. Second, they might act to constrain variability in behavior. Constraints may help the subordinate by clarifying expectancies that effort leads to rewards or by preventing the subordinate from experiencing conflict and confusion. Constraints may also be counterproductive to the extent that they restrict initiative or prevent increases in effort from being associated positively with rewards. Third, environmental factors may serve as rewards for achieving desired performance. For example, it is possible for the subordinate to receive the necessary cues to do his job, and the needed rewards for satisfaction, from sources other than the leader (e.g., co-workers in the primary work group). The effect of the leader on subordinates' motivation then will be a function of how deficient the environment is with respect to motivational stimuli, constraints, or rewards.

With respect to the environment, the theory asserts that when goals, and paths to desired goals, are apparent because of the routine nature of the task, clear group norms, or objective controls of the formal authority systems, attempts by the leader to clarify paths and goals will be redundant and will be seen by subordinates as an imposition of unnecessarily close control. Although such control may increase performance by preventing soldiering or malingering, it will also result in decreased satisfaction (see Figure 13-1). Further, with respect to the work environment, the theory asserts that the more dissatisfying the task the more the subordinates will resent behavior by the leader directed at increasing productivity or enforcing compliance to organizational rules and procedures.

Finally, with respect to environmental variables, the theory states that leader behavior will be motivational to the extent that it helps subordinates cope with environmental uncertainties, threat from others, or sources of frustration. Such leader behavior is predicted to increase subordinates' satisfaction with the job context and to be motivational to the extent that it increases the subordinates' expectations that their effort will lead to valued rewards.

The above propositions and specification of situational contingencies provide a heuristic framework on which to base future research which will hopefully lead to a more fully developed explicit formal theory of leadership. Figure 13-2 presents a summary of the theory. These propositions, while admittedly tentative, are hoped to provide managers with some insights concerning the effects of their own leader behavior and that of others.

The theory has been tested in a limited number of studies, and the results have generated considerable empirical support for our ideas. They also suggest areas in which the theory requires revision. The following is a brief review of these studies.

EMPIRICAL SUPPORT

Leader Directiveness

Leader directiveness has been found to have a positive correlation with satisfaction and expectancies of subordinates who are engaged in ambiguous tasks and to have a negative correlation with satisfaction and expectancies of subordinates engaged in clear tasks. These findings are as predicted by the theory and have been replicated in seven organizations (House, 1971; House and Dessler, 1974; Szilagyi and Sims, 1974; Dermer, 1974; Smetana, 1974). These findings suggest that when task demands are

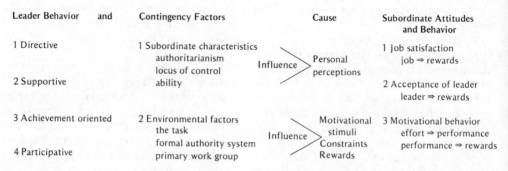

Leader Behavior	and	Contingency Factors		Cause	Subordinate Attitudes and Behavior
1 Directive		1 Subordinate characteristics authoritarianism locus of control	Influence	Personal perceptions	1 Job satisfaction job ⇒ rewards
2 Supportive		ability			2 Acceptance of leader leader ⇒ rewards
3 Achievement oriented		2 Environmental factors the task	Influence	Motivational stimuli	3 Motivational behavior effort ⇒ performance
4 Participative		formal authority system primary work group		Constraints Rewards	performance ⇒ rewards

Fig. 13-2. Summary of Path-Goal Relationships

ambiguous, or when the organization procedures, rules, and policies are not clear, a leader who behaves in a directive manner complements the tasks and the organization by providing the necessary guidance and psychological structure for subordinates. When task demands are clear to subordinates, however, leader directiveness is seen more as a hindrance.

Other studies, however, fail to confirm all of these findings (Weed, Mitchell, and Smyser, 1974; Dermer and Siegel, 1973; Schuler, 1973; Downey *et al.*, 1974; Stinson and Johnson, 1974). A study by Dessler (1973) suggests a resolution to these conflicting findings. Dessler found that for subordinates at the lower organizational levels of a manufacturing firm who were doing routine-repetitive-unambiguous tasks, directive leadership was preferred by closed-minded-dogmatic-authoritarian subordinates, and nondirective leadership was preferred by nonauthoritarian-opened-minded-subordinates. However, for subordinates at higher organizational levels doing nonroutine-ambiguous-tasks, directive leadership was preferred for both authoritarian and nonauthoritarian subordinates.

Thus, Dessler found that two contingency factors appear to operate simultaneously: subordinate task ambiguity, and degree of subordinate authoritarianism. When measured in combination the findings are as predicted by the theory. When the subor-

dinate's personality is not taken into account, however, task ambiguity does not always operate as a contingency variable as predicted by the theory. House, Burill, and Dessler (unpublished) recently found a similar interaction between subordinate authoritarianism and task ambiguity in a second manufacturing firm, thus adding confidence in Dessler's original findings.

Supportive Leadership

The theory hypothesizes that supportive leadership will have its most positive effect on subordinate satisfaction for subordinates who work on stressful, frustrating, or dissatisfying tasks. This hypothesis has been tested in ten samples of employees (House, 1971; House and Dessler, 1974; Szalagyi and Sims, 1974; Stinson and Johnson, 1974; Schuler, 1973; Downey *et al.*, 1974; Weed *et al.*, 1974). In only one of these studies was the hypothesis disconfirmed (Szalagyi and Sims, 1974). Despite some inconsistency in research on supportive leadership, the evidence is sufficiently positive to suggest that managers should be alert to the critical need for supportive leadership under conditions where tasks are dissatisfying, frustrating, or stressful to subordinates.

Achievement-oriented Leadership

The theory hypothesizes that achievement-oriented leadership will cause subordinates to strive for higher standards of performance and to have more confidence in the ability to meet challenging goals. A recent unpublished study by House, Valency, and Van der Krabben provides a partial test of this hypothesis among white-collar employees in service organizations. For subordinates performing ambiguous-nonrepetitive tasks they found a positive relation between the amount of achievement orientation of the leader and subordinates' expectancy that their effort will result in effective performance. Stated less technically, for subordinates performing ambiguous-nonrepetitive tasks, the higher the achievement orientation of the leader the more the subordinates were confident that their efforts would pay off in effective performance. For subordinates performing moderately unambiguous-repetitive tasks there was no significant relationship between achievement-oriented leadership and subordinate expectancies that their effort would lead to effective performance. This finding held in four separate organizations.

Two plausible interpretations may be used to explain these data. First, people who select ambiguous, non-repetitive tasks may be different from those who select a repetitive job because of their personality and may therefore be more responsive to an achievement-oriented leader. A second explanation is that achievement orientation only affects expectancies in ambiguous situations because there is more flexibility and autonomy in such tasks. Subordinates in such tasks are therefore more likely to be able to change in response to such leadership style. Neither of the above interpretations has been tested to date. However, additional research is currently under way to investigate these relationships.

Participative Leadership

In theorizing about the effects of participative leadership it is necessary to ask about the specific characteristics of subordinates and the specific characteristics of their situation that would cause participative leadership to be viewed as satisfying and instrumental to effective performance.

Mitchell (1973) recently described at least four ways in which a participative leadership style would impact on subordinate attitudes and behavior as predicted by expectancy theory. First, a participative climate should increase the clarity of organizational contingencies. Through participation in decision-making, subordinates should learn what leads to what. From a path-goal viewpoint participation would lead to greater clarity of the paths to various goals. A second impact of participation would be that subordinates should hopefully select goals they highly value. If one participates in decisions about various goals it makes sense that he would select goals he wants. Thus, participation would increase the correspondence between organization and subordinate goals. Third, we can see how participation would increase the individual's control over what happens to him on the job. If our motivation is higher (based on the preceding two points), then having greater autonomy and ability to carry out our intentions should lead to increased effort and performance. Finally, under a participative system, pressure toward high performance should come from sources other than just the leader or the organization. More specifically, when people participate in the decision process they become more ego-involved. The decisions made are in some part their own. Further, their peers know what is expected, and the social pressure has a greater impact. Thus, motivation to perform well stems from internal and social factors as well as from formal external ones.

A number of investigations prior to the above formulation supported the idea that participation appears to be helpful (Tosi, 1970; Sadler, 1970. Wexley *et al.*, 1973); and Mitchell (1973) presents a number of recent studies that support the above four points. It is also true, however, that we would expect the relation between a participative style and subordinate behavior to be moderated by both the personality characteristics of the subordinate and the situational demands. Studies by Tannenbaum and Allport (1956) and Vroom (1959) have shown that subordinates who prefer autonomy and self-control respond more positively to participative leadership in terms of both satisfaction and performance than do subordinates who do not have such preferences. In addition, the studies mentioned earlier by Runyon (1973) and Mitchell *et al.* (1974) showed that subordinates who were external in their orientation (i.e., believed that what happened to them was generally attributable to chance or luck) were less satisfied with a participative style of leadership than were internal subordinates.

House (1974) has also reviewed these studies in an attempt to explain the ways in which the situation or environment moderates the relation between participation and subordinate attitudes and behavior. His analysis suggests that where participative leadership is positively related to satisfaction, regardless of the predispositions of subordinates, the tasks of the subjects appear to be ambiguous and ego-involving. In the studies in which the subject's personality or predispositions moderates the effect of participative leadership, the tasks of the subjects are inferred to be highly routine and/or non-ego-involving tasks.

House reasoned from this analysis that the task may have an overriding effect on the relation between leader participation and subordinate responses, and that individual predispositions or personality characteristics of subordinates may have an effect only under some tasks. It was assumed that, when task demands are ambiguous, the subordinates will have a need to reduce the ambiguity. Further, it was assumed that when task demands are ambiguous, participative problem-solving between the leader and the subordinate will result in more effective decisions than when the task demands are unambiguous. Finally, it was assumed that

when the subordinates are ego-involved in their tasks, they will be more likely to want to have a say in the decisions that effect them when they are not ego-involved. Given these assumptions, the following hypotheses were formulated to account for the conflicting findings reviewed above:

1. When subjects are highly ego-involved in a decision or a task, and the decision or task demands are ambiguous, participative leadership will have a positive effect on the satisfaction and motivation of the subordinate, *regardless* of the subordinate's predisposition toward self-control, authoritarianism, or need for independence.
2. When subordinates are not ego-involved in their tasks and the task demands are clear, subordinates who are not authoritarian, and who have high needs for independence and self-control, will respond favorably to participative leadership, and their opposite personality types will respond less favorably.

These hypotheses were derived on the basis of path-goal theorizing. That is, the rationale that guided the analysis of prior studies was that both task characteristics and characteristics of subordinates interact to determine the effect of a specific kind of leader behavior on the satisfaction, expectancies, and performance of subordinates. To date, one major investigation (Schuler, 1974) has supported some of these predictions. The subjects were 354 employees in an industrial manufacturing organization, and personality variables, the amount of participative leadership, task ambiguity, and job satisfaction were assessed. As expected, in non-repetitive ego-involving tasks, employees (regardless of their personality) were more satisfied under a participative style than a non-participative style. In repetitive tasks that were less ego-involving, however, the amount of authoritarianism of subordinates moderated the relation between leadership style and satisfaction. Specifically, low-authoritarian subordinates were *more satisfied* under a non-participative style. These findings are exactly as the theory would predict. Thus, the theory is shown to have promise in reconciling a set of confusing and contradictory findings with respect to participative leadership.

SUMMARY AND CONCLUSIONS

We have attempted to describe what we believe is a useful theoretical framework for understanding the effect of leadership behavior on subordinate satisfaction and motivation. Most theorists today have moved away from the simplistic notions that all effective leaders have a certain set of personality traits or that the situation completely determines performance. Some researchers have presented rather complex attempts at matching certain types of leaders with certain types of situations (for example, the paper by Fiedler in this book). But we believe that a path-goal approach goes one step further. It not only suggests what type of style may be most effective in a given situation; it also attempts to explain *why* it is most effective.

We are optimistic about the future outlook for leadership research. With the guidance of path-goal theorizing, future research is expected to unravel many of the confusing puzzles about the reasons for and the effects of leader behavior that have heretofore not been solved. We would, however, add a word of caution. The theory, and the research on it, are relatively new to the literature of organizational behavior. Consequently, the theory is offered more as a tool for directing research and stimulating insight than as a proven guide for managerial action.

REFERENCES

Atkinson, J. W., and Raynor, J. O. *Motivation and achievement*. Washington, D.C.: V. H. Winston and Sons, 1974.

Dansereau, F., Jr., Cashman, J., and Graen, G. Instrumentality theory and equity theory as complementary approaches in predicting the relationship of leadership and turnover among managers. *Organizational Behavior and Human Performance*, 1973, 10, 184-200.

Dermer, J. D., and Siegel, J. P. A test of path-goal theory: disconfirming evidence and a critique. Faculty of Management Studies, University of Toronto, (Mimeographed) 1973.

Dermer, J. D. Supervisory behavior and budget motivation. Working paper, W. P. Sloan School of Management, Massachusetts Institute of Technology, Cambridge, Mass., 1974.

Dessler, G. An investigation of the path-goal theory of leadership. Ph.D. diss., Bernard M. Baruch College, City University of New York, 1973.

Downey, H. K., Sheridan, J. E., and Slocum, J. W., Jr. Analysis of relationships among leader behavior, subordinate job performance and satisfaction: A path-goal approach. Unpublished paper, 1974.

Evans, M. G. The effects of supervisory behavior on the path-goal relationship. *Organizational Behavior and Human Performance*, 1970, 55, 277-98.

Evans, M. G. Extensions of a path-goal theory of motivation. *Journal of Applied Psychology*, 1974, 59, 172-78.

Graen, G., Dansereau, F., Jr., and Minami, T., Disfunctional leadership styles. *Organizational Behavior and Human Performance*, 1972(a), 7, 216-36.

Graen, G., Dansereau, F., Jr., and Minami, T., An empirical test of the man-in-the-middle hypothesis among executives in a hierarchical organization employing a unit analysis. *Organizational Behavior and Human Performance*, 1972(b), 8, 262-85.

Hammer, T.H., and Dachler, H.T. The process of supervision in the context of motivation theory. Research Report No. 3, Department of Psychology, University of Maryland, 1973.

Haythorn, W., Couch, A., Haefner, D., Langham, P., and Carter, L. The effects of varying combinations of authoritarian and equalitarian leaders and followers. *Journal of Abnormal Social Psychology*, 1956, 53, 210-19.

Hill, W. A., and Hughes, D. Variations in leader behavior as a function of task type.

Organization Behavior and Human Performance, 1974, 11, 83-96.

Hill, W.A., and Ruhe, J.A. Attitudes and behavior of black and white supervisors in problem-solving groups. *Organization Behavior and Human Performance* (in press).

House, R. J. A path-goal theory of leader effectiveness. *Administrative Science Quarterly*, 16, 3 (September 1971), 321-38.

House, R.J. Notes on the path-goal theory of leadership. Faculty of Management Studies, University of Toronto, May 1974.

House, R. J., and Dessler, G. The path-goal theory of leadership: some post hoc and a priori tests. In Hunt, J. G. (Ed.), *Contingency approaches to leadership.* Carbondale, Ill.: Southern Illinois University Press, 1974.

House, R. J., Shapiro, H. J., and Wahba, M. A. Expectancy theory as a predictor of work behavior and attitude, a re-evaluation of empirical evidence. *Decision Sciences*, 1974, 5, 3, 54-77.

House, R. J., Valency, A., and Van der Krabben, R. Some tests and extensions of the path-goal theory of leadership. Unpublished paper, 1974.

Mitchell, T. R. Expectancy model of job satisfaction, occupational preference, and effort: A theoretical, methodological, and empirical appraisal. *Psychological Bulletin,* 1974, 81, 1053-77.

Mitchell, T. R., Smyser, C. R., and Weed, S. E. Locus of control: supervision and work satisfaction. Technical Report No. 74-56. Seattle: University of Washington, 1974.

Mitchell, T. R. Motivation and participation: an integration. *Academy of Management Journal*, 1973, 16, 4, 660-79.

Nebeker, D. M., and Mitchell, T. R. Leader behavior: An expectancy theory approach. *Organizational Behavior and Human Performance*, 1974, 11, 355-67.

Runyon, K. E. Some interactions between personality variables and management styles. *Journal of Applied Psychology*, 1973, 57, 3, 288-94.

Sadler, J., Leadership style, confidence in management and job satisfacation. *Journal of Applied Behavioral Sciences*, 1970, 6, 3-19.

Schuler, R. S. A path-goal theory of leadership: an empirical investigation. Ph.D. diss., Michigan State University, East Lansing, Mich., 1973.

Schuler, R. S. Leader participation, task structure, and subordinate authoritarianism. Unpublished paper, Cleveland State University, 1974.

Smetana, R. W. The relationship between managerial behavior and subordinate attitudes in motivation: a contribution to a behavioral theory of leadership. Ph.D. diss., Wayne State University, Detroit, 1974.

Stinson, J. E., and Johnson, T. W. The path-goal theory of leadership: a partial test and suggested refinement. *Proceedings*, 7th Annual Conference of the Mid-West Division of the Academy of Management, Kent, Ohio, April 1974, 18-36.

Stogdill, R. M. *Managers, employees, organization.* Bureau of Business Research, Division of Research, College of Commerce and Administration. Columbus: Ohio State University, 1965.

Szalagyi, A. D., and Sims, H. P. An exploration of the path-goal theory of leadership in a health care environment. *Academy of Management Journal*, 1974, 17, 622-34.

Tannenbaum, A. S., and Allport, F. H. Personality structure and group structure: an interpretive study of their relationship through an event-structure hypothesis. *Journal of Abnormal and Social Psychology*, 1956, 53, 272-80.

Tosi, H. A re-examination of personality as a determinant of the effects of participation. *Personnel Psychology*, 1970, 23, 91-99.

Vroom, V. H. Some personality determinants of the effects of participation. *Journal of Abnormal and Social Psychology*, 1959, 59, 322-27.

Weed, S. E., Mitchell, T. R., and Smyser, C. R. A test of House's path-goal theory of leadership in an organizational setting. Paper presented at Western Psychological Association, 1974.

Wexley, K. N., Singh, J. P., and Yukl, G. A. Subordinate personality as a moderator of the effects of participation in three types of appraisal interviews. *Journal of Applied Psychology*, 1973, 83, 1, 54-59.

3

ORGANIZATION STRUCTURE, TECHNOLOGY, AND ENVIRONMENT

Formal organizations are the dominant type of institution in today's highly specialized, technological, and interdependent society. An organization can be defined as the patterned relationships and activities of a large group of people who are attempting to achieve some common purpose. The structure of an organization is unlike that of a biological organism or a machine, because it consists of relatively stable and enduring patterns of events and processes instead of physical parts. Organizational processes include such things as communication, decision-making, planning, control, conflict resolution, leadership, production, adaptation, and system maintenance. Of course, organizations are linked to the world of concrete things such as buildings, equipment and people, but the organization can remain intact even though these physical things are changed (Katz and Kahn, 1966.) The structure of an organization can be described in terms of a number of separate but interrelated dimensions such as organization size, vertical differentiation (i.e., number of levels in the authority hierarchy), horizontal differentiation (i.e., degree and complexity of sub unit specialization), centralization of authority, and formalization (i.e., standardization of procedures and degree of role specialization).

The study of organizations is an interdisciplinary effort involving diverse fields such as anthropology, economics, management, political science, psychology, and sociology. Behavioral scientists from these various fields have proposed organization theories to describe and explain the structure and processes of organizations. Over the years there has been a gradual convergence of these theories, as well as a general increase in the level of theoretical sophistication and complexity. The article by Perrow summarizes the history of organization theory from the early part of the twentieth century until the present time. A description of various organization theories is also provided in the article by Lichtman and Hunt. The scope of their review is narrower, but they provide a more detailed description of the major theories of personality and organization.

Both these articles begin with a description of traditional or classical organization theories, including "scientific management," "administrative management," and "bureaucracy." The proponents of these early theories attempted to formulate general principles of effective organizing that would be applicable to all kinds of organizations. In the bureaucratic and mechanistic organization they prescribed, there is a high degree of job simplification and specialization; jobs are grouped into specialized subunits according to function or purpose; coordination is achieved through a hierarchy of administrative positions with a clear chain of command; authority to make major decisions is centralized at the top of the hierarchy; the communication network coincides with the hierarchical structure; and the behavior of lower-level personnel is controlled by detailed rules and operating procedures in conjunction with economic rewards and punishments. Two basic assumptions are implicit in this type of organization. The first assumption is that most members of the organization dislike work, avoid responsibility, lack ambition, prefer to be directed, and are motivated primarily by desire for economic gain and security (McGregor, 1960). The second assumption is that the goals and environment of the organization are relatively stable over time, and there is little uncertainty or variation in the tasks performed by the organization.

Since the famous Hawthorne studies (Roethlisberger and Dickson, 1939), the classical organization theories have come under attack. Some critics have argued that the classical theories ignore the "informal" organization and do not take into account important phenomena in organizations such as conflict over goals and priorities, the influence of informal groups (e.g., work-group restriction of production), sources of leader influence other than position power (e.g., referent and expert power), and communication occurring outside of the formal communication network (e.g., the "grapevine").

McGregor (1960) questioned the negative assumptions about human nature and proposed that completely different assumptions are more valid. According to McGregor, work is as natural as play; workers have higher-order needs such as esteem and self-actualization; and workers are capable of self-direction and creativity. McGregor and other "humanistic" organization theorists like Argyris (1964) and Likert (1967) have claimed that bureaucratic-mechanistic organizations stifle the psychological growth of most organization members and lead to a number of dysfunctional consequences. For example, excessive job simplification leads to employee frustration, apathy, or hostility, and excessive formalization results in a focus on rules rather than on goals, as well as prolonged delays in action ("red tape"). These humanistic organization theorists proposed that organizations should be designed in a more flexible and "organic" manner with less formalization, centralization of authority, and job simplification. They advocated the use of supportive leadership, job enrichment, group action, and participation of subordinates in decision-making.

The primary focus of the humanistic organization theorists was the compatibility of organization structure with member personality, which may reflect the fact that these theorists were psychologists. Organization theorists from other disciplines, including Burns and Stalker (1961), Hall (1972), Hickson *et al.* (1969), Lawrence and Lorsch (1969), Perrow (1967), Thompson (1967), and Woodward (1965), have been more concerned with the relationship of organization structure to the environment and technology of the organization. Most of these theorists have conducted comparative studies of many organizations in order to gain a greater understanding of the reasons for structural variations across organizations and the consequences of these variations in terms of organizational effectiveness. The results of their research suggest that there is no single form or organization that is best for all situations, and both the classical and humanistic organization theorists have neglected some important implications of the organization's technology and environment.

The article by Hickson, Pugh, and Pheysey provides an example of research conducted to determine how various structural dimensions of an organization are related to each other and to the technology used by the organization. They compare their results to those found in an earlier study by Woodward (1964) and attempt to reconcile the discrepancies between the two studies. The relationship between technology and organization structure is examined further in the article by Hunt. He considers various definitions of technology, reviews some of the comparative research on technology, and discusses the implications of this research for the design of effective organizations.

The next selection, by Lorsch, summarizes the results of research conducted by Lawrence and Lorsch (1969) on the relationship between the structure of an organization and environmental conditions. Lorsch describes a conceptual framework developed to analyze organizations in terms of the structural requirements posed by the degree of uncertainty and instability in various parts of an organization's environment. The degree of differentiation necessary for effective functioning of organization subunits facing different environmental conditions, and the kind of integrating mechanisms necessary to achieve coordination and management of conflict among these subunits, are the central elements of this conceptual framework.

The final article in this section, by Walker and Lorsch, shows how the Lawrence and Lorsch (1969) theory can be used to analyze the consequences of grouping jobs into departments by function or product. The classical theorists proposed that this choice should depend upon which type of departmentalization maximizes the efficient and economical utilization of equipment and technical knowledge, while allowing effective control and coordination. Walker and Lorsch suggest that the choice between product and functional departmentalization should also take into account the amount of differentiation (i.e., differences in time and goal orientation and formalization) among subunits that is required for the organization to perform effectively its multiple tasks and cope with its environment. The appropriate communication and integrating mechanisms for achieving coordination among these differentiated subunits should also be taken into account. Walker and Lorsch describe a study comparing two plants, one organized by product and the other by function. Observed differences between plants in conflict management, employee attitudes, and production effectiveness are summarized and discussed.

REFERENCES AND SUGGESTED READINGS

Argyris, C. *Integrating the individual and the organization.* New York: Wiley, 1964.

Argyris, C. Personality and organization theory revisited. *Administrative Science Quarterly*, 1973, 18, 141-67.

Burns, T. and Stalker, G. M. *The management of innovation.* London: Tavistock Publications, 1961.

Hall, R. H. *Organizations: Structure and process.* Englewood Cliffs, N.J.: Prentice-Hall, 1972.

Hickson, D. J., Pugh, D. S., and Pheysey, D. C. Operations technology and organization structure. *Administrative Science Quarterly*, 1969, 17, 378-97.

Katz, D., and Kahn, R. L. *The social psychology of organizations.* New York: Wiley, 1966.

Lawrence, P. R., and Lorsch, J. W. *Organization and environment.* Homewood, Ill.: Irwin, 1969.

Likert, R. *The human organization.* New York: McGraw-Hill, 1967.

Massie, J. L. Management theory. In J. G. March (Ed.), *Handbook of organizations.* Chicago: Rand McNally, 1965.

McGregor, D. M. *The human side of interprise.* New York: McGraw-Hill, 1960.

Perrow, C. A framework for the comparative analysis of organizations. *American Sociological Review*, 1967, 32, 194-209.

Roethlisberger, F. J., and Dickson, W. J. *Management and the worker.* Cambridge, Mass.: Harvard University Press, 1939.

Thompson, J. D. *Organizations in action.* New York: McGraw-Hill, 1967.

Woodward, J. *Industrial organisation: Theory and practice.* New York: Oxford University Press, 1965.

14

The Short and Glorious History
of Organizational Theory

CHARLES PERROW

From the beginning, the forces of light and the forces of darkness have polarized the field of organizational analysis, and the struggle has been protracted and inconclusive. The forces of darkness have been represented by the mechanical school of organizational theory—those who treat the organization as a machine. This school characterizes organizations in terms of such things as:

> centralized authority
> clear lines of authority
> specialization and expertise
> marked division of labor
> rules and regulations
> clear separation of staff and line.

The forces of light, which by mid-twentieth century came to be characterized as the human relations school, emphasizes people rather than machines, accommodations rather than machine-like precision, and draws its inspiration from biological systems rather than engineering systems. It has emphasized such things as:

> delegation of authority
> employee autonomy
> trust and openness
> concerns with the "whole person"
> interpersonal dynamics.

THE RISE AND FALL OF SCIENTIFIC MANAGEMENT

The forces of darkness formulated their position first, starting in the early part of this century. They have been characterized as the scientific management or classical management school. This school started by parading simple-minded injunctions to plan ahead, keep records, write down policies, specialize, be decisive, and keep your span of control to about six people. These injunctions were needed as firms grew in size and complexity, since there were few models around beyond the railroads, the military, and the Catholic Church to guide organizations. And their injunctions worked. Executives began to delegate, reduce their span of control, keep records, and specialize. Planning ahead still is difficult, it seems, and the modern equivalent is Management by Objectives.

But many things intruded to make these simple-minded injunctions less relevant:

Reprinted, by permission of the publisher, from *Organizational Dynamics*, Summer 1973. ©1973 by AMACOM, a division of American Management Association.

1. Labor became a more critical factor in the firm. As the technology increased in sophistication it took longer to train people, and more varied and specialized skills were needed. Thus, labor turnover cost more and recruitment became more selective. As a consequence, labor's power increased. Unions and strikes appeared. Management adjusted by beginning to speak of a cooperative system of capital, management, and labor. The machine model began to lose its relevancy.

2. The increasing complexity of markets, variability of products, increasing number of branch plants, and changes in technology all required more adaptive organization. The scientific management school was ill-equipped to deal with rapid change. It had presumed that once the proper structure was achieved the firm could run forever without much tampering. By the late 1930s, people began writing about adaptation and change in industry from an organizational point of view and had to abandon some of the principles of scientific management.

3. Political, social, and cultural changes meant new expectations regarding the proper way to treat people. The dark, satanic mills needed at the least a white-washing. Child labor and the brutality of supervision in many enterprises became no longer permissible. Even managers could not be expected to accept the authoritarian patterns of leadership that prevailed in the small firm run by the founding father.

4. As mergers and growth proceeded apace and the firm could no longer be viewed as the shadow of one man (the founding entrepeneur), a search for methods of selecting good leadership became a preoccupation. A good, clear, mechanical structure would no longer suffice. Instead, firms had to search for the qualities of leadership that could fill the large footsteps of the entrepreneur. They tacitly had to admit that something other than either "sound principles" or "dynamic leadership" was needed. The search for leadership traits implied that leaders were made, not just born, that the matter was complex, and that several skills were involved.

ENTER HUMAN RELATIONS

From the beginning, individual voices were raised against the implications of the scientific management school. "Bureaucracy" had always been a dirty word, and the job design efforts of Frederick Taylor were even the subject of a congressional investigation. But no effective counterforce developed until 1938, when a business executive with academic talents named Chester Barnard proposed the first new theory of organizations: Organizations are cooperative systems, not the products of mechanical engineering. He stressed natural groups within the organization, upward communication, authority from below rather than from above, and leaders who functioned as a cohesive force. With the spectre of labor unrest and the Great Depression upon him, Barnard's emphasis on the cooperative nature of organizations was well-timed. The year following the publication of his *Functions of the Executive* (1938) saw the publication of F. J. Roethlisberger and William Dickson's *Management and the Worker*, reporting on the first large-scale empirical investigation of productivity and social relations. The research, most of it conducted in the Hawthorne plant of the Western Electric Company during a period in which the workforce was reduced, highlighted the role of informal groups, work restriction norms, the value of decent, humane leadership, and the role of psychological manipulation of employees through the counseling system. World War II intervened, but after the war the human relations movement, building on the insights of Barnard and the Hawthorne studies, came into its own.

The first step was a search for the traits of good leadership. It went on furiously at university centers but at first failed to produce more than a list of Boy Scout maxims: A good leader was kind, courteous, loyal, courageous, etc. We suspected as much. However, the studies did turn up a distinction between "consideration," or employee-centered aspects of leadership, and job-centered, technical aspects labeled "initiating structure." Both were important, but the former received most of the attention and the latter went undeveloped. The former led directly to an examination of group processes, an investigation that has culminated in T-group programs and is moving forward still with encounter groups. Meanwhile, in England, the Tavistock Institute sensed the importance of the influence of the kind of task a group had to perform on the social relations within the group. The first important study, conducted among coal miners, showed that job simplification and specialization did not work under conditions of uncertainty and nonroutine tasks.

As this work flourished and spread, more adventurous theorists began to extend it beyond work groups to organizations as a whole. We now knew that there were a number of things that were bad for the morale and loyalty of groups—routine tasks, submission to authority, specialization of task, segregation of task sequence, ignorance of the goals of the firm, centralized decision making, and so on. If these were bad for groups, they were likely to be bad for groups of groups—i.e., for organizations. So people like Warren Bennis began talking about innovative, rapidly changing organizations that were made up of temporary leadership and role assignments, and democratic access to the goals of the firm. If rapidly changing technologies and unstable, turbulent environments were to characterize industry, then the structure of firms should be temporary and decentralized. The forces of light, of freedom, autonomy, change, humanity, creativity, and democracy were winning. Scientific management survived only in outdated text books. If the evangelizing of some of the human relations school theorists were excessive, and if Likert's

System 4 or MacGregor's Theory Y or Blake's 9 X 9 evaded us, at least there was a rationale for confusion, disorganization, scrambling, and stress: Systems should be temporary.

BUREAUCRACY'S COMEBACK

Meanwhile, in another part of the management forest, the mechanistic school was gathering its forces and preparing to outflank the forces of light. First came the numbers men—the linear programmers, the budget experts, and the financial analysts—with their PERT systems and cost-benefit analyses. From another world, unburdened by most of the scientific management ideology and untouched by the human relations school, they began to parcel things out and give some meaning to those truisms, "plan ahead" and "keep records." Armed with emerging systems concepts, they carried the "mechanistic" analogy to its fullest—and it was very productive. Their work still goes on, largely untroubled by organizational theory; the theory, it seems clear, will have to adjust to them, rather than the other way around.

Then the words of Max Weber, first translated from the German in the 1940s—he wrote around 1910, incredibly—began to find their way into social science thought. At first, with his celebration of the efficiency of bureaucracy, he was received with only reluctant respect, and even with hostility. All writers were against bureaucracy. But it turned out, surprisingly, that managers were not. When asked, they acknowledge that they preferred clear lines of communication, clear specifications of authority and responsibility, and clear knowledge of whom they were responsible to. They were as wont to say "there ought to be a rule about this," as to say "there are too many rules around here," as wont to say "next week we've got to get organized," as to say "there is too much red tape." Gradually, studies began to show that bureaucratic organizations could change faster than nonbureaucratic ones, and that morale could be higher where there was clear evidence of bureaucracy.

What was this thing, then? Weber had showed us, for example, that bureaucracy was the most effective way of ridding organizations of favoritism, arbitrary authority, discrimination, payola and kickbacks, and yes, even incompetence. His model stressed expertise, and the favorite or the boss's nephew or the guy who burned up resources to make his performance look good was *not* the one with expertise. Rules could be changed; they could be dropped in exceptional circumstances; job security promoted more innovation. The sins of bureaucracy began to look like the sins of failing to follow its principles.

ENTER POWER, CONFLICT, AND DECISIONS

But another discipline began to intrude upon the confident work and increasingly elaborate models of the human relations theorists (largely social psychologists) and the uneasy toying with bureaucracy of the "structionalists" (largely sociologists). Both tended to study economic organizations. A few, like Philip Selznick, were noting conflict and differences in goals (perhaps because he was studying a public agency, the Tennessee Valley Authority), but most ignored conflict or treated it as a pathological manifestation of breakdowns in communication or the ego trips of unreconstructed managers.

But in the world of political parties, pressure groups, and legislative bodies, conflict was not only rampant, but to be expected—it was even functional. This was the domain of the political scientists. They kept talking about power, making it a legitimate concern for analysis. There was an open acknowledgement of "manipulation." These were political scientists who were behaviorally" inclined—studying and recording behavior rather than constitutions and

formal systems of government—and they came to a much more complex view of organized activity. It spilled over into the area of economic organizations, with the help of some economists like R. A. Gordon and some sociologists who were studying conflicting goals of treatment and custody in prisons and mental hospitals.

The presence of legitimately conflicting goals and techniques of preserving and using power did not, of course, sit well with a cooperative systems view of organizations. But it also puzzled the bureaucratic school (and what was left of the old scientific management school), for the impressive Weberian principles were designed to settle questions of power through organizational design and to keep conflict out through reliance on rational-legal authority and systems of careers, expertise, and hierarchy. But power was being overtly contested and exercised in covert ways, and conflict was bursting out all over, and even being creative.

Gradually, in the second half of the 1950s and in the next decade, the political-science view infiltrated both schools. Conflict could be healthy, even in a cooperative system, said the human relationists; it was the mode of resolution that counted, rather than prevention. Power became reconceptualized as "influence," and the distribution was less important, said Arnold Tannenbaum, than the total amount. For the bureaucratic school—never a clearly defined group of people, and largely without any clear ideology—it was easier to just absorb the new data and theories as something else to be thrown into the pot. That is to say, they floundered, writing books that went from topic to topic, without a clear view of organizations, or better yet, producing "readers" and leaving students to sort it all out.

Buried in the political science viewpoint was a sleeper that only gradually began to undermine the dominant views. This was the idea, largely found in the work of Herbert

Simon and James March, that because man was so limited—in intelligence, reasoning powers, information at his disposal, time available, and means of ordering his preferences clearly—he generally seized on the first acceptable alternative when deciding, rather than looking for the best; that he rarely changed things unless they really got bad, and even then he continued to try what had worked before; that he limited his search for solutions to well-worn paths and traditional sources of information and established ideas; that he was wont to remain preoccupied with routine, thus preventing innovation. They called these characteristics "cognitive limits on rationality" and spoke of "satisficing" rather than maximizing or optimizing. It is now called the "decision making" school, and is concerned with the basic question of how people make decisions.

This view had some rather unusual implications. It suggested that if managers were so limited, then they could be easily controlled. What was necessary was not to give direct orders (on the assumption that subordinates were idiots without expertise) or to leave them to their own devices (on the assumption that they were supermen who would somehow know what was best for the organization, how to coordinate with all the other supermen, how to anticipate market changes, etc.). It was necessary to control only the *premises* of their decisions. Left to themselves, with those premises set, they could be predicted to rely on precedent, keep things stable and smooth, and respond to signals that reinforce the behavior desired of them.

To control the premises of decision making, March and Simon outline a variety of devices, all of which are familiar to you, but some of which you may not have seen before in quite this light. For example, organizations develop vocabularies, and this means that certain kinds of information are highlighted, and others are screened out —just as Eskimos (and skiers) distinguish

many varieties of snow, while Londoners see only one. This is a form of attention-directing. Another is the reward system. Change the bonus for salesmen and you can shift them from volume selling to steady-account selling, or to selling quality products or new products. If you want to channel good people into a different function (because, for example, sales should no longer be the critical function as the market changes, but engineering applications should), you may have to promote mediocre people in the unrewarded function in order to signal to the good people in the rewarded one that the game has changed. You cannot expect most people to make such decisions on their own because of the cognitive limits on their rationality, nor will you succeed by giving direct orders, because you yourself probably do not know whom to order where. You presume that once the signals are clear and the new sets of alternatives are manifest, they have enough ability to make the decision but you have had to change the premises for their decisions about their career lines.

It would take too long to go through the dozen or so devices, covering a range of decision areas (March and Simon are not that clear or systematic about them, themselves, so I have summarized them in my own book), but I think the message is clear.

It was becoming clear to the human relations school, and to the bureaucratic school. The human relationists had begun to speak of changing stimuli rather than changing personality. They had begun to see that the rewards that can change behavior can well be prestige, money, comfort, etc., rather than trust, openness, self-insight, and so on. The alternative to supportive relations need not be punishment, since behavior can best be changed by rewarding approved behavior rather than by punishing disapproved behavior. They were finding that although leadership may be centralized, it can function best through indirect and unobtrusive means such as changing the premises on which decisions are made, thus giving the impression that the subordinate is actually making a decision when he has only been switched to a different set of alternatives. The implications of this work were also beginning to filter into the human relations school through an emphasis on behavioral psychology (the modern version of the much maligned stimulus-response school) that was supplanting personality theory (Freudian in its roots, and drawing heavily, in the human relations school, on Maslow).

For the bureaucratic school, this new line of thought reduced the heavy weight placed upon the bony structure of bureaucracy by highlighting the muscle and flesh that make these bones move. A single chain of command, precise division of labor, and clear lines of communication are simply not enough in themselves. Control can be achieved by using alternative communication channels, depending on the situation; by increasing or decreasing the static or "noise" in the system; by creating organizational myths and organizational vocabularies that allow only selective bits of information to enter the system; and through monitoring performance through indirect means rather than direct surveillance. Weber was all right for a starter, but organizations had changed vastly, and the leaders needed many more means of control and more subtle means of manipulation than they did at the turn of the century.

THE TECHNOLOGICAL QUALIFICATION

By now the forces of darkness and forces of light had moved respectively from midnight and noon to about 4 A.M. and 8 P.M. But any convergence or resolution would have to be on yet new terms, for soon after the political science tradition had begun to infiltrate the established schools, another blow struck both of the major positions. Working quite independently of the Tavistock Group, with its emphasis on sociotech-

nical systems, and before the work of Burns and Stalker on mechanistic and organic firms, Joan Woodward was trying to see whether the classical scientific principles of organization made any sense in her survey of a hundred firms in South Essex. She tripped and stumbled over a piece of gold in the process. She picked up the gold, labeled it "technology," and made sense out of her otherwise hopeless data. Job-shop firms, mass-production firms, and continuous-process firms all had quite different structures because the type of tasks, or the "technology," was different. Somewhat later, researchers in America were coming to very similar conclusions based on studies of hospitals, juvenile correctional institutions, and industrial firms. Bureaucracy appeared to be the best form of organization for routine operations; temporary work groups, decentralization, and emphasis on interpersonal processes appeared to work best for nonroutine operations. A raft of studies appeared and are still appearing, all trying to show how the nature of the task affects the structure of the organization.

This severely complicated things for the human relations school, since it suggested that openness and trust, while good things in themselves, did not have much impact, or perhaps were not even possible in some kinds of work situations. The prescriptions that were being handed out would have to be drastically qualified. What might work for nonroutine, high-status, interesting, and challenging jobs performed by highly educated people might not be relevant or even beneficial for the vast majority of jobs and people.

It also forced the upholders of the revised bureaucratic theory to qualify their recommendations, since research and development units should obviously be run differently from mass-production units, and the difference between both of these and highly programmed and highly sophisticated continuous-process firms was obscure in terms of bureaucratic theory. But the bureaucratic school perhaps came out on top, because the forces of evil—authority, structure, division of labor, etc.—no longer looked evil, even if they were not applicable to a minority of industrial units.

The emphasis on technology raised other questions, however. A can company might be quite routine, and a plastics division nonroutine, but there were both routine and nonroutine units within each. How should they be integrated if the prescription were followed that, say, production should be bureaucratized and R & D not? James Thompson began spelling out different forms of interdependence among units in organizations, and Paul Lawrence and Jay Lorsch looked closely at the nature of integrating mechanisms. Lawrence and Lorsch found that firms performed best when the differences between units were *maximized* (in contrast to both the human relations and the bureaucratic school), as long as the integrating mechanisms stood half-way between the two—being neither strongly bureaucratic nor nonroutine. They also noted that attempts at participative management in routine situations were counterproductive, that the environments of some kinds of organizations were far from turbulent and customers did not want innovations and changes, that cost reduction, price and efficiency were trivial considerations in some firms, and so on. The technical insight was demolishing our comfortable truths right and left. They were also being questioned from another quarter.

ENTER GOALS, ENVIRONMENTS, AND SYSTEMS

The final seam was being mined by the sociologists while all this went on. This was the concern with organizational goals and the environment. Borrowing from the political scientists to some extent, but pushing ahead on their own, this "institutional school" came to see that goals were not fixed; conflicting goals could be pursued

simultaneously, if there were enough slack resources, or sequentially (growth for the next four years, then cost-cutting and profit-taking for the next four); that goals were up for grabs in organizations, and units fought over them. Goals were, of course, not what they seemed to be, the important ones were quite unofficial; history played a big role; and assuming profit as the pre-eminent goal explained almost nothing about a firm's behavior.

They also did case studies that linked the organization to the web of influence of the environment; that showed how unique organizations were in many respects (so that, once again, there was no one best way to do things for all organizations); how organizations were embedded in their own history, making change difficult. Most striking of all, perhaps, the case studies revealed that the stated goals usually were not the real ones; the official leaders usually were not the real ones; the official leaders usually were not the powerful ones; claims of effectiveness and efficiency were deceptive or even untrue; the public interest was not being served; political influences were pervasive; favoritism, discrimination, and sheer corruption were commonplace. The accumulation of these studies presented quite a pill for either the forces of light or darkness to swallow, since it was hard to see how training sessions or interpersonal skills were relevant to these problems, and it was also clear that the vaunted efficiency of bureaucracy was hardly in evidence. What could they make of this wad of case studies?

We are still sorting it out. In one sense, the Weberian model is upheld because organizations are not, *by nature*, cooperative systems; top managers must exercise a great deal of effort to control them. But if organizations are tools in the hands of leaders, they may be very recalcitrant ones. Like the broom in the story of the sorcerer's apprentice, they occasionally get out of hand. If conflicting goals, bargaining, and unofficial leadership exists, where is the structure of Weberian bones and Simonian muscle? To what extent are organizations tools, and to what extent are they products of the varied interests and group strivings of their members? Does it vary by organization, in terms of some typological alchemy we have not discovered? We don't know. But at any rate, the bureaucratic model suffers again; it simply has not reckoned on the role of the environment. There are enormous sources of variations that the neat, though by now quite complex, neo-Weberian model could not account for.

The human relations model has also been badly shaken by the findings of the institutional school, for it was wont to assume that goals were given and unproblematical, and that anything that promoted harmony and efficiency for an organization also was good for society. Human relationists assumed that the problems created by organizations were largely limited to the psychological consequences of poor interpersonal relations within them, rather than their impact on the environment. Could the organization really promote the psychological health of its members when by necessity it had to define psychological health in terms of the goals of the organization itself? The neo-Weberian model at least called manipulation "manipulation" and was skeptical of claims about autonomy and self-realization.

But on one thing all the varied schools of organizational analysis now seemed to be agreed: organizations are systems—indeed, they are open systems. As the growth of the field has forced ever more variables into our consciousness, flat claims of predictive power are beginning to decrease and research has become bewilderingly complex. Even consulting groups need more than one or two tools in their kit-bag as the software multiplies.

The systems view is intuitively simple. Everything is related to everything else, though in uneven degrees of tension and reciprocity. Every unit, organization, department, or work group takes in resources, transforms them, and sends them out, and thus interacts with the larger system. The psychological, sociological, and cultural aspects of units interact. The systems view was explicit in the institutional work, since they tried to study whole organizations; it became explicit in the human relations school, because they were so concerned with the interactions of people. The political science and technology viewpoints also had to come to this realization, since they deal with parts affecting each other (sales affecting production; technology affecting structure).

But as intuitively simple as it is, the systems view has been difficult to put into practical use. We still find ourselves ignoring the tenets of the open-systems view, possibly because of the cognitive limits on our rationality. General systems theory itself had not lived up to its heady predictions; it remains rather nebulous. But at least there is a model for calling us to account and for stretching our minds, our research tools, and our troubled nostrums.

SOME CONCLUSIONS

Where does all this leave us? We might summarize the prescriptions and proscriptions for management very roughly as follows:

1. A great deal of the "variance" in a firm's behavior depends on the environment. We have become more realistic about the limited range of change that can be induced through internal efforts. The goals of organizations, including those of profit and efficiency, vary greatly among industries and vary systematically by industries. This suggests that the impact of better management by itself will be limited, since so much will depend on market forces, competition, legislation, nature of the work force, available technologies and innovations, and so on. Another source of variation is, obviously, the history of the firm and its industry and its traditions.

2. A fair amount of variation in both firms and industries is due to the type of work done in the organization—the technology. We are now fairly confident in recommending that if work is predictable and routine, the necessary arrangement for getting the work done can be highly structured, and one can use a good deal of bureaucratic theory in accomplishing this. If it is not predictable, if it is nonroutine and there is a good deal of uncertainty as to how to do a job, then one had better utilize the theories that emphasize autonomy, temporary groups, multiple lines of authority and communications, and so on. We also know that this distinction is important when organizing different parts of an organization.

We are also getting a grasp on the question of what is the most critical function in different types of organizations. For some organizations it is production; for others, marketing; for still others, development. Furthermore, firms go through phases whereby the initial development of a market or a product or manufacturing process or accounting scheme may require a non-bureaucratic structure, but once it comes on stream, the structure should change to reflect the changed character of the work.

3. In keeping with this, management should be advised that the attempt to produce change in an organization through managerial grids, sensitivity training, and even job enrichment and job enlargement is likely to be fairly ineffective for all but a few organizations. The critical reviews of research in all these fields show that there is no scientific evidence to support the claims of the proponents of these various methods; that research has told us a great deal about social psychology, but little about how to apply the highly complex findings to actual situations. The key word is *selectivity:* We have no broad-spectrum antibiotics for interpersonal relations. Of course, managers should be sensitive, decent, kind, courteous, and courageous, but we have known that for some time now, and beyond a minimal threshold level, the payoff is hard to measure. The various attempts to make work and interpersonal relations more humane and stimulating should be applauded, but we should not confuse this with solving problems of structure, or as the equivalent of decentralization or participatory democracy.

4. The burning cry in all organizations is for "good leadership," but we have learned that beyond a threshold level of adequacy it is extremely difficult to know what good leadership is. The hundreds of scientific studies of this phenomenon come to one general conclusion: Leadership is highly variable or "contingent" upon a large variety of important variables such as nature of task, size of the group, length of time the group has existed, type of personnel within the group and their relationships with each other, and amount of pressure the group is under. It does not seem likely that we'll be able to devise a way to select the best leader for a particular situation. Even if we could, that situation would probably change in a short time and thus would require a somewhat different type of leader.

Furthermore, we are beginning to realize that leadership involves more than smoothing the paths of human interaction. What has rarely been studied in this area is the wisdom or even the technical adequacy of a leader's decision. A leader does more than lead people; he also makes decisions about the allocation of resources, type of technology to be used, the nature of the market, and so on. This aspect of leadership remains very obscure, but it is obviously crucial.

5. If we cannot solve our problems through good human relations or through good leadership, what are we then left with? The literature suggests that changing the structures of organizations might be the most effective and certainly the quickest and cheapest method. However, we are now sophisticated enough to know that changing the formal structure by itself is not likely to produce the desired changes. In addition,

one must be aware of a large range of subtle, unobtrusive, and even covert processes and change devices that exist. If inspection procedures are not working, we are now unlikely to rush in with sensitivity training, nor would we send down authoritative communications telling people to do a better job. We are more likely to find out where the authority really lies, whether the degree of specialization is adequate, what the rules and regulations are, and so on, but even this very likely will not be enough.

According to the neo-Weberian bureaucratic model, it has been influenced by work on decision-making and behavioral psychology, we should find out how to manipulate the reward structure, change the premises of the decision-makers through finer controls on the information received and the expectations generated, search for interdepartmental conflicts that prevent better inspection procedures from being followed, and after manipulating these variables, sit back and wait for two or three months for them to take hold. This is complicated and hardly as dramatic as many of the solutions currently being peddled, but I think the weight of organizational theory is in its favor.

We have probably learned more, over several decades of research and theory, about the things that do *not* work (even though some of them obviously *should* have worked), than we have about things that do work. On balance, this is an important gain and should not discourage us. As you know, organizations are extremely complicated. To have as much knowledge as we do have in a fledgling discipline that has had to borrow from the diverse tools and concepts of psychology, sociology, economics, engineering, biology, history, and even anthropology is not really so bad.

REFERENCES

This paper is an adaptation of the discussion to be found in Charles Perrow, *Complex Organizations: A Critical Essay*, Scott, Foresman, Glenview, Ill., 1972. All the points made in this paper are discussed thoroughly in that volume.

The best overview and discussion of classical management theory, and its changes over time is by Joseph Massie—"Management Theory" in the *Handbook of Organizations* edited by James March, Rand McNally, Chicago, 1965, pp. 387-422.

The best discussion of the changing justifications for managerial rule and worker obedience as they are related to changes in technology, etc., can be found in Reinhard Bendix's *Work and Authority in Industry*, Wiley, New York, 1956. See especially the chapter on the American experience.

Some of the leading lights of the classical view—F.W. Taylor, Col. Urwick, and Henry Fayol—are briefly discussed in *Writers on Organizations* by D.S. Pugh, D.J. Hickson, and C.R. Hinings, Penguin, 1971. This brief, readable, and useful book also contains selections from many other schools that I discuss, including Weber, Woodward, Cyert and March, Simon, the Hawthorne Investigations, and the Human Relations Movement as represented by Argyris, Herzberg, Likert, McGregor, and Blake and Mouton.

As good a place as any to start examining the human relations tradition is Rensis Likert, *The Human Organization*, McGraw-Hill, New York, 1967. See also his *New Patterns of Management*, McGraw-Hill, 1961.

The Buck Rogers school of organizational theory is best represented by Warren Bennis. See his *Changing Organizations*, McGraw-Hill, 1966, and his book with Philip Slater, *The Temporary Society*, Harper & Row, New York, 1968. Much of this work is linked into more general studies, e.g., Alvin Toffler's very popular paperback *Future Shock*, Random House, 1970, and Bantam Paperbacks, or Zibigniew Brzezinsky's *Between Two Ages: America's Role in the Technitronic Era*, Viking Press, New York, 1970. One of the first intimations of the new type of environment and firm and still perhaps the most perceptive is to be found in the volume by Tom Burns, and G. Stalker, *The Management of Innovation*, Tavistock, London, 1961, where they distinguished between "organic" and "mechanistic" systems. The introduction, which is not very long, is an excellent and very tight summary of the book.

The political science tradition came in through three important works. First, Herbert Simon's *Administrative Behavior*, Macmillan, New York, 1948, followed by the second half of James March and Herbert Simon's *Organizations*, Wiley, New York, 1958, then Richard M. Cyert and James March's *A Behavioral Theory of the Firm*, Prentice-Hall, Englewood Cliffs, N.J., 1963. All three of these books are fairly rough going, though chapters 1, 2, 3, and 6 of the last volume are fairly short and accessible. A quite interesting book in this tradition, though somewhat heavy-going, is Michael Crozier's *The Bureaucratic Phenomenon*, University of Chicago, and Tavistock Publications, 1964. This is a striking description of power in organizations, though there is a somewhat dubious attempt to link organization processes in France to the cultural traits of the French people.

The book by Joan Woodward *Industrial Organisation: Theory and Practice*, Oxford University Press, London, 1965, is still very much worth reading. A fairly popular attempt to discuss the implications for this for management can be found in my own book *Organizational Analysis: A Sociological*

View, Tavistock, 1970, chapters 2 and 3. The impact of technology on structure is still fairly controversial. A number of technical studies have found both support and nonsupport, largely because the concept is defined so differently, but there is general agreement that different structures and leadership techniques are needed for different situations. For studies that support and document this viewpoint see James Thompson, *Organizations in Action*, McGraw-Hill, 1967, and Paul Lawrence and Jay Lorsch, *Organizations and Environment*, Harvard University Press, Cambridge, Mass., 1967.

The best single work on the relation between the organization and the environment and one of the most readable books in the field is Philip Selznick's short volume *Leadership in Administration*, Row, Peterson, Evanston, Ill., 1957. But the large number of these studies are scattered about. I have summarized several in my *Complex Organizations: A Critical Essay*.

Lastly, the most elaborate and persuasive argument for a systems view of organizations is found in the first 100 pages of the book by Daniel Katz and Robert Kahn, *The Social Psychology of Organizations*, Wiley, 1966. It is not easy reading, however.

15

Personality and Organization Theory:
A Review of Some Conceptual Literature

CARY M. LICHTMAN and RAYMOND G. HUNT

When viewing the phenomena of human behavior, it has been a custom among social scientists to debate the relative importance to it of individual characteristics and properties of the social situation. Sometimes they hide from the problem, and, of course, accommodations have been sought, but the question still divides "personalists" and "situationalists" despite the efforts of a growing school of "interactionist" peacemakers (see Hollander and Hunt, 1967, especially Sections I and III, for fuller discussion of these issues).

Theories of organization, dealing as they do with human collective undertakings, could hardly expect to escape the conceptual fall-out from this "debate." Nor have they. And because we believe a theory of organization can be no better than the assumptions it makes about the human personality, we propose to review and comment on the ways different theories have chosen to resolve (or evade) the issue of relating persons and organizations.

In this discussion we construe organizations, after W. R. Scott (1964), as "collectivities . . . established for the pursuit of relatively specific objectives on a more or

less continuous basis" (p. 488). Although organizational policies and structures may be elaborated separately from their memberships, people populate and work them, and the interplay of people and structures defines the phenomena of organization (see Hollander and Hunt, 1967, pp. 352-53).

Early theories of social organization emphasized the more general sociological conviction that the social structure was the primary determinant of differential human characteristics. Classical organization theorists, therefore, proposed that these structural determinants be utilized in the design of organizations to maximize human potential and organizational efficiency. Some two decades later, however, the so-called neoclassical organization theorists offered models based on the personalistic views of psychology. Reacting to early sociological notions, this school of thought rejected the formal organizational structure as of small importance and placed the locus of the organization within the phenomenal fields of its individual incumbents. Then, reacting in turn to the one-sidedness of these two earlier approaches, many modern organization theorists acknowledged the value

Reprinted from *Psychological Bulletin*, 1971, 76, 271-94, by permission of the authors and the publisher.

of each and attempted to integrate them into a unitary systemic conceptual scheme. Thus, modern organization theory (cf. Scott, 1961) proposes that human behavior in organizational settings can be understood in terms of three elements: (a) the stated design of functions, that is, the requirements of the organization; (b) the characteristics of people who populate the organization, that is, the attributes they bring with them into the organization, including those derived from other social affiliations; (c) the relations between the organization's defined properties and the characteristics of people who populate it. The last element is a system concept that provides for prospects of organization-level emergents and is a hallmark of "modern" organization theory.

In their entirety, particular theories of organization do not always fit neatly into any one of these categories. The limited conceptual scope of some theories obviously places them with either the structural or personalistic camps; others seem to be a combination of both, without necessarily being full-fledged systemic theories. Grouping conceptual formulations into categories may not always do maximum justice to many of their nuances, but it does help to integrate the diverse ideas contained in the organizational literature. And the task of grouping theories becomes somewhat simpler if the classification is done, as we have tried to do here, according to the actual content of particular theoretical statements rather than what their authors claim to be the domain of their conceptualizations.

VARIETIES OF THEORY

For classificatory purposes we elected to employ four categories instead of the traditional three. The first two sections of this discussion deal in sequence with *traditional structural approaches* and *modern structural approaches* to organizational behavior. What the old and new structural theories have in common is the use of a global theory of personality as a premise upon which an organizational structure is designed. "All men are thus," they say, "and organizational theory and practice had best take account of such truths" (Quinn and Kahn, 1967, p. 451). In the case of traditional structuralists (classical organization theorists) the grounding assumption is that man is lazy, untrustworthy, and works only for money. The resulting organizational design suggested by this assumption, of course, has been of the bureaucratic variety, and the motivational presuppositions of traditional structuralism still underly much modern "incentive" theory and associated modes of compensating performance (cf. Opsahl and Dunnette, 1966).

Modern structural theorists follow quite the same logic, although basing it on a different initial premise. They argue that all men are interested in self-actualizing or realizing their full potential, and to allow for this they recommend a looser, more decentralized structure than did the bureaucrats. Both views are logically committed to the position that since people share certain important characteristics, differences in people or performance can best be explained in terms of differential positional occupancy in the organizational structure. The implication of this typology is that theorists such as Argyris and McGregor (and some others as well), who have usually been considered personalistic theorists, emerge as structural theorists in the present context.

The third section of the discussion deals with those theories that emphasize the *personalistic approach* to the understanding of organizational behavior. In this category are viewpoints that stress individual cognitive attributes, human experience, and individual differences as behavioral determinants. Some of these assume that employees act as individuals, while others assume that individual behavior is mediated by informal groups. In either case, however, the bias is in the direction of personalism or "psychologism" rather than "sociologism" or structuralism.

The fourth section deals with *integrative approaches* to organizations, which attempt to synthesize the various one-sided views into a single framework represented to be a more accurate model of organizational functioning.

Traditional Structural Approaches

Probably the most ambitious attempt to deal with the social-psychological aspects of the social structure was that of Marx (cf. 1887; or more particularly the collection of writings, 1964). Marx was concerned with properties of the social environment as they influence the characteristics of people who populated that environment. In this view, social stratification is seen collectively in the form of ideology; the stratification system is a way of organizing the social order. Ideology, then, is an expression of the stratification system and develops after the stratification system is established.

Thus, for Marx, the individual is influenced entirely by the social order and has no important characteristics aside from the system of which he is a part. The only way to change people is to change the society.

Following Marx's lead, Durkheim (1902) maintained that once a society establishes a division of labor, the properties of that society can be defined independently of people. The characteristics of people can be examined as a function of the categories to which they belong. In other words, people can be characterized as a function of the structural properties of society.

Ironically, then, the earlier sociological writings of theorists such as Marx and Durkheim can be seen to provide a broad theoretical base for classical organization theorists who founded such schools of organizational thought as scientific management, administrative management, and bureaucracy. By implication the Marxes and Durkheims introduced questions of distinctions between organization theory and personality theory, whose solutions still tend to elude us (cf. Hunt, 1969b).

Scientific Management

In his scientific management, Taylor (1911) set out to study organizations with "scientific precepts." He was interested primarily in work performance, and his goal was to integrate properties of the man with properties of the job. To this end, Taylor worked out procedures, by means of time and method studies, that would utilize less energy and yield more work. This view (and its complements, e.g., Gilbreth, 1911) shows little concern with the worker as a person; rather, the worker was seen as an extension of the job. So far as the model was concerned, the worker simply had no life outside his job or separate from his tasks. The implications of this "ascribed status" have been illuminated by Daniel Bell (1956). And it is interesting to note in passing that many Tayloristic polemics are today re-echoed in passionate debates about "computerism." What was written before about Taylor and scientific management is being written again about the inhumanity of the computer (cf., e.g., Simon, 1965).

In the Tayloristic model, work gets done by providing employees with work routines (or programs). There is no point, thought Taylor, in having men work at less than capacity because the work is poorly organized (the man-machine concept). The assembly line, therefore, can be run as fast as people can work, and time-method studies can be used to discover how fast people can work. In other words, experiments could be performed to discover the *one best method* or *best conditions* for doing the job.

Apart from a kind of Calvinist work-ethic and a trust in monetary inducements, Taylor had no motivational terms in his models. Motivation was largely assumed as an intrinsic moral matter. Furthermore, the "essential ability to work" was simply taken as given (cf. Neff, 1968, pp. 5-11, for a pointed discussion of this idea). But, if motivation and ability tended to be treated as intrinsic, organizational operation was viewed as dependent on extrinsic control.

For Taylor, the organization was an authority structure to be described in terms of *span of control*. This was the key to organizational design and created a system based on a centralized pyramidal authority structure. Taylor's plan was to devise a rational structure based on an authority hierarchy, with varying support functions (clerical, research, and development, etc.) where and when necessary—the line-staff notion. Thus, for Taylor, the guiding principle of organization was the span of control (or the authority structure), with components laid out in terms of vertical line and lateral staff.

According to Taylor, the organization could then be specified in terms of organizational charts (authority and line-staff) and job specifications. This was the organization, the *formal system*. Nothing else mattered. The organization was thus defined in terms of scientific principles used to describe the formal system.

Confined almost exclusively to the vantage point of top management, Taylor's view of the organization suffers from a severe lack of conceptual richness. Furthermore,

Scientific management achieves conceptual closure of the organization by assuming that goals are known, tasks are repetitive, output from production processes somehow disappears, and resources in uniform qualities are available. (Thompson, 1967, p. 5)

Administrative Management

The administrative management views fostered by Gulick and Urwick (1937) stressed the structural relationships among production, personnel, supply, and other service units of the organization. Here again the emphasis is on efficiency, and many Tayloristic principles are invoked. Efficiency is maximized by task specialization and the grouping of similar tasks into departments. Responsibility is fixed according to such principles as span of control or delegation and by insuring adequate control over employees so that action conforms to plans.

The assumption in this view is that a master plan is known so that specialization, departmentalization, and control can be determined rationally. (Simon, 1957, for one, has criticized this view by enumerating the difficulties in attaining agreement with and constancy in master plans.)

Like its relative, scientific management, administrative management commonly ignores the organization's environment and boundary functions necessary to transact matters of organizational survival with that environment.

We might interject at this point the observation that reviews of scientific management concepts frequently convey a not altogether accurate sense of ancient history. To be sure, there have been sequences of appearance and development, but the scientific management movement is hardly dead, even if it appears more often now in the form of computer-oriented management science exercises in model building, operations research, cost-benefit analysis, etc. Moreover, it often disguises itself today in a more dynamic "systems" terminology and posture, sometimes leaving behind many of its earlier oversimplifications (cf. Haberstroh, 1965; Koontz, 1962). In anticipation, the same cautionary comment might be made about the human relations tradition (discussed below), which sometimes is painted as if it were solely a manifestation of the 1930s and 1940s. However, unlike Australopithicus (or Chè), it lives (cf., e.g., Whyte, 1969—note expecially p. 708).

Bureaucracy

Similar in many ways to the above views, bureaucracy (cf. Mouzelis, 1967; Weber, 1947) focuses on staffing and structure as a means of dealing with clients and disposing of cases—and the achievement of efficiency. In this view, efficiency is maximized by organizing offices according to jurisdiction and hierarchical position, appointing experts to offices, utilizing procedural devices for work situations, the promulgation of rules governing behavior of positional incumbents, providing differential rewards by office to provide incentive and patterns for career advancement (Quinn and Kahn, 1967; Thompson, 1967). As with other structural theories of organization, Weber felt that the proper use of rules, rewards, and punishments could render the human component negligible by divorcing the individual's private life from his role as an officeholder. Once more the significance of individual identify was uncomprehended: indeed, the belief was widely implicit that "workers," unlike managers and other "good" people, had none.

The static nature of the organization as described by Weber inspired numerous eloquent attacks on bureaucratic theory. Notable among these were the criticisms suggested by Merton (1957) and Gouldner (1954), dealing with the unintended consequences of bureaucratic rule enforcement. Merton argued that reliance on depersonalized relations and strict enforcement of rules and jurisdictions in order to reduce human variability lead to rigid behavior on the part of position incumbents. This rigidity, based on the need to defend individual actions, leads to reliance on organizational precedent and use of the most easily invoked rule in dealings with clients. Often, however, the rule most easily invoked is least appropriate to the client's case. The client's challenge of the bureaucrat's judgment serves only to increase his drive to defend his actions and thence to increasingly rigid and inappropriate behavior.

In a somewhat similar vein, Gouldner (1954) pointed out an additional self-defeating consequence of reliance, stemming from demands for control, on the use of general and impersonal rules. He argued that the use of such rules offers little incentive for employees to do any more than the minimum amount of work that will avoid punishment. When management discovers that productivity has fallen behind goals, pressure is placed on supervisors to supervise

more closely. This serves to increase the visibility of power relations within the work group and leads to even more dogged determination on the part of the workers to do as little as possible.

Thompson (1961) added that bureaucracies tend to attract monocratic types to supervisory positions who tend to enhance feelings of helplessness and insecurity in subordinates. Jasinski (1956) has found even more problems with the overreliance on efficiency controls. He specified seven: wasted time, higher maintenance costs, figure "fudging," low morale, impaired labor recruitment, higher unit costs, and lowered product quality. Schlesinger has provided an especially amusing account of bureaucratic blundering and job protectiveness in the United States Department of State in his book *A Thousand Days* (1956), and Bell (1956) has penned a scathing indictment of the Tayloristic-bureaucratic "cult of efficiency."

Other writers (e.g., Argyris, 1964; Bennis, 1969; Haire, 1963) have objected to bureaucratic theory because it is based on the assumption that man is lazy and not to be trusted. They further object to the accompanying moral nction of the intrinsic goodness of work and the punishment orientation implicit in classical theory. These critics agree that classical models of organization serve to stifle workers in their quest for "psychological success."

Argyris (1964), for example, has argued that to the degree that the dictates of classical theory are followed in an organization, the lower-level employee will suffer because

few of his abilities will be used . . . [he] will tend to experience a sense of dependence and submissiveness toward his superior because decisions of whether or not he works, how much he shall be paid, and so on, will be largely under his superior's control . . . [and] the worker will tend to experience a decreasing sense of self-responsibility and self-control. (pp. 38-39)

Although most of the critics of classical organization theory view bureaucracy as either an ideal type or an undifferentiated lump, Hall (1963) has shown that the major discussants of bureaucracy cannot themselves completely agree on a list of definitive characteristics. Furthermore, in an empirical study, Hall demonstrated that organizations that are highly bureaucratized on one dimension may not be so on another. The dimensions studied by Hall were hierarchy of authority, division of labor, system of rules, system of procedures, impersonality, and emphasis on technical competence; other variables have been dealt with by Woodward (1965), Perrow (1967), and Harvey (1968) with comparable results. Clearly, then, bureaucracy exists in degrees, and there are very few so-called bureaucracies conforming in all ways to an ideal type. Nevertheless, most of the critical writing in this area tends to view it as an all-or-none phenomenon. The conclusion to be drawn is that classical organization theory is often used as a straw man or figurative foil for both critical virtuosos and theorists advancing alternative models.

Modern Structural Views

Sharing the same general rationale of organizational design as the traditional structural theorists– that the organization must be designed to fit the nature of people—the modern structural theorists, by altering their assumptions concerning people, have proposed alternative designs to bureaucracy. Instead of assuming as did classical theorists, that all workers are motivated by rational economic factors, modern structuralists undertake to view the worker as a total human being striving for self-improvement, self-expression, autonomy, recognition, or what-not. It is further assumed that these strivings exist in equal amounts in all people but that their expression depends on the degree to which the social structure is able to accommodate such strivings.

The model used by this approach is nicely exemplified in Merton's (1957) reformulation of the concept of *anomie*. The problem for Merton was to explain why the frequency of deviant behavior varies in different social structures. He viewed the task as one of locating groups which typically engage in deviant behavior (or maladjustive behavior from the societal viewpoint) as *normal* responses to the social situation in which they find themselves.

Specifically, Merton argued that certain cultural axioms prescribing the means and ends of success have been well internalized by virtually all members of American society. He defined success as the attainment of wealth and stature, and the means to this end are hard, honest work, and no horseplay. The culture, however, while vigorously stressing the ends, provides a social structure that severely limits access to the means. Anomie arises from the conflict between the goals that a culture sets up and the ineffectiveness of the prescribed means for attaining these goals. The incidence of this conflict is differentially observable in various strata of society, being more pronounced where an individual's position is weakened by the structure of society. Thus, people occupying positions in the lower social strata are more likely to be anomic as evidenced by criminal or ritualistic life styles employed as a means of coping with or defending against structural restrictions. The solution to problems of deviance then, of course, is to work at modifying the societal structure to allow for more freedom of legitimate goal attainment for incumbents of lower social strata (Gordon, 1964).

Several organization theorists have applied similar logic to social organizations. They maintain that all people have certain important common needs and that the structure of the organization interferes with the expression of these needs, especially for incumbents of positions low in the organization's hierarchy. This restrictiveness results in coping and adaptive responses such as minimal productivity, sabotage, low morale and job satisfaction. Most of these theorists acknowledge the existence of individual differences, but they proceed to build their models as if these differences are of no account.

The immediate influences on these views rest with the Hawthorne studies (discussed later) and Maslow's (1954) theoretical formulations emphasizing man's inherent need to use his capacities and skills in a mature and productive way. Maslow specified a need hierarchy common to all normal people and consisting, in ascending order, of safety and survival needs, social needs, ego needs, autonomy needs, and self-actualization needs. A higher-level need cannot be satisfied until the needs below it in the hierarchy have been served. Maslow argued that it is universally true that all manner of human activity is an attempt to work upward in the hierarchy. Using this basic notion, modern structural theorists feel that since membership in a work organization is a central fact in men's lives, it is to the best interest of the organization and the people in it to alter the organization's structure to allow for the human quest for self-actualization.

Among the major advocates of this view is Argyris (1957, 1964), whose chief premise was that there is a lack of fit between requirements of bureaucratic organizations (the formal structure) and the needs of individual members to achieve "psychological success." Argyris wrote:

[Our] selection of the individual who aspires toward psychological success is not an arbitrary one . . . [T]here is an increasing number of psychologists who believe that self-esteem, self-acceptance, and psychological success are some of the most central factors that constitute individual mental health in our culture. If we are able to understand better how one may enhance the opportunity for individual psychological success, we believe that this will contribute toward individual mental health. (1964, pp. 36-37)

As evidence for his premise, Argyris cited a number of empirical studies showing that workers at the lower end of the organizational hierarchy, as opposed to those at higher levels, suffer from poorer mental health, lower job satisfaction, lower levels of self-esteem, feelings of insecurity, and other related variables. The resulting feelings of dependence, subordination, and passivity on the part of the workers can only result in "frustration, failure, short-term perspective, and conflict" (1964, p. 40).

Further, Argyris took the position that an organization operated on classical premises suffers inefficiency to the extent that employees waste energy by engaging in activities of a compulsive, defensive nature. Thus, there is less human energy available for genuine productivity. As an outline for a solution, Argyris proposed a "mix model" in which "changes in the organization toward increasing opportunity for psychological success and self-esteem be made as long as we are able to show that they are decreasing the unproductive compulsive activities" (1964, p. 147). Argyris is quick to point out that this does not necessarily imply a people-centered organization, because self-esteem is strongly coupled with responsibility to others. Furthermore, organizational changes designed to accommodate psychological success should continue only so long as the organization can more efficiently achieve its objectives, maintain its internal system, and adapt to its environment.

Argyris' view, then, contains a powerful belief in the reality of the forces exerted on individuals by an organizational structure. Since personality is considered a constant, individual differences can only be explained in terms of differential positional incumbency, and, indeed, the lower organizational levels are seen as the most restricting with respect to human need satisfaction.

McGregor (1960) embraced a similar view when he proposed "Theory Y" as a general solution to the problem of organizational improvement. Theory Y represents a set of assumptions about human motivation, based on Maslow's need hierarchy, which he felt should serve as a basis for organizational design. McGregor argued:

Above all, the assumptions of Theory Y point up the fact that the limits of human collaboration in the organizational setting are not limits of human nature but of management's ingenuity in discovering how to realize the potential represented by its human resources. Theory X offers management an easy rationalization for ineffective organizational performance: It is due to the nature of human resources with which we must work. Theory Y, on the other hand, places problems squarely in the lap of management. If employees are lazy, indifferent, unwilling to take responsibility, intransigent, uncreative, uncooperative, Theory Y implies that the causes lie in management's methods of organization and control. (p. 48)

In other words, the structure of the organization is responsible for difficult employees, and an alteration in this structure is called for.

Other theorists have, in whole or in part, fostered a similar point of view. Likert (1961, 1967) did so by arguing that "System 4" (trust and participation) is the only leadership style which can yield maximum effectiveness. Gellerman (1963) posited competence and power as general motives and suggested that the structure take these into account. And Blake and his co-workers (cf. Blake and Mouton, 1968) also proposed a "one best" route to managerial effectiveness—the 9-9 theory.

The solutions proposed by the several writers holding to modern structural viewpoints suggest reordering organization away from bureaucratic designs so that they will allow for participative decision making, face-to-face work groups, mutual confidence between superior and subordinate, job enlargement, increased responsibility at lower positions, and so on.

The modern structural theorists have met with criticism on two main grounds: Their global personality assumptions and their propensity to blame the structure of the organization for all of its ills. Examples of the first type of criticism have emanated from the pen of Strauss (1963, 1968). Strauss felt that the notions of such people as Argyris (1959), Herzberg, Mausner, and Snyderman (1959), Maier (1955), Maslow (1954), and McGregor (1960) are laden with an inner-directed academic bias in which righteous professors impose their own values on members of population segments who may have quite a different idea of self-development. J. K. Galbraith (1967), however, felt that modern structural theorists seem to feel that if workers gain most of their satisfactions away from their jobs, then the organization has somehow failed in both efficiency and elementary humanism and must, of necessity, be restructured. Strauss (1963) continued by asserting that the injudicious use of power-equalization practices may actually adversely affect the security needs of those workers who are not prepared for the added responsibilities that accompany an expanded role. Indeed, a closely related phenomenon figured prominently as a source of disturbance in Levinson, Price, Munden, Mandel, and Solley's Midland Utilities study (1962). Further, power-equalization techniques may be more expensive to employ than they are worth in highly programmed situations where simply adequate performance or keeping up with the assembly line is all that is required (cf. Perrow, 1967, for a discussion of this and related matters in a wider context of reviewing relations between technology and organization). Moreover, like their traditional counterparts, the modern structuralists are susceptible to criticism for their advocacy of "one best way" notions, albeit this time applied mostly to managerial methods (cf. Fiedler, 1965).

Sayles and Strauss (1966) maintained that the personality versus organization model is most applicable to employees who do highly skilled or creative work in large companies (e.g., research and development scientists, industrial designers—people similar to the model builders). For the workers who must perform jobs that are more difficult to make intrinsically interesting, Sayles and Strauss (1966) predicted a re-emergence of the kind of leisure-based culture characteristic of ancient Greece and Rome. It is too late, they feel, four our society to revert to a production system based on individual craftsmanship. Katz and Kahn (1966) have pointed out, for instance, that a good many mass-produced automobiles can be bought for the price of one Rolls Royce. As noted above, Galbraith (1967), too, has voiced similar sentiments, although Bell (1956), while acknowledging the trend, has expressed skepticism as to whether there can be adequate substitutes for loss of satisfaction from work.

At any rate, a challenge to the structural suppositions of the human relations theorists has come from an extensive review of the empirical literature by Porter and Lawler (1965). These authors studied the literature pertaining to seven aspects of organizational structure: Organizational levels, line and staff hierarchies, span of control, subunit size, total organization size, hierarchical steepness, and degree of centralization or decentralization; they concluded:

Five of the seven properties of organization structure (span of control and centralization/decentralization being the two possible exceptions) have been shown to have some kind of significant relationship to either job attitudes or job behavior, or to both of these types of variables. However, . . . experimental "proof" of cause-effect relationships between structure and employee attitudes and behavior is elusive and almost nonexistent. (p. 47)

[T]here are already enough indications in the literature to support a greater research effort to investigate the interactions among structural properties of organizations in their relationship to employees' job behavior and attitudes. Too much previous theorizing in the area of organizations has neglected such

interaction possibilities and hence, there has been an unfortunate tendency to over-simplify vastly the effects of particular variables. Organizations appear to be much too complex for a given variable to have a consistent unidirectional effect across a wide variety of types of conditions. (p. 48)

Similar sentiments relative to the contingent nature of organizational processes have become commonplace in the literature. And their pertinence is underscored by recent work on determinants of formal organization structure and the impact of formal structures on member characteristics (cf., e.g., Hickson, Pugh, and Pheysey, 1969; Whyte, 1969, especially chapter 3). Structural properties of organizations surely "seep into" their members, as Udy (1965) stated, but the reverse is also true, and, in any case, the relations usually are not simple.

Other criticisms have also been leveled against the human relations structuralists. Pugh (1966) has noted that the theorists reacting against the classical school seem to have an implicit bias against formal organization. Leavitt (1962) felt that much organizational restructuring based on human relations philosophies has been done on the principle of defeating Taylorism and has too often thrown out the baby with the bath water. Leavitt felt, in particular, that the over-reaction against classical theories has served to impede the salutary introduction of principles from communication and information theory into organizational design. Hunt and Lichtman[1] have cautioned managers against giving their employees the impression that productivity is somehow not important; in the first place, it is not true; second, it only serves to confuse employees and may create stress in those places where a human relations orientation is supposed to relieve it. And Katzell (1962) has cited

1. Hunt, R. G., and Lichtman, C. M. Concepts and strategies for training work supervisors as employee counselors. Buffalo, N. Y.: State University of New York, 1969.

evidence of conventional organizations that seemed to be functioning perfectly well and of human relations programs that were rejected by workers.

It would seem, then, that current structural theories with emphases on human relations have made many of the same errors of theoretical presumption as did the classical theorists against whom they were ostensibly reacting. Notably, their assumptions of global personality characteristics give their theories the same one-sided, closed system, quality of the classical theories. They have a way of proposing the one *best* solution to the efficiency of all organizations and the *one best way* to motivate all members. Their view then is not only simplistically one-sided, but unidirectional: Effects flow almost entirely from the organization's properties to the individual. As compared with modern varieties, traditional structuralism might, however, be said to hold a somewhat friendlier attitude toward organizations and a somewhat less humanistic one toward its members. Traditional structuralists tend to see organizations as societal benefactors needful only of augmented efficiency, whereas the modernists look upon the organization as a more oppressive agency suitable for reform. In either case, however, the believe prevails that apt structuring of the features of the organization will allow the individual's natural inclinations to issue forth as more effective performance. (And Taylor was as convinced as anybody that this would be accompanied by happier workers.)

In his discussion of "work as a psychological problem," Neff (1968), however, argued that it is evident that people exist who cannot (or will not) work effectively under even the best of conditions. The question he raised under the rubric of the "work personality" is, in essence, What psychological characteristics are requisite to entry and performance in "work rules"? (cf. also Dawis, Lofquist, and Weiss, 1968).

Personalistic Views

Although global theories of personality have been of benefit to organization and management theory—especially their implications for organizational design—they are often difficult to study in a precise empirical manner, and they do not provide sufficient differential predictive power to be useful by themselves for an understanding of organizational behavior. As a result, many students of organizations have chosen to concentrate their theoretical and empirical efforts on the discovery of the influence of more particularized measures of personality. Schein (1965) commented:

Man is not only complex, but also highly variable; he has many motives which are arranged in some sort of hierarchy of importance to him, but this hierarchy is subject to change from time to time and situation to situation; furthermore, motives interact and combine complex motive patterns (for example, since money can facilitate self-actualization, for some people economic strivings are equivalent to self-actualization). Man is capable of learning new motives through his organizational experiences . . . and . . . is the result of a complex interaction between initial needs and organizational experiences. Man's motives in different organizations or different subparts of the same organization may be different. . . . Man can become productively involved with organizations on the basis of many different kinds of motives . . . . (p. 60)

Many of the same points have been made by Hunt (1969a) in discussion of the role of profit in business affairs. In any event, the general assumption of the personalistic view is that people react to their organization on the basis of their perceptions of it. These perceptions are based on people's needs, motives, and values. Therefore, to understand human behavior in organizations, one must understand how individuals differ with respect to personalistic variables; to change organizations, one must alter the perceptions of people. The impetus to this view rests largely with the writings of Kurt Lewin and the Hawthorne group.

Lewin's field theory and his group dynamics work (cf. Lewin, 1951) prefigured more than one important contemporary pattern of organizational analysis. The group dynamics research, of course, was one of the roots of T-grouping, while field theory per se constituted one of the early gestures in psychology toward a systemlike interpretation of individual and group behavior. Among other things, for instance, Lewin argued that action was no simple outcome from mechanical stimulus-response linkages, but was a complex resultant of coacting mutually influential elements coalescing as dynamically shifting momentary fields of force in a psychological environment, the life space.

Broadly phenomenological in orientation, Lewin held the characteristics of the life space to be indefinable apart from the cognitions of the person-actor; overt behavior was construed as essentially derivative from fields of force consequent upon modes of organization of that cognitive space. Through his cognitive contributions, the actor is thus viewed as active in the behavioral process and not as just a passive recipient of discrete stimuli. Indeed, in the Lewinian scheme, although constrained ecologically, the frame of behavior was phenomenal; the life space was a perceptual or experiential creation. Furthermore, little room was left for examining the accuracy of perception. The field of behavior was, so to say, principally "intra-psychic."

Now, if an organization has no properties aside from people's perceptions of it based on their needs, values, and attitudes, it can have no real structure because it cannot exist independently of its particular time-relative membership (cf. Hunt, 1968). The process of organizational analysis must then consist largely of personnel assessments and identification of ad hoc liaisons; organizational change must consist solely in the changing of people. Such a premise is fundamental (if implicit) to what may be termed "clinical" approaches to organization development (e.g., those associated with T-group perspectives; cf. Schein and Bennis, 1965).

About the same time as Lewin was writing, the Hawthorne or Western Electric studies (Mayo, 1933; Roethlisberger and Dickson, 1939) were being conducted. Although originally conceived as a test of Taylorism—a search for the one best level of illumination, among others things—the findings indicated that there was no one best level. Rather, workers stepped up production at all levels. The Hawthorne studies became important principally because the investigators went on to ask *why* there was no relation between illumination and output, and the studies conducted to discover the answer led to neoclassical organization theory.

From their studies the investigators concluded that friendship patterns were the heart of organization. They subsequently advocated human relations as a set of techniques by which people could be motivated. By maintaining that the organization is what is perceived by the employees to be the case, the proponents of neoclassical organization theory abandoned the formal structural notions of the classical theorists. The important system was no longer the formal organizational structure, but the informal relations at all organizational levels. What had traditionally been called the formal structure, then, was nothing but the manifestation of the workings of the informal system (or else somebody's idealization of it).

As the Hawthorne researchers saw it, however, the implications for management did not lie in any gross restructuring of the organization, but rather in a program of individual counseling designed to change the perceptions of individual workers toward the organization. The classic studies of Coch and French (1948) and Lewin (1958) were direct offshoots of this line of thinking. In both of these studies the persuasive potential of informal group membership was used as a vehicle for changing people's perceptions of the structure *as it is;* there was no intention of changing the basic structure of the system, there was only the attempt to get people to accept it. Although this new approach came to be called participative management, the fact was that management had no intention of altering the organization —only of changing people's attitudes toward work. Among others, Bell (1956) has been vocal about the "manipulative" qualities of human relations operations, and recently even Bennis (1970) has commented on this tendency.

Individuals and Informal Groups

The Hawthorne researchers have been subject to sweeping critique. Carey (1967) has argued that their conclusions neither followed from nor were they supportable from their data; if anything, they demonstrated exactly what they maintained had been disproven. Yet, be that as it may, few more influential works could be found—they ushered in an era. But as Katz (1965) has pointed out, the Hawthorne studies led to the demise of the notion of economic man without, however, actually making social organization the focus of analysis. The Hawthorne studies argued that man is motivated by a good deal more than monetary self-interest; indeed, that the worker's peer group could actually guide a man away from his own self-interest by establishing a norm of restricted output. Although the group factor in work situations was emphasized, and the concept of social system introduced, an individual focus was retained. The function of the group, in this view, was to relieve the boredom of the individual.

Roy (1960), however, has argued that the function of the group is a good deal more than that. The work-group culture reaches outside the organization by defining the social reality not only of the work situation but also of the worker's place in the larger society. The work group as an informal structure, argued Roy, provides a continuity between life outside and inside the organization. This general position has received wide support in the literature (e.g., Bennis and Shepard, 1965; Festinger, 1950; Walker, 1958).

Likert (1961, 1967) typifies the group dynamics approach in his advocacy of group decision processes at all levels. He proposed a type of organizational structure consisting of many overlapping groups that extend across adjacent management levels. Each foreman, for example, would be a member not only of the work group but also a full-fledged member of the next higher supervisory level. Thus, the supervisor in one group is a subordinate in the next, and so on, at successive levels. Horizontal as well as vertical linkages are built into this system. The emphasis is clearly on groups rather than on individuals. "An organization will function best when its personnel function not as individuals but as members of highly effective work groups with high performance goals" (Likert, 1961, p. 105). Likert felt that employee participation in decision-making, when accomplished according to his "linking pin" notion, will not reduce supervisory influence (a view shared by Tannenbaum, 1966), but rather will serve to change the attitudes of work-group members to better conform to organizational goals. Moreover, like others of its genre, Likert's solutions to organizational problems rarely carry important implications of a basic structural order; indeed, by and large they presume a generally bureaucratic system and speak mainly to operations within in (cf. Bennis, 1970).

Despite contemporary recognition of the influence of informal groups on the formal organization, many modern theorists have preferred to limit the domain of their analysis to individual experience. Vroom

(1964), for instance, has recently applied Lewin's general theory of personality to the study of organizational behavior, hypothesizing performance to be a function of the worker's perception of the abilities required by the job, the degree to which the person perceives himself as having these abilities, and the degree to which he values the possession of such abilities. Vroom, thus, stressed the affective consequences of the degree of consistency between a person's performance and his self-concept. In this view a person is motivated to perform effectively when effective performance is consistent with his conception of his abilities and with the value he places on them. Porter and Lawler (1968) have similarly hypothesized that managerial performance is a function of the perceived value of the reward, the probability that effort will bring the reward, and the accuracy of role perceptions. Smith and Cranny (1968) have presented a similar formulation, and March and Simon (1958) and Cyert and March (1963) have also stressed personalistic variables in their individual decision-making models of organizations. They have used such expressions as "the perceived consequence of evoked alternatives," "the expected value of reward," placing the locus of the organization within the individuals who populate it.

Katz (1964) has posited that the motivation to produce and motivation to belong are orthogonal dimensions, and this independence helps to explain the corresponding lack of relationship between job satisfaction and productivity. Bass (1965) argued that it is not necessary to study workers with reference to any basic needs or tensions; rather, there is just as much predictive power to be had by restricting research to "organizationally relevant" motivational dispositions. Task orientation, self-orientation, and interpersonal orientation are the three proposed by Bass. These and some related ideas have been well summarized by Quinn and Kahn (1967).

In his book *Eupsychian Management*, Maslow (1965) took a more radical view by arguing that work in itself has a kind of symbiotic quality. Satisfaction can indeed be gotten out of good work, but this is not a social or socially derived (ego) need. Rather, work is a primitive need independent of social need satisfaction and can be intrinsically interesting. In principle, Maslow's view is not altogether unlike that of Bell (1956), which we have cited, or of Herzberg *et al.* (1959), who have claimed that the only true job satisfaction can come out of work itself. Good working conditions and satisfactory social relationships around the job can only serve to make the job tolerable.

A review of the literature concerned with studies of individual worker differences was written by Smith and Cranny (1968) and provides further evidence for the value of such research. In sum, recognizing the inadequacies of classical organization theory, many writers have turned the coin and concentrated their theoretical efforts toward evaluating the role of the individual and the work group as a determinant. They have also encouraged an individual differences approach to the study of organizational behavior, by proposing intrapersonal dimensions along which people may vary. An especially clear illustration of this can be found in Hackman's recent (1969) reworking of the Herzberg two-factor notions about work motivation.

But this view is no less one-sided than the structural approaches because it has little to say about the formal organization. Any comprehensive theory of organizational behavior, of necessity, has to integrate the formal structure, the processes occurring within individuals, and the function of informal groups (cf. Hunt, 1968; Perrow, 1967).

The solution, according to Scott (1961), lies in the remembrance that the main problem with the structural and personalistic views was not one of inaccuracy but rather incompleteness and shortsightedness. In neither approach is there adequate integration among the numerous facets of human behavior studied by it. The task of the modern organization theorist, therefore, is to combine the several views into a more accurate model of organizational functioning.

Mechanic (1963) has championed the use of the multivariable or "eclectic" approach to organizational studies, as opposed to "one-sided" approaches committed to a single view of human nature. He maintained that one-sided approaches tend to encourage strong partisanship to a particular view and thus engender misunderstandings, communication difficulties, unjustified attacks, while they also discourage interdisciplinary cooperation.

However, if "one-sided" analysis is defined openly as a strategy of approach rather than a dogmatic assertion of priority, the dialogue between theories may be improved and communication and cross-fertilization may be preserved at the same time ... [W]hile it may be valuable to urge antieclecticism in theory building, it is essential to urge eclecticism in the use of research approaches and methodologies. Perhaps the most significant recent trend in organization studies is the utilization of various modes of data collection in the same study. (Mechanic, 1963, pp. 172-73)

The virtues of the one-sided versus the eclectic approach depend, in part, on the purposes of the theorist. If his purpose is to convince bureaucratic managers of the advantages of human relations practices, there is probably no harm in taking a more extreme personalistic view of human behavior in organizations; presumably, the target is already familiar with the operations of formal rules. If, however, the theorist's intent is to build an accurate and workable general model of organizational functioning, then it is clear that none of the one-sided views proposed to date can do that job. The next section deals with some approaches to the discovery of a general solution to the organizational dilemma.

Integrating Approaches

Increasing disenchantment with the myriad of one-sided and normative approaches to organization theory has led many writers to favor the use of alternative models. Such models typically represent attempts to integrate existing approaches and/or reflect the influence of situational factors on organizational functioning. Katzell, for example, wrote:

[B]y concerning themselves with certain preselected dependent variables ... and not with others that are relevant to the system, by relying heavily on unproven assumptions, and by their tendency to generalize rather than paying due attention to surrounding circumstances, such theories typically take the form of a blueprint or master plan which is prescribed as the one best way to organize and manage all work. (1962, p. 104)

Katzell felt that many factors must be taken into account before it can be decided what organizational policies and practices are likely to work best. As a starting point, he suggested five such parameters:

1. The first parameter mentioned by Katzell is size, or the number of interdependent organizational members. Hickson et al. (1969) have also given prominence to size factors in their analyses of determinants of structure. Indik (1963) reviewed the literature relating organizational size to member participation in terms of absence and turnover (a finding which calls to mind Barker's ecological studies of schools, cf., e.g., 1963). In another paper, Indik (1965) interpreted these findings by positing that larger organizations contain more potential and necessary communication linkages among members, rendering adequate communication more difficult to achieve. The result of inadequate communication among members serves to decrease interpersonal attractiveness and, in turn, member participation rates. Porter and Lawler (1965) also reviewed the literature on organizational size and concluded that

although job satisfaction and morale tend to be lower in large organizations, the general findings relevant to this area are neither reliable nor clear. These authors felt that perhaps subunit size is a more crucial determinant of employee reactions that is total organization size. Woodward (1965), too, has pressed for a more differentiated concept of size, stressing the importance of indexing size by reference to the size of managerial subsystems. There is clearly a need for more research in this area.[2]

2. The degree of interaction and interdependence is another parameter suggested as important by Katzell. Katz and Kahn (1966) have theorized that the degree of task interdependence is an important consideration in choosing the appropriate authority structure for an organization. They argued that where such interdependence is high, where creative requirements are minimal, and where identification with organizational goals is not required, a hierarchical authority structure, with its implication of close supervision, is indicated. Where the opposite circumstances obtain, a more democratic alternative should be used for maximum efficiency. Vroom and Mann (1960) have proposed that differences in work-group task interdependence account for the choice of autocratic supervisors by some groups and democratic supervisors by others.

More generally, Hackman[3] has shown the importance of task structure to patterns of group interaction; Sommer (1967, 1968) has demonstrated the pervasive influence of broader ecological factors in group (and, by inference, organization) processes, and W. F. Whyte (1969) may be consulted for a wide-ranging discussion of various aspects and implications of "the structuring of the work environment" (cf. especially chapter 3). Hunt (1970) has discussed at length the organizational significance of task uncertainty and has identified distinctive modes of structural adaptation to it. Relatedly, Haberstroh (1965) provided a review of the role of information systems in task modeling and organizational design. He noted, for instance, that "the coherence and unity of an organization is intimately related to its information system" (p. 1192). Therefore, he maintained, variations in such systems will precipitate "major [organizational] repercussions." Haberstroh promoted the idea of close and explicit integration of information systems and task models (cf. also Cleland and King, 1968; Glans, Grad, Holstein, Meyers, and Schmidt, 1968).

3. Another variable to be considered is the personalities of organization members. Their motivations, expectations, abilities, and other personal qualities seem to be of paramount importance in determining policies and practices of organizations. Employee satisfactions and attitudes have been linked to subcultural differences (Katzell, Barrett, and Parker, 1961) and cross-cultural differences (French, Israel, and Ås, 1960), as well as to individual difference measures (Smith and Cranny, 1968) and patterns of immediate supervision (Ronan, 1970).

4. The degree of congruence or disparity between organizational goals and the needs and goals of the members is a fourth factor to be considered as a determinant of organizational design. Katz and Kahn (1966) distinguished between two types of goal internalization that might be aroused in an employee. The first of these occurs when the employee identifies with the job itself and is, therefore, conducive to high quantity and high quality role performance. Job identification is exemplified by the craftsman or

2. Recently Blau (1970) has published a systematic theory relating organization size and structural differentiation that could prove a productive guide for such research. He touches on various nuances of both dimensions, but his "basic generalizations are (a) increasing organizational size generates differentiation along various lines at decelerating rates; and (b) differentiation enlarges the administrative component in organizations to effect coordination [Abstract, p. 201]."
3. Hackman, J. R. Functions of group interaction. Paper presented at Colloquium of the State University of New York, Buffalo, October 1969.

scientist who delights in the work he does and is rewarded by the opportunity to express his abilities and to make his own decisions. Although morale and satisfaction are well-linked to the variety and challenge of the job and the gratifications that accrue to workers, such individual craftsmanship is infeasible and expensive to apply to many positions in a company concerned with the mass production of consumer goods and also in some service operations. One solution is to eliminate dull assembly-line jobs through automation (cf. Bell, 1956, for a useful general discussion of this issue). Mann and Hoffman (1960) and Blauner (1964) have argued that after automation has occurred, the remaining jobs provide more freedom, responsibility, and dignity. The result is a decrease rather than an increase in worker alienation.

The second type of identification proposed by Katz and Kahn occurs through internalization of organizational goals rather than through the job itself. This type of motivation is associated with value expression and self-identification. In industrial organizations this type of internalization is usually found among management personnel, although in voluntary organizations it may extend to the rank and file. Katz and Kahn argued, however, that complete internalization of organizational goals is less common than two types of partial internalization. The first of these concerns general organizational purposes that are not unique to a particular organization. A scientist, for example, may internalize the research values of his profession and, to the extent that the organization that employs him shares similar goals, coincidence in worker and organizational goals will occur. However, the scientist could work in many other organizations just as easily. The same, of course, could be said of teachers and other professions whose attachments to particular organizations are derivative and chiefly as a simple locus of occupational activity.

The other subtype proposed by Katz and Kahn is the internalization of subsystem goals and values. Since one's own organization unit is often more visible to him and is frequently his immediate source of reward, it is often easier to internalize the smaller unit goal than that of the entire organization. This often leads to the aggrandizement effect (Caplow and McGee, 1958; Morane, 1967), that is, tendencies to rate one's subsystem higher than outsiders do. This may lead in turn to empire building, parochialism, petty jealousies, and factionalism within the organization. Thus, depending on which tendencies are involved, a high degree of goal internalization on the part of employees may not always be a bed of roses for the organization; but, in general, it is clear that the degree and variety of employee identification can have a profound influence on organizational policy and practice.

5. Katzell's final parameter has to do with who in the organization has the necessary ability and motivation to take action that will further its objectives. Rubin and Hunt (1969) have discussed this matter with special reference to what they called "mission identification." After reviewing some of the literature on supervision, Katzell observed that

the best way to organize and manage work is heavily conditioned by those in the organization who have the knowledge and motivation to get the job done. More specifically, it would seem necessary to mold the organizational system so that it maximizes freedom of action and initiative for those who can and will take effective action, while eliciting compliance, support, or noninterference from others. Depending on the organizational loci of expertise and dedication, the appropriate work system may vary widely from situation to situation. (1962, p. 107)

Katzell concluded that "the sheer number of variables that can be used to describe organizations is staggering" (1962, p. 105) and that ways must be found to work with them meaningfully (and we have hardly even mentioned technological variables: cf. Hunt, 1970). One way to do this, he proposed (not surprisingly), is to discover the genotypic dimensions that underlie phenotypic complexities.

It is the recognition of the vast number and complexity of organizational variables that has been responsible for a decided shift in emphasis on the part of many organization theorists over the past decade or so. Perhaps it is more accurate to say that recognition of the complexity of the facts of social structure and social organization was responsible for the belated development of the psychological approach to the study of organizations. Until perhaps two decades ago the social sciences lacked the conceptual tools for dealing with many important facets of social life (Katz and Kahn, 1966). With the introduction of the biological notion of an open system (von Bertalanffy, 1950) into the social sciences (Miller, 1968; Morane, 1967) came a practicable possibility for integrating the plethora of one-sided views of social organizations.

Social Systems

Among the earliest and most generally useful systemic theories of organizational behavior was the theory put forth by Homans (1950). Homans commenced by positing that any social system exists in a three-part environment: a *physical* environment (geography, climate, etc.), a *cultural* environment (the norms and values and goals of the society at large), and a *technological* environment (the state of knowledge and instrumentation available to the system). At the next level the social system itself has certain requirements and goals that are translated into specified activities and interactions for members of the system. The behavior required by the system or determined by its environment is called the *external* system by Homans. For example, in a work organization, manage-

ment constitutes a large element of the external system by making decisions that bring certain people together in particular ways, for instance, through job specifications, work methods, prescribed layouts, and selection of personnel.

Although the people brought together by the management may be strangers at first, they eventually come to know one another, develop cliques and friendships, socialize on and off the job, help one another in their work, agree to restrict production, and so on. They now have another basis on which to associate, one that modifies and influences their behavior over and above (and perhaps instead of) the effects of the external system. The new form of behavior comes about as a reaction to the demands of the external system. Homans called this phenomenon the *internal system*.

Homans further specified that the elements of a social system can be sorted into three categories which contain aspects of both the internal and external systems: *activities* (the things people do, the acts they perform), *interactions* (activities that link people together so that the activity of one person has an effect on the activity of another), and *sentiments* (internal psychological states, e.g., emotions, feelings, beliefs, values). Homans postulated that activities, interactions, and sentiments are mutually dependent on one another so that a change in any one will produce a change in the others. For example, positive sentiments between two people lead to increased interaction, or vice versa. Homans further argued that the internal and external systems are mutually dependent; for instance, technology influences interaction, which affects informal relationships. Conversely, the Hawthorne studies demonstrated how the informal system influenced "formal" production quotas.

Lastly, the two systems and the environment are mutually dependent. The environment may change the formal organizations (e.g., through federal and state legislation, union activities), which, in turn, will serve to alter informal organizational relations. Contained in Homans's formulations is the explicit recognition that a social organization, at any point in time, is the outcome of a pattern of interactions between the organization's stated requirements, its environment, and the characteristics of the people who populate it. It ties the emergent system of people's actual everyday behavior to organizations and the external system of formal plans, culture, and other groups that mold emergent behavior.

A more recent comprehensive discussion of organizations as open social systems is *The Social Psychology of Organizations* in which Katz and Kahn (1966) give precision to many concepts of organization by including them as part of a formal model within which a concept is defined partly in terms of its relations to other concepts.

At the outset of their book, Katz and Kahn discuss nine common characteristics of open systems:

1. Open systems, like biological organisms, must import some form of energy from the environment in order to survive.

2. Open systems contain a through-put process by which the imported energy is transformed; the through-put of an organization may be the creation of a new product, the providing of a service, the modification or treatment of human beings, etc.

3. "Open systems export some product into the environment, whether it be the invention of an inquiring mind or a bridge constructed by an engineering firm." (p. 20)

4. An open system consists of cycles of events. The product exported to the environment furnishes sources of energy renewal for the input so that the cycle may be repeated. It is important to note in this context that the structure of a social system

is to be found in an interrelated set of events which return upon themselves to complete and renew a cycle of activities. It is events rather than

things which are structured, so that social structure is a dynamic rather than a static concept. (p. 21)

5. Open systems are further characterized by negative entropy. An open system imports more energy from its environment than it expends; it can thus store energy to counter entropic forces.

6. Energic inputs, which become transformed or altered by the through-put, are not the only form of system inputs. Information inputs, negative feedback, and the coding process are inputs of an informative character and serve to provide the system with information concerning its own functioning in relation to its environment.

7. An open system is characterized by a steady state and dynamic homeostasis. This does not imply a motionless or true equilibrium, but rather a force that seeks to preserve a constant ratio between the parts of the system. Thus, when one element in the system changes, forces are exerted to preserve the character of the system by the proportional alteration of all other elements. Thus, as with living organisms, organizational evolution is a symmetrical process.

8. Open systems become more differentiated and elaborated over time. Diffuse global patterns give way to more specialized functions.

9. Finally, open systems are characterized by the principle of equifinality. There is no *one best way* for a system to reach a given final state from a particular initial state. Contrariwise, given similar initial states, open systems may reach quite different final states. In short, there are a variety of paths between any two given points in a system's existence.

The underlying notion of open-system theory is that everything that does or can happen is dependent on everything else that does or can happen; that is, all events are correlated. Thus, the concept of cause and effect is discarded. While a closed system uses up all its energy in the through-put process and becomes simpler over time as a result of entropic processes, an open system has a permeable boundary that allows it to draw sustenance from its environment. Newcomb (1959) has written:

I have chosen to emphasize "system properties" rather than single variables which contribute to them, and consequently none of the variables has an enduring status either as independent or as dependent . . . a change in one system variable is likely (under certain conditions) to be followed by a specified change in another system variable, but according to others a change in the second is a precondition for a change in the first. (p. 388)

All elements of the system change when the value of any one is changed. That is, there is a redistribution of energy through some form of equilibration process. An open system is, therefore, dynamic; it is expending energy, and, as a result, it is in process and ongoing. (Doubtless the most wide-ranging treatment of system concepts and applications will be found in Buckley's 1968 compendium.)

The open-system model has also been vigorously advanced by the Tavistock group (e.g., Rice, 1963; Trist, Higgin, Murray, and Pollack, 1963) who have combined it with the less general concept of the sociotechnical system. The purpose of the sociotechnical concept is to bring into the same framework both the ideal efficiency of the system and the practicability of attaining the ideal with human beings and realistic conditions of work. Any productive organization, in this view, is the result of the interaction between technology and the system of relationships between those who perform the jobs (the social system). Each system influences the other (cf. Hunt, 1970, for a detailed discussion of these relations). This notion, of course, is not unlike Homans's.

However, the Tavistock group, by adding the notion of a sociotechnical system to the open-system model, served thereby to add recognition of the importance of the channels of interaction between the organization and its environment. Thus, the organization

suffers constraints from two sources. On the one hand, the environment controls raw material, labor, money, and so on, all at the input side, while the output of the organization depends on such variables as consumer preferences, the state of the economy, and government regulation. And if that is not enough, additional constraints are imposed on the organization by the expectations, values, and norms of its human incumbents.

Of utmost importance in this model, however, is the notion that human capacities, preferences, and expectations are not necessarily personalistic elements, but may be influenced by experiences within the organization. Thus, the functions of personnel selection and organizational design are of *equal* importance—human behavior in organizations is the result of the interaction between formal role requirements and the nature of people (cf. Hunt, 1967).

In a more recent volume from the Tavistock Institute, Miller and Rice (1967) have employed a boundary model as a framework for examining problems of organizational control (see also Tannenbaum, 1968). The focus of this model is to make a distinction between the boundaries of the activity system ("that complex of activities which is required to complete the process of transforming an intake into an output" [p. 6]) task group (comprising those individuals employed in an activity system), and sentient group ("being the group to which individuals are prepared to commit themselves and on which they depend for emotional support" [p. 253]). Miller and Rice presented various organizational models that represent different degrees of coincidence between task, sentient, and administrative boundaries and evaluate each in terms of their ability to control task performance, to ensure the commitment of members to the organizational objectives, and to regulate relations between task and sentient systems.

One of the major hypotheses posited by Miller and Rice is that in organizations in which task and sentient groups coincide on a more or less permanent basis, only short-term effectiveness can be achieved. "In the longer term such groups can inhibit change and hence can lead eventually to deterioration of performance and, in consequence, to social and psychological deprivation rather than to satisfaction" (p. 253). As an alternative, Miller and Rice promoted temporary project systems as a general solution. These authors felt that such temporary work groups (such as an airline flight crew) will discourage the formation of group standards detrimental to organization efficiency, while providing sufficient social relationships to satisfy relevant employee needs. Bennis and Slater (1968), of course, have made of such ideas as these a basis for general societal design.

In a related vein, Crozier (1964) has argued that for a given organization there is no such thing as *a* structure; rather, each organization may best be characterized as an aggregate of structures, for instance, a power structure, a communication structure, or a friendship structure. Thus, an organizational member may be seen as occupying a variety of positions with respect to the various structures in which he is included. In Crozier's view, such dimensions as work flow and dependence, as well as those mentioned above, may reveal numerous relationships not accounted for by the formal structure.

The recognition by the open-system model of the legion of variables and relationships affecting the behavior of social systems need not, however, imply that such phenomena are randomly distributed throughout an organization; they tend to be specialized by location. For example, Parsons (1960) has proposed that organizations exhibit three distinct levels of responsibility and control—technical, managerial, and institutional.

In his view, an organization contains substructures that exert forces to maintain a specific category of functions necessary to organizational survival. The technical or pro-duction structures are primarily concerned with the through-put of the organization—the processing or conversion of the input—and strive to achieve technical proficiency. The managerial structure services the technical subsystem by procuring necessary resources for the input and by mediating between the technical structure and the environmental elements to which the product will be exported. The managerial level controls or administers the technical substructure (not necessarily unilaterally or even unidirectionally, it should be noted) by deciding such matters as what the business of the organization shall be, the scale of its operations, and employment and purchasing policy.

Finally, the organization itself is part of a wider social system, which is the source of higher level support for the organization's goals. Although an organization may be relatively independent with regard to its formal controls, it must depend on its environment for meaning, legitimation, and resources. The over-all responsibility for maintaining a favorable environment for the organization lies at the institutional level.

Parsons further argued that at each of the two points of articulation between the three levels there is a qualitative break in the simple continuity of line authority because the functions at each level are qualitatively different. The difference is one of kind, not degree. Organizational survival consists of the adequate functioning of these three levels as well as adequate interaction. If any level withholds its contribution, the system is dissipate.

Katz and Kahn (1966) have expanded Parson's notion by offering a somewhat finer articulation of basic organizational substructures. Production structures are concerned with the work that gets done; supportive structures procure the input, dispose of the output, and deal with institutional relations; maintenance structures promote adequate role performances; adaptive subsystems serve to change the organization in line with a changing environment; and managerial subsystems direct, adjudicate, and control the several subsystems and activities of the organization.

The upshot of this line of thinking is that since these basic substructures are interdependent, a change in any one will bear implications of change for the others: For instance, differences in technology will make for differences at the managerial, supportive, and other levels; differences in environment will, in turn, place different demands on the productive, managerial, supportive, and other levels (cf. Hunt, 1970; Udy, 1965).

Thus a strong case has been made by several recent theories of organization for the recognition of the nature of the interaction between a social system and its environment, on the one hand, and its people on the other. By the use of the open-system model as a framework and conceptual language for describing organizations there is the possibility for a more thorough (but also more complex) understanding of organizational behavior:

It is too soon to predict whether this approach will become a dominant guide to empirical work or whether "system" will become merely the latest "in" word among organizational psychologists. (Quinn and Kahn, 1967, p. 461)

Contribution of Role Theory

In years past, the mind-body problem was a leading topic for philosophical discussion. For many, the tenability of the mind-body model depended on discovering the precise locus of the meeting of the two. The contemporary person-environment dilemma has prompted a similar search for a conceptual meeting point for social structural forces and individual personalistic forces. Programmatically, at least, probably the most satisfactory solution came about when Linton (1936) gave the notion of *role* a central place in the social sciences. Introduced to social psychology by Newcomb (1950), this concept has been explicated and advanced by such writers as Merton (1957), Shibutani (1961), Banton (1965), and Sarbin and Allen (1968). Until rather recently, however, the concept of role occupied only a secondary position among social science concepts, partly because earlier sociological and anthropological role notions tended to focus solely upon structural influences on personality. The advent of systems approaches to the study of large groups, however, gave the concept of role a new lease on life by balancing it with the personalistic forces that have traditionally been the concern of psychology.

Somewhere within the action system that is the functioning organization, structural and personal forces jointly draw a bead, as it were, on the individual, controlling his performances. And we have now reached the point of development in role concepts where, in their exemplary analysis of organizations, Katz and Kahn (1966) proposed role concepts as:

the major means for linking the individual and organizational levels of research and theory; it is at once the building block of social systems and the summation of the requirements with which such systems confront their members as individuals. (p. 197)

Highlighting distinctions between structure and person while concerned with their integration, Hunt (1967) pointed out that a social system may be viewed conceptually as an interlocking complex of positions (the structural aspect), or functional divisions of labor, which are to be populated by people who are expected to fulfill certain behavior requirements and possess certain personal attributes associated with each position. Since a social system is a system of interdependent activities, positions within a social structure exist in relationships with certain other positions. Thus, the "rights and duties" of a particular *focal position* exist with respect to a *counterposition*.

This complementary contrast is, of course, a function basically of the complex patterns of behavior organized around these positions and embodying the relevant mutual expectations (the rights and duties) *vis à vis* one another held by occupants of positions. It is possible, therefore, to regard social process as an interaction of positions patterned in terms of these complementary expectations which are themselves called *roles*. (p. 259)

Thus, role and its personalistic correlate, identity, represent the implications of social position incumbency and can be comprehensively described only with reference to other roles, which bear a complementary relation to the focal role.

We cannot explicate the ideas here, but we can say simply that since persons occupy multiple positions in life and are only partly involved in any single position they occupy, they have multiple identities that combine in various ways to affect their views and the enactments of their singular roles, And, whatever else may be involved, the modes of a man's participation in structured social intercourse will be reflected in his concept of himself and in the fabric of his personality.

The essential point, then, is not simply that role serves a linking function; more than that. In its modern forms, it exemplifies and operationalizes the merging of social and individual phenomena heretofore treated separatistically. Roles are undoubtedly social phenomena. However, they are not only external "demands," they are dynamic interactional processes carried out by individuals who color their performances personal. By way of reciprocity, however, through their identity implications roles become operationally integral to individual personality. Thus, roles more than link the individual and the social (or structural)—they unite them.

Role Conflict

Cyert and MacCrimmon (1968) made some of these same points, in their discussion of organizational processes, and accorded a prominent place to role concepts. In particular, they identified organizational roles as points of linkage and also as principal sources of conflict between individuals and organizations. In the study cited earlier, Hunt (1967) explicated five role varieties that are helpful in conceptualizing role differentiation. These focus attention on the interplay of patterns of expectation and performance within the role system. The importance of the distinctions he draws between aspects of role-taking is that a lack of fit between any of them will result in some degree of role conflict, the effects of which have been the topic of two relatively recent major organizational studies and resulting theories.

Gross, Mason, and McEachern (1958) studied the perception and resolution of role conflict among school superintendents. They focused on both interrole conflicts (resulting from the occupancy of multiple positions) and intrarole conflicts (resulting from the perception of conflicting sent-roles[4] vis-à-vis a single focal position). On the basis of their data, they concluded that there were three major cognitive styles employed by superintendents in the resolution of perceived role conflict.

The first style they called the *moral* orientation. Individuals in this category give most weight to evaluating the legitimacy of the conflicting expectations or the *right* of others to hold such expectations. With minimal attention to the likelihood of sanctions for nonconformity, this style emphasizes conformity to the demand seen as most legitimate. The second type of orientation is called *expedient*. Priority here is given to a consideration of the sanctions others will bring to bear if the individual does not conform to their expectations. The resolution style in this case is to minimize negative

4. Communications by persons intended to influence the role behavior of others (cf. Kahn, Wolfe, Quinn, Snoek, and Rosenthal, 1964).

sanctions involved in the role-conflict situation. The nature of the right of others to hold particular expectations is not nearly so important in this case as the perceived severity of the probable sanctions. This superintendent, therefore, will choose to conform to the expectations of those whose sanctions he fears most. *Moral expedient* is the third orientation toward role conflict resolution. Here no primacy is given to the dimensions of legitimacy or sanctions; rather, both are considered equally in choosing a course of resolution.

Among the numerous empirical findings of these authors was the high job satisfaction reported among superintendents who perceived agreement between the sent-role from the school board and their own role stereotypes. What is probably conceptually more important was the consistent finding of Gross *et al.* (1958) that the effects of role conflict on job satisfaction and expressions of worry among the superintendents were mediated by the characteristic anxiety level of the individual. Implicit in this finding is the notion that personality may be the result of an interaction of social structural conditions and personalistic dispositions. The difficulty in this particular study is that Gross and his colleagues dealt only with perceptions of role conflict and did not attempt to deal with the accuracy of perception. So the social structure is not truly represented in their research.

Clearly the most ambitious attempt to employ the role concept in organizational studies is that of Kahn *et al.* (1964). Borrowing Merton's (1957) formulation of a role set, these authors built a model that is specifically designed to integrate properties of a social structure with characteristics of people who populate it. They called their model a role episode and posited that it consists of a series of events. Specifically, role pressures emanate from members of the role set—the discrepancy between their own expectations and their evaluations of how well the focal person's behavior measures up.

Members of the role set attempt to reduce this discrepancy by exerting pressures on the focal person to adjust his behavior to conform with their expectations. These pressures induce perceptual and cognitive experiences in the focal person that can lead to certain adjustive or maladjustive responses. The role-senders monitor any subsequent behavior of the focal person and reward him if they are satisfied with his adjustment or exert further pressures if they are not. This is a cyclic, ongoing process.

Role conflict and ambiguity may thus occur in two ways. In the first case it may occur as a property of the social structure where, in fact, the sent-roles from role-set members exert pressures for various mutually exclusive behaviors on the part of the focal person (cf. also Hunt, 1967). Role ambiguity exists where the sent-role expectations lack sufficient clarity to be translated into behavior by the focal person. The second variety of role conflict occurs at the perceptual level and may or may not correspond with an actual state of affairs. Thus the focal person may not perceive conflict where it actually exists, or he may perceive it where it does not exist, or he may perceive it where it does indeed exist.

Furthermore, Kahn and his associates hypothesized that the degree of structural and perceived role conflict varies as a function of several enduring organizational and personal characteristics. For example, organizational positions vary in their vulnerability to conflicting expectations. Typically, the less structured and explicit the job requirement, the closer the position is to the boundary of the organization, and the larger the number of bosses, subordinates, and equals associated with a given position, the greater is the likelihood that role conflict (and the tensions and frustrations, which may occur as a result of its experience) will vary with such personalistic dispositions as needs for cognition, tolerance of ambiguity, neurotic anxiety, or need achievement.

Thus, these authors posited that the

degree of role conflict and its relation to individual experience and reactions is highly conditional and depends on numerous organizational and personal attributes. Furthermore, variables such as job satisfaction and general mental health are anchored, via the role-set concept, to both the social structure and individual dispositions. These authors have further contributed to knowledge by operationalizing and testing their hypotheses—successfully.

The theories and data of the Kahn *et al.* (1964) study and the Gross *et al.* (1958) study have seriously challenged many old and static notions of organizational behavior. They have demonstrated crucial functions of personalistic dispositions as mediators between formal system requirements and individual outcomes. In other words, neither can stand alone as a comprehensive explanation of human behavior in organizations. Furthermore, they have provided evidence of the inadequacy of the personality versus organization hypothesis. While Gross *et al.* have shown that simply holding a high-ranking position does not render a man free from emotional problems, Kahn *et al,* have provided data comparing six hierarchical organizational levels and showing that tension induced by role strain increases with increasing rank. Since role conflict is linked with emotional reactions and mental health in general, it is apparently true that if the right measures are chosen, management positions may not be as rosy as the personality-organization theorists hold. Kahn *et al.* have clearly shown that the organizational locus of emotional maladjustment can occur anywhere in an organization and is not necessarily restricted to unskilled or low level workers. Employee reactions apparently depend on the nature of the organization, the nature of the job, and the nature of the person. It seems plain that Katzell's (1962) thesis warrants being taken seriously (and Quinn and Kahn's 1967, as well). It is neither meaningful nor useful to promote normative, one-sided theories intended to account for all organizational situations. There is good evidence that organizational behavior is the outcome of a variety of highly conditional and highly contingent relationships and situations. Future theory will need to build on the foundations of those premises.

REFERENCES

Argyris, C. *Personality and organization.* New York: Harper, 1957.

Argyris, C. Understanding human behavior in organizations: One viewpoint. In M. Haire (Ed.), *Modern organization theory.* New York: Wiley, 1959.

Argyris, C. *Integrating the individual and the organization.* New York: Wiley, 1964.

Banton, M. *Roles.* New York: Basic Books, 1965.

Barker, R. G. On the nature of the environment. *Journal of Social Issues*, 1963, 19, 17-38.

Bass, B. M. *Organizational psychology.* Boston: Allyn & Bacon, 1965.

Bell, D. *Work and its discontents.* Boston: Beacon Press, 1956.

Bennis, W. G. Organizational developments and the fate of bureaucracy. In L.L. Cummings and W.E. Scott (Eds.), *Organizational behavior and human performance.* Homewood, Ill.: Irwin-Dorsey, 1969.

Bennis, W. G., Organic Populism. *Psychology Today*, 1970, 3, 48-71.

Bennis, W.G., and Shepard, H. A theory of group development. *Human Relations*, 1965, 9, 415-57.

Bennis, W.G., and Slater, P.E. *The temporary society.* New York: Harper & Row, 1968.

Blake, R. R., and Mouton, J. *Corporate excellence through grid organizational development.* Houston, Tex.: Gulf Corporation, 1968.

Blau, P. A formal theory of differentiation in organizations. *American Sociological Review*, 1970, 35, 201-19.

Blauner, R. *Alienation and freedom: The factory worker and his industry.* Chicago: University of Chicago Press, 1964.

Buckley, W. (Ed.) *Modern systems research for the behavioral scientist*. Chicago: Aldine, 1968.

Caplow, T., and McGee, R. *The academic marketplace*. New York: Basic Books, 1958.

Carey, A. The Hawthorne studies: A radical criticism. *American Sociological Review*, 1967, 32, 403-17.

Cleland, D. I., and King, W. R. *Systems analysis and project management*. New York: McGraw-Hill, 1968.

Coch, L., and French, J. R. P. Overcoming resistance to change. *Human Relations*, 1948, 1, 512-33.

Crozier, M. *The bureaucratic phenomenon*. Chicago: University of Chicago Press, 1964.

Cyert, R. M., and McCrimmon, K. R. Organizations. In G. Lindzey and E. Aronson (Eds.), *Handbook of social psychology*. Vol. 1, 2nd ed. Boston: Addison-Wesley, 1968.

Cyert, R. M., and March, J. G. *A behavioral theory of the firm*. Englewood Cliffs, N.J.: Prentice-Hall, 1963.

Dawis, R. V., Lofquist, L. H., and Weiss, D. J. A theory of work adjustment. *Minnesota Studies in Vocational Rehabilitation*, 1968, 23, Bulletin 47.

Durkheim, E. *De la division du travail social*. [Division of labor in society] (Trans. G. Simpson; New York: Macmillan, 1933, 1947). Paris: F. Alcan, 1902.

Festinger, L. Informal social communication. *Psychological Review*, 1950, 57, 271-82.

Fiedler, F. E. Engineer the job to fit the manager. *Harvard Business Review*, 1965, 43, 115-22.

French, J. R. P., Israel, J., and Ås, D. An experiment on participation in a Norwegian factory. *Human Relations*, 1960, 13, 3-19.

Galbraith, J. K. *The new industrial state*. Boston: Houghton Mifflin, 1967.

Gellerman, S.W. *Motivation and productivity*. New York: American Management Association, 1963.

Gilbreth, F. B. *Motion study*. New York: Van Nostrand, 1911.

Glans, T. B., Grad, B., Holstein, D., Meyers, W. E., and Schmidt, R. N. *Management systems*. New York: Holt, Rinehart & Winston, 1968.

Gordon, M. M. *Assimilation in American life: The role of race, religion, and national origins*. New York: Oxford, 1964.

Gouldner, A.W. *Patterns of industrial bureaucracy*. New York: Free Press, 1954.

Gross, N., Mason, W. S., and McEachern, A.W. *Explorations in role analysis*. New York: Wiley, 1958.

Gulick, L., and Urwick, F. L. (Eds.) *Papers on the science of administration*. New York: Institute of Public Administration, 1937.

systems analysis. In J. March (Ed.), *Handbook of organizations*. Chicago: Rand McNally, 1965.

Hackman, R. *The motivated working adult*. New York: American Management Association, 1969.

Haire, M. Philosophy of organizations. In D.M. Bowerman and F.M. Fillerup (Eds.), *Management: Organization and planning*. New York: McGraw-Hill, 1963.

Hall, R. The concept of bureaucracy: An empirical assessment. *American Journal of Sociology*, 1963, 69, 32-40.

Harvey, E. Technology and the structure of organizations. *American Sociological Review*, 1968, 33, 247-59.

Herzberg, F., Mausner, B., and Snyderman, B. *The motivation to work*. 2nd ed. New York: Wiley, 1959.

Hickson, D. J., Pugh, D. S., and Pheysey, D. C. Operations technology and organization structure. *Administrative Science Quarterly*, 1969, 17, 378-97.

Hollander, E. P., and Hunt, R.G. (Eds.) *Current perspectives in social psychology*. New York: Oxford, 1967.

Homans, G. C. *The human group*. New York: Harcourt, Brace & World, 1950.

Hunt, R. G. Role and role conflict. In E.P. Hollander and R. G. Hunt (Eds.), *Current perspectives in social psychology*. 2nd ed. New York: Oxford, 1965.

Hunt, R. G. An essay on the profit motive. *Defense Management Journal*, 1969, 5, 6-11. (a)

Hunt, R. G. Review of R.C. Hackman, *The*

Motivated Working Adult. Administrative Science Quarterly, 1969, 14, 614-15. (b)

Hunt, R. G. Technology and organization. *Academy of Management Journal*, 1970, 13, 235-53.

Indik, B. P. Some effects of organization size on member attitudes and behavior. *Human Relations*, 1963, 16, 369-84.

Indik, B. P. Organization size and member participation: Some empirical tests of alternative explanations. *Human Relations*, 1965, 18, 339-50.

Jasinski, F. J. Use and misuses of efficiency controls. *Harvard Business Review*, 1956, 34, 105-12.

Kahn, R. L., Wolfe, D. M., Quinn, R. P., Snoek, J. D., and Rosenthal, R. A. *Organizational stress: Studies in role conflict and ambiguity*. New York: Wiley, 1964.

Katz, D. The motivational basis of organizational behavior. *Behavioral Science*, 1964, 9, 131-46.

Katz, D., and Kahn, R. L. *The social psychology of organizations*. New York: Wiley, 1966.

Katz, F. E. Explaining informal work groups in complex organizations: The case for autonomy in structure. *Administrative Science Quarterly*, 1965, 10, 204-21.

Katzell, R. A. Contrasting systems of work organization. *American Psychologist*, 1962, 17, 102-8.

Katzell, R. A., Barrett, R. S., and Parker, T. C. Job satisfaction, job performance, and situational characteristics. *Journal of Applied Psychology*, 1961, 45, 65-72.

Koontz, H. Making sense of management theory. *Harvard Business Review*, 1962, 40, 25.

Leavitt, H. J. Unhuman organizations. *Harvard Business Review*, 1962, 40, 90-98.

Levinson, H., Price, C. R., Munden, K. J., Mandel, H. J., and Solley, C. M. *Men, management and mental health*. Cambridge: Harvard University Press, 1962.

Lewin, K. *Field theory in social science*. New York: Harper, 1951.

Lewin, K. Group decision and social change. In E. Maccoby, T. Newcomb, and E. Hartley (Eds.), *Readings in social psychology*. 3rd ed. New York: Holt, Rinehart & Winston, 1958.

Likert, R. *New patterns of management*. New York: McGraw-Hill, 1961.

Likert, R. *The human organization*. New York: McGraw-Hill, 1967.

Linton, R. *The study of man*. New York: Appleton-Century, 1936.

Maier, N. *Psychology in industry*. Boston: Houghton Mifflin, 1955.

Mann, F. C., and Hoffman, L. R. *Automation and the worker: A study of social change in power plants*. New York: Holt, 1960.

March, J. G., and Simon, H. A. *Organizations*. New York: Wiley, 1958.

Marx, K. *Capital*. London: Allen & Unwin, 1887. (Translation reproduced and supplemented, 1943.)

Marx, K. *Selected writings in sociology and social philosophy*. (Ed. and Trans. T. B. Bottomore and M. Rubel) New York: McGraw-Hill, 1964.

Maslow, A. H. *Motivation and personality*. New York: Harper, 1954.

Maslow, A. H. *Eupsychian management*. Homewood, Ill.: Irwin-Dorsey, 1965.

Mayo, E. *The human problems of industrial civilization*. New York: Macmillan, 1933.

McGregor, D. *The human side of enterprise*. New York: McGraw-Hill, 1960.

Mechanic, D. Some considerations in the methodology of organizational studies. In H. Leavitt (Ed.), *The social science of organizations*. Englewood Cliffs, N.J.: Prentice-Hall, 1963.

Merton, R. K. *Social theory and social structure*. Rev. ed. New York: Free Press, 1957.

Miller, E. J., and Rice, A. K. *Systems of organization: The control of task and sentient boundaries*. London: Tavistock, 1967.

Miller, J. G. *Living systems*. New York: Wiley, 1968.

Morane, J. H. *A sociology of human systems*. New York: Appleton-Century-Crofts, 1967.

Mouzelis, N. P. *Organization and bureaucracy*. Chicago: Aldine, 1967.

Neff, W. S. *Work and human behavior*. New York: Atherton, 1968.

Newcomb, T. M. *Social psychology*. New York: Dryden, 1950.

Newcomb, T. M. Individual systems of orientation. In S. Koch (Ed.). *Psychology: A study of a science*. Vol. 3. New York: McGraw-Hill, 1959.

Opsahl, R. L., and Dunnette, M. D. The role of financial compensation in industrial motivation. *Psychological Bulletin*, 1966, 66, 94-118.

Parsons, T. *Structure and process in modern societies*. New York: Free Press, 1960.

Perrow, C. A framework for the comparative analysis of organizations. *American Sociological Review*, 1967, 32, 194-209.

Porter, L. W., and Lawler, E. E. Properties of organization structure in relation to job attitudes and job behavior. *Psychological Bulletin*, 1965, 64, 23-51.

Porter, L. W., and Lawler, E. E. *Managerial attitudes and performance*. Homewood, Ill.: Irwin-Dorsey, 1968.

Pugh, D. S. Modern organization theory: A psychological and sociological study. *Psychological Bulletin*, 1966, 66, 235-51.

Quinn, A. P., and Kahn, R. L. Organizational psychology. *Annual Review of Psychology*, 1967, 18, 437-66.

Rice, A. K. *The enterprise and its environment*. London: Tavistock, 1963.

Roethlisberger, F. J., and Dickson, W. J. *Management and the worker*. Cambridge: Harvard University Press, 1939.

Ronan, W. W. Individual and situational variables relating to job satisfaction. *Journal of Applied Psychology Monograph*, 1970, 54, No. 1, Pt. 2.

Roy, D. F. Banana time: Job satisfaction and informal interaction. *Human Organization*, 1960, 18, 158-68.

Rubin, I., and Hunt, R. G. *Some aspects of managerial control in interpenetrating systems: The case of government-industry relations*. Tech. Rep. No. 7. State University of New York at Buffalo: Grant NGR 33-015-061, National Aeronautics and Space Administration, July 1969.

Sarbin, T. R., and Allen, V. L. Role theory. G. Lindzey and E. Aronson (Eds.), *Handbook of social psychology*. Vol. 1. 2nd ed. Boston: Addison-Wesley, 1968.

Sayles, L., and Strauss, G. *Human behavior in organizations*. Englewood Cliffs, N.J.: Prentice-Hall, 1966.

Schein, E. H. *Organizational psychology*. Englewood Cliffs, N.J.: Prentice-Hall, 1965.

Schein, E. H., and Bennis, W. G. *Personal and organizational change through group methods: The laboratory approach*. New York: Wiley, 1965.

Schlesinger, A. *A thousand days*. Boston: Houghton Mifflin, 1965.

Scott, W. G. Organizational theory: An overview and an appraisal. *Academy of Management Journal*, 1961, 4, 7-27.

Scott, W. R. Theory of organizations. In R.E.L. Farris (Ed.), *Handbook of modern sociology*. Chicago: Rand McNally, 1964.

Shibutani, T. *Society and personality*. Englewood Cliffs, N.J.: Prentice-Hall, 1961.

Simon, H. *Administrative behavior*. 2nd ed. New York: Macmillan, 1957.

Simon, H. *The shape of automation for men and management*. New York: Harper & Row, 1965.

Smith, P. E., and Cranny, C. J. Psychology of men at work. *Annual Review of psychology*, 1968, 19, 467-96.

Sommer, R. Small group ecology. *Psychological Bulletin*, 1967, 67, 145-52.

Sommer, R. *Personal space*. Englewood Cliffs, N.J.: Prentice-Hall, 1968.

Strauss, G. Some notes on power equalization. In H. Leavitt (Ed.), *The social science of organizations*. Englewood Cliffs, N.J.: Prentice-Hall, 1963.

Strauss, G. Human relations—1968 style. *Industrial Relations*, 1968, 7, 262-72.

Tannenbaum, A. S. *Social psychology of the work organization*. Belmont, Calif.: Wadsworth, 1966.

Tannenbaum, A. S. *Control in organizations*. New York: McGraw-Hill, 1968.

Taylor, F. W. *Scientific management*. New York: Harper & Row, 1911.

Thompson, J. D. *Organizations in action*. York: McGraw-Hill, 1967.

Thompson, V. *Modern organization*. New York: Knopf, 1961.

Trist, E. L., Higgin, G. W., Murray, H., and Pollack, A. B. *Organizational choice*. London: Tavistock, 1963.

Udy, S. H. The comparative analysis of organizations. In J. March (Ed.), *Handbook of organizations*. Chicago: Rand McNally, 1965.

von Bertalanffy, L. The theory of open systems in physics and biology. *Science*, 1950, 111, 23-38.

Vroom, V. H. *Work and motivation*. New York: Wiley, 1964.

Vroom, V. H., and Mann, F. Leader authoritarianism and employee attitudes. *Personnel Psychology*, 1960, 13, 125-140.

Walker, C. R. Life in the automatic factory. *Harvard Business Review*, 1958, 36, 111-19.

Weber, M. *Theory of social and economic organization*. (Trans. by A. M. Henderson and T. Parsons of Pt. I, *Wirtschaft und Gesellschaft*) New York: Oxford, 1947. (2nd ed., Free Press, 1964.)

Whyte, W. F. *Organization behavior: Theory and application*. Homewood, Ill.: Irwin-Dorsey, 1969.

Woodward, J. *Industrial organisation: Theory and practice*. London: Oxford, 1965.

16
Organization Structure:
Is Technology the Key?

DAVID HICKSON, DEREK PUGH, and DIANA PHEYSEY

Does technology determine organization? Is the form of organization in a chemical plant, for instance, dictated by the fact that it *is* a chemical plant—that is, by its highly automated equipment and continuous flow process? And is the organization of a batch production engineering factory shaped by the way its work is done—that is, by its rows of machine tools and its varying batches?

This is a contentious question which bears on the basis of management practice, as it affects and is affected by the framework of organization through which managers work. For it also asks how far do the number of levels of management, the centralization of major job decisions, the proliferation of standard procedures, the development of specialist "service" sections, and the many other features of the structure of an organization depend on its technology?

When senior managers from very different kinds of undertakings meet at conferences or in airport lounges, they frequently find they share many common problems. There are some of the same headaches in an oil refinery as in a jobbing shop. This broad area of shared problems has been the stimulus to the efforts made over the years by managers

and by consultants to agree on and to commit to writing general principles of management. Such principles include clear lines of authority and responsibility (one man, one boss), limited spans of control (for effective supervision) and so on.

The need for general principles has always been especially pressing in management education as a foundation for teaching about general management. Small wonder, then, that when Joan Woodward's booklet *Management and Technology* was published by HMSO in 1958 it generated wide discussion. Indeed, the discussion actively continues, revived by the appearance in 1965 of her expanded version *Industrial Organisation* (Oxford University Press). For she and her colleagues at South-East Essex Technical College saw things differently. To them there was no one best form of organization. The principles which had been evolved might well apply in large batch and mass production firms, for they rested primarily on the experience of managers and consultants in this range of technology. But outside this range, in the unit/jobbing and process technologies, different principles might be required.

Reprinted from *Personnel Management*, 1970, 2 (2), 21-26, by permission of the publisher, Mercury House Business Publications, Ltd.

To quote from the 1958 booklet, "It was possible to trace a cause and effect relationship between a system of production and its associated organizational pattern and, as a result, to predict what the organizational requirements of a firm are likely to be, given its *production system*."

Woodward took this view as a result of comparing as many as eighty firms on a unit and small batch, large batch and mass, and flow process classification. She found, for example, that the line of command from the chief executive of each firm was shortest in unit and small batch firms, lengthened in large batch and mass, and was longest in process firms. Another example of this relationship was the ratio of managers to total personnel, which also increased from unit up to process technology.

In contrast, it appeared that the spans of control of the first-line production supervisors were widest in large batch and mass production (averaging 46), but dropped away in unit and small batch on the one side (to average 22) and in process on the other (to average 14). Other suggested examples of this pattern were clear definition of duties and amount of paperwork, which were also greatest in large batch/mass technology.

FRESH RESEARCH IN THE MIDLANDS

In 1961, seven years after Woodward had studied South-East Essex, the Industrial Administration Research Unit at what is now the University of Aston in Birmingham embarked on a new program of organizational research under the leadership of Derek Pugh. This included a fresh examination of the relationship between the technology of organizations and their structures.

Some years of work were devoted to devising more accurate and reliable means of comparing structural features than had hitherto existed. Forms of measurement were used which enabled numerical scores to be assigned to organizations to denote their structural and other characteristics. Organi-

zations could thus be given a score for their degree of development of specialist jobs—a specialized roles score. This would be high where there were specialists in many functions such as finance, personnel, transport, buying, etc., and low where there were few. Likewise, organizations could be scored on the extent to which they had standardized routine procedures, formalized documentation and centralization/decentralization of major decisions. (This work is fully described by Pugh, Hickson, Hinings and Turner in "Dimensions of Organisational Structure," *Administrative Science Quarterly*, June, 1968, Vol. 13, No. 1, pp. 64-105.)

Fifty-two diverse organizations were studied. Among them were thirty-one manufacturing units, ranging through vehicles and vehicle components, various engineering works, foodstuffs, glass, domestic appliances, toys, etc. The problem was to find and to express a common denominator in the technologies of these manufacturing units, in terms which their production systems might be contrasted and compared.

MEASUREMENT OF TECHNOLOGY

Woodward had used the conventional production engineering unit/mass/process distinction, subdivided into ten categories (and slightly altered in her 1965 book). With this as a starting point, a measure of *production continuity* was worked out in the form shown in Table 16-1. It attempts to be more precisely defined than the Woodward headings, though it still leaves a lot to be desired.

One basic problem in devising this measure was "How small is a small batch?" This difficulty impedes comparison of different factories which have different batches of different products. It was tackled by introducing the criterion of time. Whether batches fell into the "small" or "large" categories was decided by the frequency with which equipment was reset; for example, batches were called "small" if resetting occurred once or more each week. The

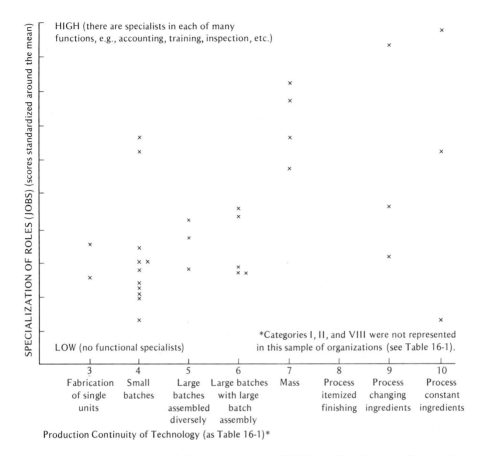

Fig. 16-1. Technology and Role (Job) Specialization on 31 Midlands Manufacturing Organizations

intervals selected were arbitrary and, though useful on these Midlands organizations, are flexible and might be adjusted for other organizations and other purposes.

Once the thirty-one manufacturing organizations were placed on this scale of production continuity they could be given scores; high scores implying continuous flow process with largely constant materials, low scores implying sporadic workflow piece by piece. Technologies were then related to structures with the aid of the new scoring methods.

Did the organizations with the most continuous production technologies have the widest range of specialist jobs? One way of finding out is to plot the scores of the thirty-one organizations on production continuity against their scores on role (job) specialization. As can be seen in Figure 16-1, there is some possible relationship between production continuity and specialized roles. Organizations with process technologies which score high on production continuity may well have the greatest role specialization, but not always by any means.

However, plotting *size* against role specialization produces a much more positive result (see Figure 16-2). The biggest organizations, that is those with the most employees, do

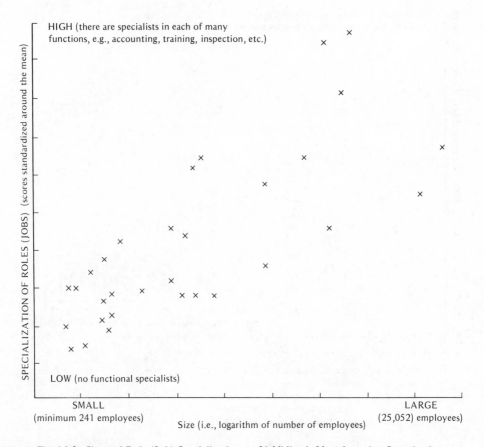

Fig. 16-2. Size and Role (Job) Specialization on 31 Midlands Manufacturing Organizations

indeed tend to have the greatest proliferation of specialist control and service sections, that is the highest specialized role scores. Role specialization scores of, say, sixty or seventy indicate that organizations scoring this high will probably have jobs for specialists in buying, in stock control, transport and despatch, wages, costing and other aspects of finance, in training, employment, and various other personnel activities, in different sections of sales and marketing, perhaps in market research, in work study or operations research in production control, and so on, and so on. Smaller organizations do not have all these and therefore score

lower. The association between size and role specialization is strong enough to string out the scores plotted on the graph from the lower left to the top right.

This pattern immediately implies a strong relationship between the two factors plotted, that is, a co-relation between them. The degree of correlation can be more precisely expressed by calculating a correlation coefficient. The strong relationship between size and role specialization in Figure 16-2 is expressed by a ("product-moment") coefficient of 0.83, but the moderate relationship between the production continuity of technology and specialized roles in Figure 16-1 gives a coefficient of 0.52—it can be shown to be partly due to the effects of size, in any case.

Table 16-2 lists a number of representative correlation coefficients between several features of organization and technology, size, and "dependence." High coefficients show an association between the two factors concerned. *Exact* fit between the two (so that organizations with high scores on one would have equivalently high scores on the other, low scorers would score low on both, and so on) would produce a coefficient of 1.00. This never occurs in this sort of work, and the highest coefficient is the 0.83 reflecting Figure 16-2 (Table 16-2, column 2). If there were no association whatever between two factors the coefficient would be 0.00, as it is between Centralization of Decisions and Production Continuity (Table 16-2, column 1).

Few Links with Technology

Table 16-2 shows that relationships between technology and organizational features are few and slight, and are dwarfed by the links that organization has with other factors such as size and "dependence." In column 1, the relationships between organizational features and production continuity (the unit/batch-mass/process measure) are small, for the apparent link with specialized roles (0.52) shrinks away when subjected to further analysis, taking account of size differences.

It is not column 1, technology, that is impressive, but column 2, size. The features of organization shown are overwhelmingly associated with the size of the organization. The bigger the organization, the more people get specialized jobs, are constrained by standard procedures, and have to cope with paperwork; though, on the other hand, some of those at lower levels can take more official decisions.

This last, centralization versus decentralization, is even more affected by "indepen-

dence" (Table 16-2, column 3). The independence measure denotes how far a unit of organization depends on other units (either inside or outside the same parent group) for services or materials; and whether it is a relatively small part of a large parent group or is independent. The correlation shows that it is being dependent on external units, and not the technology used, which is mainly associated with having centralized decisions.

This result immediately aroused interest. It had been anticipated that the form of organization *would* be broadly tied to the kind of technology, particularly because of Woodward's findings. Now this was *not* necessarily so.

What is more, using a second independently developed measure of technology called Workflow Integration, it was *still* not so. This second measure yielded much the same outcome, as Table 16-2 shows in its fourth column. Correlations with it are insignificant compared with those with size, with independence, and with other factors such as geographical dispersion and producing to customer specification which are not shown in the table. In other words, these factors have more to do with organization than has technology.

The Workflow Integration measure has affinities with the Production Continuity scale, but it is not based on the unit/batch-mass/process notion as such. It is an entirely fresh development by the Research Unit at Aston which combines a series of fundamental ideas in the production engineering field. These include the degree of mechanization and automation in the equipment used; the rigidity or flexibility of the sequence of operations carried out by the equipment in terms of the feasibility of re-routing work, the versatility of the equipment, the availability of buffer stocks between operating stages, etc.; the sequential linking or otherwise of manufacturing departments; and how far the standard of what is done can be

Table 16-1. Production Continuity—a Further Operationalization of Woodward's Classification of Production Systems

	Woodward Classification	Scale of Production Continuity	31 Manufacturing Organizations
Unit and small batch	I. Production of simple units to customers' orders	Simple units=units basically *single-piece*, not assemblies, produced one by one.	0
Unit and small batch	II. Production of technically complex units	Complex units=*assemblies*, produced one by one.	0
Unit and small batch	III. Fabrication of large equipment in stages	*Fabrication* one by one, in which workpeople come to the unit of output (which moves about very infrequently) rather than the unit moves around to different workpeople.	2
Unit and small batch	IV. Production of small batches	Small batches=equipment reset every week or, more often, for outputs measured in *items*.	11
Large batch and mass	V. Production of components in large batches subsequently assembled diversely	Large batches=equipment reset at intervals longer than a week for outputs measured in items: BUT items *assembled diversely* (i.e., variety of assembly sequences, including assembly by unit and/or small batch methods).	3
Large batch and mass	VI. Production of large batches, assembly line type	Large batches, as no V, but with *large batch assembly*.	5
Large batch and mass	VII. Mass production	Mass=*batch size, measured* in items, is indefinite (i.e., a change of batch requires decisions on (a) design modification, (b) re-tooling, which are beyond the normal authority of the line production management and production planning to vary production programmes).	4
Process	VIII. Process production combined with the preparation of a product for sale by large-batch or mass-production methods	Process=throughputs measured by weight or volume: BUT outputs become *items at finishing stage*.	0
Process	IX. Process production of chemicals in batches	Process, but *ingredients* (i.e., recipes) *of the throughputs change periodically*.	3
Process	X. Continuous flow production of liquids, gases, and solid shapes	Process, but *constant ingredients* (i.e., recipe change is beyond the normal authority of the line production management and production planning to vary production programmes).	3

*The Predominant Technology of an organization was assessed, giving particular weight to its highest degree of "continuity."

Table 16-2. Relationships Between Features of Organization and Selected Factors, as Indicated by Correlation Coefficients (Product-Moment)

	Technology: Production Continuity	Size: Log. of Number of Employees	Independence	Technology: Workflow Integration
	(1)	(2)	(3)	(4)
Some features of organization				
Specialized roles (degree of specialized differentiation of jobs)	0·52*	0·83*	0·04	0·25
Standardized procedures (degree of standardized routine)	0·35	0·65*	−0·12	0·19
Formalized documentation (degree of formal records and paperwork)	0·27	0·67*	−0·09	0·04
Centralization of decisions (degree of concentration of authority in a controlling board or with chief executive)	0·00	−0·47*	−0·54*	−0·05

*Beyond 99 per cent level of confidence.

Table 16-3

Summary of type of items used, in combination, to constitute the measure of workflow integration

A highly Workflow Integrated technology is signified by:

(a) Automatic repeat-cycle equipment, selfadjusting.
(b) Single-purpose equipment.
(c) Fixed "line" or sequence of operations.
(d) Single input point at commencement of "line."
(e) No waiting time between operations.
(f) No "buffer stocks" between operations.
(g) Breakdown anywhere stops workflow immediately.
(h) Outputs of workflow (production) segments/departments become inputs of others, i.e., flow from department to department throughout.
(i) Operations evaluated by measurement techniques against precise specifications.

A technology low in Workflow Integration is at the opposite extremes on these items.

exactly evaluated. These constituents of the measure are listed in Table 16-3.

A high score on Workflow Integration means that the organization has a substantial proportion of fairly automated equipment, through which there is a fixed order of operations or processes—so that a breakdown may hold up the entire plant—with operations evaluated by measurement against precise standards. A low score means the opposite. *Again, these aspects of an organization's technology have little or nothing to do with its organizational features.* If, using two measures which between them represent much of an organization's technical system, no connection is found between technology and forms of organization, what then? Can this be reconciled with the opposing conclusions reached by Woodward? What of the stress in management teaching over the last decade on applying principles of organization only with due attention to differences in the technologies employed? Perhaps after all, technology can be ignored.

SEVEN ORGANIZATIONAL FEATURES

Further exhaustive search of the data on the thirty-one Birmingham organizations revealed connections between either or both the technology measures, and seven organizational features previously considered to be of secondary interest only. These were:

1. Subordinate/first-line supervisor ratio.
Proportions of total employees in:
2. Inspection
3. Maintenance
4. Production control
5. Transport and despatch
6. Employment aspects of personnel
7. Buying and stocks.

The ways in which these link with the two technology measures are shown in Figures 16-3(a), (b), and (c). These show smoothed curves which simplify and exaggerate the relationships and are merely illustrative.

The ratio of subordinates to first-line supervisors is the only point at which the Woodward results in South-East Essex and the Aston teams' results agree exactly. Supervisors have most subordinates in the middle of the Production Continuity range, the large batch/mass production stage (Figure 16-3(a)). This is where each foreman often has forty or fifty workers turning out large quantities of standard items: whereas in jobbing or in process plants he has a smaller group.

Hence the proportions of employees in inspection work and in maintenance work are also greatest at the large batch stage, and lower in both unit production and processing (Figure 16-3(b)).

Figure 16-3(c) shows the proportion in transport and despatch work rising as technology is more integrated, that is, more automated with fixed sequences of operations and precise measurement. This is probably due to the greater proportionate numbers of full-time operators of mechanical handling equipment and drivers of special-purpose lorries often required to cope with the volume of output. The sharp reversal of the trend when technology becomes highly integrated suggests that these personnel can be dispensed with at an advanced stage of mechanization.

But the proportions in employment and in buying and stocks fall away in more integrated technologies, apparently again reflecting the relatively smaller numbers of personnel and/or of job classifications, and less complex materials' problems.

The detailed examination of these seven features is interesting, but it is of much less consequence than their implications taken as a whole. What is distinctive about them, as against the range of organizational characteristics *not* related to technology?

The first-mentioned characteristic, ratio of subordinates to first-line supervisors, is an element of organization at the level of the operative and his immediate boss. Obviously the number of men a supervisor requires to run a row of lathes differs from the number he requires to run the more continuous integrated workflow of an automatic transfer machine. Thus subordinate/supervisor ratio is an aspect of organization which reflects activities directly bound up with the technology itself. And this is true also of the next four characteristics, the proportions in inspection, maintenance, production control, and transport and despatch. It is the variety of equipment and products in batch production which demands larger numbers of inspectors and of maintenance personnel; unit and process technologies are less demanding in this respect. It is the complexity of technology both in variety of equipment and in sequences of operations which requires relatively large numbers of production control personnel outside the more automatic process-type technologies. The numbers in transport are linked to the means of handling.

The point is made more clearly by the contrast with, say, activities such as accounting or market research which are not directly implicated in the work technology itself—and in the research results show no connection with the technological factors.

In this light, it may be suggested that the

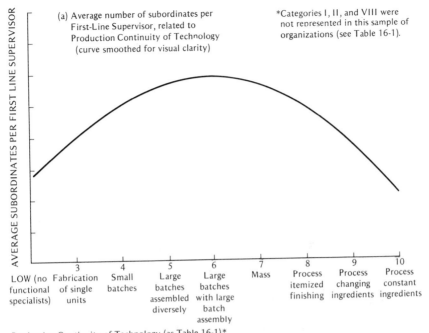

Fig. 16-3(a). Some Features of Organization That Are Related to the Technology of Production

connections between the workflow integration measure of technology and the proportions engaged in employment and in buying and stocks may be due to the intermediate position of these activities. They are closer to the production work itself than is, say, accounting: but not so close as, say, inspection.

So among the extensive range of organizational features studied, *only those directly centered on the production workflow itself show any connection with technology*: these are all "job-counts" of employees on production-linked activies.

But if these findings contradict Woodward's case for more widely-ranging technological effects, who is right? Are the constraints that technology places upon organization specifically limited, or are they all-pervasive? Do these two pieces of research make sense?

The critical clue comes from the differences in the sizes of the organizations studied by Woodward compared with those studied by the Industrial Administration Research Unit at Aston. Woodward's organizations were smaller. They ranged from 100 employees upwards, whereas the organizations in the Midlands were from 250 upwards, and included more giant multi-thousand units.

SMALLER VERSUS LARGER ORGANIZATIONS

In short, smaller organizations were found to be affected throughout by technology (Woodward). It affected the numbers of specialists employed, the definition of duties and responsibilities, the amount of paperwork, the length of the line of command, the span of control of the chief executive, etc., as well as the subordinate/supervisor ratio. In larger organizations—the research reported here—technology affected only characteristics directly centered on the pro-

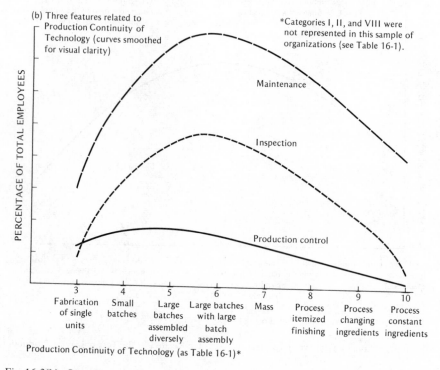

(b) Three features related to Production Continuity of Technology (curves smoothed for visual clarity)

*Categories I, II, and VIII were not represented in this sample of organizations (see Table 16-1).

Maintenance

Inspection

Production control

PERCENTAGE OF TOTAL EMPLOYEES

Production Continuity of Technology (as Table 16-1)*

3	4	5	6	7	8	9	10
Fabrication of single units	Small batches	Large batches assembled diversely	Large batches with large batch assembly	Mass	Process itemized finishing	Process changing ingredients	Process constant ingredients

Fig. 16-3(b). Some Features of Organization That Are Related to the Technology of Production

duction workflow, such as numbers of employees in certain tasks.

This does make sense. In smaller organizations, *everyone* is close to the "shop-floor," and organizational responses to the problems of size have not begun to show. For example, it *does* make all the difference whether technology is small batch and flexible, and non-integrated, as against being process-type with fixed integrated flow sequences. In batch technologies, the attempt to sustain orderly systems of work among varieties of personnel on multifarious jobs with multiple materials and components may well require written definition of duties and responsibilities, written communication between sections, and short lines of command, so that senior management are drawn directly into the daily production problems by their foremen. In process technologies,

longer lines of command, more delegation, and less concern over exact job definition are possible.

In larger organizations, managers and administrators are buffered from the technology itself by the specialist departments, the standard procedures, and the formalized paperwork that size as such brings with it. Whether ·it is the manager in a big-batch production machine-tool factory, the manager in a big, highly mechanized food processing works, or the manager in a big flow-technology chemical plant, each has much the same organizational scene before him. Each is confronted by a phalanx of specialist departments; each promulgates —and himself obeys—standard procedures, rules and regulations; each has a similar pile of booklets, forms, reports and what-not to cope with.

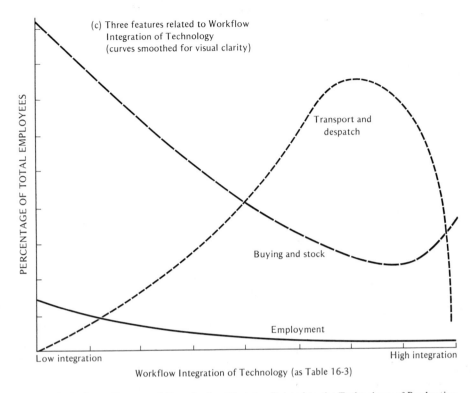

(c) Three features related to Workflow
Integration of Technology
(curves smoothed for visual clarity)

PERCENTAGE OF TOTAL EMPLOYEES

Transport and
despatch

Buying and stock

Employment

Low integration

High integration

Workflow Integration of Technology (as Table 16-3)

Fig. 16-3(c). Some Features of Organization That Are Related to the Technology of Production

They may differ in other respects. For instance, their organization's relative standing in its owning group, and whether it is independent or publicly owned, will affect how far they may take major decisions themselves or must refer upwards. But differences in *technology* do not affect them that much. These differences are mainly felt much closer to the "shop-floor."

THE MEANING FOR MANAGEMENT

If this research is well-founded, what does it mean for managers, for management, for management education? It means that the view taken over the past decade must be revised once again. Until then, the drive for generalized principles of management organization had gone forward. Then Woodward forced a recognition of the importance of technological differences. The research at

Aston now suggests that at those levels of larger organizations closely implicated in the problems of the shop-floor itself, and in smaller organizations where this applies to most aspects, technology does make a real difference to management organization and practice.

But technology does not necessarily affect the more remote administrative and hierarchical structure of larger organizations. In these organizations, principles may well be soundly applied at the general management level irrespective of technology. The early management theorists were not altogether deluding us.*

*A detailed account of the research work upon which this article is based has been published in the *Administrative Science Quarterly*, September 1969, vol. 14, no. 2.

17

Technology and Organization

RAYMOND G. HUNT[1]

In order to solve practical problems of organizational design, it is necessary initially to understand the many differences between types of organizations and the reasons that these differences exist. The fact that these aspects have not been considered until the mid-1960s is reflected by the independence of developments in organizational design and theory until this time.[2] However, recent progress in comparative analysis of organizations, together with integrative theory building, gives promise of altering this state of affairs, especially regarding the appreciation of technology as a main basis for differentiating organizational varieties and explaining organizational processes.

These recent developments are the foundation for this paper; first, we will outline the ways in which organizations may be classified, and then we will appraise the current understanding of the relationship between technology and organizational design.

CLASSIFYING ORGANIZATIONS

To be useful, a schema for distinguishing organizations must identify cogent parameters or dimensions that cut across particular cases and provide a basis for ordering those cases, even if it is only on a yes-no basis. Different schemas will be useful for different purposes, but since every organization can be construed as having: (1) a function in society; (2) a pattern of input; (3) a pattern of output; (4) a set of procedures for converting inputs into outputs (something to which we shall apply the term "throughput"[3]); and (5) a pattern according to which it is put together, it follows that any organization could be classified on any or all

1. Preparation of this paper was assisted by NASA Grant NGR 33-015-061.
2. R. M. Cyert and J. G. March, Organizational design. In W. W. Cooper, H. J. Leavitt, and M. W. Shelly (Eds.), *New perspectives in organization research* (New York: Wiley, 1964), chap. 29, p. 558.

3. In this usage we are following the example of D. Katz and R. Kahn, *The social psychology of organizations* (New York: Wiley, 1966).

Reprinted from *Academy of Management Journal*, 1970, 13, 235-52, by permission of the authors and the Academy of Management.

of these bases. Indeed, allowing for some mixed cases and some ambiguous ones, examples of all five kinds of classification can be found.

Classification by Social Function

In Chapter 5 of their remarkable book, Katz and Kahn[4] present a "typology" or organizations based on "first-order" and "second-order factors." First-order factors describe "genotypic functions" that differentiate among all kinds of organizational systems and subsystems. Thus, in Katz and Kahn's typology there are productive or economic organizations (e.g., factories); maintenance organizations (e.g., those, like schools, specialized to socialize people); adaptive organizations (e.g., research labs); and managerial or political organizations. These first-order distinctions have to do principally with the part played by the organization in the larger society; thus, they can claim kinship with Parsons's social function criteria.[5] With regard to actual organizations, of course, these categories are not mutually exclusive. A particular organization could fall into more than one class: AT&T may be mainly an economic organization, but in its research labs it contains adaptive organizations.

Defined by its contributions to the larger social system, an organization's social function, unlike the other four of its facets, has to do with its *relations* with the society as a whole, not just with its own characteristics. Talking of an organization's social functions is to treat it (the organization) not so much as an integral system, but as a subsystem of a larger system. One might therefore infer that this essentially *exogenous* criterion for classification is different from and independent of the others. Katz and Kahn obviously think so with their distinction between first- and second-order factors (see also Pugh, note 10

below).[6] To be sure, an organization's social function is likely to influence its perceived social value which, in turn, may affect its access to societal resources, including technological ones which may help shape its other characteristics. But any such linkages depend entirely on the organization's embeddedness in the larger societal system. In any event, these linkages are complex and clearly not direct.

For very general purposes, classification by social function can be helpful. However, the variability within functional types is too great for them to afford much analytic power.[7] Katz and Kahn are aware of this, of course, as their positing of second-order factors implies. These second-order factors have more to do with input, output, or conversion methods (throughput), or else with design features.

Classification by Form or Pattern

Pattern denotes the discernible "phenomenology" or anatomy of an organization—its characteristics or properties *qua* organization. This aspect of organizations we shall herein reference by the term "structure," or, when construed in a purposive sense, "design."

With its functional traditions, American scholarship has tended to pay more attention to operational than to structural properties of organization.[8] To be sure, structure is only revealed in the functions of organizations,[9] but structure there is nevertheless. We mean by it the varied patterns of interaction, intended or otherwise, that characterize an organization. To the degree these

4. *Ibid.*
5. T. Parsons, *Structure and process in modern societies* (Glencoe, Ill.: Free Press, 1960).

6. D. Katz and R. Kahn, *Social psychology,* Dimension of organization structure, *Administrative Science Quarterly* (1968), 13, 65-105.
7. See, C. A. Perrow, A framework for the comparative analysis of organizations, *American Sociological Review,* 1967, 32, 195-208.
8. See, R. G. Hunt, Review of systems of organization by E. J. Miller and A. K. Rice, *Administrative Science Quarterly,* 1968, 13, 360-62.
9. D. Katz and R. Kahn, *Social psychology,* chap. 1.

patterns are codified or standardized, we can speak of the organization as being formal. And "formal organizational structure" can be defined in terms of prescriptions regarding lines of authority, divisions of labor, and allocations of resources[10] that often can be found memorialized in such things as organization charts, job descriptions, and budgetary formulae. Such pointers are far from infallible guides to organizational reality, but even so it is essential to recognize that the nature of the formal organization has much to do with limiting and shaping organizational life (including whatever "informal" processes may be spawned therein). Moreover, the idea of formal structure is fundamental to rational organization design.

Our concept of structure in substance and in spirit approximates Anthony's idea of "system" as distinct from "process."[11] The latter has to do with the actual events and decisions that transpire within the organization, whereas the former represents the formal and informal framework within which these are done—the "formula," as it were, according to which the organization's tasks are specified, interrelated, performed, and controlled, Obviously this formula can be either explicit or not explicit.

As for the use of structural criteria for classifying organizations, it has long been traditional[12] to distinguish three basic forms of organization design:

1. line organization;
2. functional organization; and
3. line-staff organization.

In line organizations everybody does essentially the same kind of work under the more or less immediate authority of a "man at the top." Some degree of internal specialization may lead to departmentalization of line organizations, but this does not necessarily change their fundamentals.

Pure functional organizations are scarce, apparently because they are based on the sensible but hard to implement idea that since it is difficult to combine all necessary managerial-supervisory skills in single individuals, it is wise to organize around functions—skills, activities, etc.—rather than people. The desire to include functional specialists within an organization while retaining unity of command is the basis for the widespread "compromise" development of line-staff organizations wherein supporting specialists work through particular line managers.

It is obviously possible to combine these models in various ways and mention might be made of such special cases as project organizations (which, in a sense, are temporary, special-purpose, line organizations) and matrix organizations (which are meldings of project and functional models calculated to satisfy institutional needs for permanence). Furthermore, other structural classifications are possible. Pugh *et al.* stress a multidimensional characterization built around performance regulation, centralization of authority, and the degree to which operations are controlled by line management rather than by impersonal records and procedures generated from staff offices.[13] Burns and Stalker's well known distinction between "organic" and "mechanistic" management patterns is another somewhat similar example.[14] Organic organizations are characterized by less formalized definitions of jobs, by more stress on flexibility and adaptability, and by communication networks involving more consultation than command. Mechanistic organizations are more rigidly specialized functionally, and in general, de-

---

10. See D. S. Pugh *et al.*, Dimensions; W. F. Whyte, *Organizational behavior: Theory and application* (Homewood, Ill.: Irwin-Dorsey, 1969).
11. R. N. Anthony, *Planning and control systems* (Cambridge, Mass.: Harvard University Press, 1965).
12. See J. Woodward, *Industrial organisation: Theory and practice* (London: Oxford University Press, 1965).

13. D. S. Pugh *et al.*, Dimensions.
14. T. Burns and G. M. Stalker, *The management of innovation* (London: Tavistock Publications, 1961).

fine an opposite pole on an organic-mechanistic continuum. Finally, of course, distinctions between bureaucratic and non-bureaucratic organizations exemplify the classificatory use of structural or design criteria.[15]

Classification by Output

Classifying organizations according to their output is a common practice that may involve one of two emphases. One, the kind or type of output (i.e., the product), is a standard basis for defining industries (e.g., automobile, motion pictures, etc.) and is too familiar to require further comment. But, output can also be viewed from the standpoint of the quantity or volume of whatever it is that is produced. For example, Woodward, although she thought of it more as a direct expression of technology, used to good effect classification of industrial firms as unit, small-batch, large-batch, and mass production.[16] The immediate meaning of unit, batch, and mass production is plain: it describes a scale of production quantities ranging from one of a kind through a few to very many.

W. F. Whyte makes use of these same distinctions, but only as subcategories within a broader, more heterogeneous system of classes.[17] Whyte's primary breakdown of organizations into "office, service, manufacturing, and continuous process" varieties clearly employs criteria other than output. Indeed it makes use of just about all criteria save social function. Office and service classes, for instance, appear to be distinguishable on the basis of the nature of their outputs, but they (and surely manufacturing and continuous processing) are classifications that also make use of other bases for

categorization, notably throughout processes and, possibly, input as well.

Classification by Input

Distinctions between organizations based on input rest on contrasts regarding the raw materials on which the system works. The possibilities here are at least as numerous as the vast number offered to classifications based on output. One input distinction that has received special attention in the literature, however, is that between organizations (such as prisons, schools, employment agencies) that deal mainly with people and those organizations that operate chiefly on things, objects, hardware, or the like. Erving Goffman has provided some especially exotic discussions of "people-processing" systems, and the topic is capable of generating more than a little emotion. It is doubtless that such systems differ from others, if for no other reason than because their raw materials are "reactive" instead of passive. In fact, this reactivity can itself be made a basis for a distinction between organizations by focusing on the form of feedback controlling the system's operations. We shall illustrate this in the next section.

In the meantime, take notice of Thompson and Bates' use of a "ratio of mechanization to professionalization" to distinguish organizations.[19] By this they mean the extent to which technology is represented in human or nonhuman resources. But whether this is truly a classification based on input is questionable for, if Thompson and Bates stress the *locus* of technology, the notions of mechanization and professionalization seem to link the distinction closely to technology itself.

15. See, e.g., D. Katz and R. Kahn, *Social psychology*, chap. 5; N. P. Mouzelis, *Organization and bureaucracy* (Chicago: Aldine, 1967); W. F. Whyte, *Organizational behavior*, chap. 1; W. Bennis, Beyond bureaucracy, *Transaction*, 1965, 2, 31-35.
16. J. Woodward, *Industrial organisation*.
17. W. F. Whyte, *Organizational behavior*.

18. E. Goffman, *Asylums* (Garden City, N.Y.: Doubleday/Anchor, 1961).
19. J. D. Thompson and F. L. Bates, Technology, organization, and administration, *Administrative Science Quarterly*, 1957, 2, 325-42.

Classification by Throughput

Conversion processes or throughput are the various things done, with or without tools and machines, to transform inputs into outputs. The term "technology" is usually applied to these processes.[20] Our own definition of technology encompasses the three facets of technology (1) operations, (2) materials, and (3) knowledge, differentiated by Hickson et al.,[21] and includes the sequencing of activities involved in the conversion processes, thereby including what Whyte, among others, refers to as "work flow."[22]

A straightforward throughput classification might be exemplified by J. D. Thompson's distinction between long-linked, mediating, and intensive technologies.[23] The first of these includes conversion processes (like those found in automobile assembly plants) involving serially interdependent operations, standard products, and constant, repetitive work rates. Mediating technologies link clients who "are or wish to be interdependent (as banks link depositors and lenders)." These, too, commonly employ standardization along with bureaucratic formats. Intensive technologies are those involving application of a variety of techniques to the change of some specific object, in which actual operations are determined by feedback from the object itself. This is clearly a "custom technology," and includes such examples as hospitals, schools, research projects, and tailor shops. Obviously a single organization might include within itself multiple technologies.

We have already mentioned that Whyte's classification of organizations included an admixture of output and throughput criteria; the same was true of Woodward's classification. Along with other categories defined by output, both Whyte and Woodward include in their schemas a "continuous process" category (e.g., a fully automated oil refinery) that indexes technology rather than output.[24]

It must be evident that input and output systems, as well as throughput systems, can be described in terms of the processes or technologies by which they are implemented. That is, the operations by which inputs—raw materials—are introduced into a system describe a technology, and the same is true on the output (product) side. This fact, plus the other consideration that conversion processes in an organization must be relative to the input and output to and from the system (e.g., knowledge of the raw materials and product specifications) strongly suggest that the input-conversion-output cycle represents a single basic technological sequence or organizational substrate. Thus, the crucial consideration may not be the particular properties of the inputs or the outputs *per se*, but the technologies according to which they are accomplished.[25] In any case, it seems clear that input, output, and technology (throughput) are inextricably joined. Taken together they constitute the basic *endogenous* operational properties of organizations and, when actualized, collectively describe what Anthony calls organizational "process" (or function) as distinguished from structure (system).[26]

There is, of course, nothing in these unifying assertions to preclude variation in technological manifestations at different

---

20. For a useful discussion of definitional issues, see D. J. Hickson, D. S. Pugh, and D. C. Pheysey, Operations technology and organization structure: An empirical reappraisal, *Administrative Science Quarterly*, 1969, 14, 378-97.
21. *Ibid.*
22. W. F. Whyte, *Organizational behavior.*
23. J. D. Thompson, *Organizations in action* (New York: McGraw-Hill, 1967).

24. W. F. Whyte, *Organizational behavior*; Woodward, *Industrial organisation.* Notice might be taken of Hickson *et al.'s* incorporation of this category, along with unit production, mass production, and the others, into a throughput scale of "production continuity" (see Hickson *et al.*, Operations technology).
25. For a related discussion with different conclusions see Hickson *et al.*, *ibid.*, p. 380.
26. R. N. Anthony, *Planning and control systems.*

points in the process cycle. Input and conversion operations might be highly routinized, for example, but output methods (e.g., marketing) might be quite non-routine.[27] And certainly nothing prevents separate analyses of respective technological features of input, output, or conversion subsystems. The point here is that input and output criteria for classifying organizations may be structurally significant only insofar as they indirectly index technological phenomena.

Another thing that may have been evident in our exposition is the difficulty one has treating technology or process without making reference to structural or design aspects of the organization (see, e.g., the allusion to bureaucratic formats in the presentation above of Thompson's "mediating" technology). This is no accident of discursive formats. Indeed, we have taken notice of Anthony's proposition that system (structure) represents the formulae for organizational processes (input-thoughput-output).[28] Certainly the two dimensions are intimately entwined, even if the nature and degree of that intimacy may not yet be altogether clear; furthermore, they are both technologies. Conversion processes, or, more generally, modes of production, constitute what Olsen has called "material technologies." He has described modes of organization as "social technologies."[29] Thus, from Anthony's perspective, exploring relations between "technology" and "organiza-tion" resolves itself into an analysis of relations between system and process. From Olsen's standpoint, this amounts to tracing the linkages between material and social technologies. We should hardly be surprised to find a good deal of interdependence in these relationships. Indeed, the expectation is implicit in the now common characterization of organizations as sociotechnical systems. In a manner of speaking, then, describing relations between technology and organizational forms amounts to an extended definition of the meaning of the concept of the sociotechnical system. With that observation, a more explicit overview of technology and organizational patterns is in order.

TECHNOLOGY
AND ORGANIZATION DESIGN

Beginning at least with Veblen and Marx, material technology has been regularly proposed as a major influence on organizational phenomena. Indications of its broad significance can be found in Toynbee's demonstration of changing forms of English social organization as new industrial technologies emerged during the eighteenth and nineteenth centuries. Margaret Mead has provided vivid portrayals of interrelations between technological advances and social patterns.[30] More recently, Dubin[31] has nominated technology as the single most important determinant of work behavior, and Mouzelis[32] has spoken at length of the determining effect of technological structures and processes on organizational interaction. Stinchcombe, too, in context with

27. Distinctions could be drawn, but throughout this discussion we shall use the basic terms "routine" (or "routinized") and "program" ("programmed") more or less interchangably to mean the extent to which an organization's tasks can and have been specified and prescribed—formalized. Programming performance (as, to take an extreme example, in a robot) is difficult when tasks are vague, variable, or complicated, but the process can be generally regarded (with neither approval nor disapproval) as a broad organizational means of reducing operational uncertainty by eliminating operator discretion.
28. Anthony, *Planning and control systems.*
29. M. E. Olsen, *The process of social organization* (New York: Holt, Rinehart & Winston, 1968).

30. A. Toynbee, *The industrial revolution* (Boston: Beacon, 1956); M. Mead (Ed.), *Cultural patterns and technological change* (New York: New American Library, 1955).
31. R. Dubin, *The world of work* (Englewood Cliffs, N. J.: Prentice-Hall, 1958).
32. N. P. Mouzelis, *Organization and bureaucracy.*
33. A. L. Stinchcombe, Social structure and organization." In, J. G. March (Ed.), *Handbook of organizations* (Chicago: Rand McNally, 1965), pp. 142-94).

his discussion of "motives for organizing," mentions technology among the basic variables affecting organizing capacity,[33] and Olsen lists material technology as one of four primary factors underlying forms of social organization (the other three are the natural environment, population, and the human being).[34] Finally, in his excellent review of comparative studies, Udy points out two basic "casual mechanisms" that shape organizations. One operates via people to affect structures, and the other is *ecological* and deals with how activity is limited and channeled.[35] Together with the "social setting," which we are disregarding here, technology can be construed as imposing ecological limits on organizational propproperties.

In somewhat the same way, social technology can be looked upon as constraining material technology, as in the case of cultural or organizational resistance to change[36] or as in the extent to which a system is attuned to the receipt of inputs regarding new material technologies. Burns and Stalker, to cite a pertinent instance, found that firms adapting successfully to the electronics industry were characterized by a more global task model and a different communication process for innovative information than were the less successful ones. In the adaptive firms, technological or market information was introduced to reprogram routine operations, thus enhancing flexibility in a technologically changing environment.[37]

To undergird these contentions, a significant empirical literature has now emerged relating technology to various organizational matters. The most noteworthy examples are probably Woodward's seminal

studies.[38] Her work and other relevant investigations have been well reviewed by Perrow, J. D. Thompson, and Hickson *et al.*, so there is no need for repetition here.[39] It will be sufficient to observe that, although the nature, degree, and conditions of its effect remain controversial,[40] technology has been shown to affect structure, to shape interaction, and to influence the personal characteristics of organizational members.[41]

Yet, as late as 1964, W. R. Scott felt constrained to mark the infrequency with which technological variables had been built into theory.[42] The reasons for this seem to reside partly in a preoccupation of organizational scholars with nonstructural human relations or "informal" processes[43] and partly from the fact that, although technological phenomena were widely recognized and sometimes even categorized, until recently there literally were no technological *variables* to build into theory.[44] Perhaps what is most important in the technology-organization literature of the past few years, therefore, aside from empirical explication, is that it has begun to give form to conceptualizations of managable technological variables or dimensions. Prominent in this connection have been the work of Bell, Harvey, Perrow, Whyte, and Pugh and Hickson.

The Technology Variable

It will be recalled from our earlier discussion

---

34. M. E Olsen, *Social organization.*
35. S. H. Udy, The comparative analysis of organizations. In J. G. March (Ed.), *Handbook of organizations,* pp. 678-710.
36. See, e.g., M. Mead, *Cultural patterns,* for illustrations of such cultural disinclinations.
37. T. Burns and G. M. Stalker, *Management of innovation.*

38. J. Woodward, *Industrial organisation.*
39. C. A. Perrow, Framework for comparative analysis; J. D. Thompson, Organizations in action; D. S. Hickson, *et al.,* Operations technology.
40. Illumination of the controversy can perhaps best be found in Hickson *et al.,* Operations technology.
41. One example of this last point, which is here mentioned only incidentally, may be found in R. Blauner's studies of alienation, e.g., *Alienation and freedom* (Chicago: University of Chicago Press, 1964).
42. W. R. Scott, Theory of organizations. In R. E. L. Faris (Ed.), *Handbook of modern sociology* (Chicago: Rand McNally, 1964), pp. 485-530.
43. See N. P. Mouzelis, *Organization and bureaucracy,* for further discussion of this point.
44. W. F. Whyte, *Organizational behavior* (chap. 3).

that productive as it was empirically, the technology variable was ambiguous in Woodward's classification scheme. She regarded her entire scheme as a direct index of technology, even as a scale of technological complexity ranging from unit to mass to process modes of production. Harvey, however, has quite reasonably pointed out that the complexity scale could equally well be the reverse.[45] And Woodward's own findings that unit production and continuous process organizations tended to exhibit many common characteristics that contrasted sharply with other kinds of organizations, could imply a "circular" interpretation of the technological dimension underlying her classification.

The precise mechanisms linking technologies with organizational forms are still problematical in the literature, but, as a generality, the critical technological element to which organizational structure must respond seems best conceptualized as *complexity*. This is something that unit production organizations, for instance, may have in at least as long a supply as their continuous process counterparts—a moment's reflection on the many esoteric one-of-a-kind products produced under the American space program vindicates that assertion. To state it simply, this view of correlation between organization and technology signifies that the concrete manifestations of technology are less important than the essential complexity underlying them. Having said that, however, it is necessary to acknowledge immediately that complexity is an elusive concept that takes many forms.

Bell, for instance, has dealt explicitly with the matter of complexity and structure in his study of spans of control (ratios of personnel to supervisors) in a large hospital.[46] He defined complexity as:

a. The degree of predictability of work demands;
b. The discretion provided for in a position; and
c. The responsibility of the job holder (construed as the time lapse between decision and its supervisory review or assessment).

Bell then showed that as complexity increased with regard to either subordinates' or supervisors' roles, the span of control decreased.

Harvey, using Woodward's work as a point of departure, prefers to speak of a complexity dimension ranging from technical diffuseness ("made to orderness") to specificity.[47] He argues that one needs to take account not only of the *form* of technology (as Woodward tried to do), but also the amount of "changefulness" *within* a form. As he puts it: A unit production firm might produce the same thing most of the time and thus be "specific." Or, it might vary its outputs and be "diffuse." Harvey postulated that whether the organization is specific or diffuse, it will have differential implications for its structural characteristics. He conceived three "sociotechnical types" (marriages of technology and internal organizational structure): (1) diffuse, (2) intermediate, and (3) specific (defined in terms of frequency of product change), and showed that when compared with specific types, diffuse types had fewer specialized subunits, fewer levels of authority, a lower ratio of managers and supervisors to total personnel, and a lessened degree of performance program specification.

Drawing mainly on the work of Woodward, Harvey, and Bell, together with his own experience, Whyte has gone about the detailed application of technological concepts to analysis of that basic organizational element, the span of control, asking what factors are responsible for its variations. He concludes that there are five factors:

45. E. Harvey, Technology and the structure of organizations, *American Sociological Review*, 1968, 33, 247-59.
46. G. D. Bell, Determinants of span of control, *American Journal of Sociology, 1967, 73, 90-101.*

47. E. Harvey, Technology and the structure.

1. The complexity (in Bell's sense) of the job for the supervisor and subordinate;
2. The visibility of results from performing the work;
3. The interdependence and need for coordination among tasks;
4. The degree to which interdependent activities require human rather than mechanical control; and
5. The kinds of personnel required by the technology.[48]

Probably the most searching attempts at conceptualizing technology and relating it to organizational processes can be found in Perrow's work with his contingent, two-dimensional model that elaborates a distinction between routine and nonroutine technologies.[49] Perrow's emphasis is on classifying technologies regarding the frequency with which exceptional cases[50] are encountered and with reference to the nature of the search process (for solutions) that ensues when exceptions (problems) do occur. Using this general model, he relates task-structure to analogous control/coordination processes involving variations in individual or group discretion and the nature of the feedback mechanisms controlling performance (i.e., their degree of "programming"). Perrow also distinguishes three functional areas in management: (1) design and planning, (2) technical control and support of product, and (3) the supervision of production and marketing, each of which he ties in with the technological and task dimensions described. Finally, in a tentative way, Perrow undertakes to relate nontask-related (i.e., informal) interaction to the basic model.

In a later paper Perrow refined his basic model and extended it to connect with the psychological processes of its human operatives.[51] He stresses a kind of "cognitive" conception of technology working as a system of cues (that may vary in clarity), which signal the initiation of performance routines (that also may vary in their degree of explicit "programming") and involve provision for handling exceptions that may be procedurally more or less routinized. The notable feature of this construction is that regardless of how complicated or elaborate, a system may be viewed as technologically routine to the extent that:

1. The signals that initiate its processes are unambiguous;
2. The performance processes so cued are programmed; and
3. When faced with exceptions not covered by regular performance routines, search processes and problem-solving methods are programmed.

The properties of technology emphasized by other writers (e.g., Harvey's "changefulness" or Whyte's "human" versus "mechanical" control) can probably be treated in Perrow's formulation as either sources of cognitive complexity (exceptions) or as proxies for it.

Perrow's cognitive constructions rather closely parallel the much more general cybernetic model of human problem-solving due to Miller, Galanter, and Pribram.[52] These authors construe individual performance in relation to a cognitive Test-Operate-Test-Exit (TOTE) model which is based on the notion of "plan." A plan is defined as any hierarchical process controlling the sequence in which a set of operations is performed. They discuss a variety of ways

48. W. F. Whyte, *Organizational behavior.*
49. C. A. Perrow, Framework for comparative analysis.
50. I.e., tasks, decisions, etc., not covered, or perceived to be covered, by existing performance programs. Such exceptions define problems for which organizational solutions must be sought if the system is to function, or at least if it is to function smoothly.

51. C. A. Perrow, Technology and structural changes in business firms. Paper presented at First World Congress, International Industrial Relations Assn., Geneva, September 1967.
52. G. A. Miller, E. Galanter, and K. H. Pribram, *Plans and the structure of behavior* (New York: Holt, Rinehart and Winston, 1960).

that plans may differ (communicability, source, detail, flexibility, etc.) and discuss also plans for searching and solving, distinguishing between systematic and heuristic varieties.

Very briefly, their idea is that people have images of reality and an array of plans for dealing with it. As information in the form of environmental signals flows into a human performance system, it is "tested" for fit with existing plans which then may be put into operation. Results of action are appraised via feedback from the performance, and the system moves on either to another performance segment or, if a problem has arisen, to a more or less standardized search routine. Of course, the system could cycle into a search routine immediately if the initial "test" yielded no suitable performance program.

From Miller, Galanter, and Pribram's presentation it is evident that when a search plan exists one may not even be aware of it, although it is necessary to perceive the exception—it is the function of the TOTE unit to guarantee that. Thus, regardless of how complicated it may be materially, at the behavioral level, technology can be defined in terms of an ordered set of skills or habits that differ mainly in their degree of routinization, integration, or mechanization. Complicated material technologies may be more difficult to program and they may place greater demands on human resources, but be that as it may, what counts operationally is behavioral routinization. We may say, then, that technological complexity is a function of the frequency with which problems (exceptions) confront organizational operations and the practical difficulty and degree of individual discretion or judgment required in resolving or finding solutions to them.

Performance vs. Problem-Solving System

It may be concluded from the foregoing that it is not material technology, *per se*, that presents organizational challenges, but the nature of the behavioral and problem-solving tasks confronting those operating the system at all its various levels. The extent to which an organization's task systems can be programmed and operational uncertainty thereby eliminated seem to be the critical circumstances. However, no performance program can anticipate every contingency; exceptions will occur. Even if it can be reduced, operational uncertainty cannot be totally eliminated. Consequently, as Perrow has maintained, the decisive structural determinants are apt to be associated with the handling of exceptions to task programs. The frequency of such exceptions, of course, will not be unrelated to material technology, but it still may not parallel it closely—very complicated material technologies may, for instance, be highly programmed. But, in any event, the more crucial consideration would seem to be the importance of exceptions to the viability of the organization and how these exceptions can be handled by it.

If paradoxical, then, it seems nevertheless reasonable to assume that the more a system depends upon its performance programs to control its outputs, the more seriously it must view exceptions to their application or breakdowns in their operation and, hence, the more it must be geared to deal with them if and when they occur. If problem-solving processes are routinized along with task performance, one could expect a different kind of organization from the one that would result when they are not. In an unpublished paper, Perrow has presented some data consistent with such an expectation.[53]

If this is sensible, a potential basis for the similarity found by Woodward between unit production and process organizations is discoverable via the simple expedient of conceiving, somewhat after the fashion of Burns

53. C. A. Perrow, Working paper on technology and structure (University of Wisconsin, 1970), mimeo.

and Stalker,[54] of two quite different kinds of organization: one geared chiefly to performance (as in a mass-production factory or a modern bank) and the other one geared to problem-solving (as in a hospital or a design and development enterprise). In a unit production firm, the system deals almost entirely with exceptions, and its problem-solving modes are likely to be unroutinized, especially if it is technologically diffuse.[55] In automated continuous process organizations, whether exceptions are frequent or not, they will be critical when they occur so that such systems, too, are likely to be structured as problem-solving or troubleshooting affairs. Thus, both unit production organizations (at any rate diffuse ones involved with complicated material technologies) and continuous process varieties are likely to be similarly structured—as organic problem-solving systems. Other operations, facing fewer exceptions and less vitally affected by ones that occur or are equipped with simple routines for solving the problems that ensue from them, are likely to be differently structured—as mechanistic performance systems. We shall not now go into the matter further, but it does seem likely that over the long run firms may tend to organize more and more as performance systems, whether or not it is good for them to do so.[56]

Organizational-Level Analysis of Technology and Structure

So far we have talked of relations between technology and structure mostly at the so-called level of the organization, treating the system largely as a unitary entity. Yet, we have mentioned the frequent internal technological diversity of organizations—a fact that confronts organization-level analyses with thorny problems. In addition to complicating life, it prompts serious questions about suitable units of system analysis, for there is no inherent reason to expect technologically diverse organizations to be any less diverse structurally. Therefore, assessments of technology-structure correlations might profit from being based on homogeneous organizational subsystems instead of "forcing" aggregated total systems into statistically defined "types." Or, a system-level alternative might be to devise suitable indexes of technological diversity for use either as independent variables or as "test factors."

To illustrate the force of this point: it is possible that the reason Hickson et al. found stronger relations between organizational size and structure than between technology and structure (leaving aside their definition of technology), is that size may well be correlated with diversity.[57] Small unit production firms (missing from Hickson et al.'s research) are likely to be technologically more homogeneous (in the cognitive sense described above) than are very large firms (which were heavily represented in the Hickson et al. investigation). While no evidence exists bearing on the matter, actually, Hickson et al.'s attempts to reconcile their findings with Woodward's are not too different from the present thesis. In any event, the issue is one which deserves attention in future research.

Designing Organizational Structures

The design of an organization refers to the composition of its structure; moreover, "design" implies a purposive formulation legitimized by an organization's formal authority.[58] Certainly, presumptions of or-

---

54. T. Burns and G. M. Stalker, *Management of innovation.*
55. For data regarding this point, see E. Harvey, Technology and structure.
56. Pertinent discussions of processes of bureaucratization can be found in N. P. Mouzelis, *Organization and bureaucracy,* and in M. E. Olsen, *Social organization,"* chap. 17.

57. D. J. Hickson *et al.,* Operations technology.
58. See C. J. Haberstroh, Organization design and systems analysis. In J. G. March (Ed.), *Handbook of organizations,* pp. 1171-1213.

ganizational rationality implicit in the idea of design connote a sense of organizational construction which is neatly adapted by managerial plan to the objectives and circumstances (technological or other) of a particular organization, adaptations optimized by careful analyses and the systematic application of "principles" of organization and management theory. Yet curiously enough, in her extensive studies, Woodward found firms, both successful and unsuccessful, to vary markedly in "organization consciousness." Even among firms "in which production systems were basically the same," considerable differences could be found regarding the extent to which they tried "to rationalize their production, in their awareness of technical developments, and in their use of techniques such as work study, methods engineering, and operations research."[59]

Woodward was led to the view that conscious organizational planning rarely is based on technical considerations; that it amounts mostly to implicit recognition of technologically constrained situational demands; and that it represents the institutionalization of prevailing organizational realities. Woodward did find process-type firms to be successful a little more often than any other kind, but, by and large she discovered that successful firms were mostly those organizations which were *typical* of their technological types. Successful large-batch firms, for instance, tended to be mechanistic (in Burns and Stalker's sense), whereas other successful firms tended to be organic. And, the same organizational characteristic associated with success among large-batch firms—formalization of roles—augured failure among process types. But, in Woodward's studies, the organizational designing was so "unconscious" that most managers were not even aware of how their organizations compared structurally with others.

Findings like Woodward's suggest that planning is either absent (which it often surely is) or that it is more apparent than real (coming to little more than formalization of what already is). Undoubtedly, much ostensible organizational analysis and design does represent a sort of managerial doodling instigated by external affiliations,[60] motivated by managers' desires to display virtuousity, or motivated by their needs to "keep up with the Joneses." This analysis and design may also depend heavily upon having time to think about such things—on organizational "slack," as Perrow put it.[61] Furthermore, Blau, Scott, and V. A. Thompson have suggested that organizational elaboration often arises simply from desires on the part of those in power either to evade unpleasant tasks or to bolster the prevailing status structure,[62] or from some other consideration (e.g., empire-building) quite extraneous to technical requirements of organizational tasks.

Still, Woodward found, too, that "organic" firms tended as a group to be low in organization-consciousness, thus implying that these things may not depend altogether on managerial caprice. And, while organization-consciousness was not always a mark of "mechanistic" orientations—organization charts sometimes poorly reflected what actually happened in the firm—consciousness did not seem to be altogether random regarding technology. In short, some technologies seem to prompt more concern with design than others. It follows that they would, from arguments like Udy's; that the salience of technology as an influence upon structure will decrease with its flexibility and that mechanization of technology will enhance the salience of group structure[63] —a proposition fully consistent with Cyert and March's assertion that questions of organiza-

---

59. J. Woodward, *Industrial organisation*, p. 42,

60. See *ibid.*, p. 21.
61. C. A. Perrow, Comparative analysis.
62. P. Blau and W. R. Scott, *Formal organizations* (San Francisco: Chandler, 1962); V. A. Thompson. *Modern organization* (New York: Knopf, 1961).
63. S. H. Udy, Analysis of organizations.

tional design are meaningful only when alternative modes of performance exist.[64]

These issues have been well reviewed by J. D. Thompson, who offers an array of propositions relating technology to organizational operations and thence to rational organizational design.[65] His book nicely illustrates both how operations depend on technology and how various principles of organizational design implicitly assume sustaining technologies. The latter is a matter of overarching significance highlighted by Woodward's finding that success was associated with "textbook" management applications only among large-batch concerns;[66] this suggests the conclusion that management theory has been largely based on this technological model, without this fact having been understood. If that is true, application of standard managerial precepts in other technological contexts is likely to yield less than salutary consequences. Miller and Rice have made this point, commenting that classical theories of organization drew mainly on experience in industries representing only a narrow technological range.[67] They add that their own experiences support Woodward's implication that the models and principles derived do not fit either process or unit production industries. Hickson *et al.* have also argued the relativity of design precepts to technological environments, though they appear to believe this is because technology is relevant mostly at "shop-floor levels" and, therefore, chiefly in small organizations "where nothing is far removed from the workflow itself."[68]

In any case, it follows, as Perrow also has said,[69] that there can probably be no "one best" organizational structure or managerial

orientation—not participative management, not bureaucracy, not any single fashionable methodology. In this regard, one might call to mind Fiedler's persuasive arguments that effective leadership entails an adaption of "style" to organizational context.[70] In the same way, organizational success depends fundamentally upon meshing design (social technology) with the material technology out of which emerge the organizaton's tasks. It may be, as Woodward's work suggests, that organizations tend as a "natural" process to shape themselves into at least a loose match of technologies, but that does not mean that management design activity is irrelevant or that management ought to become passive and desist from efforts to plan and enhance operational effectiveness.[71] What follows is only that it must acknowledge the technological imperative.[72] Social and material technology must be mutually adapted in system designs. Admittedly, until more adequately differentiated social technological models become available from comparative studies this will be hard to do. But, who ever said management was easy?

CONCLUDING OBSERVATIONS

We have distinguished between two fundamentally different models for organization—performance and problem-solving. Analogous in conception to Burns and Stalker's mechanistic and organic management models, this distinction has the virtue of making management methods the means to ends—e.g., problem-solving—rather than inherently good or bad things. In any event, we have also suggested that most management theories pertain to performance models, not to

64. R. M. Cyert and J. G. March, Organization design.
65. J. D. Thompson, Organizations in action.
66. J. Woodward, *Industrial organisation.*
67. E. J. Miller and A. K. Rice, *Systems of organization* (London: Tavistock, 1967).
68. D. J. Hickson *et al.,* Operations technology, p. 396.
69. C. A. Perrow, Comparative analysis.

70. F. E. Fiedler, *A theory of leadership effectiveness* (New York: McGraw-Hill, 1967).
71. I am indebted to John D. Senger for pointing out the possible analogy between this "natural" process and Darwinian evolution of form and its attendant costs. Managerial manipulation of organizational forms then might be considered an attempt to reduce the costs of evolutionary development, even if it might not always succeed.
72. See Hickson, Operations technology.

problem-solving models of organization, but that, for various reasons, organizations tend to evolve toward performance models; i.e., they endeavor to increase routinization. It may be, as Olsen says, that such tendencies arise from the organization's continual efforts to rationalize its functioning in order to achieve its goals more effectively,[73] but nevertheless there are many times when such movement is premature and disfunctional. Consequently, it will sometimes require deliberate managerial effort to resist such evolution when it would compromise the flexibility and creativity of the system and defeat effective goal achievement.

Probably nowhere is this maxim more applicable than in research and development environments (whether in industry, universities, or wherever). Decentralized, organically operated project organizations have been effective vehicles for accomplishing goals in such contexts, but the moral of our story, paradoxically perhaps, is that centralized authority may be necessary to preserve their adaptive integrity in the face of "natural" forces toward bureaucratization. Udy, for instance, hypothesized that technological "complexity" stimulates concerns for coordination that tend to lead toward elaboration and formalization of administration.[74] Furthermore, the generation of inflexibility occasioned by predilections toward "empire-building" within projects and by dispositions to assimilate project organizations to functional (or administrative) divisions are familiar experiences in research and development environments.[75]

Finally, we should close by commenting that nothing in the foregoing should be interpreted to preclude various kinds of performance or information programming. Nor should it foreclose use of searching methods for systems analysis; the basic message is that these things must be employed in the service of a fundamental problem-solving model of organization. In brief, they should be means to ends and not devices for transforming the organizational design or for reducing it to some tepid least common denominator. One unfortunate (or fortunate, depending on your view) consequence of this policy, of course, is that it leaves the organization in a condition of heavy dependence on the commitment and competence of the people who run it—or at least those who manage it.

SUMMARY

Various means of classifying organizations are reviewed and the relevance of technology to the structure of organization is discussed. Developments in the operationalization of technological variables are traced, and the implications for purposive organizational planning considered. Emphasis is placed on a "cognitive" interpretation of technological complexity and on the role of uncertainty as a basic constraint upon organizational design. Two basically distinct organizational models are differentiated: one is oriented toward problem-solving and the other toward performance. It is concluded that most management theories pertain to the latter and not the former, and various consequences of that judgment are considered.

73. M. E. Olsen, *Social organization*, pp. 300-1.
74. S. H. Udy, Analysis of organizations.
75. See C. J. Haberstroh, Organization design, pp. 1208-9, for a brief discussion of these issues.

18

Introduction to the Structural Design of Organizations

JAY W. LORSCH

Our purpose is to introduce you to a useful way of thinking about the structural design of organizations, and to make you aware that the structure of an organization is not an immutable given, but rather a set of complex variables about which managers can exercise considerable choice.

DEFINITION OF STRUCTURAL DESIGN

It is useful to make a distinction between the basic structure and the operating mechanisms which implement and reinforce this basic structure.[1] Design of the *basic structure* involves such central issues as how the work of the organization will be divided and assigned among positions, groups, departments, divisions, etc., and how the coordination necessary to accomplish total organizational objectives will be achieved. Choices made about these issues are usually publicized in organization charts and job descriptions. If we recognize that behavior in

1. I am indebted to my colleague Larry E. Greiner, for suggesting this conceptual distinction.

an organization is influenced by a system of variables (technical, individual, social and organizational inputs), it is obvious that such formal documents are only one method of signaling to individuals what behavior is expected of them. Nevertheless, this method is important because it is so widely used by managers to define and communicate their expectations of other organization members.

Managers also can reinforce the intent of their basic structural design through what we call *operating mechanisms*. Operating mechanisms include such factors as control procedures, information systems, reward and appraisal systems, standardized rules and procedures, and even spatial arrangements. These structural variables can be used to more clearly signal to organizational members what is expected of them, to motivate them toward their assigned part of the organization's goal, and, as necessary, to encourage them to undertake collaborative activity. While our central focus is on the basic structure, we shall have more to say about these operating mechanisms later.

Reprinted with permission from J. W. Lorsch, "Introduction to the Structural Design of Organizations," in *Organizational Structure and Design*, G. W. Dalton, P. R. Lawrence, and J. W. Lorsch (Eds.) (Homewood, Ill.: Richard D. Irwin, Inc., 1970). © pp. 1-16.

CONVENTIONAL APPROACHES TO STRUCTURAL DESIGN

In the past, the most widely used ideas about structural design were those developed by a group of organization theorists who have been labeled the *classicists*.[2] Fayol, Gulick, Urwick, Mooney and their colleagues and successors drew heavily on their own experience in early twentieth-century organizations and on the industrial engineering ideas of Frederick J. Taylor. While a detailed review of these ideas is beyond our scope, we can briefly summarize the central features of their "principles of organization."

With regard to the division of work, most of the authors recommended dividing up the work by function (i.e., sales, manufacturing, engineering, etc.). The one exception was Gulick, who suggested that the work of an organization could be divided on several bases: by function; by product; by territory; by time. In any case these writers emphasized economic and technical efficiency. The only human variable given major attention was the limited intellectual capacity of the individual. To cope with this limitation, division of labor was advocated. Each individual would have a narrow task which, given his limited capacity, he could accomplish in the most technically efficient manner. While these ideas are based on the simplistic assumption that man is motivated only by money and will do as he is directed, they still persist and are widely used as a basis for making decisions about organization structure.

According to these writers, coordination was not a major problem. Work was to be divided so that the subgoals of various units would add up to the over-all organizational goals. Any remaining coordinating issues would be handled through the management hierarchy. Since people followed the direction of their superiors, the management hierarchy was the only coordinating device necessary.

While this approach has been widely used, it has severe limitations. First, it provides little help in designing a task with intrinsic motivation. Second, it is of limited value in dealing with the multiple levels of division of work in most large organizations. Third, managers have become more aware that the management hierarchy is not sufficient as a mechanism to achieve the coordination required in an organization. The goals of individuals and units do not automatically add up to the total goals of the organization.

Because of these shortcomings, other organizational theorists, most of whom were psychologists or social psychologists, began conducting research into these issues and have more recently come up with a second set of prescriptions which, while less widely applied, are sufficiently used to be worthy of mention. Perhaps the most concise statement of these ideas is offered by Likert.[3] This approach considers the motivational and collaborative issues left unattended by the classical theorists. While these behavioral scientists do not deal explicitly with the issue of division of labor, they do implicitly suggest that jobs should be divided to give the individual meaningful work over which he can have some feeling of control and influence. According to this view, the individual is motivated by self-actualization, and it follows that he will seek more complicated

2. Henri Fayol, *Industrial and general administration*, Part II, chap. 1, General principles of organization; chap. 2, Elements of administration. (Paris: Dunod, 1925); Luther Gulick, Notes on the theory of organization, in Luther Gulick and Lyndall F. Urwick (Eds.); *Papers on the science of administration* (New York: Institute of Public Administration, Columbia University, 1937); Lyndall F. Urwick, Organization as a technical problem, *ibid.*; James D. Mooney, The principles of organization, *ibid.*

3. Rensis Likert, *The human organization* (New York: McGraw-Hill, 1968). See also Douglas McGregor, *The human side of enterprise* (McGraw-Hill, 1960).

and engaging jobs. This must be taken into account in the division of work. The individual is also motivated by social needs and it is therefore important, according to Likert, to structure the organization so that each individual belongs to a cohesive work group in which participation in decision-making is the accepted norm.

While this approach offers no explicit recommendation about how to divide up the work of an organization to provide self-actualizing work and group membership, it is very explicit about how to achieve collaboration or coordinated effort. This is done by linking work groups together by members who hold overlapping membership in two or more groups. This "linking pin" individual is a key figure in the organization, since it is through him that information about group objectives and decisions is transmitted and conflicting viewpoints are resolved.

One shortcoming of this approach is the implicit assumption that all individuals are motivated by similar needs. No attention is focused on the important differences in individual needs. A second problem is, because of either the needs of organization members or the nature of the task, linking pin and participative decision-making practices are often impractical. For example, some managers find it difficult because of their own predispositions to involve subordinates in all decisions. Similarly, some tasks require decisions for which the information is not available to all the members of the work group.

Both of these approaches described above are subject to a more general criticism. While each offers a particular prescription about how to design the basic structure of an organization, both approaches are offered as the one best way to organize. To the readers who have already been exposed to a systemic conceptual framework, it should be obvious that any blanket prescription is an oversimplification. As the recent title of a book on organization theory states, "It all depends."[4] Furthermore, recent research which utilizes the systemic approach suggests that the choices made in designing a basic structure depend on the task and human inputs involved.

A SYSTEMIC APPROACH TO THE DESIGN OF ORGANIZATION STRUCTURE

Two recent studies point to the validity of this conclusion. Burns and Stalker, in their pioneering study of firms in both a dynamic, changing industry and a more established, stable industry, report that there were important structural differences between the successful firms in each industry.[5] In the stable industry, successful organizations tended to be what the authors called "mechanistic." There was more reliance on formal rules and procedures. Decisions were made at the higher levels of the organization. The spans of supervisory control were narrow. In the more dynamic industry, the authors characterized the effective organizations as "organic." Spans of supervisory control were wider; less attention was paid to formal procedures; and more decisions were reached at the lower levels of the organization. The second study was conducted by Joan Woodward.[6] She found that economically successful organizations in industries with different production technologies were characterized by different organization structures. For example, successful firms in industries with a unit or job-shop technology had wider spans of supervisory control and fewer hierarchical levels than did successful firms with continuous process technologies.

While both of these studies consider the structure of an organization as one variable

4. Harvey Sherman, *It all depends: A pragmatic approach to organization* (Tuscaloosa: University of Alabama Press, 1966).
5. T. Burns and G. M. Stalker, *The management of innovation* (London: Tavistock Publications, 1961).
6. Joan Woodward, *Industrial organisation: Theory and practice* (Oxford: Oxford University Press, 1965).

in a system affecting behavior in organizations, they do not provide a conceptual framework which is sufficiently comprehensive for analyzing and solving structural design problems. A more recent study by Lawrence and Lorsch builds on the basic idea of Woodward, Burns, and Stalker, and others, and provides a more comprehensive analytic framework for working on structural design problems.[7]

DIFFERENTIATION AND INTEGRATION

Before describing the analytic framework which Lawrence and Lorsch have developed, it is important to emphasize three points.[8] First, this conceptual scheme is based on an empirical study of ten organizations with varying levels of economic performance in three different industrial environments (plastics, consumer foods, standardized containers), and these findings have been corroborated by research in several additional settings. Second, this conceptual model does not provide a prescription for the one best way to organize. Instead, it provides a framework for thinking about structural design issues based on the demands of the organization's particular market and technological environment. Third, this set of concepts can be used to analyze the structural design which seems to best fit an organization's environment. These concepts can also be used to understand the organization's current strengths and weaknesses and to help determine what design changes will move a particular organization toward a better fit with the demands of its specific environment.

As we begin this discussion, we must first define two of the central concepts in this framework. First, *differentiation* is defined as *the differences in cognitive and emotional orientations among managers in different functional departments, and the differences in formal structure among these departments.* Rather than thinking of division of work as only affecting the economies and efficiencies of task performance, as did the classicists, Lawrence and Lorsch recognized that each unit was itself a subsystem in which members would develop particular orientations and structural patterns, depending on their task and their predispositions. Since different units were working with different parts of the organization's environment [e.g., market, scientific techno-economic (manufacturing) variables], these units would develop differentiation to some degree or other, depending upon the specific environment.

The second concept which we want to define is *integration— the quality of the state of collaboration that exists among departments that are required to achieve unity of effort by the environment.*

As we have already indicated, different environments require varying degrees of differentiation among organizational units. Basically, the extent of organizational differentiation depends upon the *certainty or uncertainty of the environment* and its *diversity or homogeneity*. Rather than being concerned with the environment as a single entity, the authors recognized that complex organizations—those with more than one unit—actually segment their environments into parts. The authors then identified the relative certainty of the parts of any environment. For example, each of the ten organizations was dealing with a market subenvironment (the task of the sales organization), a techno-economic subenvironment (the task of the manufacturing unit) and a scientific subenvironment (the task of the research of design unit).

Each of these subenvironments within any one industry had a different degree of certainty of information about what needed

7. P. R. Lawrence and J. W. Lorsch, *Organization and environment: Managing differentiation and integration* (Boston: Division of Research, Harvard Graduate School of Business Administration, 1967).
8. A more complete statement of their findings may be found in *Organization and environment*.

Fig. 18-1

Uncertainty of environmental sector	High	Moderate	Low
Extent of formalized unit structure	Low	Medium	High
Interpersonal orientation*	Task	Social	Task
Time orientation	Long	Medium	Short

*This curvilinear relation between the members' interpersonal orientation in a task-oriented/social-oriented continuum is consistent with the work of Fred E. Fiedler, *Technical Report No. 10* (Urbana, Ill.: Group Effectiveness Research Laboratory, Department of Psychology, University of Illinois, May 1962).

to be done. How similar or different these parts of any environment were on the certainty-uncertainty continuum determined whether that environment was relatively homogeneous or diverse. For example, in one of the environments studied, the container industry, all parts of the environment were relatively certain and the environment was characterized as homogeneous. On the other hand, in a second environment, the plastics industry, the parts of the environment ranged from a highly certain techno-economic sector to a very uncertain scientific subenvironment and the total environment was characterized as more diverse. As suggested above, the degree of differentiation in an effective organization was found to be related to the diversity of the environment. Thus, in the economically effective container industry there was less differentiation than in an effective plastic organization. The less effective organizations in these industries did not meet the environmental demand for differentiation so well.

We can now summarize the general relationship the authors found between the certainty of the subenvironment a unit is dealing with and three of the unit characteristics along which differentiation was measured (Figure 18-1).

The fourth characteristic of units along which differentiation was measured—goal orientation—was not related to the certainty of the environment, but instead to the goals inherent in each part of the environment— e.g., the market (customer service, competitive action, etc.); techno-economic (costs, quality, efficient schedules, etc.); science

(discovery of new knowledge; utilization of technical talent, etc.).

We can quote from the original study for a more detailed picture of how the varying degrees of differentiation manifest themselves in the high-performing organizations in two of the three industries studied.[9]

To illustrate the varying states of differentiation among these three organizations, we can use hypothetical encounters among managers in both the plastics and the container high-performing organizations. In the plastics organization we might find a sales manager discussing a potential new product with a fundamental research scientist and an integrator. In this discussion the sales manager is concerned with the needs of the customer. What performance characteristics must a new product have to perform in the customer's machinery? How much can the customer afford to pay? How long can the material be stored without deteriorating? Further, our sales manager, while talking about these matters, may be thinking about more pressing current problems. Should he lower the price on an existing product? Did the material shipped to another customer meet his specifications? Is he going to meet this quarter's sales targets?

In contrast, our fundamental scientist is concerned about a different order of problems. Will this new project provide a scientific challenge? To get the desired result, could he change the molecular structure of a known material without affecting its

9. *Ibid.*, pp. 134-36.

stability? What difficulties will he encounter in solving these problems? Will this be a more interesting project to work on than another he heard about last week? Will he receive some professional recognition if he is successful in solving the problem? Thus our sales manager and our fundamental scientist not only have quite different goal orientations, but they are thinking about different time dimensions—the sales manager about what's going on today and in the next few months; the scientist, how he will spend the next few years.

But these are not the only ways in which these two specialists are different. The sales manager may be outgoing and concerned with maintaining a warm, friendly relationship with the scientist. He may be put off because the scientist seems withdrawn and disinclined to talk about anything other than the problems in which he is interested. He may also be annoyed that the scientist seems to have such freedom in choosing what he will work on. Furthermore, the scientist is probably often late for appointments, which, from the salesman's point of view, is no way to run a business. Our scientist, for his part, may feel uncomfortable because the salesman seems to be pressing for immediate answers to technical questions that will take a long time to investigate. All these discomforts are concrete manifestations of the relatively wide differences between these two men in respect to their working and thinking styles and the departmental structures to which each is accustomed.

Between these different points of view stands our integrator. If he is effective, he will understand, and to some extent share, the viewpoints of both specialists and will be working to help them communicate with each other. We do not want to dwell on his role at this point, but the mere fact that he is present is a result of the great differences among specialists in his organization.

In the high-performing container organization we might find a research scientist meeting with a plant manager to determine how to solve a quality problem. The plant manager talks about getting the problem solved as quickly as possible, in order to reduce the spoilage rate. He is probably thinking about how this problem will affect his ability to meet the current production schedule and to operate within cost constraints. The researcher is also seeking an immediate answer to the problem. He is concerned not with its theoretical niceties, but with how he can find an immediate applied solution. (Research in this industry tended to focus on short-term process development.) What adjustments in materials or machine procedures can he suggest to get the desired effect? In fact, these specialists may share a concern with finding the most feasible solution. They also operate in a similar, short-term time dimension. The differences in their inter-personal styles are also not too large. Both are primarily concerned with getting the job done, and neither finds the other's style of behavior strange. They are also accustomed to quite similar organizational practices. Both see that they are rewarded for quite specific short-run accomplishments, and both might be feeling similar pressures from their superiors to get the job done. In essence, these two specialists, while somewhat different in their thinking and behavior patterns, would not find it uncomfortable or difficult to work together in seeking a joint solution to a problem. Thus they would need no integrator.

The authors summarize this approach as follows: "These two hypothetical examples show clearly that the differentiation in the [effective] plastics organization is much greater than in the equally effective container concern. The high-performing food organization fell between the extremes of differentiation represented by the other two organizations."[10]

But the environment of an organization imposes requirements other than differen-

10. *Ibid.*, p. 137.

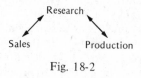

Fig. 18-2

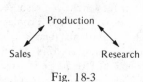

Fig. 18-3

tiation upon the organization. One of these is the *dominant competitive issue*. In the plastics and food environment, this was the issue of innovating new products and processes; for the container industry the dominant issue was the scheduling and allocation of production facilities to meet market demands.

The dominant competitive issue was also related to the final environmental characteristic of interest to the authors—the pattern and degree of integration required among units. In all three environments the tightness of integration required was found to be identical. However, there was an important difference in the pattern around which this integration was occurring. In plastics and foods, where innovative issues are dominant, the tight integration was required between sales and research and production and research. In the container industry, the tight integration was required between production and sales and between production and research.

The authors report that in each industry the high-performing organizations achieved more effective integration around these critical interdependencies than their less effective competitor. Thus, the effective organization more satisfactorily met the demands of its environment for both differentiation and integration than did the less effective organization(s) in the same environment.

This finding is particularly interesting,

because the authors found a strong inverse relationship between differentiation and integration within any one organization. When highly interdependent units are highly differentiated, it is more difficult to achieve integration among them than when members of the units have similar ways of thinking and behaving. This antagonistic relationship is illustrated by Figure 18-4, taken from the original study.[11]

Thus, we are presented with an interesting paradox: effective organizations in a given environment achieve more differentiation *and* more integration, but these two states are basically antagonistic. How does an organization get both? The authors found that two related factors made this possible.

First, when an organization is both highly differentiated and well integrated, it is necessary for the organization to develop more complicated mechanisms for achieving integration. Of course the basic organizational device for achieving integration is the management hierarchy. In an organization such as the effective container firm, with relatively low differentiation, the authors found that the hierarchy, along with formal plans and controls, was sufficient to achieve the required integration. However, the effective plastics and food organizations, faced with a requirement for both high differentiation and close integration, developed other supplemental integrating devices. These included individual coordinators (integrators), cross-unit teams, and even whole departments of integrators—individuals whose basic contribution is achieving integration among units. The integrative devices present in the high-performing organization in each environment are summarized in Figure 18-5.

The authors point out that while the effective organization always had integrative devices which were sufficient to handle both the differentiation and integration required, often the less effective firm also had appro-

11. *Ibid.*, Figure II–2, p. 48.

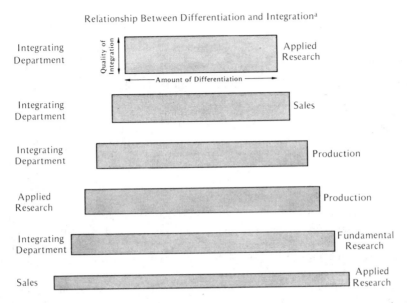

Relationship Between Differentiation and Integration[a]

a. This is a schematic representation of the relationship among departments in one organization. The longer the bar, the more differentiation; the wider the bar, the better the integration. This relationship held between pairs of units in all six organizations.

Fig. 18-4

Fig. 18-5. Introduction to the Structural Design of Organizations
(environmental factors and organizational characteristics of effective organizations)

Industry	Environment diversity	Actual differentiation	Actual integration	Integrative Devices		Conflict Management Variables	
				Type of integrative devices	Special integrating personnel as % of total management	Hierarchical influence	Unit having high influence
Plastics	high	high	high	Teams, roles departments, hierarchy, plans and procedures	22%*	Evenly distributed	Integrating unit
Foods	moderate	moderate	high	Roles, plans, hierarchy, procedures	17%*	Evenly distributed	Sales and research
Container	low	low	high	Hierarchy, plans and procedures	0%*	Top high, bottom low	Sales

*This proportion was constant for the high and low performer within these industries.

priate integrative devices. Thus, the integrative devices alone do not explain why the more effective firms were able to achieve the required states of differentiation and integration while the less effective firms did not.

A second set of factors seems to account for this difference. This is the behavior pattern used within the organization to manage intergroup conflict. As individuals with different points of view attempt to attain unity of effort, conflicts inevitably arise. How well the organization does in achieving integration in the face of differentiation is very dependent upon how the individuals involved resolve their conflicts. Lawrence and Lorsch's findings indicate that the behavior which leads to effective conflict resolution in certain respects varies with environmental demands, but in other respects shows no such variations.

Those conflict-management factors which vary with environmental influence include the pattern of power or influence among groups and at various levels of the management hierarchy of each group. In the high-performing organizations where conflict was managed effectively, influence was concentrated at the level within each group where the information relevant to the decision was also present. The exact level in any unit depended upon the certainty of information in its part of the particular environment. For example, in the research units of the effective plastics organization, because of the uncertainty of knowledge, influence was concentrated at the lowest management level. In the production unit of this same plastics organization, where environmental information was more certain, influence was concentrated at a higher level of the management hierarchy. Because of the diversity of this environment, the hierarchical influence in this organization was distributed differently among different levels in each function. The same was true of the effective food organization for similar reasons. However, in the container organization, dealing with more certain and more homogeneous environment, the information could be effici-

ently gathered by upper levels of management in all functions. Thus, hierarchical influence in this organization was concentrated at the top in all units.

The required pattern of influence among units also varied with environmental requirements. In the effective organization the unit(s) which had the central knowledge about environmental conditions related to the dominant strategic variable was the one with the most influence. For instance, in the effective plastics organization, where a separate integrating unit had been established, this group had the highest influence because it was in a position to have information about the various parts of the environment, all of which were important in achieving innovation. In the food organization, where the dominant issue was also innovation, the situation was slightly different. Here no integrating department had been established, because the differentiation required was not as high as in the plastics environment. Also because of the consumer products involved, the dominant knowledge was in the market and scientific sectors of the environment. Therefore, the sales and research units had similar high levels of power in relation to the production unit. In the container industry the dominant issue of customer service meant that the sales unit must call the tune, and this unit did have the highest influence.

The two factors which led to effective resolution under all environmental conditions were the mode of conflict resolution, and the basis from which high influence was derived. In high-performing organizations in all environments, it was found that conflict was managed by involved individuals who dealt openly with the conflict and worked a problem until a resolution was reached which best met total organizational goals. In the effective organizations, there was more of a tendency to *confront* conflict instead of using raw power to *force* one party's compliance or instead of *smoothing* over the conflict by agreeing to disagree.

In all the high-performing organizations,

the authors also found that the individuals primarily involved in resolving conflict, whether they were a common superior in the hierarchy or persons in special integrating positions, had influence based to a large extent on their perceived competence and knowledge. This was in contrast to the less effective organizations where such persons usually drew their power solely from their position or from their control over scarce resources. The persons centrally involved in achieving integration in the high-performing organizations were followed not only because they had formal positional authority, but also because they were seen as knowledgeable about the issues which had to be resolved.

In those organizations where special integrators existed, Lawrence and Lorsch found one additional conflict-management factor which seemed important. In the effective organizations, such integrators had orientations which were balanced between those of the groups whose efforts they were integrating. This made it possible for them to understand and communicate with each of the groups concerned. In the less effective organizations, these integrators tended to have one-sided orientations. They thought and acted like sales personnel or like researchers and this made it difficult for them to work with other groups.

All of these conflict-management variables taken together suggest why the effective organizations in each environment were able to achieve the differentiation and integration required by the particular environment when less effective firms were not able to do so. These conflict management practices were the glue which held the differentiated units together as they worked toward integrated goals.

To summarize, then, the Lawrence and Lorsch study provides a set of research findings and concepts which enable us to understand what characteristics an organization must have to be effective in a particular set of environmental circumstances. This study directs our attention to the environmental demands placed on the organization in terms of the degree of differentiation, the pattern and degree of integration, integrative mechanisms, and conflict management behaviors. Those factors in the study which varied among high-performing organizations in the three environments studied are summarized in Figure 18-5.

With this summary of the findings of this study, we now want to examine briefly how these ideas can be put to use to work on the issues of structural design.

APPLYING THESE CONCEPTS TO STRUCTURAL DESIGN

As we consider these concepts as they apply to structural design decisions, we will also suggest the sequence of structural subproblems. While these subproblems are stated as discrete issues, the reader should be aware that in practice it is necessary to move back and forth among them as one thinks about the whole problem of structural design in a given organization. We will look first at the design of the basic structure and then at the necessary operating mechanisms.

Grouping activities into units is the logical first step in designing a basic structure. The differentiation and integration concepts focus our attention on two criteria for making decisions about grouping activity. First, units which will have similar orientations and tasks should be grouped together, both because they can reinforce each other's common concerns to achieve the needed differentiation and because this will simplify the coordinating task of the common boss. Second, units which are required to integrate their activities closely should be grouped together, because the common superior can then work to achieve the required integration through the management hierarchy. Therefore units which have a requirement for both low differentiation and tight integration, should be grouped together. However, when some units are low in differentiation but are not highly interdependent, the choice about grouping becomes more complex. In these cases, we must use our judgment to determine which criterion—low differentiation or high integration—we want to optimize in grouping activities.

Designing integrative devices is the second step in determining the basic structure. As we suggested above, the grouping of activities itself has an effect upon the design of integrative devices. A primary integrative device in any organization is the management hierarchy. In grouping activities, we are essentially making choices about which units we want to integrate through the hierarchy. However, as the Lawrence and Lorsch findings suggest, even after the units are grouped and decisions have been made about where the hierarchy can be used to achieve integration, we are still left with the question of what other integrating devices are desirable and necessary. Their findings suggest that as the environment requires more differentiation and tighter integration it is necessary to build supplemental integrating mechanisms such as integrating departments or cross-functional teams into the organization. This study also suggests that these special devices should be built into the organization in such a way that they facilitate the interaction of integrators with functional specialists who have the relevant knowledge to contribute to joint decisions. Alternatively, they may also need to facilitate the direct interaction among functional specialists who have the necessary knowledge to contribute to these joint decisions.

Structuring the individual units is a third step in the design process. Here the emphasis is on operating mechanisms, which will be consistent with the unit task and the needs of its members. Issues of individual motivation are particularly relevant here.[12] In addition, the Lawrence and Lorsch findings underline the importance of designing mea-

surement and reward procedures to encourage orientations which are appropriate to the unit task. Similarly, reliance on formal rules and standardized procedures should be consistent with the task. Finally, the unit hierarchy and spans of control should be designed not only to provide the intra-unit coordination required by the task, but also to encourage involvement in decision-making at the level where the relevant information is available.

Other Operating Mechanisms

In addition to the operating mechanisms within each unit, it is necessary to consider operating mechanisms which are applied across the whole organization. Do rewards and measurements encourage collaboration around the critical integrative issues? Do they demand consistency and conformity among units where more differentiation is required? Again, issues of individual rewards and motivation should be helpful here, but we must also realize that some operating mechanisms must be built to encourage differentiation, while others are necessary to encourage integration. We must understand the environmental demands on the organization so that reward and measurement systems can be designed to encourage both the differentiated and integrated behavior required.

Factors Affecting Conflict Management

Finally, we should consider the effect of the basic structure and the operating mechanisms on conflict resolution. The basic structure should assign responsibility for cross-functional liaison to individuals who have the relevant knowledge. If individuals who have such knowledge are formally assigned the responsibility for joint decision making, there is the highest probability they will develop the power necessary to resolve conflict effectively. A second issue is related to operating mechanisms. Do they induce unnecessary conflict? Do they cause organi-

12. See G. W. Dalton and P. R. Lawrence, *Organizational motivation and control* (Homewood, Ill.: Irwin, 1970).

zation members to see conflicts as win-lose rather than integrative? Is so, can they be altered to encourage more integrative problem solving?

Finally, there is the issue of training and its impact on conflict-resolving behavior. While this topic could lead into a long discussion of organizational change, it is useful to mention here that some forms of laboratory training and education may be helpful to encourage the confrontation of conflict.[13] The ideas we have been discussing may be helpful in identifying which organization members are so involved in

conflict management that such training might be useful.

SUMMARY

In this introduction we have explored the approaches available to solving structural design problems. In concluding, we offer a word of caution. Our understanding of organizations as systems is new and it is growing rapidly. The ideas which are presented here will certainly be modified and improved. But as crude as they are, they represent better tools than the principles which have been relied on in the past. These ideas clearly move us in a new and promising direction—that of tailoring the organization to its environment and to the complex needs of its members.

13. See G. W. Dalton and P. R. Lawrence, *Organizational motivation and control* (Homewood, Ill.: Irwin, 1970).

19

Organizational Choice : Product vs. Function

ARTHUR H. WALKER and JAY W. LORSCH

Of all the issues facing a manager as he thinks about the form of his organization, one of the thorniest is the question of whether to group activities primarily by product or by function. Should all specialists in a given function be grouped under a common boss, regardless of differences in products they are involved in, or should the various functional specialists working on a single product be grouped together under the same superior?

In talks with managers we have repeatedly heard them anguishing over this choice. For example, recently a divisional vice president of a major U.S. corporation was contemplating a major organizational change. After long study, he made this revealing observation to his subordinate managers:

"We still don't know which choice will be the best one. Should the research, engineering, marketing, and production people be grouped separately in departments for each function? Or would it be better to have them grouped together in product departments, each department dealing with a particular product group?

"We were organized by product up until a few years ago. Then we consolidated our organization into specialized functional departments, each dealing with all of our products. Now I'm wondering if we wouldn't be better off to divide our operations again into product units. Either way I can see advantages and disadvantages, trade-offs. What criteria should I use? How can we predict what the outcomes will be if we change?"

Companies that have made a choice often feel confident that they have resolved this dilemma. Consider the case of a large advertising agency that consolidated its copy, art, and television personnel into a "total creative department." Previously they had reported to group heads in their areas of specialization. In a memo to employees the company explained the move:

"Formation of the 'total creative' department completely tears down the walls between art, copy, and television people. Behind this move is the realization that for best results all creative people, regardless of their particular specialty, must work together under the most intimate relationship as total advertising people, trying to solve creative problems together from start to finish.

"The new department will be broken into

Reprinted from *Harvard Business Review*, 1968 (November-December), 129-38, by permission of the publisher. © 1968 by the President and Fellows of Harvard College.

five groups reporting to the senior vice president and creative director, each under the direction of an associate creative director. Each group will be responsible for art, television, and copy in their accounts."

But our experience is that such reorganizations often are only temporary. The issues involved are so complex that many managements oscillate between these two choices or try to effect some compromise between them.

In this article we shall explore—from the viewpoint of the behavioral scientist—some of the criteria that have been used in the past to make these choices, and present ideas from recent studies that suggest more relevant criteria for making the decision. We hope to provide a way of thinking about these problems that will lead to the most sensible decisions for the accomplishment of organizational goals.

The dilemma of product versus function is by no means new; managers have been facing the same basic question for decades. As large corporations like Du Pont and General Motors grew, they found it necessary to divide their activities among product divisions.[1] Following World War II, as companies expanded their sales of existing products and added new products and businesses, many of them implemented a transition from functional organizations handling a number of different products to independently managed product divisions. These changes raised problems concerning divisionalization, decentralization, corporate staff activities, and the like.

As the product divisions grew and prospered, many companies extended the idea of product organization further down in their organizations under such labels as "the unit management concept." Today most of the attention is still being directed to these changes and innovations *within* product or market areas below the divisional level.

today within product divisions. The reader

We are focusing therefore on these organizational issues at the middle and lower echelons of management, particularly on the crucial questions being faced by managers today within product divisions. The reader should note, however, that a discussion of these issues is immensely complicated by the fact that a choice at one level of the corporate structure affects the choices and criteria for choice at other levels. Nonetheless, the ideas we suggest in this article are directly relevant to organizational choice at any level.

ELEMENTS TO CONSIDER

To understand more fully the factors that make these issues so difficult, it is useful to review the criteria often relied on in making this decision. Typically, managers have used technical and economic criteria. They ask themselves, for instance, "Which choice will minimize payroll costs?" Or, "Which will best utilize equipment and specialists?" This approach not only makes real sense in the traditional logic of management, but it has strong support from the classical school of organization theorists. Luther Gulick, for example, used it in arguing for organization by function:

It guarantees the maximum utilization of up-to-date technical skill and . . . makes it possible in each case to make use of the most effective divisions of work and specialization. . . . [It] makes possible also the economies of the maximum use of labor-saving machinery and mass production . . . . [It] encourages coordination in all of the technical and skilled work of the enterprise . . . . [It] furnishes an excellent approach to the development of central coordination and control.[2]

In pointing to the advantages of the product

1. For a historical study of the organizational structure of U.S. corporations, see Alfred D. Chandler, Jr., *Strategy and structure* (Cambridge, Mass.: M.I.T. Press, 1962).

2. Luther Gulick, Notes on the theory of organization, in *Papers on the science of administration*, ed. by Luther Gulick and Lyndall F. Urwick (New York: New York Institute of Public Administration, 1937), pp. 23-24.

basis of organization, two other classical theorists used the same approach:

Product or product line is an important basis for departmentalizing, because it permits the maximum use of personal skills and specialized knowledge, facilitates the employment of specialized capital and makes easier a certain type of coordination.[3]

In sum, these writers on organization suggested that the manager should make the choice based on three criteria:
1. Which approach permits the maximum use of special technical knowldge?
2. Which provides the most efficient utilization of machinery and equipment?
3. Which provides the best hope of obtaining the required control and coordination?

There is nothing fundamentally wrong with these criteria as far as they go, and, of course, managers have been using them. But they fail to recognize the complex set of trade-offs involved in these decisions. As a consequence, managers make changes that produce unanticipated results and may even reduce the effectiveness of their organization. For example:

A major manufacturer of corrugated containers a few years ago shifted from a product basis to a functional basis. The rationale for the decision was that it would lead to improved control of production costs and efficiencies in production and marketing. While the organization did accomplish these aims, it found itself less able to obtain coordination among its local sales and production units. The functional specialists now reported to the top officers in charge of production and sales, and there was no mechanism for one person to coordinate their work below the level of division management. As a result, the company encoun-

tered numerous problems and unresolved conflicts among functions and later returned to the product form.

This example pinpoints the major trade-off that the traditional criteria omit. Developing highly specialized functional units makes it difficult to achieve coordination or integration among these units. On the other hand, having product units as the basis for organization promotes collaboration between specialists, but the functional specialists feel less identification with functional goals.

Behaviorists' Findings

We now turn to some new behavioral science approaches to designing organization structure. Recent studies[4] have highlighted three other important factors about specialization and coordination:

As we have suggested, the classical theorists saw specialization in terms of grouping similar activities, skills, or even equipment. They did not look at its psychological and social consequences. Recently, behavioral scientists (including the authors) have found that there is an important relationship between a unit's or individual's assigned activities and the unit members' patterns of thought and behavior. Functional specialists tend to develop patterns of behavior and thought that are in tune with the demands of their jobs and their prior training, and as a result these specialists (e.g., industrial engineers and production supervisors) have different ideas and orientation about what is important in getting the job done. This is called *differentiation*, which simply means the differences in behavior and thought patterns that develop among different specialists in relation to their respective tasks. Differentiation is necessary for functional

3. Harold D. Koontz and C. J. O'Donnell, *Principles of management.* 2nd ed. (New York: McGraw-Hill, 1959), p. 111.

4. See Paul R. Lawrence and Jay W. Lorsch, *Organization and environment* (Boston: Division of Research, Harvard Business School, 1967); and Eric J. Miller and A. K. Rice, *Systems of organization* (London: Tavistock Publications, 1967).

specialists to perform their jobs effectively.

Differentiation is closely related to achievement of coordination, or what behavioral scientists call *integration*. This means collaboration between specialized units or individuals. Recent studies have demonstrated that there is an inverse relationship between differentiation and integration: the more two functional specialists (or their units) differ in their patterns of behavior and thought, the more difficult it is to bring about integration between them. Nevertheless, this research has indicated, achievement of both differentiation and integration is essential if organizations are to perform effectively.

While achievement of both differentiation and integration is possible, it can occur only when well-developed means of communication among specialists exist in the organization and when the specialists are effective in resolving the inevitable cross-functional conflicts.

These recent studies, then, point to certain related questions that managers must consider when they choose between a product or functional basis of organization:

1. How will the choice affect differentiation among specialists? Will it allow the necessary differences in viewpoint to develop so that specialized tasks can be performed effectively?

2. How does the decision affect the prospects of accomplishing integration? Will it lead, for instance, to greater differentiation, which will increase the problems of achieving integration?

3. How will the decision affect the ability of organization members to communicate with each other, resolve conflicts, and reach the necessary joint decisions?

There appears to be a connection between the appropriate extent of differentiation and integration and the organization's effectiveness in accomplishing its economic goals. What the appropriate pattern is depends on the nature of external factors—markets,

technology, and so on—facing the organization, as well as the goals themselves. The question of how the organizational pattern will affect individual members is equally complex. Management must consider how much stress will be associated with a certain pattern and whether such stress should be a serious concern.

To explore in more detail the significance of modern approaches to organizational structuring, we shall describe one recent study conducted in two manufacturing plants—one organized by *product*, the other on a *functional* basis.[5]

PLANT F and PLANT P

The two plants where this study was conducted were selected because they were closely matched in several ways. They were making the same product; their markets, technology, and even raw materials were identical. The parent companies were also similar: both were large, national corporations that developed, manufactured, and marketed many consumer products. In each case divisional and corporate headquarters were located more than a hundred miles from the facilities studied. The plants were separated from other structures at the same site, where other company products were made.

Both plants had very similar management styles. They stressed their desire to foster employees' initiative and autonomy and placed great reliance on selection of well-qualified department heads. They also identified explicitly the same two objectives. The first was to formulate, package, and ship the products to minimum time at specified levels of quality and at minimum cost—that is, within existing capabilities. The second was to improve the capabilities of the plant.

In each plant there were identical functional specialists involved with the manufac-

5. Arthur H. Walker, *Behavioral consequences of contrasting patterns of organization* (Boston: Harvard Business School, Ph.D. diss., 1967).

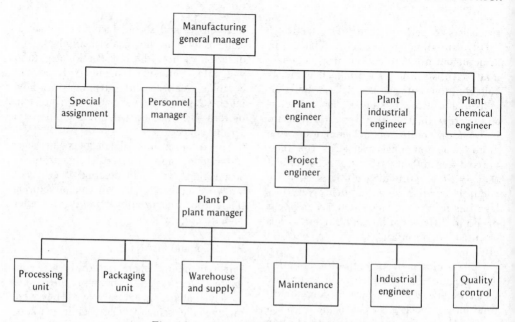

Fig. 19-1. Organizational Chart at Plant F

turing units and packing unit, as well as quality control, planning and scheduling, warehousing, industrial engineering, and plant engineering. In Plant F (with the *functional* basis of organization), only the manufacturing departments and the planning and scheduling function reported to the plant manager responsible for the product (see Figure 19-1). All other functional specialists reported to the staff of the divisional manufacturing manager, who was also responsible for plants manufacturing other products. At Plant P (with the *product* basis of organization), all functional specialists with the exception of plant engineering reported to the plant manager (see Figure 19-2).

State of Differentiation

In studying differentiation, it is useful to focus on the functional specialists' differences in outlook in terms of:

Orientation toward goals;
Orientation toward time;
Perception of the formality of organization.

Goal orientation. The basis of organization in the two plants had a marked effect on the specialists' differentiated goal orientations. In Plant F they focused sharply on their specialized goals and objectives. For example, quality control specialists were concerned almost exclusively with meeting quality standards, industrial engineers with methods improvements and cost reduction, and scheduling specialists with how to meet schedule requirements. An industrial engineer in Plant F indicated this intensive interest in his own activity:

"We have 150 projects worth close to a million dollars in annual savings. I guess I've completed some that save as much as $90,000 a year. Right now I'm working on cutting departmental costs. You need a hard shell in this work. No one likes to have his costs cut, but that is my job."

That these intense concerns with specialized objectives were expected is illustrated by the apologetic tone of a comment on production goals by an engineering supervisor at Plant F:

"At times we become too much involved

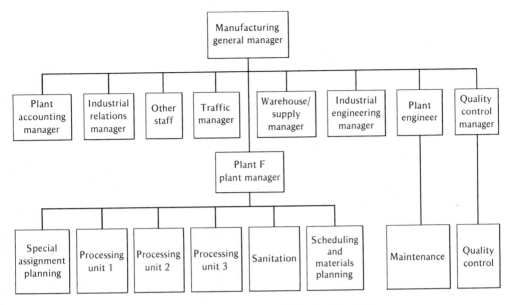

Fig. 19-2. Organizational Chart at Plant P

in production. It causes a change in heart. We are interested in production, but not at the expense of our own standards of performance. If we get too much involved, then we may become compromised."

A final illustration is when production employees stood watching while members of the maintenance department worked to start a new production line, and a production supervisor remarked:

"I hope that they get that line going soon. Right now, however, my hands are tied. Maintenance has the job. I can only wait. My people have to wait, too."

This intense concern with one set of goals is analogous to a rifle shot; in a manner of speaking, each specialist took aim at one set of goals and fired at it. Moreover, the specialists identified closely with their counterparts in other plants and at divisional headquarters. As one engineer put it:

"We carry the ball for them (the central office). We carry a project through and get it working right."

At Plant P the functional specialists' goals

were more diffuse—like buckshot. Each specialist was concerned not only with his own goals, but also with the operation of the entire plant. For example, in contrast in the Plant F production supervisor's attitude about maintenance, a Plant P maintenance manager said, under similar circumstances:

"We're all interested in the same thing. If I can help, I'm willing. If I have a mechanical problem, there is no member of the operating department who wouldn't go out of his way to solve it."

Additional evidence of this more diffuse orientation toward goals is provided by comments such as these which came from Plant P engineers and managers:

"We are here for a reason—to run this place the best way we know how. There is no reluctance to be open and frank despite various backgrounds and ages."

"The changeovers tell the story. Everyone shows willingness to dig in. The whole plant turns out to do cleaning up."

Because the functional specialists at Plant F focused on their individual goals, they had relatively wide differences in goals and objectives. Plant P's structure, on the other hand, seemed to make functional specialists more aware of common product goals and reduced differences in goal orientation. Yet, as we shall see, this lesser differentiation did not hamper their performance.

Time orientation. The two organizational bases had the opposite effect, however, on the time orientation of functional managers. At Plant F, the specialists shared a concern with short-term issues (mostly daily problems). The time orientation of specialists at Plant P was more differentiated. For example, its production managers concentrated on routine matters, while planning and industrial engineering focused on issues that needed solution within a week, and quality control specialists worried about even longer-term problems.

The reason is not difficult to find. Since Plant P's organization led its managers to identify with product goals, those who could contribute to the solution of longer-term problems became involved in these activities. In Plant F, where each unit focused on its own goals, there was more of a tendency to worry about getting daily progress. On the average, employees of Plant P reported devoting 30 per cent of their time to daily problems, while at Plant F this figure was 49 per cent. We shall have more to say shortly about how these factors influenced the results achieved in the two plants.

Organizational formality. In the study, the formality of organizational structure in each functional activity was measured by three criteria:

1. Clarity of definition of job responsibilities;
2. Clarity of dividing lines between jobs;
3. Importance of rules and procedures.

It was found that at Plant F there were fewer differences among functional activities in the formality of organization structure than at Plant P. Plant F employees reported that a uniform degree of structure existed across functional specialties; job responsibilities were well defined, and the distinctions between jobs were clear. Similarly, rules and procedures were extensively relied on. At Plant P, on the other hand, substantial differences in the formality of organization existed. Plant engineers and industrial engineers, for example, were rather vague about their responsibilities and about the dividing line between their jobs and other jobs. Similarly, they reported relatively low reliance on rules and procedures. Production managers, on the other hand, noted that their jobs were well defined and that rules and procedures were more important to them.

The effects of these two bases of organization on differentiation along these three dimensions are summarized in Figure 19-3. Over-all, differentiation was greater between functional specialists at Plant P than at Plant F.

Integration Achieved

While the study found that both plants experienced some problems in accomplishing integration, these difficulties were more noticeable at Plant F. Collaboration between maintenance and production personnel and between production and scheduling was a problem there. In Plant P the only relationship where integration was unsatisfactory was that between production and quality control specialists. Thus Plant P seemed to be getting slightly better integration in spite of the greater differentiation among specialists in that organization. Since differentiation and integration are basically antagonistic, the only way managers at Plant P could get both was by being effective at communication and conflict resolution. They were better at this than were managers at Plant F.

Communication patterns. In Plant P, communication among employees was more frequent, less formal, and more often of a

Fig. 19-3. Differentiation in Plants F and P

Dimensions of differentiation	Plant F	Plant P
Goal orientation	More differentiated and focused	Less differentiated and more diffuse
Time orientation	Less differentiated and shorter term	More differentiated and longer term
Formality of structure	Less differentiated, with more formality	More differentiated, with less formality

face-to-face nature than was the case with Plant F personnel. One Plant P employee volunteered:

"Communications are no problem around here. You can say it. You can get an answer."

Members of Plant F did not reflect such positive feelings. They were heard to say:

"Why didn't they tell me this was going to happen? Now they've shut down the line."

"When we get the information, it is usually too late to do any real planning. We just do our best."

The formal boundaries outlining positions that were more prevalent at Plant F appeared to act as a damper on communication. The encounters observed were often a succession of two-man conversations, even though more than two may have been involved in a problem. The telephone and written memoranda were more often employed than at Plant P, where spontaneous meetings involving several persons were frequent, usually in the cafeteria.

Dealing with conflict. In both plants, *confrontation* of conflict was reported to be more typical than either the use of power to *force* one's own position or an attempt to *smooth* conflict by "agreeing to disagree." There was strong evidence, nevertheless, that in Plant P managers were coming to grips with conflicts more directly than in Plant F. Managers at Plant F reported that more conflicts were being smoothed over. They

worried that issues were often not getting settled. As they put it:

"We have too many nice guys here."

"If you can't resolve an issue, you go to the plant manager. But we don't like to bother him often with small matters. We should be able to settle them ourselves. The trouble is we don't. So it dies."

Thus, by ignoring conflict in the hope it would go away, or by passing it to a higher level, managers at Plant F often tried to smooth over their differences. While use of the management hierarchy is one acceptable way to resolve conflict, so many disagreements at Plant F were pushed upstairs that the hierarchy became overloaded and could not handle all the problems facing it. So it responded by dealing with only the more immediate and pressing ones.

At Plant P the managers uniformly reported that they resolved conflicts themselves. There was no evidence that conflicts were being avoided or smoothed over. As one manager said:

"We don't let problems wait very long. There's no sense to it. And besides, we get together frequently and have plenty of chances to discuss differences over a cup of coffee."

As this remark suggests, the quicker resolution of conflict was closely related to the open and informal communication pattern prevailing at Plant P. In spite of greater differentiation in time orientation and structure, then, Plant P managers were able to achieve more satisfactory integration because they could communicate and resolve conflict effectively.

Performance and Attitudes

Before drawing some conclusions from the study of these two plants, it is important to make two more relevant comparisons between them—their effectiveness in terms of the goals set for them and the attitudes of employees.

Plant performance. As we noted before, the managements of the two plants were aiming at the same two objectives:

1. Maximizing current output within existing capabilities;
2. Improving the capabilities of the plant.

Of the two facilities, Plant F met the first objective more effectively; it was achieving a higher production rate with greater efficiency and at less cost than was Plant P. In terms of the second objective, however, Plant P was clearly superior to Plant F; the former's productivity had increased by 23 per cent from 1963 to 1966 compared with the latter's increment of only 3 per cent. One key manager at Plant F commented:

"There has been a three- or four-year effort to improve our capability. Our expectations have simply not been achieved. The improvement in performance is just not there. We are still where we were three years ago. But our targets for improvements are realistic."

By contrast, a key manager at Plant P observed:

"Our crews have held steady, yet our volume is up. Our quality is consistently better, too."

Another said:

"We are continuing to look for and find ways to improve and consolidate jobs."

Employee attitudes. Here, too, the two organizations offer a contrast, but the contrast presents a paradoxical situation. Key personnel at Plant P appeared to be more deeply involved in their work than did managers at Plant F, and they admitted more often to feeling stress and pressure than did their opposite numbers at Plant F. But Plant F managers expressed more satisfaction with their work than did those at Plant P; they liked the company and their jobs more than did managers at Plant P.

Why Plant P managers felt more involved and had a higher level of stress, but were less satisfied than Plant F managers, can best be explained by linking these findings with the others we have reported.

Study Summary

The characteristics of these two organizations are summarized in Figure 19-4. The nature of the organization at Plant F seemed to suit its stable but high rate of efficiency. Its specialists concentrated on their own goals and performed well, on the whole. The jobs were well defined and managers worked within procedures and rules. The managers were concerned primarily with short-term matters. They were not particularly effective in communicating with each other and in resolving conflict. But this was not very important to achieve steady, good performance, since the coordination necessary to meet this objective could be achieved through plans and procedures and through the manufacturing technology itself.

As long as top management did not exert much pressure to improve performance dramatically, the plant's managerial hierarchy was able to resolve the few conflicts arising from daily operations. And as long as the organization avoided extensive problem-solving, a great deal of personal contact was not very important. It is not surprising therefore that the managers were satisfied and felt relatively little pressure. They attended strictly to their own duties, remained uninvolved, and got the job done. For them, this combination was satisfying. And higher management was pleased with the facility's production efficiency.

Fig. 19-4. Observed Characteristics of the Two Organizations

Characteristics	Plant F	Plant P
Differentiation	Less differentiation except in ogal orientation	Greater differentiation in structure and time orientation
Integration	Somewhat less effective	More effective
Conflict management	Confrontation, but also "smoothing over" and avoidance; rather restricted communication pattern	Confrontation of conflict; open, face-to-face communication
Effectiveness	Efficient, stable production; but less successful in improving plant capabilities	Successful in improving plant capabilities, but less effective in stable production
Employee attitudes	Prevalent feeling of satisfaction, but less feeling of stress and involvement	Prevalent feeling of stress and involvement, but less satisfaction

The atmosphere at Plant P, in contrast, was well suited to the goal of improving plant capabilities, which it did very well. There was less differentiation between goals, since the functional specialists to a degree shared the product goals. Obviously, one danger in this form of organization is the potential attraction of specialist managers to total goals to the extent that they lose sight of their particular goals and become less effective in their jobs. But this was not a serious problem at Plant P.

Moreover, there was considerable differentiation in time orientation and structure; some specialists worked at the routine and programmed tasks in operating the plant, while others concentrated on longer-term problems to improve manufacturing capability. The latter group was less constrained by formal procedures and job definitions, and this atmosphere was conducive to problem solving. The longer-time orientation of some specialists, however, appeared to divert their attention from maintaining schedules and productivity. This was a contributing factor to Plant P's less effective current performance.

In spite of the higher degree of differen-

tiation in these dimensions, Plant P managers were able to achieve the integration necessary to solve problems that hindered plant capability. Their shared goals and a common boss encouraged them to deal directly with each other and confront their conflicts. Given this pattern, it is not surprising that they felt very involved in their jobs. Also they were under stress because of their great involvement in their jobs. This stress could lead to dissatisfaction with their situation. Satisfaction for its own sake, however, may not be very important; there was no evidence of higher turnover of managers at Plant P.

Obviously, in comparing the performance of these two plants operating with similar technologies and in the same market, we might predict that, because of its greater ability to improve plant capabilities, Plant P eventually will reach a performance level at least as high as Plant F's. While this might occur in time, it should not obscure one important point: the functional organization seems to lead to better results in a situation where stable performance of a routine task is desired, while the product organization leads to better results in situations where the task is less predictable and requires innovative problem-solving.

CLUES FOR MANAGERS

How can the manager concerned with the function-versus-product decision use these ideas to guide him in making the appropriate choice? The essential step is identifying the demands of the task confronting the organization.

Is it a routine, repetitive task? It is one where integration can be achieved by plan and conflict-managed through the hierarchy? This was the way the task was implicitly defined at Plant F. If this is the nature of the task, or, to put in another way, if management is satisfied with this definition of the task, then the functional organization is quite appropriate. While it allows less differentiation in time orientation and structure, it does encourage differentiation in goal orientation. This combination is important for specialists to work effectively in their jobs.

Perhaps even more important, the functional structure also seems to permit a degree of integration sufficient to get the organization's work done. Much of this can be accomplished through paper systems and through the hardware of the production line itself. Conflict that comes up can more safely be dealt with through the management hierarchy, since the difficulties of resolving conflict are less acute. This is so because the tasks provide less opportunity for conflict and because the specialists have less differentiated viewpoints to overcome. This form of organization is less psychologically demanding for the individuals involved.

On the other hand, if the task is of a problem-solving nature, or if management defines it this way, the product organization seems to be more appropriate. This is especially true where there is a need for tight integration among specialists. As illustrated at Plant P, the product organization form allows the greater differentiation in time

orientation and structure that specialists need to attack problems. While encouraging identification with superordinate goals, this organizational form does allow enough differentiation in goals for specialists to make their contributions.

Even more important, to identify with product ends and have a common boss encourages employees to deal constructively with conflict, communicate directly and openly with each other, and confront their differences, so they can collaborate effectively. Greater stress and less satisfaction for the individual may be unavoidable, but it is a small price to pay for the involvement that accompanies it.

The manager's problem in choosing between product and functional forms is complicated by the fact that in each organization there are routine tasks and tasks requiring problem solving, jobs requiring little interdependence among specialists and jobs requiring a great deal. Faced with these mixtures, many companies have adopted various compromises between product and functional bases. They include (in ascending order of structural complexity):

1. The use of cross-functional teams to facilitate integration. These teams provide some opportunity for communication and conflict resolution and also a degree of the common identification with product goals that characterizes the product organization. At the same time, they retain the differentiation provided by the functional organization.

2. The appointment of full-time integrators or coordinators around a product. These product managers or project managers encourage the functional specialists to become committed to product goals and help resolve conflicts between them. The specialists still retain their primary identification with their functions.[6]

3. The "matrix" or grid organization,

6. See Paul R. Lawrence and Jay W. Lorsch, "New management job: The integrator," HBR, 1967 (November-December), p. 142.

which combines the product and functional forms by overlaying them. Some managers wear functional hats and are involved in the day-to-day, more routine activities. Naturally, they identify with functional goals. Others, wearing product or project hats, identify with total product goals and are more involved in the problem-solving activity required to copy with long-range issues and to achieve cross-functional coordination.

These compromises are becoming popular because they enable companies to deal with multiple tasks simultaneously. But we do not propose them as a panacea, because they make sense only for those situations where the differentiation and integration required by the sum of all the tasks make a middle approach necessary. Further, the complexity of interpersonal plus organizational relationships in these forms and the ambiguity associated with them make them difficult to administer effectively and psychologically demanding on the persons involved.

In our view, the only solution to the product-versus-function dilemma lies in analysis of the multiple tasks that must be performed, the differences between specialists, the integration that must be achieved, and the mechanisms and behavior required to resolve conflict and arrive at these states of differentiation and integration. This analysis provides the best hope of making a correct product or function choice or of arriving at some appropriate compromise solution.

4

ORGANIZATION DEVELOPMENT AND CONFLICT MANAGEMENT

The term "organization development" ("OD") has been used to describe a variety of change programs in organizations. These change programs are broader in scope than the training methods discussed in Section VII or the motivational techniques discussed in Section I, although an OD program may include training and motivational techniques such as T-groups and job enrichment. The general objective of organization development is to improve the problem-solving and conflict-resolution processes of the organization. The targets of the change effort are usually groups rather than individuals, but changes in individual attitudes and values may be involved, as well as improvement in interpersonal competence and diagnostic skill. Changes in organization structure may or may not be included as part of an OD program and are usually secondary in importance.

An OD program is usually an organization-wide or large-scale effort rather than being limited to one small subunit of the organization. The program is usually a long-range, rather than a short-range, effort. Finally, organization development is usually guided by a behavioral science consultant who is not a regular member of the organization being changed (French and Bell, 1973).

The basic tactic used in organization development is some type of "intervention" designed to bring about changes in the organization. While some of the interventions originated with the action research conducted by Kurt Lewin and his associates in the 1940s, many innovations and refinements have occurred in recent years. The assumptions underlying most OD interventions reflect an optimistic, positive view of human nature. People are assumed to have drives toward psychological growth and self-actualization and to be capable of positive change in personality and values. It is also assumed that the effectiveness of work groups can be improved by expression of emotions and openness of communication, as well as by considerable participation of members in the problem-solving and decision-making processes of the group. The selection by French and Bell provides an overview of the large variety of OD interventions currently in use. The major types of interventions are briefly described, and some recommendations for "better structuring" of intervention activities are suggested. For a more detailed description of OD interventions, the reader is referred to the books by French and Bell (1973), Beckhard (1969), and Schein (1969).

Only a limited amount of empirical data has been collected on the effectiveness of OD programs. Most evaluations have been case studies without rigorous measurement of attitudes and performance. The article by Bowers is probably the most comprehensive and elaborate evaluation of OD interventions to date. Bowers analyzed data from more than 14,000 respondents in 23 organizations in which various types of OD interventions were carried out. Interventions such as survey feedback, interpersonal process consultation, task process consultaton, and team training were compared with each other and with control groups in which there was no systematic change effort. The criteria for evaluating the interventions were changes in organization climate, leadership behavior, and job satisfaction. Bowers interprets the results and discusses the implications of differences found in the effectiveness of the interventions.

One assumption of most OD proponents is that an organization is a system with continuous interaction among component subsystems and with the external environment. Because of the interdependency of processes within organizations, one part of the system cannot be changed without important consequences for the interrelated parts. A change program may fail if the complete set of interactions and feedback effects is not anticipated in the planning of the change program. A "systems approach" to OD may dictate that the usual interventions into group and intergroup processes must be accompanied by supporting changes in such things as the organization structure, the personnel subsystem (e.g., selection, training, performance appraisal), and the budgetary and control processes.

The article by Beer and Huse presents an organizational model portraying the complex interaction among systems variables and describes an OD program that was carried out using a systems approach. Beer and Huse describes how an OD effort in one subunit of the organization can lead to the gradual emergence of a "change culture" that induces receptiveness to change in other subunits. Some new insights about the conditions facilitating a successful OD effort are presented, and some commonly held assumptions about OD are questioned.

Another systems approach to organizational change is described in the article by Bowers and Seashore. They describe briefly the OD program and its short-run consequences in terms of improved employee motivation and satisfaction, as well as increased organizational profitability. Their primary interest, however, was not the short-run changes but the durability of the changes after the OD program was formally completed. Therefore, additional data were collected four and one-half years later. Seashore and Bowers interpret these data and discuss the importance of a systems approach for preventing retrogression.

The reduction of conflict within or between organization subunits is a major objective of some OD interventions. Subjects like conflict and power have only recently begun to receive the attention they deserve in the literature on organizational behavior. Two important questions are the determinants of conflict in organizations and the effectiveness of different methods of reacting to conflict. The article by Walton and Dutton is concerned with both these questions. Walton and Dutton present a general model of interdepartmental conflict and review the relevant literature on conflict in organizations. They summarize the implications of their model for developing a strategy of conflict management, which includes use of some types of OD interventions. For a more elaborate treatment of OD interventions used for conflict resolution, the reader is referred to Walton (1969) and Fisher (1972).

REFERENCES AND SUGGESTED READINGS

Beckhard, R. Organization development: Strategies and models. Reading, Mass.: Addison-Wesley, 1969.

Bennis, W. G. Organization development: Its nature, origins, and prospects. Reading, Mass.: Addison-Wesley, 1969.

Blake, R. R., and Mouton, J. S. Building a dynamic corporation through GRID organization development. Reading, Mass.: Addison-Wesley, 1969.

Fisher, R. J. Third-party consultation: A method for the study and resolution of conflict. Journal of Conflict Resolution, 1972, 16, 67-94.

French, W. L., and Bell, C. H. Organization development. Englewood Cliffs, N.J.: Prentice-Hall, 1973.

Litterer, J. A. Conflict in organizations: A re-examination. Academy of Management Journal, 1966, 9, 178-86.

Pondy, L. Varieties of organizational conflict. Administrative Science Quarterly, 1969, 14, 499-505.

Schein, E. H. Process consultation: Its role in organization development. Reading, Mass.: Addison-Wesley, 1969.

Schmidt, S. M., and Kochan, T. A. Conflict: Toward conceptual clarity. Administrative Science Quarterly, 1972, 17, 359-70.

Walton, R. E. Interpersonal peacemaking: Its role in organization development. Reading, Mass.: Addison-Wesley, 1969.

20

OD Interventions - An Overview

WENDELL L. FRENCH and CECIL H. BELL, JR.

The term "OD interventions" refers to the range of planned programmatic activities clients and consultants participate in during the course of an organization development program. These activities are designed to improve the organization's functioning through enabling organization members better to manage their team and organization culture. OD interventions constitute the continually evolving technology—the methods and techniques—of the practice of organization development. Knowing the OD intervention armamentarium and knowing the rationale underlying the use of different interventions contributes substantially to understanding the philosophy, assumptions, nature, and processes of organization development. In this chapter we look at issues, definitions, rationale, and several classificatory schemata related to interventions.

A DEFINITION OF OD INTERVENTIONS

The term "OD interventions" is currently being used in several different ways. On the one hand, this seems to be due to confusion and lack of definition; on the other hand, it is due to the fact that it quite accurately (if not precisely) refers to several orders of meaning in terms of level of abstraction. Is an OD intervention something that someone does to an organization, or is it something that is going on, that is, an activity? It is both. We prefer, however, that emphasis be placed on the activity nature of interventions; interventions are "things that happen," activities, in an organization's life.

One use of the term that is common with practitioners and laymen alike is that an intervention is something the outside consultant does to the client system. The major shortcomings of this definition are, first, that it does not provide for the client system doing something to itself without the assistance of an external, or even internal, consultant; and, second, it denies the joint collaboration that takes place between consultant and client. In OD programs, individuals and units within the organization often initiate activities designed to improve their functioning and do so on their own. These activities can clearly constitute OD interventions.

The term is often used to refer to any

From Wendell L. French and Cecil H. Bell, Jr., *Organization development: Behavioral science interventions for organization improvement*. © 1973, pp. 97-111. Reprinted by permission of Prentice-Hall, Inc., Englewood Cliffs, N.J.

learning technique or method available to the practitioner. Thus, any one of the extant methods available, what Burke and Hornstein call "the social technology of OD,"[1] is an intervention according to this use. (These techniques are available both to the client system and to consultants.) This is probably the most common use, and it is an appropriate one. The technology of OD consists of educational activities, methods, and techniques; some "things to do" and "things to be sure not to do"; questionnaires, observation and interview schedules, and so forth. Any of these can appropriately be considered an intervention when it is used to bring about organization improvement.

Common usage also finds the term applied to the following different levels of activities:

A single task, say, a two-hour decision-making exercise;

A sequence or series of related tasks designed around some theme or objective; for example, Beckhard's *confrontation meeting* is a series of tasks designed to surface an organization's major problems, determine the priorities for solving the problems, and assign responsibilities for actions;[2]

A "family" of activities that are related but may be quite different, for example, the set of activities called team-building interventions, are a wide variety of diverse activities all designed to improve a team's effectiveness as a unit, and the activities may relate to ways to perform the task better or to ways to improve the relations between the team members;

The over-all plan for relating and integrating the organization improvement activities that an organization might be engaged in over a period of years (this is generally referred to as the *intervention strategy*, the

strategy of intervention, or the *OD strategy* of the organization development program).

All of these are correct uses of the term intervention, but they relate to different levels of abstraction and can thus be confusing at times.

Finally, to give our definition of the term: OD interventions are *sets of structured activities* in which selected organizational units (target groups or individuals) engage with a task or a sequence of tasks where the task goals are related directly or indirectly to organizational improvement. Interventions constitute the action thrust of organization development; they "make things happen" and are "what's happening."

The OD practitioner is a professional versed in the theory and practice of organization development. He brings four sets of attributes to the organizational setting: a set of values; a set of assumptions about man, organizations, and interpersonal relationships; a set of goals and objectives for himself and for the organization and its members; and a set of structured activities that are the *means* to implementing his values, assumptions, and goals. These activities are what we mean by the word *intervention*.

A BRIEF WORD ABOUT THE NATURE OF OD INTERVENTIONS

Many of the characteristics ascribed to OD inhere also in OD interventions. The foundations and characteristics of the OD process are as follows: it is data based and experience based, with emphasis on action, diagnosis, and goal setting; it frequently utilizes work teams as target groups; it rests on a systems approach to organizations; it is a normative-re-educative strategy of changing; and it is an ongoing process. In this chapter we deal explicitly with OD interventions, covering some new materials and some old materials in a new way.

OD interventions are structured activities of selected target groups. Some "secrets" of

1. W. W. Burke and H. A. Hornstein, Introduction to *"The social technology of organization development,"* prepublication copy, 1971, p. 1.
2. Richard Beckhard, The Confrontation Meeting, *Harvard Business Review,* 1967 (March-April 1967), 45, 149-53.

OD are contained in this statement, because there are "better" ways and "worse" ways to structure activities in order for learning and change to take place. OD practitioners know how to structure activities in the "better" ways through attending to the following points:

Structure the activity so that the relevant people are there. The relevant people are those affected by the problem or the opportunity. For example, if the goal is improved team effectiveness, have the whole team engage in the activities. If the goal is improved relations between two separate work groups, have both work groups present. If the goal is to build some linkages with some special group, say, the industrial relations people, have them there and have the linking people from the home group there.

This preplanning of the group composition is a necessary feature of properly structuring the activity.

Structure the activity so that it is (1) problem oriented or opportunity oriented and (2) oriented to the problems and opportunities generated by the clients themselves. Solving problems and capitalizing on opportunities are involving, interesting, and enjoyable tasks for most people, whether it is due to a desire for competence or mastery (as suggested by White[3]), or a desire to achieve (as suggested by McClelland[4]), or whatever. This is especially true when the issues to be worked on have been defined by the client. There is built-in support and involvement, and there is a real payoff when clients are solving issues that they have stated have highest priority.

Structure the activity so that the goal is clear and the way to reach the goal is clear.

3. R. W. White, Motivation reconsidered: The concept of competence, *Psychological Review,* 1959, 66, 297-334.
4. D. C. McClelland, J. W. Atkinson, R. A. Clark, and E. L. Lowell, *The achievement motive* (New York: Appleton-Century-Crofts, 1953).

Few things demotivate an individual as much as not knowing what he is working toward and not knowing how what he is doing contributes to goal attainment. Both of these points are part of structuring the activity properly. (Parenthetically, the goals will be important goals for the individuals if the second point above is followed.)

Structure the activity so that there is a high probability of successful goal attainment. Implicit in this point is the warning that expectations of practitioners and clients should be realistic. But more than that, manageable, attainable objectives once achieved produce feelings of success, competence, and potency for the people involved. This, in turn, raises aspiration levels and feelings of self- and group-worth. The task can still be hard, complicated, taxing—but it should be attainable. And if there is failure to accomplish the goal, the reasons for this should be clear so they can be avoided in the future.

Structure the activity so that it contains both experience-based learning and conceptual/cognitive/theoretical-based learning. New learnings gained through experience are made a permanent part of the individual's repertoire when they are augmented (and "cemented") through conceptual material that puts the experience into a broader framework of theory and behavior. Relating the experience to conceptual models, theories, and other experiences and beliefs helps the learning to become integrated for the individual.

Structure the climate of the activity so that individuals are "freed up" rather than anxious or defensive. Setting the climate of interventions so that people expect "to learn together" and "to look at practices in an experimenting way so that we can select better procedures" is what we mean by climate setting.

Structure the activity so that the participants learn both how to solve a particular problem and "learn how to learn" at the same time. This may mean scheduling in time for reflecting on the activity and teasing out learnings that occurred; it may mean devoting as much as half the activity to one focus and half to the other.

Structure the activity so that individuals can learn about both *task* and *process*. The task is what the group is working on, that is, the stated agenda items. The term process, as used here, refers to *how* the group is working and *what else is going on* as the task is being worked on. This includes the group's processes and dynamics, individual styles of interacting and behaving, etc. Learning to be skillful in working in both of these areas is a powerful tool. Activities structured to focus on both aspects result in learnings on both aspects.

Structure the activity so that individuals are engaged as whole persons, not segmented persons. This means that role demands, thoughts, beliefs, feelings, and strivings should all be called into play, not just one or two of these. Integrating disparate parts of individuals in an organizational world where differentiation in terms of role, feelings, thoughts is common probably enhances the individual's ability to cope and grow.

These features are integral characteristics of OD interventions and also of the practitioner's practice theory of organization development. Little attention is given to characteristics of structuring activities in the literature, but knowledge of them helps to take some of the mystery out of interventions and may also be helpful to people who are just beginning to practice OD.

A different approach to the nature of OD interventions is provided by Warren Bennis when he lists the major interventions in terms of their underlying themes.[5] He describes the following kinds of interventions:

5. *Organization development: Its nature, origins, and prospects* (Reading, Mass.: Addison-Wesley 1969), pp. 37-39. We have paraphrased and interpreted his list extensively.

1. *discrepancy intervention*, which calls attention to a contradiction in action or attitudes that then leads to exploration;

2. *theory intervention*, where behavioral science knowledge and theory are used to explain present behavior and assumptions underlying the behavior;

3. *procedural intervention*, which represents a critiquing of how something is being done to determine whether the best methods are being used;

4. *relationship intervention*, which focuses attention on interpersonal relationships (particularly those where there are strong negative feelings) and surfaces the issues for exploration and possible resolution;

5. *experimentation intervention*, in which two different action plans are tested for their consequences before a final decision on one is made;

6. *dilemma intervention*, in which an imposed or emergent dilemma is used to force close examination of the possible choices involved and the assumptions underlying them;

7. *perspective intervention*, which draws attention away from immediate actions and demands and allows a look at historical background, context, and future objectives in order to assess whether or not the actions are "still on target";

8. *organization structure intervention*, which calls for examination and evaluation of structural causes for organizational ineffectiveness; and

9. *cultural intervention*, which examines traditions, precedents, and practices—the fabric of the organization's culture—in a direct, focused approach.

Bennis' typology helps to provide a more thorough understanding of the nature of OD interventions while at the same time affording a classification scheme against which specific activities may be compared.

The nature of OD interventions—the structured activities designed to bring about system improvement—is complex and multi-faceted. But certain themes recur in many interventions, the dynamics of the intervention process itself are becoming better understood, and there is a growing body of concepts that relates to the process of planned change. Considerable understanding of the nature of OD interventions is available to practitioners and clients alike as a result of this process. Just as an example, and to close this section on a serendipitous note: the *decision* to participate in an OD intervention may itself be a cause of organizational improvement. Just making the decision will signal to the members involved that the culture is changing, that new ideas and new ways of doing things are becoming more of a possibility and reality. This signal may itself cause changes in the direction of improvement. Our evaluation techniques and our theories of the intervention process are not sophisticated enough to handle such interactional complexities. That is for future practitioners at future times.

THE MAJOR FAMILIES OF OD INTERVENTIONS

Not all OD programs contain all the possible intervention activities, but a wide range of activities is available to the practitioner. As we see it, the following are the major "families" or types of OD interventions.

Diagnostic Activities: fact-finding activities designed to ascertain the state of the system, the status of a problem, the "way things are." Available methods range from projective devices like "build a collage that represents for you your place in this organization" to the more traditional data-collection methods of interviews, questionnaires, surveys, and meetings.

Team-building Activities: activities designed to enhance the effective operation of system teams. They may relate to task issues, such as the way things are done, the needed skills to accomplish tasks, the resource allocations necessary for task accomplishment; or they may relate to the nature and quality of the relationships between the team members or between members and the leader. Again, a wide range of activities is possible. In addition, consideration is given to the different kinds of teams that may exist in the organization, such as formal work teams, temporary task-force teams, and newly constituted teams.

Intergroup Activities: activities designed to improve effectiveness of interdependent groups. They focus on joint activities and the output of the groups considered as a single system rather than as two subsystems. When two groups are involved, the activities are generally designated intergroup or interface activities; when more than two groups are involved, the activities are often called *organizational mirroring*.

Survey-Feedback Activities: related to and similar to the diagnostic activities mentioned above in that they are a large component of those activities. However, they are important enough in their own right to be considered separately. These activities center around actively working the data produced by a survey and designing action plans based on the survey data.

Education and Training Activities: activities designed to improve skills, abilities, and knowledge of individuals. There are several activities available and several approaches possible. For example, the individual can be educated in isolation from his work group (say, in a T-group comprised of strangers), or he can be educated in relation to his work group (say, when a work team learns how better to manage interpersonal conflict). The activities may be directed toward technical skills required for effective task performance or may be directed toward improving interpersonal competence. The activities may be directed toward leadership issues, responsibilities and functions of group members, decision-making, problem-solving, goal-setting and planning, etc.

Technostructural Activities: activities designed to improve the effectiveness of the technical or structural inputs and constraints affecting individuals or groups. The activities may take the form of (1) experimenting with new organization structures and evaluating their effectiveness in terms of specific goals; (2) devising new ways to bring technical resources to bear on problems.

Process Consultation Activities: activities on the part of the consultant "which help the client to perceive, understand, and act upon process events which occur in the client's environment."[6] These activities perhaps more accurately describe an approach, a consulting mode in which the client is given insight into the human processes in organizations and taught skills in diagnosing and managing them. Primary emphasis is on processes such as communications, leader and member roles in groups, problem-solving and decision-making, group norms and group growth, leadership and authority, and intergroup cooperation and competition. Emphasis is also placed upon learning how to diagnose and develop the necessary skills to be effective in dealing with these processes.

Grid Organization Development Activities: activities invented and franchised by Robert Blake and Jane Mouton, which comprise a six-phase change model involving the total organization.[7] Internal resources are developed to conduct most of the programs which may take from three to five years to complete. The model starts with upgrading individual managers' skills and leadership abilities, moves to team-improvement activities, then to intergroup relations activities. Later phases include corporate planning for improvement, developing implementation tactics, and concluding with an evaluation phase assessing change in the organization culture and looking toward future directions.

Third-Party Peacemaking Activities: activities conducted by a skilled consultant (the *third party*), which are designed to "help two members of an organization manage their interpersonal conflict."[8] They are based on confrontation tactics and an understanding of the processes involved in conflict and conflict resolution.

Coaching and Counseling Activities: activities that entail the consultant or other organization members working with individuals to help them (1) define learning goals; (2) learn how others see their behavior; (3) learn new modes of behavior to see if these help them to achieve their goals better. A central feature of this activity is the non-evaluative feedback given by others to an individual. A second feature is the joint exploration of alternative behaviors.

Life- and Career-Planning Activities: activities that enable individuals to focus on their life and career objectives and how they might go about achieving them. Structured activities lead to production of life and career inventories, discussions of goals and objectives, and assessment of capabilities, needed additional training, and areas of strength and deficiency.

Planning and Goal-Setting Activities: activities that include theory and experience in planning and goal setting, utilizing problem-solving models, planning paradigms, ideal organization versus real organization "discrepancy" models, and the like. The goal of all of them is to improve these skills at the levels of the individual group, and total organization.

Each of these families of interventions has many activities and exercises included in it. They all rely on inputs of both conceptual

6. E. H. Schein, *Process consultation* (Reading, Mass.: Addison-Wesley, 1969), p. 9.

7. R. R. Blake and J. S. Mouton, *Building a dynamic corporation through organization development* (Reading, Mass.: Addison-Wesley, 1969). A treatise showing how grid organization development programs operate.

8. R. W. Walton, *Interpersonal peacemaking: Confrontation and third-party consultation* (Reading, Mass.: Addison-Wesley, 1969), p. 1. This entire book is devoted to an explication of this specialized intervention technique.

material and actual experience with the phenomenon being studied. Some of the families are directed toward specific targets, problems, or processes. For example, the team-building activities are specific to intact work teams, while the life-planning activities are directed to individuals, although this latter activity takes place in group settings. Some interventions are problem-specific: examples of this are the third-party peace-making activities and the goal-setting activities. Some activities are process-specific— that is, specific to selected processes: an example of this is the intergroup activities in which the processes involved in managing interfaces are explored. Examples of important interventions that in themselves do not constitute a family are the confrontation meeting, sensitivity training, force field analysis, and the role analysis technique (RAT).

SOME CLASSIFICATION SCHEMATA FOR OD INTERVENTIONS

There are many possible ways to classify OD interventions. Several have already been given: the families of interventions represent one approach, and Bennis' types of interventions represent another approach. Our desire is to construct several classificatory schemata showing interventions from several perspectives. In this way, we can better accomplish our objective of examining OD from a kaleidoscopic rather than from a microscopic point of view.

One way to gain a perspective of OD interventions is to form a typology of interventions based on the following questions:

1. Is the intervention directed primarily toward individual learning, insight, and skill building or toward group learning?

2. Does the intervention focus on *task* or *process* issues? (Task is what is being done; process is how it is accomplished, including how people are relating to each other and what processes and dynamics are occurring.) A four-quadrant typology constructed by

using these two questions is shown in Figure 20-1.

This classification scheme presents one approximation of the categories of various interventions; it is difficult to pinpoint the interventions precisely because a single intervention may have the attributes of more than one of the quadrants. Interventions simply are not mutually exclusive; there is great overlap of emphasis and the activity will frequently focus on, say, task at one time and process at a later time. Generally, however, the interventions may be viewed as belonging predominantly in the quadrant in which they are placed. It is thus possible to see that the interventions do differ from each other in terms of major emphasis.

Another way to view interventions is to see them as *designed to improve the effectiveness of a given organizational unit.* Given different organizational targets, what interventions are most commonly used to improve their effectiveness? This is shown in Figure 20-2. The elasticity of different interventions really becomes apparent in this figure, with many interventions being placed in several categories.

Examination of Figures 20-1 and 20-2 reveals redundancy and overlap in that specific interventions and activities appear in several classification categories. This may be confusing to the reader who is new to the area of organization development, but it nevertheless reflects the use to which various interventions are put. Perhaps a positive feature of the redundancy is that it suggests patterns among the interventions that the practitioner knows but that may not be readily apparent to the layman. Some of these patterns become more apparent in Figure 20-3.

Another conceptual scheme for categorizing the OD interventions rests on an attempt to determine the central, probably underlying causal mechanisms of the intervention, that is, the underlying dynamics of the intervention that probably are the cause of its efficacy. This scheme is more contro-

Individual vs. Group Dimension

	Focus on the Individual	Focus on the Group

Focus on Task Issues	Role-analysis technique
	
	Education: technical skills;
	    also decision-making, problem-solving,
	    goal-setting, and planning
	
	Career planning
	
	Grid OD phase 1 (see also below)
	
	Possibly job enrichment and Management by
	    Objectives (MBO)
		Technostructural changes
		
		Survey feedback (see also below)
		
		Confrontation meeting
		
		Team-building sessions
		
		Intergroup activities
		
		Grid OD phases 2, 3 (see also below)

Focus on Process Issues	Life planning
	
	Process consultation with
	    coaching and counseling of individuals
	
	Education: group dynamics,
	    planned change
	
	Stranger T-groups
	
	Third-party peacemaking
	
	Grid OD phase 1
		Survey feedback
		
		Team-building sessions
		
		Intergroup activities
		
		Process consultation
		
		Family T-group
		
		Grid OD phases 2, 3

Task vs. Process Dimension

Fig. 20-1. OD Interventions Classified by Two Independent Dimensions: Individual-Group and Task-Process

versial: different authors might hypothesize different causal dynamics. This is due partly to the relative paucity of theory and research on interventions. But the practitioner chooses and categorizes interventions on the basis of assumed underlying dynamics of change and learning, and it might therefore be helpful to present a tentative classification scheme based on these mechanisms.

Several hypothesized causal mechanisms inherent in OD interventions may lead to change and learning. These causal mechanisms are found to greater and lesser degrees in different interventions, and it is probable that the efficacy of the different interventions therefore rests on different causes. Some features of different interventions that may be causally related to learning and change are presented below. These are used to construct Figure 20-3.

Feedback: This refers to learning new data about oneself, others, group processes, or organizational dynamics—data that one did not previously take active account of. Feedback refers to activities and processes that "reflect" or "mirror" an objective picture of the real world. Awareness of this "new information" may lead to change if the feedback is not too threatening.

Awareness of Changing Sociocultural Norms: Often people modify their behavior, attitudes, values, etc., when they become aware of changes in the norms that are helping to determine their behavior. Thus, awareness of new norms has change potential because the individual will adjust his behavior to bring it in line with the new norms. The awareness that "this is a new ball game" or that "we're now playing with a new set of rules" is here hypothesized to be a cause of changes in individual behavior.

Target Group	Types of Interventions
Interventions designed to improve the effectiveness of INDIVIDUALS	Life- and career-planning activities Role analysis technique Coaching and counseling T-group (sensitivity training) Education and training to increase skills, knowledge in the areas of technical task needs, relationship skills, process skills, decision-making, problem-solving, planning, goal-setting skills Grid OD phase 1
Interventions designed to improve the effectiveness of DYADS/TRIADS	Process consultation Third-party peacemaking Grid OD phases 1, 2
Interventions designed to improve the effectiveness of TEAMS & GROUPS	Team building — Task directed — Process directed Family T-group Survey feedback Process consultation Role analysis technique "Start-up" team-building activities Education in decision-making, problem-solving, planning, goal-setting in group settings
Interventions designed to improve the effectiveness of INTERGROUP RELATIONS	Intergroup activities — Process directed — Task directed Organizational mirroring Technostructural interventions Process consultation Third-party peacemaking at group level Grid OD phase 3 Survey feedback
Interventions designed to improve the effectiveness of the TOTAL ORGANIZATION	Technostructural activities Confrontation meetings Strategic planning activities Grid OD phase 4, 5, 6 Survey feedback

Fig. 20-2. Typology of OD Interventions Based on Target Groups

Increased Interaction and Communication: Increasing interaction and communication between individuals and groups may in and of itself effect changes in attitudes and behavior. Homans, for example, suggests that increased interaction leads to increased positive sentiments.[9] Individuals and groups in isolation tend to develop "tunnel vision" or "autism," according to Murphy.[10] Increasing communication probably counteracts this tendency. Increased communication allows one to check his perceptions to see if they are socially validated and shared.

Confrontation: This term refers to sur-

9. George C. Homans, *The human group* (New York: Harcourt, Brace, 1950).

10. G. Murphy, The freeing of intelligence, *Psychological Bulletin*, 1945, 42, 1-19.

Hypothesized Change Mechanism	Interventions Based Primarily on the Change Mechanism
Feedback	Survey feedback T-group Process consultation Organization mirroring Grid OD instruments
Awareness of changing sociocultural norms	Team building T-group Intergroup interface sessions First three phases of Grid OD
Increased interaction and communication	Survey feedback Intergroup interface sessions Third-party peacemaking Organizational mirroring Management by objectives Team building Technostructural changes
Confrontation and working for resolution of differences	Third-party peacemaking Intergroup interface sessions Coaching and counseling individuals Confrontation meetings Organizational mirroring
Education through: (1) New knowledge (2) Skill practice	Career and life planning Team building Goal-setting, decision-making, problem-solving, planning activities T-group Process consultation

Fig. 20-3. Intervention Typology Based on Principal Emphasis of Intervention in Relation to Different Hypothesized Change Mechanisms

facing and addressing differences in beliefs, feelings, attitudes, values, or norms to remove obstacles to effective interaction. Confrontation is a process that actively seeks to discern real differences that are "getting in the way," surface those issues, and work on the issues in a constructive way. Many obstacles to growth and learning exist; they continue to exist when they are not actively looked at and examined.

Education: This refers to activities designed to upgrade (1) knowledge and concepts, (2) outmoded beliefs and attitudes, (3) skills. In organization development the

education may be directed toward increasing these three components in several content areas: task achievement, human and social relationships and behavior, organizational dynamics and processes, and processes of managing and directing change. Education has long been an accepted change technique.

Some interventions emphasize one mechanism of· change over others. A tentative typology based on these principal underlying change mechanisms is presented in Figure 20-3.

This classification scheme, while differentiating between interventions, also shows the many multiple emphases that are found in many of the activities. We are only beginning to understand the underlying mechanisms of change in interventions. As that knowledge increases, greater precision in the selection of intervention activities will be possible. The issue seems to be statable as follows: OD does in fact work; why it works is less well known and understood.

We find that another convenient classificatory scheme can be formed by categorizing OD interventions into those directed toward team improvement, toward improving intergroup relations, and toward the level of the total organization and those interventions that focus directly on personal, interpersonal, and group processes. This scheme is similar to the typology based on target groups presented in Figure 20-2, but separates out the "process" interventions for special attention.

As a final note, in addition to knowledge about various interventions and knowledge about the appropriateness and timeliness of interventions, the OD practitioner is cognizant of the many dimensions inherent in each particular activity. Since an intervention contains the possibility for going in many directions, the practitioner attends to the range of alternatives in his own inputs. For example, in a team-building meeting, the practitioner will have various dimensions in his head that guide his inputs and contributions. These dimensions can be explained through looking at the questions the practitioner may be asking himself:

We are dealing with individual behavior right now; how can this learning be translated to learning for the group?

We are dealing with group phenomena right now; how can this learning be translated to learning for the individuals?

We are focusing on task competencies and requirements; how do these relate to process issues and understanding of the group's dynamics?

We have just learned about a phenomenon by experiencing it; what theoretical or conceptual material would augment this learning?

We are dealing with issues and forces impinging on this group from outside the group; what activities must be designed to facilitate more appropriate handling of these interface issues?

We are dealing with an old problem in a new way; does that signal a change in the sociocultural norms of this group, and are the members aware of it?

We are diagnosing areas of interpersonal and intergroup conflict; what interventions are appropriate to deal with these issues?

SUMMARY

In this chapter we have taken an overview of OD interventions—the sets of structured activities in which selected organizational units (target groups or individuals) engage with a task or a sequence of tasks where task goals are related directly or indirectly to organizational improvement. Different definitions of OD interventions were discussed. The nature of interventions and several classifications of them were presented to gain a picture of interventions from several different perspectives. . . .

21

OD Techniques and Their
Results in 23 Organizations:
The Michigan ICL Study

DAVID G. BOWERS[1]

In 1966, staff members of the University of Michigan's Institute for Social Research launched a five-year program of organizational projects, the Inter-Company Longitudinal Study (ICLS). This ambitious undertaking addressed itself to a number of substantive questions of organizational behavior and change research within a framework containing the following features:

1. *Continuity of site* (over a period of one or more years);

2. *Use of a common survey instrument* (as a benchmark measure of the functioning of the human organization);

3. *Organizational development as a beneficial tool* (to increase payoff to participating firms and to ensure the presence of constructive movement for research purposes);

4. *Research on organizational change techniques* (to permit the acquisition of systematic knowledge about the comparative effect of a number of possible interventions).

1. The research upon which this article is based was supported by Office of Naval Research Contract N00014-67-A-0181. The cooperation and help of that agency is hereby gratefully acknowledged.

After an initial year of instrument development, staff acquisition, and pilot projects, the main phase of the study began. The hopes and aims sketched in the four precepts listed above were in varying degrees brought to fulfillment. Continuity of site proved to be greater than has been the case in the great majority of previous studies: most organizations remained committed to and involved in an ICLS project for at least two years. They did not, however, endure for the full five years (although some may well ultimately do so).

A common instrument, the Survey of Organizations questionnaire, was developed and refined. It has been used, in one of its editions, in each site- and date-collection wave. Most participating organizations underwent at least two measurement waves using that instrument, with some form of change, development, or intervention occurring in the interval between the two; some had as many as five successive measurements. Relevant portions of this instrument generated the substance of the data examined in this article.

All organizations, with the exception of a very few in which no action plan was intended and in which none evolved, under-

Reprinted by special permission from *Journal of Applied Behavioral Science*, 1973, 9, 21-43. © 1973 by the NTL Institute for Applied Behavioral Science.

took some program of organizational development; as we shall see, the specific nature of the activity varied from one site to another.

Organizational change research is an uncharted territory in many aspects, and the research staff has had, of necessity, to feel its way along quite gradually. Many of the findings are only now slowly entering into the professional purview. As the reader can imagine, content analysis of five years of documents and multivariate analysis of a mountain of quantitative data is a lengthy, difficult task. I wish to forewarn the reader who anticipates a detailed chronicling of intervention strategies that I will present less of that than he (or I) might wish. Instead, my present purpose is an overview of results from this study's large number of cases and their possibilities for comparative analysis.

At the end of five years, work in some form has been underway in 31 organizations (plants or separate marketing regions) in 15 companies. Data from 23 of these organizations in 10 companies are included in the present analysis. Six organizations, in four companies, were excluded because no repeat measurements have as yet been obtained. One company was excluded because it was primarily involved in an ancillary activity unrelated to organizational research and change of the kind considered here.

The 23 organizations comprise 14,812 persons, in white-collar and blue-collar positions, and constitute a wide array of industries—paper, chemicals, petroleum refining, aluminum, automobiles, household products, and insurance, in the areas of continuous process manufacturing, assembly-line manufacturing, components fabrication, marketing, and research and development.

CHANGE TREATMENTS TO BE COMPARED

Six forms of intervention can be identified as having occurred in one or more of the 23 organizations. For the most part they are not "pure" treatments, since nearly all involved at least some form of return of tabulated survey data. Nevertheless, they are sufficiently different from one another to have been the sources of conflicts between the change agents who used them and to have been regarded as different by the client systems who experienced them.

Survey Feedback

No authoritative volume has as yet been written about this development technique, although a number of article-length references exist.[2]

Many persons mistakenly believe that survey feedback consists of a rather superficial handing back of tabulated numbers and percentages, and little else.

On the contrary, when employed with skill and experience, it becomes a sophisticated tool for using the data as a springboard to development. In the sites classified as having received *survey feedback* as a change treatment, this treatment formed the principal substance of the intervention. Data were tabulated for each group engaged in the project, as well as for each combination of groups that represented an area of responsibility in the organizational pyramid. Data appeared in the format shown in Figure 21-1.

Each supervisor and manager received a tabulation of this sort containing data from the responses of his own immediate subordinates; the measures, descriptions of their basis, and meaning; and suggestions concerning their interpretation and use. A resource person, from ISR or the client system's own staff, usually counseled privately with the supervisor-recipient about the contents of the package and then arranged a time when the supervisor could meet with his subordinates to discuss the findings and their implications. The resource

2. See Bowers and Franklin (1972) for a discussion of the theoretical rationale for this treatment.

Fig. 21-1. Typical Format of Survey Feedback Tabulation

```
***************************
* GROUP NUMBER 99999 *
***************************
```

	PERCENTAGE DISTRIBUTION						STD.	
ITEM	(1)	(2)	(3)	(4)	(5)	MEAN	DEV.	N
7 Co uses new work methods	8	0	17	42	25	3.82	1.11	11
8 Co interest in welfare	8	8	17	25	33	3.73	1.29	11
22 Disagreemts wked thru	0	8	50	17	8	3.30	0.78	10
38 Objectives set jointly	17	8	25	17	17	3.10	1.37	10

person ordinarily agreed to attend that meeting in order to help the participants with the technical aspects of the tabulations and the process aspects of the discussion.

Feedback procedures typically vary from site to site, and did so within the ICLS sites that received this treatment. In certain instances, a "waterfall" pattern, in which the feedback process is substantially completed at superordinate levels before moving to subordinate groups, was adopted. In other instances, feedback to all groups and echelons was more or less simultaneous.

Time and space do not permit a lengthy discussion of the various forms which feedback may take. It should be stated, however, that an effective survey feedback operation helps an organization's groups move from a discussion of the tabulated perceptions, through a cataloguing of their implications, to commitment to solutions to the problems identified and defined by the discussion.

This technique has long been associated with organizational development and change work conducted by the Institute for Social Research and was considered at the outset of this study as likely to constitute a more or less standard tool. That it was not as universally employed as this statement might suggest forms the basis for its identification as a distinct treatment.

Interpersonal Process Consultation

This treatment bears at least some resemblance to what Schein (1969) has termed "Process Consultation." The change agent most closely identified with this treatment attaches great importance to developing, within the client groups themselves, a capacity for forming and implementing their own change program. Considerable importance is attached to the change agent's establishing himself from the outset as a trustworthy, helpful adjunct to the group's own process. A great deal of effort and emphasis is placed on his catalyzing a process of surfacing data in areas customarily not plumbed in work organizations (attitudes, feelings, individual needs, reasons for conflict, informal processes, and so on). In behavioral specifics, the change agent employs the posing of questions to group members; process-analysis periods; feedback of observations or feelings; agenda-setting, review, and appropriateness-testing procedures; and occasional conceptual inputs on interpersonal topics. Work is sometimes undertaken with members singly, but more often in natural workgroupings. Human, rather than technical, processes are generally assumed to have primacy for organizational effectiveness.

Task Process Consultation

This treatment is oriented very closely to task objectives and the specific interpersonal processes associated with them. A change agent who adheres to this pattern typically begins by analyzing a client unit's work-task situation privately, after extensive interviews concerning its objectives, potential resources, and the organizational forces blocking its progress. He consults privately with the supervisor at frequent intervals to establish rapport and to gain commitment to objectives and desired future courses of action. He sets the stage for client-group discussions by introducing select bits of data or by having another person do so. He encourages group discussion and serves as a process observer, but also uses role playing, some substantive inputs at timely points, as well as nondirective counseling techniques, to guide the discussion toward commitment to desired courses of action.

Laboratory Training

As practiced within ICLS projects, this intervention technique more nearly approximates the interpersonal relations laboratory than the intrapsychic or personal growth session. A "family group" design was followed almost exclusively, with the entire laboratory lasting from three days to two weeks, depending upon circumstances and organizational schedule requirements. Sessions were ordinarily conducted at a motel or resort away from the usual work place. Experiential exercises (e.g., the NASA Game or "Moon Problem," the Ten-Dollar Exercise, the Tower-Building Problem) were interspersed with unstructured discussion time. During the years of the study, a number of terms were used by those conducting the training to describe it. Initially it was referred to as "T-group Training"; in later years it was termed "Team Development Training," or simply "Team Training." The content, however, remained relatively constant in kind, if not in exact substance. The change agents who conducted the training were not novices; on the contrary, they had had many years of experience in conducting it and were judged by those familiar with their work to be competent.

Data Handback

Not truly a change treatment, this forms instead a control or comparison condition. In certain sites no real survey feedback work was conducted. Data were tabulated and returned in envelopes to the appropriate supervisor, but no effort was made to encourage group problem-solving discussions concerning those data. Nor did any other treatment occur in these sites.

No Treatment

In a few sites, data were tabulated and returned to the appropriate top or staff manager but were not shared by him with relevant managers and supervisors. They were instead filed away in a cabinet. Since no other development activities were undertaken in these sites, it seems justifiable to classify them as having had no treatment at all.

Survey Feedback was earlier described as the "principal substance of the intervention" in sites labeled as such in the study. It was also stated that some form of tabulated survey data was returned to someone in all sites. Both statements are true. A system is classified in this article as having received Survey Feedback as its treatment when survey feedback, *and that alone* was used, both with capstone groups (those groups at the top management rungs of the organizational ladder) and with all groups below them which were involved in the project. Where Interpersonal Process Consultation, Task Process Consultation, or Laboratory Training are the reported treatments, the principal intervention *with the capstone groups* consisted of that particular treatment. These groups, along with all other participating groups in their organization, also received tabulated data, and ordinarily spent a varying amount of time discussing it.[3] Change agents who used these treat-

3. All items were in each instance returned to group participants. Thus, although selective attention may have occurred, treatments do not differ in the particular data returned.

ments characteristically placed survey feedback work in a distinctly secondary role. In some instances, after a few brief and sometimes superficial sessions, groups were encouraged to move on to the "real" change activity; in other instances, the nonfeedback activity began before survey data were made available, and the data were used only occasionally (perhaps by the change agent himself) to underscore a point or a development. Data feedback, to the extent that it went on at all, was often left in these sites to partially trained, and normally overloaded, internal resource persons, who were often more attracted to the more glamorous activities modeled by the external change agent.

Thus events, schedules and the personal style preference of the change agents combined to produce a contrast between sites in which Survey Feedback was truly and thoroughly conducted at all levels and without other treatments, and sites in which a rather half-hearted effort at data discussion was overshadowed by other treatments with capstone groups.

Finally, a word must be said about the way in which organizations came to receive different treatments. In a true experiment, assignment to treatment category is random. No pretense can be made that a purely random assignment procedure was employed in this multicompany study. Still, if not random, it appears to have been less than systematic. Change treatment was determined on a basis having little, if anything, to do with the nature of the client system; it was instead determined by change agent preference, i.e., by the preferred and customary techniques of the change agent assigned to the site. In short, treatment was determined by change agent selection, which was in turn determined by sheer availability at the time of contract.

MEASUREMENT AND ANALYSIS PROCEDURES

The dependent variables in the analyses reported below are measures of organiza-tional functioning obtained from repeated administrations (ordinarily one year apart) of the Survey of Organizations questionnaire (Taylor and Bowers, 1972), particularly the 16 critical indices that constitute the core of that instrument. The content of this instrument was originally developed from the many studies which ISR had conducted over the years prior to 1966. Subsequently the content of this questionnaire has been subjected to a number of analyses, employing both smallest-space analysis and hierarchical cluster analysis, which suggest that the total may really comprise the limited number of multi-item indices employed in this present study. Six are measures of the organizational conditions that surround any particular focal group to form the environment within which it must live. These conditions, outside and especially above a particular manager's group, are really nothing more than the perceived accumulated effects of the ways in which other groups function. Helpful or harmful policies, for example, are the output of higher-echelon groups with good or poor leadership, respectively. We call these accumulated effects *organizational climate*, and attach to that term essentially the same meaning given it by Evan (1968), i.e., a concrete phenomenon reflecting a social-psychological reality, shared by people related to the organization, and having its impact on organizational behavior. We do *not* imply by the term the alternative meaning sometimes given it, that of a general flow of behavior and feeling with a group (cf. Halpin, 1966).

Four other indices measure managerial leadership behavior of an interpersonal (support and interaction facilitation) and task (goal emphasis and work facilitation) nature. Four similar measures tap the peer leadership area, and together these eight measures reflect what has come to be called the "Four-Factor" theory of leaderhip (Bowers and Seashore, 1966; Taylor and Bowers, 1972). The remaining two measures tap Group Process and Satisfaction, respectively.

High scores on these 16 measures, for any organization or group, are considered to be reasonably reflective of a general state of organizational effectiveness; lower scores, of a less effective state. The content of the measures, like their place in a conceptual scheme, is based upon the Likert "meta-theory" of the human organization as a social system (Likert, 1961, 1967), which itself represents an integration of a large array of empirical findings. The questionnaire has been subjected to extensive analyses, and the healthy and inquisitive skeptic is directed to Taylor and Bowers (1972), where both reliability and validity data are presented in considerable detail. For present purposes, a brief summary of content and reliability is presented in Table 21-1. Evidence concerning validity is perhaps best summarized by the following statement, taken from the basic reference:

Fairly clear evidence exists that the *Survey of Organizations* measures relate appropriately to both efficiency and attendance criteria. Relationships to efficiency extend across all four time periods and reach levels as high as .80. Relationships to attendance attain only slightly lower levels, and, where data are available, show every sign of extending across all time periods.[4]

Relationships to other criteria present patterns which are far less definitive. In the case of Product Quality, no clear pattern emerges at all. In the Human Cost area, organizational climate seems to have appropriate and significant relationships to all three measures available for analysis: minor injuries, physical health, and grievance rate (Taylor and Bowers, 1972).

Two successive measures are considered simultaneously for the analyses to be reported here: those preceding and following (a year later) the occurrence of a particular change treatment. In certain instances, index measures for the premeasure or the post-

measure are considered separately, and are therefore reported as arithmetic means on a five-point Likert scale (high score = desirable condition, low score = undesirable condition). In other instances, change itself is the focal concern; for these purposes, the first (or pre-) measures have been subtracted from the second (or post-) measures. Thus a "positive" change score indicates enhanced effectiveness; a "negative" score, deterioration.

The balance of the article considers findings which, within the confines of the ICLS setting, help answer the following research questions:

1. Were the treatments differentially effective in producing change in organizational functioning, as measured by the Survey of Organizations questionnaire?

2. What is the relationship between change in organizational climate and the effects of these various treatments?

RESULTS

We begin with a consideration of change or gain scores for each of the 16 critical indices for each treatment, presented in Table 21-2. The reader may note that, for each treatment, two sets of scores are given for each variable category. One comparison is labeled "Whole Systems," and refers to grand response mean gain scores for all respondents combined within organizations receiving that treatment for the first and second waves of measurement (ordinarily one year apart). The other comparison is labeled "Capstone Groups" and refers, within the Interpersonal Process Consultation, Task Process Consultation, and Laboratory Training treatments, to persons in groups that actually received that particular treatment. For comparison purposes, persons in groups of a similar nature (ordinarily the top management groups) are presented for the Survey Feedback, Data Handback, and No Treatment clusters.

The findings presented in Table 21-2 may be summarized as follows:

---

4. A "time period" is a period of approximately four consecutive months; four such periods, covering an 18-month time span, are used in the validation analyses.

Table 21-1. Summary of Content and Reliability of 16 Indices of the Survey of
Organizations Questionnaire

Area—Measure	Description	No. of Items	Internal Consistency Reliability Coefficient
ORGANIZATIONAL CLIMATE			
Human resources primacy	Whether the climate indicates that people, their talents, skills, and motivation are considered to be one of the organization's most important assets	3	.80
Communication flow	Whether information flows effectively upward, downward, and laterally in the organization	3	.78
Motivational climate	Whether conditions and relationships in the environment are generally encouraging or discouraging to effective work	3	.80
Decision-making practices	How decisions are made in the organization: whether they are made effectively, at the right levels, and based upon all the available information	4	.79
Technological readiness	Whether the equipment and resources are up to date, efficient, and well maintained	2	.58
Lower-level influence	Whether lowest-level supervisors and employees feel they have influence on what goes on in their department	2	.70
MANAGERIAL LEADERSHIP			
Support	Behavior toward subordinates that lets them know they are worthwhile persons doing useful work	3	.94
Interaction facilitation	Team building, behavior that encourages subordinates to develop close, cooperative working relationships with one another	2	.89
Goal emphasis	Behavior that stimulates a contagious enthusiasm for doing a good job (*not* pressure)	2	.85
Work facilitation	Behavior that removes roadblocks to doing a good job	3	.88

Area–Measure	Description	No. of Items	Internal Consistency Reliability Coefficient
PEER LEADERSHIP			
Support	Behavior by subordinates toward one another that enhances their mutual feeling of being worthwhile persons doing useful work	3	.87
Interaction facilitation	Behavior by subordinates toward one another that encourages the development of close, cooperative working relationships	3	.87
Goal emphasis	Behavior by subordinates toward one another that stimulates a mutually contagious enthusiasm for doing a good job	2	.70
Work facilitation	Behavior that is mutually helpful; helping each other remove roadblocks to doing a good job	3	.89
GROUP PROCESS	How the group functions; does it plan and coordinate its efforts, make decisions and solve problems, know how to do its job, share information; is it motivated to meet its objectives, is it adaptable, is there confidence and trust among its members?	7	.94
SATISFACTION	Whether employees are satisfied with economic and related rewards, adequacy of their immediate supervisor, effectiveness of the organization, compatibility with fellow employees, present and future progress within the organization, and their job as a whole	7	.87

1. *Laboratory Training* is associated with negative change in organizational climate for both capstone groups and systems as a whole. Although group process improves at both levels, peer support declines for capstone groups, and both peer and managerial support decline for the systems in which these groups are located, as does over-all satisfaction.

2. *Interpersonal Process Consultation* contains so few cases within capstone groups, and the changes are of such a (low) magnitude, that firm conclusions cannot be drawn. For their systems *in toto*, however, 7

Table 21-2. Changes in Questionnaire Indices, from First to Second Survey Waves, by Variable and Change Treatment

| | Treatment | | | | | | | | | | | |
| Area—Measure | Laboratory training | | Interpersonal process consultation | | Task process consultation | | Survey feedback | | Data handback | | No treatment | |
	Caps. Gps N = 116	Whole Sys. N = 3417	Caps. Gps N = 12	Whole Sys. N = 3788	Caps. Gps N = 38	Whole Sys. N = 1847	Caps. Gps N = 85	Whole Sys. N = 3893	Caps. Gps N = 55	Whole Sys. N = 932	Caps. Gps N = 51	Whole Sys. N = 935
Organizational Climate												
Human resources primary	−.42*	−.18*	+.10	−.02	−.04	−.17*	+.35*	+.15*	+.13	−.05	−.59*	−.61*
Communication flow	−.19*	−.12*	+.10	+.12*	+.16	−.06	+.22*	+.15*	+.23*	−.12*	−.02	−.06
Motivational conditions	−.13*	−.12*	−.22	+.02	+.03	−.04	+.24*	+.01	+.04	−.16*	−.09	−.09
Decision-making practices	−.15*	−.13*	−.17	+.03	+.21*	−.14*	+.30*	+.17*	+.04	.00	−.32*	−.52*
Technological readiness	−.01	+.13*	−.25	−.07	+.02	−.11*	+.39*	+.05	+.02	−.08	NA†	NA†
Lower-level influence	+.03	−.10*	−.23	+.05	+.11	+.03	+.26*	+.01	−.33*	−.18*	−.47*	−.23*
Managerial Leadership												
Support	−.10	−.11*	+.31	+.11*	−.11	−.19*	+.07	+.18*	+.18	+.01	−.16	−.32*
Interaction facilitation	−.04	+.02	−.05	+.20*	+.07	.00	+.11	+.36*	+.27*	+.15*	+.21*	.00
Goal emphasis	+.11	−.06	−.13	+.08	+.09	−.06	.00	+.17*	+.21*	+.06	−.11	−.11*
Work facilitation	+.12	−.08	+.29	+.21*	−.09	−.05	+.17	+.27*	+.33*	+.15*	−.09	−.16*
Peer Leadership												
Support	−.20*	−.11*	−.24	+.02	+.17	−.13*	+.29*	+.06	−.01	+.03	−.19*	−.23*
Interaction facilitation	+.09	−.04	−.07	+.12*	+.08	−.06	+.30*	+.20*	+.06	+.20*	−.04	−.11*
Goal emphasis	−.05	.00	+.08	+.12*	+.22	−.02	+.21*	+.14*	+.15	+.12*	+.04	−.12*
Work facilitation	+.07	+.03	−.17	+.15*	+.04	−.03	+.36*	+.19*	+.09	+.20*	−.02	−.08
Group Process	+.20*	+.27*	−.05	+.01	−.03	−.06	+.28*	+.21*	−.14	−.21*	NA†	NA†
Satisfaction	−.09	−.15*	−.04	+.04	+.32*	−.03	+.17*	+.09	+.07	−.02	−.07	−.23*

*Change large enough to be statistically significant at or beyond .05 level of confidence.
†Measures omitted in edition of questionnaire used in these sites.

of the 16 measures reflect significant, positive changes, largely in the managerial and peer leadership areas. Organizational climate, group process, and satisfaction measures change scarcely at all.

3. *Task Process Consultation* is associated with little significant change among capstone groups; only two measures (Decision-Making Practices, Satisfaction) change, both in a positive direction. For whole systems, however, all significant changes are negative, and a majority of them occur in the area of organizational climate. Considering that the two measures of support (managerial and peer) also show a significant decline, the pattern shows at least some resemblance to that observed in conjunction with Laboratory Training.

4. *Survey Feedback* reflects positive and significant changes for capstone groups in every area except managerial leadership. For whole systems, 11 of the 16 measures show positive, statistically significant change. No measure, for either capstone groups or whole systems, reflects negative change.

5. *Data Handback* is associated in capstone groups with improved communication flow but a decline in the amount of influence attributed to lower organizational levels. Managerial leadership generally improves in these groups; all other measures show essentially no change. For their systems *in toto*, organizational climate is viewed as becoming worse, while peer leadership and some aspects of managerial leadership improve.

6. *No Treatment*, as a "treatment," is associated with general negative change for capstone groups and whole systems.

There are, therefore, clear differences in reported change among treatment categories. It would be premature, however, to discuss substantive implications of these results before considering the possible impact of several methodological or situational factors.

Regression Toward the Mean

One such factor is the familiar argument concerning "regression toward the mean." Although clients were assigned on a staff-availability basis, it is conceivable that client systems were assigned to change agents (and therefore to treatments) in a way which coincided with their initial positions on the characteristics measured. If so, and if regression toward the mean accounts for the observed results, we would expect those initially below the mean to exhibit positive change (toward the mean) and those initially above the mean to exhibit negative change (also toward the mean). We would also expect them to reflect significant differences at the outset; that is, to have been different from one another in the premeasure in ways congruent with a regression explanation. Table 21-3 presents an analysis of variance test of the differences among treatment categories at the time of the premeasure, and Table 21-4 shows a simple categorization of significant changes in terms of their consistency or inconsistency with a regression hypothesis.

There are clearly significant differences at the outset. Inspection of the treatment means shows that these differences do not, however, coincide with what would be expected if some form of regression toward the mean were to account for the contrasting results obtained with the various treatments. Task Process Consultation sites, which began the effort around mid-range of the comparative distribution, show scarcely any change, and that which does occur is mixed as to its possible regression effects. Interpersonal Process Consultation and Data Handback treatment sites did, in fact, begin the change process from a somewhat lower scale point. Although capstone groups in Data Handback reflect a pattern in Table 21-4 that might suggest consistency with a regression hypothesis, the pattern for whole systems in this treatment is mixed, and that for whole systems in Interpersonal Process Consultation is clearly contrary to the hypothesis.

The contrary pattern presented by both Laboratory Training and Survey Feedback is

Table 21-3. Intertreatment Differences in Premeasures

Area—Measure	F	p	Laboratory training	Interpersonal process consultation	Task process consultation	Survey feedback	Data handback	No treatment
					Treatments—Capstone Groups ($df = 5,350$)			
Organizational Climate								
Human resources primacy	10.97	.001	4.00	3.46	3.92	3.80	3.46	4.46
Communication flow	4.94	.001	3.74	3.28	3.74	3.75	3.33	3.93
Motivational conditions	6.83	.001	3.92	3.64	3.98	3.86	3.47	4.20
Decision-making practices	6.94	.001	3.28	3.11	3.49	3.53	2.90	3.60
Technological readiness	2.09	N.S.	3.64	4.50	3.86	3.69	3.64	N.A.
Lower-level influences	3.34	.01	2.96	2.54	2.97	2.96	2.86	3.43
Managerial Leadership								
Support	5.02	.001	4.17	4.05	4.26	4.45	3.85	4.42
Interaction facilitation	8.93	.001	3.99	3.49	4.12	4.11	3.25	3.90
Goal emphasis	5.73	.001	4.14	4.08	4.41	4.49	3.85	4.40
Work facilitation	6.53	.001	3.38	3.21	3.68	3.70	3.10	3.79
Peer Leadership								
Support	5.34	.001	4.09	4.06	3.76	3.91	3.87	4.38
Interaction facilitation	2.55	.05	3.45	3.17	3.31	3.53	3.16	3.71
Goal emphasis	1.70	N.S.	3.63	3.46	3.38	3.61	3.44	3.78
Work facilitation	1.69	N.S.	3.00	3.19	3.14	3.21	2.96	3.32
Group Process	5.54	.001	3.52	4.00	3.74	4.00	3.63	N.A.
Satisfaction	4.68	.001	3.99	3.88	3.99	4.22	3.78	4.32

Table 21-3. Intertreatment Differences in Premeasures (Continued)

			Treatments—Whole Systems ($df = 5$, inf.)					
Organizational Climate								
Human resources primacy	236.78	.001	3.00	3.28	3.65	3.17	2.93	4.01
Communication Flow	110.09	.001	2.94	2.98	3.27	2.94	2.96	3.57
Motivational Conditions	99.25	.001	3.23	3.31	3.56	3.25	3.10	3.77
Decision-making practices	164.16	.001	2.73	2.84	3.13	2.68	2.47	3.38
Technological Readiness	342.60	.001	2.80	3.47	3.70	3.37	3.53	N.A.
Lower-level influences	61.81	.001	2.56	2.48	2.68	2.50	2.37	3.01
Managerial Leadership								
Support	83.15	.001	3.78	3.84	4.04	3.82	3.77	4.44
Interaction facilitation	33.44	.001	3.20	3.20	3.37	3.11	2.98	3.48
Goal emphasis	50.52	.001	3.72	3.75	3.86	3.66	3.57	4.16
Work facilitation	75.13	.001	3.15	3.19	3.32	3.17	2.99	3.74
Peer Leadership								
Support	51.97	.001	3.84	3.83	3.89	3.73	3.80	4.20
Interaction facilitation	44.98	.001	3.16	3.18	3.19	2.96	2.91	3.40
Goal emphasis	41.19	.001	3.30	3.36	3.36	3.21	3.15	3.60
Work facilitation	34.65	.001	3.10	3.20	3.12	2.98	2.85	3.22
Group process	95.33	.001	3.28	3.56	3.59	3.63	3.56	N.A.
Satisfaction	61.65	.001	3.60	3.73	3.74	3.68	3.51	4.07

Table 21-4. Consistency of Significant Changes with a Regression Hypothesis, by Change Treatment

Treatment	No. Consistent with Regression Hypothesis	No. Inconsistent with Regression Hypothesis
Laboratory Training		
Capstone	1	5
Whole systems	1	9
Interpersonal Process Consult.		
Capstone	0	0
Whole systems	0	7
Task Process Consult.		
Capstone	0	2
Whole systems	3	2
Survey Feedback		
Capstone	0	12
Whole systems	0	11
Data Handback		
Capstone	4	1
Whole systems	5	4
No Treatment		
Capstone	1	4
Whole systems	10	0

even stronger. Laboratory Training, which began below the mean of the array and which would therefore be expected to show improvement, in fact declined. Survey Feedback, which started above the array mean and would be expected on a "regression toward the mean" hypothesis to decline, showed improvement.

Only in the case of whole systems experiencing No Treatment is there some substantial evidence for the regression hypothesis. In terms of the most striking differences in changes associated with various treatments it therefore seems reasonable to reject the hypothesis that they represent regression-toward-the-mean, methodological artifacts.

Organizational Climate as a Mediating Factor

Still another possible explanation of the findings centers around the role played by organizational climate in conjunction with attempts at intervention. A quite plausible argument can be made (and indeed was made at the time, particularly by individuals

connected with the Laboratory Training sites) that basically autocratic and punitive practices and policies contribute to an organizational climate that masks the true effects of the change treatment. Thus, the argument goes, if organizational climate could be controlled, the effects of the treatment on group member leadership behavior would show themselves to be positive.

What could not be controlled in the course of the projects can be controlled at least reasonably well by an analytic strategy employing Multiple Classification Analysis, which produces estimates of the effect of each of several predictors alone, after controlling for the effects of all others (Andrews, Morgan, and Sonquist, 1967). Table 21-5 shows change scores for the eight leadership indices, adjusted to remove the effects of organizational climate change.[5]

5. The technical report from which this analysis was drawn used workgroup means, not individual scores, as the analysis units. Thus the gain scores reported in Table 21-5 differ slightly from those reported in Table 21-2. The pattern, however, is substantially the same.

Table 21-5. Mean Workgroup Change Scores, Adjusted To Remove Effects of Organizational Climate Change, by Leadership Measure, by Treatment

	Treatment											
	N = 167 Lab. Training		N = 298 Interpersonal Process Consultation		N = 109 Task Process Consultation		N = 112 Survey Feedback		N = 98 Data Handback		N = 104 No Treatment	
Area—Measure	Unadjusted	Adjusted	Unadjusted	Adjusted	Unadjusted	Adjusted	Unadjusted	Adjusted	Unadjusted	Adjusted	Unadjusted	Adjusted
Managerial Leadership												
Support	-.15*	-.04	+.12*	+.04	-.25*	-.22	+.13	+.05	+.03	+.07	-.25*	-.18*
Interaction facilitation	+.07	+.20*	+.23*	+.13*	+.03	+.07	+.43*	+.33*	+.14	+.18*	+.05	+.14*
Goal emphasis	-.02	+.09	+.13*	+.05	-.09	-.06	+.14	+.06	+.06	+.09	-.08	-.01
Work facilitation	-.01	+.11*	+.22*	+.13*	-.09	-.05	+.24*	+.15	+.16*	+.21*	-.13*	-.05
Peer Leadership												
Support	-.17*	-.11*	+.06	+.01	-.18*	-.17*	.00	-.06	+.07	+.08	-.22*	-.17*
Interaction facilitation	-.01	+.11	+.16*	+.06	-.09	-.06	+.17*	+.08	+.20*	+.24*	-.12	-.03
Goal emphasis	-.04	+.05	+.15*	+.08*	-.06	-.04	+.10	+.04	+.16*	+.20*	-.10	-.03
Work facilitation	+.05	+.15*	+.24*	+.16*	-.10	-.08	+.25*	+.18*	+.22*	+.26*	-.05	+.02

*Statistically significant at .01 level of confidence.

The results indicate considerable merit to the argument that the impact of a treatment is in part contingent upon the organizational climate in which it occurs, particularly in the case of Laboratory Training. The significant decline in managerial support present in the unadjusted scores disappears when adjustment is made for organizational climate, and the changes for managerial interaction facilitation and work facilitation, as well as for peer work facilitation, become positive. Only peer support remains significant and negative, although a decline in magnitude is apparent there as well.

Data Handback also benefits somewhat from controlling for level of organizational climate, with previously significant, positive changes increasing slightly in magnitude, and one additional measure attaining significance.

The remaining treatments (Interpersonal and Task Process Consultation, Survey Feedback, and No Treatment) show slight reduction in effects as a result of controlling for the effects of organizational climate.

SPURIOUS EFFECTS IN SURVEY FEEDBACK

An additional issue potentially affecting interpretation must be at least acknowledged before discussion of the overall implications of the findings. As an intervention technique, Survey Feedback usually employs the same instrument as a development tool that it uses to measure changes in the dependent variables. Therefore, the argument may be made, the results are likely to be confounded.

On reflection, this question breaks down into two separate issues:

1. the possibility that the feedback process subtly teaches organizational members how to respond to the questionnaire;

2. the greater likelihood that issues tapped by the instrument will receive more attention during the work or change activities which intervene between pre- and postmeasures than will other issues.

The "subtle education" issue seems plausible on the surface, but with close examination proves less reasonable in the present setting. First, at least as employed within ICLS, questionnaires were administered by members of the ISR project staff, who literally took them to the sites and returned them to Ann Arbor. Large stocks of questionnairs left for scrutiny, memorization, or "boning up" were not available to member-participants. Second, the questionnaire contains over a hundred items, and only a shorthand identification of the question stems appears on the computer print-out employed in feedback. Third, the tabulation sheets for any group or organization show considerable variation in response among members, as well as variation among the responses of any single respondent. Fourth, organizations of the type included in this study undergo a great deal of member rotation and turnover. Fifth, a substantial amount of evidence (not reported here) obtained from more detailed analyses within organizations reflects the construct validity of the measured changes. Changes in questionnaire indices relate differentially to one another in ways congruent with chronicled events in the project's history, with reports of change agents and top managers (obtained by content-analyzed interviews), and with performance measures from the operating records of the firm.

All in all, then, in order for the observed effects in the present study to represent a "subtle education" in how to respond, either an educative capability that would make organizational development itself obsolete or a conspiracy of organizational members so large and complex as to be mind-boggling would have had to occur.

Consider: the invisible hand guiding such a process would have had to build into the memory banks of hundreds—often thousands—of persons (many of them relatively uneducated) exactly that correct combination of responses which would square with all or most of the appropriate comparisons internal to the data themselves, with data from operating records, and with events during the interim which had been flagged by project staff members. It would have had to accomplish this without inducing an undifferentiated, across-the-board rise in response positiveness, while taking into account a large percentage of members who were new to the setting. Finally, it would have had to arrange all of this some six to eight months after the overwhelming majority of persons within the organization had seen the instrument or any data tabulated from it!

The second problem, that greater attention is likely to be paid during the intervention to issues reflected in the survey rather than to issues not reflected in the survey, is not to be denied, but rather acknowledged. In its most basic form, this is not a "problem" (in the sense of something which distorts or obfuscates). Instead, it is the heart of the change process for any system attempting to adapt to changes in its environment by a process of information inputs concerning the effect of mid-course corrections. This so-called problem appears in any change treatment and any evaluation or self-monitoring system geared to corrective input short of ultimate survival or destruction.

Having said this, we must also acknowledge that a measuring instrument fails to the extent that it is parochial in content. It may well be, for example, that the questionnaire used in this study omits content areas of great significance for organizational effectiveness—areas which are targeted by non-Survey Feedback treatments. If that is the case, however, it becomes an error of omission, not of commission. Errors of commission only appear if the instrument or the meta-theory on which they are based are themselves invalid. To the extent that the questionnaire taps what it purports to tap, and to the extent that those characteristics *do* relate to valid outcomes, its use as an assessment device is appropriate.

THOUGHTS ABOUT THE IMPLICATIONS OF THESE FINDINGS

Although these findings emphasize the differences present among the several treatments, all the application methods used in the present study appear to be quite climate-impacted. If the organizational climate is not changing positively, none of the treatments show any likelihood of substantially enhancing supportive behavior, whether by managers or by peers, or of enhancing goal emphasis by managers. Similarly, the problem-solving behavioral combination of interaction facilitation and work facilitation, as well as mutual goal emphasis by peers, seems climate-prone, in the sense that it is enhanced by positive shifts in climate, and harmed by negative shifts.

In the sites and projects included in the present study, Laboratory Training clearly suffers from an organizational climate that is *becoming* harsher and more barren.[6] This may, in fact, explain the discrepancy between findings in the present study and findings reported elsewhere: it may be that laboratory-like, experiential learning is successful in organizations whose climate is, or is becoming, positive (e.g., a Harwood or a TRW; cf. Marrow, Bowers, and Seashore, 1967; or Davis, 1967), but unsuccessful in organizations whose superstructure is, or is becoming, more autocratic and punitive.

Survey Feedback, on the other hand, is the only treatment in the present study associated with large, across-the-board, positive changes in organizational climate. Controlling for these changes tends to *reduce* the raw, significant, and positive change observed in Survey Feedback sites for managerial and peer leadership variables. By way of contrast, Data Handback shows an increase, not a decrease, in positive change in

6. It is worth noting that it is the *change* in climate, not its original state, which seems impactful. Laboratory Training and Survey Feedback, for example, are almost identical in climate at the outset, but change differentially.

managerial and peer variables when change in organizational climate is controlled statistically. In both treatments, the data format, content of the tabulation, and nature of the recipients are the same. Why, then, do we find a difference? The reason may be that the Survey Feedback process, in combination with the data, produces an attention to those issues related to organizational climate that must change if the system itself is to change. In fact, considering the intrinsic nature of the other treatments, it seems at least plausible that Survey Feedback is the only treatment of those considered which is likely to attend to these system-level issues in anything like a comprehensive form. Although the issue whether treatment itself effects climate change remains truly unanswered within these present data, a technical report (Bowers, 1971) investigates this particular problem and produces evidence to suggest that it does. In any event, more research on this question is needed; if treatments do not affect organizational climate positively or if other ways of accomplishing that end are not available, the present findings suggest that one would be best off following the rather barren practice of simply tabulating the data and handing them back!

Little more can be added at this point by way of interpreting the present findings. At the very least, they indicate that the different intervention strategies employed in ICLS had somewhat different outcomes. Beyond this, however, they add a degree of credence to the argument advanced by some that organizational change is a complex, systems-level problem in organizational adaptation, not merely an additive end-product of participation in particular development activities.

REFERENCES

Andrews, F., Morgan, J., and Sonquist, J. *Multiple classification analysis.* Ann Arbor, Mich.: Institute for Social Research, 1967.

Bowers, D. Development techniques and organizational climate: An evaluation of the comparative importance of two potential forces for organization change. Technical Report, Office of Naval Research, 1971.

Bowers, D., and Franklin, J. Survey-guided development: Using human resources measurement in organizational change. *Journal of Contemporary Business,* 1972, 1, 43-55.

Bowers, D., and Seashore, S. Predicting organizational effectiveness with a four-factor theory of leadership. *Administrative Science Quarterly,* 1966, 11, 238-63.

Davis, S. An organic problem-solving method of organizational change. *Journal of Applied Behavioral Science,* 1967, 3, 3-21.

Evan, W. A systems model of organizational climate. In R. Tagiuri and G. Litwin (Eds.), *Organizational climate.* Boston: Harvard University Press, 1968.

Halpin, A.W. *Theory and research in administration.* New York: Macmillan, 1966.

Likert, R. *New patterns of management.* New York: McGraw-Hill, 1961.

Likert, R. *The human organization.* New York: McGraw-Hill, 1967.

Marrow, A., Bowers, D., and Seashore, S. *Management by participation.* New York: Harper & Row, 1967.

Schein, E. Process consultation: Its role in organization development. In E. Schein, W. Bennis, and R. Beckhard (Eds.), *Organization development.* Reading, Mass.: Addison-Wesley, 1969.

Taylor, J., and Bowers, D. *The survey of organizations: A machine-scored standardized questionnaire instrument.* Ann Arbor: Institute for Social Research, 1972.

22

A Systems Approach to
Organization Development

MICHAEL BEER and EDGAR F. HUSE[1]

INTRODUCTION AND HISTORICAL PERSPECTIVE

Although the plant has since grown considerably, at the beginning of the change effort there were approximately 35 hourly employees, mostly women; some 15 weekly-salaried technical and clerical personnel; and approximately eight professional and managerial personnel, who were paid monthly.

Some particulars about this plant which need to be considered in generalizing the results obtained in this study to other organizations follow: (1) the products are complex; (2) the operation is primarily assembly, as opposed to fabrication; (3) a majority of factory workers are women; (4) the organization is nonunion; and (5) the organization is relatively small. In other

words, approaches which might work with female assembly workers in a nonunion plant might not have the same impact with male union workers in a plant utilizing a different technology.

Because the organization was relatively new when this organization development effort started, it did not have a well-established historical culture and set of norms. It was in its formative stages, and crucial decisions were in the making concerning the technology in the plant (means of production), methods of setting production standards and controls, personnel practices and policies, managerial practices and philosophy, and the like. For example, at the time of our entry this was one of the relatively few nonunionized plants in an organization having about fifty geographically separate plants. Thus, an opportunity existed to do work in a plant which had not yet completely internalized the practice and traditions of older plants and of the corporation as a whole.

Since I've been working here, my husband is a much better supervisor in *his* plant. I tell him what he should do to make his people

1. Based on a paper presented as part of a symposium entitled "Organizational Change," at American Psychological Association convention, Washington, D. C., September 3, 1969. The authors would like to acknowledge the innovative and far-sighted approaches to management implemented by the managers and supervisors of the organization described. Particular thanks are due to J. G. Sabin, C. F. Wheatley, and J. Johnson. Many others were and are involved, and we thank them also.

more interested in what they are doing—based on what *our* supervisors do here. (*Assembly Worker*)

I hate to say it, but I think that I could be off the manufacturing floor for a month and my girls would still make the manufacturing schedule. (*First-Line Supervisor*)

The comments above were gathered in one plant of a large company which, for several years, has been the focus of a successful systems approach to organizational development (OD) at all levels. It is important to point out at the outset that no single OD approach was used with this plant. Rather, in the systems approach, a wide variety of behavioral science concepts concerning organizational change and effective management were operationalized.

This article is written to provide the reader with an understanding of the systems organizational model that guided our efforts as change agents; to describe the varied approaches used for organizational change; and to describe the results and what we have learned about the process of change and its prospects in large, complex organizations. Rather than consigning the conclusions to the end, we shall underscore our major findings as we proceed through the sections of the case study.

The organizational development program took place in a plant designing and manufacturing complex instruments for medical and laboratory use.

Through the efforts of the personnel supervisor, enough interest existed initially for our holding a series of seminars which contrasted traditional approaches with newer approaches based on behavioral research findings and theory. Although these seminars never succeeded in getting an explicit decision on the pattern of management that would prevail in the plant (indeed, as will be discussed later, there was considerable resistance to "theory"), they did start to unfreeze the managerial group (which was steeped in the tradition of the parent organization) sufficiently to commit themselves to "trying" some new approaches on a very limited basis. This constituted much less than commitment to a new pattern of management, but it did open the door to experimentation and examination.

Overworked Theories

A number of practitioners of OD stress the importance of top management commitment to OD if such a program is to be successful. As one author puts it, "Without such support, we have found no program of this kind can ever succeed . . . . First, we worked with top managers to help them fully understand . . . . This proved vital, not only in helping their understanding of the concepts but also in earning their commitment to the program" (Roche and MacKinnon, 1970). In the same vein, Beckhard (1969) and Blake and Mouton (1969) stress that OD must be planned and managed from the top down.

Certainly no one would dispute the proposition that top management commitment to OD is highly valuable and helpful. However, our experience in this study [*Finding 1*] indicates that *a clear-cut commitment at the top of the organizational unit to a particular OD approach is not necessary for a development program to succeed*. Indeed, an attempt to obtain too strong a commitment from top management in the early stages may be threatening enough to cause the withdrawal of any commitment to planned change, especially since the concept of OD and its technologies (e.g., Theory Y, job enrichment, sensitivity training, and the like) are foreign and threatening to the established beliefs of many managers.

Moreover, we found [*Finding 2*] that *total top management understanding of where the OD process will lead and the state of the organization at the end is not necessary for successful programs to take place*. Indeed, given the current state of the art, the OD practitioner himself may not have a clear view of the road ahead, except in very general terms.

What *is* necessary is that someone in a strategic position feel the need for change and improvement. In our plant, that person was the personnel supervisor. Although the plant manager was mildly interested in the initial stages, he was mainly submitting to pressures from the personnel man. Throughout his tenure in the plant, the plant manager's commitment and interest mildly increased, but he was never a strong proponent nor the most skilled manager in some of the new approaches. Furthermore, the plant manager's "boss" never fully knew what was going on in the plant nor did he ever commit himself in any way to the OD program. We now believe that it is possible to change a relatively autonomous unit of a larger organization without the total commitment or understanding of top management in that unit and, in larger and more complex organizations, even without their knowledge.

Initial Commitment to New Approaches

In addition to felt need, the second essential condition is that there be, somewhere in the organization, some initial commitment to experimentation, application, and evaluation of new approaches to present problems. A case study report by the second author (Huse, 1965) describes a successful OD program that took place because a middle manager in a large organization felt the need for change and requested help. He could not have cared less about specific OD principles. He simply wanted help in improving his organization. Davis (1967) points out, in his now classic case study, that top management was not really involved at the beginning and that a majority of the effort was expended in "on-the-job" situations, working out real problems with the people who are involved with them."

Of course, it is obvious that top management support of both theory and practice makes it easier for the change agent; conversely, the lack of such support increases the risk involved for consultants and managers, and causes other systems problems, as we shall discuss later in this article. Furthermore, the conditions of a felt need, a strong and self-sufficient commitment to change, and relative unit autonomy are needed. What we *are* saying is that the commonly heard dicta that one must start at the top and that top management must be committed to a set of normative principles are overworked. *Change can and does begin at lower levels in an organization* [*Finding 3*].

A CONCEPTUAL MODEL

If the client system and its management in this case did not (need to) have specific OD concepts in mind, who did? The change agents did.

It is important that the change agent have in mind an organizational model and a flexible set of normative concepts about management with a systems orientation. The organization model should be general and reflect the complex *interactive* nature of systems variables. The concepts must be updated and changed as new research findings become available and as more is learned about the functioning of the client system, the environment in which the client system operates, and the effects of changes made in the client system. That is, of course, an iterative procedure.

Figure 22-1 represents the model of organizational change which guided our efforts. This model has some basic characteristics which must be understood if we are to see how it can shape the planning of a change effort. It represents an organization as an open system engaged in a conversion process. Employee needs, expectations, and abilities are among the raw materials (inputs) with which a manager must work to achieve his objectives.

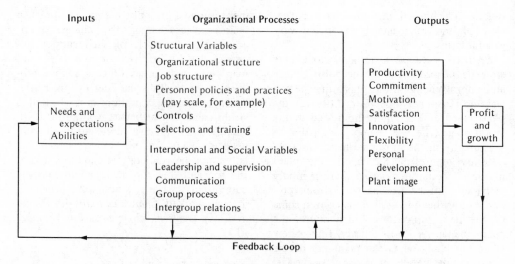

Fig. 22-1. Systems Model of an Organization

Organizations have many processes. Figure 22-1 includes only the more important ones in general terms, and these exist at both the structural and interpersonal levels. Leadership and communication, for example, are two of the interpersonal dimensions which serve to pull together, integrate, and shape the behavior of organizational members. They convert into effort and attitudes the potential brought to the organization in the form of needs and abilities of individuals. The structure or formalized dimensions of the organization obviously cannot exist independently of the interpersonal variables, but they are different from the interpersonal variables in terms of their susceptibility to managerial control, the means by which they might be changed, and the timing of their change. Previous literature on organizational change has emphasized interpersonal variables; more recent literature (Lawrence and Lorsch, 1969) has emphasized structural variables. It is our opinion, based upon experience, that both interpersonal and structural variables are crucial to effective organizational change. The effects of organizational design or managerial control systems on employees have been researched and

documented but are still insufficiently understood. For example, we are convinced that an operant conditioning model can be used to understand the behavior of managers with respect to controls. "Beating" goals and looking good on standard measures are like food pellets to the manager.

In the output column, we have listed multiple outcomes. These are not completely independent, but they are conceptually distinctive enough in their relationship to the organizational process variables that it is useful to think of them individually. It is the optimization of the organizational outputs that leads to long-term profitability and growth for employees and the organization. Other final outcomes could be listed if we were discussing organizations with different objectives.

Inherent in this model are several basic notions: An organization is an open system which, from the human point of view, converts individual needs and expectations into outputs. Organizational outputs can be increased by improving the quality of the input. An example of this would be the selection of people with higher levels of ability and needs. However, because there are costs associated with selecting personnel of higher quality, we might say that efficiency has not increased. The organization may improve its performance, but this gain has been obtained only because the input, i.e., the quality of personnel has improved, not because there has been a change in the manner in which the organization *utilizes* its human resources.

Since organizations are open systems, organizational performance can also improve by unleashing more of the potential inherent in the human resources. If you will, outputs will increase because we have made the conversion process more efficient. This can be done, for example, by designing organizational processes which better fit the organization's environment or by changing organizational processes so that human resources can be fully unleashed and brought to bear on the task and objectives of the organization. The adjustment of organizational processes to reflect more accurately the needs of the environment and of the persons in it is one of the key objectives of our organizational development program.

Figure 22-1[2] does not cover some of the more traditional but vitally important concepts of an organization as a total system. For example, capital budgets, the R & D thrust of an organization, overhead or indirect budgets, and the marketing direction of an organization are extremely important aspects which need to be considered. Blake and Mouton (1969) have developed the Corporate Excellence Rubric as a means of assessing the health of the organization through a traditional functional framework. Furthermore, current research (Lawrence and Lorsch, 1969) points up the fact that the differentiation of functional units has a tremendous influence upon the effectiveness of an organization. However, for purposes of brevity, these aspects are not covered in this article.

Mechanisms of Change

We chose an eclectic approach to create change in the organizational processes listed in Figure 22-1, with the basic belief that a variety of approaches to change should be used with the plant in question. The primary mechanism was consulting, counseling, and feedback by a team of four. The primary change agents were the personnel man within the organization (there have been four different ones since the OD effort began); Beer as an external-to-the-plant agent but internal to the organization, and Huse as the outside change agent. The fourth member of the team was a research assistant whose responsibility it was to interview and gather data in the client system for diagnostic and feedback uses by the change agents.[3]

We began a basic strategy of establishing working relationships with individuals at all levels of the organization. We operated as resource persons who could be used to solve specific problems or initiate small experiments in management; we tried to encourage someone or some organizational component to start implementing the concepts inherent in our model of an organization. Managers gained familiarity with these ideas through consultation and, to a much lesser extent and without full understanding, from the initial few seminars that we held. The main ingredients were a problem or a desire to change and improve, combined with action recommendations from the change agents. Soon there were a few individuals throughout the organization who began, with our help, to apply some new approaches. Because most of these approaches were successful, the result was increased motivation to change. To a degree, nothing succeeds like success!

Models for Learning

There are at least two basic models for

2. Cf. the traditional aspects included in the conceptual model developed by Huse (1969).

3. We should like to acknowledge the help and participation of Mrs. Gloria Gery and Miss Joan Doolittle in the data-gathering phase.

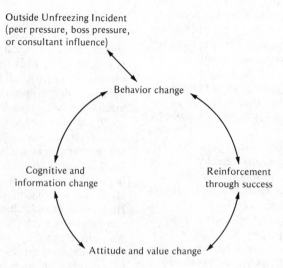

Fig. 22-2. The Learning Process

learning. The traditional method, that of the classroom and seminar, stresses theory and cognitive concepts before action. As Argyris (1967) points out, "The traditional educational models emphasize substance, rationality . . . ." However, a number of authors (Bartlett, 1967; Bradford, 1964; Schein and Bennis, 1965) make the point that behavior is another place to start. For example, Huse (1966) has shown that one's own facts are "much more powerful instruments of change than facts or principles generated and presented by an outside 'expert.' " The process of change in this OD effort started with behavioral recommendations, was followed by appropriate reinforcement and feedback, and then proceeded to attitudinal and cognitive changes.

Figure 22-2 summarizes the basic concept from our experience. *Effective and permanent adult learning [Finding 4] comes after the individual has experimented with new approaches and received appropriate feedback in the on-the-job situation.* This approach is analogous to, but somewhat different from, the here-and-now learning in the T-group.

In other words, a manager might have a problem. Without discussing theory, the change agent might make some recommendations relating to the specific situation at hand. If, in the here-and-now, the manager was successful in the attempt to solve the problem, this would lead to another try, as well as a change in his attitude toward OD. This approach capitalizes upon the powerful here-and-now influence which the job and the organizational climate can have upon the individual. Indeed, such changes can occur without *any* knowledge of theory.

Either model of learning can probably work to produce change in the individual. However, if one starts with cognitive facts and theory (as in seminars), this may be less effective and less authentic than starting with the individual's own here-and-now behavior in the ongoing job situation. In any case, the process is a cyclic one, involving behavior, attitudes, and cognition, each reinforcing the other. In our case, there was an early resistance to seminars and the presentation of "Theory." However, after behavior and attitude changes occurred, there began to be more and more requests for cognitive inputs through reading, seminars, and the like. It is at this later stage that seminars and "theory inputs" would seem to be of most value.

That learning starts with behavior and personal experience has been one of the most important things we have learned as we have worked to effect organizational change. The process is quite similar to what is intended to happen in laboratory training. What have we found [*Finding 5*] is that *the operating, ongoing organization may, indeed, be the best "laboratory" for learning.* This knowledge may save us from an overreliance upon sensitivity training described by Bennis (1968) when he states that "when you read the pages of this Journal, you cannot but think that we're a one-product outfit with a 100 per cent foolproof patent medicine." This finding may also be the answer in dealing with Campbell and Dunnette's (1968) conclusions that "while T-group training seems to produce observable changes in behavior, the utility of these changes for the performance of individuals in their organizational roles remains to be demonstrated."

The unfreezing process. What triggers an individual to unfreeze and to allow the process to begin, if it is not "theory"? First, there are some individuals who are ready to change behavior as soon as the opportunity presents itself in the form of an outside change agent. These are people who seem to be aware of problems and have a desire to work on them. Sometimes all that they need are some suggestions or recommendations as to different approaches or methods they may try. If their experiences are successful, they become change leaders in their own right. *They then [Finding 6] are natural targets for the change agent, since they become opinion leaders that help shape a culture that influences others in the organization to begin to experiment and try out new behaviors.* As Davis (1967) points out, it is necessary to "provide a situation which

could initiate the process of freeing up these potential multipliers from the organizational and personal constraints which . . . kept them from responding effectively to their awareness of the problems." Davis used "strangers" and "cousins" laboratories. In our case, the unfreezing process was done almost exclusively in the immediate job context.

An early example of the development of change leaders in our work with this company was the successful joint effort of an engineer and a supervisor to redesign a hotplate assembly operation which would eliminate an assembly line and give each worker total responsibility for the assembly of a particular product. It resulted in a productivity increase of close to 50 per cent, a drop in rejects from 23 per cent, controllable rejects to close to 1 per cent, and a reduction in absenteeism from about 8 per cent to less than 1 per cent in a few months. Not all the early experiments were successful, but mistakes were treated as part of the experiential learning process.

As some in the organization changed and moved ahead by trying out new behaviors, others watched and waited but were eventually influenced by the culture. An example of late changers so influenced was the supervisor of Materials Control, who watched for two years what was going on in the plant but basically disagreed with the concepts of OD. Then he began to feel pressure to change because his peers were trying new things and he was not. He began by experimenting with enriching his secretary's job and found, in his own words, that "she was doing three times as much, enjoying it more, and giving me more time to manage." When he found that this experiment in managerial behavior had "paid off," he began to take a more active interest in OD. His next step was to completely reorganize his department to push decision making down the ladder, to utilize a team approach, and to enrich jobs. He supervised four sections: purchasing, inventory control, plant scheduling, and expediting. Reorganization of Materials Control was around product line teams. Each group had total project responsibility for their own product lines, including the four functions described above. We moved slowly and discussed with him alternative ways of going about the structural change. When he made the change, his subordinates were prepared and ready. The results were clear: In a three-month period of time (with the volume of business remaining steady), the parts shortage list was reduced from 14 I.B.M. pages to less than a page. In other words, although he was a late-changer in terms of the developing culture, his later actions were highly successful.

The influence of the developing culture was also documented through interviews with new employees coming into the plant. The perception by production employees that this was a "different" place to work occurred almost immediately, and changes in behavior of management personnel were clear by the second month.

In other words, while seminars and survey feedback techniques were used in our work with this plant, the initial and most crucial changes were achieved through a work-centered, consulting-counseling approach, e.g., through discussion with managers and others about work-related problems, following the model of adult learning described earlier.

So much for the manner in which the unfreezing process occurred and some of our learning about this process. What were some of the normative concepts applied and why? A brief overview of our approaches and findings follows.

A NORMATIVE MODEL

Communications

In this phase we attempted to open up communications at all levels. We started monthly meetings at every level of the organization, as well as a weekly meeting between the plant manager and a sample of production and clerical employees. The aim was to institutionalize the meetings to serve as a means for exchanging information and ideas about what had happened and what needed to happen. The meetings, especially between first-line supervisors and production workers, began primarily as one-way communications downward. Little by little, qualitative changes occurred and the meetings shifted to two-way communications about quality, schedules and production problems. This effort to communicate (which was also extended through many other approaches) was an entire year in attaining success. It was an agonizingly slow process of change. In retrospect, this was a critical period during which trust was building and a culture conducive to further change was developing. Out of this, we concluded [*Finding 7*] that *organizational change occurs in stages: a stage of unfreezing and trust building, a take-off stage when observable change occurs, and a stabilization stage. Then the cycle iterates.* In addition to the communication type of meeting described above, confrontation meetings between departments were also held (Blake, Shepard, and Mouton, 1964). These, too, improved relationships between departments, over time.

Job Enrichment

A second area of change was in job structure, primarily through the use of job enrichment, or, as it has been called in the plant, "the total job concept." We have already discussed the importance of the job for psychological growth and development—our findings in this area parallel those of Ford (1969). Our first experience of tearing down a hotplate assembly line has already been discussed. This was followed by similar job enrichment efforts in other areas. In one department, girls individually assemble instruments containing thousands of parts and costing several thousand dollars. The change here allowed production workers to have greater responsibility for quality checks and calibration (instead of trained technicians). In another case, the changeover involved an instrument which had been produced for several years. Here, production was increased by 17 per cent with a corresponding increase in quality; absenteeism was reduced by more than 50 per cent.

The plant is presently engaged in completely removing quality control inspection from some departments, leaving final inspection to the workers themselves. In other departments, workers have been organized into autonomous workgroups with total responsibility for scheduling, assembly, training, and some quality control inspection (the source for the supervisor's laudatory quote at the beginning of this case study). Changes in these areas have evolved out of an attempt to utilize the positive forces of cohesive workgroups. However, like Ford (1969), we have found that not everyone in the assembly workforce responds positively to such changes, although a high majority do so over time.

Mutual goal setting has also been widely adopted. Instead of standards established by engineering (a direction in which the plant was heading when we started), goals for each department are derived from the plant goal, and individual goals for the week or month are developed in individual departments through discussions between the boss and subordinates. Our interview data clearly show that in this way workers understand how their individual goals fit into the plant goal structure and can work on their own without close supervision for long periods of time.

Changes toward a pay process more clearly based on merit (including appraisals for hourly and weekly salaried clerical and technical employees as well as for managerial and professional personnel) were made to reinforce and legitimate an escalating climate of work involvement. More and more employees are now involved in questions of production, quality, department layout, and

methods. Assembly workers give department tours to visitors, including vice presidents. Organization-wide technical and product information sessions are held. Concerned more with strategy than with daily problems, the top team has for some time molded itself into a business team, meeting periodically to discuss future plans.

More recently, changes in organizational structure are taking place to move a functionally oriented organization to a matrix organization, using concepts derived directly from Lawrence and Lorsch (1969). This involves, among other approaches, the use of "integrators" at varying levels within the organization.

Systems Interaction

A systems approach requires that mutually consistent changes in *all* subsystems be made in affecting the organizational processes listed in our model. In other words, [*Finding 8*] *multiple changes in the subsystems are needed for the individual employee to change behavior and perceptions of his role.* For example, participative supervision should be accompanied by redesign of jobs to allow more responsibility, by a pay system that recognizes performance, by a communication system that is truly open, and by corresponding changes in other subsystems throughout the organization. Past attempts to change organizations through a nonsystems approach, e.g., through such single media as supervisory training or sensitivity training, have had limited success because other key leverage points have not been changed in the total system. Further, an attempt to change one subsystem too quickly or too drastically can have severely harmful results, as pointed out in the "Hovey and Beard Company" case (Lawrence, Bailey, Katz, Seiler, Orth, Clark, Barnes, and Turner, 1961). Whether structural *or* interpersonal changes should take precedence in a given period of time depends upon the readiness of the system to change

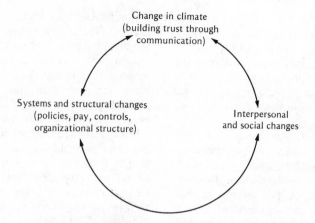

Fig. 22-3. The Sequence of Organizational Change

and the key leverage points. The key concept [*Finding 9*] is that *structural and interpersonal systems changes must reinforce and legitimate each other.* Figure 3 presents this concept. The change can be in either direction in the model.

We also learned [*Finding 10*] that *systems changes set off additional interactive processes in which changes in organizational functioning increase not only outputs but also develop the latent abilities of people.* We have concluded that the real potential in organizational development lies in setting in motion such a positive snowball of change, growth, and development. For example, as assembly workers took on additional responsibility they became more and more concerned about the total organization and product. "Mini-gripes" turned into "mega-gripes," indicating a change in the maturity of the assembly workers (Huse and Price, 1970). At the same time, this freed up management personnel to be less concerned about daily assignments and more concerned about long-range planning.

To illustrate this, at the beginning of the OD effort, the organization had a plant manager, a production superintendent, and three first-line supervisors, or a total of five supervisory personnel in the direct manufacturing line. As the assembly line workers took on more responsibility, the five have been reduced to three (the plant manager and two first-line supervisors). The number of inspection and quality control personnel has also been reduced.

A Subsystem Within the Larger Organization

Up to this point in the case study we have been considering the plant as a system in its own right. However, changes set in motion here have also provided the first step in a larger plan for change and development to occur in the parent corporation (consisting of some 50 plants). As a subsystem within the larger system, this plant was to serve as a model for the rest of the corporation—as an example of how change should be planned and implemented. It was our hope that the systems approach to change would create such a clearly different culture in this plant that it would become visible to the rest of the corporation; that people from other segments of the larger organization would visit and become interested in trying similar models and mechanisms of change. Our hopes have been realized. Indeed, both authors are now applying OD concepts to other areas of the organization.

Influence is also exerted upward, with greater acceptance of these concepts by

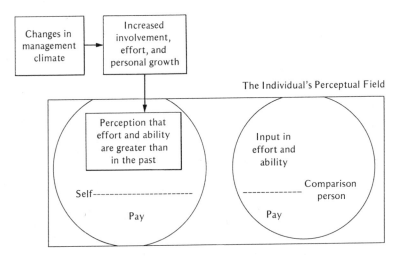

Fig. 22-4. Equity Model

individuals at higher levels in the organization [Finding 11]. It is our perception that changes in organizational subsystems can have strong influences on the larger culture if the change is planned and publicized; if seed personnel are transferred to other parts of the system; if a network of change agents is clearly identified; and if careful planning goes into where and how change resources are to be used. Once again, top management commitment is not a necessary commitment for evolutionary change in a complex, multidivision, multilocation organization. (*Sometimes*, the tail begins to wag the dog.)

Subsystem Difficulties

However, this change process may cause some difficulties in the area of interface between the smaller subsystem and the larger system. For example, the increased responsibilities, commitment, and involvement represented by job enrichment for assembly workers are not adequately represented in the normal job evaluation program for factory workers and are difficult to handle adequately within the larger system. So pay and pay system changes must be modified to fit modern OD concepts. Figure

22-4 is a model which shows the effects of change in climate on individual model perceptions of equity in pay.

In addition to the larger system difficulties over wage plans, there still exists a great deal of controversy as to the importance of pay as a motivator (or dissatisfier). For example, Walton (1967) takes a basically pessimistic approach about participation through the informal approach, as opposed to the more formal approaches embodied in the Scanlon Plan (Lesieur, 1958), which "stress the economic rewards which can come from [formal] participation." On the other hand, Paul, Robertson, and Herzberg (1969) review a number of job enrichment projects and report: "In no instance did management face a demand of this kind [higher pay or better conditions] as a result of changes made in the studies." In a recent review of the Scanlon Plan (Lesieur and Puckett, 1969), the authors point out that Scanlon's first application did not involve the use of financial incentives but, rather, a common sharing between management and employees of problems, goals, and ideas. Indeed, Ford (1969) reports on the results of a series of job enrichment studies without ever mentioning the words "pay" or "salary." In the plant described in this case, no significant pressures for higher pay have been felt to date. However, there has been sufficient opportunity for promotion of hourly employees to higher level jobs as the plant has grown.

It is certainly not within the scope of this article to handle the controversy regarding the place of pay as a motivator. We do want to make the point that standard corporate job evaluation plans are only one instance of the difficulties of interface between the client plant as a subsystem and the larger system. In our experience, these and other areas have been minor rather than major problems, but they have been problems.

Changes in Consumption of Research Findings

An important by-product of our experience has been [*Finding 12*] that *the client system eventually becomes a sophisticated consumer of new research findings in the behavioral sciences.* As mentioned earlier, there was early resistance to "theory"; but as the program progressed, there was increasing desire for "theory." We also found that a flexible and adaptable organization is more likely to translate theory into new policies and actions. Perhaps this is where behavioral scientists may have gone wrong in the past. We may have saturated our client systems with sophisticated research studies before the culture was ready to absorb them. This would suggest that a more effective approach may be carefully planned stages of evolution from an action orientation to an action-research orientation to a research orientation. This implies a long-range plan for change that we often talk about but rarely execute with respect to the changes in organizations that we seek as behavioral scientists.

RESULTS OF THE ORGANIZATIONAL DEVELOPMENT PROGRAM

To a great extent we have tried to share with

you our results and findings throughout the article. In addition, we are retesting these concepts in several other plants. In retrospect, how much change really occurred at the client plant, and how effective have been the new approaches introduced? We have only partial answers since a control plant did not exist and since the plant was relatively new; no historical data existed against which to compare performance. However, considerable data do exist to support the thesis that change has occurred and that new managerial approaches have created an effective organization. (In addition, the second author is conducting ongoing research in another plant in the organization which has historical data. Before- and aftermeasures have already shown dramatic change: e.g., reduction in manufacturing costs for the plant of 40 to 45 per cent.)

Extensive interviews by the researcher and detailed notes and observations by the change agents indicate considerable improvement after our work with this plant. Communication is open, workers feel informed, jobs are interesting and challenging, and goals are mutually set and accomplished.

In each of the output dimensions, positive changes have occurred which we think, but cannot always prove, would not have occurred without the OD effort. Turnover has been considerably reduced; specific changes in job structure, organizational change, or group process have resulted in measurable productivity changes of up to 50 per cent. Recent changes in the Instrument Department have resulted in productivity and quality improvements. We have witnessed the significant changes in maturity and motivation which have taken place among the assembly workers. A change to a project team structure in the Materials Control Department led to a reduction of the weekly parts shortages. Following the findings of Lawrence and Lorsch (1969), the use of "integrators" and project teams has significantly reduced the time necessary for new product development, introduction, and manufacture. A fuller evaluation of the integrator role and the project organization as it affects intergroup relations and new product development is reported elsewhere (Beer, Pieters, Marcus, and Hundert, 1971).

Several recent incidents in the plant are evidence of the effect of the changes and bear repeating. An order called for in seven days and requiring extraordinary cooperation on the part of a temporary team of production workers was completed in fewer than seven days. A threatened layoff was handled with candor and openness and resulted in volunteers among some of the secondary wage earners.

New employees and managers now transferred into the plant are immediately struck by the differences between the "climate" of this plant and other locations. They report more openness, greater involvement by employees, more communication, and more interesting jobs. Even visitors are struck immediately by the differences. For example, one of the authors has on several occasions taken graduate students on field trips to the plant. After the tour, the consensus is, "You've told us about it, but I had to see it for myself before I would believe it." Managers transferred or promoted out of the plant to other locations report "cultural shock."

SUMMARY AND CONCLUSIONS

The Medfield Project (as it can now be labeled) has been an experiment in a systems approach to organizational development at two systems levels. On the one hand, we have regarded the plant as a system in and of itself. On the other hand, we have regarded the plant as a subsystem within a larger organization. As such a subsystem, we wanted it to serve as a model for the rest of the organization. Indeed, as a result of this study, OD work is going forward elsewhere in the parent company and will be reported in forthcoming articles.

Although we have shared our findings with you throughout the article, it seems wise now to summarize them for your convenience, so that they may be generalized to other organizations and climates.

Findings

1. A clear-cut commitment to a particular OD approach is not necessary (although desirable) for a successful OD program to succeed.

2. Total top-management understanding of where the OD process will lead and the state of the organization at the end is not necessary for organizational change to occur.

3. Change can and does begin at lower levels in the organization.

4. Effective and permanent adult learning comes after the individual has experimented with new approaches and received appropriate feedback in the on-the-job situation.

5. Rather than the T-group, the operating, ongoing organization may be the best "laboratory" for learning, with fewer problems in transfer of training.

6. Internal change leaders are natural targets for the change agent, since they become influence leaders and help to shape the culture.

7. Organizational change occurs in stages: a stage of unfreezing and trust building, a take-off stage when observable change occurs, and a stabilization stage. Then the cycle iterates.

8. Multiple changes in the subsystems are needed for the individual employee to change behavior and perceptions of his role.

9. Structural and interpersonal systems changes must reinforce and legitimate each other.

10. Systems changes set off additional interactive processes in which changes in organizational functioning not only increase outputs but also develop the latent abilities of people.

11. Influence is also exerted upward, with greater acceptance of these concepts by individuals at higher levels in the organization.

12. The client system eventually becomes a sophisticated consumer of new research findings in the behavioral sciences.

Perhaps the most important and far-reaching conclusion is that as organizational psychologists we have viewed our role too narrowly and with an insufficient historical and change perspective. Our research studies tend to be static rather than dynamic. We need to do a better job of developing a theory and technology of changing and to develop a flexible set of concepts which will change as we experiment with and socially engineer organizations. We are suggesting a stronger action orientation for our field and less of a natural science orientation. We must be less timid about helping organizations to change themselves. We must create a positive snowball of organizational change followed by changes in needs and expectations of organizational members, followed again by further organizational change. The objective of change agents should be to develop an evolving system that maintains reasonable internal consistency while staying relevant to and anticipating changes and adaptation to the outside environment. As behavioral scientists and change agents, we must help organizations begin to "become."

REFERENCES

Argyris, C. On the future of laboratory training. *Journal of Applied Behavioral Science*, 1967, 3 (2), 153-83.

Bartlett, A. C. Changing behavior as a means to increased efficiency. *Journal of Applied Behavioral Science*, 1967, 3 (3), 381-403.

Beckhard, R. *Organization development: Strategies and models.* Reading, Mass.: Addison-Wesley, 1969.

Beer, M., Pieters, G. R., Marcus, S. H., and Hundert, A.T. Improving integration between functional groups: A case in organization change and implications for theory and practice. Symposium presented at American Psychological Association convention, Washington, D.C., September 1971.

Bennis, W. G. The case study—I. Introduction. *Journal of Applied Behavioral Science.* 1968, 4 (2), 227-231.

Blake, R. R., and Mouton, J. S. *Building a dynamic corporation through grid organization development.* Reading, Mass.: Addison-Wesley, 1969.

Blake, R. R., Shepard, H. A., and Mouton, J.S. *Managing intergroup conflict in industry.* Houston, Tex.: Gulf, 1964.

Bradford, L. P. Membership and the learning process. In L. P. Bradford, J. R. Gibb, and K. D. Benne (Eds.), *T-group theory and laboratory method: Innovation in re-education.* New York: Wiley, 1964.

Campbell, J. P., and Dunnette, M. D. Effectiveness of T-group experiences in managerial training and development. *Psychological Bulletin*, 1968 (August), 70, (2), 73-104.

Davis, S. A. An organic problem-solving method of organizational change. *Journal of Applied Behavioral Science*, 1967, 3 (1), 3-21.

Ford, R. N. *Motivation through the work itself.* New York: American Management Association, 1969.

Huse, E. F. The behavioral scientist in the shop. *Personnel*, 1965 (May/June), 42 (3), 50-57.

Huse, E. F. Putting in a management development program that works. *California Management Review*, (Winter) 1966, 73-80.

Huse, E. F., and Price, P. S. The relationship between maturity and motivation in varied work groups. *Proceedings* of the Seventieth Annual Convention of the American Psychological Association, September, 1970.

Lawrence, P. R., and Lorsch, J. W. *Organization and environment.* Homewood, Ill.: Irwin, 1969.

Lawrence, P. R., Bailey, J. C., Katz, R. L., Seiler, J. A., Orth, C. D. III, Clark, J. V., Barnes, L. B., and Turner, A. N. *Organizational behavior and administration.* Homewood, Ill.: Irwin-Dorsey, 1961.

Lesieur, F. G. (Ed.) *The Scanlon plan: A frontier in labor-management cooperation.* Cambridge, Mass.: M.I.T. Press, 1958.

Lesieur, F. G., and Puckett, E. S. The Scanlon plan has proved itself. *Harvard Business Review*, 1969 (September/October), 47, 109-18.

Paul, W. J., Robertson, K. B., and Herzberg, F. Job enrichment pays off. *Harvard Business Review*. 1969 (March/April), 47 (2) 61-78.

Roche, W. J., and MacKinnon, N. L. Motivating people with meaningful work. *Harvard Business Review*, 1970 (May/June), 48 (3), 97-110.

Schein, E. H., and Bennis, W. G. *Personal and organizational change through group methods: The laboratory approach*. New York: Wiley, 1965.

Walton, R. E. Contrasting designs for participative systems. *Personnel Administration*, 1967 (November/December), 30 (6), 35-41.

23
Durability of Organizational Change

STANLEY E. SEASHORE and DAVID G. BOWERS[1]

The aim of this article is to add a modest footnote to the growing literature concerning planned change in the structure and function of formal organizations. The question asked is whether changes that have been planned, successfully introduced, and confirmed by measurements, over but a relatively short span of time, can survive as permanent features of the organization. Will such a changed organization become stabilized in its new state, or will it continue the direction and pace of change, or perhaps revert to its earlier state?

This report will include a brief review of an earlier effort to change an organization, a presentation of some new data about the present state of the organization, and some first speculations about the meaning of psychological and social phenomena in formal organizations.

BACKGROUND

The earlier events against which our new

1. Presidential Address by Stanley E. Seashore presented to the Division of Industrial Psychology (Division 14) at the annual meeting of the American Psychological Association, Washington, D.C., September 1969.

data are to be set are reported rather fully elsewhere (Marrow, Bowers, and Seashore, 1967). A brief review of the essential facts will set the stage.

In late 1961 the Harwood company purchased its major competitor, the Weldon company. This brought under common ownership and general management two organizations remarkably similar in certain features and remarkably different in others. Both made and marketed similar products using equipment and manufacturing processes of a like kind; were of similar size in terms of business volume and number of employees; served similar and partially overlapping markets; were family-owned and owner-managed firms; and had similar histories of growth and enjoyed high reputation in the trade.

The differences between the two organizations are of particular interest. The Harwood company had earned some prominence and respect for their efforts over many years to operate the organization as a participative system with high value given to individual and organizational development, as well as to effective performance. The Weldon company had for years been managed in a

Reprinted from *American Psychologist*, 1970, 25, 227-33, by permission of the authors and the publisher.

fashion that prevails in the garment industry, with a highly centralized, authoritarian philosophy and with secondary concern for individual development and organizational maintenance. The two organizations were, in 1962, rather extreme examples from the continuum vaguely defined by the terms authoritarian versus participative. Measurements in both firms in 1962 confirmed that the difference was not merely impressionistic, but was represented in quantitative assessments of the organizational processes for planning, coordination, communication, motivation, and work performance, and was represented as well in member attitudes. The two firms were also sharply contrasting in their performance in 1962, even though over a longer span of years their business accomplishments had been similar. In 1962 Weldon in sharp contrast to Harwood, was losing money, experiencing high costs, generating many errors of strategy and work performance, suffering from member disaffection with consequent high absenteeism and high turnover. Weldon, despite its technical, fiscal, and market strengths, was near the point of disaster.

The new owners set out on a program to rebuild the Weldon enterprise according to the model of the Harwood company. The ultimate aim was to make the Weldon firm a viable and profitable economic unit within a short period of time. A rather strenuous and costly program was envisioned, including some modernization of the plant, improved layout and flow of work, improvements in records and production control methods, and product simplification, as well as changes in the human organization. The renewal program concerning the organization itself concerns us here.

The approach to organizational change can be characterized briefly in three respects: (a) the conception of the organizational characteristics to be sought; (b) the conception of processes for changing persons and organizational systems; and (c) the linking of the social system to the work system.

The guiding assumptions or "philosophy" on which the change program was based included elements such as the following:

1. It was assumed that employees would have to gain a realistic sense of security in their jobs and that this security would have to arise basically out of their own successful efforts to improve their organization and their performance, not out of some bargained assurances.

2. The introduction of substantial change in the work environment requires that employees have confidence in the technical competence and humane values of the managers and supervisors; this confidence can be earned only if it is reciprocated by placing confidence in the employees.

3. In a situation of rapid change it is particularly necessary to use procedures of participation in the planning and control of the work and of the changes; such procedures are needed at all levels of the organization.

4. The rebuilding of an organization may require an input of technical resources and capital on a substantial scale—not unlike the investments required to rework a technology or control system of a factory.

5. Management involves skills and attitudes that can be defined, taught, and learned, and these skills and attitudes need not be confined to high rank staff; each member of the organization, at least in some limited degree, must learn to help manage his own work and that of others related to him.

6. Guidelines such as these are not readily understood and accepted unless they can be linked to concrete events and to the rational requirements of the work to be done and the problems to be solved.

The conception of change processes incorporated in the rebuilding of the Weldon organization emphasized the application of multiple and compatible change forces. The physical improvements in work resources and conditions were to be accompanied by informational clarity, enhanced motivation through rewards, and ample skill training and practice. That is, change was to be introduced simultaneously at the situational, cognitive, motivational, and behavioral levels so that each would support the others.

The linking of the social organization to the work system was to be accomplished through efforts, however limited, to design work places, work flows, information flows, and the like in a manner not merely compatible with but integral with the associated social organization and organizational processes.

The program of rebuilding the organization was carried out by the local management with substantial assistance and stimulation from the new owners and from a variety of consultants, including psychologists. The general planning and guidance of the program were influenced primarily by Alfred Marrow, Board Chairman of the Harwood Corporation and Fellow of Division 14. The role of the Institute for Social Research was not that of change agent, but rather that of observing, recording, measuring, and analyzing the course of events and the change that resulted.

The change program was successful in important respects. Within two years there occurred improvements in employee satisfactions, motivations, and work performance. The organization took on characteristics of an adaptive, self-controlling, participative system. The firm as a business unit moved from a position of loss to one of profit. At the end of 1964, after two years of change effort, the factory was abandoned as a research site, the rate of input of capital and external manpower into the change program diminished substantially, and the factory and its organization were expected to settle down to something like a "normal" state.

EXPECTATIONS ABOUT CHANGE

From the start of this organizational change program there was a concern about the long-run consequences of the program, and there was uncertainty about the permanence of change. The following quotations from our earlier report illustrate the intentions, hopes, and doubts (Marrow et al., 1967):

... the whole organization, from the plant manager down to the production workers, were taken into an exercise in joint problem-solving through participative methods in groups, with a view toward making such procedures a normal part of the management system of the plant [p. 69].

The refreezing of Weldon in a new and more effective state is not regarded as a permanent thing, but as another stage in the evolution and continuous adaptation of the organization. Some features of the conversion plan explicitly include the provision of built-in capacities for easier change in the future [p. 232].

Will the changes at Weldon last? The only evidence we have at the present time is that the change from a predominantly "authoritative" to a dominantly "consultative" type of management organization persisted for at least two years in the view of the managers and supervisors involved. Surely there exist forces toward a reversion to the old Weldon form of organizational life; it remains an uncertainty whether they will or will not win out over the new forces toward consolidation of change and further change of the intended kinds. (p. 244)

In mid-1969, four and one-half years after the termination of the intensive change program, Dr. Bowers and I invited ourselves back to the Weldon plant for a follow-up measurement of the state of the organization. This remeasurement consisted of a one-day visit to the plant by a research assistant who administered questionnaires to managers, supervisors, and a sample of the employees.[2] In addition, certain information was abstracted from the firm's records, and the views of the plant manager were solicited

2. The assistance of Edith Wessner is acknowledged.

Table 23-1. Changes in Job Attitudes

Item	1962 %	1964 %	1969 %
Company better than most	22	28	36
Own work satisfying	77	84	91
Satisfied with pay system	22	27	28
Company tries to maintain earnings	26	44	41
Satisfied with supervisor	64	54	54
Like fellow employees	85	86	85
Group cohesivesness	25	25	30
Plan to stay indefinitely	72	87	66
Expect future improvement in situation	23	31	43

as to changes that had taken place and possible reasons for change. We can turn directly to a few tables and figures representing the changes and the situation as of 1969.

RESULTS

First, we present some data from the production employees. Table 23-1 shows selected items from our questionnaire survey bearing on the issue of whether there has occurred a decline, a rise, or a stabilization of the attitudes, satisfactions, and optimism of the employees. The table shows the percentage of employees giving the two most favorable responses, of five offered, to each question. The columns represent the result in 1962 before the change program began, in 1964 at the conclusion of the formal change effort, and in 1969.

The general picture is one of the maintenance of earlier gains in the favorability of employee attitudes or the further improvement in attitudes. This observation holds for seven of the nine indicators. The remaining two deserve brief special comment.

Satisfaction with supervisors declined during the period of the active change program but has remained relatively high and constant since 1964. The initial decline

is viewed as a consequence of the substantial change in the supervisors' role during the active change program. During that period, the supervisors acquired substantially more responsibility and authority as well as some new activities and duties that are thought to have removed the supervisors from a peerlike to a superior status relationship with the operators which they retain now. This interpretation is of course speculative but made before the 1969 data were in hand.

The decline in the proportion of employees planning to stay on indefinitely is rather difficult to assess. The rise between 1962 and 1964 can be attributed to the improvement in pay and working conditions in that period. The subsequent decline is to be accounted for, partly, by the fact of recent production expansion and the presence on the payroll of a relatively larger number of turnover-prone short-service employees. One might also speculate that rising prosperity during the period might have increased the attractiveness of marriage, child bearing, or retirement for these female employees. In any case, the decline in the percentage committed to long job tenure appears to be at odds with the general rise in job satisfactions and in the marked rise in optimism about the future improvement in the Weldon situation. We should add that the decline in percentage committed to long tenure is confirmed by the fact of a moderate rise in actual turnover rates in recent months.

Table 23-2 shows a few selected items bearing on the question whether the rise in satisfactions and expectations is accompanied by some loss in productivity concerns and task orientation. The data, again, are from employee questionnaire responses (except for the last line) and show changes from 1962 to 1964, and then to 1969.

Five of the indicators reflect a rise in level of task orientation and production concern since the end of the formal change program. The remaining items are not negative, but merely indeterminate. There is clearly a rise

Table 23-2. Change in Task-Orientation Indicators

Item	1962 %	1964 %	1969 %
Company quick to improve methods	18	24	31
Company good at planning	22	26	35
Not delayed by poor services	76	79	90
Produce what rates call for	44	67	53
Expect own productivity to improve	63	55	62
Peers approve of high producers	58	58	66
Closeness of task supervision	38	27	47
Desired closeness of supervision	57	52	64
Mean productivity (% of standard)	87	114	?

in recent years in the percentage of employees who say the firm is quick to improve work methods, good at planning, provides efficient service (maintenance, supplies, scheduling), who report that their peers approve of high producers, and who themselves desire frequent and ready access to supervisory help. Two sets of data require special comment.

The data on productivity, three lines in the table, should be considered as a set. The numbers show that the self-report of "Nearly always producing what the rates call for" rose substantially during the active change program, and this is confirmed by the actual productivity records of the firm as shown in the last line "Mean productivity against standard." During the same period, the percentage of employees expecting a further gain in their own productivity declined, as it should have considering that more employees were approaching the firm's hoped-for level of high productivity and earnings. By 1969 there was some decline in the percentage reporting high productivity and a corresponding rise in the percentage

expecting a future rise in their productivity; this pair of related changes appears to reflect the presence on the staff of an increasing number of relatively new employees not yet up to the level of skill and performance they may reasonably expect to attain. There is a crucial item of missing data in the last line of the table; for technical reasons, we have not been able to calculate the current actual productivity rate in a form that allows confident comparisons with the earlier figures. Our best estimate is that productivity has been stable with a slight decline in recent months arising from the recent introduction of additional inexperienced employees.

Attention is also suggested to the pair of lines in Table 23-2 concerning closeness of supervision. At all three times of measurement, these production workers desired more close supervision than they actually experienced; these employees, unlike those in some other organizations, see their supervisors to be potentially helpful in improving productivity and increasing piece-rate earnings. The decline in experienced closeness of supervision during the period 1962-64 matches other evidence to be presented later that during this period there was a substantial change in the supervisors' role that diverted the supervisors from immediate floor supervision and left a temporary partial shortage of this service to production workers. The figures show that by 1969 this supervisory deficit had been recouped and more. This sustains our general view that during the years following the Weldon change program there has been not a decline in concern for task performance among employees and in the organizational system generally but rather a further gain in task orientation.

The change in supervisory behavior mentioned earlier is shown in Figure 23-1. We attempted at the three points in time to measure the extent to which supervisors, in the view of employees, engaged in behaviors we categorize as "supportive," "goal empha-

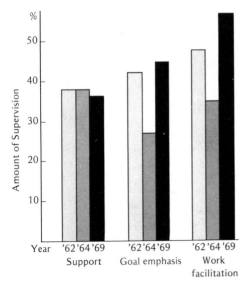

Fig. 23-1. Change in Three Dimensions of Supervisory Leadership Behavior

sizing," and "work facilitating." (Two additional dimensions of leader behavior that we now use in describing organizations are not represented here because they were not yet identified in 1962; we chose to continue use of the initial measurement methods rather than to update them.)

Figure 23-1 shows that the amount of supervisory supportiveness experienced by employees remained constant during the 1962-64 period and has risen slightly since then. Goal emphasis and work facilitation both dropped during the active change program, for reasons mentioned earlier, and have since risen above their 1962 levels. These data sustain our belief that the Weldon organization since 1964 has increased its expression of concern for production goals and its provision of conditions for effective work performance, and at no cost of declining concern for employee attitudes and satisfactions.

One more set of data from the employees is pertinent here, namely, their description of the amount and hierarchical distribution of control in the Weldon organization. One

of the explicit aims of the change program was that of increasing the total amount of control and of altering the distribution of control so that lower rank people—supervisors and operators—would have some added degree of control. This was accomplished during the change program period to a very limited and nonsignificant degree. Subsequent changes have been in the direction intended and more substantial in degree. The data are shown in Figure 23-2. In 1969, compared with the earlier periods, there is more control being exercised in total, with a notable increment in the case of the headquarters staff, a further small decline for the local plant management, and increments for the supervisors and for the employees. There appears to have been a change of modest degree, more or less as hoped for, and there has clearly not been a reversion to the original condition of concentrated control in the hands of the plant manager.

We turn now to some indicators of the state of the Weldon organization from the views of the supervisors and managers. The

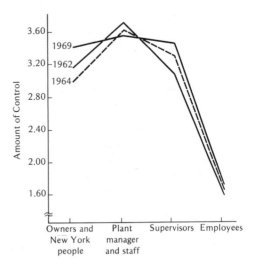

Fig. 23-2. Change in Amount and Hierarchical Distribution of Control

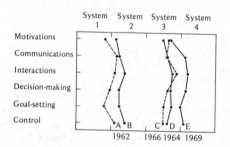

Fig. 23-3. Change in Profile of Organizational Characteristics

data presented in Figure 23-3 are derived from Likert's assessment instrument "Profile of Organizational and Performance Characteristics" (Likert, 1961, 1967). Most readers will have some acquaintance with this instrument and the theory and research data that it expresses, but a brief characterization might be helpful. The instrument used is a 43-item graphic-scale rating form that allows the respondent to describe his own organization as it presently functions and as he ideally would like it to function. The items are so chosen and arranged that the respondent may report a syndrome of organizational characteristics that locates the organization on a scale ranging from "authoritative" to "participative." Likert discerns four regions of this scale, named Systems 1, 2, 3, and 4, with word labels ranging from "Authoritarian" through "Benevolent Authoritarian" and "Consultative" to "Participative." The conception is analogous to McGregor's "Theory X" and "Theory Y" scale, and also to Blake's two-dimensioned matrix. To put it somewhat disrespectfully, the bad guys are thought to have and to prefer System 1 organizations while good guys aspire to and approach the System 4 state. The results for Weldon, 1962, 1964, and 1969 are represented in Figure 23-3.

At the left of the field are two graph lines showing the state of the Weldon organization in 1962, first as rated by the Institute for Social Research research team from interview protocols and observations, and

next and somewhat more favorably as rated by the supervisors and managers on the scene. Weldon at that time was described to be autocratic—in some respects rather harshly autocratic and in some respects more benevolently autocratic. The state of the organization in 1964 and in 1966 is represented in the next two lines. These data are from supervisors and managers; they indicate a pattern of change that is substantial in magnitude and wholly compatible with the intentions embodied in the Weldon change program. There was no regression toward the earlier state during the 1964-66 period. The right-hand line represents the results of our 1969 assessment; it shows that in the view of the managers and supervisors at Weldon, the organization has progressed still further toward their ideal of a participative organizational system.

A final remark should be made about measured changes in Weldon before we turn to a consideration of the meaning of these data. Some readers will be interested in business outcomes as well as in the attitudes and behavior of the members of the organization. Briefly, Weldon moved from a position of substantial capital loss in 1962 to substantial return on investment in 1964; this direction of change in profitability has continued through 1968, the last year of record. Employee earnings which rose substantially between 1962 and 1964 have been sustained at a relatively high level. During the period since 1964 there have been substantial gains in efficiency and volume for the factory as a whole. New products and work methods have been introduced. By such business indicators, Weldon is a successful organization.

DURABLE CHANGE

The evidence we must weigh, although somewhat mixed and with a few contrary elements, appears to sustain the conclusion that the Weldon organization, far from reverting to its prior condition, has during recent years made additional progress toward the organizational goals envisioned by the owners and managers in 1962, and envisioned as well by supervisors and production employees at a somewhat later time. This outcome invites speculations about the psychological and social forces that are at work.

We confess a brief regret that there was not an opposite outcome, for we are rather better equipped with ideas about organizational stability and regression than we are with ideas about organizational change and continuing development. For example, before the data became available, we were prepared to make some remarks about the "Hawthorne effect"—about the superficiality and transient quality of organizational and behavioral changes induced under conditions of external attention and pressure; but it boggles the mind to think of a "Hawthorne effect" persisting for over eight years among people half of whom were not on the scene at the time of the original change. Similarly, we were prepared to make wise remarks about cultural forces, habits, and the natural predilection of managers for nonparticipative methods; these we thought would help explain a reversion to the prevailing conditions in organizations. We were prepared to assert that in the absence of contrary environmental forces, external influences, and purposive continuing change efforts of a vigorous kind, an organization would migrate back to some more primitive form of organizational life.

Clearly we need to appeal to other ideas than these. We are, all of us, ill prepared to do so. Two recent and fairly comprehensive reviews of organizational change strategies (Leavitt, 1965; Shepard, 1965) say nothing about the permanence or continuation of change processes except for a remark by Shepard that "change in the direction of collaboration-consensus patterns [participative patterns] ... facilitates growth, change and adaptation to new environmental challenges and opportunities" (p. 1141).

A first explanatory idea rests on the possibility that the heavy investment of external talent, money, and effort that characterized the original change period at Weldon has been continued during the subsequent years. We are assured that this is not the case. There has indeed been some additional use of external consultants, but at a modest rate that is considered normal and permanent. There has indeed been further improvement and change in the work system and the production facilities, but at no more than a permanently sustainable rate. There has indeed been a continuation of certain organizational activities introduced as part of the original change program, but these are regarded as normal operating procedure and not as special change efforts. Economic conditions have been favorable to the firm, but they were also favorable at the distressed time preceding the change of ownership in 1962.

We believe that there are three other lines of explanation that do bear scrutiny. These thoughts about the Weldon experience are not offered with any sense of great insight or of conceptual innovation. They are offered only as suggestions for lines of inquiry and emphasis in future organizational research. The first concerns the provision of "lock-in" devices that make difficult the reversal of the original change.

It was mentioned earlier that the original change program contained some notions of seeking mutually reinforcing change actions across the psychological, organizational, and technological domains. A central idea was to make structural changes in the organization that matched the work system and that did not violate reasonable assumptions about the values and motives of individual members. For example, the revitalized piece-rate pay system was viewed to be viable only if sustained by the provision of assured services that allowed high earnings, a revision of the record and information flow system that assured instant supervisory response to low earnings, and a moderating of the prior job assignment system so that a production employee could become skilled in the work assigned. The idea of systemic consistency is surely an elementary one, no more than common sense—a habit of thought for those who have learned to view the factory as a total system in which all elements are interdependent. The interdependence of elements tends to preserve, to enhance, and to "lock in" the central characteristics of the system and thus to prevent retrogression.

A second factor in Weldon's continuation of intended change might lie in the earlier legitimation of concern about organizational processes. This is speculative, for we have no ready way to assess the extent to which there was implanted the habit of deliberate and self-conscious examination of the potential side effects of the many policy and operating decisions, usually technical or economic in origin, that arise daily. One of the fragmenting features of many organizations is the tendency to isolate problems, to treat them as if they could be optimally resolved without reference to their broader context. An organization habituated at all levels to think about, discuss openly, and to weigh properly the full range of elements in the organizational system might well have unusual capacities for self-maintenance and self-development.

A third possible explanation of the maintenance of the changes at Weldon and their further development under conditions of limited continuing external influence might lie in the inherent merit of the participative organizational model. Could it be that people who have experienced a taste of it get hooked, know what they want, and lend their effort to maintaining it? A glance at the newspaper headlines on almost any day will suggest that some of our fellow citizens do not like what they are experiencing in formal organizations and have thoughts of having something better, by force if necessary.

REFERENCES

Leavitt, H. J. Applied organizational change in industry. In J. G. March (Ed.), *Handbook of organizations*. Chicago: Rand McNally, 1965.

Likert, R. *New patterns of management*. New York: McGraw-Hill, 1961.

Likert, R. *The human organization*. New York: McGraw-Hill, 1967.

Marrow, A. J., Bowers, D. G., and Seashore, S. E. *Management by participation*. New York: Harper & Row, 1967.

Shepard, H. A. Changing interpersonal and intergroup relationships in organizations. In J. G. March (Ed.), *Handbook of organizations*. Chicago: Rand McNally, 1965.

24

The Management of
Interdepartmental Conflict:
A Model and Review

RICHARD E. WALTON and JOHN M. DUTTON

Horizontal interactions are seldom shown on the organizational chart, but transactions along this dimension are often at least as important as vertical interactions (Simpson, 1959; Landsberger, 1961; Burns and Stalker, 1961). This paper presents a general model of interdepartmental conflict and its management, together with a review of the relevant literature.[1] The model includes five sets of related variables: antecedents to conflict, attributes of the lateral relationship, management of the interface, consequences of the relationship, and responses of higher executives. Figure 24-1 shows the general relationship among these sets of variables.

The general model is postulated as applicable to all lateral relations between any two organizational units (departments, divisions, sections, and so on) that engage in any type of transaction, including joint decision making, exchanging information, providing expertise or advice, and auditing or inspecting.

1. This research was supported by a grant from the McKinsey Foundation for Management Research, Inc.

ANTECEDENTS TO INTERUNIT CONFLICT AND COLLABORATION

Manifest conflict results largely from factors which originate outside the particular lateral relationship under consideration or which antedate the relationship. Hypotheses and models that use external factors to predict lateral relations have been advanced by March and Simon (1958), Thompson (1961), Caplow (1964), Lawrence and Lorsch (1967a, b) and Pondy (1967). The present model describes nine major types of antecedents: mutual dependence, asymmetries, rewards, organizational differentiation, role dissatisfaction, ambiguities, common resources, communication obstacles, and personal skills and traits.

Mutual Task Dependence

Mutual task dependence is the key variable in the relevance of the interunit conflict model in general and the impact of the postulated conflict antecedents in particular. Task dependence is the extent to which two units depend upon each other for assistance, information, compliance, or other coordinative acts in the performance of their respec-

Reprinted from *Administrative Science Quarterly*, 1969, 14, 73-84, by permission of the publisher and the authors.

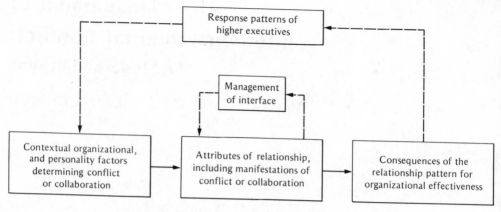

Fig. 24-1.   General Model of Interunit Conflict

tive tasks. It is assumed here that dependence is mutual and can range from low to high. Asymmetry in the interdependence is treated later.

According to Miller (1959), the more performance of one unit depends on the performance of all other units, the more likely is the system to perform without external control. Other studies, however, Dutton and Walton (1966), for example, indicate that task interdependence not only provides an incentive for collaboration, but also presents an occasion for conflict and the means for bargaining over interdepartmental issues. A related factor, task overload, has similarly mixed potential for conflict and collaboration. Overload conditions may intensify the problem of scarce resources and lead to bargaining; may increase tension, frustration, and aggression; and may decrease the time available for the social interactions that would enable the units to contain their conflict. On the other hand, overload may place a premium on mutual assistance. The net directional effects of high task interdependence and overload are therefore uncertain.

Other implications of the extent of mutual task dependence are more predictable. High task interdependence and overload tend to heighten the intensity of either interunit antagonisms or friendliness, increase the

magnitude of the consequences of unit conflict for organizational performance, and contribute to the difficulty of changing an ongoing pattern.

Task-related Asymmetries

Symmetrical interdependence and symmetrical patterns of initiation between units promote collaboration; asymmetrical interdependence leads to conflict. For example, in a study by Dalton (1959), a staff group resented the asymmetries in their relationship with line groups. The staff group had to understand the problems of the line groups, had to get along with them, promote their ideas, and justify their existence; but none of these relations were reciprocal requirements imposed on the line groups. Strauss (1962) reported that asymmetrical high dependence of purchasing agents on another group led them to make more attempts to influence the terms of requisitions they received and thereby force interaction to flow both ways.

The adverse effects of asymmetrical conditions are sometimes related to the fact that one unit has little incentive to coordinate. The more dependent unit may try to increase the incentive of the more independent unit to cooperate by interfering with their task performance. The assumption is that once the independent unit is made aware of their need for the cooperation of the dependent unit (i.e., to desist from interfering acts), they will behave more cooperatively (supply the assistance necessary). This tactic may indeed achieve its purpose, and the conflict-interfering acts may cease; but frequently interference elicits a retaliatory response.

Conflict is also produced by differences in the way units are ranked along various dimensions of organizational status, namely direction of initiation of action, prestige, power, and knowledge. Seiler (1963) studied in an organization in which it was generally agreed that research had more prestige than engineering and engineering had more prestige than production. When the sequential pattern of initiation and influence followed this status ordering, it was accepted. However, where a lower-status industrial engineering group needed to direct the higher-status research group to carry out routine tests, the result was a breakdown in relationships between the departments.

Inconsistency between the distribution of knowledge among departments and the lateral influence patterns are also a source of conflict. Lawrence and Lorsch (1967a) advanced the idea that the more the influence of each unit is consistent with key competitive factors, the more effectively will interunit issues be resolved. They noted that in container firms, customer delivery and product quality were crucial for competitive success; therefore, sales and production were required to have the most influence in the resolution of interunit conflict. By contrast, in the food industry, where market expertise and food science were essential, sales and research were required to be the more influential. Landsberger (1961) also found that the locus of power among three plants in the same industry was affected by their different market positions.

Zald (1962) in a study of correctional institutions offered a power-balance proposition about the effect of relative power: assuming task interdependence and divergent values among three units (teachers, cottage parents, and social service workers), conflict is most likely to occur between units that are unable to control the situation and those perceived as being in control. He found that the patterns of conflict among these three units were generally consistent with predictions based on this power-balance hypothesis.

Performance Criteria and Rewards

Interunit conflict results when each of the interdependent departments has responsibility for only one side of a dilemma embedded in organizational tasks. Dutton and Walton (1966) noted that the preference of production units for long, economical runs conflicted with the preference of sales units for quick delivery to good customers. Dalton (1959) observed that staff units valued change, because that was one way they proved their worth; whereas line units valued stability, because change reflected unfavorably upon them or inconvenienced them. Also, staff units were strongly committed to preserving the integrity of control and rule systems, whereas line personnel believed they could be more effective by flexible reinterpretation of control and incentive schemes, and by ignoring many discipline and safety violations. A study by Strauss (1962) showed that engineers preferred to order brand items, whereas purchasing agents sought specifications suitable for several vendors. Similar instances abound. Landsberger (1961) postulated several basic dilemmas which probably underlie many interdepartmental differences: flexibility versus stability; criteria for short-run versus long-run performance; emphasis on measurable results versus attention to intangible results; maximizing organizational goals versus responding to other societal needs.

Although the dilemmas may be inherent in the total task, the reward system designed by management can serve either to sharpen or to blunt their divisive effects: the more the evaluations and rewards of higher man-

agement emphasize the separate performance of each department rather than their
combined performance, the more conflict.

Close, one-to-one supervisory styles have
generally been assumed to promote more
conflict among peers than general supervision in which the superior also deals with
subordinates as a group (Likert, 1961). One
might speculate that group supervisory patterns are taken to indicate emphasis on
group rather than individual performance
criteria; and that group patterns allow the
supervisor to observe the process and to
reward cooperative acts.

Organizational Differentiation

Litwak (1961) postulated that uniform tasks
require a bureaucratic type of organization,
characterized by impersonality of relations,
prior specification of job authority, emphasis on hierarchical authority, separation of
policy and administration, and emphasis on
general rules and specialization; whereas
nonuniform tasks require a human-relations
organization with the contrasting characteristics. In contemporary society, most
large-scale organizations have to deal with
both uniform and nonuniform tasks, and
must combine these contradictory forms of
social relations into a professional model.
Litwak regards the inclusions of these
contradictory forms as a source of organizational conflict.

Lawrence and Lorsch (1967a) emphasized
the effects of differentiation. Where each
unit (such as research, sales, or production)
performs a different type of task and copes
with a different segment of the environment,
the units will develop significant internal
differences. Such units may differ from each
other (a) in the degree of structure, that is,
tightness of rules, narrowness of span of
supervisory control, frequency and specificity of performance review; and in the
orientation of its members; (b) toward the
environment, such as, new scientific knowledge versus customer problems and market
opportunities versus costs of raw materials

and processing; (c) toward time, such as
planning time perspective; and (d) toward
other people, such as, openness and permissiveness of interpersonal relationships.
Lawrence and Lorsch measured these differences in six plastics organizations with the
results shown in Table 24-1.

Lawrence and Lorsch believe this fourfold
differentiation is largely a response to the
degree of uncertainty in the environments of
the different departments. They use a notion
of optimum degree of differentiation, which
depends upon the task environments. Thus,
either overdifferentiation or underdifferen-
tiation has implications for the coordinative
processes. Although greater differentiation
apparently results in more *potential* for
conflict, these authors do not assume that
more manifest conflict will automatically
result. In their study of six plastics organizations, the degree of integration did not, in
fact, vary strictly with the degree of differentiation.

Role Dissatisfaction

Role dissatisfaction, stemming from a
variety of sources, can be a source of
conflict. Blocking status aspirations in purchasing agents (Strauss, 1962) and in staff
members (Dalton, 1959) led to conflict with
other units. In these cases, professionals felt
they lacked recognition and opportunities
for advancement. Similarly, White (1961)
stated that members might feel that the
growth of their units and its external status
did not meet their needs, and therefore
might enter another unit or withdraw from
contacts which were painful reminders of
the lack of status. Where one unit informally
reports on the activities of another unit,
resentment can occur, as with staff units
reporting to management on production
irregularities (Dalton, 1959). Argyris (1964)
and Dalton (1959) both argued that role
dissatisfaction and conflict followed where
one unit with the same or less status set
standards for another.

Where there is role dissatisfaction, am-

Table 24-1. Differences Related to Environment of Departments*

Departments	Orientation toward environment	Orientation toward time	Degree of formality in departmental structure	Permissiveness versus directiveness in orientation toward others
Applied research	Techno-economic	Long	Medium	Medium
Sales	Market	Short	High	Low
Production	Techno-economic	Short	High	High

*After Lawrence and Lorsch (1967)

biguities in the definition of work responsibilities further increase the likelihood of interunit conflict. Landsberger (1961) pointed out that ambiguities tempted the dissatisfied unit to engage in offensive maneuvers so as to improve its lot, and thus induced other units to engage in defensive maneuvers.

Role dissatisfaction and ambiguity are related to more basic organizational variables, including growth rate, organizational level, and hierarchical differences. Organizational growth appears to have offsetting consequences. Slower rates of organizational growth and of opportunities for promotion increase role dissatisfaction, but are also accompanied by fewer ambiguities. Interfaces higher in the organization are more likely to be marked by conflict to redefine departmental responsibilities. At the higher levels, jurisdictional boundaries are less clear (Pondy, 1967), and the participants perceive more opportunity to achieve some restructuring. Steep and heavily emphasized hierarchical differences in status, power, and rewards were seen by Thompson (1961) as responsible for some lateral conflict, because these factors tended to activate and to legitimate individual aspiration for increased status and power and tended to lead to increased upward orientation toward the desires of one's superiors, rather than to problem orientation and increased horizontal coordination.

Ambiguities

In addition to its interaction with role dissatisfaction, ambiguity contributes to interunit conflict in several other ways. Difficulty in assigning credit or blame between two departments increases the likelihood of conflict between units. Dalton (1959) attributed part of the staff-line conflict he observed to the fact that although improvements required collaboration between line and staff units, it was later difficult to assess the contribution of each unit. Similarly, disputes resulted between production and sales units, when it could not be determined which department made a mistake (Dutton and Walton, 1966).

Low routinization and uncertainty of means to goals increase the potential for interunit conflict. This proposition is supported by Zald (1962) in his study of interunit conflict in five correctional institutions. Similarly, ambiguity in the criteria used to evaluate the performance of a unit may also create tension, frustration, and conflict (Kahn, Wolfe, et al., 1964). Organization planning, which includes clarity of rule definition, correlated positively with measures of lateral coordination and problem solving in a study of ten hospitals by Georgopoulos and Mann (1962).

Dependence on Common Resources

Conflict potential exists when two units depend upon a common pool of scarce organizational resources, such as, physical space, equipment, manpower, operating funds, capital funds, central staff resources, and centralized services (e.g., typing and drafting). If the two units have interdependent tasks, the competition for scarce resources will tend to decrease interunit problem solving and coordination. Also, if competition for scarce resources is not mediated by some third unit and they must agree on their allocation, they will come into direct conflict.

Communication Obstacles

Semantic difficulties can impede communications essential for cooperation. Strauss (1964) observed that differences in training of purchasing agents and engineers contributed to their conflicts. March and Simon (1958) stated that organizational channeling of information introduced bias.

Common experience reduces communication barriers and provides common referents. Miller (1959) proposed that the less units know about each other's job, the less collaboration, and that lack of knowledge can lead to unreasonable interunit demands through ignorance. Cozer (1956) argued that accommodation is especially dependent on knowledge of the power of the other unit.

Personal Skills and Traits

Walton and McKersie (1965), reviewing experimental studies, found that certain personality attributes, such as high authoritarianism, high dogmatism, and low self-esteem, increased conflict behavior. Kahn *et al.* (1964: 256) found that in objective role conflict persons who scored lower on neurotic anxiety scales tended to depart more from "cordial, congenial, trusting, respecting, and understanding relations," and introverts tended to lose their confidence, trust, and respect for work associates more than extroverts.

Most interunit relationships are mixed-motive situations, which require high behavioral flexibility to manage optimally. A person with a narrower range of behavioral skills is less likely to exploit the integrative potential fully in an interunit relationship. He may either engage in bargaining to the exclusion of collaborative problem solving, or withdraw or become passive (Walton and

McKersie, 1966). Dalton (1959) and Thompson (1960) found that personal dissimilarities, such as, background, values, education, age, social patterns lowered the probability of interpersonal rapport between unit representatives, and in turn decreased the amount of collaboration between their respective units. Personal status incongruities between departmental representatives, that is, the degree to which they differed in rank orderings in various status dimensions (such as length of service, age, education, ethnicity, esteem in eyes of superiors, pay and so on) increase the tendency for conflict (Dutton and Walton, 1966).

Personal satisfaction with the internal climate of one's unit decreases the likelihood that a member will initiate interunit conflict. Seiler (1963) observed that in one firm, constructive handling of interdepartmental differences occurred in part because the members of each department derived social satisfaction from their work associates, had high job interest and good opportunities for promotions, and were not in conflict with each other.

INTERDEPARTMENTAL RELATIONSHIP

Tactics of Conflict and Indicators of Collaboration

The literature on interdepartmental relations has been most vivid in its description of manifest conflict and collaboration processes. Dalton (1959) observed that staff units were encouraged by top management to monitor and report on the activities of line units, and the line units retaliated by resisting the ideas of the staff units and discouraging their promotions. He also observed power struggles between line units and documented the conflict tactics of coalitions, distortion of information, and misappropriation of resources.

Strauss (1962) observed the tactics of purchasing agents who wished to increase their authority and influence over decisions shared with engineering and production. The

Table 24-2. Components and Characteristics of Contrasting Types of Lateral Relationship*

Component	Type of Lateral Relationship	
	Integrative	Distributive
Form of joint decision process	Problem-solving: free exchange of information, conscientious accuracy in transmitting information	Bargaining: careful rationing, and deliberate distortion of information.
Structure of interaction and framework of decision	Flexible, informal, open	Rigid, formal, circumscribed
Attitudes toward other unit	Positive attitudes: trust, friendliness, inclusion of other unit	Negative attitudes: suspicion, hostility, dissociation from other unit

*After Walton (1966)

purchasing agents made restrictive rules for the other units, evaded their rules, relied on personal contacts and persuasion to subvert the other units, and altered organization structure.

Focusing on positive relations, Georgopoulos and Mann (1962) used coordination as their broadest concept, which included "the extent to which the various interdependent parts of an organization function each according to the needs and requirements of the other parts of the total system. In a study of ten hospitals, they found that over-all coordination correlated positively with (a) shared expectations, (b) absence of intraorganizational tension, (c) awareness of problems and solving of problems, and (d) ease of communication.

System Characteristics of an Interunit Relationship

Attempting to incorporate aspects of the approaches just described, Walton (1966) developed a theory which also explains the system dynamics of conflict and collaboration in the interunit relationship. Three components of the relationship are considered: (a) exchange of information in the joint decision process, (b) structure of interunit interactions and decision making, and (c) attitudes toward the other unit. Two opposite types of relationships, "integrative" and "distributive," are postulated as fre-

quently encountered systems of interunit behavior (see Table 24-2). This particular model now appears to be most applicable to lateral relations where the dominant transaction at the interface is joint decision making; where there is relative symmetry in interdependency; and where the transactions required are relatively frequent and important.

In the most general sense, the chain of assumptions underlying Walton's systems theory of lateral relationships (and explaining the distributive syndrome, in particular) is as follows: First, an antecedent, say goal competition between participants engaged in joint decision making, induces the units to engage in concealment and distortion tactics in their exchange of information, such that joint decision making takes on the character of bargaining. Second, in order to ration and distort information effectively and systematically, a unit will attempt to place limitations on the interactions and other behavior of their counterpart in order to make them more predictable and keep them within certain boundaries. Third, the way information is handled (concealment, distortion, etc.) and the way interactions are patterned (circumscribed, rigid, etc.) results in suspicion and hostility. Furthermore, these negative attitudes have a feedback effect which tends to reinforce the same interaction structure and information-handling pattern.

Regardless of the antecedents, the theory hypothesizes that the conflict relationship will become fixed as a result of: the tendency to generalize a conflictful orientation to the many areas of interunit decision making, the self-reinforcing nature of the various elements of a relationship pattern, the reciprocal nature of a conflictful orientation between units, and the tendency toward socialization and institutionalization of these orientations within a unit.

The individual propositions contained in the model are generally supported by a review of the relevant literature in experimental social psychology (Walton, 1966). The hypothesized variations of attributes of a relationship are also generally supported by a comparative field study of production-sales relationships in six plants (Walton, Dutton, and Fitch, 1966). The hypothesized dominant cause-effect relationships among process, structure, and attitude are anecdotally supported in a comparison of two plants (Dutton and Walton, 1966).

The theory suggests that the total lateral relationship is influenced or determined by contextual factors operating first upon the way the parties exchange information, with the effects on interaction structure and interunit trust as subsequent reactions. However, although the process of exchanging information may be the most frequent determinant, it is not exclusively the point of entry in the lateral relationship. For instance, personality and status may first influence attitudes such as trust and friendliness, in which case the pattern of information exchange and interaction structure are a secondary reaction.

MANAGEMENT OF THE INTERFACE

The relationship between units is largely a function of the conflict potential inherent in the factors already discussed; but it is also subject to control by the participants, their effectiveness depending upon how much conscious effort they invest in management of the interface and the appropriateness of the techniques they use.

Interface conflict will be managed best where the attention devoted to interface management corresponds to the degree of differentiation between departments. Lawrence and Lorsch (1967a) compared integrative devices used by three high-performing organizations selected from industries with high, medium, and low differentiation. The most differentiated firm had the most elaborate array of interface management techniques, including a separate integrative department with the primary purpose of coordinating the basic functional units, permanent teams consisting of representatives of members from functional units together with the integrative department, direct contact across hierarchies at all levels, procedures for appeal to a common superior, and a coordination system involving written communications. As expected, when all three organizations were compared, the same rank order obtained for the differentiation scores as for the degree of elaboration of integrative devices. Explicit conflict-resolution mechanisms can be overelaborate, however. For example, a formal coordinative unit was used between slightly differentiated units in a *low*-performing unit. Lawrence and Lorsch concluded that the units were not sufficiently differentiated to justify the coordinative unit, and the result was that the superfluous unit added noise to the system, actually decreasing coordination.

In their comparison of six plastics firms, Lawrence and Lorsch found that three factors promoted effective resolution of interdepartmental conflict and thus high organizational performance. First, where there is a separate coordinating person or unit, the coordinating unit will be most effective if its degree of structure and the goal, time, and interpersonal orientations of its personnel are intermediate between those of the units linked. Second, where there is a separate coordinating unit, conflict resolution will be more effective if its personnel have relatively high influence based on perceived expertise, and if they are evaluated and rewarded on over-all performance measures embracing the activities of the several departments. Third, interunit cooperation will be more effectively achieved and over-all organizational performance will be higher to the extent that managers openly confront differences rather than smooth them over or force decisions. The more subtle aspects of confrontation are discussed by Schmidt and Tannenbaum (1960) and Walton (1968), who analyze the advantages and risks of confronting differences, the timing and skill required, as well as the conditions under which confrontation is most appropriate.

Seiler (1963) also observed techniques for management of interunit conflict. A department may keep its own records, so as to reduce requests for information and thus avoid distasteful contact; a junior member may be assigned as the liaison person, where his presence will not arouse status conflict; and inventories may be introduced to reduce scheduling interdependence.

CONSEQUENCES OF INTERUNIT CONFLICT

The manifest characteristics of interunit conflict include: a competitive orientation, bargaining and restrictions on information, circumscribed interaction patterns, and antagonistic feelings. To determine whether the conflict has an adverse effect on organizational performance, one must assess the consequences of these characteristics. Whether a competitive orientation is in fact energizing or debilitating for members of the unit will depend in part on the personalities of the participants. For some, competition is motivating and arouses energies not otherwise available for organizational tasks; for others conflict is a major threat. Whether competitive energy will contribute to over-all performance depends upon whether a unit can improve its performance without interfering with the performance of another unit.

Another factor governing the motivational effect of conflict is the degree of symmetry in tactics between units. Crozier (1961) reported that managers who were not able to retaliate when conflict was initiated responded by withdrawing commitment from their job. Seiler (1963) postulated that internal social stability, value sharing between units, and a legitimate authority hierarchy between units were important in influencing whether interunit competition would result in destructive conflict.

According to Strauss (1964), the competitive orientation that accompanies conflict behavior may also contribute to a system of checks and balances, increase the availability of new ideas to compete with established ones, and decrease the type of collusion among middle managers that deprives higher-level top management of information.

It seems reasonable to assume that the more important the interdependence, the more a restriction or interunit information becomes damaging. When a lateral relationship involves joint decision making, each unit can bias the decisions in its own favor by controlling information relevant to these decisions. Even minor concealment or distortion can be of great importance, if the decisions are key ones.

The structural attributes of a conflictful relationship are not necessarily variable in the lateral relationship, as for example, the number of liaison contacts between departments, which may be specified by higher authorities. Whether a structural attribute has a positive or an adverse effect on over-all performance depends on factors other than structure. For example, in a conflictful pattern more problems are referred to the superiors. On the one hand, referral may overload a superior; on the other, a superior may find himself more informed about operations and subordinates. Similarly, referral of problems requiring new policy may also be organizationally useful. Also the inability of a decision-making pair to change decision rules or apply them flexibly may result in decisions that are not innovative. However, given the larger network of task relationships in which the pair is embedded, the inflexibility may produce a degree of predictability, which is valuable for some other reason.

Channeling all interunit interactions through a few liaison persons in a conflict syndrome often reduces over-all performance; for where other persons are either affected by an interunit decision or have potentially relevant information or opinions, ignoring their contribution decreases the quality of the decisions and lowers the commitment to decisions.

Apart from their influence on the quality of decisions, the attributes of an interunit relationship may impinge upon coordinative activities. For example, a tendency to avoid contact can result in implementation that lacks coordination. The seriousness of the effect of conflict in decreasing the rate of interaction between the units therefore depends in part upon how much coordination is required to implement joint decisions.

Conflict relationships involve stereotyping and include *attitudes* of low friendliness, low trust, and low respect. Such attitudes indirectly affect performance. For example, low trust limits the flow of relevant task information and decreases coordinative interactions. Furthermore, some persons experience psychological strain when other persons dislike or distrust them. Dalton (1959: 95) reported that staff men were shocked by the need to engage in conflict that required them to use their interpersonal skills as much as their academic skills. The stress of this interpersonal or intergroup climate may result in higher turnover or withdrawal from interdepartmental relations.

A positive by-product of interunit rivalry is more unit cohesion, which contributes to cooperation within the unit. Each unit may become more receptive to directives from their own hierarchy; but sometimes the centralization of control within the unit

Table 24-3. Consequences of Interunit Conflict

Attributes of conflictful lateral relationships	Illustrative consequences
Competition in general	Motivates or debilitates
	Provides checks and balances
Concealment and distortion	Lowers quality of decisions
Channeled interunit contacts	Enhances stability in the system
Rigidity, formality in decision procedures	Enhances stability in the system
	Lowers adaptability to change
Appeals to superiors for decisions	Provides more contact for superiors
	May increase or decrease quality of decisions
Decreased rate of interunit interaction	Hinders coordination and implementation of tasks
Low trust, suspicion, hostility	Psychological strain and turnover of personnel or decrease in individual performance

causes frustration in subordinates (Seiler, 1963). Competition may serve as a useful training device. Managers' insight into how the respective goals of interdependent units contribute to over-all goals may be sharpened. Negotiating and policy-making skills of prospective top managers may be increased, and tolerance of unavoidable conflict may be developed.

Some of the postulated relationships between attributes of a conflictful syndrome and consequences for over-all performance are shown in Table 24-3. Each of the relationships is subject to limiting conditions, some of which were noted earlier. The point being made is that conclusions about the effect of a generally competitive or conflictful relationship can only be made on the basis of an analysis of the specific components of the pattern together with an analysis of the task. Comparative field data are needed to evaluate the validity of the concept of an optimum degree of competitiveness and rivalry. The optimum might be expected to vary, depending upon the type of interunit interdependence, the type of work of each unit, and the personalities of unit representatives.

RESPONSES OF HIGHER EXECUTIVES

Response Tendencies of Executives

The response of executives refers to how superiors react to information about subordinate organizational units; that is, to low performance and attributes of the interunit relationship itself. Here "low performance" means inadequate productivity, low adaptability, or inability of the units to conserve their human and other resources.

A manager's response is a combination of his habitual patterns, emotional reactions, and deliberate responses. This idiosyncratic element in the system of interunit conflict shown in Figure 24-1 is a major problem in developing a general explanatory or predictive model of the total system. For the same reason, however, it is an opportunity for improving the interunit relationship. Several automatic responses to low performance can be noted for illustration. If the joint performance of two units is considered inadequate, higher executives may place particular emphasis on observable, short-run measures of performance for each subunit. Thus, poor performance, whatever its source, may lead to the very rewards, controls, and styles of supervision here shown to be antecedents to conflict. If the relationships hypothesized are valid, reinforcing feedback will lead to more interunit conflict and still lower performance. White (1961) reported that higher executives who were dissatisfied with the performance of subordinate units frequently responded by reorganizing the units. The feelings of status depreciation or power deprivation and the ambiguity which frequently follow a reorganization may increase the potential for conflict.

Executive Responses in Relation to Model

The model has implications both for determining what needs changing and for developing a strategy for achieving the change. Executive responses can either reinforce and intensify a conflict pattern, or create pressures to change it. Much depends upon how sophisticated a diagnostic model the manager uses. Ideally he would take into account all the valid implications of a model of the antecedents, dynamics, and consequences of conflict.

The model as a diagnostic tool. Cause-and-effect relationships can be traced back through the model as follows:

1. Are there manifestations of conflict or low collaboration in the lateral relationship? If not, this interunit conflict model is not relevant. If so, determine the particular aspects of the relationship processes that are impinging upon performance; for instance, distortion of information, infrequent interaction, and lack of mutual assistance.

2. Are these dysfunctional elements of the conflict process inherent in a competitive interunit relationship? If not, determine how the management activities at the interface are inadequate, and whether these can be modified by suggesting or requiring changes in them. If they are, determine what particular contextual variables are responsible for the competitive orientation; for example, scarce resources, competitive reward system, asymmetrical task interdependence, or personalities of key liaison personnel.

3. Which of the contextual factors that create the interunit conflict are not inherent in the technology or are not essential parts of the administrative apparatus? Determine which of these might be modified to have a significant influence on the relationship.

An exhaustive treatment of the factors which are instrumental in altering a conflictful interunit relationship and which executives can modify would review the entire model. Instead, only a few relevant executive responses that have been treated in the literature are considered.

Thompson (1960) identified three areas of executive response: First, "Within limits, administrative allocations (or rewards, status symbols, resources, etc.) determine the relative deprivation experienced by organizational members, and thereby control potential conflict inherent in modern technologies" (p. 392). Second, "To the extent that recruitment and selection procedures limit or maintain it within manageable pattern, the organization can manage the potential conflict in latent role diversity" (p. 394). By latent role diversity, Thompson means differences in socioeconomic status, ethnic background, and so on. Third, "By varying the distinctiveness of the organization, the proportion of members exposed, and the frequency and regularity of their exposure, the organization gains a measure of control over conflict stemming from potential reactions to competing pressures" (p. 396). Here he is referring to organizational conflict induced by ideas or pressures from the organization's environment.

Landsberger (1961) states that horizontal differences in authority can be more strongly supported by organizational logic, and need be less dependent on arbitrary fiat than vertical authority. On the other hand, differences in lateral authority are less obvious and are less likely to be stated explicitly, and therefore tend toward conflict. Consequently, one executive response is to make explicit rules allocating final authority for decisions or interunit activities, so as to depersonalize the order. A related response is for higher executives to develop rules to cover an increasing proportion of interunit transactions, and thereby confine decisions to exceptional situations, a practice noted by both Brown (1960) and Landsberger (1961).

Pondy (1967) refers to other devices which are not only available to those who manage the interface, but which can also be included in the executive response repertory: reducing dependence on common resources, transfer pricing between units, loosening schedules, or introducing buffer inventories. Litwak (1961) suggests many "mechanisms or segregation," used to reduce the conflict generated by contradictory social forms which modern organizations must incorporate, including stricter role separation between those for whom affect and those for whom strict objectivity is important; physical separation, such as moving the research facility away from the production facility; and transferral occupations, such as engineers who maintain involvement with a product from research to production stages.

Implications of the model for change of strategy. Ideally, higher executives would develop a strategy for modifying the level of interunit conflict and collaboration which not only acts on the problem diagnosed, but also takes into account the self-perpetuating characteristics of conflict relationships. The analysis of the dynamics of lateral relationship not only underscored the self-reinforcing tendencies of conflictful processes of information exchange, interaction patterns, and attitudes between units; it is also stressed the reciprocal and regenerative tendencies of conflictful approaches to the interface.

These self-reinforcing, regenerative, and reciprocal tendencies lead to persistence of a conflict process; therefore, higher management needs to engage in activities designed to replace existing patterns. Blake, Shepard and Mouton (1964), and Walton (1968) have outlined theories and techniques of third-party consulting interventions. The underlying assumption is that the units must find a new culture in which to view and understand each other. Various techniques of re-education can be used to change intergroup perceptions based on stereotypes, misunderstanding the intention of others, and past history of hostile relations. Thus, whether higher executives conclude that basic contextual factors or techniques for interface management need to be modified, change effort will be effective only if it includes some interventions which help change the existing pattern.

CONCLUSIONS

Several features of the model of interunit conflict deserve emphasis: First, no *a priori* assumption is made that interunit conflict should be reduced. Second, the model recognizes a large number of potential determinants of conflict and conflict-reinforcement syndromes. Third, the model incorporates contextual and structural factors emphasized by sociologists and economists, as well as interpersonal interaction phenomena studied by social psychologists. These approaches are integrated in the explanatory model and in the action implications of the model. Fourth, the model of the internal dynamics of the relationship particularly throws light on the problems of unfreezing the existing patterns. Fifth, the ability to manage interunit conflict is shown to require sophistication in executive response.

REFERENCES

Argyris, Chris. *Integrating the individual and the organization.* New York: Wiley, 1964.

Blake, R. R., Shephard, H. A., and Mouton, J. S. *Intergroup conflict in organizations.* Ann Arbor: Foundation for Research on Human Behavior, 1964.

Brown, Wilfred. *Explorations in management.* London: Tavistock, 1960.

Burns, T., and Stalker, G. M. *The management of innovation.* London: Tavistock, 1961.

Caplow, T. *Principles of organization.* New York: Harcourt, Brace and World, 1964.

Cozer, L. A. *The functions of social conflict.* Glencoe, Ill.: Free Press, 1956.

Crozier, Michel. Human relations at the management level in a bureaucratic system of organization. *Human Organization,* 1961, 20, 51-64.

Dalton, M. *Men who manage.* New York: Wiley, 1959.

Dutton, J. M., and Walton, R. E. Interdepartmental conflict and cooperation: two contrasting studies. *Human Organization,* 1966, 25, 207-20.

Georgopoulos, B., and Mann, F. *The community general hospital.* New York: Macmillan, 1962.

Kahn, R. L., Wolfe, D. M., Quinn, R. P., Snoek, J. D., and Rosenthal, R. A. *Organizational stress: Studies in role conflict and ambiguity.* New York: Wiley, 1964.

Landsberger, H. A. The horizontal dimension in a bureaucracy. *Administrative Science Quarterly,* 1961, 6, 298-333.

Lawrence, P. R., and Lorsch, J. W. *Organization and environment.* Boston: Division of Research, Graduate School of Business Administration, Harvard University, 1967a.

Lawrence, P. R., and Lorsch, J. W. Differentiation and integration in complex organizations. *Administrative Science Quarterly,* 1967b, 12, 1-47.

Likert, R. *New patterns of management.* New York: McGraw-Hill, 1961.

Litwak, E. Models of bureaucracy which permit conflict. *American Journal of Sociology,* 1961, 67, 177-84.

March, J. G., and Simon, H. A. *Organizations.* New York: Wiley, 1958.

Miller, E. J. Technology, territory and time. *Human Relations,* 1959, 12, 243-72.

Pondy, L. R. Organizational conflict: Concepts and models. *Administrative Science Quarterly,* 1967, 12, 296-320.

Schmidt, W. and Tannenbaum, R. The management of differences. *Harvard Business Review,* 1960 (November/December), 38, 107-15.

Seiler, J. A. Diagnosing interdepartmental conflict. *Harvard Business Review,* 1963 (September/October), 41, 121-32.

Simpson, R. L. Vertical and horizontal communication in formal organization. *Administrative Science Quarterly,* 1959, 4, 188-96.

Strauss, G. Tactics of lateral relationship: The purchasing agent. *Administrative Science Quarterly,* 1962, 7, 161-86.

Strauss, G. Work-flow frictions, interfunctional rivalry, and professionalism: A case study of purchasing agents. *Human Organization,* 1964, 23, 137-49.

Thompson, J. D. Organizational management of conflict. *Administrative Science Quarterly*, 1960, 4, 389-409.

Thompson, V. A. *Modern organization*. New York: Alfred A. Knopf, 1961.

Walton, R. E. Theory of conflict in lateral organizational relationships. In J. R. Lawrence (Ed.), *Operational research and the social sciences*. London: Tavistock, 1966, 409-28.

Walton, R. E., Dutton, J. M., and Fitch, H. G. and basic third-party roles. *Journal of Applied Behavioral Sciences*, 1968.

Walton, R. E. Dutton, J. M., and Fitch, H. G. A study of conflict in the process, structure, and attitudes of lateral relationships. In Haberstroh and Rubenstein

(Eds.), *Some theories of organization*. Rev. ed. Homewood, Ill.: Irwin, 1966, 444-65.

Walton, R. E., and McKersie, R. B. *A behavioral theory of labor negotiations*. New York: McGraw-Hill, 1965.

Walton, R.E., and McKersie, R.B. Behavioral dilemmas in mixed-motive decision making. *Behavioral Science*, 1966, 11, 370-84.

White, J. Management conflict and social structure. *American Journal of Sociology*, 1961, 67, 185-91.

Zald, M. N. Power balance and staff conflict in correctional institutions. *Administrative Science Quarterly*, 1962, 7, 22-49.

5

PERFORMANCE APPRAISAL
AND MANAGEMENT BY OBJECTIVES

Nearly every phase of industrial-organizational psychology depends upon the development of dependable measures of worker proficiency. These measures (also called performance criteria) aid management in making various personnel decisions concerning transfers, wage increases, layoffs, and promotions. Performance measures are used also as criteria for evaluating the effectiveness of various selection devices (e. g., tests and interviews), training programs, incentive systems, and organization development programs. Finally, performance data can be communicated to workers for the purpose of improving their subsequent job performance via goal setting.

The first article in this section, by Schmidt and Kaplan, discusses one of the oldest problems involved in the development and use of performance criteria. The problem is that for most jobs there is more than one measure of job success. That is, a number of criterion measures such as work quantity, work quality, absenteeism, and accidents are usually available. When making personnel decisions or using these criterion measures in any other manner, it is necessary to decide whether to use them separately or to combine them into a single index of over-all worker effectiveness.

The major advocates of using multiple criteria (e.g., Ghiselli, Guion, and Dunnett) argue that unless there is a high positive intercorrelation among criterion measures, they are measuring different things and therefore cannot be combined meaningfully. Moreover, these advocates of multiple criteria view the validation process as a vehicle for increased understanding of what our tests really measure and of the behaviors involved in each criterion element. They argue that by combining criterion measures much valuable information is lost.

On the other hand, advocates of the composite criterion (e.g., Toops, Nagle, and Brogden and Taylor) argue that since all criterion elements are related to some underlying economic construct, these criteria can be combined into a composite without concern for their intercorrelations. They point out that, even when criterion elements are used separately in the test-validation process, the criteria must eventually be combined subjectively when personnel decisions are made. Advocates of the composite criterion believe that it makes more sense to use an objective, formalized weighting procedure at the outset. The paper by Schmidt and Kaplan clearly presents the arguments for and against each position and discusses some of the assumptions underlying the arguments. Schmidt and Kaplan bravely attempt to resolve the controversy by presenting a compromise approach.

The many different measures of worker proficiency in industrial-organizational psychology can be classified into two main categories: objective criteria and subjective criteria. Objective criteria such as absenteeism, quality of work, and accidents can be determined by simply counting the number of days employees miss work, the number of unacceptable units they produce, and the number of accidents they report during a certain span of time. Subjective criteria are ratings or judgments of employees' job proficiency made by their supervisors, peers, subordinates, or outside observers. Since all subjective criteria depend upon human judgment and opinion, they are subject to certain kinds of error likely to be found in the rating process.

There are many different rating methods by which the rater can appraise the efficiency of workers (McCormick and Tiffin, 1974). Examples of widely used rating methods are the following: graphic rating scales, paired comparisons, ranking, forced-choice, checklists, and the critical-incident technique. In the article by Oberg the strengths and weaknesses of several rating methods and performance appraisal techniques are discussed. Each of these methods attempts to reduce human error in some way. No one method is completely free of flaws, and each method has its own combination of strengths and weaknesses. Oberg shows how each appraisal technique can be used singly or in combination for various purposes such as worker motivation, organization development, and personnel decisions. Oberg contends that performance appraisal can be made considerably more effective if organizations carefully choose the appraisal techniques that fit the company's particular purposes.

One approach not mentioned by Oberg is the procedure suggested by Smith and Kendall (1963) for the development of behaviorally anchored rating scales. The first step in the development of such scales is the generation of job dimensions and the behavioral incidents exemplifying each dimension. This is typically done by consensus of the persons who will eventually use the scales. By participating in the development of the scales, it is believed that raters will be more inclined to complete the ratings carefully and honestly, especially since all of the dimensions and incidents are expressed in their own words, not in the terminology of the psychologist.

In the second step an independent group of individuals attempts to assign each incident to the dimension that it illustrates. Those incidents which are so ambiguous that they are not consistently assigned to the same dimension are discarded. The final step involves the scaling of the incidents belonging to each dimension, the elimination of incidents too vague to be accurately scaled, and the rewording of incidents in terms of expected behaviors rather than actual behaviors. Raters who use the completed scale indicate for each dimension what behavior they would "expect" of the individual being evaluated. According to Smith and Kendall, use of expected behaviors reduces central tendency, reduces faking, and makes the judgment easier for the rater.

Such scales have been developed for rating the performance of department store managers (Dunnette, Campbell, Arvey, and Hellervik, 1973), nurses (Smith and Kendall, 1963), grocery store clerks (Folgi, Hulin, and Blood, 1971), and the motivation of engineers (Landy and Guion, 1970). The article by Harari and Zedeck presents a clear description of the steps involved in the development of behaviorally anchored rating scales for evaluating the teaching effectiveness of university professors. Use of such scales is a possible solution to the controversial problem of evaluating faculty teaching in colleges and universities.

The next reading, by Miner, reviews in capsule form much of the current research on the management-appraisal process. There are many potential influences on the quality of managerial appraisals that can arise from various sources such as the characteristics of the rater, the number of raters used, and the manager characteristics being rated. Miner discusses these and other influences on managerial evaluations and suggests some feasible solutions.

The next article in this section, by Brummet, Pyle, and Flamholtz, discusses a human-resource accounting system derived from the earlier work of Rensis Likert (1967) and his colleagues. The authors point out that conventional corporate accounting statements fail to take into consideration the organization's current state of human assets and fluctuations in the human asset condition. The authors contend that a need exists to develop an organizational accounting system which will provide management with the following information regarding both its human and non-human assets: (1) resource acquisition and development, (2) resource maintenance or condition, and (3) resource utilization. The model presented is intended to provide this information to management by measuring investment, causal, intervening, end-result, and return on investment variables.

"Management by Objectives" (MBO) was first publicized by Drucker (1954) in his book entitled *Patterns of Management*. According to Drucker, every manager in an organization should have specified goals that coincide with the goals of upper-level management, and should be able to participate in the setting of their own goals and those of higher-level management. McGregor (1960) also favored the use of MBO, but saw it more as a solution to the problems of the traditional managerial performance appraisal program.

Most authorities would agree that MBO involves three basic elements: (1) the formation and communication of organizational goals; (2) the involvement and participation of subordinates in the setting of their own goals; and (3) the periodic and final review of performance in relation to these goals. The article by Tosi and Carroll gives an excellent overview of the MBO approach. They discuss the basic elements of MBO, the relationship of MBO to employee motivation and compensation, and the strengths and weaknesses of MBO. The next article, by Tosi, Rizzo, and Carroll covers in detail the problems and techniques involved in setting goals and action plans for specific managers and organizational units. It also describes the difficulties of measuring the attainment of certain objectives and offers possible solutions.

The final article, by Meyer, Kay, and French, summarizes a series of studies conducted at the General Electric Company. They first describe a study that attempted to determine how criticism, praise, and mutual-goal setting during an appraisal interview affect subordinates' subsequent job performance, attitudes, and defensiveness. Based on their findings, Meyer, Kay, and French developed a program called "Work Planning and Review" which is basically a form of MBO. They then describe a study comparing their MBO program to a modified version of the traditional performance-appraisal program used by the company.

REFERENCES AND SELECTED READINGS

Carroll, S. J., Jr., and Tosi, H. L., Jr. *Management by objectives: applications and research* New York: Macmillan, 1973.

Campbell, J. P., Dunnette, M.D., Arvey, R. D., and Hellervik, L. V. The development and evaluation of behaviorally based rating scales. *Journal of Applied Psychology*, 1973, 57, 15-22.

Drucker, P. F. *The practice of management.* New York: Harper & Row, 1954.

Flanagan, J. C. The critical incident technique. *Psychological Bulletin,* 1954, 51, 327-58.

Folgi, L., Hulin, C. L., and Blood, M. R. Development of first-level behavioral job criteria. *Journal of Applied Psychology,* 1971, 55, 3-8.

Landy, F., and Guion, R. M. Development of scales for the measurement of work motivation. *Organizational Behavior and Human Performance,* 1970, 5, 93-103.

Likert, R. *The human organization.* New York: McGraw-Hill, 1967.

McCormick, E. J., and Tiffin, J. *Industrial psychology,* Englewood Cliffs, N.J.: Prentice-Hall, 1974.

McGregor, D. *The human side of enterprise.* New York: McGraw-Hill, 1960.

Odiorne, G. S. Management by objectives: A system of managerial leadership. New York: Pitman, 1965.

Smith P. C., and Kendall, L. M. Retranslation of expectations: An approach to the construction of unambiguous anchors for rating scales. *Journal of Applied Psychology,* 1963, 47, 149-55.

25

Composite vs. Multiple Criteria:

A Review and Resolution of the Controversy

FRANK L. SCHMIDT AND LEON B. KAPLAN

There has been a controversy of long standing in industrial psychology between the
advocates of the single composite criterion
and those favoring multiple criteria. Earlier
writers on this problem tended to favor the
composite criterion concept (Toops, 1944;
Brogden and Taylor, 1950; Nagle, 1953),
and this doctrine remained essentially un-
challenged until the second half of the
fifties. Then, starting in 1956, a series of
statements by a number of well-known
industrial psychologists appeared seriously
questioning the utility of this concept and
concluded that, in most cases, the use of
multiple criteria was to be preferred to the
use of the traditional composite (Ghiselli,
1956; Guion, 1961, 1965, pp. 114-19; Dunnette, 1963a, 1963b). To date, this controversy has not been satisfactorily resolved, as
is obvious from the cautious and rather
indecisive treatment the question receives in
most standard texts in industrial psychology
(Tiffin and McCormick, 1965, pp. 47-54,
Blum and Naylor, 1968, pp. 184-93). The
purpose of this paper is to set forth the basic
arguments advanced for each position, to
explore the assumptions underlying these
arguments, and, finally, to offer a practical
and conceptual resolution of the controversy.

ARGUMENTS FOR COMPOSITE CRITERION

The basic contention of the advocates of the
composite criterion is that the criterion
should provide a measure of the overall
"success" or "value-to-the-organization" of
the individual—because such an index is
needed to compare and make decisions
about individuals (Toops, 1944; Thorndike,
1948, p. 125; Brogden and Taylor, 1950;
Nagle, 1953). They maintain that, even if
the criterion elements are used separately in
validation, they must be combined in some
way when decisions are made about individuals (cf. particularly Toops, 1944, and Tiffin
and McCormick, 1965, p. 52; also, Brogden,
1967, personal communication).

If, adopting the multiple criteria approach and following Ghiselli's (1956) suggestion, the decision-maker conceptualizes
each individual's performance as a point in
multidimensional space, where the dimensions represent criterion elements, it is maintained that he has no basis for preferring one
individual over another—unless he somehow
collapses the various criterion scores onto
one dimension. This he usually does subjectively, thus obscuring the relative sizes of the
weights placed on the criterion elements. A

Reprinted from *Personnel Psychology*, 1971, 24, 419-34, by permission of the authors and Personnel
Psychology, Inc.

formal weighting into a composite makes known the absolute and relative sizes of the weights used and, in addition, insures that they will be stable across occasions and decision-makers. It is also contended that the formal solution makes explicit the basis of decisions as to the relative importance of the criterion elements (Brogden and Taylor, 1950). It can thus be seen that the advocates of the composte criterion view the multiple criteria approach as evading rather than solving the weighting problem.

ARGUMENTS FOR MULTIPLE CRITERIA

The basic contention of those favoring multiple criteria is that measures of different variables should not be combined. Cattell (1957, p. 11) puts it thus: "Ten men and two bottles of beer cannot be added to give the same total as two men and ten bottles of beer." If criterion elements display low positive, zero, or low negative correlations with one another, then they are obviously measuring different variables, and weighting them into a composite result in scores that are so ambiguous as to be uninterpretable.

Very different patterns of scores on the criterion elements can result in the same composite score. The worker who is slow and accurate in assembly work, for example, may achieve the same composite criterion score as another worker who works fast but makes more errors. It is maintained that since these two patterns of work behavior are so different in nature, it makes no sense to assign them the same composite score (Ghiselli, 1956; Dunnette, 1963a; Guion, 1965, pp. 113-14). The ambiguity of composite scores is much reduced, of course, by high intercorrelations among the criterion elements, but the advocates of multiple criteria cite many studies which indicate very strongly that, even in the case of relatively low-level jobs, performance is often, if not typically, multidimensional

(Seashore, Indik, and Georgopoulos, 1960; Peres, 1962; Ghiselli, 1960).[1]

For higher level jobs, such as that of scientist or college professor, there is evidence that performance is even more complex, with up to 15 relatively independent factors emerging (Taylor, Smith, Ghiselin, and Ellison, 1961; Taylor, Price, Richards, and Jacobson, 1964). On such jobs, it would appear that there would be a very large number of performance patterns that could result in the same composite criterion score.

Those favoring multiple criteria view the composite criterion as not only virtually uninterpretable in most cases, but also as an impediment to progress in practical prediction. Dunnette (1963b) suggests that the use of composite criteria may go far in explaining the failure of industrial psychology to break through the ceiling of about .50 on validity coefficients pointed out by Hull over 50 years ago (Hull, 1928). Ghiselli (1956) makes the same implication, and even Tiffin and McCormick (1965, p. 51), who identify with neither side in this controversy, suggest that one cannot "reasonably expect" to identify, for a given ambiguous composite criterion score, a common set of personal characteristics associated with that score.

ASSUMPTIONS UNDERLYING THE TWO POSITIONS

Nature of the Construct Represented by the Criterion Measure

Underlying the arguments for a composite

1. Performance on some jobs has also been shown to be "dynamic," i.e., to change in apparent factorial composition over time (Ghiselli and Haire, 1960; Fleishman and Fructer, 1960; Bass, 1962). In addition, Prien (1966) has pointed out that changes in organizational needs and goals can change the nature of the criteria of success in individual jobs within the organization. Criterial dynamism is an important problem in industrial psychology, meriting much more research than has been devoted to it to date. However, our concern here is with what Ghiselli (1956) refers to as "static dimensionality"—dimensionality without respect to time.

criterion is the assumption, often unarticulated, that the criterion should represent an economic, rather than a behavioral, construct. The economic nature of this dimension is often obscured by the use of such terms as "overall success" (Toops, 1944), "performance on the task" (Thorndike, 1948, p. 125), "overall contribution" (Nagle, 1953), and "overall value of the individual in the job" (Gaylord and Brogden, 1964). The basic criterion of "relevancy," discussed by these writers, is defined in a number of superficially different ways, all of which ultimately relate the criterion measure to an underlying economic dimension. Thus Nagle (1953, p. 274) defines relevancy as "the extent to which an index of success (criterion) is related to the true order of success in the given activity." Thorndike (1948, p. 125) states that a criterion measure is relevant "as far as the knowledge, skills, and basic aptitudes required for success on it are the same as those required for performance of the ultimate goal." Tiffin and McCormick (1965, p. 44) define relevance as "the extent to which criterion measures of different individuals are meaningful in terms of the objectives for which such measures are derived."

In most organizations, the objectives or "ultimate goals" are economic in nature. Certainly this is true for industrial firms, whose general objective is to make money. Even in the case of nonprofit organizations and governmental agencies, the general objective is to deliver services as efficiently as possible, all other things equal—and efficiency is measured in terms of economic units. Brogden and Taylor (1950) are most explicit in advocating that criteria be economic in nature, stating that "the criterion should measure the contribution of the individual to the overall efficiency of the organization." They recommend that such contributions be measured, whenever possible, in dollars and cents—by means of the application of cost accounting concepts and procedures to the individual job behaviors of the employee. They are quite definite in stating that it is the economic end products of job behaviors, and not the behaviors themselves, that the criterion measure should assess:

In job analysis for criterion purposes we believe that a clearcut distinction must be made between the end products of a given job and the job processes that lead to these end products. It may be pertinent to such other legitimate objectives of job analysis as training or position classification to study the exact sequence of operations in the production of the finished product. The skills needed, the tools used, and the methods employed may all be needed for this purpose. Such information does not, however, give a direct answer to the major question, "How much does the employee produce and how good is it?" (Brogden and Taylor, 1950, p. 141)

By contrast, the assumption, often implicit, that the criterion should represent a behavioral or psychological construct is the basis of all the arguments in favor of multiple criteria. This assumption is rather clear in the following statement:

Even a very low level of aspiration in prediction requires that the *behavior* on our scale be operationally defined to have some homogeneity, and defined in such a way which will not permit its confusion with an essentially different kind of behavior. (Cattell, 1957, p. 11; italics added)

Ghiselli (1956) states that attempts to justify combining criterion elements into a composite rest on the assumption of a general factor in job performance. Since this general factor can be shown not to exist in many, if not most cases, he advises that criterion elements be used separately rather than combined. The general factor to which he refers is certainly behavioral or psychological in nature. Otherwise, he would be putting himself in the position of denying the ubiquity of the economic factor in "relevant" criterion elements. Similarly, Dunnette (1963) states that high intercorrelations among criterion elements can be taken as justification for a composite criterion, and, conversely, lack of correlation among elements argues for multiple criterion.

Again, the common variance represented by the intercorrelations must reflect a unitary behavioral factor. Guion (1965, p. 114) writes that if the criterion elements to be combined are "essentially similar," the resultant composite is "psychologically sensible." A "psychologically sensible" criterion composite is, it seems obvious, one that is behaviorally homogenous, or nearly so. Haire (1960) states that criterion measures should represent behavioral and psychological variables, suggesting that lack of progress in the improvement of validities may be due to the use of criterion measures representing business or economic constructs.

Primary Goals of the Validation Process

The partisans of these two positions differ in their basic assumptions as to the primary purpose of the validation process itself. Those favoring the composite criterion are assuming, usually implicitly, that the validation process is initiated and carried out only for practical and economic reasons. While some are rather vague on this point (Toops, 1944; Nagle, 1953), Brogden and Taylor (1950, p. 138) could hardly be more explicit:

. . . the only functions of the criterion are (a) to establish the basis for choosing the "best" battery from the experimental predictors, and (b) to provide an estimate of the validity of that battery.

None of those favoring composite criteria

mention the attainment of increased understanding of the psychological and behavioral processes involved in various tasks as a goal of the validation process.

By contrast, the advocates of multiple criteria view increased understanding as an important goal of the validation process, perhaps co-equal with the practical and economic goals. Dunnette (1963a, 1963b), for example, postulates that validation goals should include increased understanding both of what the test scores measure and of the behaviors involved in each criterion element. Using the term "description" rather than understanding, Ghiselli (1956) makes a similar appeal. This emphasis on understanding is undoubtedly the factor which has led to the concept of the criterion as a measure of a behavioral and/or psychological construct. The goal of the search for understanding is a theory (or theories) of work behavior; theories of human behavior are cast in terms of psychological and behavioral, not economic, constructs.

Both Dunnette (1963a) and Guion (1965, pp. 115–16) advance validation models designed to aid in the attainment of understanding. For purposes of the present discussion, the important thing about these models is the fact that they both depict predictors as predicting a number of intermediate criterion measures which are behavioral and homogenous in nature. These behavioral measures are then, in effect, used in turn to predict the practical, economic outcomes, referred to by Dunnette as "consequences to the organization" and by Guion as "the observable consequence."

EVALUATION OF THE ARGUMENTS

The Composite as Necessary for Decisions

What can be said of the contention that an over-all criterion of some sort is necessary in order to make decisions about individuals? Apparently only two of the advocates of multiple criteria have addressed themselves to this problem; neither has satisfactorily answered the argument. As noted earlier, Ghiselli (1956) suggests that each individual be conceptualized as a point in N-dimensional space, where the N dimensions are the criterion elements. He further indicates that perhaps the space should be divided into parts and "that portion of the space in which the individual is most likely to fall could be estimated by the discriminate function." But he admits that the problem of deciding which portions of the space are relatively more desirable is unsolved. It can easily be seen that the process of rank ordering the various portions of the criterion space in over all desirability is identical with the process of combining the criterion elements into an overall composite. Thus Ghiselli's solution to the problem of the practical use of multiple criteria takes him back to a composite.

Guion (1961) argues that the criterion elements are best kept separate during the validation process and then, during the actual selection process, subjectively weighted into a composite for each individual when decisions are made. This procedure, he contends, moves the reliance on judgment to a "more sensible place" in the employment procedure. The decision-maker can then make his decisions about the relative importance of the criterion elements for each individual at the time of selection or rejection.

As pointed out by those favoring the composite criterion, there are a number of shortcomings inherent in approaches of this general nature: (a) neither the basis for the assignment of the weights nor the actual weights are made explicit; (b) the relative sizes of the weights are unknown; and (c) the reliability of the weights is unknown. In addition, use of subjective weights means that the efficacy of the selection program can not be evaluated independently of the individual making these judgments. The adequacy of the selection program depends heavily on the adequacy of the decision-maker in assigning subjective criterion weights. If the program is evaluated with this judge included as an element of the system, the evaluation can not be generalized to other judges.

The Combining of Uncorrelated Variables

Next, consider the argument that the weighting of uncorrelated variables into a composite results in an ambiguous, essentially meaningless score. This argument asserts, in effect, that such composite criteria do not represent meaningful behavioral or psychological constructs. Combining into a single composite implies that there is a single underlying dimension in job performance, but it does not, in itself, imply that this single underlying dimension is behavioral or psychological in nature. A composite criterion may represent very well an underlying economic dimension, while at the same time being virtually meaningless from a behavioral point of view.

Now, as Brogden and Taylor (1950) point out, when the criterion elements are all "relevant" measures of economic variables, they can be combined into a composite without regard to their intercorrelations. Even if these intercorrelations are zero and/or negative, the criterion elements are, by definition, positively related to the underlying economic construct and hence are measures of the same variable. Thus, assuming equal units in the criterion elements, if two employees have the same composite criterion score but have achieved this score by means of different patterns of scores on the various criterion elements, there is no construct ambiguity. Both composite scores represent the same point along a unidimensional economic scale. The problem arises from the fact that those discussing the question of criterion element intercorrelations have failed to distinguish explicitly between criterion measures that represent economic constructs and criterion measures that represent behavioral or psychological constructs.[2] As a result, the advocates of multiple criteria have, in general, failed to recognize the possibility that, in certain contexts, behaviorally meaningless composite criteria can be quite useful from a practical point of view.

In these contexts, it may make economic sense to use psychological predictors to predict economic measures, even though there is no basis in psychological theory for doing so. Such a procedure can be seen to be well within the American tradition of empiricism in the behavioral sciences, especially as this tradition is found in the applied behavioral sciences (Tyler, 1965, 129-33) and, as such, should not be viewed as in any way illegitimate. Furthermore, there is even a rationale, in terms of factor theory, that can be offered for such a procedure, as we shall see below.

The Argument to Validity

What is to be said of the argument that the factorial complexity of most composite criteria leads to lower validity coefficients? Discussions of factorial heterogeneity and resultant ambiguity seem to be limited to the criterion. None of the advocates of multiple criteria, in discussing this question, address themselves to the problem of factorial complexity in the predictors, despite the fact that most tests are, in fact, far from factorially unitary (Guilford, 1954, p. 356). It is difficult to see how increased factorial purity in the criterion can lead to higher correlations with heterogenous tests. In fact, psychometric considerations predict exactly the opposite outcome.

The validity coefficient, in terms of factor theory, is given the same factor space for predictors and criterion elements, the sum of the cross products of the factor loadings of the test, and the criterion on their common underlying factors (Magnusson, 1966, p. 193; Guilford, 1954, p. 356). From this it can be seen that if the predictor is factorially complex, its validity can be higher for a factorially complex criterion than for a factorially unitary criterion. For example, if the test loads on (uncorrelated) factors 1, 2, 3, 4, and 5 with values of .50, .40, .30, .50, and .30, respectively, and the homogeneous criterion loads only on factor 1 with value .90, the validity of the predictor is .45. If the criterion is now made a factorially complex composite with, say, loadings of .50, .20, .60, .40, and .00 on factors 1 through 5, respectively, then the validity of the test becomes .71.[3] Thus, it can be seen that increased heterogeneity in the criterion can lead to increased validity when the predictor is factorially complex.

When the predictor is highly homogeneous, making the criterion more heterogeneous will reduce validity, assuming the reliability of the criterion measure remains constant, unless initial validity is zero and one of the factors added to the criterion is the factor represented by the test. Conversely, relatively large validity coefficients are possible when both homogenous tests and homogenous criteria are employed and both represent the same factor. (In such a case,

---

2. Guion (1961) distinguishes between "behavioral data" and "result-of-behavior data" as criterion measures, and Dunnette (1963b) distinguishes between "behavior" and "consequences of behavior," but neither recognizes or develops this distinction as one between the measurement of behavioral constructs, on the one hand, and the measurement of economic constructs, on the other.

3. Note that in each case the sum of the squared factor loadings in the criterion is .81, the per cent of total variance in the criterion measure that is true variance, i.e., the reliability of the measure. (For the sake of simplification, we are assuming that there is no specific variance in the measure.) Reliability is held constant when the factorial composition of the criterion is changed. For a fuller explanation, see Magnusson (1966, pp. 187-92) or Guilford (1954, pp. 356 ff.).

For the sake of simplication, we assume uncorrelated factors. The model holds equally well in the case of correlated factors, but is considerably more cumbersome mathematically.

continuing the assumption of no specific variance in our measures, the validity coefficient is the product of the square roots of their reliabilities, i.e., $\sqrt{r_{11}}\sqrt{r_{22}}$.) However, there is nothing to indicate that the ceiling on such validity coefficients is any higher than that holding for the case in which both predictor and criterion are heterogenous.[4]

It is clear from this discussion that the contention that the factorial complexity and resultant ambiguity that characterizes many composite criterion measures acts to depress the size of obtained validity coefficients has little conceptual justification. Thus, there is, apparently, no real basis for the hope that the use of factorially pure or homogenous criteria will, per se, lead to increases in the magnitudes of validity coefficients.

The controversy over heterogeneity in the criterion is analogous to the controversy of long standing between the advocates of "rationally" constructed, homogenous predictors and those who prefer "empirically" constructed, heterogenous predictors. Some writers (Travers, 1951; Guion, 1965, pp. 201-2; Guilford, 1954, p. 356; Nunnally, 1967, pp. 245-50) have disparaged the use of multifactor predictors, constructed by item analysis against an external criterion, as lacking in rationale and as incapable of leading to "progress in prediction." Others have preferred this approach as more practical and useful than the construction and use of homogenous predictors (Strong, 1943, p. 73; Dunnette, 1966, pp. 43-46; Albright, Glennon, and Smith, 1963). In general, the literature indicates a certain degree of superiority in size of validity coefficients for the heterogenous, empirically constructed predictors (cf. Wallace, 1965; Clark, 1966, pp. 69-112; Campbell et al., 1968).

The Argument to Understanding

The contention that composite criteria, un-

like multiple criteria, do not and cannot lead to understanding of psychological and behavioral processes is probably the most persuasive of the arguments for multiple criteria; indeed, it may be the only persuasive argument. But despite this fact, the multiple criteria advocates have failed to develop this line of reasoning fully. They have not, in general, explicitly recognized the fact that the degree of understanding attainable is a function of the predictor as well as the criterion end of the prediction equation (Guion, 1961, 1965, pp. 114-16; Dunnette, 1963a, 1963b; Ghiselli, 1956). The understanding that can be attained from homogenous criteria when the predictor or predictors are heterogenous is limited. In such a situation, the ambiguity and uninterpretability of the criterion scores have been eliminated or much reduced, but the predictor scores remain psychologically ambiguous.

To illustrate, if the correlation of a given test with a given unifactor criterion element is, say, .30, then one knows that one of the psychological factors measured by the test corresponds, at least to some extent, to the behavioral factor measured by the homogenous criterion element.[5] The knowledge that a certain portion of the variance of the test reflects a given, known behavioral factor represents a degree of understanding. But it is not possible, given the heterogeneity of the test, to ascertain which set of items within the test is measuring this factor. The fuller understanding and insight that could result from a careful examination of this subset of items is not possible.

Dunnette's position with respect to this problem is especially curious. On the one

---

4. Ceilings on validity are lower when either the criterion or the predictor is homogenous, while the other is heterogenous.

5. In fact, following the factor model, one can compute the loading of the test on the factor of which the criterion element is a (imperfect) measure. Let the proportion of the variance in the criterion element which reflects this factor = .81. Let X = the loading of the test on this factor. Then
$\sqrt{.81}\ X = .30$
$.90\ X = .30$
$X = .333.$

hand, he advocates the use of homogenous multiple criteria as a method of gaining "understanding of the meaning of our test scores" (Dunnette, 1963a); on the other hand, he is one of the most enthusiastic advocates of heterogenous, empirically constructed tests (Dunnette, 1966, pp. 43-46). Guion, by contrast, takes a strong position in favor of the use of homogenous predictor tests (Guion, 1965, pp. 202-3), but he does not discuss the relation between this question and the question of the use of multiple, homogenous criteria as a method of increasing understanding of work behavior. Nunnally (1965, pp. 245-50) vigorously condemns the use of heterogenous, empirically constructed tests in criterion prediction as not leading to understanding, but he does not suggest that factorially complex criteria be subdivided into homogenous criterion elements to further enhance the possibilities for understanding.

In short, those psychologists concerned with conditions necessary for the attainment of understanding in the validation process have concentrated on either the predictor or the criterion end of the prediction equation, but none have attempted to integrate simultaneously into their treatment of this problem the factorial compositions of the variables on both ends of the equation.

To sum up, it would appear that the use of both homogenous criteria and homogenous predictors holds the most promise as a method of attaining some degree of insight into the nature of job behaviors. If the unambiguous scores of a unifactor test correlate with a unifactor criterion measure, the size of this correlation indicates the extent to which the psychological trait measured by the test is associated with a specific kind of job behavior. It is clearly interpretable and can potentially be employed in the construction of a theory of job behavior.

GOALS OF THE VALIDATION PROCESS

As discussed earlier, those favoring composite criterion measures have generally assumed that the goals of the validation process are essentially limited to the practical and economic. This assumption appears difficult to defend. It seems to mean asking far too little of the validation process; it seems to mean asking too little of industrial psychology as a discipline. It is interesting to note that the advocates of the composite criterion, i.e., the criterion as representing an economic dimension, wrote, for the most part, during the 1940s and early 1950s, before industrial psychology was as established and accepted in the industrial and governmental sectors as it is today (Toops, 1944; Nagle, 1950; Brogden and Taylor, 1950). They wrote for a young and somewhat insecure profession, anxious to prove its value in the "real," i.e., economic, world. By contrast, the advocates of multiple criteria, i.e., criteria as representing behavioral constructs, emerged more recently, most within the last 10 to 15 years, a period during which the profession has enjoyed rather wide acceptance (Ghiselli, 1956; Dunnette, 1963a; Guion, 1961, 1965, pp. 113-15).

The quest for understanding, once perhaps an unaffordable luxury, is coming to be viewed more and more as a basic necessity for the survival and advancement of the field (Wallace, 1965; Blum and Naylor, 1968, pp. 193-94; Dunnette, 1963b; Guion, 1961, 1965b). The essential question seems to be whether industrial psychology shall be conceived of as a technology seeking application or as a science seeking to delineate general principles of human behavior in the economic sector of life (Guion, 1965b; Pugh, 1966). The growing consensus seems to be that the discipline should definitely not limit itself to the former and that the latter concept should become an important part of the definition of our area.

Pugh (1966) states that the traditional tendency of industrial psychology to define its concerns and problems in terms of "economic and management problems" rather than in terms of psychological problems has hindered the development of the discipline. Guion (1965b) criticized the "narrow view" of industrial psychology as a "management tool" employed mostly for industrial "fire-fighting." He recommends that the success or failure of industrial psychology be "measured on the scales of psychology, not those of industry." Haire (1960) makes a similar appeal. Wallace (1965) calls for the construction and use of criteria with construct validity as a means of achieving understanding, and urges the use of such criterion measures even when they are not relevant to "management's ultimate goals," i.e., economic goals. Criterion measures with theoretical relevance should not replace the economically relevant measures, he suggests, but rather should be used along with them. Wallace's recommendations are especially significant in that he has long been identified with the purely empirical, practical approach to test validation, an orientation which he has come to feel is "approaching the end of its tether" (Wallace, 1965). Along with Blum and Naylor (1968, pp. 193-194), Wallace suggests that industrial psychologists loosen somewhat their grip on the specific empirical criterion measure and begin to theorize in terms of behavioral constructs. Later, he says, operational definitions can be constructed for the constructs.

Thus it seems obvious that understanding is today viewed in industrial psychology as a legitimate goal of the validation process and that this goal is intimately bound up with the question of the nature of the criterion measure. As Wallace (1965) sums up: ". . . the answer to the question 'Criteria for what?' must always include—for understanding!"

RESOLUTION

It would appear that two very different conceptions of the validation process—both legitimate for their own purposes—emerge from the discussion up to this point. The first is applicable to situations in which goals are limited to the practical and economic. This conception allows for factorial complexity in both the predictors and the criteria. The goal is the largest possible validity coefficient, and as we have seen, heterogeneity on both ends of the prediction equation does not impair the attainment of this goal.

Criterion elements can be, and, in fact, at some point must be, weighted into a composite irrespective of their intercorrelations. If all criterion elements are considered to be measures of a single underlying economic construct, the resulting composite unambiguously represents the economic construct and is interpretable as such. If the criterion elements are conceived of as measures of essentially uncorrelated behavioral variables, then the factor theory of validity provides a model to account for the resulting validity coefficients. This approach, stemming from the American tradition of empiricism in applied social science, might be referred to as the "test validation" concept of the validation process.

The other concept of the validation process which this discussion has brought to light might be referred to as the "validation research" approach. This conception of the validation process is applicable to situations in which increased understanding is the primary or only goal. This model, in its ideal form, calls for —homogeneity in both predictors and criterion measures, these being the circumstances under which the potentialities for contribution to understanding are maximal. In practice, this concept must be flexible enough to include situations in which relative homogeneity exists on one end of the prediction equation but not on both.[6] As we have seen, this approach is

6. Under these conditions, when it is the predictors that are univocal, it can be seen that the criterion need not be multiple. In composite form, it is viewed as an initially uninterpretable, factorially complex behavioral measure which is to be clarified somewhat by examination of its correlations with the unifactor predictor or predictors.

capable of yielding some degree of understanding.

Other methods and techniques for the attainment of understanding, such as the subgrouping approaches recommended by Dunnette (1963b) and Owens (1968), are easily integrated into this concept of the validation process. Since the resulting predictions are not to be employed in the making of practical decisions about individuals, there is no necessity for weighting the criterion elements into a composite.

The majority of industrial psychologists will probably not find either of these models entirely satisfactory, and, indeed, they are introduced here for heuristic purposes rather than as normative standards. The typical practicing industrial psychologist probably seeks both economic and psychological ends in the validation process. From the point of view of the criterion end of the prediction equation, the implication of this fact is that he should, ideally, weight criterion elements, regardless of their intercorrelations, into a composite representing an economic construct in order to achieve his practical goals, and, at the same time, he should analyze the relationships between predictors and separate criterion elements in order to achieve his psychological goals. It is this sort of approach, and this sort of concept of the validation process, that embodies the ideal that we have set up for ourselves as applied psychologists—the ideal of the scientist-professional.

REFERENCES

Albright, L. E., Glennon, J. R., and Smith, W. J. *The use of psychological tests in industry.* Cleveland: Howard Allen, 1963.

Bass, B. Further evidence on the dynamic character of criteria. *Personnel Psychology,* 1962, 15, 93-97.

Bellows, R. M. Procedures for evaluating vocational criteria. *Journal of Applied Psychology,* 1941, 25, 499-513.

Blum, M. L., and Naylor, J. C. *Industrial psychology.* New York: Harper & Row, 1968.

Brogden, H. E. Personal communication, 1967.

Brogden, H. E., and Taylor, E. K. The dollar criterion—applying the cost accounting concept to criterion construction. *Personnel Psychology,* 1950, 3, 133-67.

Campbell, D. P., Borgen, F. H., Eastes, S. H., Johansson, C. B., and Peterson, R. A. A set of basic interest scales for the Strong Vocational Interest Blank for Men. *Journal of Applied Psychology Monograph,* 52, 1968.

Cattell, R. B. *Personality and motivation: Structure and measurement.* New York: Harcourt, Brace and World, 1957.

Clark, K. E. *The vocational interests of nonprofessional men.* Minneapolis: University of Minnesota Press, 1966.

Dunnette, M. D. A note on the criterion. *Journal of Applied Psychology,* 1963, 47, 251-54. (a)

Dunnette, M. D. A modified model for test validation and selection research. *Journal of Applied Psychology,* 1963, 47, 317-23. (b)

Dunnette, M. D. President's message. *The Industrial Psychologist,* 1966, 4, 1-2.

Dunnette, M. D. *Personnel selection and placement.* Belmont, Calif.: Wadsworth 1966.

Fleishman, E. A., and Fruchter, B. Factor structure and predictability of successive stages of learning Morse code, *Journal of Applied Psychology,* 1960, 44, 97-101.

Gaylord, R. H., and Brogden, H. E. Optimal weighting of unreliable criterion elements. *Educational and Psychological Measurement,* 1964, 24, 529-33.

Ghiselli, E. E. Dimensional problems of criteria. *Journal of Applied Psychology,* 1956, 40, 1-4.

Ghiselli, E. E., and Haire, M. The validation of selection tests in the light of the dynamic characteristics of criteria. *Personnel Psychology,* 1960, 13, 225-31.

Guilford, J. P. *Psychometric methods.* New York: McGraw-Hill, 1954.

Guion, R. M. *Personnel testing.* New York: McGraw-Hill, 1965.

Guion, R. M. Criterion measurement and personnel judgment. *Personnel Psychology,* 1961, 14, 141-49.

Guion, R. M. Industrial psychology as an

academic discipline. *American Psychologist*, 1965, 20, 815-21.

Haire, M. Business is too important to be studied only by economists. *American Psychologist*, 1960, 15, 271-72.

Hull, C. L. *Aptitude testing*. New York: World Book Co., 1928.

Magnusson, D. *Test theory*. London: Addison-Wesley, 1966.

Nagle, B. F. Criterion development. *Personnel Psychology*, 1953, 6, 271-89.

Nunnally, J. C. *Psychometric theory*. New York: McGraw-Hill, 1967.

Owens, W. A. Toward one discipline of scientific psychology. *American Psychologist*, 1968, 23, 782-85.

Peres, S. H. Performance dimensions of supervisory positions *Personnel Psychology*, 1962, 15, 405-10.

Prien, E. P. Dynamic character of criteria: organizational change. *Journal of Applied Psychology*, 1966, 50, 501-4.

Pugh, D. S. Modern organizational theory: a psychological and sociological study. *Psychological Bulletin*, 1966, 66, 235-37.

Seashore, S. E., Indik, B. P., and Georgopoulos, B. S. Relationships among criteria of job performance. *Journal of Applied Psychology*, 1960, 44, 195-202.

Strong, E. K. *Vocational interests of men and women*. Stanford, Calif.: Stanford University Press, 1943.

Taylor, C. W., Smith, W. R., Ghiselin, B., and Ellison, R. Explorations in the measurement and prediction of contributions of one sample of scientists. ASD-TR-61-96, Personnel Laboratory, Lackland Air Force Base, Texas, 1961.

Taylor, C. W., Price, P. B., Richards, J. M., and Jacobson, T. L. An investigation of the criterion problem for a medical school faculty. *Journal of Applied Psychology*, 1964, 48, 294-301.

Thorndike, R. L. *Personnel selection*. New York: Wiley, 1948.

Tiffin, J., and McCormick, E. J. *Industrial psychology*. 5th ed. Englewood Cliffs, N.J.: Prentice-Hall, 1965.

Toops, H. A. The criterion. *Educational and Psychological Measurement*, 1944, 4, 271-97.

Travers, R. M. W. Rational hypotheses in the construction of tests. *Educational and Psychological Measurement*, 1951, 11, 128-37.

Tyler, Leona E. *The psychology of human differences*. New York: Appleton-Century-Crofts, 1965.

Wallace, S. R. Criteria for what? *American Psychologist*, 1965, 20, 411-17.

26
Make Performance Appraisal Relevant

WINSTON OBERG

These frequently voiced goals of performance appraisal programs underscore the importance of such programs to any ongoing business organization:

Help or prod supervisors to observe their subordinates more closely and to do a better coaching job;

Motivate employees by providing feedback on how they are doing;

Provide back-up data for management decisions concerning merit increases, transfers, dismissals, and so on;

Improve organization development by identifying people with promotion potential and pinpointing development needs;

Establish a research and reference base for personnel decisions.

It has been estimated that over three-fourths of U.S. companies now have performance appraisal programs.[1]

In actual practice, however, formal performance appraisal programs have often yielded unsatisfactory and disappointing results, as the growing body of critical literature attests.[2] Some critics even suggest that we abandon performance appraisal as a lost hope, and they point to scores of problems and pitfalls as evidence.

But considering the potential of appraisal programs, the issue should not be whether to scrap them; rather, it should be how to make them better. I have found that one reason for failures is that companies often select indiscriminately from the wide battery of available performance appraisal techniques without really thinking about which particular technique is best suited to a particular appraisal objective.

For example, the most commonly used appraisal techniques include:

1. See W. R. Spriegel and Edwin W. Mumma, *Merit Rating of Supervisors and Executives* (Austin, Bureau of Business Research, University of Texas, 1961); and Richard V. Miller, "Merit Rating in Industry: A Survey of Current Practices and Problems," ILR Research, Fall 1959.

2. See, for example, Douglas McGregor, "An Uneasy Look at Performance Appraisal," HBR May-June 1957, p. 89; Paul H. Thompson and Gene W. Dalton, "Performance Appraisals Managers Beware," HBR January–February 1970, p. 149; and Albert W. Schrader, "Let's Abolish the Annual Performance Review," *Management of Personnel Quarterly*, Fall 1969, p. 293.

Reprinted from *Harvard Business Review*, 1972 (January-February), 61-67, by permission of the publisher.

1. Essay appraisal;
2. Graphic rating scale;
3. Field review;
4. Forced-choice rating;
5. Critical incident appraisal;
6. Management-by-objectives approach;
7. Work-standards approach.
8. Ranking methods;
9. Assessment centers.

Each of these has its own combination of strengths and weaknesses, and none is able to achieve all of the purposes for which management institutes performance appraisal systems. Nor is any one technique able to evade all of the pitfalls. The best anyone can hope to do is to match an appropriate appraisal method to a particular performance appraisal goal.

In this article I shall attempt to lay the groundwork for such a matching effort. First, I shall review some familiar pitfalls in appraisal programs; then, against this background, I shall assess the strengths and weaknesses of the nine commonly used appraisal techniques. In the last section I shall match the organizational objectives listed at the outset of this article with the techniques best suited to achieving them.

SOME COMMON PITFALLS

Obstacles to the success of formal performance appraisal programs should be familiar to most managers, either from painful personal experience or from the growing body of critical literature. Here are the most troublesome and frequently cited drawbacks:

Performance appraisal programs demand too much from supervisors. Formal performance appraisals obviously require at least periodic supervisor observation of subordinates' performance. However, the typical first-line supervisor can hardly know, in a very adequate way, just what each of 20, 30, or more subordinates is doing.

Standards and ratings tend to vary widely and, often, unfairly. Some raters are tough, others are lenient. Some departments have highly competent people; others have less competent people. Consequently, employees subject to less competition or lenient ratings can receive higher appraisals than equally competent or superior associates.

Personal values and bias can replace organizational standards. An appraiser may not lack standards, but the standards he uses are sometimes the wrong ones. For example, unfairly low ratings may be given to valued subordinates so they will not be promoted out of the rater's department. More often, however, outright bias dictates favored treatment for some employees.

Because of lack of communication, employees may not know how they are rated. The standards by which employees think they are being judged are sometimes different from those their superiors actually use. No performance appraisal system can be very effective for management decisions, organization development, or any other purpose until the people being appraised know what is expected of them and by what criteria they are being judged.

Appraisal techniques tend to be used as performance panaceas. If a worker lacks the basic ability or has not been given the necessary training for his job, it is neither reasonable to try to stimulate adequate performance through performance appraisals, nor fair to base salary, dismissal, or other negative decisions on such an appraisal. No appraisal program can substitute for sound selection, placement, and training programs. Poor performance represents someone else's failure.

In many cases, the validity of ratings is reduced by supervisory resistance to making the ratings. Rather than confront their less effective subordinates with negative ratings, negative feedback in appraisal interviews, and below-average salary increases, supervisors often take the more comfortable way out and give average or above-average ratings to inferior performers.

Performance appraisal ratings can boomerang when communicated to employees. Negative feedback (i.e., criticism) not only fails to motivate the typical employee, but also can cause him to perform worse.[3] Only those employees who have a high degree of self-esteem appear to be stimulated by criticism to improve their performance.

Performance appraisals interfere with the more constructive coaching relationship that should exist between a superior and his subordinates. Performance appraisal interviews tend to emphasize the superior position of the supervisor by placing him in the role of judge, thus countering his equally important role of teacher and coach. This is particularly damaging in organizations that are attempting to maintain a more participative organizational climate.

A LOOK AT METHODS

The foregoing list of major program pitfalls represents a formidable challenge, even considering the available battery of appraisal techniques. But attempting to avoid these pitfalls by doing away with appraisals themselves is like trying to solve the problems of life by committing suicide. The more logical task is to identify those appraisal practices that are (a) most likely to achieve a particular objective and (b) least vulnerable to the obstacles already discussed.

Before relating the specific techniques to the goals of performance appraisal stated at the outset of the article, I shall briefly review each, taking them more or less in an order of increasing complexity. The best-known techniques will be treated most briefly.

1. Essay appraisal

In its simplest form, this technique asks the rater to write a paragraph or more covering an individual's strengths, weaknesses, poten-

tial, and so on. In most selection situations, particularly those involving professional, sales, or managerial positions, essay appraisals from former employers, teachers, or associates carry significant weight. The assumption seems to be that an honest and informed statement—either by word of mouth or in writing—from someone who knows a man well, is fully as valid as more formal and more complicated methods.

The biggest drawback to essay appraisals is their variability in length and content. Moreover, since different essays touch on different aspects of a man's performance or personal qualifications, essay ratings are difficult to combine or compare. For comparability, some type of more formal method, like the graphic rating scale, is desirable.

2. Graphic rating scale

This technique may not yield the depth of an essay appraisal, but it is more consistent and reliable. Typically, a graphic scale assesses a person on the quality and quantity of his work (is he outstanding, above average, average, or unsatisfactory?) and on a variety of other factors that vary with the job but usually include personal traits like reliability and cooperation. It may also include specific performance items like oral and written communication.

The graphic scale has come under frequent attack, but remains the most widely used rating method. In a classic comparison between the "old-fashioned" graphic scale and the much more sophisticated forced-choice technique, the former proved to be fully as valid as the best of the forced-choice forms, and better than most of them.[4] It is also cheaper to develop and more acceptable to raters than the forced-choice form. For many purposes there is no need to use anything more complicated than a graphic

---

3. See Herbert H. Meyer, Emanuel Kay, and John R.P. French, Jr., "Split Roles in Performance Appraisal," HBR January-February 1965, p. 123.

4. James Berkshire and Richard Highland, "Forced-choice performance rating on a methodological study," *Personnel Psychology,* Autumn 1953, p. 355.

scale supplemented by a few essay questions.

3. Field review

When there is reason to suspect rater bias, when some raters appear to be using higher standards than others, or when comparability of ratings is essential, essay or graphic ratings are often combined with a systematic review process. The field review is one of several techniques for doing this. A member of the personnel or central administrative staff meets with small groups of raters from each supervisory unit and goes over each employee's rating with them to (a) identify areas of inter-rater disagreement, (b) help the group arrive at a consensus, and (c) determine that each rater conceives the standards similarly.

This group-judgment technique tends to be more fair and more valid than individual ratings and permits the central staff to develop an awareness of the varying degrees of leniency or severity—as well as bias—exhibited by raters in different departments. On the negative side, the process is very time consuming.

4. Forced-choice rating

Like the field review, this technique was developed to reduce bias and establish objective standards of comparison between individuals, but it does not involve the intervention of a third party. Although there are many variations of this method, the most common one asks raters to choose from among groups of statements those which *best* fit the individual being rated and those which *least* fit him. The statements are then weighted or scored, very much the way a psychological test is scored. People with high scores are, by definition, the better employees; those with low scores are the poorer ones. Since the rater does not know what the scoring weights for each statement are, in theory at least, he cannot play favorites. He simply describes his people, and someone in the personnel department applies the scoring weights to determine who gets the best rating.

The rationale behind this technique is difficult to fault. It is the same rationale used in developing selection test batteries. In practice, however, the forced-choice method tends to irritate raters, who feel they are not being trusted. They want to say openly how they rate someone and not be second-guessed or tricked into making "honest" appraisals.

A few clever raters have even found ways to beat the system. When they want to give average employee Harry Smith a high rating, they simply describe the best employee they know. If the best employee is Elliott Jones, they describe Jones on Smith's forced-choice form. Thus, Smith gets a good rating and hopefully a raise.

An additional drawback is the difficulty and cost of developing forms. Consequently, the technique is usually limited to middle- and lower-management levels where the jobs are sufficiently similar to make standard or common forms feasible.

Finally, forced-choice forms tend to be of little value—and probably have a negative effect—when used in performance appraisal interviews.

5. Critical incident appraisal

The discussion of ratings with employees has, in many companies, proved to be a traumatic experience for supervisors. Some have learned from bitter experience what General Electric later documented; people who receive honest but negative feedback are typically not motivated to do better—and often do worse—after the appraisal interview.[5] Consequently, supervisors tend to avoid such interviews, or if forced to hold them, avoid giving negative ratings when the ratings have to be shown to the employee.

One stumbling block has no doubt been the unsatisfactory rating form used. Typically, these are graphic scales that often include rather vague traits like initiative, cooperativeness, reliability, and even per-

---

5. Meyer, Kay, and French, *op. cit.*

sonality. Discussing these with an employee can be difficult.

The critical incident technique looks like a natural to some people for performance review interviews, because it gives a supervisor actual, factual incidents to discuss with an employee. Supervisors are asked to keep a record, a "little black book," on each employee and to record actual incidents of positive or negative behavior. For example:

Bob Mitchell, who has been rated as somewhat unreliable, fails to meet several deadlines during the appraisal period. His supervisor makes a note of these incidents and is now prepared with hard, factual data:

"Bob, I rated you down on reliability because, on three different occasions over the last two months, you told me you would do something and you didn't do it. You remember six weeks ago when I. . . ."

Instead of arguing over traits, the discussion now deals with actual behavior. Possibly, Bob has misunderstood the supervisor or has good reasons for his apparent "unreliability." If so, he now has an opportunity to respond. His performance, not his personality, is being criticized. He knows specifically how to perform differently if he wants to be rated higher the next time. Of course, Bob might feel the supervisor was using unfairly high standards in evaluating his performance. But at least he would know just what those standards are.

There are, however, several drawbacks to this approach. It requires that supervisors jot down incidents on a daily or, at the very least, a weekly basis. This can become a chore. Furthermore, the critical incident rating technique need not, but may, cause a supervisor to delay feedback to employees. And it is hardly desirable to wait six months or a year to confront an employee with a misdeed or mistake.

Finally, the supervisor sets the standards. If they seem unfair to a subordinate, might he not be more motivated if he at least has some say in setting, or at least agreeing to, the standards against which he is judged?

6. Management by objectives

To avoid, or to deal with, the feeling that they are being judged by unfairly high standards, employees in some organizations are being asked to set—or help set—their own performance goals. Within the past five or six years, MBO has become something of a fad and is so familiar to most managers that I will not dwell on it here.

It should be noted, however, that when MBO is applied to lower organizational levels, employees do not always want to be involved in their own goal setting. As Arthur N. Turner and Paul R. Lawrence discovered, many do not want self-direction or autonomy.[6] As a result, more coercive variations of MBO are becoming increasingly common, and some critics see MBO drifting into a kind of manipulative form of management in which pseudo-participation substitutes for the real thing. Employees are consulted, but management ends up imposing its standards and its objectives.[7]

Some organizations, therefore, are introducing a work-standards approach to goal setting in which the goals are openly set by management. In fact, there appears to be something of a vogue in the setting of such work standards in white-collar and service areas.

7. Work-standards approach

Instead of asking employees to set their own performance goals, many organizations set measured daily work standards. In short, the work-standards technique establishes work and staffing targets aimed at improving productivity. When realistically used, it can make possible an objective and accurate appraisal of the work of employees and supervisors.

To be effective, the standards must be visible and fair. Hence a good deal of time is

6. *Industrial Jobs and the Worker* (Boston, Division of Research, Harvard Business School, 1965).
7. See, for example, Harry Levinson, "Management by Whose Objectives?" HBR July-August 1970, p. 125.

spent observing employees on the job, simplifying and improving the job where possible, and attempting to arrive at realistic output standards.

It is not clear, in every case, that work standards have been integrated with an organization's performance appraisal program. However, since the work-standards program provides each employee with a more or less complete set of his job duties, it would seem only natural that supervisors will eventually relate performance appraisal and interview comments to these duties. I would expect this to happen increasingly where work standards exist. The use of work standards should make performance interviews less threatening than the use of personal, more subjective standards alone.

The most serious drawback appears to be the problem of comparability. If people are evaluated on different standards, how can the ratings be brought together for comparison purposes when decisions have to be made on promotions or on salary increases? For these purposes some form of ranking is necessary.

8. Ranking methods

For comparative purposes, particularly when it is necessary to compare people who work for different supervisors, individual statements, ratings, or appraisal forms are not particularly useful. Instead, it is necessary to recognize that comparisons involve an overall subjective judgment to which a host of additional facts and impressions must somehow be added. There is no single form or way to do this.

Comparing people in different units for the purpose of, say, choosing a service supervisor or determining the relative size of salary increases for different supervisors, requires subjective judgment, not statistics. The best approach appears to be a ranking technique involving pooled judgment. The two most effective methods are alternation ranking and paired comparison ranking.

Alternation ranking: In this method, the names of employees are listed on the left-hand side of a sheet of paper—preferably in random order. If the rankings are for salary purposes, a supervisor is asked to choose the "most valuable" employee on the list, cross his name off, and put it at the top of the column on the right-hand side of the sheet. Next, he selects the "least valuable" employee on the list, crosses his name off, and puts it at the bottom of the right-hand column. The ranker then selects the "most valuable" person from the remaining list, crosses his name off and enters it below the top name on the right-hand list, and so on.

Paired-comparison ranking: This technique is probably just as accurate as alternation ranking and might be more so. But with large numbers of employees it becomes extremely time consuming and cumbersome.

To illustrate the method, let us say we have five employees: Mr. Abbott, Mr. Barnes, Mr. Cox, Mr. Drew, and Mr. Eliot. We list their names on the left-hand side of the sheet. We compare Abbott with Barnes on whatever criterion we have chosen, say, present value to the organization. If we feel Abbott is more valuable than Barnes, we put a tally beside Abbott's name. We then compare Abbott with Cox, with Drew, and with Eliot. The process is repeated for each individual. The man with the most tallies is the most valuable person, at least in the eyes of the rater; the man with no tallies at all is regarded as the least valuable person.

Both ranking techniques, particularly when combined with multiple rankings (i.e., when two or more people are asked to make independent rankings of the same work group and their lists are averaged), are among the best available for generating valid order-of-merit rankings for salary administration purposes.

9. Assessment centers

So far, we have been talking about assessing past performance. What about the assessment of future performance or potential? In any placement decision and even more so in promotion decisions, some prediciton of future performance is necessary. How can this kind of prediction be made most validly and most fairly?

One widely used rule of thumb is that "what a man has done is the best predictor of what he will do in the future." But suppose you are picking a man to be a supervisor and this person has never held supervisory responsibility? Or suppose you are selecting a man for a job from among a group of candidates, none of whom has done the job or one like it? In these situations, many organizations use assessment centers to predict future performance more accurately.

Typically, individuals from different departments are brought together to spend two or three days working on individual and group assignments similar to the ones they will be handling if they are promoted. The pooled judgment of observers—sometimes derived by paired comparison or alternation ranking—leads to an order-of-merit ranking for each participant. Less structured, subjective judgments are also made.

There is a good deal of evidence that people chosen by assessment center methods work out better than those not chosen by these methods.[8] The center also makes it possible for people who are working for departments of low status or low visibliity in an organization to become visible and, in the competitive situation of an assessment center, show how they stack up against people from more well-known departments. This has the effect of equalizing opportunity, improving morale, and enlarging the pool of possible promotion candidates.

FITTING PRACTICE TO PURPOSE

In the foregoing analysis, I have tried to

show that each performance appraisal technique has its own combination of strengths and weaknesses. The success of any program that makes use of these techniques will largely depend on how they are used relative to the goals of that program.

For example, goal-setting and work-standards methods will be most effective for objective coaching, counseling, and motivational purposes, but some form of critical incident appraisal is better when a supervisor's personal judgment and criticism are necessary.

Comparisons of individuals, especially in win-lose situations when only one person can be promoted or only a limited number can be given large salary increases, necessitate a still different approach. Each person should be rated on the same form, which must be a simple as possible, probably involving essay and graphic responses. Then order-of-merit rankings and final averaging should follow. To be more explicit, here are the appraisal goals listed at the outset of this article and the techniques best suited to them.

Help or prod supervisors to observe their subordinates more closely and to do a better coaching job. The critical incident appraisal appears to be ideal for this purpose, if supervisors can be convinced they should take the time to look for, and record, significant events. Time delays, however, are a major drawback to this technique and should be kept as short as possible. Still, over the longer term, a supervisor will gain a better knowledge of his own performance standards, including his possible biases, as he reviews the incidents he has recorded. He may even decide to change or reweight his own criteria.

Another technique that is useful for coaching purposes is, of course, MBO. Like the critical incident method, it focuses on actual behavior and actual results which can be discussed objectively and constructively, with little or no need for a supervisor to "play God."

8. See, for example, Robert C. Albrook, "Spot executives early," *Fortune,* July 1968, p. 106; and William C. Byham, "Assessment centers for spotting future managers," HBR July-August 1970, p. 150.

Motivate employees by providing feedback on how they are doing. The MBO approach, if it involves real participation, appears to be most likely to lead to an inner commitment to improved performance. However, the work-standards approach can also motivate, although in a more coercive way. If organizations staff to meet their work standards, the work force is reduced and people are compelled to work harder.

The former technique is more "democratic," while the latter technique is more "autocratic." Both can be effective; both make use of specific work goals or targets and both provide for knowledge of results.

If performance appraisal information is to be communicated to subordinates, either in writing or in an interview, the two most effective techniques are the management-by-objectives approach and the critical incident method. The latter, by communicating not only factual data but also the flavor of a supervisor's own values and biases, can be effective in an area where objective work standards or quantitative goals are not available.

Provide back-up data for management decisions concerning merit increases, promotions, transfers, dismissals, and so on. Most decisions involving employees require a comparison of people doing very different kinds of work. In this respect, the more specifically job-related techniques like management by objectives or work standards are not appropriate, or, if used, must be supplemented by less restricted methods.

For promotion to supervisory positions, the forced-choice rating form, if carefully developed and validated, could prove best. But the difficulty and cost of developing such a form and the resistance of raters to its use render it impractical except in large organizations.

Companies faced with the problem of selecting promotable men from a number of departments or divisions might consider using an assessment center. This minimizes the bias resulting from differences in departmental "visibility" and enlarges the pool of potential promotables.

The best appraisal method for most other management decisions will probably involve a very simple kind of graphic form or a combined graphic and essay form. If this is supplemented by the use of field reviews, it will be measurably strengthened. Following the individual appraisals, groups of supervisors should then be asked to rank the people they have rated, using a technique like alternation ranking or paired comparison. Pooled or averaged rankings will then tend to cancel out the most extreme forms of bias and should yield fair and valid order-of-merit lists.

Improve organization development by identifying people with promotion potential and pinpointing development needs. Comparison of people for promotion purposes has already been discussed. However, identification of training and development needs will probably best—and most simply—come from the essay part of the combined graphic/essay rating form recommended for the previous goal.

Establish a reference and research base for personnel decisions. For this goal, the simplest form is the best form. A graphic/essay combination is adequate for most reference purposes. But order-of-merit salary rankings should be used to develop criterion groups of good and poor performers.

CONCLUSION

Formal systems for appraising performance are neither worthless nor evil, as some critics have implied. Nor are they panaceas, as many managers might wish. A formal appraisal system is, at the very least, a commendable attempt to make visible, and hence improvable, a set of essential organization activities. Personal judgments about employee performance are inescapable, and subjective values and fallible human perception are always involved. Formal appraisal systems, to the degree that they bring these perceptions and values into the open, make it possible for at least some of the inherent bias and error to be recognized and remedied.

By improving the probability that good performance will be recognized and rewarded and poor performance corrected, a sound appraisal system can contribute both to organizational morale and organizational performance. Moreover, the alternative to a bad appraisal program need not be no appraisal program at all, as some critics have suggested. It can and ought to be a better appraisal program. And the first step in that direction is a thoughtful matching of practice to purpose.

27

Development of Behaviorally Anchored Scales
for the Evaluation of Faculty Teaching

OREN HARARI and SHELDON ZEDECK

An increasing number of articles are being devoted to the analysis and evaluation of college teaching. Generally, two questions have been posed: (a) Is it possible to identify independent dimensions of "teaching ability?" (b) Is it possible to develop a reliable, valid measure of "teaching ability?" The first question has received a great deal of attention and has usually been studied through factor analyses (cf. Hildebrand, Wilson, and Dienst, 1971) or by discriminant function analysis of students' ratings of professors (Field, Simpkins, Browne, and Rich, 1971). The results of these analyses, however, are open to question. Current student evaluation forms are often ambiguous, verbose, disorganized, and arbitrarily developed. They consist of global behavioral measures and vague trait descriptions. As a result, the forms tend to be unreliable and very susceptible to response biases. Different ways of investigating the original two questions are necessary.

A rigorous and comprehensive project conducted by Hildebrand *et al.* (1971) demonstrated some innovative procedures. First, two evaluation forms were empirically (rather than arbitrarily) developed whose items

met objective criteria (e.g., each item on one form discriminated between best and worst teachers at the .001 level). Second, items were developed and judged by students rather than by faculty members. The evaluation forms, however, still contain vague, global behaviors and trait descriptions. Also, the use of a simple 5-point scale for each item is not a conducive means for eliminating response biases such as leniency and central tendency. As in past studies, independent dimensions were obtained from factor analysis of the evaluation form. However, the weaknesses of the evaluation form suggest that results of the analyses be viewed cautiously. Finally, the forms by Hildebrand *et al.* attempt, as do most forms, to encompass the teaching of all university disciplines. Yet, it is unlikely that all, or even most, disciplines require identical patterns of teacher behavior. By its very nature, an evaluation form for all disciplines is not conducive to specific behavior and trait descriptions. Specific items, and possibly even dimensions of teaching ability, that are appropriate for the teaching of psychology may be quite inappropriate for the teaching of art, philosophy, physics, etc.

Reprinted from *Journal of Applied Psychology*, 1973, 58, 261-65, by permission of the authors and the publisher. ©1973 by the American Psychological Association.

One approach to the development of an evaluation or appraisal form that reduces the weaknesses inherent in most forms is the procedure suggested by Smith and Kendall (1963) for the construction of behaviorally anchored rating scales. The procedure involves the development of dimensions and items of performance criteria by independent groups and it has several advantages for the development of teaching evaluation forms: (a) members of the rater population, students, construct the scales; (b) conceptually independent dimensions are obtained which elicit consensus among raters as to the construct validity and exhaustiveness of the broad areas of performance that should be evaluated; (c) specific behavioral incidents, which retain *student terminology*, are used as anchor points on each dimension scale and thereby eliminate gross performance descriptions and many response biases; and (d) in actual use, students document ratings with specific incidents that they have observed, a procedure which favors honest and conscientious ratings. The purpose of the present study is to develop behaviorally anchored rating scales for the evaluation of the teaching ability of psychology professors.

METHOD

Subjects

Subjects were 231 male and female undergraduate students at the University of California, Berkeley, each of whom was enrolled in at least one psychology course, lower or upper division, when participating in the study. The sample included both psychology majors and nonmajors.

Procedure

The development of the scales utilized three independent stages. Subjects in each stage were exposed to a detailed explanation of the entire project before performing any task.

Stage 1: Generation of dimensions and behaviors. Stage 1 (n = 38) consisted of two conferences. In Conference 1 (n = 28), subjects divided themselves into four groups of seven members each. Each group was instructed to identify and define independent (yet exhaustive) dimensions of the "teaching ability" of psychology instructors. After each group completed its task, two volunteers from each group convened with the first author to integrate and edit the work of the four groups. The resulting dimensions and definitions were presented to all students for approval. Students were then instructed to provide behavioral incidents for each dimension. The necessity for very specific examples based on the students' experiences was stressed. Examples of acceptable and unacceptable items were discussed. Each student provided three critical incidents, reflecting good, average, or poor teaching performance, for each dimension.

The purpose of Conference 2 (n = 10) was to review the dimensions obtained in Conference 1 and to supplement the work, if necessary, with additional dimensions or behavioral examples.

Stage 2: Reallocation of behaviors. An independent group of students (n = 54) was provided with a list of the behavioral examples (randomly ordered) and a list of the dimensions and definitions generated in Stage 1. Students assigned each item to the dimension that the example was thought to illustrate. Examples that were not assigned to a dimension by 60 per cent of the students were eliminated from additional analyses. Effectively, ambiguous examples were eliminated because of lack of consensus as to which dimensions the examples illustrated.

Stage 3: Assignment of values. Students (n = 139) were provided with dimension lists with corresponding items that met the criterion established in Stage 2. Scale values ranging from 1 to 7 (reflecting very poor to very good performance) were assigned by the students to each example in the respective dimension. Items with standard deviations greater than 1.50 (the same criterion used by Fogli, Hulin, and Blood, 1971, and Smith and Kendall, 1963) were eliminated from further consideration. Effectively, the retained examples elicited agreement as to the type of performance illustrated and the degree to which the behavior represented poor to good performance on a 7-point scale.

The behavioral examples that were used as anchors in the final evaluation form were reworded from actual behaviors to expected behaviors. That is, a statement such as "This professor tells the class to read chapters 3, 4, and 5 of the text and then lectures about material in chapters 7, 8, and 9" was reworded to, "The professor *could be expected to* tell . . . chapters 7, 8, and 9." According to Smith and Kendall (1963), the rationale for this step is twofold: (a) the anchors become so concrete that, in view of previous peer group consensus in developing the scales, central tendency or judging effects should be minimized, and (b) the anchors become so verifiable that a rater's insight, judgment, and values are potentially challenged if subsequent ratee behavior would fail to confirm the rater's prediction. A third advantage of this step is that the rater should find it easy to compare the types of behaviors illustrated in the anchors with similar behaviors that the ratee has either demonstrated in the past or could be expected to demonstrate in the future.

RESULTS AND DISCUSSION

The synthesis of the four groups' work in Conference 1, Stage 1, resulted in seven dimensions: *depth of knowledge, delivery, organization, interpersonal relationships with students, relevance, testing and grading, and inspiration and motivation.* The review of the behavioral examples after Conference 1 indicated that the testing and grading dimensions should be split into two distinct dimensions, *"testing"* and *"grading."* Many examples for the original dimension were confounded because specific testing behavior and specific grading behavior were usually combined in the same example.

One of the tasks assigned to Conference 2 was to develop critical incidents for the two new dimensions. However, a discussion of Conference 1's work indicated that still another dimension, *assignments and work*

load, should also be added. Each student in Conference 2 provided three critical incidents for this dimension as well.

A review of the pool of all examples generated in both conferences resulted in the modification or elimination of vague, global, or incomprehensible items and the addition of extra items, especially items illustrating ordinary or mediocre teaching performance. The final pool consisted of 310 critical incidents. After Stage 2 (reallocation of behaviors), the number of behavioral incidents was reduced to 231. After Stage 3 (assignment of values), the number of behavioral items was reduced to 199. The number of behavioral incidents which appeared as anchors on the final form were 78. Descriptive data appear in Table 27-1.

Table 27-1 indicates that nearly all the items in each dimension met the standard deviation criterion of 1.50. Many items with standard deviations below 1.50 were not included in the final scales because their mean scores were similar to other items (with standard deviations below 1.50) on the same dimension. The items that were selected for the final scales represented a wide range of behaviors in terms of mean values and met subjective criteria of brevity, clarity, and contrast in subject matter with other items.

The interpersonal relationships and relevance dimensions each required the accepting of one item with standard deviations of 1.54 and 1.52, respectively, so as to provide anchors for the scale areas representing mediocre performance. As Landy and Guion (1970) observed, the problem of obtaining critical incidents for ordinary or mediocre performance often arises when developing behaviorally anchored scales. In the present study, students in Stage 1 had difficulty generating acceptable critical incidents for mediocre performance. Furthermore, results of Stage 3 showed that a given dimension would invariably contain few items which had mean values between 3.5 and 4.5, and even those items often had larger standard

Table 27-1. Descriptive Statistics of Dimensions

Dimension	No. items after Stage 2	Range of *SD* for Stage 3	No. items which met 1.50 criterion	No. anchors on final scale	Range of means on final scale	Range of *SD* on final scale
Depth of knowledge	20	.91-1.50	19	9	1.44-6.35	.91-1.36
Delivery	32	.85-1.51	31	9	1.45-6.40	.85-1.09
Organization	20	.94-1.69	18	7	1.90-6.21	1.00-1.13
Interpersonal relations with students	42	.86-1.54	41	10	1.32-6.51	.86-1.54
Relevance	20	.65-1.92	15	8	1.38-6.06	.65-1.52
Testing	31	.95-2.03	21	9	1.71-5.83	1.03-1.47
Grading	25	1.11-1.90	13	8	1.63-5.97	1.15-1.49
Assignment and work load	18	.85-1.78	16	8	1.65-6.09	.85-1.36
Ability to motivate	23	.91-1.39	23	10	1.60-6.35	.96-1.39

deviations than items that received mean values below 3.5 or above 4.5. As an extreme example, there are no anchors between the means 2.88 and 5.65 in the organization dimension because the standard deviations of the few items which fell within that range of means were simply too large to be acceptable.

This difficulty in obtaining behaviors of medium value may be a function of the instructions and the connotations of the words "average" or "mediocre." Though students were asked for examples of good, poor, and mediocre performance, the request was for *critical incidents*. Emphasis on critical incidents may preclude the opportunity for noncritical, mediocre examples. Perhaps other adjectives than average or mediocre should be used, for example, satisfactory or acceptable; or another strategy may be to ask for examples that range from good to poor without specifying a midpoint.

Table 27-2 shows one scale which appeared in the final evaluation forms—interpersonal relations with students.

A few comments on the *testing* and *grading* dimensions may be appropriate. The results of Stage 3 indicate some conflict among students as to the position of testing and grading in a university. First, the standard deviation of items on these dimensions, especially grading, were on the whole larger

than those of other dimensions. Second, items that described professors who do not test or grade, or who give everyone As, or who allow students to test or grade themselves received means between 3.5 and 4.5 and large standard deviations. The moderate values and large standard deviations indicate that students are divided with respect to the types of performance certain grading and/or testing procedures reflect. On the other hand, there was substantial agreement as to what *poor* testing and grading practices are. Not only did Stage 3 contain more items illustrating poor testing and grading practices than good testing and grading practices, but students showed more agreement in evaluating those items which they identified as poor performance. These results may be due to (a) greater exposure to poor testing and grading procedures than good procedures, or (b) selective recall of negative personal evaluation. These possibilities should be examined in future research.

A general inspection of the scales reveals that there might be two components to teaching ability. The scales of depth of knowledge, delivery, organization, interpersonal relations, relevance, and inspiration and motivation could be considered *intrinsic* factors. That is, these components are the input of the instructor; the what and how he wants to make the course. In contrast, the scales of testing, grading, and assignments and work load could be considered *extrinsic*

Table 27-2. Interpersonal Relations with Students—the Professor's Rapport with and Sensitivity to Students

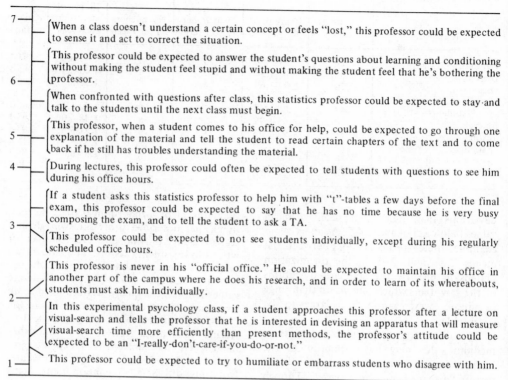

7 — When a class doesn't understand a certain concept or feels "lost," this professor could be expected to sense it and act to correct the situation.

This professor could be expected to answer the student's questions about learning and conditioning without making the student feel stupid and without making the student feel that he's bothering the professor.

6 —

When confronted with questions after class, this statistics professor could be expected to stay and talk to the students until the next class must begin.

5 — This professor, when a student comes to his office for help, could be expected to go through one explanation of the material and tell the student to read certain chapters of the text and to come back if he still has troubles understanding the material.

4 — During lectures, this professor could often be expected to tell students with questions to see him during his office hours.

If a student asks this statistics professor to help him with "t"-tables a few days before the final exam, this professor could be expected to say that he has no time because he is very busy composing the exam, and to tell the student to ask a TA.

3 —

This professor could be expected to not see students individually, except during his regularly scheduled office hours.

This professor is never in his "official office." He could be expected to maintain his office in another part of the campus where he does his research, and in order to learn of its whereabouts, students must ask him individually.

2 —

In this experimental psychology class, if a student approaches this professor after a lecture on visual-search and tells the professor that he is interested in devising an apparatus that will measure visual-search time more efficiently than present methods, the professor's attitude could be expected to be an "I-really-don't-care-if-you-do-or-not."

1 — This professor could be expected to try to humiliate or embarrass students who disagree with him.

components. These scales are the outputs to the student; the relatively tangible product the student receives.

Of relevance to this categorization is data provided by faculty ($n = 10$) in the Psychology Department. Faculty were requested to provide values to the items (same task required of students in Stage 3) developed by the students. Rank-order correlations between student and faculty values for only those items retained on each scale indicated 1.00 or near 1.00 correlations on all scales, except testing, grading, and assignments and work load. In other words, faculty and students agreed on the rank-order value of the behaviors for the intrinsic components

but disagreed on the value of the items for the extrinsic scales.

In general, the form is concise, clearly organized, and since the student provides only nine ratings, easy to fill out, check, and review. The form can be supplemented with space for an overall evaluation of the professor or with questions concerned with the characteristics of a particular course. Conversely, the form may be shortened: a dimension(s) may be deleted from the form when it is inappropriate; for example, students rating a professor who does not give examinations would use a form with only eight dimensions.

In addition, all of the examples obtained

through this procedure can be used as standards of good, mediocre, and poor teaching in a training course. The examples with low standard deviations reflect agreed upon behavior and can form the basis for a much needed course in training of future college instructors.

In conclusion, the literature suggests: (a) Students are competent and mature raters who separate good teaching from showmanship and popularity (cf. Kent, 1966). The present study seems to support this generalization. (b) Efficient and scientific assessment of a professor's teaching is impossible without systematic student opinion as a primary source of the assessment (Slobin and Nichols, 1969). We agree and suggest that student opinion be a key input for evaluation of faculty teaching and for development of scales for this purpose.

REFERENCES

Field, T. W., Simpkins, W. S., Browne, R. K., and Rich, P. Identifying patterns of teacher behavior from student evaluations. *Journal of Applied Psychology,* 1971, 55, 466-69.

Fogli, L., Hulin, C. L., and Blood, M. R. Development of first-level behavioral job criteria. *Journal of Applied Psychology,* 1971, 55, 3-8.

Hildebrand, M. H., Wilson, R. C., and Dienst, E. R. *Evaluating university teaching.* Berkeley: University of California, Center for Research and Development in Higher Education, 1971.

Kent, L. Student evaluation of teaching. *Educational Record,* 1966, 47, 376-406.

Landy, F., and Guion, R. M. Development of scales for the measurement of work motivation. *Organizational Behavior and Human Performance,* 1970, 5, 93-103.

Slobin, D. I., and Nichols, D. G. Student rating of teaching, *Improving College and University Teaching,* 1969, 17, 244-48.

Smith, P. C., and Kendall, L. M. Retranslation of expectations: An approach to the construction of unambiguous anchors for rating scales. *Journal of Applied Psychology,* 1963, 47, 149-55.

28

Management Appraisal:

A Capsule Review and Current References

JOHN B. MINER

Does a supervisor appraise your performance? Is this appraisal written, formal, and permanent? Does it affect your performance? Are you a manager who must appraise subordinates and write up these appraisals? Has the company recently instituted a system of appraisal and development by objectives? The chances are that you answered "yes" to many or all of these questions, for approximately 80 per cent of all U.S. companies have a formal management appraisal system (10); the shift is away from appraisal of the rank and file (42). (The numbers in parentheses apply to the current references listed at the end of the article.)

Many of these companies, and most of the managers being appraised, are unsatisfied with their formal appraisal system. This is a justifiable position, for the whole concept is in a state of flux—new approaches, new plans, and new methods. With this constant change, where is a manager to turn for guidance?

For most of us, management appraisal is extraordinarily difficult. It is hard to pass judgment on a fellow man, especially if that judgment will become a permanent part of his company record, affecting his future. The procedure is further complicated by the absence of needed facts and of widely accepted theories. Yet the attainment of any organization's goals requires that the performance of our managers be measured, compared, and recorded. Growth requires that potential be evaluated. These requirements can best be met by a thoughtfully adopted formal appraisal system, one that best conforms to current knowledge and theory.

The purposes of this article are to provide this knowledge and theory in capsule form, and to provide a reference to current work. I have done this by asking—and answering—questions, those most frequently asked about the evaluation of executives.

What are the relative merits of appraisals made by superiors, peers, subordinates, and the man himself?

Appraisals made by superiors, peers, subordinates, or the man himself all have merit, but for different qualities. About 98 per cent of all evaluation forms are designed to be completed by the immediate superior. This approach appears to have widespread acceptance, and subordinates usually prefer it (21).

Reprinted from *Business Horizons*, 1968 (October), 83-96, by permission of the author and the publisher.

There is ample evidence that ratings made by peers differ considerably from those made by superiors. The results of a study conducted at North American Aviation (39) indicate that two levels of supervision agree reasonably well; superiors and co-workers do not. Co-workers apparently consider somewhat different factors and, on the average, give higher ratings.

Similar discrepancies occur when self-ratings are compared with those of superiors. While various levels of supervision tend to agree, superior and self-ratings rarely do (34). Self-ratings emphasize getting along with others as important for success, while superiors stress initiative and work knowledge (21). Furthermore, self-ratings are usually inflated (32).

There is reason to believe that self-interest can influence peer, subordinate, and self-ratings to the point where the evaluations may lack organizational relevance. Where favorable results have been reported with these techniques, it has been almost exclusively in an artificial research setting. It seems likely that their use as the *primary* element of a regular on-going appraisal system would produce somewhat different results, and that mutual and/or self-protection could well become a more important consideration that the profitability of the company (2).

Although these findings seem to argue strongly for appraisal by superiors, certain additional facts contradict this conclusion. For one, many companies use a management-by-objectives approach, which has a strong participative component. Managers have a say in setting their own objectives and in determining whether these objectives have been met. This is really self-rating. Experimental evidence from studies at General Electric indicates that such participation in the appraisal situation can contribute to more effective performance (12). Thus, at least for purposes of management development, self-rating of a kind has some value.

Peer rating has also received significant support from recent research. A study utilizing middle-level managers at IBM indicates quite clearly that those men rated high by other managers at the same level were more likely to be promoted (36). It seems entirely possible that at the middle and upper levels of management, where organizational commitment is often high, objective peer evaluations that are relatively free of protective bias can be obtained. Such evaluations may well prove particularly valuable in the identification of leadership potential, just as self-evaluations appear to be most useful for developmental purposes. The Air Force is currently experimenting rather extensively with peer ratings, working on the theory that they are particularly significant in the measurement of potential.

A recent proposal favors a combination appraisal process utilizing superior, peer, and self-ratings (19). The advantages are considerable. The knowledge that ratings by superiors are also being obtained reduces bias in the two; these can capitalize on their unique observational opportunities. The match, or correlation, between the different types of ratings provides a measure of integrated perception among different people in the company, and thus of the capacity to concentrate effort behind goals (29). To the extent that peer and self-ratings support superior ratings, acceptance is likely, and personnel actions, such as promotion and firing, can be carried out without resistance. To the extent they do not, resistance is likely to develop. Furthermore, self-ratings and peer ratings are available for purposes of development and the identification of potential. Finally, special attention can be focused on those individuals whose ratings differ sharply. An appraisal involving high superior and self-ratings combined with very low peer ratings is clearly not the same as one with high ratings from all three sources. Yet, if superior evaluations only are obtained, significant aspects of the situation may go undetected.

The major advantage for the three-rating

approach is that it provides a wealth of information about the individual and the organization, and pulls together a number of schools of thought on appraisals. All in all, it appears to be *the* approach to management appraisal of the future. Development of such complex programs and effective utilization of the information made available will, however, require expertise beyond that currently available in many companies.

Are there advantages in using more than one rater?

Research shows consistently that using more than one rater is advantageous. The best evidence comes from studies conducted by the U.S. Army (4), which indicate a clear superiority for the average of ratings made by several individuals over those made by only one person.

The rationale behind averaging ratings from the same type of source—superiors, peers, or subordinates—is that an average tends to reduce the impact of any single biased rating. For example, in one study, managers who were found to be particularly considerate and kind to their subordinates also gave them high ratings (17). When averaged with the evaluations of more production-oriented managers, such lenient ratings have less impact on the final appraisal.

However, the availability of raters with access to a sufficiently large sample of work behaviors can limit the number of raters who should be used. Increasing the size of the rating group by adding people who are not really qualified to evaluate and who, therefore, will give erroneous data defeats the value of the averaging process. One of the potential values of peer and subordinate appraisals is the availability of a large number of individuals who can qualify as raters because of their particularly good opportunities for observation.

What is the value of rating reviews by a hierarchical superior of the rater?

Various provisions for reviews by the direct-line superior of a rater are a common feature of appraisal systems (21). In the U.S. Army procedure, there are in essence two reviews— one by the indorser, who also makes his own rating, and one by the reviewer, who merely indicates that a review has been made. Thus, the original rater has his evaluations scrutinized twice, the indorser once (7).

A review procedure may operate in a number of ways. One approach requires the rater to present his evaluations orally to a review board of superiors (37). In other cases, as with the military, only the written forms are reviewed at higher levels. A reviewer may have the authority to change evaluations directly without any consultation, to personally require the rater to make changes, to advise on changes, or merely to indicate disagreement. Under appropriate circumstances, such a review does appear to contribute to evaluation quality (2). Ideally, adequate knowledge of a manager's performance exists at several hierarchical levels above him. In this case, the best approach is to pass the appraisals upward so that each manager can make his evaluation either independently, as in the case of the immediate superior, or with knowledge only of what those below him think. This chain of evaluation should stop when it reaches a level in the hierarchy where adequate knowledge of performance does not exist; there is little point in including a reviewer who does not also rate. If such an individual has no basis for evaluating a man, nothing is gained by adding his signature to a form. If he does have a basis, his ratings should be averaged with the others.

This rater-indorser chain approach has an advantage in that each manager, except the one at the top, knows that his evaluations will be scrutinized. The approach also provides for multiple ratings under conditions that protect against undue influence from a superior who may have the least adequate basis for appraisal. The information flow is upward from what can be presumed to be the most knowledgeable individual to the least, rather than the reverse. The use of such an approach assumes that a superior will not change or influence his subordinates' ratings in any way. Evidence indicates that, when actual changes at higher levels are permitted, they do nothing to improve the evaluation process. The superior can, however, disagree in his own ratings and thus mitigate the effects of what he feels is an error.

Should management appraisals be made at the same time as salary recommendations?
The real problem here is not whether management appraisals and salary recommendations should be made together, although traditionally this is the way it is done. Rather, the problem is to find some method of avoiding the common tendency to decide on salary first and then adjust the performance ratings to fit. Because salary is in practice influenced by many factors other than merit, the ratings are frequently distorted.

I cannot locate any research that bears directly on the question. Nonetheless, studies at General Electric clearly indicate that feeding back information on salary actions along with management appraisal data is not desirable insofar as motivational and developmental goals are concerned (24). Criticism tied directly to pay action produces so much defensiveness that there is little prospect of learning. Energies focus primarily on self-protection rather than self-improvement (33).

Separating appraisals and salary actions in time is one way of reducing distortion, but many managers unquestionably do prefer to couple them. An approach that would overcome bias and still allow both decisions to be made simultaneously would clearly be helpful. A means of changing perceptions—of the process of salary administration and of the appraisal process—seems called for. Although evidence is lacking, I believe this change could be achieved through a training program, provided the content of the program truly represented top management philosophies. The training would consider merit as well as various factors that inevitably influence salary actions—the labor market, previous salary history, budgetary limitations, equity considerations, and rate ranges. The training would also consider sources of bias in appraisal. Possibly, with such an approach, pay and performance could be separated in the manager's mind at least as effectively as with elapsed time.

What are the pros and cons of feedback from the rater to the man being rated?
Usually, the results of appraisals are given to the man who has been evaluated; this may be done in a number of different ways and with varying amounts of detail (21). But the question is whether it should be done at all. An adequate answer requires two kinds of information: the effect of the feedback on the ratings and the effect of the feedback on the man who has been rated.

1. Feedback and ratings

A Lockheed Aircraft study (40) provides the best example of how the feedback requirement may influence ratings. The regular evaluations, which were not revealed to subordinates, were followed in two weeks by a second appraisal, which included discussions of the ratings with the men. The mean score for the 485 men involved rose dramatically—from an initial 60 to 84 out of a possible 100. Apparently, when faced with the prospect of making face-to-face negative comments, many managers avoided the problem by inflating their ratings.

This problem has plagued the Armed Forces for years (7). Although direct feedback by the superior is not required by law, the legal structrue does indicate that an officer may inspect the evaluations in his file and that under certain conditions he may appeal. Anticipating that efficiency reports may be inspected, raters tend to make favorable statements. A variety of techniques including forced choice, forced distribution, and critical incidents have been introduced with little success over the years to deal with the inflation of ratings.

Thus, where valid ratings are necessary for salary administration, promotion, transfer, discharge, and evaluation of selection procedures, feedback is not desirable. It is particularly important to avoid optional feedback, in which a manager does as he pleases. Under such circumstances, managers who plan to discuss their evaluations with subordinates will inflate them; those who do no plan to discuss their evaluations will not inflate them. As a result, the two types of ratings will actually be on different scales. Assuming the existence of single scale under these circumstances will not only result in injustice to the individual, but will produce decisions detrimental to the organization as well.

2. Feedback and the man rated

The major source of information on the motivational or developmental effects of feedback is a series of studies conducted at General Electric (12, 16, 24). The findings of this research on the dynamics of the feedback interview are summarized as follows:

Criticism tends to have a negative impact on achievement of goals.

Praise has little effect, either positive or negative.

Performance tends to improve when specific objectives are established.

Defensiveness as a consequence of criticism results in inferior performance.

Coaching is best done on a day-to-day basis and in direct association with specific acts, not once a year.

Mutual goal setting by superior and subordinate yields positive results.

Interviews intended primarily to improve performance should not at the same time deal with salary and promotion.

Participation by the subordinate in establishing his own performance goals yields favorable results.

Separate performance evaluations are required for different purposes.

Generally, the results of the General Electric research seem to provide appropriate guides for action. Nonetheless, subsequent research has raised some doubts about the value of goal setting as it is actually done within the context of the management-by-objectives approach (22).

Feedback can be an effective motivational and developmental tool, but often it is not. Whether systematic appraisal interviews should be attempted depends on the approach taken and the skill of the interviewer. Clearly, feedback can do more harm than good. Ideally, a feedback interview should be goal oriented and should take a problem-solving approach, but this is not easy to do. Getting a manager to agree on a set of objectives and standards is one thing; getting him to recognize where and why he has fallen short in his performance is quite another (25). However, the requisite skill can be developed in many managers through training (23, 31).

Based on the evidence currently available, the appropriate conclusion seems to be that only those ratings made specifically for motivational or developmental purposes should ever be fed back, and then only by a fully trained and skilled interviewer. Feedback has tremendous potential for harm as well as good. It *can* be a major source of managerial turnover.

On what types of characteristics should managers be rated?
In selecting the types of characteristics on which to rate a manager, it is most important to include only those that manifest themselves in the work situation. The rating factors should be firmly anchored in behavior that characteristically occurs on the job and that influences performance (10). There is a tendency to include a variety of traits that do not meet these requirements. Often rating scales deal with aspects of "good" and "bad" people that cannot be

adequately judged from job contact alone, or that matter little, if at all, in effective performance. In this connection, it is well to note that it is not always the "good" people who do well. One study found that an intense sense of honesty and ethics almost guaranteed failure in a particular type of sales job (26).

Ratings should also deal with characteristics that can be described clearly so all raters will have the same kinds of behavior in mind (2). Considerable evidence indicates that certain personality traits, such as "character" and "aggressiveness," are viewed so nebulously that agreement is almost impossible on whether people possess them. Generally, the closer the factors are to job behavior and results, the more raters will agree in their evaluations.

How can ratings be spread out along a scale most successfully?

One approach to spreading out ratings is the forced distribution technique, which is a variant of ranking. However, rather than having as many categories as there are managers to be rated, the number of categories is predetermined, as is the percentage of the men to be placed in each category. In theory, the technique, like ranking, has considerable appeal. In practice, however, it presents so many difficulties that, at least for *management* appraisal, it cannot be recommended. One problem is that the percentages are meaningless unless a large group is to be rated by a single manager. Where spans of control are limited, this condition is not met. Furthermore, there is the difficulty of combining groups. Is the lower 10 per cent of one group likely to be at the same performance level as the lower 10 per cent of another? This problem also occurs with ranking, of course.

Furthermore, raters tend to resist forced distribution (42). The result is a continuing conflict between those responsible for administering the appraisal system and the managers doing the rating. In the end, either

the ratings are adjusted to fit the required percentage distribution, with great potential for error (17), or the forced distribution technique is abandoned entirely.

Given the conclusion that forced distribution techniques are not satisfactory for management appraisal, what other procedures are available to produce a meaningful spread of ratings along a scale? The armed services have faced this problem continually over the years. As indicated previously, since the man rated has ready access to the armed service efficiency reports, scores tend to pile up at the high end of the scales. In the late 1940s and early 1950s, two rather complex procedures were developed to deal with this problem. The forced choice approach was introduced by the Army and then adopted by the Air Force, which subsequently developed the critical incident technique to replace it. Neither approach proved successful (9). Forced choice failed because rating officers resisted a procedure that made it difficult, if not impossible, for them to determine how they had actually rated a man. In addition, leniency was not entirely overcome. The critical incident approach proved too complicated, too time consuming, resulted in too much concern with the final score, and did not really solve the leniency problem. In both cases, resistance from rating officers in the field was sufficient to terminate use of the technique. Research evidence indicates that graphic rating scales are actually just as valid as these more complex procedures (4).

All this does not mean that steps cannot be taken to produce a satisfactory spread of ratings. The following procedures used in business organizations have proved successful in extending this range:

Maintain security so evaluations are not available to the men rated or fed back to them (40).

Avoid ambiguous descriptions of the characteristics to be rated and of steps on the scale; the rater must have a clear understanding of exactly what job behaviors he is to consider (3).

Carry out training aimed at providing an understanding of the desirability of a wide range of scores (20). Particular stress should be placed on getting overly considerate managers, who want more than anything else to help their men, to spread their ratings out. These are the raters who typically have the smallest ranges (17).

If these three conditions are met, and an adequate number of steps or levels exist in the scale, the usual graphic rating scale should yield a satisfactory spread of scores and should prove the most generally useful (2).

Does a tendency to stress recent events serve to bias ratings?
Studies indicate, as many have hypothesized, that specific instances of effective or ineffective behavior occurring shortly before evaluations unduly affect the ratings (10). Apparently, raters remember recent events more vividly and, therefore, weigh them more heavily.

This situation suggests the need for relatively frequent ratings—at least every three to six months. Averaging such evaluations to yield a running appraisal score will minimize the effects of any recent events. Another antidote involves keeping managers aware of this problem; some managers might be induced to keep notes on performance throughout the rating period and then to review these at appraisal time. All of this, of course, represents another training area.

Is there any method of communicating information regarding an appraisal system that will ensure consistency of application?
Evidence on the value of introducing an educational process as an integral part of a total appraisal system is consistently positive. Normally, this process is based on the spoken word, but, on occasion, it may utilize written materials as well. Some uses of these procedures have already been noted, but additional features of the communication problem should be mentioned.

Studies indicate that training can serve to increase the agreement between different raters, reduce bias (40), increase accuracy generally, prevent inflation of scores (5), and spread out the rating distribution (20). In general, training sessions should be conducted by a person qualified as an expert on management appraisal and familiar with the details of the particular system in use. There should be an opportunity for considerable discussion and some practice with the rating forms. Various sources of error and bias, as well as factors that will make the ratings most useful, need primary attention (41).

Despite the consistently favorable evidence, a great many companies do not build training procedures into their appraisal systems. In fact, a lack of adequate training is the major problem of most programs (21). In addition, there is reason to believe that many programs that have succumbed to widespread managerial resistance could have survived had they been introduced with adequate training. Group sessions, which are usually used, may be supplemented with some individual assistance at the time the ratings are made. Also, manuals containing information similar to the training program have proved useful (5).

What can be done to overcome the resistance to appraisal systems?
Many people have a negative view of the whole process of evaluating performance. This feeling appears related to fear of low ratings, if an appraisal system is instituted and survives, and also to a strong belief in the seniority principle (30). Evidence shows that less effective managers tend to be the ones most opposed to performance appraisal (14). Furthermore, many managers, in addition to rank-and-file employees, strongly believe seniority is the best guide for making personnel decisions.

As a result of these factors, and perhaps others, any management appraisal system will encounter some resistance. This resistance may block the initiation of a program, but it is particularly likely to manifest itself once a program is instituted and there is something to shoot at. Resistance will vary, depending on the values predominant in the company, and it may relate rather specifically to certain kinds of approaches.

Obviously, the greater the resistance the more those who are instituting the program will have to move toward those who will do the rating and the more the management group as a whole will have to be involved in developing the system. These approaches demonstrate the willingness of those who will be using the data to do part of the work to ensure a successful program. The alternative procedure involves inducing the raters to come to the users of the data. This procedure is entirely satisfactory where acceptance is high, but, where it is not, merely mailing out forms along with directives and follow-up memoranda will only increase negative feeling. Another successful approach is to have large numbers of managers participate in the construction of the system itself (2). This can be done if managers are used both as a source for developing items and as judges of proposals (38).

The need for special procedures to help overcome resistance will vary, depending on the nature of the program. Many managers tend to resist feeding back appraisal results, for instance. Thus, acceptance problems may be anticipated when this is required. Many managers strongly dislike peer and subordinate ratings (2). Thus, the use of a three-rating system along the lines noted previously may require special attention. Forced choice and forced distribution procedures are known to be sources of resistance and, accordingly, require more than the usual efforts to develop favorable attitudes.

How can potential be evaluated and what factors predict potential?
To determine a method for evaluating potential and the characteristics that indicate potential, research must show that some measure did in fact predict success in

management over a considerable period of time after the original measurement. The following discussion is restricted entirely to studies of this kind. Predictions made by managers are considered first, then predictions by psychologists.

1. Managerial prediction

The difficulty with using ratings of potential for advancement is that they are available and known, and quite obviously can influence a man's career entirely apart from his actual competence. Even with this bias included, results with these potential ratings by superiors are not impressive. Clearly, a great many individuals identified in this manner as having high potential do not advance very far (11). In one study, departments within a single company varied considerably in the extent to which potential ratings predicted even the first promotion after appraisal (29). Results like these have led some writers to conclude that the evaluation of potential is beyond the scope of the usual management appraisal system and that the matter should be left to specialists (35). Many ratings of potential are believed to be merely the inverse of the manager's age and thus convey little new information.

The armed forces have carried out most of the research on the predictive value of ratings by superiors, usually with relatively short intervals between the initial predictions and the subsequent measurement of success (18). The correlations obtained are not impressive. These findings contrast sharply with those for peer ratings, which offer much better predictions of potential. Why this difference exists between superior and peer predictions is a matter of conjecture at the present time.

2. Psychological prediction

A considerable amount of predictive research has used psychological techniques. Some studies utilize separate measures like psychological tests or biographical inventories; others use the over-all evaluations of psychologists derived from a combination of sources, including interviews, observation of behavior, and tests. In general, tests of intelligence and mental abilities do seem to predict success. However, in many highly selected managerial groups, intelligence tests are not very helpful in identifying potential, because all the managers score at such a high level. At the foreman level, intelligence tests are more effective as indicators of subsequent performance (18).

Psychological tests in the personality area have produced uneven results when used individually. In a number of cases, they have not proved useful (18), yet exceptions do exist. In general, measures of such characteristics as dominance, self-confidence, and persuasiveness are most useful (10).

Consistently positive results have been obtained with the Miner Sentence Completion Scale in a series of predictive studies (27). This measure was designed specifically for predicting success in management. Although the test discriminates most effectively at the graduate level, it can identify individuals with managerial potential as early as the third year of college (28).

A considerable amount of research has used biographical inventories containing questions similar to those found in application blanks. This research has produced sufficiently positive results to recommend the approach (10, 18). However, companies tend to keep the specific results of these studies secret, so that managerial candidates do not learn the "right" answers. Thus, studies aimed at establishing those factors that are predictive in a given company must be carried out individually. Nonetheless, published research does show that a prior pattern of success is likely to be predictive of subsequent success.

Results with comprehensive evaluations by psychologists using a variety of source data are also encouraging, despite significant failures. Studies using this approach have predicted success over a period as long as seven years (1, 8).

A related approach, even more comprehensive in that managers are studied over a period of days with a whole host of techniques, is the assessment center. AT&T has conducted much of the research with this technique under the title of "The Management Progress Study." Staff assessments of potential for advancement derived from these assessment situations have consistently proved predictive of promotion and salary progress over periods up to eight years (6). These assessments were not made available to those making promotion and compensation decisons. Research indicates that those who have moved up most rapidly are more intelligent and more active, control their feelings more, are more nonconforming, exhibit a greater work orientation (6), are more independent, desire more leadership, and have stronger achievement motivation (13). Although this type of approach is extremely expensive relative to the usual psychological evaluation (15), it appears to yield even higher correlations with later success in management jobs.

There is reason to believe that any psychological approach is likely to be effective only to the extent it is attuned to the value and reward structures of the particular organization (29). Thus, the development of psychological predictors to identify potential within a given company must involve a complex interaction between analysis of the individual and analysis of the organization. Such an interaction involving both individual assessment and social psychological research seems to provide the best guide for management appraisal systems of the future.

REFERENCES

1. Albrecht, P. A., Glaser, E. M., and Marks, J. Validation of a multiple-assessment procedure for managerial personnel. *Journal of Applied Psychology*, 1964, 48, 351-60.
2. Barrett, R. S. *Performance rating.* Chicago: Science Research Associates, 1966.
3. Barrett, R. S., Taylor, E. K., Parker, J.

W., and Martins, L. Rating scale content. I: Scale information and supervisory ratings. *Personnel Psychology,* 1958, 11, 333-46.

4. Bayroff, A. G., Haggerty, H. R., and Rundquist, E. A. Validity of ratings as related to rating techniques and conditions. *Personnel Psychology*, 1954, 7, 93-113.

5. Bittner, R. Developing an industrial merit rating procedure. *Personnel Psychology*, 1948, 1, 403-32.

6. Bray, D. W., and Grant, D. L. The assessment center in the measurement of potential for business management. *Psychological Monographs*, 1966, 80, 1-27.

7. Brooks, W. W., An analysis and evaluation of the officer performance appraisal system in the United States Army. M.S. thesis, George Washington University, 1966.

8. Dicken, C. F., and Black, J. D. Predictive validity of psychometric evaluations of supervisors. *Journal of Applied Psychology*, 1965, 49, 34-47.

9. Druit, C. A. An analysis of military officer evaluation systems using principles presently advanced by authorities in this field. M.A. thesis, Ohio State University, 1964.

10. Dunnette, M. D., Lawler, E. E., Campbell, J. P., and Weick, K. E. Identification and enhancement of managerial effectiveness. Richardson Foundation Survey Report, 1966.

11. Ferguson, L. L. Better management of managers' careers. *Harvard Business Review*, 1966, 44, 139-52.

12. French, J. R. P., Kay, E., and Meyer, H. H. Participation and the appraisal system. *Human Relations*, 1966, 19, 3-20.

13. Grant, D. L., Katkovsky, W., and Bray, D. W. Contributions of projective techniques to assessment of managerial potential. *Journal of Applied Psychology*, 1967, 41, 226-32.

14. Gruenfeld, L. W., and Weissenberg, P. Supervisory characteristics and attitudes toward performance appraisals. *Personnel Psychology*, 1966, 19, 143-51.

15. Hardesty, D. L., and Jones, W. S. Characteristics of judged high-potential

management personnel—the operations of an industrial assessment center. *Personnel Psychology*, 1968, 21, 85-98.

16. Kay, E., Meyer, H. H., and French J. R. P. Effects of threat in a performance appraisal interview. *Journal of Applied Psychology*, 1865, 49, 311-17.

17. Klores, M. S. Rater bias in forced-distribution performance ratings. *Personnel Psychology*, 1966, 19, 411-21.

18. Korman, A. K. The prediction of managerial performance: A review. *Personnel Psychology*, 1968, 21, 259-322.

19. Lawler, E. E. The multitrait-multirater approach to measuring managerial job performance. *Journal of Applied Psychology*, 1967, 51, 369-81.

20. Levine, J., and Butler, J. Lecture vs. group decision in changing behavior. *Journal of Applied Psychology*, 1952, 36, 29-33.

21. Lopez, F. M. Evaluating employee performance. Chicago: Public Personnel Association, 1968.

22. Mendleson, J. L. Manager goal setting: An exploration into its meaning and measurement, D.B.A. thesis, Michigan State University, 1967.

23. Meyer, H. H., and Walker, W. B. A study of factors relating to the effectiveness of a performance appraisal program. *Personnel Psychology*, 1961, 14, 291-98.

24. Meyer, H. H., Kay, E., and French, J. R. P. Split roles in performance appraisal. *Harvard Business Review*, 1965, 43, 123-29.

25. Michael, J. M. Problem situations in performance counselling. *Personnel*, 1965, 42, 16-22.

26. Miner, J. B. Personality and ability factors in sales performance. *Journal of Applied Psychology*, 1962, 46, 6-13.

27. Miner, J. B. *Studies in management education*. New York: Springer Pub. Co., 1965.

28. Miner, J. B. The early identification of managerial talent. *Personnel and Guidance Journal*, 1968, 46, 586-91.

29. Miner, J. B. Bridging the gulf in organizational performance. *Harvard Business Review*, 1968, 46, 102-10.

30. Miner, J. B. *Personnel and industrial relations—a managerial approach*. New York: Macmillan, 1969.

31. Moon, C. G., and Hariton, T. Evaluating an appraisal and feedback training program. *Personnel,* 1958, *35,* 36-41.

32. Parker, J. W., Taylor, E. K., Barrett, R. S., and Martens, L. Rating scale content: III. Relationships between supervisory and self-ratings. *Personnel Psychology,* 1959, *12,* 49-63.

33. Patton, A. Executive motivation: How it is changing. *Management Review,* 1968, *57,* 4-20.

34. Prien, E. P., and Liske, R. E. Assessments of higher level personnel: III. Rating criteria: A comparative analysis of supervisor ratings and incumbent self-ratings of job performance. *Personnel Psychology,* 1962, *15,* 187-94.

35. Richards, K. E. A new concept of performance appraisal. *Journal of Business,* 1959, *32,* 229-43.

36. Roadman, H. E. An industrial use of peer ratings. *Journal of Applied Psychology,* 1964, *48,* 211-14.

37. Rowland, V. K. Management inventory and development. *Personnel,* 1951, *28,* 12-22.

38. Smith, P. C., and Kendall, L. M. Retranslation of expectations: An approach to the construction of unambiguous anchors for rating scales. *Journal of Applied Psychology,* 1963, *47,* 149-55.

39. Springer, D. Ratings of candidates for promotion by co-workers and supervisors. *Journal of Applied Psychology,* 1953, *37,* 347-51.

40. Stockford, L., and Bissell, H. W. Factors involved in establishing a merit-rating scale. *Personnel,* 1949, *26,* 94-116.

41. Tiffin, J., and McCormick, E. J. *Industrial psychology.* 5th ed. Englewood Cliffs, N.J.: Prentice-Hall, 1965.

42. Whisler, T. L., and Harper, S. F. *Performance appraisal.* New York: Holt, Rinehart & Winston, 1962.

29

Human Resource Accounting in Industry

R. LEE BRUMMET, ERIC FLAMHOLTZ, and WILLIAM C. PYLE

INVESTMENTS IN THE BUSINESS ENTERPRISE

Investments are expenditures made for the purpose of providing future benefits beyond the current accounting period. If a firm purchases a new plant with an expected useful life of fifty years, it is treated as an investment on the corporate balance sheet, and is depreciated over its useful life. If the structure should be destroyed or become obsolete, it would lose its service potential and be written off the books as a loss that would be reflected as an offset against earnings on the company's statement of income.

Firms also make investment in *human* assets. Costs are incurred in recruiting, hiring, training, and developing people as individual employees and as members of viable interacting organizational groups. Furthermore, investments are made in building favorable relationships with *external* human resources such as customers, suppliers, and creditors. Although such expenditures are made to develop future service potential, conventional accounting practice assigns such costs to the "expense" classification,

which, by definition, assumes that they have no value to the firm beyond the current accounting year.

For this reason human assets do not normally appear on corporate balance sheets, nor are changes in these assets reflected on statements of corporate income. Thus, conventional accounting statements may conceal significant changes in the condition of the firm's unrecognized human assets. In fact, *favorable* performance may be reported when human resources are actually being liquidated.[1] If people are treated abusively in an effort to generate more production, short-term profits may be derived through liquidation of the firm's organizational assets. If product quality is reduced, immediate gains may be made at the expense of customer-loyalty assets.

A need exists, therefore, to develop an organizational accounting or information system that will reflect the current condition of and changes in the firm's human assets. Some accountants have recognized such a need, but measurement difficulties pose

1. Rensis Likert, *The human organization: Its management and value*. New York: McGraw-Hill, 1967, pp. 101-15.

Reprinted from *Personnel Administration*, 1969 (July-August), 34-46, by permission of the International Personnel Management Association.

problems for them. As early as 1922, William A. Paton observed:

> In the business enterprise, a well-organized and loyal personnel may be a much more important "asset" than a stock of merchandise . . . . At present there seems to be no way of measuring such factors in terms of the dollar; hence, they cannot be recognized as specific economic assets. But let us, accordingly, admit the serious limitations of the conventional balance sheet as a statement of financial condition.[2]

Why have industry and the accounting profession steadfastly neglected accounting for human resources? The answer may be found, partly, in the perpetuation of accounting practices which trace their origins to an early period in our industrial history when human resource investments were relatively low. In more recent years, however, those occupational classifications exhibiting the highest rates of growth, such as managerial and technical groupings, are those that require the greatest investment in human resources.[3] In addition, rising organizational complexity has created new demands for developing more sophisticated interaction capabilities and skills within industry.[4] These and other factors, coupled with persistent shortages in highly skilled occupational groupings, increase the need for a data-based scientific approach to the management of human resources.

RESOURCE MANAGEMENT AND INFORMATION NEEDS

Although oversimplified, management may be viewed as a process of *acquisition and development, maintenance,* and *utilization* of a "resource mix" to achieve organiza-

2. W. A. Paton, *Accounting theory*. New York: Ronald Press, 1922, pp. 486-87.
3. U.S. Bureau of the Census, *Historical statistics of the United States: Colonial times to 1957,* Washington, D.C., 1960, pp. 74-75; 202-14.
4. Likert, *op. cit.,* pp. 156-60.

tional objectives, as suggested in Figure 29-1. Accounting and information systems contribute to this process by identifying, measuring, and communicating economic information to permit informed judgments and decisions in the management of the resource mix. Management needs information regarding: (1) resource acquisition and development, (2) resource maintenance or condition, and (3) resource utilization.

Resource acquisition and development information

Organizations acquire a wide variety of resources to achieve their purposes. Investments are undertaken in those resources that offer the greatest potential returns to the enterprise given an acceptable degree of risk. Calculation of resource acquisition and development costs, therefore, is necessary not only for investment planning but also for determining differential returns that accrue to those investments. The *resource acquisition and development information needs* reflect themselves along two dimensions: (1) the need for measurement of *outlay costs* when assets are actually acquired, and (2) the need for estimating the *replacement cost* of these investments in the event that they should expire.

Resource maintenance or condition information

Investments are undertaken in resources with the objective of creating new capabilities, levels of competency, types of behavior, forms of organization, and other conditions which will facilitate achieving organizational objectives. An information need exists, therefore, to ascertain the degree to which investments in resources actually produce and sustain the desired new capabilities, levels of competency, types of behavior, and forms or organization.

Resource utilization information

Once new capabilities, levels of competency, and other "system states" are achieved, *resource utilization information* needs become more salient. Management should

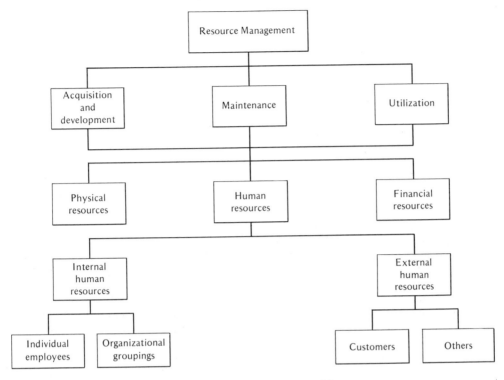

Fig. 29-1. The Process of Resource Management

know the degree to which changes in resource conditions or "system states" are translated into organizational performance. The answer to this question is reflected in the rate of return on the investments which created the new "system state" or resource condition.

Conventional Accounting and Informational Needs

Conventional accounting or information systems answer these three basic information needs for *non-human resources*. Measurement of investment in plant and equipment fulfills the "acquisition information need." Over time, these assets are depreciated, and new investments are recorded. The current "book values" of such investments reflect, at least in theory, the "resource condition" of the organization's physical assets. Finally, "utilization information needs" are supplied in the form of return on investment calculations.

Unfortunately, conventional accounting systems do not answer these three basic information needs for human assets. The objective of our research effort, therefore, is to develop a body of human resource accounting theory and techniques which will, at least in part, alleviate these information deficiencies.

HUMAN RESOURCE ACCOUNTING-MODEL

The development of human resource accounting in the business enterprise derives from the pioneering work of Rensis Likert and his colleagues at the University of Michigan's Institute for Social Research. For more than two decades, their research studies have revealed that relationships exist between certain variable constructs and organizational performance. *"Causal variables,"* such as organizational structure and patterns of management behavior have been shown to affect *"intervening variables"* such as employee loyalties, attitudes, perceptions, and motivations, which in turn have been shown to affect *"end-result variables"* such as productivity, costs, and earnings.[5] Furthermore, research by Likert and Seashore indicates that time lags of two years or more often exist between changes in the "causal variables" and resultant changes in the "end-result variables."[6]

As seen in Figure 29-2, Likert's three variable models have been adopted into a human resource accounting model with the addition of two variable constructs— *"Investment variables"* and *"return on investment variables."* Why have these new variable classifications been added? All business firms wish to improve organizational performance. In doing so, however, a more crucial question is, *how much* will performance be improved and *what will it cost.* When a firm invests in new capital equipment, the costs of various alternatives are estimated for each along with projected rates of return. For example, one piece of equipment may cost $75,000 and have an estimated rate of return of 20 per cent, while another may cost $100,000 with a return estimate of 15 per cent.

An important objective of our research is to extend capital budgeting concepts to the firm's human resources. If the company invests $50,000 in a new training program, what is the anticipated return? If the firm invests $75,000 in an organizational develop-

5. Ibid.
6. Likert, R., and Seashore, S., Making cost control work. *Harvard Business Review*, November-December 1963, pp. 96-108.

ment program, what return will accrue to that investment?

An important objective of our research is to extend capital-budgeting concepts to the firm's human resources. If the company invests $50,000 in a new training program, what is the anticipated return? If the firm invests $75,000 in an organizational development program, what return will accrue to that investment?

HUMAN RESOURCE ACCOUNTING VARIABLES AND ORGANIZATIONAL INFORMATION NEEDS

Investment Variables

Investments in both non-human assets are recorded in dollar units and are measured to fulfill the *resource acquisition and development information* needs of management through indentification of investment *outlay costs* and *replacement costs.* Conventional accounting practice now identifies *non-human* resource investments, at least on an outlay cost basis. In January 1968 a human-resource accounting system was operationalized at the R. G. Barry Corporation to measure "individual employee" investments. Development work is now in progress to provide a system for identifying "organizational investments."

Causal variables

Causal variables (see Figure 29-2) are independent variables that management may alter to affect the course of developments within the organization. These variables include the type and condition of plant and equipment, and the type and level of employee competency, managerial behavior, organizational structure, and related factors. As suggested by the arrows in Figure 29-2, the state of the "individual employee causal variables" is more likely to *directly* affect the "end-result variables" (e.g., productivity, costs, and product quality) than the "organizational causal variables," whose

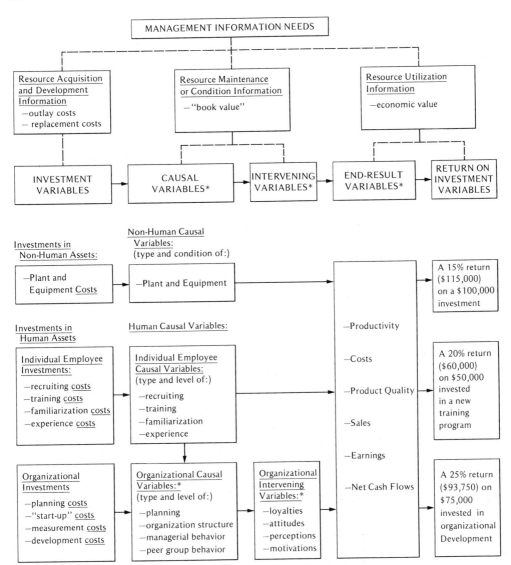

*A more complete listing of variables is found in R. Likert, *The Human Organization: Its Management and Value, Appendix III.*

Fig. 29-2. A Human Resource Accounting Model (with examples of variables)

effects tend to pass through a series of "intervening variables," which will be discussed shortly.

Causal variables are measured to supply the "resource maintenance or condition information" needs of management. Both dollar and socio-psychological based measurements may be employed to reflect the condition of the causal variables. Conventional accounting practice now provides "non-human causal variable" data in the form of asset book values which, at least in theory, reflect the current state of those assets. A similar system for measuring "individual employee causal variables" has been implemented at the R. G. Barry Corporation. Questionnaire survey techniques developed by the Institute for Social Research are being employed to measure "organizational causal variables."

Intervening variables

As stated above, the effect of "organizational causal variables" may not be directly reflected in the "end-result variables." Time lags of two years or more have been observed between changes in these "causal variables" and resultant changes in the "end-result variables." The effects of changes in "organizational causal variables" have been traced through a series of *intervening variables,* which include employee loyalties, attitudes, perceptions, and motivations.

"Intervening variables" are not measured in dollar units but in terms of responses to socio-pyschological questionnaire items along a 1-to-5 point scale. Measurements of these "intervening variables" are directed toward the "resource maintenance or condition information" needs of the organization. Conventional accounting systems do not measure "intervening variables."

End-result variables and Return on Investment variables

End-result variables are dependent variables that reflect the achievements of the organization. The particular "end-result variables" for a given enterprise are a function of performance objectives that have been defined by that organization. These may include the level of productivity, costs, product quality, sales, earnings, net cash flows, employee health and satisfaction, and related factors.

"End-result variables" are normally measured in economic based units, but they may also be reflected in socio-psychological terms, as in the case of employee satisfaction. Changes in "end-result variables" may be associated with variations in "investment," "causal," and "intervening" variables through multiple correlation analyses of data collected in each of the variable classifications over an extended period of time. In this fashion, "end-result variables" may be expressed in the form of *"return on investment variables"* where a particular change in the "end-result variables" can be significantly associated with a particular "investment variable" change. For example, if $75,000 were invested in an organizational development program, and a $93,750 change in predetermined "end-result variables" was observed, a return of 25 per cent would be realized on the investment. Such analyses may be employed to improve the allocation of organizational resources by indicating which investment patterns should be increased, reduced, or maintained at their current level.

Ultimately it may be possible to place a current valuation on the firm's human resources through a process of discounting estimates of future "end-result variables," using time lags and relations that have been observed among the variable classifications. The results of this valuation may be cross-checked with the patterns of unexpired costs that are recorded in the human asset accounts.

HUMAN RESOURCE ACCOUNTING IMPLEMENTATION OBJECTIVES

The ultimate objective of the research is to develop an integrated accounting function which fulfills basic information needs with respect to physical, financial, and human resources both internal and external to the organization. As an intermediate objective we are concentrating on the development of an *internal human resource* accounting capability. This research effort divides itself into three functions:

1. development of a human-resource

accounting system according to the model presented above;

2. *development of managerial applications of human-resource accounting which fulfill basic organizational information needs;*

3. *analysis of the behavioral impact of human-resource accounting on people.*

These objectives are being pursued in a five-year inter-company research program that has been initiated by the University of Michigan's Institute for Social Research and Graduate School of Business Administration in cooperation with participating corporations.[7]

Since October 1966, the University of Michigan has been engaged, along with the management of the R. G. Barry Corporation, in development of what is believed to be the first human resource accounting system. The Barry Corporation's 1,250 employees manufacture a variety of personal comfort items including foam-cushioned slippers, chair pads, robes, and other leisure wear, and marketed in department stores and other retail outlets under brand names such as Angel Treds, Dearfoams, Kush-ons, and Gustave. The corporate headquarters and four production facilities are in Columbus, Ohio. Several other plants, warehouses, and sales offices are located across the country. The firm has expanded from a sales volume of about $5 ½ million in 1962 to more than $16 million in 1967.

The first phase of a human resource accounting system became operational at the R. G. Barry Corporation during January 1968. This system measures investments undertaken in the firm's some 96 members of management, on both *outlay cost* and *replacement cost* bases. An account structure applicable to organizational investments

7. This research will be described in greater depth in a monograph now being prepared by the authors, and planned for publication in 1969 by the Bureau of Business Research of the Graduate School of Business Administration, The University of Michigan.

is now being developed. In the future the Barry Corporation plans to extend human-resource accounting to other occupational classifications in the firm and eventually to its customer resources. A model of an outlay-cost measurement system is presented in Figure 29-3.

MEASUREMENT OF INVESTMENT VARIABLES AND CAUSAL VARIABLES

An outlay-cost measurement system

Investments in human resources may be measured in terms of outlay costs. *Outlay costs* are sacrifices incurred by the firm in the form of out-of-pocket expenditures associated with a particular human-resource investment. These are measured in terms of *non-salary* and *salary* costs. Examples of the former include travel costs in support of recruiting or training, and tuition charges for management development programs. The latter would include employee salary allocations during an investment period. If an executive attends a two-week management seminar, his salary for this time period should be viewed as part of the investment, in addition to the tuition and travel costs. If during the first year of tenure with a firm, 30 per cent of a new manager's time is devoted to familiarization with company policy, precedents, organization structure, interaction patterns, and the like, 30 per cent of his salary should be recorded as an outlay cost associated with the familiarization investment.

At the R. G. Barry Corporation, instruments have been designed to measure investments undertaken in *individual managers* for each of the functional accounts indicated in Figure 29-3. To qualify as assets, specific expenditures must meet the test of offering service potential beyond the current accounting period in relation to long term written corporate objectives. Charges to the functional accounts are also entered in "individualized accounts" for each man-

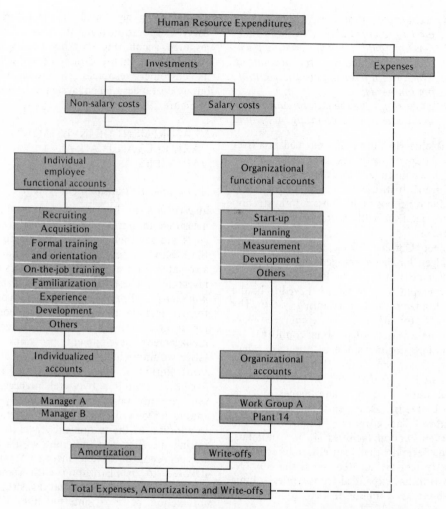

Fig. 29-3. Model of an Outlay Cost Measurement System

ager. With a few modifications, the individual manager account structure will also be applied to other occupational groupings within the firm. However, it is not contemplated that "individualized accounts" will be developed for factory and clerical personnel.

Procedures have also been designed to record investment expirations. Asset accounts are amortized on two bases: (1) *maximum life* and (2) *expected life*. Functional investments are separately identified in each manager's account and are

amortized according to the *maximum life* of each investment type. For example, recruiting and acquisition costs provide benefits to the firm so long as an employee remains with the organization. The *maximum life* of this investment would be the normal retirement age less the employee's age when hired. If *maximum life* were relied on exclusively for amortization, asset accounts would be overstated since employees frequently leave the firm prior to the "normal" retirement age. To assure a more realistic statement of assets, maximum life amortization periods are adjusted to expected life by application of weighted probabilities which reflect a particular individual's likelihood of remaining until normal retirement based upon his age, tenure, organizational level, marital status, job satisfaction, and related factors. *Expected life* periods are employed in the amortization of the functional accounts.

The question may be raised why amortization is computed on *two* bases and not just "expected life." The reason is that "maximum life" provides a relatively uniform standard against which turnover losses may be viewed. Moreover, "expected life" may, to some degree, be influenced by the organization through variation of such factors as job satisfaction.[8] For this reason, a firm should not adhere too rigidly to a particular expected life standard. In addition, amortization of "individualized accounts" on a maximum life basis offers certain psychological benefits. If an individual's account is amortized solely on *expected life,* his account will approach a zero balance as his tenure nears the end of the "expected life" period when many years of useful service may yet remain. For this reason "individualized accounts" are amortized on a *maximum life* basis while the "functional accounts" identifying grouped managerial investments are amortized on an *expected life* basis. The latter basis is reflected in the investment balances shown on the firm's balance sheet and in the adjustment to income shown on the income statement.

Specific measurement instruments have been designed to record human asset losses resulting from turnover, obsolescence, and health deteriorations. Turnover is immediately identifiable; however, obsolescence is much more elusive. For this reason individual employee asset accounts are reviewed quarterly for obsolescence by each supervisor. Review also occurs when an employee is transferred to a new position. Accounts are also adjusted for known health deteriorations in proportion to the seriousness of the impairment as reflected in actuarial data.

As suggested in Figure 29-3, an outlay-cost measurement system designed to record *organizational investments* is now being developed at the R. G. Barry Corporation. Investments are undertaken in human resources *over and above* those made in *individual employees as individuals.* Organizational "start-up" costs are reflected in heavy individual employee investments and in production below standard during the initial period when the organization is building and developing group interaction patterns for the first time. Additional investments are also made in the form of organizational planning. Furthermore, periodic measurement of organizational causal and intervening variables are in themselves investments in the organization when they lead to development activities which improve the functioning of the enterprise as an interacting system. Finally, investments are undertaken in the organization which cannot be readily traced to individual employees. A portion of the operating costs of the personnel department, company library, health service, safety department, and similar departments may be traced to activities which offer long term benefits to the organization.

Charges made to the "organizational functional accounts" will also be allocated to appropriate entities such as work groups, plants, divisions, or the enterprise as a whole. In addition, a capability is being developed to reflect expirations which occur in these accounts. Many "organizational investments" differ *in kind* from "individual employee investments" which lose their usefulness to the firm when a particular individual leaves the firm. For example, benefits could be derived indefinitely from costs incurred in molding the organization

8. Where relationships between the level of job satisfaction and expected tenure can be identified, turnover losses may be calculated in dollar terms and predicted for varying levels of job satisfaction, as a function of measured changes in causal and intervening variables.

into a system of effective interacting groups despite a moderate level of individual employee turnover within the system. This suggests the possibility that some organizational investments may be non-depreciable.

This would not, however, preclude the possibility of expiration. If, for example, an enterprise invests $50,000 in an organizational development program which succeeds in improving employee attitudes and motivations by a measurable amount, subsequent deterioration in those attitudes and motivations could justify a write-off of the original investment.

A replacement-cost measurement system

The outlay cost system described above is designed to record human resource investments, obsolescence, and losses as they are actually incurred. These data, however, only partially fulfill the "resource acquisition information" needs of the organization. For planning purposes, the *positional replacement cost* of human resources becomes more salient. Positional replacement costs are the outlay costs (recruiting, training, etc.,) which would be incurred if an incumbent should leave his position. The human resource accounting system which has been installed at the R. G. Barry Corporation has the capability of supplying average positional replacement cost data for each manager. These positional replacement cost data reflect annual adjustments for price level changes. The system also records "compositional" investment changes since some investments undertaken in the past will not be repeated and, conversely, others not made in the past will be undertaken in the future. For these and other reasons, positional replacement cost may be less than, equal to, or greater than historical outlay cost.

Appropriate measurement units

As noted above, "investment variables" are measured exclusively in dollar units. How-

ever, "causal variables" may be measured in either dollar or socio-psychologically based units. For example, the current condition of the firm's plant and equipment (a "causal variable") should be reflected in its current book value, although other indicators may be employed. Similarly, the *current condition* of the company's "individual employee investments" (a "causal variable") should be reflected in the book values recorded in the functional asset accounts discussed above. However, other indicators are being developed as cross-checks. Socio-psychological survey questions are being derived to measure employee perceptions of the current condition of "individual employee causal variables" such as the quality of recruiting and training. Trends in these data will be checked against trends in the individual employee asset account balances. Socio-psychological data may suggest more realistic amortization procedures for "individual employee investments." The current condition of "organizational causal variables" may also be reflected in the current book value of "organizational investments." However, socio-psychological survey instruments may prove more reliable here in view of the fact that managerial behavior (a "causal variable") may be altered independently of cost outlays.

Measurement of other variables

"Intervening variable" measurements have been undertaken at the R. G. Barry Corporation and additional surveys are planned. However, an accumulation of several years' data will be required before meaningful "return on investment variables" may be calculated.

MANAGERIAL APPLICATIONS OF HUMAN RESOURCE ACCOUNTING

Human resource accounting system applications should be directed toward fulfilling the three basic organizational information

Fig. 29-4. Balance Sheets

	Dec. 31, 1966	Dec. 31, 1967
ASSETS		
Current Assets (cash, etc.)	$1,000,000	$1,500,000
Plant and Equipment	8,000,000	8,000,000
Investment in Individual Employees (recruiting, training, development, etc.)	750,000	850,000
Organizational Investments (start-up, planning, development, etc.)	900,000	700,000
TOTAL ASSETS	$10,650,000	$11,050,000
EQUITIES		
Liabilities	$2,000,000	$2,000,000
Owner's Equity:		
Stock	6,000,000	6,000,000
Retained Earnings (including investment in human resources)	2,650,000	3,050,000
TOTAL EQUITIES	$10,650,000	$11,050,000

INCOME STATEMENT

Year Ending December 31, 1967

Sales		$2,000,000
Expenses		1,500,000
Net Income		$ 500,000
Adjustment for change in investment in human resources		
—Individual employee adjustment	+$100,000	
—Organizational adjustment	−$200,000	−100,000
Adjusted Net Income		$ 400,000

needs: (1) resource acquisition and development information; (2) resource maintenance or condition information; and (3) resource utilization information. Inasmuch as the human resource accounting system at the R. G. Barry Corporation is in an early stage of development, its potential applications can only be stated in provisional terms at this time.

It is contemplated that the system will generate two types of data: (1) information integrated with conventional accounting statements, and (2) information presented independently of these statements.

Data integrated with conventional statements

One of the first reports generated by the system is a *balance sheet* indicating the firm's investment in human resources. The corporate *income statement* will also be affected to the degree that there is a net change in the firm's investment in human resources during the reporting period. This situation is exemplified in Figure 29-4. The two balance sheets indicate that a hypothetical company experienced a *net increase* in its investment in *individual employees* during the period. This change, taken by itself, would result in a positive adjustment to the firm's net income[9] of $100,000. However, this firm also experienced a *net decline* in its organizational investments during the period. (This could result, for example, from a plant's being closed in one location and its operations' being moved to another state.) This change, taken by itself, would result in a negative net income adjustment of $200,000. When the two changes are taken together, a negative adjustment of $100,000 is reflected in the firm's net income.

Preliminary data generated by the human-resource accounting system at the R. G. Barry Corporation indicate that the replacement investment of their some 96 managers is approximately $1,000,000, while the current "book value" is about $600,000. The firm invests around $3,000 in a first-line supervisor and upwards of $30,000 in top management personnel.

Other human resource accounting reports

A wide variety of additional reports may be generated by a human-resource accounting system. Periodic comparative data for different work groups, plants, and divisions could contrast human resource investment changes during reporting periods. Turnover losses may also be quantified and analyzed according to such factors as employee job satisfaction, age, occupation, tenure and the like. Special purpose reports can be prepared to evaluate various organizational alternatives which require investments in human resources. To increase production capacity, for example, should a firm expand its existing plant or construct a new facility? For each alternative these reports could indicate projected new investments, write-offs, and the effect on net cash flows. Once a particular alternative is chosen, actual investment, write-offs and cash flows may be contrasted against projections. As patterns

of return on investments in human resources become apparent, the firm will learn which investment types should be increased, reduced, or maintained at their current level.

THE BEHAVIORAL IMPACT OF HUMAN RESOURCE ACCOUNTING

The ultimate success of any accounting system is determined by its impact on the behavior of people. Where the goals of employees and the organization are reasonably consistent, data may be employed as a problem solving tool to achieve organizational objectives. However, the social science literature is replete with evidence of the distortions which may be introduced into an information system when individual and organizational goals are not congruent.[10] For this reason, an integral part of human resource accounting research will focus on determining the behavioral impact of an operational human resource accounting system on employees. Socio-psychological survey instruments supplemented by personal interviews will be employed to assess the impact. These data will, in turn, be utilized to design organizational development activities which will facilitate installation and sustained operation of the human resource accounting system.

CONCLUSIONS

Human resource accounting is now in an early stage, and a host of problems remain to be resolved before a fully developed system can become operational. The initial results are encouraging, however, as many beneficial results may be derived prior to full-scale operation. Investments in human resources may be determined at a relatively early stage. The techniques developed to measure these assets may be employed also in extended

9. The net income that would be indicated without a human resource accounting system.

10. Argyris, C., Human problems with budgets, *Harvard Business Review*, January-February 1953, 97-110; Whyte, W. F., *Money and motivation*, New York: Harper & Row, 1955.

organizational and manpower planning that underlie and sustain corporate growth. Even before return on investment data become available, measurement of trends and rates of change in "causal" and "intervening" variable data may suggest new behaviors and investment routes which will improve organizational effectiveness.

30

Management by Objectives

HENRY L. TOSI AND STEPHEN CARROLL

Since Drucker (1954) and McGregor (1960) made statements about management by objectives, organizations of all types have made increasing use of this method. While most of the early discussions of MBO emphasized its use as a tool for the development of more objective criteria for performance evaluation, it has become apparent that subordinate participation in goal setting has resulted in greater levels of ego involvement, increased motivation, and increased planning behavior, all of which have an effect upon performance.

These advantages stemmed from the process of setting goals and using them, in place of personality traits and characteristics for evaluation of performance. Management by objectives has been described as a general process in which "The superior and the subordinate manager of an organization jointly define its common goals, define each individual's major areas of responsibility in terms of the results expected of him and use these measures as guides for operating the unit and assessing the contribution of each of its members" (Odiorne, 1965).

The logic of MBO is, indeed, attractive.

There is an intrinsic desirability to a method that motivates performance and enhances measurement while at the same time increases the participation and involvement of subordinates.

THE ELEMENTS OF MBO

There are three basic aspects of MBO which will affect its success: (1) goals and goal setting, (2) participation and involvement of subordinates, (3) feedback and performance evaluation.

Goals and goal setting. A number of studies[1] have clearly demonstrated that when an individual or group has a specific goal, there is higher performance than when the goals are general, or have not been set. Generally, high performance can be associated with higher individual or group goals. A number of

---

1. See for instance J. F. Bryan, and E. A. Locke, Goal setting as a means of increasing motivation, *Journal of Applied Psychology*, 1967, 51, 274-77; E. A. Locke, "Motivational effects of knowledge of results: Knowledge or Goal Setting?" *Journal of Applied Psychology*, 1967, 51, 324-29.

Reprinted from *Personnel Administration*, 1970 (July-August), 44-48, by permission of the International Personnel Management Association.

studies[2] also suggest that performance improvement occurs when an individual is successful in achieving past goals. When there is previous goal success, the individual is more likely to set higher goals in future periods, and he is more likely to attain them.

Participation. There have been a number of diverse findings about the relationship of participation in decision-making and productivity. These apparently contradictory findings have been resolved by concluding that if the subordinate perceives the participation to be legitimate, it will have positive effects on productivity. In addition, participation does seem to have an effect on the degree of acceptance of decisions reached mutually. There is also evidence[3] that involvement and participation are correlated positively with the level of job satisfaction.

Feedback. Both laboratory and field research have demonstrated that relatively clear, unambiguous feedback increases problem solving capacities of groups and improves the performance of individuals.[4] Positive attitudes, increased confidence in decisions, and greater certainties of superior's expectations were found to be related

to communications which clarified roles and role expectancies with more and better information.

Feedback, in the form of formal appraisal in a work setting, when based on relatively objective performance standards, tends to be related to a more positive orientation by subordinates of the amount of supervision their boss exercises. Positive actions are more likely to be taken by subordinates when feedback is viewed as supportive and is objectively based.

MBO AND EMPLOYEE MOTIVATION

Studies of the MBO process in organizations strongly suggest that changes in performance and attitude, which seem positive and desirable, appear to be associated with how it is formally implemented. The implementation of MBO alters the expectations of organization members about performance appraisal and evaluation. These expectations, if not met, may affect the degree of acceptance of the MBO approach. (See Raia, 1965; Tosi and Carroll, 1968.)

This problem may be resolved, to some degree, through proper setting of objectives and use of the MBO process. We believe that certain minimal conditions must prevail if MBO is to have its motivational effect:

Goal clarity and relevance. Few managers would quarrel with the notion that organizational goals should be made known to the members. Individual perceptions of the goal are important here. Tosi and Carroll (1968) have suggested some dimensions of goals which need to be communicated to members. First, goals should represent the unit's needs. The members must be aware of the importance of the goals. The development of relatively objective criteria increases the perception of goal clarity. If goals have these properties, they are more likely to have effects upon the individual working toward them.

Managerial use and support. "Top management support" is important for the success

2. See R. R. Lockette, *The effect of level of aspiration upon the learning of skills.* Ph.D. diss., University of Illinois, 1956; G. K. Yacorzynski, Degree of effort: III. Relationship to the level of aspiration, *Journal of Experimental Psychology*, 1941, 30, 407-13; M. Horowitz, *et al., Motivational effects of alternative decision making processes in groups*, Bureau of Education Research, University of Illinois, 1953.
3. Vroom, Victor. *Some personality determinants of the effects of participation*, Englewood Cliffs, N. J.: Prentice-Hall; Tosi, Henry, A reexamination of some personality determinants of the effects of participation, *Personnel Psychology* (forthcoming).
4. See J. A. Wertz, Antoinetti, and S. R. Wallace, The effect of home office contact on sales performance, *Personnel Psychology*, 1954, 7, 381-84; E. E. Smith, The effects of clear and unclear role expectations on group productivity and effectiveness, *Journal of Abnormal and Social Psychology*, 1957, 55, 213-17; and H. Leavitt and A. Mueller, Some effects of feedback on communication, *Human Relations*, 1951, 4, 401-10.

of any program. The best evidence of support is the use of the technique by the manager himself. Formulating goals, discussing them with subordinates, and providing feedback based on these goals will have substantially greater effect on a subordinate than simply saying "this has the support of top management."

Many managers mistakenly feel the verbalization of support for a policy is adequate enough. They send a memo to subordinates stating that top management wishes a program to be implemented. This, obviously, does not insure compliance. "Do as I say, not as I do" will not work. Verbalized policy support must be reinforced by the individual's perception of the superior's action and behavior in using an objective approach. It is of little or no use to support MBO philosophy orally and not use it!

The need for feedback. While a number of studies have concluded that goals have a greater impact on performance than just feedback alone we do not believe it to be an either/or situation. Feedback about well-developed goals seems a fundamental requirement for behavior change. It may be that the subordinate's perception of the specificity, objectivity, and frequency of feedback is interpreted as a measure of the superior's support of an objectives approach.

Some other cautions. There are other significant points that cut across those made above: there are personal as well as organization constraints which must be taken into consideration in the development of goals. The organizational unit and the organization level affect the nature of the goals which can, and will, be set. Goals at lower levels may be more precise and probably more objectively measured. The goals of one functional area, engineering for instance, may be much more general than those of another, say, the marketing department.

MBO AND THE COMPENSATION PROCESS

If, as McClelland (1961) suggests, individuals high in need achievement will expend more effort in reaching challenging goals irrespective of external rewards associated with goal accomplishment, MBO may supplement or complement standard compensation procedures. Tying MBO into the financial reward system could have a handsome pay-off. It is for this reason that we suggest how information obtained from MBO can be used in making improved compensation decisions.

INTERNAL WAGE ADMINISTRATION

MBO can be of assistance in developing salary differentials within a particular job class. By assessing the level of difficulty and contribution of the goals for a particular job and comparing them with similar jobs, better determination of the appropriateness of basic compensation differentials may be made.

MBO may be useful in providing information about changes in job requirements which may necessitate re-evaluation and adjustment of compensation levels for different positions. By observing changes in objectives over time, changes in job requirements may be detected which could lead to revisions in compensation schedules.

The objectives approach can aid in determining supplementary compensation levels such as stock options, bonus plans, and administration of profit sharing plans. This type of compensation is usually given when performance exceeds the normal position requirements. A properly developed objectives approach will take into account both normal job duties as well as goals and activities which extend beyond them. The extent to which an incumbent is able to achieve these non-routine objectives should be one, but perhaps not the only, factor in ranking unit members in order of their additional contribution to group effectiveness. It will provide a sound basis for determining what the level of supplemental compensation should be. Needless to say, goals which extend beyond normal job requirements should contribute importantly to organizational success.

A possible problem needs to be noted here. When goals go substantially beyond the current job requirements it may be due to the individual's initiative and aggressiveness. If this happens, it may be more appropriate strategy to change the position of the individual, not to redefine his job and change his compensation levels. A method must be developed which takes this possibility into consideration, as well as the fact that different managers will have different goals. This does not seem to be the appropriate place to detail such a device. A weighing approach which considers the capability of the manager, the difficulty of the goal, and its importance to the unit might resolve this problem.

PERFORMANCE-LINKED REWARDS

If goals are developed properly, their achievement may be more readily associated with an individual so that appropriate individual rewards may be given. The *goal statement* is the heart of the "objectives approach." It is a description of the boss's expectancies which will be used in the feedback and evaluation process. It is a communicative artifact which spells out, for both the boss and the subordinate, the objectives *and* the manner in which they will be obtained. It should *contain two elements,* the *desired goal level* and the *activities* required to achieve that level of performance. This not only permits a comparison of performance against some criterion, but also allows determination of whether or not events, which are presumed to lead to goal achievement, have taken place if appropriate criteria are not available.

This has important implications for the problems of assessment, evaluation, and compensation. Some goals may be neither measurable nor adequately verifiable. Yet, intuitively we know what must be done to achieve them. If this is the case, and we have distinguished between goals and activities, we can at least determine whether activities which are presumed to lead to desired ends have taken place.

It is important to recognize the distinction between measuring the achievement of a goal level and determining whether or not an event presumed to lead to goal achievement has taken place. If we are unable to quantify or specify a goal level in a meaningful way, then we must simply assume that the desired level will be achieved if a particular event, or set of activities, has taken place. For example, it is very difficult to find measurable criteria to assess a manager's capability in developing subordinates; yet we can determine if he has provided them with development opportunities. If they have participated in seminars, attended meetings or gone to school it may be *assumed* that the development activities are properly conducted.

PROMISES AND PROBLEMS

By its very nature, MBO seems to be a promising vehicle for linking performance to the evaluation process and the reward system in order to encourage both job satisfaction and productivity. It appears that higher performance and motivation is most likely when there is a link between performance and the reward systems (Tosi and Carroll, 1968; Porter and Lawler, 1968). It may be that this link can be achieved through the process of feedback regarding goal achievement and the association of rewards and sanctions to achievement. Goal attainment should be organizationally reinforced, and the reinforcement should be different for individuals, as a function of their own attainment. The use of an "objectives" approach in conjunction with a compensation program may also result in less dissatisfaction with the allocation of compensation increases made. Certainly there is virtually universal agreement among managers that rewards should go for actual accomplishments rather than for irrelevant personal characteristics and political or social standing.

There may be problems arising from the use of MBO and its emphasis on goals and goal achievement. Many organizations have adopted the objectives approach because it seems to be a better appraisal device, and they have used it primarily in this manner. But, an appraisal system should furnish information needed to make other personnel decisions, such as promotion and transfer. Information furnished by the objectives approach may not be adequate for these purposes. Accomplishment of goals at a lower level job may be a good indicator of capability in the current job and/or level of motivation, but not of the individual's abilities to perform at higher levels or responsibility, especially if the requirements on the higher level job are much different from the current position.

Conversely, goals accomplished at a lower level may be indicative of promotability to a particular high-level job if there is high goal congruence between the two positions. At any rate, there is certainly no reason to rely strictly upon the objectives approach for these decisions. It can be used along with other criteria, such as assessment of traits, when this is deemed an important dimension by the decision-makers. Another potential difficulty should be pointed out. If the objectives approach becomes the basic vehicle for the determination of compensation increases, then managers may quickly learn to "beat the system." Unless higher level managers are skilled in the use of MBO, subordinates may set objectives which have high probabilities of achievement, refraining from setting high risk goals. When any system becomes too formalized, managers learn how to beat it, and those using it become more concerned with simply meeting the formal benefits for both the individual and the organization; [and the results] are probably no different from earlier more traditional methods of appraisal.

The "objectives approach" seems to be a practical way of motivating organization members, but it is not an easy path to follow. It requires a considerable amount of time and energy of *all managers,* in addition to extensive organization support, to make it work. MBO may lose some of its mystique, value, importance, and significance when it must be translated into a formal policy requirement. It is too easy to consider a formal MBO program as merely another thorn in the manager's side, with no positive gains for implementing it. To succeed, an MBO program must be relevant, applicable, helpful, and receive organization support and reinforcement. One way in which this can be done is to link it to other elements of the structural system which reinforce behavior, such as compensation and reward programs.

REFERENCES

Drucker, Peter. *The practice of management.* New York: Harper and Bros., 1954.

McClelland, D. C. *The achieving society.* Princeton: Van Nostrand, 1961.

McGregor, Douglas. *The human side of enterprise.* New York: McGraw-Hill, 1960.

Odiorne, George. *Management by objectives.* New York: Pitman, 1965.

Porter, Lyman, and Lawler, Edward, E. *Managerial attitudes and performance.* Homewood, Ill.: Irwin, 1968.

Raia, Anthony. Goal setting and self control. *Journal of Management Studies.* II-I, 1965 (Feburary), 34-35.

Tosi, H., and Carroll, S. Managerial reactions to management by objectives. *Academy of Management Journal,* 1968 (December), 415-26.

31

Setting Goals in Management by Objectives

HENRY L. TOSI, JOHN R. RIZZO, AND STEPHEN J. CARROLL

Management by objectives (MBO) is a process in which members of complex organizations, working in conjunction with one another, identify common goals and coordinate their efforts toward achieving them. It emphasizes the future and change, since an objective or goal is an end state, or a condition to be achieved or have in effect at some future time. The emphasis is on where the organization is going—the what and the how of its intended accomplishments. Objectives can be thought of as statements of purpose and direction, formalized into a system of management. They may be long-range or short-range. They may be general, to provide direction to an entire organization, or they may be highly specific to provide detailed direction for a given individual.

One purpose of MBO is to facilitate the derivation of specific from general objectives, seeing to it that objectives at all levels in the organization are meaningfully located structurally and linked to each other. Sets of objectives for an organizational unit are the bases which determine its activities. *A set of objectives for an individual determines his job,* and can be thought of as a different way to provide a job description. Once objectives are determined and assumed by organizational units and by individuals, it is possible to work out the means of performance required for accomplishing the objectives. Methods of achieving objectives, resources required, timing, interactions with others, control, and evaluation must have continuing attention.

Objectives may or may not require change. The goal or end-state may be one of insuring that no change occurs—for example, an important recurring organizational operation. However, the emphasis still remains on change and the future, and "no change" conditions can be thought of as making finer change discriminations in the management process. However, MBO is deemed most appropriate in situations where activities tend not to be recurring or repetitious, where change toward new or improved conditions is sought. Typically, these would be innovative endeavors, problem-solving situations, improvements, and personal development.

Objectives may originate at any point in the

organization structure. Quite naturally, they should be derived from the general purposes of the organization, and consistent with its philosophy, policies, and plans. It is beyond the scope of this paper to discuss the details of policy formulation and planning. Rather, it is recognized that these activities take place and that the setting of objectives can, and often does, occur in concern and consonance with them. For example, plans can specify the phasing and timing of organizational operations, out of which are derived objectives for those involved in implementing them. Objectives are not considered as substitutes for plans, but rather as a basis for developing them. Stating objectives accomplishes the following:

1. Document expectations in superior-subordinate relationship regarding what is to be done and the level of attainment for the period covered by the goal;
2. Provide members with a firmer base for developing and integrating plans and personal and departmental activity;
3. Serve as the basis for feedback and evaluation of subordinates' performance;
4. Provide for coordination and timing of individual and unit activities;
5. Draw attention to the need for control of key organizational functions;
6. Provide a basis for work-related rewards as opposed to personality-based systems;
7. Emphasize change, improvement, and growth of the organization and the individual.

OBJECTIVES AS
MEANS-END DISTINCTIONS

The formulation of objectives throughout an organization represents a kind of means-end analysis, which is an attempt to factor general requirements into specific activities. Means-end analysis starts with "the general goal to be achieved, (2) discovering a set of means, very generally specified, for accomplishing this goal, (3) taking each of these means, in turn, as a new sub-goal and

discovering a more detailed set of means for achieving it, etc."[1]

MBO is predicated on this concept. It is assumed that a means-end analysis can occur with a degree of precision and accuracy. The end represents a condition or situation that is desired, a purpose to be achieved. Here, the concept of *end* is equated with *goal* or *objective*. Objectives may represent required inputs to other sectors of the organization. They may be specific achievement levels, such as product costs, sales volume, and so on. They may also be completed projects. For instance, the market research department may seek to complete a sales forecast by a particular date so that the production facilities may be properly coordinated with market demands. Objectives, or end states, are attained through the performance of some activity. These activities are the *means* to achieve the *end* it is important to distinguish between ends and means in the use of the "objectives approach," since there are implications for measurement and assessment which will be discussed later in the paper.

It is obvious that a malfunction or break in such a process may lead to major problems in implementing management by objectives. It is for this reason that commitment, effort, support, and use by top management is critical at all levels to obtain consensus of objectives, cooperation in achievement, and the use of objectives as criteria for evaluation. But there are some problems in doing this. This paper is directed toward these: stating objectives, areas they should cover, the question of measurement, as well as some suggestions for dealing with them.

The Objective

The objectives for any position should reflect the means-end distinction discussed earlier. The first critical phase of objec-

1. J. March and H. Simon, *Organizations* (New York: Wiley, 1958), p. 191.

tives-setting is the statement which describes the end state sought. It should be:

Clear, concise and unambiguous;
Accurate in terms of the true end state or condition sought;
Consistent with policies, procedures, and plans as they apply to the unit;
Within the competence of the man, or represent a reasonable learning and developmental experience for him;
Interesting, motivating, and/or challenging whenever possible.

Some examples of goal statements might be written as: increase sales by 10 per cent; reduce manufacturing costs by 5 per cent; reduce customer complaints; increase sales by 5 per cent by December 1; increase quality within a 5 per cent increase in production control costs; develop understanding and implementation of computer techniques among subordinates.

Notice that these goal statements have at least two key components. First, each clearly suggests an *area of activity* in which accomplishment occurs. Second, some clearly specify a level of achievement, the quantity or deadlines to be met. We will refer to the desired level of achievement as *performance level*. The need for this distinction is obvious. It indicates the evaluation criterion by specifying the *level* or the condition which should exist. This has clear implications for both measurement and appraisal. Before discussing these implications, however, a more detailed examination of the scope and types of objectives in the MBO process is required.

Scope and Type of Objectives

It would be difficult to conceive of developing objectives for a manager which would cover each and every area of responsibility. The structure of most jobs is simply too complex. Yet once objectives are set for a position, they should comprise the major description of the job, and their achievement in light of what is known about total job

requirements should be assessed. A sense of interference or conflict between objectives and other job requirements should be prevented.

Two major types of objectives may be delineated: *performance* objectives and *personal development* objectives.[2] *Performance objectives* refer mainly to those goals and activities that relate to the individual's position assignment. *Personal development* goals have to do with increasing the individual's skills, competence, or potential. Delineating types of objectives in this manner, more importantly, allows for an assessment of how MBO is being used and what emphases are deriving from it. For instance:

Once all objectives are set for a person, a basis exists to ensure that there is a "balance" of different types, that he is problem solving, developing, and maintaining critical functions.

Some estimates can be made regarding the importance of objectives and consequences of failure to achieve them. For example, a man who fails on a difficult creative objective should not be evaluated the same as one who fails to maintain a critical recurring operation.

Performance Objectives

This type is derived directly from the job assignment, from the major areas of responsibility and activity of the individual that he must sustain or manage. Among them would be the maintenance of recurring or routine activities, the solving of problems, or the creation of innovative ideas, products, services, and the like. Some of these may take on the form of special activities or projects not normally part of the job. That is, even though they are part of the normal job requirements, they are goals which may take on special importance for a number of

2. These categories are similar to those proposed by Odiorne. See his *Management by objectives* (New York: Pitman, 1964), esp. chaps. 7, 8, and 9.

reasons—emergencies, changes in priorities, or simply management decisions.

A special activity for one position may be routine for another. A special project goal for a lower-level manager might be a routine goal for his boss. Developing a computer-based information system for personnel records may be a highly creative objective for the personnel department, yet should probably be considered a routine goal for a systems analysis group.

DISCRETIONARY AREAS AND OTHER PROBLEMS

By its very nature, organization imposes restrictions on individuals. The structure of an organization defines legitimate areas of influence and decision making for an individual. Specialization and definition of function tend to limit decisions and activities to those defined for the incumbent.

If the objectives process is intended to, and does, facilitate subordinate participation and involvement, we must recognize the implicit nature of power. A lower-level manager cannot *legitimately* influence goal levels and action plans in areas in which he has no discretion, unless he has the *approval of his superior*. Therefore, it is necessary to spell out areas in which the subordinate has some latitude so that he knows what his decision limits are. Otherwise he may be misled into believing that he can participate in departmental and organizational decisions which have been defined, either procedurally or by managerial fiat, as being outside his discretion area. When you expect to participate and then cannot, negative consequences may occur. It is for this reason that it is important to determine and *communicate to the subordinate* what these discretion areas are.

One way to define discretion areas is to determine whether an individual should influence means or ends. If the activity operates primarily across the boundaries of the organization and is affected by conditions beyond its control, then the individual charged with performing it may be in a better position to determine both the goals

(or ends) and the most appropriate manner to achieve them. For instance, the marketing executives in constant touch with the external environment are in a better position to determine possible sales penetration and programs than others in the organization. However, not having discretion over goal levels should not preclude involvement in goal setting. Here the MBO process should focus on developing the best *means* (later called action plans) for goal attainment.

High levels of skill and technology required in a particular function may make the specialist better able than a nontechnical person to assess what can be done in a technical field. Thus, he should be involved in determining goal levels, as well as in carrying out activities. This is not to suggest that organizational constraints and requirements be entirely removed. Budget limitations, sales quotas, and production requirements are boundaries or restrictions which may not be removed but may have to be made more flexible.

If performance levels are set, for any reason, at higher organization levels, then there is little option but to focus on the determination of the "best" activities to achieve these levels. Internal definition of goal levels will most probably be for activities which function primarily within the boundaries of the organization. The assumption, of course, is that the one defining the objective, or level, is either competent to do so or must because of its critical importance.

An important limitation on discretion is organizational level. The lower the organizational level, the more and more narrow the zone of a manager's discretion. That is, the manager at the lower levels is responsible for fewer, more specific, and more measurable activities and can commit smaller quantities of resources than those at higher levels.[3]

Another factor which causes variation in

3. H. Tosi and S. Carroll, Some structural factors related to goal influence in the management by objectives process, *Business Topics*, 1969 (Spring), 45-50.

the discretion range for a particular job is the changing competency levels of the incumbent. A person learning a job may need more guidance from the superior. However, as his skills increase, the superior may spend less time since the subordinate can capably handle more activities and make more decisions. The objectives approach, incidentally, may help the superior make assessments of the subordinate's competence to expand the decision area. As a subordinate becomes more successful in achieving goals, additional and more challenging goals within the parameters of the job could be added. When the incumbent can perform these adequately, then consideration should be given to possible promotion and transfer.

What about those decision areas beyond the discretion limits? We are not suggesting that the subordinate should have no part in these decisions. His role may be contributing information and assistance, such as providing inputs to the decision-making process of the superior, which the superior may choose to accept or reject. But this type of activity must be differentiated from *goal setting participation,* in which the individual has something to say about the final shape and form of the goals and activities. However, discretion boundaries are not rigid. While a particular decision may fall within the discretion range under normal circumstances, emergencies might develop which would result in the decision's being made by the boss. These conditions cannot be foreseen, and consequently not planned for.

PERSONAL DEVELOPMENT OBJECTIVES

First, it is important to stress that these must be based on problems or deficiencies, current or anticipated, in areas such as improvements in technical skills or interpersonal problems. They may also be directed at developing one for movement within the organization. The critical nature of these objectives lies in their potential as means to combat obsolescence under a rapid

expansion of knowledge, to prepare people for increased responsibility, and to overcome problems in organizational interactions.

Setting development goals is probably more difficult than setting performance goals, since they are personal in nature and, as such, must be handled with care and tact. This difficulty may be avoided by simply not setting them. It could be argued that they should be avoided since they are an intrusion into the individual's privacy by the boss or the organization. However, when perceived personal limitations hinder effective performance, the problem must be treated.

Thus, if at any time the superior believes an individual's limitations stand clearly in the way of the unit's goal achievement, it should be made known to the individual. He may not be aware that he is creating problems and would gladly change—if he knew. Many technically competent people have been relieved from positions because of human problems they ostensibly create. Many might have been retained had they only known that problems existed or were developing.

Personal development objectives should be a basic part of the MBO program, *when there is a need for them.* But, if they are included only to meet formal program requirements and are not problem-based, little value will obtain. Then personal improvement goals will probably be general and ambiguous, tenable only if the organization wishes to invest in "education for education's sake." For other than a philosophical or value-based justification, personal development should attack deficiencies related to performance, containing specific action proposals for solving the problems. This may be done in the following manner.

Pinpoint a problem area. Parties involved in goal setting should continually be alert to negative incidents resulting from personal incapacities. The boss is in a particularly important position for recognizing problems. When situations occur which he believes are due to either personal or technical limitations, he should be aware of who was involved, and make some determination of the cause of these problems. Other individuals in the unit may bring problems to the fore. Those with whom an individual interacts may be in a reasonably good position to judge his technical competence or to determine when problems are due to his behavior. If colleagues are continually complaining about another person, additional investigation into the problem is warranted. Perhaps the most important source of these negative incidents is the subordinate himself. He may be very aware of problems in which he is involved and by discussing them may determine those in which he has been the primary cause.

These negative incidents should be relatively significant in effect and frequency and not simply a single event that has caused some notice to be taken. This does not mean, however, that an important incident which occurs one time should be overlooked if it suggests serious deficiencies.

There are at least three areas in which personal development objectives should be set.

1. Improve interpersonal relations. Inability to maintain reasonably effective working relationships may be due to a person's lack of awareness or his inability to cooperate. This may arise from personality deficiencies or simple lack of awareness of his impact upon others. He may be unable to recognize that he is precipitating problems.

2. Improve current skills. A manager may be, for instance, unable to prepare a budget or to engage in research because he has not had adequate training in these areas or because his training is not up to date. His general performance may be acceptable, but his skills should be improved.

3. Prepare for advancement. Another possibility covers either technical or human skills required for different or higher level positions. These are truly developmental goals which focus on preparation for advancement. There are many ways in which they may be achieved. In some cases the individual may be given advanced work assignments; in others, they may be achieved by exposure in training situations to new concepts. In any event, they represent a *potential* problem area.

Assess the causes of the problem. Once it has been established that a problem exists, the cause needs to be determined. Causes should be sought jointly, a result of investigation and discussion by both the superior and subordinate after both have thought of possible causes.

The possible causes of problems may be grouped into three general categories:

1. Procedures and structure. The structure of the organization itself may induce disturbances. Interpersonal conflict may develop because of the interdependence of work activities. For instance, if formal requirements cause a delay in information transmission, those who need it may develop negative attitudes and feelings.

2. Others with whom an individual must work. Problems with subordinates or managerial peers of the goal setter may be caused by personality incompatibility or lack of certain technical skills. While this may represent an important cause of problems, it is too easy to blame negative incidents on others.

3. The person himself. The *individual* may have habits and characteristics which are not congruent with those of subordinates or colleagues. Or, he may lack the technical skills requisite to carry out certain responsibilities.

Attempting to define problems and causes facilitates converting development objectives into achievable goals. Like other objectives, they can be general (attend a sensitivity-training course or role-playing seminar), or more specific (attend XYZ course in financial planning, use PERT techniques on Project X).

Self-improvement goals may be designed to improve current performance, or may be specifically intended to develop skills required at higher levels, or in different jobs (where it may be impossible to describe the end state of affairs to be achieved because success can be determined only in the future, or in other positions).

For development objectives it is necessary simply to rely upon the determination that the action plan has been carried out and that the individual has learned something. Suppose, for instance, that a development goal for an engineer destined to be a supervisor read as follows: "To meet with members of the financial, marketing, and production groups in order to learn how product release schedules affect their areas." Currently, he may have to know little about this since he may now have little impact on product release schedules. The question is, "How do you know that the activity produced the desired learning?" You don't. At some point in time, the superior, who presumably has some knowledge in the goal area, should discuss the results of the meeting with the subordinate, emphasizing particularly the important points that should have been learned. If this is done the subordinate will have the learning experience of the meeting and the reinforcement from discussion.

There is obviously no way to determine if these activities will improve the current, or future, performance of the manager. Managerial judgment is important here. We must simply assume that the superior is able to work with the subordinate to define activities of value in future work assignments.

Finally, it should be clear that performance and development objectives may well be derived from and related to management training and development efforts. These efforts must account for current organizational problems and future needs, and treat development as an integrated organization-wide effort. MBO should therefore be integrally tied to them.

PERFORMANCE REQUIRED:
THE ACTION PLAN

Some of the problems inherent in MBO can be overcome by stating and discussing the specifics of the performance required to accomplish an objective. Earlier, the differentiation of means and ends was stressed. The goal statements reflected the ends: here, the performance or "action plan" refers to the means to accomplish an objective. It describes the manner in which it is to be attained. These means reflect alternatives which lead to the desired end and performance level.

The action plan may be brief statements, but it should summarize what is to be done. The action plan for a complex activity should be broken down into major subprograms and should represent the "best" alternative, of possibly many, which would achieve the goal level. The action plan provides an initial basis for a total action program for the individual or department. These action plans might be stated in the following manner:

For the sales increase: develop more penetration in a particular market area by increasing the number of calls to dealers there.

For the reduced manufacturing costs: analyze the overtime activities and costs and schedule more work during regular hours.

Subordinates may base their own action plans on those developed by their manager, using his plan to guide their own roles in the unit's effort. Thus, clear differentiation of means from ends can facilitate lower-level use of the objectives process.

Including both means and ends permits comparing performance with some criteria and determining if events occurred which are presumed to lead to a desired outcome. It is important to recognize the distinction between measuring an objective and determining if an event has occurred. If we are unable to quantify or specify the goal level adequately, then we simply *assume that the desired goal level will be achieved* if a particular event or set of activities takes place. For example, while it is very difficult to measure if a manager is developing the talents of subordinates by means of any hard criteria, we can determine if he has provided them with development opportunities. If they have participated in seminars, attended meetings, or gone off to school, it may be *assumed* that the development activity is being properly conducted.

Some further benefits and opportunities provided by adequate attention to an action plan are as follows:

1. Aids in search for better, more efficient methods of accomplishing the objective;

2. Provides an opportunity to test the feasibility of accomplishing the objective as stated;

3. Develops a sounder basis to estimate time or cost required and deadline for accomplishment;

4. Examines the nature and degree of reliance on other people in the organization toward coordination and support needed;

5. Uncovers anticipated snags or barriers to accomplishment;

6. Determines resources (manpower, equipment, supplies, facilities) required to accomplish the objective;

7. Facilitates control if the performance is well specified and agreed upon; reporting need occur only when problems arise in implementing. This is a form of planning ahead; when plans are sufficiently complete, only deviations from it need be communicated;

8. Identifies areas in which the superior can provide support and assistance;

9. Facilitates the delegation process.

Determine coordinating requirements and contingencies. Successful achievement or failure of an objective may depend upon the contribution and performance of other individuals or departments. Therefore, since they may be extremely critical to successful performance, they must be considered.

Some contingencies apply to all objectives and need not be documented on each. For example, delays in the availability of resources, change in support or priorities from higher management, equipment failures, delayed information or approval, and the like, which are unplanned, should relieve some responsibility for objective accomplishment.

Other contingencies, specific to the objective, should be discussed. Among these might be inadequate authority of the subordinate, lack of policy covering aspects of the objective, possible failure to gain other's cooperation, known delays in the system, and so on. Once these are uncovered, several actions are possible:

Reexamination of the objective (e.g. alteration of a deadline) when and if the contingency occurs;

Commitment of the superior to aid by overcoming or preventing the contingency;

Revision of the performance required to accomplish the objective;

Establishment of a new objective. If a contingency is serious enough, an objective aimed at overcoming the problem may be justified.

MEASUREMENT AND APPRAISAL

Management by objectives carries with it most of the familiar difficulties and complications of measurement and appraisal processes. Its emphasis on performance, as opposed to personality traits or criteria presumed related to performance, makes it potentially more effective. But this potential cannot be realized unless measurement and appraisal are reasonably valid, reliable, objective, and equitable.

Means, Ends, and Evaluation

Performance evaluations should rarely be based only on whether or not the objective was accomplished, or on the sheer number accomplished. They should include:

1. Quantitative aspects (Was cost reduced 5 per cent as planned?);

2. Qualitative aspects (Have good relations been established with Department X? Has an evaluation technique been established?);

3. Deadline considerations (Was the deadline beaten? Was it met?);

4. Proper allocation of time to given objectives;

5. Type and difficulty of objectives;

6. Creativity in overcoming obstacles;

7. Additional objectives suggested or undertaken;

8. Efficient use of resources;

9. Use of good management practices in accomplishing objectives (cost reduction, delegation, good planning, etc.);

10. Coordinative and cooperative behavior; avoidance of conflict-inducing or unethical practices, etc.

Evaluation and measurement, therefore, require considering both means and ends, being concerned with both the objective (number, type, difficulty, etc.) and the means to its achievement (cost, cooperativeness, time consumed, etc.). Unless this is done, an important opportunity to communicate expectations, feedback performance results, and setting effective goals may be lost. It must be fully understood that evaluation has obvious links to action plans, as well as to desired end states.

Further Consideration in Measurement

Some goals lend themselves more easily than others to measurement—scrap rates, production costs, sales volume, and other "hard" measures. These measures pertain most to lower organizational levels and to areas such as production, marketing, or other major functional activities of the organization, and least to most staff and specialist units. The measurement problem often reduces to finding the appropriate, agreed-upon criterion for each objective, realizing that some will apply to many situations while others are unique to a single objective.

We have already detailed the distinction between performance and personal development objectives. Another distinction relevant to the measurement problem is the difference between routine and special project objectives. Classifying objectives according to these types permits some important refinements in evaluation and control. By examining the nature of the mix of objectives for a set of positions it is possible to determine any or all of the following:

The extent to which each individual has some personal development objectives;

That sufficient problem-solving or innovative activities were forthcoming in units where they might be required;

The priorities for performance or personal development objectives.

Routine objectives are basic to the job, a core part of the job description. How should they be measured? The most appropriate method for evaluating if an individual has achieved them is first to insure that he is aware of these activities and required levels. The manager must tell the subordinate—early in the relationship—what the activities of the job are and what the desired level of performance is. Evaluation should not occur after a period of service unless there has been previous discussion of criteria.

At the same time that the criteria are being specified, acceptable tolerance limits should be developed. Measurement of the routine should be a major part of the objectives process, yet it should be of most concern *when performance falls outside acceptable levels.* Essentially, we are proposing that minimum performance levels be set for routine activities. Therefore, evaluation of routine goals is *by exception,* or when these standards are not met. Naturally, the ability to manage by exception demands good plans or clear standards from which exceptions can be specified in advance. Odiorne cites the following example:

The paymaster, for example, may report that his routine duties cluster around getting the weekly payroll out every Friday. It is agreed that the measure of exception will be zero—in other words, the boss should expect no exceptions to the diligent performance of this routine duty. Thus, the failure any week to produce the payroll on Friday will be considered an exception that calls for explanation by the subordinate. If the cause were reasonably under his control or could have been averted by extra care or effort, the absence of the payroll will be considered a failure on the part of the subordinate.[4]

What about superior performance? When a subordinate frequently exceeds the performance levels, the manager should let him know that his outstanding performance has been noticed. Positive feedback should occur, especially to let the individual know when he is performing his major job responsibilities exceptionally well.

Generally, routine job responsibilities or goals are expressed as job standards, or other "hard" performance measures. Although appraisal and evaluation essentially compare performance to the standard, this may be relatively short-sighted and suboptimal. Recall that the manager should also evaluate the activities or the manner in which performance was carried out. Often costs may be reduced by foregoing other expenditures, which may have negative long-run effects. There can be substantial distortions of behavior when only quantitative criteria are used in measurement.

Problem-solving, special project, or creative objectives are more difficult to quantify than the essentially routine. If the ends are

truly creative, determining an adequate performance level may necessarily rely on intuitive judgment. Since innovation and invention are needed in their very formulation, we cannot generally measure results in these areas adequately, or directly. It is usually possible, however, to judge if an activity has been performed appropriately even though the ends, or the performance levels, are neither quantifiable nor measurable. Furthermore, constraints may be set on the activities. We can assess that they have occurred by some specific point in time or that a specific dollar amount has been expended. Thus, we are not only concerned with whether or not events have occurred, but also within some tolerance limit such as of target dates, budget constraints, or a quality assessment by the manager. It becomes possible under these conditions to establish review points, thus giving attention to the outcomes of activities when they occur. Deliberations on these outcomes can serve to re-evaluate both objectives and means. Thus changes are possible, and both flexibility and control are assured where they appear to be most needed—where predictions, plans, and standards could not be specified or articulated in advance.

Deadlines and budget constraints can be strictly specified in some cases and not in others. A great deal depends on:

The importance of the objective;

The ability to determine the time or costs required in performance;

Whether or not written plans or objectives of other people require coordinated completion dates;

The amount of time and money the subordinate will spend on the particular objective under discussion;

The predictability of problems or barriers to accomplishment.

Discussing these constraints allows greater understanding between superiors and subordinates and establishes their use in evalua-

4. Odiorne, p. 104.

tion. Expectations become known; realities can be tested. Deadlines and costs should be viewed as "negotiable," and should be reasonably and rationally arrived at whenever possible. Deadlines especially should not be set simply to insure that action is initiated.

We wish to re-emphasize the importance of this criterion problem. A fundamental requirement for MBO is the development and use of sound criteria for evaluation, appraisal, and feedback. This is critical to achieve meaningful changes in behavior. "Hard" criteria must be used with extreme care. They are best viewed as ends or levels; they indicate nothing about attaining either. "Soft" criteria involve not a particular level of achievement, but determination that an event or condition has or has not occurred. These soft criteria are a vital and fundamental part of MBO. Without them, the approach cannot be well implemented.

To some managers, the development and communication of goals comes naturally. There are those who are able intuitively to determine and specify appropriate measures, criteria, goals, and the most satisfactory methods for achieving them. They innately sense what must be observed and measured and communicate this effectively to subordinates. This, of course, is the behavior which management by objectives seeks to develop and reinforce.

SUMMARY

Research and experience strongly support the relationships between the degree of a subordinate's acceptance of the objectives approach and his perception of its support and reinforcement from top management.[5] Organization support is critical for two reasons.

Top management may be an important reference group for lower-level managers.

Ambitious employees are likely to emulate managerial behavior. They identify with the top management and act similarly. If top management uses a particular method of managing, lower-level managers are likely to use it also.

Consistent factoring and communication of goals to lower organizational levels is necessary. The general objective of organization must be continually broken down into smaller and smaller units. The boss must learn what is expected, must communicate this to his subordinates, and must work with them to achieve these objectives. If this process breaks down at any point, then the whole approach is difficult to use.

Objectives must be written down for the entire organization, but the degree of detail and precision cannot easily be specified. This may be a matter for organizational policy and procedure, or it may be determined by mutual superior-subordinate agreement. However this is resolved, the varied aspects of objective-setting should be attended to, discussed, and resolved as fully as possible to benefit from the MBO process.

Most important is that the approach must be intrinsically built into the job of managing. It must be related to other organizational processes and procedures, such as budgeting. It should be fundamentally incorporated into planning and development activities. It should be one of the major inputs to the performance appraisal and evaluation process. If not, it is likely that unless a manager intuitively uses this approach, it is easier to do other things. There are costs involved in MBO. There must be some value or payoff which managers can recognize; otherwise they will view it as a waste of time.

5. H. Tosi and S. Carroll, Managerial reactions to management by objectives, *Academy of Management Journal*, 1968 (December), 415-26.

32

Split Roles in Performance Appraisal

HERBERT H. MEYER, EMANUEL KAY, and JOHN R. P. FRENCH, JR.

In management circles, performance appraisal is a highly interesting and provocative topic. And in business literature, too, knowledgeable people write emphatically, pro and con, on the performance appraisal question.[1] In fact, one might almost say that everybody talks and writes about it, but nobody has done any real scientific testing of it.

At the General Electric Company we felt it was important that a truly scientific study be done to test the effectiveness of our traditional performance appraisal program. Why? Simply because our own experience with performance appraisal programs had been both positive and negative. For example:

Surveys generally show that most people think the idea of performance appraisal is good. They feel that a man should know where he stands and, therefore, the manager should discuss an appraisal of his performance with him periodically.

In actual practice, however, it is the extremely rare operating manager who will employ such a program on his own initiative. Personnel specialists report that most managers carry out performance appraisal interviews only when strong control procedures are established to ensure that they do so. This is surprising because the managers have been told repeatedly that the system is intended to help them obtain improved performance from their subordinates.

We also found from interviews with employees who have had a good deal of experience with traditional performance appraisal programs that few indeed can cite examples of constructive action taken—or significant improvement achieved—which stem from suggestions received in a performance appraisal interview with their boss.

TRADITIONAL PROGRAM

Faced with such contradictory evidence, we undertook a study several years ago to determine the effectiveness of our comprehensive performance appraisal process. Spe-

1. Douglas McGregor, An uneasy look at performance appraisal, HBR May-June 1957, p. 89; Harold Mayfield, In defense of performance appraisal, HBR March-April 1960, p. 81; Alva F. Kindall and James Gatza, Positive program for performance appraisal, HBR November-December 1963, p. 153.

cial attention was focused on the interview between the subordinate and his manager, because this is the discussion which is supposed to motivate the man to improve his performance. And we found out some very interesting things—among them the following:

Criticism has a negative effect on achievement of goals.

Praise has little effect one way or the other.

Performance improves most when specific goals are established.

Defensiveness resulting from critical appraisal produces inferior performance.

Coaching should be a day-to-day, not a once-a-year, activity.

Mutual goal setting, not criticism, improves performance.

Interviews designed primarily to improve a man's performance should not at the same time weigh his salary or promotion in the balance.

Participation by the employee in the goal-setting procedure helps produce favorable results.

As you can see, the results of this original study indicated that a detailed and comprehensive annual appraisal of a subordinate's performance by his manager is decidedly of questionable value. Furthermore, as is certainly the case when the major objective of such a discussion is to motivate the subordinate to improve his performance, the traditional appraisal interview does not do the job.

In the first part of this article, we will offer readers more than this bird's-eye view of our research into performance appraisal. (We shall not, however, burden managers with details of methodology.) We will describe also the one-year follow-up experiment General Electric conducted to validate the conclusions derived from our original study. Here the traditional annual performance appraisal method was tested against a new method we developed, which we called Work Planning and Review (WP&R). As you

will see, this approach produced, under actual plant conditions, results which were decidedly superior to those afforded by the traditional performance appraisal method. Finally, we will offer evidence to support our contention that some form of WP&R might well be incorporated into other industrial personnel programs to achieve improvement in work performance.

APPRAISING APPRAISAL

In order to assure a fair test of the effectiveness of the traditional performance appraisal method, which had been widely used throughout General Electric, we conducted an intensive study of the process at a large GE plant where the performance appraisal program was judged to be good; that is, in this plant—

... appraisals had been based on job responsibilities, rather than on personal characteristics of the individuals involved;

... an intensive training program had been carried out for managers in the use of the traditional appraisal method and techniques for conducting appraisal interviews;

... the program had been given strong backing by the plant manager and had been policed diligently by the personnel staff so that over 90 per cent of the exempt employees had been appraised and interviewed annually.

This comprehensive annual performance appraisal program, as is typical, was designed to serve two major purposes. The first was to justify recommended salary action. The second, which was motivational in character, was intended to present an opportunity for the manager to review a subordinate's performance and promote discussion on needed improvements. For the latter purpose, the manager was required to draw up a specific program of plans and goals for the subordinate which would help him to improve his job performance and to qualify, hopefully, for future promotion.

Interview Modifications

Preliminary interviews with key managers and subordinates revealed the salary action issue had so dominated the annual comprehensive performance appraisal interview that neither party had been in the right frame of mind to discuss plans for improved performance. To straighten this out, we asked managers to split the traditional appraisal interview into two sessions—discussing appraisal of performance and salary action in one interview and performance improvement plans in another to be held about two weeks later. This split provided us with a better opportunity to conduct our experiment on the effects of participation in goal planning.

To enable us to test the effects of participation, we instructed half the managers to use a *high participation* approach and the other half to use a *low participation* technique. Thus:

Each of the "high" managers was instructed to ask his appraisee to prepare a set of goals for achieving improved job performance and to submit them for the manager's review and approval. The manager also was encouraged to permit the subordinate to exert as much influence as possible on the formulation of the final list of job goals agreed on in the performance improvement discussion.

The "low" managers operated in much the same way they had in our traditional appraisal program. They formulated a set of goals for the subordinate, and these goals were then reviewed in the performance improvement session. The manager was instructed to conduct this interview in such a way that his influence in the forming of the final list of job goals would be greater than the subordinate's.

Conducting the Research

There were 92 appraisees in the experimental group, representing a cross section of the exempt salaried employees in the plant. This group included engineers; engineering support technicians; foremen; and specialists in manufacturing, customer service, marketing, finance, and purchasing functions. None of the exempt men who participated as appraisees in the experiment had other exempt persons reporting to them; thus they did not serve in conflicting manager-subordinate roles.

The entire group was interviewed and asked to complete questionnaires (a) before and after the salary action interview, and (b) after the delayed second discussion with their managers about performance improvement. These interviews and questionnaires were designed to achieve three objectives:

1. Assess changes in the attitudes of individuals toward their managers and toward the appraisal system after each of the discussions.
2. Get an estimate from the appraisee of the degree to which he usually participated in decisions that affected him. (This was done in order to determine whether or not previous lack of participation affected his response to participation in the experiment.)
3. Obtain a self-appraisal from each subordinate before and after he met with his manager. (This was done in order to determine how discrepancies in these self-appraisals might affect his reaction to the appraisal interview.)

Moreover, each salary action and performance improvement discussion was observed by outsiders trained to record essentially what transpired. (Managers preferred to use neither tape recorders nor unseen observers, feeling that observers unaffiliated with the company—in this case, graduate students in applied psychological disciplines—afforded the best way of obtaining a reasonably close approximation of the normal discussions.) In the appraisal for salary action interviews, for example, the observers recorded the amount of criticism and praise employed by the manager, as well as the reactions of the appraisee to the manager's comments. In the performance improvement discussions, the observers recorded the participation of the subordinate, as well as the amount of influence he seemed to exert in establishing his future success goals.

Criticism and Defensiveness

In general, the managers completed the performance appraisal forms in a thorough and conscientious manner. Their appraisals were discussed with subordinates in interviews ranging from approximately 30 to 90 minutes in length. On the average, managers covered 32 specific performance items which, when broken down, showed positive (praise) appraisals on 19 items, and negative (criticism) on 13. Typically, praise was more often related to *general* performance characteristics, while criticism was usually focused on *specific* performance items.

The average subordinate reacted defensively to seven of the manager's criticisms during the appraisal interview (that is, he reacted defensively about 54 per cent of the time when criticized). Denial of shortcomings cited by the manager, blaming others, and various other forms of excuses were recorded by the observers as defensive reactions.

Constructive responses to criticism were *rarely* observed. In fact, the average was less than one per interview. Not too surprising, along with this, was the finding that the more criticism a man received in the performance appraisal discussion, the more defensively he reacted. Men who received an above-average number of criticisms showed more than five times as much defensive behavior as those who received a below-average number of criticisms. Subordinates who received a below-average number of criticisms, for example, reacted defensively only about one time out of three. But those who received an above-average number reacted defensively almost two times out of three.

One explanation for this defensiveness is that it seems to stem from the overrating each man tended to give to his own performance. The average employee's self-estimate

of performance *before* appraisal placed him at the 77 percentile. (Only 2 of the 92 participants estimated their performance to be below the average point on the scale.) But when the same men were asked *after* their performance appraisal discussions how they thought their bosses had rated them, the average figure given was at the 65 percentile. The great majority (75 out of 92) saw their manager's evaluation as being less favorable than their self-estimates. Obviously, to these men, the performance appraisal discussion with the manager was a deflating experience. Thus, it was not surprising that the subordinates reacted defensively in their interviews.

Criticism and Goal Achievement

Even more important is the fact that men who received an above-average number of criticisms in their performance appraisal discussions generally showed *less* goal achievement 10 to 12 weeks later than those who had received fewer criticisms. At first, we thought that this difference might be accounted for by the fact that the subordinates who received more criticisms were probably poorer performers in general. But there was little factual evidence found to support this suspicion.

It was true that those who received an above-average number of criticisms in their appraisal discussions did receive slightly lower summary ratings on over-all performance from their managers. But they did not receive proportionally lower salary increases. And the salary increases granted were *supposed* to reflect differences in job performance, according to the salary plan traditionally used in this plant. This argument, admittedly, is something less than perfect.

But it does appear clear that frequent criticism constitutes so strong a threat to self-esteem that it disrupts rather than improves subsequent performance. We expected such a disruptive threat to operate more strongly on those individuals who were already low on self-esteem, just as we expected a man who had confidence in his ability to do his job to react more constructively to criticism. Our group experiment proved these expectations to be correct.

Still further evidence that criticism has a negative effect on performance was found when we investigated areas which had been given special emphasis by the manager in his criticism. Following the appraisal discussion with the manager, each employee was asked to indicate which one aspect of his performance had been most criticized by the manager. Then, when we conducted our follow-up investigation 10 to 12 weeks later, it revealed that improvement in the most-criticized aspects of performance cited was considerably less than improvement realized in other areas!

Participation Effects

As our original research study had indicated, the effects of a high-participation level were also favorable in our group experiment. In general, here is what we found:

Subordinates who received a high-participation level in the performance interview reacted more favorably than did those who received a low-participation level. The "highs" also, in most cases, achieved a greater percentage of their improvement goals than did their "low" counterparts. For the former, the high-participation level was associated with greater mutual understanding between them and their managers, greater acceptance of job goals, a more favorable attitude toward the appraisal system, and a feeling of greater self-realization on the job.

But employees who had traditionally been accustomed to low-participation in their daily relationship with the manager did not necessarily perform better under the high-participation treatment. In fact, those men who had received a high level of criticism in their appraisal interviews actually performed better when their managers set goals for them than they did when they set their own goals, as permitted under the high-participation treatment.

In general, our experiment showed that the men who usually worked under high participation levels performed best on goals they set for themselves. Those who indicated that they usually worked under low levels performed best on goals that the manager set for them. Evidently, the man who usually does not participate in work-planning decisions considers job goals set by the manager to be more important than goals he sets for himself. The man accustomed to a high participation level, on the other hand, may have stronger motivation to achieve goals he sets for himself than to achieve those set by his manager.

Goal-setting Importance

While subordinate participation in the goal-setting process had some effect on improved performance, a much more powerful influence was whether goals were set at all. Many times in appraisal discussions, managers mentioned areas of performance where improvement was needed. Quite often these were translated into specific work plans and goals. But this was not always the case. In fact, when we looked at the one performance area which each manager had emphasized in the appraisal interview as most in need of improvement, we found that these items actually were translated into specific work plans and goals for only about 60 per cent of our experiment participants.

When performance was being measured 10 to 12 weeks after the goal-planning sessions, managers were asked to describe what results they hoped for in the way of subordinate on-the-job improvement. They did this for those important performance items that had been mentioned in the interview. Each manager was then asked to estimate on a percentage scale the degree to which his hoped-for changes had actually been observed. The average percent accomplishment estimate for those performance items that *did* get translated into goals was 65, while the percent estimate for those items that *did not* get translated into goals was about 27! Establishing specific plans and goals seemed to ensure that attention would be given to that aspect of job performance.

Summation of Findings

At the end of this experiment, we were able to draw certain tentative conclusions. These conclusions were the basis of a future research study which we will describe later. In general, we learned that:

Comprehensive annual performance appraisals are of questionable value. Certainly a major objective of the manager in traditional appraisal discussions is motivating the subordinate to improve his performance. But the evidence we gathered indicated clearly that praise tended to have no effect, perhaps because it was regarded as the sandwich which surrounded the raw meat of criticism.[2] And criticism itself brought on defensive reactions that were essentially denials of responsibility for a poor performance.

Coaching should be a day-to-day, not a once-a-year, activity. There are two main reasons for this:

1. Employees seem to accept suggestions for improved performance if they are given in a less concentrated form than is the case in comprehensive annual appraisals. As our experiment showed, employees become clearly more prone to reject criticisms as the number of criticisms mounts. This indicates that an "overload phenomenon" may be operating. In other words, each individual seems to have a tolerance level for the amount of criticism he can take. And, as this level is approached or passed, it becomes increasingly difficult for him to accept responsibility for the shortcomings pointed out.

2. Some managers reported that the traditional performance appraisal program tended to cause them to save up items where improvement was needed in order to have

2. See Richard E. Farson, Praise reappraised. HBR September-October 1963, p. 61.

enough material to conduct a comprehensive discussion of performance in the annual review. This short-circuited one of the primary purposes of the appraisal program— that of giving feedback to the subordinates as to their performance. Studies of the learning process point out that feedback is less effective if much time is allowed to elapse between the performance and the feedback. This fact alone argues for more frequent discussions between the manager and the subordinate.

Goal setting, not criticism, should be used to improve performance. One of the most significant findings in our experiment was the fact that far superior results were observed when the manager and the man *together* set specific goals to be achieved, rather than merely discussed needed improvement. Frequent reviews of progress provide natural opportunities for discussing means of improving performance *as needs occur,* and these reviews are far less threatening than the annual appraisal and salary review discussions.

Separate appraisals should be held for different purposes. Our work demonstrated that it was unrealistic to expect a single performance appraisal program to achieve every conceivable need. It seems foolish to have a manager serving in the self-conflicting role as a counselor (helping a man to improve his performance) when, at the same time, he is presiding as a judge over the same employee's salary-action case.

NEW WP&R METHOD

This intensive year-long test of the performance appraisal program indicated clearly that work-planning-and-review discussions between a man and his manager appeared to be a far more effective approach in improving job performance than was the concentrated annual performance appraisal program.

For this reason, after the findings had been announced, many GE managers adopted some form of the new WP&R program to motivate performance improvement in employees, especially those at the professional and administrative levels. Briefly described, the WP&R approach calls for periodic meetings between the manager and his subordinate. During these meetings, progress on past goals is reviewed, solutions are sought for job-related problems, and new goals are established. The intent of the method is to create a situation in which manager and subordinate can discuss job performance and needed improvements in detail without the subordinate's becoming defensive.

Basic Features

This WP&R approach differs from the traditional performance appraisal program in that:

There are more frequent discussions of performance;

There are no summary judgments or ratings made;

Salary-action discussions are held separately;

The emphasis is on mutual goal planning and problem solving.

As far as frequency is concerned, these WP&R discussions are held more often than traditional performance appraisal interviews, but are not scheduled at rigidly fixed intervals. Usually at the conclusion of one work planning session the man and manager set an approximate date for the next review. Frequency depends both on the nature of the job and on the manager's style of operating. Sometimes these WP&R discussions are held as often as once a month, whereas for other jobs and/or individuals, once every six months is more appropriate.

In these WP&R discussions, the manager and his subordinate do not deal in generalities, they consider specific, objectively defined work goals and establish the yardstick for measuring performance. These goals stem, of course, from broader departmental objectives and are defined in relation to the individual's position in the department.

Comparison Setting

After the findings of our experiment were communicated by means of reports and group meetings in the plant where the research was carried out, about half the key managers decided they would abandon the comprehensive annual performance appraisal method and adopt the new WP&R program instead. The other half were hesitant to make such a major change at the time. They decided, consequently, to continue with the traditional performance appraisal program and to try to make it more effective. This provided a natural setting for us to compare the effectiveness of the two approaches. We decided that the comparison should be made in the light of the objectives usually stated for the comprehensive annual performance appraisal program. These objectives were: (a) to provide knowledge of results to employees, (b) to justify reasons for salary action, and (c) to motivate and help employees do a better job.

The study design was simple. Before any changes were made, the exempt employees who would be affected by these programs were surveyed to provide base-line data. The WP&R program was then implemented in about half of the exempt group, with the other half continuing to use a modified version of the traditional performance appraisal program. One year later, the identical survey questionnaire was again administered in order to compare the changes that had occurred.

Attitudes and Actions

The results of this research study were quite convincing. The group that continued on the traditional performance appraisal showed no change in any of the areas measured. The WP&R group, by contrast, expressed significantly more favorable attitudes on almost all questionnaire items. Specifically, their attitudes changed in a favorable direction over the year that they participated in the new WP&R program with regard to the—

... amount of help the manager was giving them in improving performance on the job;
... degree to which the manager was receptive to new ideas and suggestions;
... ability of the manager to plan;
... extent to which the manager made use of their abilities and experience;
... degree to which they felt the goals they were shooting for were what they *should* be;
... extent to which they received help from the manager in planning for *future* job opportunities;
... value of the performance discussions they had with their managers.

In addition to these changes in attitudes, evidence was also found which showed clearly that the members of the WP&R group were much more likely to have taken specific actions to improve performance than were those who continued with the traditional performance appraisal approach.

CURRENT OBSERVATIONS

Recently we undertook still another intensive study of the WP&R program in order to learn more about the nature of these discussions and how they can be made most effective. While these observations have not been completed, some interesting findings have already come to light—especially in relation to differences between WP&R and traditional performance appraisal discussions.

Perceived Differences

For one thing, WP&R interviews are strictly man-to-man in character, rather than having a father-and-son flavor, as did so many of the traditional performance appraisals. This seems to be due to the fact that it is much more natural under the WP&R program for the subordinate to take the initiative when his performance on past goals is being

reviewed. Thus, in listening to the subordinate's review of performance, problems, and failings, the manager is automatically cast in the role of *counselor*. This role for the manager, in turn, results naturally in a problem-solving discussion.

In the traditional performance appraisal interview, on the other hand, the manager is automatically cast in the role of *judge*. The subordinate's natural reaction is to assume a defensive posture, and thus all the necessary ingredients for an argument are present.

Since the WP&R approach focuses mainly on immediate, short-term goals, some managers are concerned that longer-range, broader plans and goals might be neglected. Our data show that this concern is unfounded. In almost every case, the discussion of specific work plans and goals seems to lead naturally into a consideration of broader, longer-range plans. In fact, in a substantial percentage of these sessions, even the career plans of the subordinates are reviewed.

In general, the WP&R approach appears to be a better way of defining what is expected of an individual and how he is doing on the job. Whereas the traditional performance appraisal often results in resistance to the manager's attempts to help the subordinate, the WP&R approach brings about acceptance of such attempts.

CONCLUSION

Multiple studies conducted by the Behavioral Research Service at GE reveal that the traditional performance-appraisal method contains a number of problems:

1. Appraisal interviews attempt to accomplish the two objectives of—
... providing a written justification for salary action;
... motivating the employee to improve his work performance.
2. The two purposes are in conflict, with the result that the traditional appraisal system essentially becomes a salary discussion

in which the manager justifies the action taken.

3. The appraisal discussion has little influence on future job performance.

4. Appreciable improvement is realized only when specified goals and deadlines are mutually established and agreed on by the subordinate and his manager in an interview split away from the appraisal interview.

This evidence, coupled with other principles relating to employee motivation, gave rise to the new WP&R program, which is proving to be far more effective in improving job performance than the traditional performance appraisal method. Thus, it appears likely that companies currently relying on the comprehensive annual performance appraisal process to achieve improvement in work performance might well consider the advisability of switching to some form of work-planning-and-review in their industrial personnel programs.

6

PERSONNEL SELECTION AND EQUAL EMPLOYMENT OPPORTUNITY

One of the oldest functions performed by psychologists in industry has been the selection and placement of personnel. Since the early 1900s, industrial psychologists have used various selection devices such as interviews, application blanks, tests, and references in an attempt to predict, at the time of hiring, how successful an applicant will be on a particular job. The utility of these selection instruments is traditionally estimated by determining their predictive validity.

Predictive validity is simply the extent to which the scores obtained by job applicants on a selection device are related to the criterion scores (e.g., measures of job performance) of these same workers at some future date. The strength of this relationship is measured by a statistic known as a correlation coefficient or described by expectancy charts and/or tables. Coefficients of correlation vary between -1.00 to $+1.00$; the larger the magnitude of the correlation, the more predictive power a selection device possesses. Expectancy charts show the validity of a selection device graphically rather than statistically and are usually more meaningful and understandable to nonstatisticians.

The first reading in this section, by Korman, describes the steps involved in the traditional personnel selection model (i.e., predictive validity) for both the one predictor-one criterion and the multiple predictor-one criterion cases. Korman discusses the advantages and disadvantages of the concurrent validity model, an alternate method of test validation which uses current employees instead of job applicants as examinees. He also mentions some of the problems of the traditional model which leads the reader into the next article, by Dunnette.

According to Dunnette the traditional prediction model, which links selection devices and criteria by means of correlation coefficients, is grossly oversimplified. He contends that this model is largely responsible for the fact that one rarely obtains correlation coefficients that exceed, or even equal, 0.50. He presents a more sophisticated model, one taking into account many complexities in personnel research that up to recently have been ignored.

The model calls attention to the complex interactions between predictor groupings, types of individuals, job behavior patterns, and organizational consequences. The model makes it clear that predictors can have different levels of validity for different subgroups of individuals (e.g., racial groups). It further suggests that similar job behavior may be predictable by quite different combinations of predictors and individuals or even that the same predictors can result in the prediction of different behavior patterns for different groups of individuals. The model points out also that the same job behavior can lead to different organizational consequences depending upon different situational contexts.

Title VII of the 1964 Civil Rights Act has focused considerable attention on the problem of discrimination in personnel selection. This act and the enforced guidelines of the Equal Employment Opportunity Commission (EEOC) and the Office of Federal Contract Compliance (OFCC) make it unlawful to use any selection device that adversely affects hiring, transfer, promotion, or any other employment or membership opportunity to classes protected by the act. In short, a test cannot discriminate on the basis of race, color, religion, national origin, or sex; and the burden of proof is on the employer to show that his tests are valid and not intended or used to discriminate. As a result of recent federal and state legislation as well as investigations by the EEOC and OFCC, many employers are quite concerned about their compliance with fair-employment laws. In his article Ruch discusses several basic positions taken by employers regarding the hiring of minority groups, and evaluates each in terms of its legality. Ruch reviews the various methods of validation permissible under the OFCC Testing Order and the EEOC Guidelines, and offers five recommendations for immediate action that can help the employer hire qualified applicants and still be within the constraints of the law.

The next article, by Seligman, has been included in this section because it reviews the main functions and practices of the EEOC and OFCC and discusses the impact of the U.S. Supreme Court's ruling in the case of Griggs vs. Duke Power. Seligman argues that equal employment opportunity has turned into a system whereby the Government is imposing quotas on companies. In this controversial article he argues that the Government's desire to wipe out old-fashioned discrimination in the corporate world has resulted in an undermining of other old-fashioned notions about hiring on the basis of merit. He suggests that perfectly reasonable selection standards are now being dropped by companies as being simpler than trying to defend their validity to the Government.

In the last few years we have seen a gradual change in the attitude of the American population toward the working woman. This change has been spurred by several pieces of legislation that have focused on past inequities faced by women employees (e.g., Equal Pay Act of 1963, Title VII of the Civil Rights Act, and Executive Order 11375 of 1968). Among the trends seen today are the efforts to give women pay equal to that of men for equal work, to drop sex-role stereotypes for certain jobs (e.g., male nurses and female jockeys), and to increase the opportunity for women to reach executive positions. Despite these encouraging trends, there is still a great deal of negativism toward women in the work force, especially women aspiring to or holding management positions. The next article, by Schein, focuses on one of the reasons why so few women hold management positions. According to her results, successful middle managers are perceived by male managers to possess characteristics, temperaments, and attitudes more commonly ascribed to men in general than to women. Schein discusses these results in terms of sex-role stereotyping and organizational practices.

Although there are several techniques available to an organization for assessing an applicant's subsequent job success, the employment interview is the most widely used selection device. A survey conducted about seventeen years ago (Spriegel and James, 1958) revealed that 99 per cent of the 852 firms questioned at that time interviewed their applicants before hiring them. There is every reason to believe that the popularity of the selection interview has not subsided since this survey and that its use will continue unabated. Most personnel administrators conduct their selection interviews in a relatively unstructured manner. The questions the applicant is asked and the interviewer's evaluation of the applicant's answers vary from interviewer to interviewer and from applicant to applicant. In essence, this interview style can be described as a loosely organized, casual conversation between the interviewer and interviewee covering any topics that the interviewer desires to discuss.

In view of this lack of standardization, it is not surprising that there is little evidence confirming the reliability (i.e., agreement among interviewers' evaluations of the same applicant) and validity (i.e., ability to accurately predict subsequent job performance) of the conventional selection interview. Improvement in the reliability and validity of the traditional selection interview is urgently needed for two reasons. First, as mentioned previously, companies must now provide proof that all their selection instruments are valid predictors of job performance. Second, the efficiency of this selection device must be improved to justify its continued use in light of the rising costs of recruiting and selecting new employees. The next article, entitled "Improvements in the Selection Interview," discusses some of the influences operating during the interview that may lower its reliability and validity, and suggests several ways in which these errors can be minimized. The reader is referred to other review articles by Mayfield (1964), Ulrich and Trumbo (1965), and Wright (1969) for additional information about the employment interview.

One of the most challenging problems in organizations today is the development of valid devices for identifying, selecting, and developing managerial personnel. The last article in this section deals with the assessment center, a relatively new approach for selecting and developing individuals for managerial positions. The term "assessment center" refers to a standardized off-the-job procedure in which several different types of assessment techniques (e.g., in-basket exercises, group discussions, personal interviews, peer ratings, and business games) are used to evaluate candidates for managerial positions. A number of candidates are processed at the same time, and the final assessments are the combined judgments of several trained assessors.

American Telegraph and Telephone first used the assessment-center concept in 1956 as part of its Management Progress Study (Bray and Grant, 1966), a longitudinal research study designed to identify the variables related to management success in the Bell System. AT&T got the idea of employing assessment centers from the U.S. Office of Strategic Services (OSS, 1948), which used this technique for selecting intelligence agents during World War II. Soon after the Management Progress Study had begun, the first non-research application of the assessment center was initiated at Michigan Bell to identify potential candidates for first-line management positions. Today, AT&T affiliates throughout the United States operate their own assessment centers. Many other organizations that have seen AT&T's success with the method have also begun to use it for identifying and developing managerial candidates.

The last article in this section, by Byham, describes a typical assessment center and discusses its cost, potential problems, purposes, popularity, and validity. Readers with a special interest in assessment centers are referred to an excellent article by Huck (1973), which reviews in more detail current research on the validities of assessment centers in identifying managerial skills. For an overview of management selection methods the reader is referred to Campbell, Dunnette, Lawler, and Weick (1970).

REFERENCES AND SELECTED READINGS

Bray, D. W., and Grant, D. L. The assessment center in the measurement of potential for business management. *Psychological Monographs*, 1966, 80 (17, Whole No. 625).

Campbell, J. P., Dunnette, M. D., Lawler, E. E., and Weick, K. E. *Managerial behavior, performance, and effectiveness.* New York: McGraw-Hill, 1970.

Dunnette, M. D. *Personnel selection and placement.* Belmont, Calif.: Wadsworth, 1966.

Ghiselli, E. E. *The validity of occupational aptitude tests.* New York: Wiley, 1966.

Huck, J. R. Assessment centers: A review of the external and internal validities. *Personnel Psychology,* 1973, 26, 191-212.

Mayfield, E. C. The selection interview—a re-evaluation of published research. *Personnel Psychology*, 1973, 26, 191-212.

O. S. S. Assessment Staff. *The assessment of men.* New York: Rinehart, 1948.

Spreigel, W. R., and James, V. A. Trends in recruitment and selection practices. *Personnel*, 1958, 35, 42-48.

Ulrich, L., and Trumbo, D. The selection interview since 1949. *Psychological Bulletin*, 1965, 63, 100-116.

Wiggins, J. S. *Personality and prediction: Principles of personality assessment.* Reading, Mass.: Addison-Wesley, 1973.

Wright, O. R. Summary of research on the selection interview since 1964. *Personnel Psychology*, 1969, 22, 391-413.

33

Personnel Selection: The Traditional Models

ABRAHAM K. KORMAN

THE TRADITIONAL PERSONNEL SELECTION MODEL: PREDICTIVE VALIDITY

The major contributions which industrial psychology has made to the personnel selection process have been in two areas. One has been the development of psychological measures which predict job performance and which are available to the employing company prior to the time of hiring or rejecting, while the second has concerned itself with the development of appropriate methodologies for evaluating whether or not a given predictor is actually operating effectively, i.e., whether it is predicting the behavior which it should be predicting. Information relating to these two questions has then generally been reported to management, to be used by them in their judgment and decision-making in the way they see most fit. In this chapter we shall concern ourselves with the latter contribution by industrial psychologists.

Until recent years the latter interest and concern by industrial psychologists took a relatively standardized form, i.e., those who were interested in developing effective selection procedures did pretty much the same thing, no matter what type of company they worked for.[1] This procedure, which we shall call the "traditional personnel selection model," will be discussed below as a series of steps. As we go through it the reader will see that it makes a lot of sense and that it appears to be a highly appropriate procedure to be used in personnel selection, and, in many respects, it is. However, a more searching examination, as we shall find, indicates that the picture is not all that good and that this traditional model contains within it a series of assumptions about the nature of work and human characteristics that in today's society are, sometimes (not always), dubious at best. Hence, recent years have seen a number of suggested revisions of this traditional model, and it is these revisions with their associated benefits and disadvantages which we shall discuss in this chapter.

Step 1. The Job Analysis

The traditional personnel selection model has as its first step the study of the

1. Due to Civil Service regulations the comments which we shall make in the chapter are, in general, not applicable to Government organizations.

From Abraham K. Korman, *Industrial and Organizational Psychology.* © 1971, pp. 179-204. Reprinted by permission of Prentice-Hall, Inc., Englewood Cliffs, N.J.

characteristics and required behaviors of the job for which the selection process is being undertaken. It is obvious, of course, that one must have some understanding of the nature of the job that one wishes to select for, since not to know this would reduce all selection to a purely random, chance basis. The procedure for finding out this information (which also has value for various other organizational functions such as training, job transfer, and performance appraisal) is known as a "job analysis," and it consists, usually, of a description of the various behaviors, characteristics, and abilities required of the occupant of that job. The ways in which this information is obtained varies with the company, the job, the occupant, etc., but in essence there are two major procedures.

One way is to ask the current job occupant to describe what he does, either subjectively or along some defined dimensions. This method has some advantages. It elicits worker cooperation by bringing him in on the decision making and possibly enhances his self-esteem (with consequent implications for performance) at the same time. A second advantage is, of course, that the job occupant probably knows the job better than anybody else. At the same time, however, there is the disadvantage that the job occupant will probably be most motivated to distort, either consciously or unconsciously, his description in a favored direction. Furthermore, there is another disadvantage to this procedure in that the occupant may not be psychologically, educationally, or emotionally equipped to write an accurate description of his job duties.

Similar advantages and disadvantages attach themselves to the other major job analysis method, that of "observation." Analyzing a job by observation has the advantage of eliminating "faking" to a great extent since an observer should generally be more objective. Furthermore, the observer will also usually be a "qualified" recorder. However, the first advantage could be illu-

sory in that the job occupant may fake his performance, either consciously or subconsciously, if someone is watching him. In addition, a second possible disadvantage is that this procedure is completely inappropriate for mental "thinking" jobs and for jobs which involve a long period of time before a specific job activity is finished. (The analogy here is between the division manager who might be working on a decentralization plan taking five years as opposed to the mechanical repetitive job.) Since these "long-cycle" types of jobs are becoming increasingly the norm in our society, we might expect to see a decrease in the method of "observation" in job analysis as time goes on.

Besides the advantages and disadvantages of each of these procedures, there are problems in job analysis which are common to both (and, in fact, to any observational system involving the rating of such social objects as jobs and people, as we shall point out in our later discussion on performance appraisal methods). One set of these problems has been called the "judgment" errors and can be summarized as follows:

1. *The "halo" error.* This is the tendency to allow one characteristic of a rating object to dominate ratings along other dimensions of the object being rated. An example of this is when we are more likely to attribute intellectual qualities to a person who wears glasses than a person who does not.

2. *The "central tendency" error.* This is the tendency to rate all rating objects around the "middle" or mean of a rating continuum and not to use the extremes.

3. *The "leniency" error.* This is the tendency to rate all social objects in a relatively favorable manner and not to attribute negative aspects to them.

While there are other kinds of judgment errors besides these, these are probably the most important. How one overcomes them is a different problem, however, and about this there is little agreement. In fact there are some who argue that these may not be errors at all and that one of the only reasons they are considered as such is due to the stubborn refusal of psychologists to admit that (1) some kinds of human behavior may not be distributed according to the normal bell-shaped curve (i.e., in some cases, all people might be "good") and (2) some people may actually have all their characteristics integrally a function of their main characteristic (i.e., the halo error is not an error). This seems an extreme position to take, however. Suffice to say for our purposes here that these behaviors are probably "errors" in the traditional sense but their importance and possible remedial actions will probably vary according to the given situation.

A second problem of perhaps more serious import in job analysis is how one incorporates into a description of a job's characteristics some recognition of the fact that jobs are becoming increasingly of the type whereby the behaviors that are engaged in cannot be specified in advance but result from the characteristics of the person who happens to fulfill the role at that particular time. For example, let us look at the differences between a management role and the role of a sewing-machine operator in a dress factory. It is much simpler to specify in advance what the behavior of the latter should be than the former. In fact, it is probably very much the case that the essence of the managerial role is success in the ability to handle problems which cannot be specified or "programmed" in advance. While this difference in potential specificity of roles was always a problem for job analysts, its significance is increasing greatly because more jobs in our automated society are becoming increasingly like that of the manager and increasingly less like that of the sewing-machine operator.

It should be emphasized that we are not suggesting that we do away with the job analysis as an aid in the selection (and other manpower utilization) program. This is clearly an impossibility, since the alternative is chaos. However, it is to suggest that this is a significant problem which must be taken into account in future job analysis research.

Step 2. Hypothesis Development

The second step in the traditional model is derived from the job analysis, with this step consisting, essentially, of hypothesis generation as to the kinds of individuals who would be most likely to fit the behavioral demands of the job. This step can be a subjective one based on a subjective appraisal of the job analysis information. Hence, it can be highly dependent on the cognitive characteristics of the person developing the hypotheses. Unfortunately, we know little about the kinds of people who would be particularly good at this type of thing. Such recognition of this situation is, undoubtedly, one of the reasons the more common procedure in job analysis has been to describe jobs in terms of more objective psychological dimensions and then to verify such descriptions by either (1) testing job occupants with unambiguous tests of these dimensions, or (2) getting qualified inter-judge agreement as to the importance of the dimensions for the given job. Due to the difficulty of getting tests which are unambiguous measures of simple psychological dimensions, particularly in nonability areas, the latter verification procedure is the more common one today.

A good example of the kinds of dimension by which jobs may be described and compared with one another in terms of the requirements they call for is seen in Table 33-1. This summarizes some recent work by McCormick and his co-workers (cf. McCormick, Cunningham, and Gordon, 1967). Since these dimensions can be used in varying quantities to describe a variety of different jobs, it is obvious that this project has great potential for assisting in such personnel activities as selection, job promotions, transfers, training, etc.

Table 33-1. Dimensions of Job Behavior and Examples

1. *Decision-making and communication activities:*
   Develops budgets; supervises management personnel; verbal presentations; forecasts needs; variety of communications; personnel decisions
2. *Hierarchical person-to-person interaction:*
   Instructs; supervises students, trainees, patients, subordinates, etc; issues directives; schedules work of others; interchanges information with prospective employees, students, or trainees
3. *Skilled physical activities:*
   Skill of hand tool usage; number of hand tools used; finger manipulation; estimates size
4. *Mental vs. physical activities:*
   Positive loadings—deals with data; interprets information; intelligence; uses mathematics; clerical tasks
   Negative loadings—manual force; moves objects by hand; deals with things
5. *Responsible personal contact:*
   Persuades; interchanges information with customers, clients, patients, etc.; distractions from people seeking or giving information
6. *General physical activities:*
   Adjustment to the vertical; climbing; balancing; general physical coordination
7. *Unpleasant vs. pleasant working conditions:*
   Uncomfortable atmosphere; unclean environment
8. *Decisions affecting people:*
   Personnel decisions (promotions, trnasfers, hiring, etc.)
9. *Varied intellectual vs. structural activities:*
   Positive loadings—interpretation of information; intelligence; usage of mathematics; occupation prestige
   Negative loadings—high job structure; repetitiveness; deals with things
10. *Supervisory activities:*
    Supervises others; issues directives; number of people supervised
11. *Man-machine control activities:*
    Control operations; monitors work process; interpretation of information; responsible for physical assets
12. *Planning and decision-making:*
    Uniqueness of decisions; time span of decisions; forcasts needs; develops methods
13. *Skilled manual activities:*
    Skill of hand tool usage; finger manipulation; number of hand tools used
14. *Intellectual vs. physical activities:*
    Positive loadings—"thinking" (vs. "doing"); occupation prestige
    Negative loadings—activity domain—things; repetitiveness; job structure
15. *Body-balancing activities:*
    Adjustment to the vertical; balancing; climbing
16. *Physical vs, sedentary activities:*
    Positive loadings—standing; general force; manual force
    Negative loadings—activity domain—data
17. *Clerical activities:*
    Clerical tasks (filing, typing, shorthand, etc.)
18. *Knee-bending activities:*
    Crawling; kneeling; stooping
19. *Informative communications:*
    Giving information; instructing; issuing directives; verbal communications
20. *Communication of data:*
    Reporting; activity domain—data; interchange of information; written communication
21. *Persuasive communications:*
    Persuading; verbal presentations; negotiating
22. *Public contact activities:*
    Publicizing; information interchange with public
23. *White- vs. blue-collar situations:*
    Positive loadings—wearing presentable clothing; social obligations; occupational prestige
    Negative loadings—receiving hourly and/or overtime pay; receives close supervision

Table 33-1—*Continued*

24. *Job security vs. performance-dependent income:*
    Positive loadings—job security; occupational prestige
    Negative loadings—receives tips, commissions, hourly pay, and/or overtime pay
25. *Apparel: Optional vs. work clothes:*
    Positive loading—wears special working clothes
    Negative loading—dress left to incumbent's discretion
26. *Apparel: Formal vs. optional:*
    Positive loadings—wears presentable clothing; social obligations; occupational prestige
    Negative loading—dress left to incumbent's discretion
27. *Apparel: Specific uniform:*
    Wears specific uniform
28. *Hourly pay vs. salary:*
    Positive loading—regular salary
    Negative loading—hourly pay; overtime pay
29. *Annoying environment:*
    Noise; uncomfortable atmosphere; poor illumination; cramped work space

Source: E. J. McCormick, J. W. Cunningham, C. G. Gordon: Job dimensions based on factorial analyses of worker-oriented job variables. *Personnel Psychology,* 1967, 20, 417-30.

Step 3. Predictor Development

Once the relevant psychological and behavior variables have been hypothesized, it is time for the third step. This consists of deciding how one is to measure individual differences in job applicants on the relevant variables. The most important problem is that it is important that one choose a measure which actually measures the relevant psychological variable which one is proposing as being demanded by the job. The reasons for this are simple. If the chosen measure is not an actual measure of the relevant variable, two possible problems develop, depending on whether or not the measure is actually related to job performance. First, we may reject a good hypothesis as to the cause of good job performance in a given job and not know it. Hence, whatever else we eventually learn about the job in terms of selection and training, such knowledge must always be incomplete, perhaps seriously so. Suppose, however, that the "mistake" works; i.e., suppose we have hypothesized "sociability" as an important variable but have measured "anxiety" by mistake (without knowing it) and "anxiety" does actually predict job performance. It does not matter, the "prac-

tical" man says, that it does not measure what it is supposed to measure, since it predicts job performance and hence can be used for selection. The answer to this is that this is a wasteful, shortsighted, uneconomical attitude.[2] One reason this is so can be seen if we assume that the relevant important psychological variable is "sociability" (when it is really "anxiety"). First, all of the recommendations for managerial action in training, development, appraisal, and promotion which would follow from such a successful prediction would be based on a mistaken, erroneous belief. A second reason this attitude is an impractical one relates to the fact that jobs do change, and sometimes a variable which used to predict performance no longer does. Hence, if we find that our measure of sociability (which is really anxiety) no longer predicts job performance, we shall start looking for new predictors eliminating sociability, although a good measure of sociability might now be a good predictor on the changed job.

How does one decide, then, when a measure is actually a measure of the desired

2. Actually, this was also the implicit attitude of some practical industrial psychologists for many years. Even these, however, paid lip service to our step 3, even if they did not follow it very often.

variable? The best process for this is a procedure known as "construct validity," consisting basically of looking at all the relationships which the proposed measure of the variable has with other measured variables and then deciding whether or not these observed relationships are consistent with what they should be if the measure was really measuring what it says it is. (The judgment is, of course, a subjective one and hence must be a result of the knowledge and skills of the person making the judgment.) As an example, let us look at Table 33-2, where we have listed the results of a con-

Table 33-2. Relationships Between Ghiselli Self-Assurance Scale and Other Psychological Measures

Nature of Sample	Measure	N	Means of "Highs"[a]	N	Means of "Lows"	Significance Level[b]
Engineering students	Gough Adjective Checklist *Self-Confidence Scale*	14	52.60	20	46.60	.05
Industrial foremen	Miner *Sentence Completion Scale* (a projective test of organizational power orientation)	10	4.70	12	.60	.05
Business students	Crites *Need for Social Service* (Likert-type scale)	35	5.77	36	7.97	.05
Business students	Crites *Need for Job Freedom* (Likert-type scale)	35	9.60	36	8.22	.10
Industrial foremen	Biographical data frequency with which parents supervised their jobs and tasks (lower score = greater frequency of supervision)	15	2.93	23	2.30	.05
Industrial foremen	Biographical data frequency with which they argued with their parents during teens (higher score = greater frequency of arguments)	15	2.73	23	2.34	.05
Liberal arts students	Marlow-Crowne SD Scale[c]	89	$r = .16$			No Score
Business students	Bass *Self-Orientation* (forced-choice tetrads)	20	27.10	15	24.06	.10

Source: A. Korman: Task success, task popularity and self-esteem as influences on task liking. *Journal of Applied Psychology,* 1968, *52,* 484-90. Copyright 1968 by the American Psychological Association, and reproduced by permission.

[a]Division between "highs" and "lows" was based on the median of national norms.
[b]All significance tests are two-tailed.
[c]I am indebted to Mrs. Virginia Dunda and Mr. Charles Miller for these data.

struct validity study of a scale known as the Ghiselli Self-Assurance Scale. Defined as a measure of the extent to which people see themselves as "competent, need-satisfying, and able to deal with their problems," it can be seen in this table that the relationships with other variables are about as they should be, given this kind of definition. Were they not of this nature, then we would have a basis for inferring that the scale was not a measure of what it claimed to be.

It should be noted that the process of establishing the construct validity of an instrument is a never-ending one, and that we must continually be concerned with obtaining new information on the construct validity of our instrument since the more we know about it, the more we can have confidence that we are actually measuring what we claim we are measuring. In this sense, then, the development of the construct validity of an instrument is similar to the testing of the utility of a theory. In both cases, however, as we have emphasized throughout this book, great practical benefits ensue.

What kinds of predictors are typically chosen? As indicated above, the development of measures of characteristics that will be good predictors of performance has been a primary concern of industrial psychologists with the result that a wide variety of different measures may be used. Briefly, we may summarize them into the following categories (others besides these are possible):

1. *Ability tests.* These consist of measures of verbal and other abilities. . . .

2. *Objective personality tests.* These are measures of personality characteristics which have a relatively structured format; i.e., the individual respondent describes himself along dimensions defined by the test constructor rather than along dimensions defined by himself.

3. *Projective personality tests.* These are measures of personality characteristics which have an unstructured format and which allow the individual to respond along any dimension which he wishes and which he constructs.

4. *Objective life-history items.* These consist of questions concerning relatively objective characteristics of a person's school, work, and personal background; the rationale for these is that they are measures of various attitudinal and personal characteristics of the individual which are not measured by other means.

5. *Interviews and other judgmental assessments.* These consist of judgments by various individuals as to the extent to which the individual possesses the behavioral characteristics which are felt to be necessary for adequate job performance.

Which of these are the best? As we shall see later, this is a multidimensional question, with the answer depending on the criteria used, the occupations involved, various ethical problems, theoretical measurement problems, etc. To some extent, it is even a meaningless question, since such a question implies that one may have a choice in the given situation. Yet this may not be the case.

For example, the best predictors of job performance have consistently been ability tests. However, just as consistently, it has also been shown that their predictive effectiveness will reach only a certain point and that it is necessary to use personality test variables if one wishes to predict performance more accurately above this point, even though personality tests are generally not as effective predictors as ability tests (Guion and Gottier, 1965).[3]

For these reasons, then, our later procedure will be not to bother to make any comparative claims as to the relative fruitfulness of these kinds of measures, since all have their uses in given situations and all must be improved to the greatest extent possible. Their usefulness depends on the given prediction situation and the given prediction problem, and they must be eval-

3. Guion, R. M., and Gottier, R. F. Validity of personnel measures in personnel selection. *Personnel Psychology,* 1965, 18, 135-64.

uated as such, a procedure which constitutes the basis for our discussion here. (It should be noted, however, that there may be different ethical problems involved with each of these measures. . . .)

Step 4. Administration of Predictors to Applicant Sample

Once the measures of the relevant behaviors have been decided upon, they are administered to the applicants for the job in question. However, the measures are *not* used as a basis for selection at this time. Rather, the applicants are then selected for the job in question on the basis of whatever procedures for this process are existing at that time. The scores on the hypothesized predictor measures are filed away at this time, to be utilized in connection with step 5.

The reasoning behind this procedure can be explained quite simply. Thus, if we use the hypothesized measure as a basis for hiring, then we shall never know what the job performance would have been of those individuals with the predictor scores who were not hired. That is, if the company were to take in only those with high scores, then we would not know the eventual performance of those with low scores and vice versa. The problem is, of course, that the unselected group might have been better in job performance than the selected; something we could not know unless we gave them the opportunity.

Step 5. Relate Predictor Test Scores to Measure of Job Performance

After the applicants have been hired and been on the job for a long enough period of time to get some meaningful measure of differences in job performance, the first critical point in this process is reached. This is to relate scores on the predictor variable to the measure of job performance, i.e., the criterion.

There are two major problems which are of concern here. First, what measures of relationship should be used, and what are the advantages and disadvantages of each of these measures? Second, how shall we interpret the results found in terms of their practical significance for organizational action? These are the questions we shall attempt to answer here, discussing both where we have only *one* predictor variable for each applicant and where we have more than one predictor variable for each person.

1. *The correlation coefficient.* Undoubtedly, the most popular method for describing the relationship between two variables that has been utilized in personnel selection research has been the correlation coefficient, or r. The reasons for this are several. First, there is the element of familiarity, i.e., most industrial psychologists are quite familiar with it, having studied it as part of their graduate training. Second, it is a convenient way of summarizing a relationship into one general descriptive term. Hence, when we say that a correlation is .60, it is agreed that this means something different than when we say a correlation is .10 or $-.35$. A third reason for the great utilization of the correlation coefficient is that there is a considerable amount of theory developed around it, theory concerned with how much confidence we can have in certain obtained results, given certain assumptions. Thus, because the theory concerning the correlation coefficient is well developed, we are able to specify, given certain assumptions, the likelihood that our results are not due to "chance" or "unstable" factors and we can also estimate the degree to which our specifications will be in error. Related to both this reason and the second is a fourth advantage of using the correlation coefficient as a measure of a relationship and that is that the actual r obtained is directly convertible into a measure of predictive accuracy, the purpose of the whole selection mechanism process. Finally, and this should

not be underestimated, a fifth reason for the frequent use of r is that it constitutes part of the "mystique" of the industrial psychologist as opposed to the typical manager and thus enables the former to "look good" in this sense. This is, of course, not necessarily an advantage of r except for the benefit of the psychologist.

These advantages hold whether we are concerned with the situation when we have only one predictor variable for each applicant or, the far more common case, when we are concerned with more than one predictor in a given selection situation. In the latter situation, the correlation coefficient which is used is called the multiple correlation coefficient, as opposed to the "simple r," the measure used in the case where there is only one predictor variable. The two can be distinguished in this way:

1. For the case of one predictor-one criterion, we correlate the two variables X (the predictor) and Y (the criterion) using the appropriate formula.[4]
2. For the case of multiple predictors-one criterion, the procedure can be outlined conceptually as follows:[5]

    a. Assume four predictor variables, X_1, X_2, X_3, and X_4, and one criterion variable, Y.

    b. All the predictor variables are correlated with the criterion variable and with each other.

    c. Each predictor variable is then weighted by a statistical procedure according to the degree of its intercorrelations with the criterion and with the other predictor variables; the higher the correlation with the criterion and the lower the correlation with the other predictors, the greater the weight that specific variable has for predicting that criterion.

    d. The absolute sum of these weights are then converted, again statistically, into a

correlation coefficient called the multiple r. . . . In this case, of course, the X or predictor variable is not a single variable, but a weighted composite of the four predictor variables, with each individual's score on this composite being the average of his scores on each of the predictor variables, corrected by the weight for the variables. An example of this procedure is given in Figure 33-6.

The last statement does point to one difference between the simple and multiple r which the reader should keep in mind and which does limit to an extent the general equating of the two we have made here. This difference results because the weighting system used in developing the multiple correlation is based on *maximizing* the correlation between the predictors and criterion and all variables are weighted on this basis, whether the scores that are being weighted are based on real, valid differences between people or on chance, accidental influences on the scores. The problem is that these chance, accidental scores are counted only if they add to the level of the correlation coefficient. They are *not* counted if they decrease this level; rather, they are ignored. It is for this reason that the multiple r has a general tendency to be too high, given the nature of the scores involved. Hence, it is even more necessary in the case where the multiple r is used that the step we have called "cross-validation," which we shall discuss later, be employed.

This is not the only disadvantage in the use of r or even the most serious, since there are other problems in utilizing this procedure as a way of determining the relationship between a hypothesized predictor of job behavior and an actual measure of job behavior. One of these problems stems from the fact that r measures the extent to which two variables order a group of people similarly. The greater the similarity in ordering, the higher the r, and the greater the discrepancy in ordering of the individuals, the lower the r. The latter aspect is particularly

---

4. See any standard statistics textbook.
5. The reader may consult any standard statistics textbook for a discussion of the statistical equations of multiple r.

		(a)		(b)		(c)	
		X	Y	X_1	Y_1	X_2	Y_2
Individual	A	10	18	10	16	10	18
	B	9	16	9	18	9	16
	C	8	14	8	18	8	12
Acceptable job behavior (Y = 14 or more)							
Unacceptable job behavior							
	D	7	12	7	12	7	14
	E	6	10	6	10	6	10
	F	5	8	5	8	5	8

Fig. 33-1

important, since such discrepancies in ordering have a negative effect on r, no matter what levels of the variables we are talking about, even though in many selection situations there may be some discrepancies which are more important than others. For example, let us look at (a) in Figure 33-1. In this case, let X be a predictor (either a simple predictor or a weighted composite such as in the multiple r) and Y be *actual* job behavior, i.e., the kind of work the person will actually do. Now look at (b) and (c), both of which give examples of different kinds of predictors (X_1 and X_2) and levels of job behaviors which each predicts (Y_1 and Y_2). Both X_1 and X_2 make the same level of error and both show equal correlations with actual job performance (Y); yet X_1 is much more useful than X_2 since it errs at a level which is unimportant (i.e., high in the distribution where everybody performs well), whereas X_2 errs at a crucial point in the distribution (i.e., it predicts a poor performer to perform well and a good performer to perform poorly).

Another problem with the use of correlation as a measure of a relationship is that is assumes that a straight line best describes the relationship between the two sets of pairs [see (a) in Figure 33-1 for a good example]. Yet, it is conceivable that some predictors would not be linearly related to the criterion but curvilinearly. For example, let us suppose that we wish to use a test of intelligence to predict performance as a department store sales clerk. One might certainly assume that at least a certain level of intelligence is required to write sales slips, take returns, etc. Hence, one would predict a positive correlation between intelligence and performance, or would one? Would this relationship also be so once we sampled above the average in intelligence? Would it not be just as likely here that the relationship would turn negative, since high-intelligence people would become bored with the job? If this were so, then the relationship would be a U-shaped one, as in Figure 33-2. While most relationships studied in industry have been found to be linear ones, the possibility of the kinds of relationships we have hypothesized here has made psycholo-

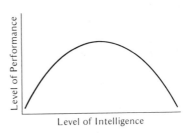

Fig. 33-2

gists increasingly wary of a blind use of r without studying the specific prediction situation.

A third problem with the use of r concerns how one actually interprets the actual figures obtained. There are two problems here. One is the tendency of some to interpret r as the proportion of predictive accuracy; e.g., and r of $+.50$ is twice as accurate as an r of $+.25$. This is *not* so. The most that can be said in this respect is that r's can be compared with one another. That is, an r of .50 is equal to an r^2 of .25 (.50 $\times$ .50) and an r of .70 is equal to an r^2 of .49 (.70 $\times$ .70), and the latter "explains" or is about twice as useful as the former. However, for the r figure itself, about all that can be said is that an r of .50 is greater than an r of .30 and so on. The second problem is the interpretation of the actual level of r itself. How much confidence can we have in it as being (1) useful in prediction and (2) a consistent, reliable relationship? Theoretically, this is a function of (1) the size of the obtained correlation and (2) the sample size. Thus, various formulas are available which provide us with a guide for determining whether a given correlation is "significant" or not (i.e., whether it is as a result of chance fluctuation or whether it really does seem to indicate a true relationship between variables). To an overwhelming extent industrial psychologists have used this concept of significance, as defined by statistical theory, as their guide to evaluating their obtained correlations for importance. There have been some objections to this, however, with the major one being that a "significant" correlation (i.e., one cited as being a "real" relationship between a given predictor and a measure of job behavior) may actually be one that is very small in actual size, if it is based on a large enough sample size. For example, a correlation of .10, based on a sample of 400, is "significant" at the .05 level of probability (i.e., there is less than 5 per cent chance that this relationship could have occurred by chance alone, given the size of the obtained relationship and the sample size). Since this correlation is only equal to about 1 per cent of predictive accuracy ($r^2 = .10 \times .10$), we can see why there have been some complaints about this concept of statistically defined significance. Surely being able to improve the accuracy in prediction 1 per cent hardly seems "significant"! As a result, Dunnette and Kirchner (1965), among others, have argued that the correlations obtained in prediction studies should be evaluated in terms of practical rather than statistical significance. While this is a laudable argument with which the author is in agreement, it must be admitted that how one translates practical significance into guides for decision-making is still a question.

Perhaps the only way of even approaching some kind of meaningful judgment as to whether a given correlation is of practical significance is to view it in terms of the specifics of a given situation, since it is these specifics which may play an important part in determining whether or not to use selection instruments at all. For example, let us contrast the sets of situations given in Figure 33-3.

Situation A	Situation B	Situation C
Job is very simple: 90% of the applicant population could perform it	Job is of medium difficulty; 45% of the applicant population could perform it	Job is of great difficulty: 10% of the applicant population could perform it

Fig. 33-3

Let us assume that we do not have any selection instruments at all and we hire all people who apply for each job; that is, we predict that *all* will succeed. The number of mistakes in prediction we shall make are as follows:

Situation A = 10% (the base rate of success is 90%)
Situation B = 55% (the base rate of success is 45%)
Situation C = 90% (the base rate of success is 10%)

Hence, if a test is to be of practical usefulness, its correlation coefficient must be higher in situation A than in situation B and much higher than in situation C, since our accuracy of prediction is so much higher in the former than the latter without the use of any selection instruments at all. (It is for this reason that selection instruments are often utilized in managerial and high-level selection which would be considered to be too low to be of practical usefulness when dealing with lower-level employees.) This, then, is one factor which enables us to interpret when a correlation coefficient is practically useful.

A second factor of significance is the selection ratio. Consider the situation where we need select only 1 of 100 applicants for a job, as opposed to one where we must select 50 of 100. Since in the first case we can take only the best, a selection instrument does not have to be very accurate in increasing our ability to predict job behavior over chance levels. It only has to be a little bit better than chance in order to help us in picking out the best person for the job. On the other hand, this is not the case in the latter situation, where we must pick out 50 and where, hence, the selection instrument must be high to be useful. The former case is called a "low selection ratio" situation and the latter, of course, a "high selection ratio" situation.

These two factors, then, the "base rate of success" (or "difficulty level" of the job) and the selection ratio in the given situation, are the major guides we have in determining the practical usefulness of a given selection instrument for any given selection question. The two are combined in making a judgment as to whether the obtained correlation coefficient is a useful one or not. To show how this may be done, Ghiselli and Brown (1955) have suggested the principles indicated in Table 33-3. (Note that "validity" in Table 33-3 means the correlation coefficient between the predictor and the criterion.)

2. *Simple and multiple cut-off systems.* To overcome some of the weaknesses of the correlation coefficient as a way of describing the relationship between the hypothesized predictors of job behavior and actual job behavior, an increasing number of psychologists have suggested the use of simple and multiple cut-off systems. These, in essence, are expectancy charts and/or tables which depict the level of job performance which is to be expected from any given level of predictor scores; cut-offs can then be developed both for simple and multiple predictors which will maximize the level of performance. An example of a simple predictor expectancy chart is given in Figure 33-4.

Although the cut-off methods do not provide convenient summary figures for describing the obtained relationships, a look at this chart indicates the obvious advantages which account for its increasing usage. It is clear and easy to interpret, thus overcoming the resistance to the correlation coefficient as a medium of communication which is frequently found among nonpsychologically trained people. A second advantage is perhaps a more technically important one in that it can be keyed to any type of relationship, linear or curvilinear, better than the correlation coefficient. Consider the example given in Figure 33-5.

If we were to compute the correlation coefficient between these variables, it would probably not be a high one due to the lack of variation in criterion performance for all those with predictor scores of 7 or above. Hence, we might discard this predictor if we

Table 33-3. Usefulness of Selection Devices When
Related to Validity, Selection Ratio, and Job Difficulty

The higher the validity of the selection device, the larger will be the proportion of selected persons who turn out to be satisfactory (e.g., with a selection ratio and job difficulty of 50%, a validity of .75 will yield 77% satisfactory workers. Under these same conditions a validity of .25 will yield only 58% satisfactory workers).

The smaller the proportion of candidates selected, the larger will be the proportion of selected persons who turn out to be satisfactory (e.g., with a validity of .50 and a job difficulty of 50%, a selection ratio of 20% will yield 78% satisfactory workers, whereas a selection ratio of 80% will yield only 57% satisfactory workers).

The easier the job, the larger will be the proportion of selected persons who turn out to be satisfactory (e.g., with a validity of .50 and a selection ratio of 50%, a job with a base success level of 80% will yield 91% satisfactory workers, but one with a base success level of 20% will yield only 31% satisfactory workers).

A selection device of lower validity when coupled with a lower selection ratio may be as effective as, or more effective than, a device of higher validity which is coupled with a higher selection ratio (e.g., for a job of 50% difficulty, with a validity of .25 and a selection ratio of 20%, the yield of successful workers will be 64%. In a job of equal difficulty, but with a validity of .75 and a selection ratio of 80%, the yield of successful workers will be 61%).

A selection device of lower validity when applied to an easier job may be as effective as, or more effective than, one of higher validity which is applied to a harder job (e.g., with a selection ratio of 50%, a validity of .25 and a job difficulty of 80%, the yield of successful workers will be 86%. With a selection ratio of 50%, a validity of .75, and a job difficulty of 20%, the yield of successful workers will only be 37%).

Source: E. Ghiselli and C. W. Brown: Personnel and industrial psychology. New York: McGraw-Hill, 1955.

were using correlation analysis. On the other hand, if we were using a cut-off system, we would have perfect prediction if we selected all those with predictor scores of 7 or more and rejected those with scores of 6 or less.

The comparative discussion is somewhat analogous but does get more complex when we talk about situations where there are multiple predictors. To review our previous comments, the reader will recall that in the multiple r situation the various predictor variables are weighted in terms of their relationships to the criterion. In essence, each individual is then assigned a score based on his scores on the predictor variables, corrected by the weights for each variable. Consider Figure 33-6, taken from our example in Figure 33-4.

One aspect which is immediately apparent and which is crucial to our discussion is that there is a variety of ways by which a person may derive a given X score on the composite variable. Hence, person A sets a score of 62 by being high on variables 2 and 3, even though he is only medium on variable 1. On the other hand, individual E is high on variable 1 but he is considerably lower on variables 2 and 3. In other words, E has "compensated" for being low on variable 2 by being higher on variable 1. This principle of "compensation" and of there being alternative ways to derive high predictor scores is the essence of the multiple correlation system.

Suppose, now, that we wanted to use a multiple cut-off system. How would this operate? Using the same sample, suppose we found that the following cut-offs for each of the variables led to the highest level of predicted performance:

Cut-off Levels

Variable X_1 = 9 or more
Variable X_2 = 6 or more
Variable X_3 = 3 or more

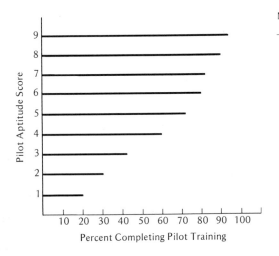

Number with this score	Approximate odds of success
14,682	9 in 10
15,286	9 in 10
24,367	8 in 10
30,066	8 in 10
31,091	7 in 10
22,827	6 in 10
11,471	4 in 10
2,239	3 in 10
904	2 in 10

Number scoring in this range	Approximate odds of staying with firm 1½ years or more
18	9 in 10
20	6 in 10
21	4 in 10
24	1 in 10

Fig. 33-4

Examples of simple cut-off systems relating test scores to job behavior. (a) Chart showing relation between pilot aptitude score and successful completion of pilot training (Psychological activities in training command AAF, *Psychological Bulletin*, 1945, 42, 46). (b) Chart showing relation between biographical "score" and length of service for female office employees (Development of a weighted application blank to aid in the selection of office employees, Research Report No. 7, *Personnel Research*, 3M Co., 1956).

Source: M. D. Dunnette and W. Kirchner: *Psychology applied to business and industry.* New York: Appleton-Century-Crofts, 1965.

According to these levels, using our previous examples, the following decisions would be made:

Individual A	=	Hire
Individual B	=	Reject
Individual C	=	Reject
Individual D	=	Hire
Individual E	=	Hire

Hence, we see that requiring each individual to be above a given level on all predictors, as in the multiple cut-off system, leads to different decisions than when we allow a person to compensate for being low on one predictor by being extra high on the other.

Which system is a better one? There is, of course, no simple answer to this. It depends

Fig. 33-5

Predictor X	Criterion Y
10	25
9	25
8	25
7	25
Acceptable performance	Unacceptable performance
6	20
5	18
4	16
3	14

on the situation. In some prediction situations it would seem that we can safely allow compensation and use the multiple r method, given the other advantages we have previously mentioned. However, it is also apparent that cut-offs may be necessary on some variables in that a low score on that given predictor cannot be compensated for by high scores on any other predictor. An example of this concerns the necessity of visual acuity for being a dentist. Unless the dentist has a high level of visual acuity, any other ability of his, verbal, manipulative, or otherwise, is not likely to be of use or value to him.

Hence, perhaps the best approach to use in the multiple predictor situation is a combination of the multiple cut-off and multiple correlation methods. The first step would be to use the multiple cut-off method for those variables where a minimum level is considered necessary and select people on that basis. After this is done, the multiple r method should be used with the remaining predictors in order to select from those remaining after the initial cut-off is made.

Step 6. Cross-Validation

The next step in the traditional personnel selection model depends on whether or not the results in step 5 look promising. Assuming that they do, the next step is to *repeat the entire procedure*, utilizing the same job, same measure of performance, same kinds of applicants, etc. The reason for this kind of procedure relates to the essentially conservative nature of the scientific endeavor in that it is felt that despite proper precautions of the type we have discussed, it is always conceivable that a single obtained result, no matter how positive the relationship, could always occur on the basis of chance factors alone. Hence, to have greater confidence in the results, one should always replicate or repeat the study. This is the purpose of the cross-validation step.

Unfortunately, it is often the case that the results of step 5 are not promising enough to continue to the cross-validation attempt. In this case, there is nothing else to do according to the traditional personnel selection model but start all over again.

Step 7. Recommendation for Selection

Finally, the last step in the procedure, assuming that step 6 works out, is to make recommendations for selection. The essential problem here is to develop a procedure as to the kinds of scores which will be acceptable for selection and to set up guidelines for the administration of such recommendations. Often such recommended guidelines may take the form of the tables given in Figure 33-4 with the desired scores outlined in some manner. Since this whole procedure is one that depends very much on the specifics

Fig. 33-6

Predictors						
	Variables				*Composite predictor*	
	X_1	X_2	X_3	X_4	*score (i.e., the X vari-*	*Level necessary*
Individual weights	3	2	1	0	*able in the multiple*	*for hiring*
					correlation equation)	*decision = 55*
Applicants						
A	10	12	8	9	62	Hire
B	6	7	15	9	47	Reject
C	13	3	11	15	56	Hire
D	9	6	8	4	47	Reject
E	13	10	3	8	62	Hire

of a given situation, we shall not bother to discuss it further here.

This, then, is the traditional personnel selection procedure in outline form. Its advantages are that it is statistically based, it attempts to limit human error, and it provides checks on the various steps along the way. Hence, it should work well, and it does *when* the implicit assumptions involved in it are met. However, the problem has been that these assumptions are being met less and less in today's world and new models and procedures in personnel selection are becoming necessary in some situations. In addition, these revised models have been designed to meet other problems which seem to be increasingly common in the process of personnel selection. Let us see, then, what some of these assumptions and problems of the traditional model are.

The first major assumption which underlies the procedures in this model is what seems to be a belief in a "static" world relating to both jobs and people. Very clearly, there is a strong assumption here that the kinds of people who apply for a given job will not change over time, nor will the characteristics of the job. Is this a reasonable assumption? It probably was in the days when our predominant organized work force consisted of blue-collar individuals engaged in semiskilled, manual factory employment, but these jobs are increas-

ingly less the case today. We now have more white-collar than blue-collar employed people and the discrepancy is increasing all the time. Since white-collar work is generally less routinized than factory work, the opportunities for innovation and job change by particular job occupants is much greater. Furthermore, an increasing number of white-collar workers are in jobs where the opportunity for job innovation and self-expression are expressly engineered into the job. In this class we may put such positions as research and managerial personnel, among others. Clearly, the assumption of the static nature of the job is difficult to meet here, and, if it is, it is done at so high a level of abstract behavioral dimensions as to make it meaningless as a guideline to specific selection.

A related argument can be made for the assumption as to the similarity of applicant populations. We live in a dynamic society and we are constantly being subjected to various legal, social, and ethical constraints on our behavior, constraints which are always changing. A good example of this is the greatly increased concern with minority-group employment and utilization, the implications for selection, training, and development of which we shall discuss in more detail later. Suffice it to say at this point that it should be obvious to all but the densest that a large company in a downtown metropolitan area is proceeding in a somewhat foolhardy manner if it assumes, without checking, that its applicant pool, particularly for low-level positions, is equivalent psychologically to the type of applicants the company had 10 or even 5 years ago.

The second major problem with this model is a fairly obvious one, that of sample size. It is clearly the case that one cannot apply this procedure unless we have a considerable number of people doing the same job, with this not changing over time. Again, one can see the remains here of a way of thinking about jobs which was adequate for the industrial world of 20 to 30 years ago but which is increasingly less so. The very essence of managerial, technical, and much other white-collar employment is their very "uniqueness" and the fact that they, and only they, do that type of work in the organization. While there are many jobs

Table 33-4. Difference in Validity According to Race

A. CORRELATIONS BETWEEN APTITUDE AND M-SCALE SUBTESTS WITH GRADE-POINT AVERAGE AS A FUNCTION OF RACE AND SEX

SAMPLE Race and Sex	Verbal Aptitude	Aptitude and M-Scale Subtests Correlated With Grade-Point Average					
		GSCI	HTI	PJCS	WRL	M Total	N
Negro							
Male	−.01	.26[a]	.14	.30[a]	.36[a]	.37[a]	104
Female	.25[a]	.46[a]	.40[a]	.34[a]	.64[a]	.55[a]	129
White							
Male	.62[a]	.50[a]	.42[a]	.32[a]	.51[a]	.50[a]	254
Female	.21[a]	.21[a]	.29[a]	.18[a]	.34[a]	.43[a]	261

B.

Predictor	Group	Correlations with Over-all Job Effectiveness
Numerical test	Total	.29[a]
	White (N = 39)	.32[a]
	Negro (N = 33)	.21
Coding test	Total	.19
	White	.04
	Negro	.48[b]
Total score	Total	.34[b]
	White	.24
	Negro	.47[b]

Sources: (A) R. L. Green and W. Farquahr: Negro academic motivation and scholastic achievement. Journal of Educational Psychology, 1965, 56, 241-43. © 1965 by the American Psychological Association, and reproduced by permission. (B) Reprinted by permission of New York University Press from Testing and fair employment: Fairness and validity of personnel tests for different ethnic groups, by James J. Kirkpatrick, Robert B. Ewen, Richard S. Barrett, and Raymond A. Katzell. © 1968 by New York University.

Note: Abbreviations used: GSCI, Generalized Situational Choice Inventory; PJCS, Preferred Job Characteristic Scale.

[a] $p < .05$
[b] $p < .01$

where this assumption still holds, it is obvious that there are many where it does not, and personnel selection procedures must be revised to take this into account.

A third problem is also a relatively obvious one and that is the amount of time involved. To develop a set of predictor instruments utilizing the traditional personnel selection model, a longitudinal study must be undertaken with *no* guarantee that the attempt will be a successful one (see step 6). This, of course, makes it a problem to sell to management.

A fourth and final problem with the procedure is not quite as obvious as this but is potentially a far more serious one. This has to do with the very clear assumption in this procedure that when we find a set of predictors of job behavior these will be equally applicable to all individuals applying for that job in terms of determing success on the job. In other words, it is assumed that if a person is to succeed on a job it is because he has the required amount of that given characteristic, and if he is to fail it is because he lacks the characteristic. There is no acknowledgment anywhere that some small subgroup of the population might succeed on the job for a different reason, and, hence, these people's unique characteristics that would enable them to succeed on the job would not be taken into account.

Consider the following:

1. 100 girls apply for a position as salesgirl.

2. 67 of these girls would use perseverance as a method of job behavior if they were hired; none would use tact.

3. 33 of these girls would use tact as a method of job behavior; none would use perseverance.

If all these girls were thrown into the same applicant pool and analyzed as a group, then the psychological variable which would come out as being of greatest predictive importance would be perseverance. Hence, all the girls who would use tact as a way of succeeding and who would succeed, if given the opportunity, are being prevented from doing so. This is unfair to these applicants, since it prevents them from obtaining a job in which they would be successful. In addition, it is also unfair to the organization, since the relationship that is obtained is lower than it would be if just the 67 girls were analyzed.

This question and the increasing recognition of the fact that people may use different routes to job success have become of great importance in recent years as a result of two factors. First, there has been a great increase in the number of jobs which allow personal innovation and differing ways of succeeding. For example, to assume that one may succeed as a research personnel psychologist only by performing experiments in the area of training and development is a foolish and dangerous process since the individual interested in personnel selection might develop a procedure of far greater benefit if given the opportunity.

A second factor is that industry is becoming increasingly concerned with the utilization of culturally deprived groups such as Blacks and Latin Americans in occupations where they were never utilized previously. The problem here is that there is some evidence which suggests that different cultural groups may succeed in various achievement situations for different reasons. Consider Table 33-4, in which we have summarized several studies of both academic and work performance (Green and Farquahr, 1965; Kirkpatrick *et al.*, 1968). The differing patterns of correlation coefficients for differing racial groups seem to support quite strongly the notion that individuals may use different patterns of variables in order to achieve effective performance and that groups with these differing tendencies may be identified *prior* to selection. The process of doing this is known as the "moderator variable" approach to personnel selection, since it involves choosing a variable (in this case race) which "moderates" or "determines" how two other variables might be related (e.g., aptitude and work achievement)....

THE CONCURRENT VALIDITY MODEL

The first major revision to be made in the traditional personnel selection model is, in some respects, not a revision at all, since its historical antecedents are at least as old. In addition, it is probably more commonly used in the industrial situation than is the traditional selection model. The reason for this is that its major purpose is to eliminate what is practically the most frustrating aspect of the traditional model, the delay between the administration of the predictor measures and the collection of job behavior measures. In essence, the concurrent validity model differs from the traditional model (which we call "predictive validity") in that it utilizes present, already working groups of employees as test groups upon which to determine whether given variables are related to job performance. In other words the procedure is very much the same as the traditional approach except that the hypothesized predictors of successful job performance are administered to those already on the job for whom job performance data are immediately available. If the expected relationships occur and are replicated in a cross-validation relationship and so on, then the measures are recommended for administrative use in selection procedures.

There is little doubt that it is because this procedure overcomes the time problem inherent in the traditional model that it became the most popular method for developing selection instruments in industrial situations. Yet, there are some who feel that despite this enormous benefit of the concurrent validity model, this advantage, when weighed in the balance, does not compensate for the very serious disadvantages entailed, disadvantages which include almost all of those in the traditional model plus several that are unique to it alone. These additional disadvantages, we shall see, are so serious that some have argued that the concurrent validity procedure should be used only as a hypothesis generator, not as a hypothesis tester (Guion, 1965).[6]

In addition to the fact that the concurrent validity procedure makes the same assumptions as the traditional model as to the static nature of the job, the constant large influx of applicants with similar characteristics, and the necessity for large numbers of individuals performing the same job, this procedure also makes the following crucial assumptions:

1. The motivational determinants of responding to a possible selection instrument such as personality tests, attitude questionnaires, etc., are the same for those already on the job as for those applying for the job.

2. Scores on a potential predictor of job behavior are not related in any systematic manner to experience on the job.

It is quite obvious that these are two very important assumptions, violations of which would destroy the validity of this whole procedure. How often are they violated? There is little systematic evidence available, but it would appear that this would depend to a great extent on the instruments being studied. For example, there are studies on record where various kinds of leadership attitudes have been studied via a concurrent validity procedure and then recommended for administrative use in selection. It seems hard to believe that attitudes in this area are not reflecting organizational experience to a great extent. Similarly, when a person with union security is asked about his motivational characteristics, it is hard to believe that the psychological determinants of his answers are similar to those of a person who has been out of work for several months.

There is a third problem associated with the concurrent validity procedure, and that

6. Guion, R. M. *Personnel testing.* New York: McGraw-Hill, 1965.

is a technical one. Consider the situation where an organization has a job category involving 40 positions but which now has 5 available openings. Who are the 35 currently on the job? Technically, they are a subgroup of those who were originally hired for that position, differing from the 5 who left in that they remained on the job. Now if we assume that, in general, the person who stays on the job or who is not fired is more competent than the one who quits or is fired, then the 35 now on the job would, in general, show less variation in job performance than the original unrestricted group of 40. If this were so, then it would be harder to find any correlation between predictor and job performance, since a correlation measures the similarity in variation between two variables and one of the variables does not have much variation. This, in turn, would depress the level of the correlation to a level perhaps lower than it would be if we had used it in a predictive validity situation.

SUMMARY

Industrial and organizational psychology has its historical beginnings as an aid to management in the selection of workers likely to be more capable in their job duties. In this process its major focuses have been in the development of a methodology for the evaluation of selection tools and the development of the selection tool itself.

Despite such historical antecedents, the field is by no means a settled one, and there is great ferment today as to the selection process, its rationale, its methods, and even its desirability. In this chapter we began our discussion of the personnel selection process by discussing and outlining the original achievement of the industrial and organizational psychologist in this area. This achievement, as we have seen, consisted primarily of the development of a rigorous methodology, quantitatively based, for the evaluation of selection tools, an achievement which became of significant value to large numbers of organizations.

Unfortunately, however, this methodology has always involved certain assumptions about the nature of organizations and the nature of the world surrounding the organization, assumptions which are increasingly difficult to meet in today's world, for at least some organizations. Hence, while this is still an appropriate methodology for personnel selection tool evaluation in many organizations and is so utilized, it is not for others. Thus, alternative procedures have been and are being developed. . . .

34

A Modified Model for Test Validation and Selection Research

MARVIN D. DUNNETTE[1]

Nearly 35 years ago, Clark Hull (1928) discussed the level of forecasting efficiency shown by the so-called modern tests of the time. He noted that the upper limit for tests was represented by validity coefficients of about .50 corresponding to a forecasting efficiency of only 13 per cent. He regarded the region of forecasting efficiency lying above this point as being inaccessible to the test batteries of the day, and he viewed with pessimism the use of test batteries for predicting occupational criteria. Hull, of course, failed to emphasize that the accuracy of practical decisions might better be assessed against zones of behavior (e.g., passing versus failing in a training program) rather than against the metrical continuum assumed in the calculation of his index of forecasting efficiency. Further, he gave no attention to the varying effects of different selection ratios on the accuracies obtainable with even rather low correlation coefficients. Even so, we should be somewhat dismayed by the fact that today our tests have still not penetrated the region of inaccessibility defined so long ago by Hull. Ghiselli's (1955)

comprehensive review of both published and unpublished studies showed average validities ranging in the .30s and low .40s; an average validity of .50 or above was a distinct rarity. These low validities have apparently led many psychologists to become disenchanted with test and selection research. Some have disappeared into other endeavors such as the study of group influences, interaction patterns, and the like. Others have sought refuge in the hypothesis testing models of statistical inference and have implied validity for tests showing *statistically* (but often not *practically*) significant differences between contrasting groups (see Dunnette and Kirchner, 1962). Nunnally (1960) comments:

We should not feel proud when we see the psychologist smile and say "the correlation is significant beyond the .01 level." Perhaps that is the most he can say, but he has no reason to smile. (p. 649)

Even less defensible, perhaps, has been the tendency for many to persist in doing selection *without* conducting selection research or test validation. The ordinary defenses for such practice run the gamut—from

1. This paper was read at the seventieth annual convention of the American Psychological Association held in St. Louis in the fall of 1962.

Reprinted from *Journal of Applied Psychology*, 1963, 47, 317-23, by permission of the author and the publisher. © 1963 by the American Psychological Association.

claiming near miracles of clinical insight in personnel assessment to the recounting of anecdotes about instances of selective accuracy (counting the "hits" and forgetting the "misses"), and finally to the old cliché that "management is well-satisfied with the methods being employed." We cannot and should not try to avoid the fact that the statistics of selection (i.e., validity coefficients) are far from gratifying and offer little support to anyone claiming to do *much* better than chance in the selection process.

It seems wise, therefore, to discuss the possibility of improving our batting average in test validation and selection research. Selection programs will go on—with or without psychologists—but I believe we now have the capability for penetrating the region of inaccessibility outlined by Hull.

First, let us examine the classic validation or prediction model. This model has sought simply to link predictors, on the one hand, with criteria, on the other, through a simple index of relationship, the correlation coefficient. Such a simple linkage of predictors and criteria is grossly oversimplified in comparison with the complexities actually involved in predicting human behavior. Most competent investigators readily recognize this fact and design their validation studies to take account of the possible complexities—job differences, criterion differences, etc.—present in the prediction situation. Even so, the appealing simplicity, false though it is, of the classic model has led many researchers to be satisfed with a correspondingly simplified design for conducting selection research. Thus, the usual validation effort has ignored the events—on the job behavior, situational differences, dynamic factors influencing definitions of success, etc.—intervening between predictor and criterion behavior. I believe that the lure of this seemingly simple model is, to a great extent, responsible for the low order of validities reported in the Ghiselli (1955) review. It is noteworthy that the studies reviewed by Ghiselli show no typical level of

prediction for any given test or type of job. In fact, there seems to be little consistency among various studies using similar tests and purporting to predict similar criteria. The review also suggests that the magnitude of validity coefficients is inversely proportional to the sample size employed in the studies. This can perhaps be explained, in part, by sampling error, but it may also be due to the relatively greater homogeneity possible within smaller groups of subjects. It appears, in other words, that the varying levels of prediction shown by the various studies are related somehow to the appropriateness (or lack thereof) of the classic prediction model for the particular set of conditions in the study being reported. It seems wise, therefore, to consider a prediction model which more fully presents the complexities which are only implied by the classic model.

Guetzkow and Forehand (1961) have suggested a modification of the classic validation model which provides a richer schematization for prediction research and which offers important implications for the direction of future research. Their model along with certain additional modifications is shown in Figure 34-1. Note that the modified prediction model takes account of the complex interactions which may occur between predictors and various predictor combinations, different groups (or types) of individuals, different behaviors on the job, and the consequences of these behaviors relative to the goals of the organization. The model permits the possibility of predictors being differentially useful for predicting the behaviors of different subsets of individuals. Further, it shows that similar job behaviors may be predictable by quite different patterns of interaction between groupings of predictors and individuals or even that the same level of performance on predictors can lead to substantially different patterns of job behavior for different individuals. Finally, the model recognizes the annoying reality that the same or similar job behaviors can, after passing through the situational filter,

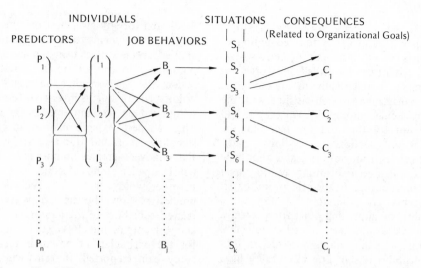

Fig. 34-1. A Modified Model for Test Validation and Selection Research

lead to quite different organizational consequences.

This modified and more complex prediction model leads to a number of important considerations involving the emphases to be followed by future validation research:

First, we must be willing to back off a step or two from global measures of occupational effectiveness—ratings, volume of output, and other so-called criteria of organizational worth, and do a more careful job of studying actual job behavior—with particular focus on behavioral or stylistic variations among different individuals with the same jobs. Most previous validation research has been overly concerned with predicting organizational consequences without first determining the nature of possible linkages between such consequences and differences in actual job behavior. It is true that industrial psychologists should continue to be concerned about predicting organizational consequences. Certainly, the modified model implies no lessening of such an interest. What is hoped, however, is that the more careful analysis of the behavioral correlates of differences in organizational consequences will lead to broader understanding

of them and, eventually, to their more accurate prediction.

Secondly, as implied by the point just made, the modified model demands that we give up our worship of the criterion (Dunnette, 1963). I believe that our concept of the criterion has suggested the existence of some single, all encompassing measure of occupational success against which predictors must be compared. Our modified model demands that we work with multiple measures of individual behavior and organizational consequences. I suggest therefore that we cease talking about the criterion problem and that we discard the notion of a so-called ultimate criterion. Such action should result in a research emphasis which will be less restrictive and less simple-minded and more aware of the necessity of analyzing and predicting the many facets of occupational success.

Thirdly, the modified model implies nothing concerning the form of the relationships to be expected. One of the unfortunate consequences of utilizing the classic validation model was its overemphasis on the correlation coefficient as almost the sole statistic of validation research. The notion of a simple linkage between predictor and criterion led easily to the equally simple assumption of the applicability of the linear, homoscedastic model for expressing the magnitude of relationships. Kahneman and Ghiselli (1962), in investigating relationships between 60 aptitude variables and various criteria, showed that 40 per cent of the scatter diagrams departed significantly from the linear, homoscedastic model, and 90 per cent of these departures held up on cross-validation. This is an important finding for it points up the necessity in future validation research of adopting a methodology taking account of the very great likelihood of non-linear, heteroscedastic models. Our more complex prediction model, focusing as it does on the complex linkages between predictors and consequences, implies also the necessity of adopting more complex and sophisticated tools of analysis in studying these linkages.

Fourth, and most obviously, our modified model demands that we develop a sort of typology for classifying people, tests, job situations, and behaviors according to their relative predictability. Future validation research must define the unique conditions under which certain predictors may be used for certain jobs and for certain purposes. Research studies should, therefore, be devoted to the definition of homogeneous subsets within which appropriate prediction equations may be developed and cross-validated. This idea is not particularly startling nor even new. But it has *not* been applied widely in the conduct of selection research. The modified model rather explicitly directs us to carry out such subgrouping studies in order to learn more about the complex linkages between predictors and consequences. Fortunately several studies already are available which confirm the advantages of studying differential patterns of validity for various subgroups. A brief review of some of these research approaches should illustrate the utility of applying our more complicated model to validation research.

With respect to job groupings, Dunnette and Kirchner (Dunnette, 1958; Dunnette and Kirchner, 1958, 1960) have studied the different patterns of validities obtained when careful techniques of job analysis are used to discover groupings of jobs which are relatively homogeneous in terms of actual responsibilities. Substantially different validities were obtained for engineers grouped according to functional similarities (research, development, production, and sales), salesmen (industrial and retail), and clerical employees (stenographers and clerk typists). These studies highlight the necessity of studying job differences and the differential predictability of effectiveness in various job groupings. More generally, an emphasis on the varying predictability of different job activities is inherent in the methods of synthetic validity (Balma, Ghiselli, McCormick, Primoff, and Griffin, 1959) and in the use of the J coefficient developed by Primoff (1955).

Everyone recognizes the possibility of situational effects on the validity of psychological predictions, but there is a paucity of research designed to estimate systematically the magnitude of such effects. Perhaps the best example of such research is provided by Vroom (1960). He showed that various aptitude tests (verbal and nonverbal reasoning, arithmetic reasoning) predicted ratings of job success most effectively for persons who were highly motivated. Job effectiveness in nonmotivating situations showed either no relationship or negative relationships with tested abilities. In a second study with Mann (Vroom and Mann, 1960), it was shown that the size of work groups strongly influenced employee attitudes toward their supervisors. Employees in small groups preferred democratic or equalitarian supervisors; employees in large work groups preferred authoritarian supervisors. In a significant series of studies, Porter (1962) is also investigating situational factors such as hierarchical level, firm size, and job functions as they effect managerial perceptions of their jobs. More emphasis needs to be given to these and other situational factors in validation studies, particularly as they serve to operate as moderating variables (Saunders, 1956) in behavioral predictions.

Many studies have shown different validities for different subgroups of individuals. For example, Seashore (1961) summarized a vast number of scholastic success studies which show almost uniformly that the grades of women (in both high school and college) are significantly more predictable than those of men. It is also well established that differing patterns of validity are typically obtained for subgroups differing in amounts of education and/or years of job experience. It may seem obvious that such factors as sex, education, and experience provide useful moderating variables in validation research. However, researchers also have identified variables which are much less *obvious* but which *do* make substantial differences in the patterns and magnitudes of validities obtained. For example, Grooms and Endler (1960) showed that the grades of anxious college students were much more predictable ($r = .63$) with aptitude and achievement measures than were the grades of nonanxious students ($r = .19$); and Frederiksen, Melville, and Gilbert (Frederiksen and Gilbert, 1960; Frederiksen and Melville, 1954) have shown that interest in engineering (as measured by the Strong test) has a higher validity for predicting grades for noncompulsive engineers than for compulsive ones. Berdie (1961) showed that the grades of engineering students with relatively consistent scores on an algebra test were more predictable from the total test score than were the grades of students with less consistent scores.[2] Ghiselli (1956, 1962) has developed a method for dividing persons, on

2. The algebra test of 100 items was divided into 10 subtests of equal difficulty. The measure of consistency for each student was simply the sum of squares of the deviations of his 10 scores from his mean score on all 10 subtests.

the basis of a screening test, into more and less predictable subgroups. The advantage of his method is that no a priori basis is necessary for the identification of subgroups; the method depends simply on the development of one or more predictor tests to facilitate the subgrouping process.

The identification of more and less predictable subgroups of persons, whether based on logical factors (such as sex, education, or experience) or on methods such as those employed by Berdie and Ghiselli, places a special burden on the investigator to demonstrate the stability of his results. Although the studies cited above were crossvalidated (i.e., checked on hold-out groups), the validity generalization and/or extension of such results has not often been measured. This needs to be done. The results so far reported with these methods are promising indeed, but they will take on greatly added significance when it is demonstrated that they hold up over time.

Less research has been directed at identifying subsets of predictors showing differential patterns of validity. However, Ghiselli (1960, 1962) has also contributed methodology in this area and has succeeded in significantly enhancing prediction by identifying, again through the development and use of screening tests, the particular predictor which will do the most valid job for each individual.

General approaches to the development of "types" have been made by a number of investigators. Gaier and Lee (1953) and Cronbach and Gleser (1953) summarize a variety of methods of assessing profile similarity and conclude that available indexes are simply variants of the general Pythagorean formula for the linear distance between two points in n-dimensional space. Lykken (1956) has questioned the psychological meaning of such "geometric similarity" and he proposes a method of actuarial pattern analysis which requires no assumptions concerning the form of the distribution and which defines similarity in psychological rather than geometric terms. His method consists simply of investigating criterial outcomes for subjects classified together into cells on the basis of similar test scores. In a recent study, he and Rose (Lykken and Rose, 1963) demonstrate that the method is more accurate in discriminating between neurotics and psychotics on the basis of MMPI scores than either clinicians' judgments or a statistical technique based on equations derived from a discriminant function analysis. Lykken's method of actuarial pattern analysis is the same as Toops' (1959) method of developing subgroups or "ulstriths" based on biographical and test similarities and then writing different prediction equations for each of the subgroups so identified. It is interesting to note that computers have now given us the capability for carrying out many of Toops' suggestions—which at one time were regarded as wild-eyed, idealistic, and unrealistic. McQuitty (1957, 1960, 1961) also has developed methods for discovering the diagnostic and predictive significance of various response patterns. His techniques, in addition to the methods proposed by Lykken and Toops, constitute the most extensive attack made to date on the problem of developing differentially predictable subsets or types.

These studies and methods mark the bare beginnings of efforts to take account of complexities which have been ignored by the oversimplified prediction model of the past. It appears that subgrouping of tests, people, jobs, situations, and consequences is necessary to a thorough understanding of what is going on in a prediction situation. The widespread acceptance of the modified model which we have been discussing should lead to a new and refreshing series of questions about problems of selection and placement. Instead of asking whether or not a particular selection technique (test, interview, or what have you) is any good, we will ask under *what circumstances* different techniques may be useful. What sorts of person

should be screened with each of the methods available, and how may the various subgroups of persons be identified and assigned to optimal screening devices? Finally, what job behaviors may be expected of various people and how may these behaviors be expected to aid or to detract from accomplishing different organizational objectives which may, in turn, vary according to different value systems and preferred outcomes?

What are the implications of these trends for the selection function in industry? Primarily, I believe they suggest the possibility of a new kind of selection process in the firm of the future. The selection expert of tomorrow will no longer be attempting to utilize the same procedure for all his selection problems. Instead, he will be armed with an array of prediction equations. He will have developed, through research, a wealth of evidence showing the patterns of validities for different linkages in the modified prediction model—for different predictors, candidates, jobs, and criteria. He will be a flexible operator, attentive always to the accumulating information on any given candidate, and ready to apply, at each stage, the tests and procedures shown to be optimal.

REFERENCES

Balma, M. J., Ghiselli, E. E., McCormick, E. J., Primoff, E. S., and Griffin, C. H. The development of processes for indirect or synthetic validity: A symposium. *Personnel Psychology*, 1959, 12, 395-400.

Berdie, R. F. Intra-individual variability and predictability. *Educational and Psychological Measurement*, 1961, 21, 663-76.

Cronbach, L. J., and Gleser, Goldine. Assessing similarity between profiles. *Psychological Bulletin*, 1953, 50, 456-73.

Dunnette, M. D. Validity of interviewer's ratings and psychological tests for predicting the job effectiveness of engineers. St. Paul: Minnesota Mining and Manufacturing Company, 1958. (Mimeo)

Dunnette, M. D. A note on *the* criterion. *Journal of Applied Psychology,* 1963, 47, 251-54.

Dunnette, M. D., and Kirchner, W. K. Validation of psychological tests in industry. *Personnel Administration,* 1958, 21, 20-27.

Dunnette, M. D., and Kirchner, W. K. Psychological test differences between industrial salesmen and retail salesmen. *Journal of Applied Psychology,* 1960, 44, 121-25.

Dunnette, M. D., and Kirchner, W. K. Validities, vectors, and verities. *Journal of Applied Psychology,* 1962, 46, 296-99.

Frederiksen, N., and Gilbert, A. C. Replication of a study of differential predictability. *Educational and Psychological Measurement,* 1960, 20, 759-67.

Frederiksen, N., and Melville, S. D. Differential predictability in the use of test scores. *Educational and Psychological Measurement,* 1954, 14, 647-56.

Gaier, E. L., and Lee, Marilyn. Pattern analysis: The configural approach to predictive measurement. *Psychological Bulletin,* 1953, 50, 140-48.

Ghiselli, E. E. *The measurement of occupational aptitude.* Berkeley: University of California Press, 1955.

Ghiselli, E. E. Differentiation of individuals in terms of their predictability. *Journal of Applied Psychology,* 1956, 40, 374-77.

Ghiselli, E. E. Differentiation of tests in terms of the accuracy with which they predict for a given individual. *Educational and Psychological Measurement,* 1960, 20, 675-84.

Ghiselli, E. E. The prediction of predictability and the predictability of prediction. Paper read at American Psychological Association, St. Louis, September 1962.

Grooms, R. R., and Endler, N. S. The effect of anxiety on academic achievement. *Journal of Educational Psychology,* 1960, 51, 299-304.

Guetzkow, H., and Forehand, G. A. A research strategy for partial knowledge useful in the selection of executives. In R. Taguiri (Ed.), *Research needs in executive selection.* Boston: Harvard Graduate School of Business Administration, 1961.

Hull, C. L. *Aptitude testing.* Yonkers, N. Y.: World Book, 1928.

Kahneman, D., and Ghiselli, E. E. Validity and non-linear heteroscedastic models. *Personnel Psychology,* 1962, 15, 1-11.

Lykken, D. T. A method of actuarial pattern analysis. *Psychological Bulletin,* 1956, 53, 102-7.

Lykken, D. T., and Rose, R. J. Psychological prediction from actuarial tables. *Journal of Clinical Psychology,* 1963, 19, 139-51.

McQuitty, L. L. Isolating predictor patterns associated with major criterion patterns. *Educational and Psychological Measurement,* 1957, 17, 3-42.

McQuitty, L. L. Hierarchical linkage analysis for the isolation of types. *Educational and Psychological Measurement,* 1960, 20, 55-67.

McQuitty, L. L. A method for selecting patterns to differentiate categories of people. *Educational and Psychological Measurement,* 1961, 21, 85-94.

Nunnally, J. The place of statistics in psychology. *Educational and Psychological Measurement,* 1960, 20, 641-50.

Porter, L. W. Some recent explorations in the study of management attitudes. Paper read at American Psychological Association, St. Louis, September 1962.

Primoff, E. S. *Test selection by job analysis.* Washington, D.C.: United States Civil Service Commission, Test Development Section, 1955.

Saunders, D. R. Moderator variables in prediction. *Educational and Psychological Measurement,* 1956, 16, 209-22.

Seashore, H. G. Women are more predictable than men. Presidential address, Division 17, American Psychological Association, New York, September 1961.

Toops, H. A. A research utopia in industrial psychology. *Personnel Psychology,* 1959, 12, 189-227.

Vroom, V. H. *Some personality determinants of the effects of participation.* Englewood Cliffs, N.J.: Prentice-Hall, 1960.

Vroom, V. H., and Mann, F. C. Leader authoritarianism and employee attitudes. *Personnel Psychology,* 1960, 13, 125-39.

35

The Impact on Employment Procedures
of the Supreme Court Decision
in the Duke Power Case

FLOYD L. RUCH

There are three basic positions that employers have assumed with regard to the hiring of minorities, especially Blacks. Stated in the simplest terms, these are:

1. Hire none irrespective of their qualifications.
2. Hire minorities to fill a quota or meet a goal regardless of their qualifications.
3. Hire the best qualified applicant without regard to their race, religion or sex.

EVALUATION OF HIRING PRACTICES

The first position is not only illegal but immoral, and it is poor business as well. It is immoral because it violates the individual's fundamental human right to be judged as a person; poor business practice because many competent minority group members can be found through affirmative action.

The law that makes position 1 illegal is clearly stated in Section 701 (a) of the Civil Rights Act of 1964. This section sets forth the fundamental obligations imposed on employers and declares it to be an unlawful practice:

(1) To fail or refuse to hire or to discharge any individual or otherwise to discriminate against him with respect to his compensation, terms condition or privileges of employment—because of his race, color, religion, sex or national origin; (2) to limit, segregate, or classify employees in any way that would deprive or tend to deprive any individual of employment opportunities or otherwise adversely affect his status as an employee—because of his race, color, religion, sex or national origin.

However, Title VII specifically states that there is no unlawful hiring practice: "Where the employer acts upon the results of a professionally developed ability test that is not designed or intended to be used to discriminate." The Supreme Court has more to say on this point. In the words of Chief Justice Burger, who wrote the unanimous opinion in the Duke Case:

The Act proscribes not only overt discrimination but also practices that are fair in form but discriminatory in operation. The touchstone is business necessity. If an employment practice which operates

Reprinted from *Personnel Journal*, 1971 (October), 777-83, by permission of the author and the publisher.

to exclude Negroes cannot be shown to be related to job performance, the practice is prohibited.

It is within the power of the employer to find this law as interpreted by the Supreme Court to be a boon rather than a bugaboo. The law permits him to assume position 3, namely of hiring competent individuals without regard to their race, color, religion, sex or national origin. But, if he is not alert to his problem he will eventually be forced into position 2, for a time at least. Forced, that is, into a quota system of hiring.

The Supreme Court opinion goes far to permit the employer to implement the third practice—namely, to hire the most competent of available applicants without regard to their race, religion, national origin or sex. For at another point Chief Justice Burger says:

Nothing in the Act precludes the use of testing or measuring procedures; obviously they are useful. What Congress has forbidden is giving these devices and mechanisms controlling force unless they are demonstrating a reasonable measure of job performance. Congress has not commanded that the less qualified be preferred over the better qualified simply because of minority origins. Far from disparaging job qualifications as such, Congress has made such qualifications the controlling factor, so that race, religion, nationality and sex become irrelevant.

THE BURDEN OF PROOF

There can be no doubt that the burden of proof is on the employer to show that his hiring standard is job related. This burden is the same for all hiring standards including psychological tests, personal interviews, scored and unscored application blanks, police and court records, and the findings of medical examinations.

The last sentence of Chief Justice Burger's opinion tells us loud and clear what the employer must do:

Congress has placed on the employer the burden of showing that any given requirement must have a manifest relationship to the employment in question.

This brings up the point of the kinds of proof of job relatedness that are acceptable under the law. The Supreme Court says that the EEOC Guidelines are entitled to great deference. The 1970 Guidelines have much to say on this very important point. They demand that employers using tests or other employment standards have available "data demonstrating that the test is predictive of, or significantly correlated with important elements of work behavior comprising or relevant to the job or jobs for which candidates are being evaluated."

There is no doubt that data of this nature clearly showing the test to be job related will protect the employer against a false accusation of discrimination no matter how large the number or proportion of minority group applicants rejected. At the same time, the minority group member is protected from unfair discrimination.

TYPES OF VALIDITY

There are two basic types of procedure to show validity or job relatedness: *empirical* and *rational*.

Empirical validation procedures are required by the EEOC Guidelines, when feasible. There are two forms of *empirical validation, predictive* and *concurrent*.

In the *predictive validation* design all applicants are tested prior to employment but the scores are not used in making the employment decision. Later, the scores are correlated to a measure of training or job success, to see whether those with high scores do substantially better than those with low scores. This is the most elegant method scientifically, but in the past it was not always used in its purest form because many employers held it to be costly and slow. For the small employer it is not feasible. This procedure has been followed by the Southern California Gas Company and is now being used by State Farm Insurance Company, to name just two companies with whom Psychological Services, Inc., is currently working.

In the *concurrent validation* design, present employees are tested and the job performance of those who score high is compared with that of those who score low, to see whether there are significant differences. This method has been widely used in the United States Employment Service.

The two *rational* methods of validation are permissible under the OFCC Testing Order and the EEOC Guidelines when *empirical validation* is not feasible. These are the methods of *content* and *construct* validity. Both require a thorough knowledge of job demands based on careful job analysis.

Content validity may be established by a systematic observation of the job and the test content to determine that the test contains a sampling of the knowledge, skills and other behaviors required for the successful performance of the job. Thus, a typing test is a valid measure to use in hiring stenographers, although it does not cover all of the domain of stenography. The same can be said for a shorthand test. Both, used together, give a more complete sampling.

The *construct validity* of a test is the extent to which it measures a "theoretical construct" or trait. Examples of such constructs are *verbal ability, space visualization* and *perceptual speed.* When careful job analysis shows that workers must read blueprints, a test of *space visualization* is valid as part of the employment procedure.

There are many life situations in which *content* and *construct* validities are the only ones available. A prime example is the selection of astronauts where these methods appear to have been quite effective. To rule out their use would seriously handicap the smaller employers whose work forces are not large enough to support the use of more elegant validation designs. Fortunately, Title

VII, as interpreted by EEOC, permits the use of these methods where *predictive* and *concurrent* validity studies are not feasible because of small number of employees on a particular job.

FIVE RECOMMENDATIONS FOR IMMEDIATE ACTION

Acting upon the following five recommendations will help the employer find qualified people within the constraints now imposed by law.

1. Make a detailed analysis of *all* hiring and promotion standards that are now being used. Among the many questions the employer should ask himself in doing this are the following:

> *What proportion of applicants both minority and non-minority are being rejected at each stage of the hiring process?*

The author knows of a case in which top management was highly dedicated to the concept of fair employment, but way down the line was a receptionist who turned back 50% of the applicants. When asked why, she replied: "Two reasons. I turn them away if I think they won't pass the tests or if I think the interviewer won't like them." Most of the applicants were Black. Nobody knows how many good prospects were lost.

> *The employer should ask of each hiring standard, "Why am I using this? What does it mean in terms of actual behavior on the job?"*

A good example is the high school or college diploma requirement. Take the case where the owner-manager of a large bakery who was a great believer in higher education required that his route men all have college degrees. Sometimes he had to relax this standard and take high school graduates. An analysis of the job performance of both groups showed the college graduates to be inferior to the less-educated driver-salesmen in actual sales produced. Obviously, this is a foolish and discriminatory standard.

In the Duke Power Case, the Court ruled that coal handlers may not be required to be high school graduates.

Where the standard is not job related and where it rejects a disproportionate number of Blacks, it should be discontinued. The employer loses nothing in doing so and can gain credit with EEOC for being a good guy.

2. Accurate records of why each applicant was rejected should be kept. A general notation of "not sufficiently well qualified" is not enough. Say why in such objective terms that these reasons can be validated when sufficient cases are available.

3. If a general intelligence test such as the Wonderlic or Otis is being used for hiring or promotion for jobs for which it has not been validated, this practice should be discontinued until a validation study on all of the jobs for which it is being used has been conducted. If the results of such a study are inadequate, abandon the practice and set up a more modern program.

The Wonderlic and Otis tests have been so misused that the EEOC is so set against them that evidence of validity will have to be overwhelming.

At the EEOC hearings held in Houston, Texas, in June of 1970, the following dialogue took place between EEOC Chairman Brown and Mr. LeRoy R. Johnston of the Gulf Oil Company:

Chairman Brown: Would you estimate the number of general intelligence tests?

Mr. Johnston: In the various departments, I would say three or four different types. Otis, Wonderlic, and the Bennett test for arithmetic are being used and a number of that type of tests. We are in the process of validating all our tests.

Chairman Brown: Are you aware of the fact that this Commission has determined that the Wonderlic test is discriminatory?

Mr. Johnston: No. I'm not aware of that. I have heard people suggest that. I didn't know you knew.

Chairman Brown: But we have, by *specific decision.*

Although the Otis and the Wonderlic can be valid for certain jobs, they have often been misused and have, therefore, invited close scrutiny by EEOC. It is important at this juncture to see why.

General intelligence testing as we know it today originated in the public schools of Paris, France, in the early 1900s. French educators were confronted with the problem of separating pupils who lagged behind their classmates into groups of those who were lazy and those who were dull. To resolve this problem, the Minister of Education set up a commission of which the psychologist Alfred Binet, a young professor of the then new science of psychology, was the most active. His test contained problems selected to be objectively scoreable. These problems stressed judgment and reasoning rather than rote memory. Follow-up studies showed clearly that such a test predicted an individual's ability to *learn school subjects.*

The advent of World War I confronted the United States with the huge task of mobilizing a large armed force in a country that was peaceful by tradition and ill prepared to face the German military might. Group tests were developed to speed the induction and classification of recruits. The Army Alpha Test of intelligence developed by Otis for this purpose was based on the same general philosophy as the original Binet.

Shortly after World War I, the famous Army Alpha Test was revised and restandardized by numerous psychologists, resulting in a wide variety of testing instruments available for use in business and industry. The two best known are, of course, the Otis and the Wonderlic. These are viewed critically by the EEOC for good reason.

The first tests of general intelligence, developed to predict academic success, were built around the concept that people are bright or dull in all aspects of intelligence. Research during the 1920s and 1930s, however, proved that this is not the case. Using a complex statistical method known as factor analysis, L. L. Thurstone of the University of Chicago demonstrated that there are seven varieties of intelligence. These are called unique abilities. For practical purposes we are mainly interested in five of them:

Verbal Factor (V) is the ability to absorb and disseminate information through the written and spoken word. A high level of this ability is the most identifying characteristic of top management as compared with the rank and file of employed people.

Numerical Factor (N) is the ability to perform mentally with speed and accuracy the four fundamental arithmetic operations of addition, subtraction, multiplication, and division. It is in this type of ability that actuaries and accountants excel.

Reasoning Factor (R) is the ability to put facts together to form a general principle or to apply an already-formed general principle to a particular case. Here again is an ability in which top management stands very high relative to the general population.

Space (S) is the ability to visualize the relationships of objects to one another in space. It is particularly important in occupations such as design engineering or drafting, in which a three-dimensional object is described by a two-dimensional drawing. A high level of space ability is not required in most office work.

Perceptual Speed (P) is the ability to identify rapidly and accurately similarities and differences among familiar objects. The important thing about a perceptual speed test is that the problems solved are so simple that anybody could handle them if given enough time. The score on such a test reflects the speed and accuracy with which these simple problems can be handled by the individual being tested. Perceptual speed is extremely important in all clerical occupations and is also required by the manager who must process considerable amounts of paper.

When the United States mobilized for World War II, testing procedures based on factor analysis provided a much more effective kit of tools than was available in the old general intelligence types of test. One of the outstanding achievements of World War II was the testing program of the United States Army Air Force, which employed factor-analyzed tests. The psychologists of the Air Force were so successful in selecting trainable pilots that an estimated saving of $1,000 in training costs per dollar spent in testing was made.

A properly chosen battery of tests measuring unique factors that are known to be related to the successful performance of a particular job will permit more accurate selection than is possible with the same amount of testing time required by a test of general intelligence. Studies on the Army Alpha, after which the Otis and the Wonderlic were patterned, reveal that these tests measure principally three factors—*verbal, reasoning,* and *number*—but omit other factors of great importance such as *perceptual speed* and *space*. Jobs differ in the demands they put upon people. People differ in their abilities to meet these demands. For example, a draftsman must be high in *number* and *space,* but he need not be high in *verbal.* A file clerk must be high in *perceptual speed* but need not be high in *space, verbal,* or *reasoning.* An executive must be high in many factors, especially *verbal, numerical, reasoning,* and *perceptual speed,* although he need not be high in *space* unless he is in some mechanical line.

General intelligence tests are dull tools because they contain elements unrelated to a particular job. For example, the *reasoning* factor in the Army Alpha, Otis, and Wonderlic is not highly predictive of the job performance of a file clerk. The employer who uses tests that measure factors that are not job related is breaking the law.

Another disadvantage of the general intelligence test for selection is that two individuals receiving the same total score can earn this test score in very different ways. For example, one applicant may be high in *reasoning,* low in *number,* and average in *verbal.* The other may be high in *number,* average in *reasoning* and low in *verbal.* Which one will make the better figure clerk? Obviously the second one.

This is such an important point that it is worthwhile to look at another example. Draftsmen and secretaries are about equal in general intelligence as measured by test. But draftsmen are higher in *space* and *number* factors while secretaries are higher in *perceptual speed* and *verbal.*

4. If you are not now testing, start to test new applicants with unique factor tests, but do not consider the test scores in hiring. After a significant number of cases have been hired and evaluated for job-performance criteria such as supervisor's ratings of quantity, quality, safety, judgment, learning speed, industry, etc., do a forward validation.

Failure to establish a job-related battery of validated hiring standards can eventually force the employer into a quota system.

The employer must bear in mind that the personal interview is subject to challenge if it rejects a disproportionate number of minorities unless it has been validated and found to be predictive of job success. Its results must be expressed quantitatively and validated.

5. If applicants are being tested with factored tests and there is reason to believe that the tests in use will prove to be valid, a predictive validity study on present employees using their recorded scores should be conducted. This should be done for all jobs where numbers are sufficient.

If the results are not impressive enough to meet with EEOC approval, testing should be continued without using scores in hiring until a predictive validation study on the new hires with unrestricted range of test scores has been completed. The greater the range of scores, the higher the validity

coefficients that will be obtained from job-related tests.

The procedure for setting test standards for already-employed candidates being considered for apprentice training may require a different approach because of the length of time that would be involved in waiting for the trainee to succeed or fail—that is, in waiting for the criterion to mature. In this case, test standards should be set by using the concurrent validation procedure on presently employed journeymen.

ECONOMICS OF TESTING

The savings resulting from a testing program can be very impressive. In a recent study at the Southern California Gas Company, it was found that a testing program that accepts 50 per cent of the applicants, reduced termination rates for typing clerks by 36 per cent. In the case of crewmen, the same selection ratio reduced turnover by 28 per cent. Being more selective produces an even greater reduction in turnover. These results are based on all hires found to be qualified on the basis of the employment interview alone. Obviously, testing improves the batting average over that which can be obtained by the interview alone.

What does this mean in dollars saved? A report entitled *Labor Turnover Handbook 1970,* recently released by Merchants and Manufacturers Association, gives the results of a survey in the Los Angeles area which indicates that the average cost of turnover of office and technical personnel is about $1,139 per person. This means that a company hiring a hundred people a year will save 30 per cent of $113,900 or $34,170 a year—and this is a small company. If the employer is hiring a thousand people a year, the estimated annual savings on turnover costs would be over a third of a million dollars.

But this is a small gain compared to the higher work output the employer will get by selecting the most competent applicants.

These savings will pay several times over the costs of doing the necessary test validation.

Test validation can be fairly complicated, and many employers will want professional help. They should contact the publishers of the tests they use or are thinking of using for help or for recommendation of a local expert.

What, then, is the impact of the Duke Power Case? It forces employers to evaluate more carefully all of their employment practices. This will result in dropping some old methods and trying new ones, in discarding invalid hiring standards and seeking valid ones. However, the required investment in research will pay off not only by satisfying Government requirements, but also by increasing the ability to identify in advance those employees who will perform most effectively. It also protects the minority group member in his inalienable right to be treated as an individual.

36

How "Equal Opportunity"
Turned into Employment Quotas

DANIEL SELIGMAN

Soon after it came into office, the Nixon Administration proposed that critics "watch what we do instead of listening to what we say." By this eminently reasonable standard, the Administration today might be judged to favor quotas in employment. The President repeatedly assailed them; in fact, the elimination of quotas was identified in a major campaign statement as one of ten great goals for the nation in his second term. Yet during his years in office, and with some powerful encouragment from the executive branch of the U.S. Government, quotas have taken hold in several areas of American life. The controversies about them have centered on their appearance in the construction industry and on university campuses. Oddly enough, very little attention has been paid to employment quotas in large corporations.

The omission is very odd indeed, for it is in corporate employment that quotas are having their major impact on the American labor force, and on relations between the races and sexes. Nowadays there are scarcely any companies among, say, the FORTUNE 500 that are not under pressure from the Government to hire and promote more women and minority-group members; and

many of these companies have responded to the pressure by installing what are, in effect, quota systems.

In most of the controversy over quotas, there is no real disagreement about ultimate objectives. Most educated Americans today would agree that several minorities, and women, suffer from discrimination in employment, that the discrimination is destructive and irrational, and that working to end it is a proper activity for government. Unfortunately, it is not clear what government should do—and all too clear that wise policies do not flow naturally from good intentions.

In discussions of this issue, people who don't define their terms can dither on for quite a while without getting anywhere. Let us begin, accordingly, with some definitions and distinctions. Among companies that have no intention of discriminating against women or minorities, four different postures may be discerned:

1. *Passive nondiscrimination* involves a willingness, in all decisions about hiring, promotion, and pay, to treat the races and sexes alike. However, this posture may involve a failure to recognize that past discrim-

ination leaves many prospective employees unaware of present opportunities.

2. *Pure affirmative action* involves a concerted effort to expand the pool of applicants so that no one is excluded because of past or present discrimination. At the point of decision, however, the company hires (or promotes) whoever seems most qualified, without regard to race or sex.

3. *Affirmative action with preferential hiring.* In this posture, the company not only ensures that it has a larger labor pool to draw from but systematically favors women and minority groups in the actual decisions about hiring. This might be thought of as a "soft" quota system, i.e., instead of establishing targets that absolutely must be met, the top officers of the company beef up employment of women and minority-group members to some unspecified extent by indicating that they want those groups given a break.

4. *Hard quotas.* No two ways about it—specific numbers of proportions of minority-group members must be hired.

Much of the current confusion about quotas—and the controversy about whether the Government is imposing them—derives from a failure to differentiate among several of these postures. The officials who are administering the principal federal programs tend, of course, to bristle at any suggestion that they are imposing quotas; they have been bristling with special vigor ever since the President's campaign statements on the subject. Their formulations tend to be somewhat self-serving, however. The officials turn out, when pressed, to be denying that the Government is pushing employers into posture No. 4. The real issue is No. 3, preferential hiring, which many Government agencies are indeed promoting. Meanwhile, the President and a few other Administration officials concerned with equal-employment opportunity sound as though the objective of the program is to promote pure affirmative action—posture No. 2.

THE CONCILIATORS HAVE MUSCLES

The U. S. Government's efforts to end discrimination in employment are carried out through two major programs. One was set in motion by Title VII of the Civil Rights Act of 1964, which forbids discrimination based on race, color, religion, sex, or national origin. The act established an Equal Employment Opportunity Commission, which now has two main functions. The first is enforcement: the commission may sue in a U.S. district court, on its own behalf or for other claimants, when it believes that discrimination has taken place. The EEOC has had the power to sue only since March 1972—previously it was limited to conciliation efforts—and has filed only about twenty-five suits in that time. Chairman William H. Brown III believes that when the commission gets warmed up it might be filing an average of five suits a week.

In practice, Brown suspects, not many of these are apt to be litigated; the right to go into court is useful to the EEOC mainly for the the muscle it provides in conciliation efforts. If the EEOC did get into court, it would have to prove outright discrimination; in principle, that is, an employer might comply with Title VII simply by practicing passive nondiscrimination—posture No. 1. However, the conciliation agreements extracted from those accused of discrimination typically call for more than that. Most of the agreements negotiated thus far involve preferential hiring.

The Commission's other main function is information gathering. Every enterprise with a hundred or more employees must file annually with the EEOC a form detailing the number of women and members of four different minority groups employed in each of nine different job categories, from laborers to "managers and officials." The minority groups are Negroes; Americans of Mexican, Puerto Rican, Cuban, or Spanish origin; Orientals; and American Indians (who in Alaska are deemed to include Eskimos and Aleuts). With some 260,000 forms a year to process, the EEOC is having some difficulty in staying on top of the data it is collecting. "Obviously, we can't look critically at all the reports." Brown concedes. Eventually, however, he hopes to develop some computerized procedures for finding patterns of discrimination, i.e., procedures somewhat analogous to those employed by the Internal Revenue Service in deciding which tax returns to audit.

Meanwhile, the EEOC is getting a fair amount of help from people who believe they are being discriminated against. When any complaint is received at the commission, even one with no visible substance to it, an EEOC staff member pulls the file on the company in question and looks for patterns of discrimination. In fiscal 1972 more than 30,000 charges were filed.

SPECIAL RULES FOR CONTRACTORS

The other major federal program is based on the special obligations incurred by Government contractors. This program may be traced all the way back to 1941, when President Franklin D. Roosevelt issued an executive order outlawing racial discrimination by defense contractors. Every President since Roosevelt has issued one or more orders extending the reach of the ban. It applies now to subcontractors as well as primes, to civilian as well as military purchases, and to services as well as goods. It affects every division and every subsidiary of any company with a contract worth $10,000 or more. It covers women as well as racial, religious, and ethnic minorities. And it has entailed increasingly expansive definitions of "nondiscrimination." Right now, about a quarter of a million companies, employing about a third of the U.S. labor force, are covered by the executive orders.

At the time President Nixon took office, most government contractors were operating under Executive Order 11246, which had been issued by President Johnson in September, 1965. The order, as later amended by

Johnson, required "affirmative action" by employers—but did not specify what this meant in practice. The Office of Federal Contract Compliance had never developed guidelines for determining whether contractors were in compliance. It was left to the Nixon Administration to make the program operational.

The Administration's first major decision about the program was to make it, in the marvelous label applied by the Labor Department, "result-oriented." Affirmative action could have been defined so that it required companies to incorporate certain procedures into their personnel policies—but did not require that any particular results follow from the procedures. The difficulty with this approach was that companies determined to discriminate might simply go through the motions while continuing to exclude women and minority-group members. "It just would have been to easy for them to make patsies of us," said Laurence Silberman, who was solicitor of the Labor Department at the time, and who participated in the formulation of the program. An alternative approach, which was the one essentially adopted, would require each company to set goals and timetables for hiring specified numbers of women and minority-group members; would allow the Government to review the goals to ensure that they were sufficiently ambitious; and, if they were not met, would require the company to prove that it had at least made a "good faith effort" to meet them.

This approach was certainly calculated to produce results. The difficulty was that it also seemed likely to produce *reverse* discrimination by companies fearful of losing their contracts. The Administration recognized this problem from the beginning, and agonized over it quite a lot. "No program has given me greater problems of conscience than this one," said Silberman recently, just before leaving the Labor Department to go into private law practice in the capital. In the end, however, the Administration always came back to the view that a program that didn't achieve results would be a charade—and that the only way to ensure results was to require goals and timetables.

The rules of the new game were first set forth in January 1970 in the Labor Department's Order No. 4, signed by then-Secretary George P. Shultz. At the time, it seems clear, businessmen did not pay a great deal of attention to Order No. 4. It is perhaps worth noting that the momentous changes signaled by the order had never been debated in Congress, not even during the great outpouring of civil-rights legislation in the 1960s. Anyone looking for examples of the growing autonomy of the executive branch of the federal government could do worse than focus on this quite unheralded administrative regulation.

TRYING TO BE REASONABLE

Specifically, Order No. 4 requires that every contractor have a written affirmative-action program for every one of his establishments. Every program must include a detailed report on the company's utilization of each of the four basic minorities in each of its own job categories. (A "Revised Order No. 4," issued by Secretary of Labor J. D. Hodgson in December 1971 called for reports on women, too.) Whenever there are job categories with fewer women or minority-group members "than would reasonably be expected by their availability," the contractor must establish goals for increasing their utilization.

Well, how does one determine the appropriate utilization rates? The order makes a great show of being helpful in this regard, listing eight criteria that contractors should consider in trying to answer the question. The first is "the minority population of the labor area surrounding the facility"; others include "the availability of minorities having requisite skills in an area in which the contractor can reasonably recruit," and "the degree of training which the contractor is

reasonably able to undertake as a means of making all job classes available to minorities." The criteria certainly give contractors a lot to think about, but they do not, in the end, make clear what would be a reasonable utilization rate for, say, black mechanics. A contractor focusing on this matter might find himself utterly confused about the number of blacks in town who were already trained as mechanics, the number who were "trainable," the amount he was expected to spend on training, the distance he was expected to travel to recruit, etc.

In practice, contractors are encouraged to assume that they are underutilizing women and minorities and, accordingly, they have goals and timetables just about everywhere. For example, International Business Machines Corp., which has long been a model employer so far as fair-employment practices are concerned, has goals and timetables today at every one of its 400-odd establishments in the U.S.

Because the criteria are so vague, the goal-setting procedure often becomes an exercise in collective bargaining, with the outcome dependent on the respective will and resourcefulness of the company's top executives and the Government's compliance officers. The Government is ordinarily represented in these matters by whichever of its departments is contracting for the company's services; the OFCC does some, but not much, coordinating. On the whole, the enforcement varies considerably in both fairness and effectiveness from one company to another. Furthermore, some companies deal with several different departments; Union Carbide, for example, is monitored by the Atomic Energy Commission and the Departments of Defense, Transportation, Labor, Interior, and Agriculture.

The compliance officers themselves are career civil servants, and they seem to come in all varieties. Two quite different criticisms of them are often heard. One is that they are apt to be knee-jerk liberals, persuaded in advance that the big corporation is guilty.

The other is that they have often lazily adopted the position that anything the company proposes is fine with them. Herbert Hill, the labor specialist of the National Association for the Advancement of Colored People, is prepared to regale anyone who wants to listen with tales of compliance officers who have been co-opted by corporate personnel departments. One senior official of the Labor Department who has been in a good position to observe the contract-compliance program was asked recently what he thought of these two criticisms. "They're both true," he answered, adding, after a moment's reflection, that the compliance officers also included many thoughtful and conscientious public servants.

WHAT'S HAPPENED TO MERIT?

There is no doubt that, between them, the EEOC and the contract-compliance program have transformed the way big business in the U.S. hires people. Even allowing for those co-opted compliance officers, the Government has gone a long way toward wiping out old-fashioned discrimination in the corporate universe. But it is increasingly evident that, in doing so, the government programs have undermined some other old-fashioned notions about hiring on the basis of merit.

The undermining process can be discerned in the campaigns, waged successfully by EEOC and OFCC, against certain kinds of employment standards. Employers who demand certain skills, education levels, or test-score results are presumed to be discriminating if their standards have the effect of excluding women or minority-group members. To counter this presumption, the employer must demonstrate conclusively that the skills are in fact needed for the job. If test-score results are involved, he must also demonstrate that the tests reliably predict the skills in question and, finally, that "alternative suitable . . . procedures are unavailable for his use." One argument the

employer *cannot* make is that he had no discriminatory intent in establishing the requirements. Under Title VII, as administered by the EEOC, the intent is irrelevant; it is only the effect that matters—which represents a major alteration in the law of discrimination.

The altered concept became the law of the land in March 1971, when the U.S. Supreme Court upheld the EEOC's view. and overruled a court of appeals, in *Griggs vs. Duke Power*. The company had required applicants for certain jobs to have a high-school diploma and also to score at certain levels in aptitude tests. There was no contention that Duke Power intended these standards to have a discriminatory effect, and it was agreed that they were applied impartially to blacks and whites alike. It was also agreed that the standards resulted in very few blacks being hired. The company argued that it wanted to use the standards to improve the over-all quality of its labor force; but it could not demonstrate that the standards had a direct relationship to the jobs being performed. In ruling that the standards had to be dropped, Chief Justice Warren E. Burger, who wrote the Court's opinion, upheld the EEOC's contention that Title VII "has placed on the employer the burden of showing that any given requirement must have a manifest relationship to the employment in question."

Anyone pondering the particulars of the Duke Power case would have to feel sympathy for the black workers involved. Growing up in a society that had denied them a decent education, they were unfit for many skilled jobs. When they applied to do some relatively unskilled work that they could perform, they were excluded by educational standards—which, the facts suggest, really were extraneous to the company's needs. Unfortunately, the logic of the Duke Power decision suggests that some perfectly reasonable standards are now in trouble, too. Companies that have high standards and want to defend them will immediately perceive that the ground rules, which not only place the burden of proof on the employer but require coping with some formidable-looking validation procedures, are not inviting. Many will obviously conclude that it is simpler to abolish their standards than to try justifying them.

The new law presents special management problems to the numerous companies that have traditionally hired overqualified people at entry-level jobs, expecting them to compete for the better jobs. Dr. Lloyd Cooke, who monitors Union Carbide's equal-employment-opportunity program, suggested recently that most big companies like his own could no longer assume there were a lot of highly qualified people searching out their own paths to the top. "Now we must develop upward mobility models that include training along the way."

In addition to all their problems with tests and formal standards, federal contractors often face a new kind of pressure on the informal standards they may have in mind when they hire and promote people. Revised Order No. 4 specifies: "Neither minority nor female employees should be required to possess higher qualifications than those of the lowest-qualified incumbent." The logic of this rule is inexorable, and it too implies lower standards. In any organization that has a number of people working at different levels of skill and competence—a corporate engineering staff, say, or a university economics department—whoever does the hiring would ordinarily be trying to raise the average level of performance, i.e., to bring in more people at the high end of the range. If the organization must take on applicants who are at the low end or face charges of discrimination, it can only end up lowering the average.

Professor Sidney Hook, the philosopher, has assailed the possibilities of this "fantastic" requirement in universities. "It opens the door," he has written, "to hiring persons who cannot meet *current standards of qualification* because, forsooth, a poorly qualified incumbent was hired by some fluke or perhaps ages ago when the department was struggling for recognition."

WHAT CONGRESS HAS PROSCRIBED

For reasons that are certainly understandable, neither the EEOC nor the OFCC has ever said in writing that it believed the law to require some hiring of less-qualified people. To do so would apparently conflict with some of President Nixon's animadversions against quotas. In addition, it would seem to go against the plain language of the laws in question. It is, after all, logically impossible to discriminate in favor of blacks without discriminating against some whites; thus anyone espousing preferential hiring of blacks would be bucking Section 703(a) of Title VII, in which it is deemed unlawful for an employer "to . . . classify his employees in any way which would deprive or tend to deprive any individual of employment opportunities . . . because of such individual's race, color, religion, sex or national origin." In *Griggs*, Chief Justice Burger reaffirmed the intent of the law in plain terms: "Discriminatory preference for any group, minority or majority, is precisely and only what Congress has proscribed."

In pushing preferences for women and minorities, the Government's lawyers and compliance officers repeatedly offer the assurance that "you never have to hire an unqualified person." Since unqualified persons are by definition unable to do the job, the assurance is perhaps less meaningful than it sounds. The real question is whether employers should have to hire women or minority-group members who are less qualified than other available workers.

The answer one gets in conversation with EEOC officials is clear enough. If hiring someone who is less qualified will help an employer to utilize women or minorities at proper levels, then he should do so. Chairman Brown was asked recently what an employer should do if he was presumed to be underutilizing women and there were two applicants for a job: a fairly well qualified woman and a man who was somewhat better qualified. "If it's just a question of 'somewhat better,' you should probably hire the woman," he replied.

THE LAWYER'S PREDICAMENT

How can the lawyers who run the federal programs justify preferences that seem to violate the intent of the basic statutes? Not all the lawyers would respond in the same way, but most of them would point to some court decisions at the appellate level that call for preferential hiring and even hard quotas. They would also note that the Supreme Court has declined to review these decisions. In one important case, for example, the Alabama state troopers were ordered by a federal judge to hire one black trooper for every white man hired until the over-all ratio was up to 25 per cent black. Most of the lawyers would also agree with this formulation by William J. Kilberg, the Labor Department's associate solicitor for labor relations and civil rights: "In situations where there has been a finding of discrimination, and where no other remedy is available, temporary preferential hiring is legal and appropriate."

Kilberg himself believes strongly that preferences should be limited to these special circumstances—in which it is indeed hard to argue against them. But other government lawyers view them as natural and desirable in a wide range of circumstances. They argue, for example, that it is unnecessary to require a finding of discrimination; they contend that companies underutilizing women or minority-group members are per se guilty of discrimination and that it is appropriate, in reviewing their goals and timetables, to push for some preference. Furthermore, the EEOC tends to the view that any past discrimination justifies preferences, i.e., it often fails to consider whether other remedies are available.

Last fall H.E.W.'s Office of Civil Rights made a major, but only partially successful, effort to clarify the ground rules of the contract-compliance program. J. Stanley Pottinger, who has headed the office for most of the past three years (he recently moved over to the Justice Department), put together a volume spelling out some guidelines. At the same time, somewhat confusingly, he issued a covering statement that went beyond anything in the volume. It said, "Nothing in the affirmative-action concept requires a university to employ or promote any faculty member who is less qualified than other applicants competing for that position." That statement was, and indeed still is, the only formal declaration ever issued by any contract-compliance official ruling out a requirement for hiring less-qualified job applicants.

Many contractors who read the statement took it for granted that the same rule would apply to corporate employment. Unfortunately, anyone talking about this matter to officials of the Labor Department soon discovers that they regard university hiring problems as somewhat special. There is a view that faculties have a unique need for "excellence," but that in the business world, and especially at the blue-collar level, most jobs are such that employers suffer no real hardship when "less-qualified" people are hired.

A MESSAGE TO JACK ANDERSON

Meanwhile, corporate executives tend to take it for granted that, in practice, reverse discrimination is what affirmative action is all about. Whoever it is at International Telephone & Telegraph Corp. that leaks internal memorandums to columnist Jack Anderson recently sent along one on this subject. In the passage that Anderson published, Senior Vice President John Hanway was proposing to another executive that thirty-four rather high-ranking jobs "lend themselves readily to being filled by affirmative-action candidates," i.e., they should be filled by women or minority-group members.

Companies' public declarations about affirmative action do not ordinarily propose so blatantly to prefer these groups, but the dynamics of the program more or less guarantee that there will be preferences. Revised Order No. 4 says, "Supervisors should be made to understand that their work performance is being evaluated on the basis of their equal employment opportunity efforts and results, as well as other criteria."

Supervisors are indeed getting the message. At I.B.M., for example, *every manager* is told that his annual performance evaluation—on which the prospects for promotions, raises, and bonuses critically depend—incudes a report on his success in meeting affirmative-action goals. A memo last July 5, from Chairman C. Peter McColough to all Xerox managers in the U.S. (it was later published by the company), warned that "a key element in each manager's over-all performance appraisal will be his progress in this important area. No manager should expect a satisfactory appraisal if he meets other objectives, but fails here." At Xerox, furthermore, the goals are very ambitious these days. Something like 40 per cent of all net additions to the corporate payroll last year were minority-group members.

In principle, of course, a line manager who is not meeting his targets is allowed to argue that he has made a "good faith effort" to do so. But the burden of proof will be on the manager, who knows perfectly well that the only sure-fire way to prove good faith is to meet the targets. If he succeeds, no questions will be asked about reverse discrimination; if he fails, he will automatically stir up questions about the adequacy of his efforts and perhaps about his racial tolerance too (not to mention his bonus). Obviously, then, a manager whose goals call for hiring six black salesmen during the year, and who has hired only one by Labor Day, is feeling a lot of pressure to discriminate against white applicants in the fall. "In this company," said the president of one billion-dollar enterprise recently, "a black has a better chance of being hired than a white, frankly. When he's hired, he has a better chance of being promoted. That's the only way it can be."

SOME KIND WORDS FOR ABILITY

The future of the "quotas issue" is hard to predict, for several reasons. One is the continuing blurriness of the Nixon Administration's intentions. For a while, last summer [during the 1972 campaign], these appeared to have been clarified. In August, Philip Hoffman, president of the American Jewish Committee, sent identical letters to Nixon and McGovern expressing concern about the spread of quota systems in American education and employment. Both candidates replied with letters assailing quotas. The President wrote to Hoffman:

> I share your support of affirmative efforts to ensure that all Americans have an equal chance to compete for employment opportunities, and to do so on the basis of individual ability . . . . With respect to these affirmative-action programs, . . . numerical goals . . . must not be allowed to be applied in such a fashion as to, in fact, result in the imposition of quotas.

This declaration was followed by a number of newspaper articles suggesting that the Administration was preparing to gut the affirmative-action program. The articles were wrong, however. Before the reply to Hoffman had been drafted, a number of Administration officials—they included White House special consultant (on minorities) Leonard Garment, Silberman, and Pottinger—met to discuss the program and to consider whether the time had come to change it. Specifically, they considered whether to drop the requirement for goals and timetables. And they decided, as they had in earlier reviews, to resolve their doubts in favor of standing pat.

It seems clear that the Nixon letter to Hoffman temporarily shook up some members of the equal-opportunity bureaucracy, but it doesn't seem to have led to any major changes in the way the federal program is implemented. Many executives, including some who are vigorous supporters of the program, confess to being baffled by the contrast between the President's words and the bureaucracy's actions. General Electric's man in charge of equal-employment-opportunity programs, whose name happens to be Jim Nixon, remarked recently that he kept reading in the papers that "the other Nixon" was cutting back on affirmative action, but "around here, all we see is a continuing tightening of the noose."

Perhaps the simplest explanation of that contrast between words and actions lies in the very nature of the program. It is logically possible to have goals and timetables that don't involve preferential hiring—and that happy arrangement is what the Administration keeps saying we have now. But there are built-in pressures that keep leading back to preference: the implicit presumption that employers are "underutilizing" women and minority-group members; the further presumption that this underutilization is essentially the result of discrimination; the extraordinary requirement, quite alien to our usual notions about due process, that unmet goals call for the employer to demonstrate good faith (i.e., instead of calling for the Government to prove bad faith). It seems reasonable to speculate that at some point the Administration will abandon goals and timetables, conceding that they lead in practice to preferential hiring and even quotas. Indeed, some of the program's senior officials regard the present format as temporary. Pottinger, who has spent a lot of time in recent years arguing that goals don't mean quotas, nevertheless says, "I sure hope they're not permanent."

In any case, one would have to be skeptical of the long-term future of any program with so many anomalies built into it. For a democratic society to systematically discriminate against "the majority" seems quite without precedent. To do so in the name of nondiscrimination seems mind-boggling. For humane and liberal-minded members of the society to espouse racial discrimination at all seems most remarkable.

THE CRUELTIES OF REVERSE DISCRIMINATION

One immediate threat to the program may be discerned, meanwhile, in a number of suits against corporations and universities, alleging some form of reverse discrimination. H.E.W. now has an "ombudsman" working full-time on such complaints. It seems likely that companies engaged in preferential hiring will be hit by more such suits as the realities of their programs sink in on employees and job applicants.

But even aside from all the large litigious possibilities, there are surely going to be serious problems about morale in these companies. It is very difficult for a large corporation to discriminate in favor of any group without, to some extent, stigmatizing all members of the group who work for it. G.E.'s Nixon, who is himself black, says that talk about hiring less-qualified minority-group members makes him uneasy—that "it puts the 'less-qualified' stamp on the minorities you do hire." In companies where reverse discrimination is the rule, there will be a nagging question about the real capabilities of any black man who gets a good job or promotion. The question will occur to the white applicants who didn't get the job; it will occur to customers who deal with the black man; and, of course, it will occur to the black himself. Perhaps the cruelest aspect of reverse discrimination is that it ultimately denies minority-group members who have made it on their own the satisfaction of knowing that.

In short, businessmen who are opting for preferential hiring, or who are being pushed to it by government pressure, may be deluding themselves if they think they're taking the easy way. It seems safe to say that at some point, even if the Government does not abandon its pressures for preference, more businessmen will begin resisting them. It should go without saying that the resistance will be easier, and will come with better grace, if those businessmen have otherwise made clear their opposition to any form of discrimination.

37

The Relationship Between Sex Role Stereotypes and Requisite Management Characteristics

VIRGINIA ELLEN SCHEIN[1]

Although women make up 38 per cent of the work force (Koontz, 1971), the proportion of women who occupy managerial and executive positions is markedly small. One extensive survey of industrial organizations (Women in the Work Force, 1970) revealed that 87 per cent of the companies surveyed had 5 per cent or fewer women in middle management and above.

According to Orth and Jacobs (1971), one reason for the limited number of women managers and executives is that " . . . traditional male attitudes toward women at the professional and managerial levels continue to block change" (p. 140). Bowman, Worthy, and Greyser (1965) found that of 1,000 male executives surveyed, 41 per cent expressed mildly unfavorable to strongly unfavorable attitudes toward women in management. This negative reaction to women in management suggests that sex role stereotypes may be inhibiting women from advancing in the managerial work force.

The existence of sex role stereotypes has been documented by numerous researchers

(Anastasi and Foley, 1949; Maccoby, 1966; Wylie, 1961). For example, Rosenkrantz, Vogel, Bee, Broverman, and Broverman (1968) found that among male and female college students, men were perceived as more aggressive and independent than women, whereas women were seen as more tactful, gentle, and quiet than men. In addition, these researchers found that the self-concepts of men and women were very similar to their respective stereotypes.

One way in which sex role stereotypes may impede the progress of women is through the creation of occupational sex typing. According to Merton, "occupations can be described as 'sex-typed' when a large majority of those in them are of one sex and when there is an associated normative expectation that this is how it should be [Epstein, 1970, p. 152]." Judging from the high ratio of men to women in managerial positions and the informal belief that this is how it should be, the managerial job can be classified as a masculine occupation. If so, then the managerial position would seem to require personal attributes often thought to be more characteristic of men than women. Basil (cited by Brenner, 1970), using a

1. The author would like to thank John C. Sherman for his assistance with the statistical analyses.

Reprinted from *Journal of Applied Psychology*, 1973, 57, 95-100, by permission of the author and the publisher. © 1973 by the American Psychological Association.

nationwide sample of present managers, found that the four personal characteristics rated as most important for an upper-management position were seen as more likely to be possessed by men than women. Thus, in general, sex role stereotypes may effectuate the perception of women as being less qualified than men for high-level management positions.

Also, sex role stereotypes may deter women from striving to succeed in managerial positions. In a theory of work behavior, Korman (1970) maintains that "individuals will engage in and find satisfying those behavioral roles which will maximize their sense of cognitive balance or consistency [p. 32]." If a woman's self-image incorporates aspects of the stereotypical feminine role, she may be less inclined to acquire the job characteristics or engage in the job behaviors associated with the masculine managerial position since such characteristics and behaviors are inconsistent with her self-image.

Despite the apparent influence of stereotypical attitudes on the selection, placement and promotion of women, there is a dearth of studies that analyze the operation of sex role stereotypes within organizations. Although stereotypical masculine characteristics have been found to be more socially desirable (Rosenkrantz et al., 1968) and more similar to the characteristics of the healthy adult (Broverman, Broverman, Clarkson, Rosenkrantz, and Vogel, 1970) than stereotypical feminine characteristics, Schein (1971) found a paucity of studies dealing with psychological barriers, such as sex role stereotyping, that prevent women from achieving in the work force.

Since there have been no empirical studies except for Basil's demonstrating the existence of a relationship between sex role stereotypes and the perceived requisite personal characteristics for the middle-management position, the purpose of the present study was to examine this association. Specifically, it was hypothesized that

successful middle managers are perceived to possess those characteristics, attitudes, and temperaments more commonly ascribed to men in general than to women in general. Bowman et al. found that male acceptance of women managers increases with the age of the respondent. Therefore, it was also hypothesized that the association between sex role stereotypes and requisite management characteristics would be less strong among older managers than among younger ones.

METHOD

Sample

The sample was composed of 300 middle-line male managers of various departments within nine insurance companies located throughout the United States. Their ages ranged from 24 to 64, with a median of 43 years, their years of experience as managers, from 1 to 40 years with the median being 10 years.

Measurement Instrument

In order to define both the sex role stereotypes and the characteristics of successful middle managers, three forms of a Descriptive Index were developed. All three forms contained the same descriptive terms and instructions, except that one form asked for a description of women in general (Women), one for a description of men in general (Men) and one for a description of successful middle managers (Managers).

In developing the Descriptive Index, 131 items that differentially described males and females were garnered from studies by Basil (In Brenner, 1970), Bennett and Cohen (1959), Brim (1958), and Rosenkrantz et al. (1968). Using these items, a preliminary form of the Descriptive Index was administered to 24 male and female college students. Half of the subjects were given the Women form and half the Men form. In order to maximize the differences in the descriptions of Women and Men, an analysis of all the means and standard deviations was performed and an item was eliminated if (a) its mean descriptive rating was the same for both Women and Men, (b) it was judged by the experimenter and a staff assistant independently to be similar in meaning to one or more other items but it had a smaller mean difference between descriptions of Women and Men, or (c) its variability on both forms was significantly greater than the overall mean variability.

The final form of the Descriptive Index contained 92 adjectives and descriptive terms. The instructions on the three forms of the Index were as follows:

> On the following pages you will find a series of descriptive terms commonly used to characterize people in general. Some of these terms are positive in connotation, others are negative, and some are neither very positive nor very negative.
>
> We would like you to use this list to tell us what you think (women in general, men in general, or successful middle managers) are like. In making your judgments, it may be helpful to imagine that you are about to meet a person for the first time and the only thing you know in advance is that the person is (an adult female, an adult male, or a successful middle manager). Please rate each word or phrase in terms of how characteristic it is of (women in general, men in general, or successful middle managers).

The ratings of the descriptive terms were made according to a 5-point scale, ranging from 1 (not characteristic) to 5 (characteristic), with a neutral rating of 3 (neither characteristic nor uncharacteristic).

Procedure

Within each company, a representative with research experience randomly distributed an equal number of the three forms of the Index to male managers with a salary range of approximately $12,000 to $30,000 and a minimum of one year of experience at the managerial level.

Each manager received only *one* form of the Index. The cover letter to the participants stated that the researcher was "engaged in the establishment of a Descriptive Index to be used for management development" and informed the participants that "since various forms of the questionnaire are being distributed within your company, high-quality research results can only be obtained if you do not discuss your questionnaire or responses to it with anyone in your company." The questionnaires were returned in individually sealed envelopes.

Of the total number of Descriptive Indexes distributed, 76.62 per cent or 354 out of 462 were returned. The return rates for the various forms of the Index were as follows: Women, 76.62 per cent; Men, 77.27 per cent; and Managers, 75.97 per cent. The usable number of questionnaires was reduced to 300 (88 Women, 107 Men, and 105 Managers). Questionnaires were eliminated if (a) demographic data, such as age and sex, were not indicated or (b) the questionnaires were completed by females. Of the latter, 17 out of 26 were Women forms, which accounts for the lower number of usable Women questionnaires.

RESULTS

The degree of resemblance between the descriptions of Men and Managers and between Women and Managers was determined by computing intraclass correlation coefficients (r') from two randomized groups analyses of variance (see Hays, 1963, p. 424). The classes (or groups) were the 92 descriptive items. In the first analysis, the scores *within* each class were the mean item ratings of Men and Managers, while in the second analysis, they were the mean item ratings of Women and Managers. According to Hays, the larger the value of r', the more similar do observations in the same class tend to be relative to observations in different classes. Thus, the smaller the within item variability, relative to the between item variability, the greater the similarity between the mean item ratings of either Men and Managers or Women and Managers.

Table 37-1. Analyses of Variance of Mean Item Ratings and Intraclass Coefficients

Source	df	MS	F	r'
Men and managers				
Between items	91	1.27	4.23*	.62
Within items	92	.30		
Women and managers				
Between items	91	.89	1.13	.06
Within items	92	.79		

*p <.01.

According to Table 37-1, which presents the results of the analyses of variance and the intraclass correlation coefficients, there was a large and significant resemblance between the ratings of Men and Managers ($r' = .62$) whereas there was a near zero, nonsignificant resemblance between the ratings of Women and Managers ($r' = .06$), thereby confirming the hypothesis that Managers are perceived to possess characteristics more commonly ascribed to Men than to Women.

To determine if age moderates the relationship, the total sample was divided into three age levels, with an approximately equal number of subjects distributed within each age level and within each Women, Men, and Manager group. Intraclass correlations between the mean ratings of Men and Managers and between Women and Managers were computed within each of the three age levels. According to the results, as shown in Table 37-2, the main hypothesis is less strongly supported among subjects 49 years and above than among younger subjects. Within all three age levels, there was a significant resemblance between the mean ratings of Men and Managers. Among subjects 24 to 39 years and those 40 to 48 years, there was no resemblance between

Women and Managers; however, among subjects 49 years and above there was a small but significant resemblance between the ratings of Women and those of Managers.

In addition to intraclass correlation coefficients, Pearson product moment correlation coefficients were computed in order to determine the linear relationships between the mean ratings among the three groups. According to the results, there was a significant correlation ($r = .81$, $p < .01$) between the mean ratings of Men and Managers, but the correlation between the mean ratings of Women and Managers was not significant ($r = .10$). Within all three age levels the r between Men and Managers was significant at the .01 level ($r_1 = .77$; $r_2 = .80$; $r_3 = .79$). Within the two younger groups the correlation between Women and Managers was not significant ($r_1 = .04$; $r_2 = .05$); however, there was a significant correlation between the mean ratings of Women and Managers among subjects 49 years and above ($r_3 = .23, p < .05$).

Although the determination of the degree of resemblance between the mean ratings of Men and Managers and the degree of resemblance between the mean ratings of Women and Managers was considered to be the primary test of the hypothesis, an exploratory examination of the specific descriptive items on which Women or Men

Table 37-2. Intraclass Coefficients Within Three Age Levels

Age level	Intraclass Coefficients	
	Men and managers	Women and managers
24-39 (n=113)	.60**	.01
40-49 (n=95)	.64**	.00
49 and above (n=92)	.60**	.16**

*p <.05.
**p <.01.

Table 37-3. Items Displaying Lack of Similarity Between Managers and Men

Category	Item	
Managers more similar to women than to men	Understanding	Intuitive
	Helpful	Neat
	Sophisticated	(Not) Vulgar
	Aware of feelings of others	Humanitarian Values
Sex role sterotypes not related to management characteristics	Competent	Intelligent
	Tactful	Persistent
	Creative	Curious
	Courteous	(Not) Quarrelsome
	(Not) Exhibitionist	(Not) Hasty
	(Not) Devious	(Not) Bitter
	(Not) Deceitful	(Not) Selfish
	(Not) Strong Need for Social Acceptance	
	(Not) Desire to Avoid Controversy	
	(Not) Dawdler and Pro-crastinator	
	(Not) Desire for Friend-ship	

were perceived as similar to or different from Managers was also carried out so as to obtain a better understanding of the relationship. For each of the 92 items a 3 X 3 factorial analysis of variance, incorporating the three groups (Women, Men, and Managers) and the three age levels, was performed. According to the results, there was a significant group effect for 86 of the 92 items. An alpha level of .0005 was used as the criterion of signficance; therefore, the probability of obtaining one or more spuriously significant F ratios was .045. There were no significant age effects, nor were there any significant age X group interactions.

For each of the 86 items displaying a significant group effect, Duncan's multiple range test for unequal n's (see Kramer, 1956) was used to determine the significance of the difference (alpha = .01) between the mean ratings of Men and Managers, Women and Managers, and Men and Women. The results revealed that on 60 of these 86 items, ratings of Managers were more similar to

Men than to ratings of Women; for 8 of the 86 items the ratings of Managers were more similar to those of Women than to Men; and for the remaining 18 items with significant group F ratios there was no relationship between sex role stereotypes and perceptions of managerial characteristics—both the mean ratings of Women and Men were significantly different from those of Managers, but there were no significant differences between the mean ratings of Women and Men.[2]

Items representative of the first outcome category, in which Managers were more

2. Since the 92 items are undoubtedly intercorrelated, the number of significant item differences within each of the three outcome categories should not be viewed as a test of the hypothesis. The N within each of the Women, Men, and Manager groups approximated the number of items, thereby precluding a factor analysis within groups, and a factor analysis combining the responses to the three different forms of the Descriptive Index would be misleading due to the possibility of differing factor structures within the three stimulus groups (see Nunnally, 1967).

similar to Men than to Women, were as follows: Emotionally Stable; Aggressive; Leadership Ability; Self-Reliant; (not) Uncertain; Vigorous; Desires Responsibility; (not) Frivolous; Objective; Well Informed and Direct. These items were judged to be representative of the total group of 60 items by three advanced psychology students unfamiliar with the aims of the study. Table 37-3 presents the items in the latter two outcome categories, in which the predicted direction of mean differences did not occur.

DISCUSSION

The results confirm the hypothesis that successful middle managers are perceived to possess those characteristics, attitudes, and temperaments more commonly ascribed to men in general than to women in general. This association between sex role stereotypes and perceptions of requisite management characteristics seems to account, in part, for the limited number of women in management positions, thereby underscoring the need for research on the effect of these stereotypical attitudes on actual behavior, such as organizational decision-making and individual job performance.

The results suggest that, all else being equal, the perceived similarity between the characteristics of successful middle managers and men in general increases the likelihood of a male rather than a female being selected for or promoted to a managerial position. In a study of hiring practices in colleges and universities, Fidell (1970), using hypothetical descriptions of young PhDs which were identical except for sex, found that the modal level of job offer was lower for women (assistant professor) than for men (associate professor). The present findings imply that similar types of discriminatory selection decisions occur in industrial settings.

To the extent that a woman's self-image incorporates the female sex role stereotype, this relationship would also seem to influence a woman's job behavior. For example, in a laboratory task study pairing high- and low-dominance subjects, Megargee (1969) found that where the same sex subjects or high-dominance males and low-dominance females were paired, the high-dominance subject, regardless of sex, assumed the leadership role; however, where high-dominance females were paired with low-dominance males, the high-dominance females did not assume the leadership role. In this particular pairing, evidently, assumption of the leadership role was inconsistent with the females' feminine self-image and, therefore, they preferred to maintain their cognitive consistency by not being leaders. Given the high degree of resemblance between the perceived requisite management characteristics and characteristics of men in general, women may suppress the exhibition of many managerial job attributes in order to maintain their feminine self-image. Certainly, additional research is needed to determine if this relationship between sex role stereotypes and management characteristics exists among female middle managers.

Although approximately the same degree of resemblance between the characteristics of successful middle managers and those of men in general was found within all three age levels, only subjects within the 49 and above age group perceived a resemblance between the characteristics of Managers and those of Women. This finding suggests a slight reduction of the differential stereotypical perceptions of men and women among older managers. Examination of the degree of resemblance between the characteristics of Men and Women within the three age levels supported this notion. There was no significant resemblance between Women and Men within the two younger age levels ($r'_1 = -.14$; $r'_2 = .07$), whereas there was a significant resemblance between Women and Men among the oldest group of managers ($r'_3 = .30$, $p < .05$).

Certain concomitants of age, such as experience, may somewhat reduce the perceptual 'male-typing' of the managerial job. For example, experienced managers (the r between age and managerial experience was .76) probably have had more exposure to women as managers, thereby modifying some of their stereotypical perceptions of women. Perhaps more influential to their perceptions may be the changing roles of the wives and female social peers of these older managers. According to Kreps (1971), the proportion of women in the work force increases from age 16 until early 20s, then declines sharply but rises to a second peak of participation that is reached at about age 50. Older male managers may have more interaction with women for whom the role of labor force participant is more salient than that of mother-homemaker. This age effect interpretation implies that as more women become active participants in the labor force, the increased experience with working women will reduce to some extent the relationship between sex role stereotypes and requisite management characteristics among all age groups. Consequently, this psychological barrier to women in management will be lowered, thereby affording a greater opportunity for women to enter into and advance in managerial positions.

The results disclosing certain managerial characteristics that were not synonymous with the masculine sex role stereotype indicate areas in which women presently may be more readily acceptable in and accepting of managerial positions. Examination of the items in Table 37-3 suggests that "employee-centered" or "consideration" behaviors, such as Understanding, Helpful, and Intuitive, are requisite managerial characteristics that are more commonly ascribed to women in general than to men in general. In certain situations, exhibition of these stereotypical feminine behaviors may be advantageous. For example, in an experimental study, Bond and Vinacke (1961) used a task that required coalition formation for success. Males tended to use exploitative strategies, while females tended to use accommodative techniques. For this particular task, females outperformed the males. Perhaps focusing more attention on the feminine characteristics that are related to managerial success will foster a climate of greater receptivity to women managers.

Turning again to Table 37-3 some of the perceived requisite characteristics that were not related to sex role stereotypes, such as Intelligent, Competent, and Creative, can be classified as ability or expertise factors. That expertise is perceived to be as characteristic of women as of men supports Brenner's suggestion that women can be placed in managerial positions in which expertise is an important component of authority and explains Bowman et al.'s finding that male managers perceive more opportunity for women managers in staff than in line positions. Most of the remaining items in this outcome category appear to be socially undesirable personality traits, such as Quarrelsome, Bitter, Devious, and Deceitful. These traits were less characteristic of successful managers than of either men or women, but no difference in the possession of these traits was perceived between men and women. Here, too, accentuation of the finding that certain attributes required of successful managers may be found more or less as easily among women as men may enhance the status of women in management.

REFERENCES

Anastasi, A., and Foley, J. P., Jr. *Differential psychology.* New York: Macmillan, 1949.

Bennett, E. M., and Cohen, L. R. Men and women: Personality patterns and contrasts. *Genetic Psychology Monographs,* 1959, 59, 101-55.

Bond, J. R., and Vinacke, W. E. Coalitions in mixed-sex triads. *Sociometry,* 1961, 24, 61-75.

Bowman, G. W., Worthy, N. B., and Greyser, S. A. Are women executives people? *Harvard Business Review,* 1965, 43, 14-16+.

Brenner, M. H. Management development activities for women. Paper presented at meeting of the American Psychological Association, Miami, September 1970.

Brim, O. G. Family structure and sex-role learning by children: A further analysis of Helen Koch's data. *Sociometry*, 1958, 21, 1-16.

Broverman, I. K., Broverman, D. M., Clarkson, F. E., Rosenkrantz, P. S., and Vogel, S. R. Sex-role stereotypes and clinical judgments of mental health. *Journal of Consulting and Clinical Psychology*, 1970, 34, 1-7.

Epstein, C. F. *Woman's place.* Berkeley: University of California Press, 1970.

Fidell, L. S. Empirical verification of sex discrimination in hiring practices in psychology. *American Psychologist*, 1970, 25, 1094-98.

Hays, W. L. *Statistics for psychologists.* New York: Holt, Rinehart & Winston, 1963.

Koontz, E. D. The progress of the woman worker: An unfinished story. *Issues in Industrial Society*, 1971, 2, 29-31.

Korman, A. K. Toward a hypothesis of work behavior. *Journal of Applied Psychology*, 1970, 54, 31-41.

Kramer, C. Y. Extension of multiple range tests to group means with unequal numbers of replications. *Biometrics*, 1956, 12, 307-10.

Kreps, J. *Sex in the marketplace: American women at work.* Baltimore: Johns Hopkins Press, 1971.

Maccoby, E. E. (Ed.) *The development of sex differences.* Stanford: Stanford University Press, 1966.

Megargee, E. I. Influence of sex roles on the manifestation of leadership. *Journal of Applied Psychology*, 1969, 53, 377-82.

Nunnally, J. C. *Psychometric theory.* New York: McGraw-Hill, 1967.

Orth, C. D., and Jacobs, F. Women in management: Pattern for change. *Harvard Business Review*, 1971, 49, 139-47.

Rosenkrantz, P., Vogel, S., Bee, H., Broverman, I., and Broverman, D. M. Sex-role stereotypes and self-concepts in college students. *Journal of Consulting and Clinical Psychology*, 1968, 32, 287-95.

Schein, V. E. The woman industrial psychologist: Illusion or reality? *American Psychologist*, 1971, 26, 708-12.

Women in the work force. *Management Review*, 1970, 59, 20-23.

Wylie, R. *The self concept.* Lincoln: University of Nebraska Press, 1961.

38

Improvements in the Selection Interview

ROBERT E. CARLSON, PAUL W. THAYER, EUGENE C. MAYFIELD,
and DONALD A. PETERSON

The effectiveness and utility of the selection interview has again been seriously questioned as a result of several comprehensive reviews of the research literature.[1] Not one of these classic summary reviews of the interview research literature arrived at conclusions that could be classed as optimistic when viewed from an applied standpoint. Yet none of this is new information. As early as 1915, the validity of the selection interview was empirically questioned.[2] Despite the fact that it is common knowledge that the selection interview probably contributes little in the way of validity to the selection decisions, it continues to be used. It is clear that no amount of additional evidence on the lack of validity will alter the role of the interview in selection. Future research should obviously be directed at understanding the mechanism of the interview and improving interview technology. As Schwab has stated, "Companies are not likely to abandon the use of the employment interview, nor is it necessarily desirable that they do so. But it is grossly premature to sit back comfortably and assume that employment interviews are satisfactory. It is even too early to dash off unsupported recommendations for their improvement. A great deal of research work remains, research which companies must be willing to sponsor before we can count the interview as a prime weapon in our selection arsenal."[3] This was essentially the conclusion that the Life Insurance Agency Management Association reached some six years ago. In addition, the life insurance industry, through LIAMA, took action and sponsored basic research on the selection interview.

The research reported here is an attempt to improve the use of the selection interview

1. See, for example, R. Wagner, The employment interview: A critical summary. *Personnel Psychology*, 1949, 2, 17-26.
G. W. England and D. G. Paterson, Selection and placement—The past ten years, in H. G. Heneman, Jr., *et al.* (Eds.), *Employment relations research: A summary and appraisal*. New York: Harper, 1960, pp. 43-72.
E. C. Mayfield, The selection interview: A re-evaluation of published research. *Personnel Psychology*, 1964, 17, 239-60.
L. Ulrich and D. Trumbo, The selection interview since 1949. *Psychological Bulletin*, 1965, 63, 100-116.

2. W. D. Scott, The scientific selection of salesmen. *Advertising and Selling*, 1915, 25, 5-6 and 94-96.

3. D. P. Schwab, "Why interview? A critique." *Personnel Journal*, 1969, 48 (2), 129.

Reprinted from *Personnel Journal*, 1971 (April), 268-75, by permission of the authors and the publisher.

in the life insurance industry. The role of the interview in selection presented a particularly difficult problem for the life insurance industry where each agency manager is responsible for many of the traditional personnel management functions. In addition, these agencies are scattered across the U.S. and Canada and make centralizing the selection process difficult. In order to strengthen the role of the selection system, LIAMA has been doing basic research on the selection interview for the past six years.

The research reported here is part of a long-run research program concerned with how interviewers make employment decisions. Its purpose is to try to determine the limits of an interviewer's capability in extending his judgment into the future. This summary covers the early studies in a program of research to develop interim tools and the training necessary to make the selection interview a useful selection instrument.

The first step in the interview research program was to observe and record numerous interviews, to interview in depth the interviewers on their decision process, to conduct group decision conferences where the interviewers discussed their perception of their decision process for a given taped interview, and to examine the published research on the selection interview. Based upon this information, a model of the selection interview was constructed that specified as many of the influences operating during the interview as could be determined. Initially, there appeared to be four main classes of influences operating to affect/limit the decision of the interviewer. They were:

The physical and psychological properties of the interviewee;
The physical and psychological properties of the interviewer;
The situation/environment in which the interviewer works;
The task or type of judgment the interviewer must make.

The research strategy has been to systematically manipulate and control the variables specified in the model, trying to eliminate variables that do not have any influence, trying to assess the magnitude of those variables that have an influence, and adding variables that other research has shown to be promising. The first section of this article will describe some of the research findings; the second section will describe some of the materials that have been developed; and the third section will describe the interviewer training that has been developed.

WHAT ARE SOME FINDINGS?

Structured vs. Unstructured Interviews

One question that has often been asked is, "What kind of interview is best?" What interview style—structured, where the interviewer follows a set procedure; or unstructured, where the interviewer has no set procedure and where he follows the interviewee's lead—results in more effective decisions? In this study, live interviews were used. Each interviewee was interviewed three times. Interviewers used the following three types of interviewing strategies: structured, where the interviewer asked questions only from an interview guide; semistructured, where the interviewer followed an interview guide, but could ask questions about any other areas he wished; and unstructured, where the interviewer had no interview guide and could do as he wished. The basic question involved was the consistency with which people interviewing the same interviewee could agree with each other. If the interviewers' judgments were not consistent —one interviewer saying the applicant was good and the other saying he was bad—no valid prediction of job performance could be made from interview data. Agreement among interviewers is essential if one is to say that the procedure used has the potential for validity.

The results indicated that only the structured interview generated information that enabled interviewers to agree with each other. Under structured conditions, the interviewer knew what to ask and what to do with the information he received. Moreover, the interviewer applied the same frame of reference to each applicant, since he covered the same areas for each. In the less-structured interviews, the managers received additional information, but it seemed to be unorganized and made their evaluation task more difficult. Thus, a highly-structured interview has the greatest potential for valid selection.[4]

Effect of Interviewer Experience

In the past it had been assumed that one way to become an effective interviewer was through experience. In fact, it has been hypothesized that interviewers who have had the same amount of experience would evaluate a job applicant similarly.[5] To determine whether this was indeed the case, a study was done that involved managers who had conducted differing numbers of interviews over the same time period. Managers were then compared who had similar as well as differing concentrations of interviewing experience. It was found that when evaluating the same recruits, interviewers with similar experiences did not agree with each other to any greater degree than did interviewers with differing experiences. It was concluded that interviewers benefit very little from day-to-day interviewing experience and apparently the conditions necessary for learning are not present in the day-to-day interviewer's job

situation.[6] This implied that systematic training is needed, with some feedback mechanism built into the selection procedure, to enable interviewers to learn from their experiences; the job performance predictions made by the interviewer must be compared with how the recruit actually performs on the job.

Situational Pressures

One of the situational variables studied was how pressure for results affected the evaluation of a new recruit. One large group of managers was told to assume that they were behind their recruiting quota, that it was October, and that the home office had just called. Another group was ahead of quota; for a third group, no quota situation existed. All three groups of managers evaluated descriptions of the same job applicants. It was found that being behind recruiting quota impaired the judgment of those managers. They evaluated the same recruits as actually having greater potential and said they would hire more of them than did the other two groups of managers.[7]

One more highly significant question was raised: Are all managers, regardless of experience, equally vulnerable to this kind of pressure? Managers were asked how frequently they conducted interviews. Regardless of how long the person had been a manager, those who had had a high rate of interviewing experience—many interviews in a given period of time—were less susceptible to pressures than were those with a low interviewing rate. The interviewers with less interviewing experience relied more on subjective information and reached a decision with less information. It was concluded that one way to overcome this problem of

4. R. E. Carlson, D. P. Schwab, and H. G. Heneman III. Agreement among selection interview styles. *Journal of Industrial Psychology,* 1970, (1), 8-17.
5. P. M. Rowe, Individual differences in assessment decisions. Doctoral thesis, McGill University. 1960.

6. R. E. Carlson, Selection interview decisions: The effect of interviewer experience, relative quota situation, and applicant sample on interviewer decisions. *Personnel Psychology,* 1967, 20, 259-80.
7. *Ibid.*

lack of concentrated interviewing experience was through the general use of a standardized interview procedure and intensive training in its use.

Standard of Comparison

Another condition studied was the standards managers applied in evaluating recruits. It was found, for example, that if a manager evaluated a candidate who was just average after evaluating three or four very unfavorable candidates in a row, the average one would be evaluated very favorably.[8] When managers were evaluating more than one recruit at a time, they used other recruits as a standard.[9] Each recruit was compared to all other recruits. Thus, managers did not have an absolute standard—who they thought looked good was partly determined by the persons with whom they were comparing the recruit. This indicated that some system was necessary to aid a manager in evaluating a recruit. The same system should be applicable to each recruit. This implied that some standardized evaluation system was necessary to reduce the large amount of information developed from an interview to a manageable number of constant dimensions.

Effect of Appearance

Some of the early studies utilized photographs to try to determine how much of an effect appearance had on the manager's decision. A favorably rated photograph was paired with a favorably rated personal history description and also with an unfavorably rated personal history. It was found that appearance had its greatest effect on the interviewer's final rating when it complemented the personal history information.[10] Even when appearance and personal history information were the same (both favorable or both unfavorable), the personal history information was given twice as much weight as appearance. However, the relationship is not a simple one and only emphasized the need for a more complete system to aid the manager in selection decision-making.

Effect of Interview Information on Valid Test Results

In many selection situations, valid selection tests are used in conjunction with the interview data in arriving at a selection decision. Two recent studies have investigated how the emphasis placed on valid test results (*Aptitude Index Battery*) is altered by the more subjective interview data. Managers do place great emphasis on the AIB, knowing that the score does generate a valid prediction.

However, how much weight is given to the score depends on other conditions; e.g., a low-scoring applicant is judged better if preceded by a number of poor applicants, unfavorable information is given much greater weight if it is uncovered just prior to ending the interview, etc. This finding suggested that what is needed is some system that places the interview information and other selection information in their proper perspective.[11]

Interview Accuracy

A recent study tried to determine how accurately managers can recall what an

8. R. E. Carlson, Effects of applicant sample on ratings of valid information in an employment setting. *Journal of Applied Psychology,* 1970, 54, 217-22.
9. R. E. Carlson, Selection interview decisions: The effect of mode of applicant presentation on some outcome measures. *Personnel Psychology,* 1968, 21, 193-207.

10. R. E. Carlson, The relative influence of appearance and factual written information on an interviewer's final rating. *Journal of Applied Psychology,* 1967, 51, 461-68.
11. R. E. Carlson, The effect of interview information in altering valid impressions. *Journal of Applied Psychology,* 1971, 55, 66-72.

applicant says during an interview. Prior to the interview the managers were given the interview guide, pencils, and paper, and were told to perform as if *they* were conducting the interview. A 20-minute video tape of a selection interview was played for a group of 40 managers. Following the video tape presentation, the managers were given a 20-question test. All questions were straightforward and factual. Some managers missed none, while some missed as many as 15 out of 20 items. The average number was 10 wrong. In a short 20-minute interview, half the managers could not report accurately on the information produced during the interview! On the other hand, those managers who had been following the interview guide and taking notes were quite accurate on the test; note-taking in conjunction with a guide appears to be essential.

Given that interviewers differed in the accuracy with which they were able to report what they heard, the next question appeared to be "How does this affect their evaluation?" In general it was found that those interviewers who were least accurate in their recollections rated the interviewee higher and with less variability, while the more accurate interviewers rated the interviewee average or lower and with greater variability. Thus, those interviewers who did not have the factual information at their disposal assumed that the interview was generally favorable and rated the interviewee more favorable in all areas. Those interviewers who were able to reproduce more of the factual information rated the interviewee lower and recognized his intra-individual differences by using more of the rating scale. This implied that the less accurate interviewers selected a "halo strategy" when evaluating the interviewee, while the more accurate interviewers used an individual differences strategy. Whether this is peculiar to the individual interviewer or due to the fact that the interviewer did or didn't have accurate information at his disposal is, of course, unanswerable from this data.

Can Interviewers Predict?

The ultimate purpose of the selection interview is to collect factual and attitudinal information that will enable the interviewer to make accurate and valid job behavior predictions for the interviewee. The interviewer does this by recording the factual information for an applicant, evaluating the meaning of the information in terms of what the interviewee will be able to do on the job in question, and extending these evaluations into the future in the form of job behavior predictions. The question is, "How reliably can a group of interviewers make predictions for a given interviewee?" Without high inter-interviewer agreement, the potential for interview validity is limited to a few interviewers and cannot be found in the interview process itself.

In this study, a combination of movies and audio tapes was played simulating an interview. In addition, each of the 42 manager-interviewers was given a detailed written summary of the interview. The total interview lasted almost three hours and covered the interviewee's work history, work experience, education and military experience, life insurance holdings, attitude toward the life insurance career, family life, financial soundness, social life and social mobility, and future goals and aspirations.

After hearing and seeing the interview and after studying a 20-page written summary, each interviewer was asked to make a decision either to continue the selection process or to terminate negotiations. In addition, each interviewer was asked to make a list of all the factual information he considered while making his decision. Also, the interviewer was to rate the interviewee in 31 different areas. The ratings were descriptive of the interviewee's past accomplishments, such as his job success pattern, the quantity and quality of his education, his family situation, financial knowledge and soundness, etc. Finally, the interviewers were asked to make job behavior predictions in 28 different job specific activities such as, Could he use the telephone for business purposes? Could he make cold calls? Would he keep records? Would he take direction? What about his market?

The interviewers agreed quite well with each other on which facts they reportedly considered in making their employment decision. Almost 70 per cent of the factual statements were recorded by all the interviewers. The remaining 30 per cent of the factual statements were specific to interviewers. This tended to confirm a hypothesis of Mayfield and Carlson where they postulate that the stereotypes held by interviewers consist of general as well as specific content.[12] It was concluded that interviewers do record and use similar factual information with agreement.

The interviewers agreed less well with each other on the evaluation or value placed on the facts. The median inter-interviewer correlation was .62, with a low of .07 and a high of .82. This means that the interviewers still agreed reasonably well on the evaluation—good vs. bad—quality of the information they received. They would make similar selection-rejection decisions.

The job behavior predictions of the interviewers, however, were not nearly as high in agreement. The median inter-interviewer correlation was .33 with a low of −.21 and a high of .67. This means that the interviewers do not agree with each other on how well the interviewee will perform the job of a life insurance agent in 28 different areas. In addition, those predictions that required the interviewer to extend his judgment further into the future had significantly greater inter-interviewer variability than did those predictions that could be verified in a short period of time. Thus,

interviewers can agree more with each other's predictions if the job behavior is of a more immediate nature.

These findings imply that although interviewers probably use much the same information in making a decision, they will evaluate it somewhat differently. Furthermore, the interviewers are not able to agree on how well the individual will perform on the job.

Thus, it was concluded that interviewers evaluate essentially similar things in an applicant; they agree reasonably well whether an applicant's past record is good or bad, but they cannot agree on good or bad for what. Yet here, and only here, is where the clinical function of the interviewer is difficult to replace with a scoring system. In being able to make accurate and valid job behavior predictions, the interview can pay for itself in terms of planning an applicant's early job training and as a mechanism whereby a supervisor can learn early how to manage an applicant. In order for the interviewer to be able to make accurate and valid job behavior predictions, it follows that he must have a feedback system whereby he can learn from his past experiences. Only through accurate feedback in language similar to the behavior predictions can the interviewer learn to make job behavior predictions. The results further imply that the interviewer must be equipped with a complete selection system that coordinates all the selection steps and provides the interviewer with as relevant and complete information as possible when he makes job behavior predictions.

CONCLUSIONS

These early studies in LIAMA's interview research program provided little in the way of optimism for the traditional approach to the selection interview. However, this research did indicate specific areas where improvements in selection and interview technology could be made. It did indicate

12. E. C. Mayfield and R. E. Carlson, Selection interview decisions: First results from a long-term research project. *Personnel Psychology*, 1966, 19, 41-53.

where interim improvements could be tried and evaluated while the long-term research on the interview continued.

Two major applied implications may be derived from the interview research to date. First, the selection interview should be made an integral part of an over-all selection procedure, and to accomplish this, new and additional materials are needed. The new materials should include a broad-gauge, comprehensive, structured interview guide; standardized evaluation and prediction forms that aid the interviewer in summarizing information from all steps in the selection process; and an evaluation system that provides feedback to the interviewer in language similar to the pre-employment job behavior predictions he must make. The second major applied implication is that an intensive training program for interviewers is necessary if interviewers are to initially learn enough in common to increase the probability of obtaining general validity from the selection interview. Thus, the early studies have provided specific information that has been used to change the way selection is carried out in the insurance industry.

IMPLEMENTATION: DEVELOPMENT OF A SELECTION PROCESS

As a result of and based upon the early interview research, LIAMA constructed the *Agent Selection Kit.* This is a complete agent selection procedure to be used by agency branch managers and general agents in the field. Selection begins when the agency head secures the name of a prospective recruit and ends when the new agent has been selling for six months or when negotiations or employment is terminated. Because research demonstrated the necessity of formally taking into consideration each step in the selection process, each step in the procedure is carefully placed to maximize the potential of succeeding and following steps. The *Agent Selection Kit* introduced the following new ideas to the insurance industry:

1. *Selection should more properly be viewed as manpower development.* The *Agent Selection Kit* is a completely integrated process, more properly described as manpower development; it goes beyond just selection. The assumption is that if industry is really going to have an appreciable effect on the manpower problem, it will have to think of recruiting, selection, training, and supervision as parts of a total manpower development process and not as entities by themselves. Quantity and quality of recruiting have an impact on selection—selection affects training—training capabilities, in turn, should affect selection. Unless viewed as a continuous, dependent process, maximum use cannot be made of the information the tools provide. If viewed as a complete process, the information gained from each step is carried forward to make future steps and the final decision more powerful.

2. *Organizational differences must be taken into consideration in selection.* Because the *Agent Selection Kit* is a complete selection process, it can be modified to meet company and agency differences. By clearly spelling out the philosophy and principles behind the steps in the *Agent Selection Kit,* the company and the agency head are able to evaluate what is being gained or lost by altering the steps in selection. Further, because the agency head is forced to make job behavior predictions, he can begin to consider each recruit in terms of his particular agency needs, style, and strengths. Agency differences as well as individual differences enter into the employment decision in a systematic manner.

3. *A career with any company should be entered into based on realistic job expectations.*[13] The company should know what the job recruit expects from his association

13. Life Insurance Agency Management Association, *"Realistic" job expectations and survival.* Research Report 1964-2 (File 432).

with the company. Under such a condition, the manager can make a manpower development decision that properly considers selection, early training, motivation, and supervision practices of the applicant in question. The job recruit should know what the company expects of him, how the company is going to help him accomplish these goals, and the difficulties and benefits he may encounter in undertaking the job. With such knowledge, the recruit can make more than a job decision. He can make a career decision. The creation of realistic expectations further implies that the employment decision be one of "mutual consent." Professional management of the future will not be able to rely on a slanted job presentation to attract recruits to a career in hopes that one or two applicants will succeed. Manpower development decisions will replace selection decisions. The *Agent Selection Kit* is built around the concept of "mutual consent" with respect to a career decision. There are already indications that the recruit of the future will respond to a "mutual exploration" theme, where together he and the manager will examine the individual's future in an industry. The *Agent Selection Kit* provides a systematic fact-finding procedure that appeals to the recruit.

4. *The selection interview should proceed according to a highly-structured format.* The *Agent Selection Kit* contains two self-contained structured interview guides. The first interview guide is to be used with applicants who have had extensive prior work history and concentrates on this work experience. The alternate interview guide is to be used with applicants just completing their education or military experiences and without any work experience. In addition, both interview guides cover the recruit's education, military experience, attitude toward insurance and toward the insurance agent's job, family commitments, finances,

social mobility, social life, and future goals and aspirations. The interview guides present the initial series of questions and several alternative probes. Experience and pretesting have indicated that recruits are receptive to a structured approach and that interviewers can learn to use the guides after brief, but intensive, training.

5. *Employment decisions should be based on predictions of future job behavior.* The *Agent Selection Kit* considers decision-making from the point of view of a prediction of future behavior, rather than from vague, over-all impressions of potential or character. The manager manages the agent's activity, use of the telephone, record-keeping, prospecting, etc. The *Agent Selection Kit* enables the manager to make predictions about such job behaviors.

6. *The manager should be able to learn from and correct his selection system.* The *Agent Selection Kit* procedure contains a built-in "feedback system" that enables the manager to learn from and correct his selection process. LIAMA interview research has shown that managers do not learn from the traditional approach to selection interviewing. To correct this, the *Agent Selection Kit* includes an Agent Performance Rating Form that the manager uses to compare to his final decision ratings. Discrepancies between his prediction and results point to areas in his selection and early training process that need extra effort.

IMPLEMENTATION: TRAINING IN SELECTION AND INTERVIEWING

To ensure at least uniform initial introduction to the material, LIAMA designed a three-day skill-building workshop. Three general training objectives and 16 specific behavioral objectives served as guides in setting up the training program. The first general goal was to develop in each trainee *knowledge* of selection and interview techniques; the second goal was to create favorable *attitudes* in the managers toward selection and self–confidence in their ability to conduct a technically good selection interview; and third, to develop *skill* in actually using the selection and interview materials. As a result of participating in the training, the agency heads are to actually be better at selection and interviewing than they were prior to training, to know they are better, and to be able to immediately use the new material with some skill. Thus, the goals of the training are to change attitudes as well as to develop knowledge and skill. These specifications dictated that the workshops be built around small-sized classes, class participation, and practice with standardized case material and controlled feedback.

To accomplish the goals of the training program, the first step in the workshop is to help the agency manager to understand and accept the principles behind the steps in the selection process. This helps to make the trainees receptive to discarding their current approach to selection and to accepting the new approach. Once the agency head accepts the logic of the principles on which the *Agent Selection Kit* is based, the next step is to get the trainee to recognize and question how he is currently conducting his selection process. This is accomplished through the use of edited tapes that demonstrate some of the effects of violating the selection principles. At the end of this first phase of the training, the agency heads are receptive to a new procedure and are aware of what a good procedure should contain.

The skill training that follows is designed to make the agency head more proficient in the use of the interview and evaluation procedures. The interview technique training includes taped examples, practice, and critique. The final evaluation practice sessions are extremely important to agency heads. Here the manager is asking to combine information from all the selection methods he has utilized — the interview,

reference checks, credit reports, interview with the wife, precontract training, etc. The manager practices making job behavior predictions in areas such as use of the telephone, night work, markets, prospecting activities, etc. For the first time, managers recognize that they will not be managing the recruit's character or how impressive he looks, but rather they recognize that they must manage his work activities. Managers begin to recognize that selection should try to predict the recruit's performance in these activities.

During the workshops, the participants' attitudes swing from skepticism to receptivity, from impatience with the training detail to complete acceptance. These swings in attitude are built into the schedule, since early experimental workshops showed that they were necessary to modify and solidify managers' attitudes.

The managers leave their workshop with greater knowledge, with a skill that is well along in development, and with much greater self-confidence in their selection and early training procedure that they can put into practice immediately.

THE FUTURE

The *Agent Selection Kit* was introduced to LIAMA's 300-plus member companies in 1969. By mid-1970, 40 major life insurance companies had introduced it to their general agents and managers. Obviously, at this time it is much too early to evaluate its effectiveness. However, it is currently being evaluated as part of LIAMA's research program on the selection interview. In addition, it also provides a natural field setting for further pure research on the selection interview. Thus, LIAMA's research on the interview is an example of pure research generating an improved product, which, in turn, furthers the pure research effort.

39

The Assessment Center as an Aid in Management Development

WILLIAM C. BYHAM

Assessment centers can aid an organization in the early identification of management potential and in the diagnosis of individual management development needs so that training and development efforts can be invested most efficiently. Centers can also act as a powerful stimulant to management development, providing self-insight into problem areas and identifying possible development actions. In addition, the method can increase the accuracy of initial selection of potential managers or salesmen, which will give the management development practitioner better material with which to work. More than one hundred large and small organizations are presently using this relatively new method; some of these are AT&T, IBM, Standard Oil (Ohio), Sears Roebuck, Olin, Cummins Engine, Department of Agriculture, G.E., J. C. Penney, Ford, Steinberg's, Northern Electric, Kodak, and Merrill Lynch, Pierce, Fenner and Smith. Hundreds more are actively implementing applications. Reasons for the increasing interest in the technique are threefold:

1. Accuracy of the technique has been proven in studies conducted by AT&T, IBM, Sears Roebuck, and Standard Oil (Ohio). Candidates chosen by the method have been found to be two to three times more likely to be successful at higher management levels than those promoted on the basis of supervisory judgment.

2. Time and money are saved by combining assessment and development in the same procedure. Participation in the program is an extremely powerful learning experience for both participants and the higher management assessors who observe and record the participants' behavior.

3. Management acceptance is high because the assessment center looks valid and makes sense to management. Management is impressed by the simulations of the challenges an employee will face as he or she moves up in management and by the fact that line managers usually make the judgment of potential and management development needs.

Assessment centers differ greatly in length, cost, contents, staffing, and administration, depending on the objectives of the center, the dimensions to be assessed, and the employee population. Basically an assessment center is a formal procedure

Reprinted by special permission from the December 1971 *Training and Development Journal.* ©1971 by the American Society for Training and Development, Inc.

incorporating group and individual exercises for the identification of dimensions of managerial or sales success identified as important for a particular position or level of management. It differs from other techniques in that a number of individuals are processed at the same time, trained managers who are usually not in a direct supervisory capacity conduct and evaluate the assessment, and multiple exercises are used to evaluate behavior.

TYPICAL CENTER

In a typical center aimed at identifying the potential of first-level managers for middle-level management positions, 12 participants are nominated by their immediate supervisors as having potential based on their current job performance. For two days, participants take part in exercises developed to expose behaviors deemed important in the particular organization. A participant may play a business game, complete an in-basket exercise, participate in two group discussions and in an individual exercise, and be interviewed. Six assessors observe the participants' behavior and take notes on special observation forms. After the two days of exercises, participants go back' to their jobs and the assessors spend two more days comparing their observations and making a final evaluation of each participant. A summary report is developed on each participant, outlining his or her potential and defining development action appropriate for both the organization and the individual. See Appendix A for a description of a typical two-day center.

The level of candidate assessment usually dictates the length of the center. Centers for identifying potential in non-management candidates for foreman positions often last only one day, while middle management and higher management centers can last as long as two and a half days.

Assessment centers are most popular and seem to be most valid when the position for which the individuals are being considered is quite different from their current positions, for instance, the promotion of salesmen or technicians into management or from direct supervision to middle management where he or she must manage through others. Because the new job requires different skills and abilities than the present job, it is difficult for managers to assess the candidates' managerial aptitude prior to promotion. Thus, many failures result. By simulating in an assessment center the problems and challenges of the level of management for which the individual is being considered, it is possible for management to determine the potential of the individual for the higher level position.

EARLY IDENTIFICATION

Because of the difficulty of determining supervisory skills in most non-management jobs, the greatest use of assessment centers is the identification of potential for first-level supervision. AT&T alone has assessed more than 70,000 candidates for first-level management, and about one-half of the assessment center operations in the United States are aimed at identifying supervisory potential.

Another increasing use of assessment centers is in the *early* identification of potential. There are many situations in which management potential must be identified at an early stage so various administrative actions can be taken. For example, AT&T has a program of identifying management potential in blacks and women during their second year of employment so that various compensatory training and development activities can be planned to speed them toward management. Another example is found in firms with a commission-sales salary structure which forces them to identify potential early in order to get the salesman on a track into management before high sales income makes movement impossible. Several organizations are using assessment centers for this purpose.

Increasingly, assessment centers are being used at higher levels of management; and it is in these applications that the full potential of centers for management development is achieved. There are numerous middle-management assessment centers in operation and a few centers aimed at top management positions.

INDIVIDUAL MANAGEMENT DEVELOPMENT NEEDS

Assessment center summary reports are not usually go—no-go documents. Rather they detail the strengths and weaknesses of participants on the dimensions the organization has previously identified as important to success. Examples of specific behavior at the center are provided as an aid to problem diagnosis and in the later feedback of performance to the participant. Frequently the managers/assessors will make specific developmental recommendations which are also included in the report. An example of such a report is given in Appendix B. This may go directly to management or to staff experts who add additional developmental suggestions based on the needs identified.

Most assessment centers above the bottom level of management have as their primary or strong secondary objective the building of individual development plans. This is not true at bottom-level management because many of those assessed at that level will not reach management; thus, an investment in diagnosing development needs is questionable. While some developmental diagnosis may be possible for those recommended for advancement, it is not generally a prime objective in such programs.

After a number of candidates have been processed, it is possible to use assessment data as an aid in allocating training and development expenditures and in planning new development programs. An extremely useful development-needs audit can be obtained by summarizing the needs of a number of assessed participants. Common areas of need can be identified for special priority. Information from multiple assessments can also aid in designing new programs. For instance, Kodak recently developed a new pre-foreman training program based on its early assessment experience. Insights from assessments of candidates for the position of product service center manager by the J. C. Penney Company resulted in the development of a totally new development plan. So few technically-trained candidates were found to have the necessary management potential that the company decided to change its whole approach to filling the position and developed a program to give technical training to people of proven managerial competence.

STIMULATION OF SELF-DEVELOPMENT

Participation in an assessment center is a developmental experience. As can be quickly recognized, many assessment exercises such as the in-basket, management games, and leaderless group discussions also are training exercises. Thus, to the extent that performance feedback is provided, participation in an assessment center is a developmental experience. In most centers above the lowest level of management, considerable performance feedback is provided during the assessment program. A good example of the kinds of feedback provided is the assessment center program of the Autolite Division of the Ford Motor Company. Participants take part in professionally led critiques of their performance in group activities, and they watch their performance in groups by means of videotape. After individually taking the in-basket for assessment purposes, they meet in small groups to share their decisions and actions with each other, to evaluate their reasoning, and to broaden their repertory of responses.

Even without special feedback opportunities built in, there is a great deal of evidence that most participants gain in self-insight from participating in assessment exercises and that this insight is fairly accurate. The evidence comes from comparing participant responses on self-evaluation questionnaires given after exercises with assessor evaluations. Correlations of .6 and higher based on large samples from several organizations have been found.

While self-insight gained from taking part in assessment center exercises is important, it is secondary to the insights gained from receiving feedback of the assessor observations. Almost all assessment centers provide feedback to participants. The amount and detail of the feedback vary greatly but are largely related to organizational level. Higher-level participants get much more information than lower-level participants. Career counseling and planning discussions are often combined with assessor feedback for higher-level participants. Most feedback interviewing ends in a written commitment to action on the part of the participant and sometimes the organization.

COMBINED ASSESSMENT AND TRAINING

Still another important way the assessment center can stimulate development is to combine physically an assessment program with a training program. This is sometimes done because of the sheer economics of the combination. Junior Achievement Incorporated was able to put an assessment program into the beginning of an existing two-week training program with little loss in training impact. The Huyck Corporation recently completed a series of centers in which an entire level of upper middle management was assessed. Since it is an international company, this entailed bringing in participants from Australia, South America, and Europe in addition to

participants from throughout the United States. Rather than have the participants leave after two and a half days as would be normal, they followed the regular center activities with two and a half days of training exercises. The economics of travel and facilities was such that these additional days of training could be added at slight increase in expense.

But most important as an argument for combining or closely associating training and assessment is the "unfreezing" process that occurs with assessment. As indicated above, even without formal feedback from assessors, center participants are greatly sensitized to their own shortcomings and open to development ideas and training. A number of companies have recognized the advantages of integrating training and assessment because of this unfreezing process. Most have chosen to follow the assessment with training designed to correct common problems such as group efficiency, sensitivity to others, public speaking, management skills and decision making. The ideal situation is for assessor observations to be fed back during the training period to maximize development.

ASSESSOR TRAINING

An assessor in an assessment center benefits more than the participant in terms of direct training. Between assessor training and participation as an assessor in a center, the assessor benefits in the following ways:

1. Improvement in interviewing skills;
2. Broadening of observation skills;
3. Increased appreciation of group dynamics and leadership styles;
4. New insights into behavior;
5. Strengthening of management skills through repeated working with in-basket case problems and other simulations;
6. Broadening of repertory of responses to problems;
7. Establishment of normative standards by which to evaluate performance;

8. Development of a more precise vocabulary with which to describe behavior.

While many on-the-job uses can be made of these improved skills, perhaps the greatest impact is in performance-appraisal interviewing. Extensive self-report data from assessors indicate a vast improvement in both accuracy and success of appraisal interviewing. Organizations such as G.E. feel so strongly about the many benefits from assessor training that they have increased the ratio of assessors to participants in their programs in order to expose more assessors to the experience.

Assessor training comes from a formal training program prior to the center, but principally from application of the procedures as an assessor in an assessment center. It is a unique opportunity for managers to focus on observing behavior without the normal interruptions associated with business. After observing the behavior, the assessors can compare their observations with those of other assessors and sometimes have the opportunity to repeat the observation via videotape recording. The procedures learned in assessor training are put into practice and thus stamped into the assessor's memory.

The principal focus of assessor training is usually on interviewing, observing behavior, and handling the in-basket. All exercises in an assessment center usually call for some combination of these skills. In addition, practice on all the exercises to be observed in assessment centers is usually provided. Any number of assessors can be trained at once, with assessor training for as many as 25 individuals not uncommon. Many organizations starting assessment centers initially train large numbers of managers as assessors to establish a pool from which to draw assessors. This plan has a number of other benefits which include providing a large number of management people with a quick orientation to the program so that they can most effectively use the reports generated. It

also allows the opportunity for a rough screening of the assessors so that the most skilled assessors can be used in the assessment center program.

In most centers run by large corporations, assessors serve only once. The exception is AT&T centers, where assessors work on six-month assignments. In smaller companies assessors must, by necessity, be used more often. In all situations assessors must be trained, but naturally more training is committed to the person who will serve for 20 weeks than for one week. Training for new, short-service assessors usually takes from two to five days, depending upon the complexity of the center, the importance of the assessment decision and the importance management gives to assessor training. A few organizations have cut assessor training to the point that it is more orientation than training, but this is not advisable. Training is important both for accurate results and for the assessors themselves.

ASSESSOR LEVEL

Assessors are usually line managers two or more levels above the participants nominated by their supervisors for the task. Line managers are used because:

1. They are familiar with the jobs for which the participant is being assessed and can therefore better judge the participant's aptitude.
2. Participation as an assessor is a developmental experience.
3. The involvement of line management greatly increases the acceptance of the program by other managers and by the participants themselves.
4. Exposure as an assessor increases familiarity with the program, assuring most effective use of the results.

Providing broad familiarity with an assessment program is an extremely important result. Take, for instance, the common situation found in the use of psychological test results by managers. Managers usually over-rely or under-rely on test results. They have difficulty determining the correct emphasis because they are not familiar with the tests, tester, or intent of the program. While the same lack of understanding can happen relative to an assessment center report, the involvement of line managers both in the development of the program and as assessors in the program gives a much wider basis of understanding. When a manager who has been an assessor gets the assessment report, he knows the basis for the observations and judgments and can more accurately weigh them against data on job performance and other available information.

A few organizations mix line managers and personnel department or other staff people. This decision usually results from a difficulty recruiting assessors or as a means of decreasing assessor training (the trained staff people lead the line managers in completing forms, etc.).

Even less frequently are professional psychologists used as assessors. AT&T has made occasional use of academic psychologists hired for the summer as assessors in their research centers and in the evaluation of very high levels of management. A few other organizations have done similar experimentation with professional psychologists as assessors but have discontinued the process. The little research available indicates that professionals do no better than *trained* line managers in performing their tasks. While the professional psychologists may have some superior observational skills, this is probably negated by their lack of company knowledge. A few organizations use a single professional assessor to do certain kinds of testing and interpreting of results.

VALIDITY AND RELATION TO EEOC GUIDELINES

To insure that they are getting what they have paid for, practitioners have always been concerned with the validity of selection, appraisal, and training techniques. Since the *Griggs et al. vs. Duke Power* Supreme Court Case (1971), which affirmed the guidelines on employee selection and promotion promulgated by the Equal Employment Opportunity Commission, organizations must be prepared to prove that their standards for selection and appraisal are job-related. This includes assessment centers.

Assessment centers can be shown to be job-related through their content. To the extent the center's dimensions resulted from an accurate and complete job analysis and to the extent that the exercises and procedures used accurately measured the dimensions, the procedure is valid. Center exercises often are forms of job samples just as a typing test is a job sample of a typist's job, and thus possess rational validity; they make sense. An in-basket exercise obviously meets most of the criteria for a job sample, but so also does an exercise measuring group effectiveness if given to executives who must spend a great deal of their time in meetings. Perhaps because of the reasonableness of the assessment center method to both participants and observers, no known charges of discrimination resulting from applying the assessment center method have been filed anywhere in the United States.

To prove a center job-related through its content, particular care must be taken in establishing the dimensions through a complete job analysis and in choosing the proper exercises and procedures to be sure that the desired dimensions are brought out. Research relating dimension to individual assessment center exercises conducted by Standard Oil (Ohio)[1] and AT&T[2] will help in the latter step.

The superior way of establishing job-relatedness is through statistically relating a job criterion such as performance ratings or advancement in the organization with assessment center ratings. An organization adopting the assessment center method should set up procedures to collect data so that such relationships can be investigated. In the meantime there is strong evidence from organizations more experienced with the method that the procedure is, in general, extremely valid. While validity in one organization does not necessarily mean that the procedure is valid in another, the existence of these studies would be an important consideration in any court case involving assessment centers.

There are 22 published research studies attempting to evaluate the over-all validity of assessment centers applications. Fifteen show positive results, six have such small samples as to show no results, and one study based on a very small sample indicates the assessment center process is not effective. While 15 positive studies may not seem like a massive research finding, it becomes more impressive when the extremely high quality and scientific rigor of many of the studies are considered and when the research is compared with research attempting to establish results of other management selection or development programs. Even given its recent adoption by most organizations as a management development tool, far more is known about the assessment center method than most other procedures with the exception of tests.

PURE RESEARCH STUDIES

Two excellent research studies have been conducted under conditions that meet the most rigorous experimental specifications. Both conducted by AT&T, they involve situations in which employees were processed through centers, the results not used in any way, and later progress and performance followed up. The first study involved 123 new college hires and 144 non-college first-level managers.[3] After a period of eight years, 82 per cent of the college assessees and 75 per cent of the non-college assessees who reached middle-level management were accurately identified by the center. Equally important, 88 per

cent of the college assessees and 95 per cent of the non-college assessees who were never promoted out of the first-level management were identified. Thus the assessment center was found to be valid at choosing both "comers" and "losers." This study differs from all other studies to be discussed in that AT&T used, in the main, professional psychologists as assessors and supplemented the usual assessment exercises with a number of clinical techniques.

The second study rating the title of "pure research" was conducted to validate AT&T's salesman selection assessment centers.[4] Seventy-eight newly hired system salesmen were assessed right after being hired, but management had no access to the assessment data. Later on, an experienced field review team having no knowledge of assessment center reports observed the assessees during actual sales calls and rated their performance. The validity results were particularly impressive. The assessment panel predicted that nearly one-half of the assessees would not be acceptable, and only 24 per cent of those gave acceptable sales calls compared to 68 per cent of the "acceptable" group and 100 per cent of the "more than acceptable" group. The correlation between the assessment panel global rating and the field review rating was .51, a substantial increase in prediction compared to the multiple correlation of .33 between four paper and pencil tests and the criteria. Also indicating the importance of the assessment center prediction was the finding that supervisor and trainer ratings were unrelated to job performance.

OPERATIONAL STUDIES

Most of the large organizations that have operated centers for any significant length of time have some validity data on their ongoing centers. To various extents, these studies all suffer from methodological flaws caused by the fact that use was made of the data in the organization. To the extent that

Table 39-1. Summary of the Findings

Assessed	% Rated Above Average in Job Performance in First-Level Management	% Rated as Having High-Management Potential	% Promoted
Acceptable	68	50	11
Questionable	65	40	5
Non-Acceptable	46	31	0

good performance in a center affected the criterion used—e.g., promotion—use of the criterion as a measure of validity is impaired. The extent of this contamination remains a mystery; but through various statistical and experimental design methods, most of the reported studies have minimized the effect.

Being the first to apply the technique, AT&T has also conducted the most impressive operational validity studies. An early study conducted by Michigan Bell compared an assessed group promoted to management with a group promoted before the assessment center program.[5] But unfortunately, the groups were not matched. Results revealed nearly twice as many high-performance and potential men at first-level management in assessed as in non-assessed groups.

Another study conducted by New England Bell Company compared "acceptable" and "non-acceptable" assessed groups consisting of craftsmen promoted to first-level management and first-level managers promoted to second level. The acceptable group was "definitely superior" to the non-acceptable group according to the researchers.[6] A large follow-up study,[7] using four other Bell companies, compared three groups (N = 223) of first-level candidates assessed "acceptable," "questionable" and "not acceptable" and subsequently promoted to management to non-assessed groups (N = 283) promoted before and after the assessment program.

As in the other follow-up studies, this study was also limited to recently promoted managers in the assessed group; but unlike the other studies, by denoting a "not acceptable" assessed group of those promoted the false negative rate could be determined. Moreover, by studying the two non-assessed groups, possible halo bias due to promotion *before* versus *after* the assessment center could be determined. An attempt was made to match assessed and non-assessed groups but it was not entirely successful.

While use of assessment centers obviously improved selection odds, it was by no means perfect, as is indicated by the fact that nearly 50 per cent of those thought to be non-acceptable actually succeeded on the job. This research and most other research indicate that assessment centers are better at predicting ratings of management potential and actual advancement than performance at first level. This is probably caused by the increasing importance of the management component of jobs as individuals rise in an organization. It is this management component that is most commonly and accurately measured in an assessment center.

By far the most impressive AT&T study followed up 5,943 assessees as they advanced in management.[8] The criterion was advancement above first-level management, the level at which the assessment results were used and thus felt to be relatively clear of bias. Individuals assessed "more than acceptable" were twice as likely to be promoted two or more times as individuals assessed as "acceptable" and almost ten times more likely than those rated "not acceptable." In addition it was found that the correlation of .461 was raised only minutely with the use of a mental ability test (r of .463).

Standard Oil (Ohio) validity studies include a managerial progress criterion and additionally include 12 job performance ratings and a potential rating. The findings confirm the earlier AT&T findings of the moderate validity of a center in predicting managerial performance, but its high validity coefficients substantially exceed those for performance ratings based upon the interview and projective tests.[9]

IBM Studies

IBM has conducted eleven studies of its assessment center programs. All show a positive relationship between center findings and various criteria of success with more than half of the 22 correlations being statistically significant.[10] One study[11] involved 94 lower- and middle-level managers. From job analyses of positions held, a criterion measure of progress (increase in management responsibility) was constructed, and correlations of .37 were found between the progress criterion and the global assessment rating from the center. But interestingly it was found that if statistical methods were used in combining the judgments relative to the rating dimension, the correlation climbed to .62.

Another interesting study which was almost assuredly not contaminated involved sales managers demoted after becoming first-line managers.[12] Of 46 individuals assessed as having potential for higher management and subsequently promoted, 4 per cent were demoted because of job failure. Of 71 individuals promoted in spite of the assessment center finding of low potential, 20 per cent failed.

Extremely thorough and comprehensive research has been conducted by Sears Roebuck into the validity of its assessment centers. Both their center used for the initial

selection of management trainees and their centers to assess management potential have been subjected to rigorous study which has shown most components of the center to be statistically related to various criteria of job success.[13]

NEGATIVE STUDIES

These are the principal studies established in the validity of the assessment centers. Other studies have either used such small samples or questionable methodology as not to warrant discussion.[14] The two studies which might be considered negative to assessment centers also suffer from a number of methodological problems. The first is not really a validity study, as assessment centers were used as the criterion rather than job performance. This study[15] seems to indicate that a thorough study of a participant's personnel file and an interview will provide information comparable to the results of an assessment center. If true, such a finding would be a wonderful cost saving to organizations. Methodological and other factors relative to the study make generalizations difficult.

The only study indicating that assessment centers are less valid than normal assessment procedures was based on 37 participants in an assessment center conducted by the Caterpillar Tractor Company.[16] Two groups of recently promoted first-line supervisors were studied, including 37 subjects assessed in an assessment center program and 27 subjects assessed by traditional methods, which included a review of personnel files and personal interviews with each candidate and his first-line supervisor. Using supervisor rating as a criterion, the study found that the assessed group was rated above average in performance slightly more often than the non-assessed group. But both were highly accurate.

A detailed analysis of all known validity studies relative to assessment centers can be found in "Validity of Assessment Centers" by Cohen, Moses, and Byham (in press). With the exception of the two "pure" AT&T research projects, all the studies mentioned above are subject to various biases, statistical restrictions in range, etc., which are typical of practical operational programs. Yet, putting them all together, the impact seems clear. The assessment center is a superior method of predicting management potential—compared wtih methods such as supervisor appraisals and tests.

DIFFERENTIAL VALIDITY

An important consideration is whether, like some paper and pencil tests, assessment centers are biased against minority groups and women. There is no published research on this question, but unpublished studies indicate that the final judgment of a center is equally valid for whites and blacks. Performance on individual exercises is different, but this seems to be somehow taken into consideration by the assessors. The area is definitely in need of research. In the meantime, a number of organizations have adopted a policy that two or more blacks must be in a center or none at all. They feel that being the only black out of twelve participants might put the black at a disadvantage.

Even less information is available about possible discriminatory effects on women, apparently because center administrators have observed no problems in this area. Some organizations with large work forces of women have segregated centers by sex, but most have mixed the sexes with apparently no problem. Again this is an area much in need of research.

PROBLEMS IN ASSESSMENT CENTERS

Two potential problems in using the assessment center method involve the employee who does not get nominated to the assessment center and the employee who attends and does poorly.

A philosophical weakness of most assessment center programs is the reliance on the supervisor to nominate employees for participation. Some high-potential employees may never be nominated because qualities of aggressiveness, curiosity, and intelligence that might make a person successful at higher levels of management are not always appreciated by lower-level supervision. To get around this problem, some companies use self-nomination or put everyone at a particular level of management through a program. Other organizations have experimented with nominations based on personnel department records indicating interest in advancement such as application for educational aid, etc., while IBM has investigated the use of tests to select people for attendance.[17]

Perhaps more of a concern to many managers is the attitudinal impact on those not nominated. Again no research evidence is available, but the feeling of "not getting to show what I can do" must be present in many individuals. Such feelings are not unique to assessment centers. The same feeling can be generated in those who are not tapped to attend any kind of managerial development program. Obviously anxiety is highest where the development program or assessment center is the stepping stone up in management. Self-nomination and other methods around the supervisor roadblock seem to be the only answer, but they can be expensive.

Typically the greatest concern of management is the individual who attends an assessment center and does poorly. As noted above, he usually recognizes his poor performance whether or not he receives a formal feedback. Will he look for another job where his chances are untainted by his poor assessment center performance? Research at three companies says no, while research at one says definitely yes—but maybe it is a way of clearing out the deadwood. It appears that organizations that have made a deliberate effort to avoid problems through expert handling of the feedback process and providing alternate methods of advancement (e.g., technical ladders) experience no problem.

Most organizations go to great lengths to stress that the assessment center is only one portion of the assessment process—a supplement to regular appraisal and other information. They stress that the participant has an opportunity on the job to disprove any negative insights gained from assessment. If precautions are not taken, some increase in turnover of lower-rated participants can occur. Turnover may not actually be increased—just speeded. The assessment center process speeds the realization that promotion is questionable.

ANXIETY

Anxiety at an assessment center can also be a problem. There is no doubt that the assessment process is stress-provoking and that the performance of a few participants is affected by the stress. The fact that the individual's performance may have been affected by stress is usually recognized by the assessors and taken into consideration in the final assessment judgment. Stress does not seem to be important problem.

"Crown Princesses" or "Golden Boys" can emerge from an assessment center if the organization allows special treatment of successful participants in the program. This can be good or bad. It is natural for the outstanding participants in centers to get prime developmental experiences to prepare them for positions management sees in the future. This is not making a crown prince; it is just putting the company's money where it will reap the greatest dividends. But special treatment is wrong if the individual is given special consideration on his present job. A negative effect on the morale of other

members in the unit can result if the individual is seen as being allowed to do less work because he is the "number one boy."

A frequently raised fear is that assessment centers will turn out more and more stereotyped versions of the particular organization's "organization man." The only data on this comes from IBM, which found that far from being organization men, successful participants in assessment centers were less conforming and more independent. Because the assessment center method brings out a much broader range of data about the individual than is typical from interviews and other conventional means, decision-making is not restricted to the superficial characteristics often associated with an "organization man."

COSTS

Costs vary dramatically among centers depending on the objectives of the center, number of participants and assessors, length, location, and, most of all, what is figured in costs. Organizations have come up with cost figures for their programs ranging from $5.00 a head to $500. The figures, however, cannot be compared and may be vastly misleading because they include quite different elements. The cost of assessors' time (including training), participants' time, and administrators' time (including preparing for the center and writing reports) depends on the length of the center and the amount of training given assessors. Assessor and administrator commitment can be cut markedly if training is conducted separately from assessment or when the company reaches the situation that assessors are being repeated, thus requiring no additional training.

Costs of meals and facilities can be figured based on the organization's experience conducting training programs. Programs on company premises can cost as little as

$50, while programs at a resort can cost as much as $3,000 for twelve participants, six observers, and one administrator.

Exercise costs depend on the length of the program and the nature of the exercises. They generally are between $100 and $200 for six participants. There is usually a one-time investment in reusable supplies which will run about $100. These costs assume that all exercises are purchased commercially. In actual fact, many organizations develop at least one unique exercise for their center, and some organizations prefer to have all unique exercises.

The remaining cost considerations are start-up costs. These costs depend upon the organization's needs for consulting help. Many organizations take information from articles such as this one, order exercises, and start the assessment center. Other organizations send their potential assessment center administrators to workshops on assessor training. Many others use consultants to aid in planning, assessor training, administration of several pilot programs, the initial writing of assessment center reports, and the planning of feedback interviews. Consultants can make their greatest contribution in planning a center and in assessor training.

REACHING A DECISION

Attendance at an assessment center is the best way to get a real feel for the concept. Many organizations have arranged to have key managers attend a center run by another company as a way of selling the technique. Some organizations are happy to have guests, especially during the assessor discussion portion of the program. If this is not possible, showing videotape recordings of assessment centers in operation can accomplish nearly the same result. These are available from the author. Another effective means of acquainting managers with the methods is to put them through a representative exercise or two. Managers quickly see the potential value of the kinds of behaviors that are brought out.

CONCLUSIONS

Assessment centers are relatively new as aids in identifying and developing sales and management potential, but the method shows great promise. Many previous management development techniques and instruments have had great popular success but have waned when the spotlight of empirical research was trained on them. Their effectiveness could not be proved. Assessment centers, on the other hand, came out of a basic research study, AT&T's "Management Progress Study"; and research has continued on the method in almost every organization where it has been applied. Much more research is needed both on general validity and on specific exercises and procedures used; but, on a basis of the findings to-date, one must conclude that the method works. It also has the advantage of great acceptability to management. But it does not work equally well in all circumstances and should be used selectively. Nevertheless the method should be added to the repertory of tools available to the management development practitioner.

STARTING AN ASSESSMENT CENTER

The following outline represents the principal steps in establishing an assessment center:

1. Determine objectives of program;
2. Define dimensions to be assessed;
3. Select exercises that will bring out the dimensions;
4. Design assessor training and assessment center program;
5. Announce program, inform participants and assessors, handle administrative detail;
6. Train assessors;

7. Conduct center;

8. Write summary reports on participants;

9. Feedback to participants a summary of performance at center and development actions;

10. Evaluate center;

11. Set up procedures to validate center against a criterion of job success.

While the task of starting a center may appear large and extremely time-consuming, it need not be. Numerous organizations have started operating centers less than one month after management gave the go-ahead. Like most techniques that have considerable rational appeal to management, there usually is great pressure to get the program going after it is approved.

APPENDIX A

A Typical Two-Day Assessment Center

Day 1. Orientation meeting

Management game—"Conglomerate." Forming different types of conglomerates is the goal with four-man teams of participants bartering companies to achieve their planned result. Teams set their own acquisition objectives and must plan and organize to meet them.

Background interview —A 1½ hour interview conducted by an assessor.

Group discussion—"Management Problems." Four short cases calling for various forms of management judgment are presented to groups of four participants. In one hour the group, acting as consultants, must resolve the cases and submit its recommendation in writing.

Individual fact-finding and decision-making exercise—"The Research Budget." The participant is told that he has just taken over as division manager. He is given a brief description of an incident in which his predecessor has recently turned down a request for funds to continue a research project. The research director is appealing for a reversal of the decision. The participant is given 15 minutes to ask questions to dig out the facts in the case. Following this fact-finding period, he must present his decision orally with supporting reasoning and defend it under challenge.

Day 2

In-basket exercise—"Section Manager's In-Basket." The contents of a section manager's in-basket are simulated. The participant is instructed to go through the contents, solving problems, answering questions, delegating, organizing, scheduling and planning, just as he might do if he were promoted suddenly to the position. An assessor reviews the contents of the completed in-basket and conducts a one-hour interview with the participant to gain further information.

Assigned role leaderless group discussion—"Compensation Committee." The Compensation Committee is meeting to allocate $8,000 in discretionary salary increases among six supervisory and managerial employees. Each member of the committee (participants) represents a department of the company and is instructed to "do the best he can" for the employee from his department.

Analysis, presentation, and group discussion:—"The Pretzel Factory." This financial analysis problem has the participant role-play a consultant called in to advise Carl Flowers of the C. F. Pretzel Company on two problems: what to do about a division of the company that has continually lost money, and whether the corporation should expand. Participants are given data on the company and are asked to recommend appropriate courses of action. They make their recommendation in a seven-minute presentation after which they are formed into a group to come up with a single set of recommendations.

Final Announcements

Days 3 and 4. Assessors meet to share their observations on each participant and to arrive at summary evaluations relative to each dimension sought and over-all potential and training needs.

APPENDIX B

Example of Assessment Center Summary Report

Smith's over-all performance in the Management Development Center (MDC) was average or below average on most exercises. He showed strengths in energy and initiative.

Observers see him as having some potential for a middle manager position but as requiring a great deal of development. The odds of his actually being a middle manager were seen as slim.

In the background interview, Smith was extremely open in discussing his problems and hopes in detail. He came across as a loyal, hardworking, highly-motivated person who has a strong desire to do a good job, but he is weak in creativity, initiative, independence, and leadership skills. He appeared to be tenacious and have a high stress tolerance but to be weak in problem analysis. He struck the assessor as being overwhelmed by his job, where his efforts are not bearing the fruit he would like. He may well fear for his job, given the Division's performance. Delegation seemed weak as was subordinate development. He feels that the only way to train is to teach by example. Sensing poor morale, he doesn't know how to improve it.

Smith participated energetically in the exercises and appeared to be intent on doing well. In the group discussion exercises, he showed initiative in starting the group on its task and providing initial organization. His oral communications were somewhat hampered by his use of slang, but in general he spoke in a clear, articulate, fluent manner. His voice was low in volume. On the negative side, he tended to be repetitive in speech and have a great need to summarize and then resummarize. He did not seem overly stressed by MDC.

Unfortunately, Smith's impact on exercise groups was fleeting. Others quickly took control with usually only a minor fight from Smith. Peer and self-ratings indicate he was never recognized as the group leader. His over-all contribution was usually in the middle. His principal difficulty in group exercises came from his inability to convince the group. Rather than pursue an argument until he won, he would too quickly give in.

Smith's financial-analysis presentation was excellent, but he had several flaws in his analysis. His presentation in the group discussion was weak, and he was unable to convince the group. He was an effective secretary for the group.

Questioning in the "Research Budget" fact-finding exercise was not well-organized but effective. He appeared to find decision-making difficult, but once the decision was made, he stuck to his idea. Slightly nervous, he was not stressed by the resource person.

Writing seemed to be a weak area. Smith's financial presentation was hard to read and disorganized. Similar observations were made about his creative writing assignment, and his in-basket.

In the in-basket exercise, Smith did quite poorly, failing to organize material or set priorities. He did not handle all the material and on several occasions displayed poor judgment.

Strengths

Work standards: Tried hard in every exercise; works very hard on job; does not want to personally settle for less than the best. Was disappointed by own performance as indicated by his self-evaluation.

Intelligence: Fast reader, catches on fast.

Corporate thinking: A company man, very loyal.

Integrity: Will not compromise convictions, e.g., copy-machine discussion.

Energy: Active in all exercises.

Stress tolerance: Except for management game, showed little stress.

Interest in self-development: Welcomes help; worked his way through college, willing to move. (While interest seemed very high, there was some doubt about strength of drive for self-development.)

Level of aspiration: Seems to be unhappy without winning or doing the best possible.

Weaknesses

Creativity: Not seen in approach to current job or in exercises—nothing shown in creative-writing exercise.

Leadership: After an initial positive impact, he could not influence group.

Independence: In present job, seems to do what his boss wants; same attitude expressed in in-basket where he intended to delegate up and to follow "what boss wants."

Use of delegation: Not effective on job, average in in-basket. He reports he does a lot of "crap" that should be done by subordinates.

Problem analysis: Didn't understand "conglomerate"; didn't see many of the major problems in in-basket; background interview indicates a lack of problem definition in job; did not see all facets of Pretzel Company problem.

Financial analytical ability: Below average on financial problems, e.g., missed opportunity to change product mix.

Range of interest: Seems to be restricted to marketing.

Flexibility: Seemed to approach every case and every situation the same way (was flexible in accepting ideas of others).

Temper: When he did not get his way in compensation committee discussion he became obstructionist to leader.

Mixed Findings

Impact: Good first impression—after that would not stand out in a crowd.

Oral communication skill: Fluent, articulate, talks too much, doesn't sell.

Oral presentation skill: Formal presentations good, e.g., financial presentation; informal poor, e.g., group discussion situations. Seems to depend on preparation.

Written communication skill: English ability adequate, very hard to read writing.

Salesmanship: Except for the formal financial presentation, showed little salesmanship; in the "Compensation Committee" exercise he tried for too much money, didn't convince peers; in group situations could not sell under opposition.

Sensitivity: Assessors described him variously as sensitive, very sensitive, too sensitive, and insensitive during the center. There was a general feeling that he might be soft, e.g., his delay in firing one of his subordinates he admitted should have been fired sooner. He seemed less sensitive to people, problems in in-basket, and cases than to needs of individuals in discussion groups, where on several occasions he showed good sensitivity and understanding.

Tenacity: When ego is involved or he feels there is an ethical problem, Smith can be very tenacious, e.g., fighting for doing right by customer regarding the photocopier. On the other hand, he did not follow up on points in group discussions.

Management style: Seems to talk a better story than he practices or could be determined from the interview. Expressed concern for "subordinate training" but assessor wondered how effective he is; tends to delegate up— lets people over lead him. Realizes need to be more "tough-minded."

Planning & organizing: Attempted to organize most groups but did not attempt to maintain organization. In-basket organization of work and priorities poor.

Management control: Interview indicated some weaknesses in this area: felt Smith would have a tendency to over-control too far down; but in-basket he did an above-average job of controlling, using due dates, etc.

Judgment: Showed good judgment in marketing-related problems; weak in judgment in other areas.

While Smith did poorly in many areas, it was felt that he is definitely trainable. He was seen as needing a lot of support and guidance and a supportive, understanding, fatherly supervisor, but one that would force him to make decisions. It was felt he would develop best in a highly-structured job with slowly increasing planning and organizing responsibility as his skills develop. An assignment at Homewood as a product manager might be good.

Some priority development challenges:
—management through others
—problem analysis
—organization
—administrative skills

Smith should be easy to communicate with regarding his assessment. He is extremely open and was accurate in his self-appraisals. A potential difficulty may be his insecurity, causing him to view "help" as a threat.

REFERENCES

1. Carleton, F. O., Relationships between follow-up evaluations and information developed in a management assessment center. Paper presented at the meetings of the American Psychological Association convention, Miami Beach, 1970. Finley, R. M., Jr., An evaluation of behavior predictions from projective tests given in a management assessment assessment center. Paper presented at meetings of the American Psychological Association convention, Miami Beach, 1970.

2. Bray, D. W., and Grant, D. L., The assessment center in the measurement of potential for business management. *Psychological Monographs,* 1966, 80 (17, Whole no. 625).

3. Bray and Grant, *ibid.*

4. Bray, D. W., and Campbell, R. J., Selection of salesmen by means of and assessment center. *Journal of Applied Psychology,* 1968, 52, 36-41.

5. Bray, D. W., The management progress study, *American Psychologist.* 1964, 19, 419-20.

6. Campbell, R. J., and Bray, D. W., Assessment centers: An aid in management selection, *Personnel Administration,* March-April 1967.

7. Campbell and Bray, *ibid.*

8. Moses, J. L., Assessment center performance and management progress (AT& T), Paper presented as part of symposium, "Validity of Assessment Centers," at the 79th Annual Convention of the American Psychological Association, 1971.

9. Carleton, *op. cit.*

10. Dodd, W. E., Summary of IBM assessment validations. Paper presented as part of the symposium. "Validity of Assessment Centers," at 79th Annual Convention of the American Psychological Association, 1971.

11. Wollowick, H. B., and McNamara, W. J., Relationship of the components of an assessment center to management success. *Journal of Applied Psychology,* 1969, 53, 348-52.

12. Dodd, *op. cit.*

13. Bentz, V. Jon, Validity of Sears assessment center procedures. Paper presented as part of symposium, "Validity of Assessment Centers," at 79th Annual Convention of the American Psychological Association, 1971.

14. Bender, J. M., Calvert, O. L., and Jaffe, C. L., Report on supervision selection

program, Oak Ridge Gaseous Diffusion Plant, Union Carbide Corporation, Nuclear Div., April 17, 1970 (K1789).

Schaffer, A. J., Information about assessment center for ES&D program finalists. Memorandum from Director, Personnel Div., National Office, Internal Revenue Service, September 16, 1970.

Tennessee Valley Authority, TVA's experiment in the assessment of managerial potential, undated.

15. Hinrichs, J. R., Comparison of "real life" assessments of management potential with situational exercises, paper-and-pencil ability tests, and personality inventories. *Journal of Applied Psychology,* 1969, 53, pp. 425-33.

16. Bullard, J. F., An evaluation of the assessment center approach to selecting supervisors. Mimeo report, Caterpillar Tractor Co., May 1969.

17. Dodd, W. E., and Kraut, A. I., The prediction of management assessment center performance from earlier measures of personality and sales training performance. A preliminary report, 1970 (internal company report).

7

TRAINING
AND BEHAVIOR MODIFICATION

Personnel training is the process whereby employees learn the skills, knowledge, attitudes, and behaviors necessary to perform their jobs effectively. Surveys indicate that nearly all large organizations employ some formalized training. There are at least four major reasons for its widespread popularity. First, personnel selection and placement by themselves do not usually provide organizations with new workers skillful enough to meet the demands of their job adequately. Many of these workers must learn new skills after they are hired. Second, experienced employees must sometimes be retrained because of changes in their job content due to promotions, automation, and transfers. Third, management is aware that effective programs can result in increased productivity, decreased absenteeism, reduced turnover, and greater worker satisfaction. Fourth, some organizations, unfortunately, conduct training programs merely because "it's the thing to do!"

When designing training programs, the industrial-organizational psychologist has a wide variety of methods and techniques from which to choose, each with its own unique advantages and disadvantages. Among the many training methods are: lecture, case studies, role playing, management games, programmed instruction, sensitivity training, and computer-assisted instruction. When deciding between the available methods many industrial psychologists evaluate their potential effectiveness by examining the extent to which they incorporate the principles of learning derived from experimental research. Among the best known of these traditional principles of learning are the following:

1. learning will be faster the greater the amount of reinforcement given during practice;
2. active participation by the trainee is an important condition for learning; and
3. trainees should be provided with immediate feedback regarding the adequacy of their performance during practice.

Thus, a training method would be felt to be more effective the more it gives the trainee reinforcement, active participation, and immediate feedback. A good source for this point of view is Bass and Vaughn (1966).

Others such as Gagné (1962) have questioned the usefulness of some of the well-known learning principles and have argued that these principles can seldom be applied to the practical problems of employee training. These critics oppose the evaluation of training methods solely on the basis of the learning principles. The article by Carroll, Paine, and Ivancevich provides additional insight into the problem of choosing between training methods by discussing their relative effectiveness from two points of view: the expert opinion of training directors, and the results of research. Specifically, the effectiveness of nine different training methods for achieving each of six training objectives is reviewed.

The management development technique known by such names as laboratory education, T-group training, and sensitivity training is widely used in organizations at the present time. T-group training originated in the 1940s at the National Training Laboratories in Bethel, Maine. It usually involves a group of about a dozen managers meeting together at a comfortable retreat away from their place of employment for the purpose of increasing their understanding of their own behavior, the behavior of others, and the functioning of groups. The trainees usually meet for about a week or more to have unstructured and informal group discussions during which they frankly discuss personal things about themselves and one another.

It is easy to see why the discussions often become quite emotional, and the T-group experience a traumatic one for certain individuals. The question of what participants actually gain from such experiences has been a source of much controversy in the field of industrial-organizational psychology (Argyris, Campbell, and Dunnette, 1968). The article in this section by Dunnette and Campbell reviews the objectives of T-group education and the studies evaluating its effectiveness. The student is referred to other review articles by Buchanan (1969) and Cooper and Mangham (1970) for more positive evaluations of T-group training.

Too many industrial training programs are evaluated solely on the basis of how well participants liked the program. One should be skeptical of these evaluations since participants' reactions to training programs are generally favorable regardless of the length or content of the program. When a company really wants to know how much its training efforts contribute to the achievement of organizational goals, it must conduct a controlled experimental study using relevant and objective criteria such as productivity, turnover, and absenteeism. The article by MacKinney discusses the various ways of designing training evaluation studies and the various types of criterion measures that can be used.

In recent years there has been a flurry of interest in applying the work of B. F. Skinner and other advocates of behavior modification to the field of industrial-organizational psychology. Interestingly, the application of Skinnerian or operant-conditioning principles to organizational behavior was a neglected area of research in the management and organizational literature until about 1970, for the reason that applied behavioral scientists found the humanistic theories of McGregor (1960) and Maslow (1965) considerably more palatable than Skinner's notion of human beings controlled and "manipulated" by their environment.

The application of Skinnerian ideas to the training and motivation of employees is known by various names such as behavior modification, behavior management, contingency management, operant conditioning, and positive reinforcement. Skinnerians assume that the frequency with which behaviors (i.e., operant responses) are emitted is influenced by the events that follow them. If the behavior is followed by an event that is pleasing or "positively reinforcing" to the individual, the probability of his repeating the behavior in the future will increase. Conversely, if the consequence of a behavior is displeasing or "punishing," the probability of the individual repeating the behavior is apt to diminish.

According to Skinnerians, individuals will exhibit desired behaviors (e.g., high productivity, low absenteeism, low tardiness) if they are positively reinforced for them. These rewards are most effective if they are experienced immediately after the desired responses. Punishment can be administered either in the form of some adversive stimulus (e.g., social disapproval) or in the removal of something pleasurable (e.g., shortening of the rest pause). Since the full effects of punishment are not always predictable, it is considered to be a less effective way than positive reinforcement of inducing behavior change. Finally, the frequency with which positive reinforcement follows a response affects the response probability. It is possible to reward an individual each time the response is made (i.e., continuous reinforcement) or only after some of the responses (i.e., partial reinforcement). There are many different ways in which partial reinforcement can be administered. For a more detailed discussion of Skinnerian principles and their potential applications to organizational behavior, the student is referred to articles by Nord (1969) and Jablonsky and DeVries (1972).

The next two articles in this section deal with the application of behavior modification principles to deal with some of the problems typically found in organizational settings. The article by Nord shows how two distinctly different organizations attempted to improve the attendance of their employees by making the reception of certain desired rewards contingent on exemplary attendance records. The next article discusses how the Emery Air Freight Company has used positive reinforcement to increase productivity and thereby save $3 million within three years.

Title VII of the Civil Rights Act of 1964 has had dramatic effects on the hiring and training of increasing numbers of minority group members (e.g., Afro-Americans, Mexican-Americans, American Indians), women, the physically handicapped, the mentally retarded, and the aged.

In response to this law, some companies have made efforts to hire and train those individuals labeled "hard-core unemployed" (HCU). Although definitions vary, the typical HCU individual is a member of a minority group, has been unemployed for more than a year, has never received intensive skill training, and has a sixth-grade education with a third-grade reading level and a fourth-grade math level (Adelberg, 1969). It is obvious from these characteristics that the training and retraining of the HCU is an enormous challenge for the industrial-organizational psychologist.

In the final article, Goodman, Paransky, and Salipante contend that the HCU worker operates in a complex social system that affects his expectancies about behavior-reward contingencies and the attractiveness of these rewards. These expectancies and rewards, in turn, affect his job performance and retention. The authors review the HCU literature by integrating it with the many factors of the social system that affect the behavior of the HCU worker. Based upon this research, they offer a number of observations that should be kept in mind when designing a HCU training program.

REFERENCES AND SELECTED READINGS

Adelberg, M. Industrial training of the hard-core unemployed. *Personnel,* 1969, 46, 22-27.

Argyris, C., Campbell, J. P., and Dunnette, M. D. A symposium: laboratory training. *Industrial Relations,* 1968, 8, 1-45.

Bass, B. M., and Vaughn, J. A. *Training in industry: The management of learning.* Belmont, Calif.: Wadsworth, 1966.

Buchanan, P. C. Laboratory training and organization development. *Administrative Science Quarterly,* 1969, 14, 466-79.

Campbell, D. T., and Stanley, J. C. *Experimental and quasi-experimental designs for research.* Chicago: Rand McNally, 1963.

Campbell, J. P. and Dunnette, M. D. Effectiveness of T-group experiences in managerial training and development. *Psychological Bulletin,* 1968, 70 73-104.

Cooper, C. L., and Mangham, I. L. T-group training: Before and after. *Journal of Management Studies,* 1970, 7, 224-39.

Gagné, R. M. Military training and principles of learning. *American Psychologist,* 1962, 17, 83-91.

House, R. J. T-group education and leadership effectiveness. *Personnel Psychology,* 1967, 20, 1-32.

Jablonsky, S. F., and DeVries, D. L. Operant conditioning principles extrapolated to the theory of management. *Organizational Behavior and Human Performance,* 1972, 7, 340-58.

Maslow, A. *Eupsychian management.* Homewood, Ill.: Dorsey, 1965.

McGregor, D. *The human side of enterprise.* New York: McGraw-Hill, 1960.

Nord, W. R. Beyond the teaching machine: The neglected area of operant conditioning in the theory and practice of management. *Organizational Behavior and Human Performance,* 1969, 4, 375-401.

40

The Relative Effectiveness of Training Methods:

Expert Opinion and Research

STEPHEN J. CARROLL, JR., FRANK T. PAINE, and JOHN M. IVANCEVICH

Programmed instruction, sensitivity training, computer games, television, and role playing have been widely used in training only in recent years. These newer techniques when added to the older methods of the lecture, conference method, movie films, and case study method provide the fields of training and education with a number of alternatives to use in a particular situation. While availability of resources in the form of money, time, and personnel do play a significant part in the choice of one training method or another, another important criterion must be the relative effectiveness of the training method being considered for a particular training objective.

The obvious approach for identifying the relative effectiveness of various training methods for particular training objectives would be to analyze the research data on the subject. An attempt by the authors to do this, however, identified many limitations in the research studies that were carried out and great variability in the amount of research carried out on particular training methods.

With the difficulties experienced in examining the research on the subject, the authors decided to focus on expert opinion. Therefore, a survey was conducted of the 200 training directors who worked for the companies with the largest numbers of employees as indicated on *Fortune's* list of the top 500 corporations. It was felt that the number of employees in a firm would be a rough indicator of the amount of training the organization carries out. Since the research data on the effectiveness of various training methods was available, it was also decided to compare the limited research available with the judgments of the training directors. This might provide some indication of the extent to which research results on training methods are known to training directors. In comparing ratings of effectiveness of the training directors with research, primary emphasis was placed on research studies carried out with adults in the employment situation since this would be the group most familiar to the training directors. Of course, this involves a minority of research studies done in this area. Most

Reprinted from *Personnel Psychology*, 1972, 25, 495-509, by permission of the authors and Personnel Psychology, Inc.

research studies on the effectiveness of alternative training methods have been carried out with college students.

METHOD

Questionnaire

A questionnaire was constructed which asked respondents to indicate the relative effectiveness of nine different training methods for achieving each of six training objectives. In the questionnaire, each training method was considered one at a time for the six different training objectives. In the effectiveness rating, five alternative degrees of effectiveness were used and these were scored as follows: highly effective (5), quite effective (4), moderately effective (3), limited effectiveness (2), and not effective (1).

Sample and Analysis

Two hundred questionnaires were mailed to the training directors of the two hundred firms with the largest number of employees. A follow-up letter was also used. There was a final useable return from 117 of these training directors for a return rate of 59 per cent.

The average effectiveness ratings of the various training methods for each of the six training objectives were calculated and compared to each other by means of a "t" test.

Training Methods and Training Objectives

The training methods compared by the training directors were: programmed instruction, case study, lecture method (with questions), conference or discussion method, role playing, sensitivity training (T-group), TV-lecture (lecture given to large audience over TV), movie films, business gaming (using computer or hand calculator).

The training objectives used in the study were: acquire knowledge, change in attitudes, participant acceptance, retention of

what is learned, development of interpersonal skills, development of problem-solving skills.

RESULTS

The results of the study are presented in Table 40-1. This table indicates the relative ranking of the nine training methods for each of the training objectives, the average effectiveness rating given for each training method for each objective, and whether the differences in average ratings between any two training methods are large enough to be statistically significant.

Acquisition of Knowledge

Table 40-1 indicates that the training directors rated programmed instruction highest of all training methods on effectiveness in the acquisition of knowledge. The lecture is ranked as least effective of all training methods. The mean ratings indicate the average respondent believes that programmed instruction is "quite effective" for acquiring knowledge and the lecture method has only limited effectiveness for this objective.

Research on the subject seems to support the high relative rating given to programmed instruction by the training directors for knowledge acquisition. In 20 studies which compared programmed instruction to conventional lecture and discussion in an industrial situation, it was found that immediate learning was at least 10 per cent higher under programmed instruction in seven comparisons, and there was not a practical difference between the conventional and programmed instruction in 13 comparisons (Nash, Muczyk, and Vettori, 1971). In 18 studies where programmed instruction and conventional lecture and discussion methods used in an industrial situation were compared with respect to time required to reach a certain level of proficiency, programmed instruction was

Table 40-1. Ratings of Training Directors on Effectiveness of Alternative Training Methods for Various Training Objectives

Training Method	Knowledge acquisition		Changing attitudes		Problem-solving skills		Interpersonal skills		Participant acceptance		Knowledge retention	
	Mean	Mean Rank	Mean	Mean Rank	Mean	Mean Rank	Mean	Mean Rank	Mean	Mean Rank	Mean	Mean Rank
Case study	3.56^b	2	3.43^d	4	3.69^b	1	3.02^d	4	3.80^d	2	3.48^e	2
Conference (Discussion) method	3.33^d	3	3.54^d	3	3.26^e	4	3.21^d	3	4.16^a	1	3.32^f	5
Lecture (with questions)	2.53	9	2.20^f	8	2.00	9	1.90	8	2.74	8	2.49	8
Business games	3.00	6	2.73^f	5	3.58^b	2	2.50^e	5	3.78^d	3	3.26^f	6
Movie films	3.16^g	4	2.50^f	6	2.24^g	7	2.19^g	6	3.44^g	5	2.67^h	7
Programmed instruction	4.03^a	1	2.22^h	7	2.56^f	6	2.11^g	7	3.28^g	7	3.74^a	1
Role playing	2.93	7	3.56^d	2	3.27^e	3	3.68^b	2	3.56^e	4	3.37^f	4
Sensitivity training (t group)	2.77	8	3.96^a	1	2.98^e	5	3.95^b	1	3.33^g	6	3.44^f	3
Television lecture	3.10^g	5	1.99	9	2.01	8	1.81	9	2.74	9	2.47	9

a. More effective than methods ranked 2 to 9 for this objective at .01 level of significance.
b. More effective than methods ranked 3 to 9 for this objective at .01 level of significance.
c. More effective than methods ranked 4 to 9 for this objective at .01 level of significance.
d. More effective than methods ranked 5 to 9 for this objective at .01 level of significance.
e. More effective than methods ranked 6 to 9 for this objective at .01 level of significance.
f. More effective than methods ranked 7 to 9 for this objective at .01 level of significance.
g. More effective than methods ranked 8 to 9 for this objective at .01 level of significance.
h. More effective than method ranked 9 for this objective at .01 level of significance.

superior to conventional instruction in 14 comparisons, and there were no practical differences in four studies (Nash, Muczyk, and Vettori, 1971).

A very large number of studies conducted with students also support the findings that programmed instruction is probably more effective than conventional instruction on amount of time taken to learn the material or on amount of material learned (Nash *et al.,* 1971; Schramm, 1962a). Nash and his colleagues, however, have pointed out that most of the studies involving a comparison of programmed with conventional instruction have not used a well-planned and well-carried-out conventional class as the basis for comparison (Nash *et al.,* 1971).

The very low rating given to the lecture method as compared to the discussion method by the training directors with respect to effectiveness for knowledge acquisition is not congruent with research results in a few studies carried out with adults and in many studies with students as subjects. For example, Richard Hill (1960), in a controlled study, compared three lecture classes of 233, 25, and 25 participants with twelve discussion classes made up of 22 to 28 members each and found no difference in amount learned. Andrew (1954) found a lecture approach superior to that of a discussion and a film for imparting mental health information. Four extensive reviews of the literature where the subjects were primarily college students all concluded that on the basis of research comparisons made, lecture and discussion methods are equally effective for the acquisition of knowledge (Buxton, 1956; Dietrick, 1960; Stovall, 1958; Verner and Dickinson, 1967).

The training directors also rated the television lecture as more effective than the conventional lecture. No studies were found where adults in the employment situation were compared, but the training directors' ratings are not supported by research results with students as subjects which generally show no significant differences between television lecture courses and conventional lecture courses. For example, in 32 comparisons between television and conventionally taught college students there was no difference in 29 of the comparisons (Carpenter and Greenhill, 1958). In 28 comparisons between television and conventionally taught courses at Miami (Ohio) University, only four differences were significant at or beyond the .05 level and three of these favored the conventional (Klausmeier, 1961). Schramm (1962b) in summarizing 393 studies of the amount learned in televsion courses versus conventionally taught courses found that in 65 per cent of the comparisons there were no differences, in 21 per cent of the comparisons the television approach was more effective, and in 14 per cent of the comparisons the participants in the television courses did worse.

The training directors indicated that movie films and the case method were superior to the lecture method for knowledge acquisition. In the Andrew study (1954) cited earlier, the lecture was superior to a film for imparting knowledge to adult subjects. In a well-controlled study where a class taught by the case method was compared to a class taught by a lecture-discussion approach, the case study section scored significantly higher on achievement tests (Butler, 1967).

Changing Attitudes

Table 40-1 indicates that the training directors believe that, in a relative sense, sensitivity training is the most effective way to change attitudes. They also believe that role playing, the conference method, and the case study method are more effective in changing attitudes than management games, movie films, programmed instruction, lecture, and TV. The scores given the various methods indicate that most of the training directors consider only the first four methods listed in the table as having any effectiveness in changing attitudes.

The training directors indicated that the discussion method was superior to the lecture method in changing attitudes. In two fairly well-controlled studies where the lecture and discussion approaches were compared in situations involving attitude change among adults (prisoners and executives), the discussion approach was more effective (Butler, 1966; Silber, 1962). In five controlled studies involving changes in behavior of adults, the discussion approach was more effective than the lecture method in changing behavior (Bond, 1956; Levine and Butler, 1952; Lewin, 1958). Some of these comparisons were not entirely fair to the lecture method, however, since in the discussion groups the participants were usually asked to commit themselves to future actions, while the subjects in the lecture groups were not asked to do this. In spite of this, it does appear that the discussion approach is superior to the lecture in changing attitudes and behavior as the training directors indicated.

The training directors believe that role playing can be quite effective in changing attitudes. Several studies conducted among students do show that role playing can be effective in changing attitudes (Festinger and Carlsmith, 1959; Harvey and Beverly, 1961). Role playing seems especially effective if the subjects participating in the role-playing situation are asked to take the point of view opposite to their own and to verbalize this opposite point of view to others (Culbertson, 1957; Janis and King, 1954; King and Janis, 1956; Janis and Mann, 1965).

The low rating on effectiveness given to movies and business games by the training directors may not be justified. A U.S. Army study among adults showed that attitudes could be changed by films and that at least half of the attitude changes found persisted for at least nine weeks (U.S. War Department, 1943). Another study found that participation in a business game by students significantly changed attitudes toward risk taking (Lewin and Weber, 1969). However,

this is obviously a very specific type of attitude.

The training directors rated the case method as more effective than the lecture in changing attitudes. In the one study found which made such a comparison, attitudes did change significantly more in a section where the case study approach was used than in the section of the course taught by the lecture-discussion method (Butler, 1967).

Finally, the training directors believe that sensitivity training is fairly effective in changing attitudes. Four studies using control groups have been conducted with adults where an attempt was made to see if behavior was changed as a result of sensitivity training (Boyd and Elliss, 1968; Bunker, 1965; Miles, 1965; Underwood, 1965; Valiquet, 1968). These studies did find behavioral changes as a result of sensitivity training. With respect to attitude rather than behavior change, two studies, using a "before-and-after" measure without controls and with student and adult participants, found attitude changes as a result of sensitivity training (Schutz and Allen, 1966; Smith, 1964). Although there were certain methodological deficiencies in these studies, on balance the results do indicate that sensitivity training can result in at least short-run behavioral and attitudinal change, although such change may not be related to greater job effectiveness (Campbell and Dunnette, 1968).

Problem Solving

For purposes of developing effectiveness in problem-solving skills, the training directors rated the case-study method, business games, role playing, and the conference method as having some effectiveness. In addition, these methods were rated more effective than sensitivity training, programmed instruction, movie films, the TV lecture, and the conventional lecture. These results are listed in Table 40-1.

The case-study method was rated highest in effectiveness for this training objective by the training directors, and certainly it is true that the case study is probably generally considered to be the primary means of developing problem-solving skills. Unfortunately, the research on the effectiveness of the case study as a training approach is very limited. Only a few studies were found that involved more than an attempt to obtain testimonials from course participants. Fox (1963) found that about one-third of the students exposed to case-study analysis improved significantly in their ability to handle cases, about a third made moderate improvement, and a third made no improvement. Solem (1960) found that both the case-study method and role playing were effective in learning how to derive solutions to problems, but felt that role playing better taught participants about how to gain acceptance of solutions.

There is more evidence on the effectiveness of role playing in developing problem-solving skills. In addition to the study by Solem (1960), studies by Maier (1953), Maier and Maier (1957), Maier and Hoffman (1960a; 1960b), and Maier and Solem (1952) indicate that problem-solving skills can be improved for both students and managers with the use of role playing. Two studies (Parnes and Meadow, 1959; Cohen, Whitmyre, and Funk, 1960) found that training in brainstorming could improve problem-solving ability. Brainstorming could be taught by means of role playing.

The training directors also ranked business games as being an effective training method for developing problem-solving skills. However, as with the case-study method, there is little research or analysis. Dill and Doppelt (1963) conducted a student self-report study which indicated that the students did not seem to learn much about specific problem-solving solutions or strategies that could be used in other situations. Raia (1966) found that experience with a business game did not improve the ability to handle cases. However, the comparison group used case material. Mc-

Kenney (1962) found that students in sections with games plus lectures understood the interrelationship between organizational factors better than students in sections with cases plus lectures.

Interpersonal Skills

Table 40-1 indicates that the training directors see sensitivity training and role playing as being the most effective of the training methods in developing interpersonal skills and feel the conference or discussion method and the case-study method also have some effectiveness for this objective. In general, business games, movie films, programmed instruction, and the conventional and TV lecture are not considered effective for the development of interpersonal skills.

Most of the research which has concerned itself with the effectiveness of training methods in developing interpersonal skills have been on sensitivity training. Six studies of sensitivity training indicate that participants in sensitivity training describe others in more interpersonal terms than people without such training (Campbell and Dunnette, 1968). However, research specifically measuring changes in perceptual accuracy of others as a result of sensitivity training has been inconclusive.

Some research on the development of interpersonal skills has examined role playing. A study by Bolda and Lawshe (1962) showed that role playing can be effective in increasing sensitivity to employee motivations, if the participants were involved in the role play. Another study indicated role playing effective in improving interviewing skills (Van Schacck, 1957). In addition, studies by Maier, 1953; Maier and Hoffman, 1960a, 1960b; Maier and Maier, 1957, indicate that role playing can be used to improve group leadership skills which are a form of interpersonal skills.

Participant Acceptance

As Table 40-1 indicates, the training

directors rated the conference or discussion method, the case-study method, and the use of business games as being significantly more acceptable to training course participants than movie films, sensitivity training, programmed instruction, the conventional lecture method, and the television lecture. In absolute terms the training directors seem to believe that all the methods except for the conventional and TV lecture are effective for achieving the objective of participant acceptance.

Several studies on managerial acceptance of the lecture versus the discussion approach indicate a preference among managers for the lecture or more leader-centered approach (Anderson, 1959; Filley and Reighhard, 1965; House, 1962; Mann and Mann, 1959). Two other studies of managers and a study of adults found no difference in reactions or attitudes to the use of the lecture and discussion approaches (Hill, 1960; House, 1965).

The training directors also indicated that the television lecture rated low on participant acceptance. Reviews of research by Kumata (1956 and 1960; Schramm, 1962a) indicate that television has fairly high acceptance among adults as a training method and with young children, and much lower acceptance among high-school and college students.

The training directors rated business games as high on participant acceptance. Raia (1966) found that business students in sections of a course which used a business game did not differ in attitudes toward the course from students who had sections without the business game. Rowland, Gardner, and Nealey (1970) found that only a few students participating in a business game felt the game was a valuable learning experience and attitudes toward the course were not improved as a result of the addition of the business game to it.

The training directors rated role playing as effective in participant acceptance. A series of studies in six organizations by Bolda

and Lawshe (1962) indicated fair acceptance for role playing by managerial personnel. The training directors also rated the case-study method as high on participant acceptance. A study by Fox (1963) found that attitudes toward the case-study method in the form of student testimonials were favorable. However, Castore (1951) found interest in cases dwindled after a period of exposure to them. The relatively higher rating given by the training directors to programmed instruction versus the lecture method is supported in a study conducted at IBM (Hughes and McNamara, 1961), and in a study by Neidt and Meredith (1966). It should be remembered, however, that several studies show that participant acceptance of a training approach is a function of their experience with it (Guetzkow, Kelly, and McKeachie, 1954; Harris, 1960; Hughes, 1963).

Retention of Knowledge

As Table 40-1 indicates, the training directors rate programmed instruction, the case-study method, sensitivity training, role playing, the conference method, and business gaming as significantly more effective than movie films and conventional and television lectures. These latter three training methods are also rated in absolute terms as not being effective for retention of knowledge.

There has not been much research on this topic. The research that has been completed has been primarily with college students and shown no clear superiority for the lecture or discussion methods as compared with each other (Dietrick, 1960; Verner and Dickinson, 1967), for the movie film as compared with the lecture and discussion methods (Sodnovitch and Pophorn, 1961; Vander-Meer, 1948; Verner and Dickinson, 1967), for the television lecture as compared to the conventional lecture or discussion approach (Kumata, 1960; Klausmeir, 1961), or for programmed instruction as compared to the conventional lecture or discussion methods

(Nash, Muczyk, Vettori, 1971). The research reviews generally conclude that the amount of material retained is proportional to the amount learned (Dietrick, 1960; Verner and Dickinson, 1967).

DISCUSSION

For most of the training objectives the training directors believed that about half the training methods listed were effective and the other half not very effective for the training objective stated. Furthermore, the training methods considered effective for one objective were usually considered ineffective for another objective. This seems to indicate that the training directors are properly discriminating in their evaluations of the various alternative training methods.

The training directors differ most from the research results in their ratings of effectiveness for the lecture method for various training objectives. In general the research shows that the lecture method has more effectiveness for acquiring knowledge, and for participant acceptance, than the training directors believe it has. It is not known why such a negative attitude toward the lecture method exists. Among reasons suggested for this bias against different forms of the lecture are: the current emphasis on "participation," the fact that nonspecialists can use the lecture method but not other methods, the downgrading of the lecture method by advocates of other approaches, or unsatisfactory personal experiences with the lecture approach.

The training directors may error somewhat too much toward the positive side in the evaluations of programmed instruction. While it is an effective training method, it does not seem to be as superior as the training directors believe it is (Nash et al., 1971)

With respect to particular training objectives the training directors seem to be most different from the research on participant acceptance. The evidence to date certainly would indicate that the conference or discussion method and the business games are not rated as high by participants as by the training directors. Also the lecture, conventional and TV lectures, and sensitivity training are rated higher than the training directors indicate.

The review of the literature reveals great gaps in knowledge about the effectiveness of various training methods. While a considerable amount of research has been conducted on sensitivity training, the conventional and TV lecture, and conference methods, little research has been conducted on the case-study method, the business game and role playing. In addition, much more research needs to be focused on the personal and situational factors which moderate the effectiveness of alternative training methods.

In carrying out new research studies it is important that the alternative training methods being compared are subjected to a fair evaluation. As indicated previously, we and others have noticed in several studies that although control groups were used and before-and-after measures were taken, fair comparisons were not always made between the alternative training methods studied.

REFERENCES

Anderson, R. C. Learning in discussions: A resume of the authoritarian-democratic study. *Harvard Educational Review*, 1959, 29, 201-15.

Andrew, G. A study of the effectiveness of a workshop method for mental health education. *Mental Hygiene*, 1954, 38, 267-78.

Bolda, R. A., and Lawshe, C. H. Evaluation of role playing. *Personnel Administration*, 1962, 25, 40-42.

Bond, B. W. The group discussion-decision approach: An appraisal of its use in health education. *Dissertation Abstracts*, 1956, 16, 903.

Boyd, J. B., and Elliss, J. D. *Findings of research into senior management seminars*. Toronto: The Hydro-Electric Power Commission of Toronto, 1962. Cited in J.

P. Campbell and M. D. Dunnette, Effectiveness of T-group experiences in managerial training and development. *Psychological Bulletin*, 1968, 70, 73-104.

Bunker, D. R. Individual applications of laboratory training, *Journal of Applied Behavioral Science*, 1965, 1, 131-48.

Butler, E. D. An experimental study of the case method in teaching the social foundations of education. *Dissertation Abstracts*, 1967, 27, 2912.

Butler, J. L. A study of the effectiveness of lecture versus conference teaching techniques in adult education. *Dissertation Abstracts*, 1966, 26, 3712.

Buxton, C. E. *College teaching: A psychologist's view.* New York: Harcourt Brace, 1956.

Campbell, J. P., and Dunnette, M. D. Effectiveness of T-group experiences in managerial training and development. *Psychological Bulletin*, 1968, 70, 73-104.

Carpenter, C. R., and Greenhill, L. *An investigation of closed circuit television for teaching university courses.* Instructional Television Project Report #2. University Park, Pa.: Pennsylvania State University, 1958.

Castore, G. F. Attitudes of students toward the case method of instruction in a human relations course. *Journal of Educational Research*, 1951, 45, 201-13.

Cohen, D., Whitmyre, J. W., and Funk, W. H. Effect of group cohesiveness and training upon creative thinking. *Journal of Applied Psychology*, 1960, 44, 319-22.

Culbertson, F. Modification of an emotionally held attitude through role playing. *Journal of Abnormal and Social Psychology*, 1957, 54, 230-33.

Dietrick, D. C. Review of research, in R. A. Hill, A comparative study of lecture and discussion methods. Pasadena, Calif.: The Fund for Adult Education, 1960, pp. 90-118.

Dill, W. R., and Doppelt, N. The acquisition of experience in a complex management game. *Management Science*, 1963, 10, 30-46.

Festinger, L., and Carlsmith, J. Cognitive consequences of forced compliance. *Journal of Abnormal and Social Psychology*, 1959, 58, 203-10.

Filley, A. C., and Reighard, F. H. *A preliminary survey of training attitudes and needs among actual and potential attendees at management institute programs.* Madison: University of Wisconsin, 1962. Cited in R. J. House, Managerial reactions to two methods of management training. *Personnel Psychology*, 1965, 18, 311-19.

Fox, W. M. A measure of the effectiveness of the case method in teaching human relations. *Personnel Administration,* 1963, 26, 53-57.

Guetzkow, H., Kelly, E. L., and McKeachie, W. J. An experimental comparison of recitation, discussion, and tutorial methods in college teaching. *Journal of Educational Psychology*, 1954, 45, 193-207. 193-207.

Harris, C. W. (Ed.) *Encyclopedia of educational research.* New York: Macmillan, 1960.

Harvey, O., and Beverly, G. Some personality correlates of concept change through role playing. *Journal of Abnormal and Social Psychology*, 1961, 63, 125-30.

Hill, R. A. *A comparative study of lecture and discussion methods.* Pasadena, Calif.: The Fund for Adult Education, 1960.

House, R. J. An experiment in the use of management training standards. *Journal of The Academy of Managment,* 1962, 5, 76-81.

House, R. J. Managerial reactions to two methods of management training. *Personnel Psychology*, 1965, 18, 311-19.

Hughes, J. L. Effects of changes in programmed text format and reduction in classroom time on achievement and attitudes of industrial trainees. *Journal of Programmed Instruction*, 1963, 1, 143-55.

Hughes, J. L., and McNamara, W. J. A comparative study of programmed and conventional instruction in industry. *Journal of Applied Psychology*, 1961, 45, 225-31.

Janis, I., and King, B. The influence of role playing on opinion change. *Journal of Abnormal and Social Psychology*, 1954, 49, 211-18.

Janis, I., and Mann, L. Effectiveness of emotional role-playing in modifying smoking habits and attitudes. *Journal of Experimental Research in Personality*, 1965, 1, 84-90.

King, B., and Janis, I. Comparison of the effectiveness of improvised vs. non-improvised role playing in producing opinion changes. *Human Relations,* 1956, 9, 177-86.

Klausmeier, H. J. *Learning and human abilities.* New York: Harper and Bros., 1961.

Kumata, H. *An inventory of instructional television research.* Ann Arbor, Mich: Educational Television and Radio Center, 1956.

Kumata, H. A decade of teaching by television. In W. Schramm (Ed.), *The impact of educational television.* Urbana: University of Illinois Press, 1960, 176-92.

Levine, J., and Butler, J. Lecture vs. group decision in changing behavior. *Journal of Applied Psychology,* 1952, 36, 29-33.

Lewin, A. Y., and Weber, R. L. Management game teams in education and organization research. An experiment on risk taking. *Academy of Management Journal,* 1969, 12, 49-58.

Lewin, K. Group decision and social change. In E. E. Maccoby, T. M. Newcombe, E. L. Hartley (Eds.), *Readings in social psychology.* New York: Henry Holt 1958, pp. 197-211.

McKenney, J. L. An evaluation of a business game in an MBA curriculum. *Journal of Business,* 1962, 35, 278-86.

Maier, N. R. F., and Solem, A. R. The contribution of the discussion leader to the quality of group thinking. *Human Relations,* 1952, 3, 155-74.

Maier, N. R. F. An experimental test of the effect of training on discussion leadership. *Human Relations,* 1953, 6, 161-73.

Maier, N. R. F., and Maier, R. A. An experimental test of the effects of "developmental" vs. "free" discussions on the quality of group decisions. *Journal of Applied Psychology,* 1957, 41, 320-23.

Maier, N. R. F., and Hoffman, L. R. Quality of first and second solutions in group problem solving. *Journal of Applied Psychology,* 1960, 44, 278-83. (a)

Maier, N. R. F., and Hoffman, L. R. Using trained "developmental" discussion leaders to improve further the quality of group decisions. *Journal of Applied Psychology,* 1960, 44, 247-51. (b)

Mann, J. H., and Mann, C. H. The importance of group tasks in producing group-member personality and behavior change. *Human Relations,* 1959, 221, 75-80.

Margulies, S., and Eigen, L. D. *Applied programmed instruction.* New York: Wiley, 1962.

Miles, M. B. Changes during the following laboratory training: A clinical experimental study. *Journal of Applied Behavioral Science,* 1965, 1, 215-42

Nash, A. N., Muczyk, J. P., and Vettori, F. L. The relative practical effectiveness of programmed instruction. *Personnel Psychology,* 1971, 397-418.

Neidt, C. O., and Meredith, T. Changes in attitudes of learners when programmed instruction is interpolated between two conventional instruction experiences. *Journal of Applied Psychology,* 1966, 50, 130-37.

Parnes, S. J., and Meadow. A. Effects of brainstorming instructions on creative problem solving by trained and untrained subjects, *Journal of Educational Psychology,* 1959, 50, 171-76.

Raia, A. P. A study of the educational value of management games. *Journal of Business,* 1966, 39, 339-52.

Rowland, K. M., Gardner, D. M., and Nealey, S. M. Business gaming in education and research, in *Proceedings of 13th Annual Midwest Management Conference Academy of Management.* Midwest Division, East Lansing Mich:, April, 1970.

Schramm, W. *The research on programmed instruction: An annotated bibliography.* Stanford, Calif.: Institute for Communication Research, 1962. (a)

Schramm, W. What we know about learning from instructional television, in *Educational Television—The Next Ten Years.* Stanford: Stanford University Press, 1962, 52-74. (b)

Schutz, W. C., and Allen, V. L. The effects of a T-group laboratory on interpersonal behavior. *Journal of Applied Behavioral Science,* 1966, 2, 265-86.

Silber, M. B. A comparative study of three methods of effecting attitude change. *Dissertation Abstracts, 1962, 22, 2488.*

Smith, P. N. Attitude changes associated with training in human relations. *British Journal of Social and Clinical Psychology,* 1964, 3, 104-13.

Sodnovitch, J. M., and Pophorn, W. J.

Retention value of filmed science courses. Pittsburg, Kans.: Kansas State College of Pittsburgh, 1961.

Solem, A. R. Human relations training: Comparisons of case study and role playing. *Personnel Administration,* 1960, 23, 29-37.

Stovall, T. F. Lecture vs. discussion. *Phi Delta Kappan,* 1958, 39, 255-58.

Underwood, W. J. Evaluation of laboratory method training. *Training Directors Journal,* 1965, 19, 34-40.

U. S. War Department. *What the soldier thinks: A monthly digest of war department studies on the attitudes of American troops.* Army Services Forces, Morals Services Division, I, 1943, 13.

Valiquet, I. M. Contribution to the evaluation of a management development program. M.A. thesis, Massachusetts Institute of Technology, 1964. Cited by J. P. Campbell and M. D. Dunnette, Effectiveness of T-group experiences in managerial training and development. *Psychological Bulletin,* 1968, 70, 73-104.

VanderMeer, A. W. *Relative effectiveness of exclusive film instruction, films plus study guides, and typical instructional methods. Progress Report #10.* Instructional Film Program, State College, Pa.: Pennsylvania State College, 1948.

Van Schacck, H. Jr. Naturalistic role playing: A method of interview training for student personnel administrators. *Dissertation Abstracts,* 1957, 17, 801.

Verner, C. and Dickinson, G. The lecture, an analysis and review of research. *Adult Education,* 1967, 17, 85-100.

41

Laboratory Education: Impact on People and Organizations

MARVIN D. DUNNETTE AND JOHN P. CAMPBELL

In recent years, the first author has been asked by a number of firms to play "doctor" to some of their sick organizational units. These assignments were accepted rather reluctantly because the scientific terrain for diagnosing and curing company ills due to dysfunctional behavior is still unfortunately a vast, unmapped wasteland with only a few dirt roads here and there. However, observing inner company workings from the somewhat detached stance of an outsider has led to the firm conclusion that it's very easy to get into trouble in business "without really trying." This may seem obvious to the reader, but let us pursue the point a bit further by recounting briefly some of the patterns of human and organizational behavior found in these companies.[1]

A DOCTOR TO ORGANIZATIONS

Competition and crisis. One large, nationally renowned industrial research laboratory

1. Expenses involved in the preparation of this review were supported in part under U.S. Public Health Service grant MH08563, National Science Foundation grant GS1081, and a Graduate Research and Study Grant in the Behavioral Sciences from the General Electric Foundation.

comprised of over 100 top-flight scientists and engineers encountered rough times. Interviews with key people showed that nearly everyone's morale was low; nearly everyone complained about haphazard decisions, precipitate organizational changes, and constantly changing job assignments; no one seemed to know what the over-all goals of the laboratory really were, if, indeed, any existed. The fluidity of the situation was expressed by many in the form of the grim comment: "If you run into my boss, be sure to find out his name and tell me."

Apparently the laboratory had been spoiled by its own success. Only a few years earlier, a select cadre, consisting of an inventor and a dozen applied-development men, had scored an innovating and engineering breakthrough to produce an outstanding new product. Sales of the product skyrocketed—so sharply that a whole new industry was created, and competitors moved rapidly and aggressively to penetrate the burgeoning market. With success in the marketplace came rapid expansion. The "group" expanded in about five years' time from just under 20 to nearly 300 professional and supporting personnel.

Reprinted from *Industrial Relations*, 1968, 8, 1-27, by permission of the authors and the Institute of Industrial Relations, University of California at Berkeley.

Unfortunately, the growth seemed to get out of hand. Engineers and scientists were made supervisors and managers without the benefit of either experience or training in the art of supervising and managing. The key man who had stimulated and coalesced the creative forces of his staff of a dozen retained his title of Laboratory Director, but three new levels of supervision were created between him and the people on the bench. For a time, everything went well, but this phase came to a sudden halt when a competitor's product proved suddenly to have greater marketability. Sales suddenly turned drastically downward. The resulting crisis was felt immediately in the laboratory, but it had apparently been organized only to deal with success, not crisis. Feelings of anxiety and insecurity, and haphazard thrashing about in response to external threat, became prevalent; few of the newly named managers had any clear notion of how to cope with such stress or how to take advantage of the rich intellectual resources of the laboratory personnel.

Being all things to all people. In a second firm, a serious problem grew out of ambiguous and often conflicting role expectations surrounding one of the organizational units. In the eyes of some company officials, the unit was formed for the sole purpose of servicing present and potential company customers—a kind of consulting service to develop equipment and machinery enabling customers to make optimal use of the company's products. However, in the eyes of an increasing number of other officials (among them, the unit manager's boss), the unit was to be regarded as another profit center in the company—billings for services and equipment should be sufficient to avoid the necessity for subsidies from other company divisions.

The manager of his organizational unit was caught in the middle of these sharply conflicting expectations. Unfortunately, he transmitted the same ambiguous and conflicting expectations to key people in his unit. Most of his subordinates had difficulties understanding either his verbal or written communications, and he seemed entirely unaware of both his impact on other people and of what they were trying to tell him. Because of these problems of perceptual impermeability and distorting, the manager seemed constantly embroiled in destructively belligerent interpersonal exchanges —with key officials throughout the company, with customers, and with his own subordinates.

Loss of people and the beginning of strife. A third unit is the most interesting because it presents a picture of almost total organizational disruption and stress. One of many similar units in a large-scale manufacturing operation, this unit for years had provided manufacturing know-how and managerial talent for most of the firm's other units. During 1964-67 a number of things occurred to bring about internal difficulties. First, many key people retired from the organization. Second, scores of additional key managers were transferred by the parent company to other units. The unit manager apparently replaced these losses with much less effective supervisors and managers because of lack of available talent, an inadequate supervisory selection system, and a haphazard supervisory training program. Third, manpower shortages at the rank-and-file level and unprecedented consumer demands forced an excessively high rate of overtime (ranging to 60-65 hours a week and extending over a span of three years).

About a year before we began working with this organizational unit, absenteeism at both the supervisory and rank-and-file levels became a severe problem, production quality dropped sharply, and the over-all cost of manufacturing rose excessively, exceeding the budgeted cost quotas by tens of thousands of dollars a week. In our interviews with key managers, we found an acute awareness that the plant was "in trouble," combined with an unusual willingness to point to other people or other departments as a major reason for difficulties. Communication among departments had deteriorated into backbiting and finger-pointing; many supervisors used coercive, aggressive, and derogating tactics in fruitless efforts to assure compliance. Many key officials wanted desperately to open up constructive lines of communication directed toward more rational problem-solving and mature methods of conflict resolution, but few knew how such changes could be implemented.

This organization illustrates more closely than either of the other two the pervasive and unfavorable effects of strategies which fail to give sufficient emphasis to the many steps necessary for adequate problem-solving, problem analysis, information synthesis, and cooperative group action, but instead push prematurely toward instant action based mostly on essentially incomplete information or on surface symptoms.

SOLUTION THROUGH EDUCATION?

We have gone into some detail because we believe that these three instances of organizational distress illustrate patterns of personal and organizational behavior which are common in industry.[2] Moreover, they illustrate types of behavior and organizational problems specifically in the areas of interpersonal perception, interpersonal interaction, and inter- and intragroup conflict resolution. All these, in turn, are claimed by advocates to be amenable to change through techniques of laboratory education.

By laboratory education we mean those personnel and organizational development and training courses which combine traditional training features—such as lectures, group problem-solving sessions, and role-planning—with T-group or sensitivity training techniques.[3] Laboratory education is being used more and more by industry. No national statistics are available on total volume or frequency of use, but it is clear that consumer demand is high.[4] The National Training Laboratories and the Western Training Laboratories conduct programs for hundreds of industrial managers each year. Many consulting firms now offer such training as a standard part of their bill of fare; many colleges and universities incorporate T-groups into their business, public administration, education, and psychology curricula; and a number of university institutes (e.g., Boston University's Human Relations Center and UCLA's Institute of Industrial Relations) conduct T-groups for business people. Moreover, psychologists working in companies have developed laboratory education programs for internal use by managers, and a substantial number of line managers have been trained to conduct such programs as an ongoing feature of their firms' management development efforts.[5] It is apparent that laboratory education (or a T-group) is now within easy reach of almost any manager.

Our purpose in writing this article has been to report what is known of the behavioral effects (on both people and organiza-

2. Our descriptions of these organizational units are really rather stark caricatures of the actual state of events. We departed from reality in order (1) to highlight the major points we wish to make, and (2) more important, to assure anonymity of the units we worked with.

3. For detailed accounts of the basic T-group method, see descriptions given by S. Klaw, Two weeks in a T-group, *Fortune*, 1961, 64, 114-17; A. H. Kuriloff and S. Atkins, T-group for a work team, *Journal of Applied Behavioral Science*, 1966, 2, 63-94; R. Tannenbaum, I. R. Weschler, and F. Massarik, *Leadership and organization: A behavioral science approach* (New York: McGraw-Hill, 1961); and I. R. Weschler and J. Reisel, *Inside a sensitivity training group* (Los Angeles: Institute of Industrial Relations, University of California, 1959).

4. For example, see R. J. House, T-group education and leadership effectiveness: A review of empirical literature and a critical evaluation. *Personnel Psychology*, 1967, 20, 1-32; or the latest *Information Brochure* (1967) describing the 21st annual summer laboratories sponsored by the National Training Laboratories.

5. Two examples are Dr. Seymour Levy of Pillsbury Mills in Minneapolis and Dr. Joseph McPherson of Dow Chemical Co. in Midland, Mich.

tions) of laboratory education. We have approached the task as follows: First, we have examined the difficulties of the organizations described previously in order to discover the major problems of interpersonal behavior common to them and—by extrapolation—to most other troubled organizations. Second, we consider these behavioral problems in the context of what advocates and practitioners of laboratory education claim to be their major behavioral goals. Third, we review and evaluate published research studies which have been done to assess the actual behavioral effects of laboratory education. Finally, we call attention to gaps in our present level of knowledge and offer guidelines for planning future research studies designed to fill the gaps.

ACTION, ATTACK, APATHY, ANOMIE, AND ALIENATION

Most managers in the organizations described above tended to show either apathy or belligerence. Some were consistently apathetic, others consistently belligerent, but most behaved inconsistently, ranging from apathy (withdrawal) to belligerent aggressiveness (attack) from situation to situation. They tended to spend too much time pressing for quick action in response to difficulties. More often than not, they ended up responding inappropriately and nonconstructively to the problems and threats facing them. Why?

We believe two reasons stand out. First, most were so strongly oriented toward accomplishing immediate solutions that they failed to gather data or information about problem causes. They tended to rush in with premature conclusions about causes and remedies (often fixing blame on others) in an attempt to remove opposition (or frustration) rapidly and completely. Needless to say, a few unsuccessful forays of this type would probably result either in further undifferentiated attacks or in discouragement, temporary withdrawal, and apathy.

Second, most managers in these units appeared not to trust others sufficiently to deal openly and cooperatively with them in coping with problems. They avoided those confrontations that threatened to reveal opposing viewpoints or lead to open conflict. Most seemed unwilling or unable to cope with others as individuals, to try to know them better, or "to put themselves in the other fellow's shoes."

Thus, the major patterns of individual behavior in these three ailing units involved apathy, overt belligerence, and impatience with analytical procedures for getting to know either problems or people better—symptomatic, in our opinion, of efforts to protect the ego or to save face.

Obviously, these individual behavioral tendencies were related to broader patterns of organizational behavior in these units. Our interviews and questionnaires revealed patterns of poor coordination, inefficient and inaccurate communication, and poorly defined and poorly transmitted organizational objectives. To a degree, these patterns seemed to occur simply because more constructive patterns had never been learned. Coordination, goal definition, and communications in each of the three units suffered for different reasons—extremely rapid growth and poor supervisory assignments in the first, role ambiguity in the second, and loss of key managerial talent in the third.

In each of the units, things had been going well just prior to the onset of the "sickness"; unfortunately, proper plans had not been developed nor people readied to respond analytically to crisis situations. Each organization floundered—from the top down. Clear-cut objectives (specific organizational goals, intentions, and actions) were not formulated and could not, therefore, be communicated—even if sound methods for coordination and communication had been available. The tendency to meet threat by fighting or fleeing characterized each organization's behavior as well as that of the individuals making it up, and this yielded finally to a deteriorating downward spiral of threat-induced fear eliciting inappropriate (self-defeating) and precipitate organizational and individual actions, followed by suspicion, alienation, deepening crisis, further nonconstructive counteractions, and so on.

BEHAVIORAL NEEDS AND THE GOALS OF LABORATORY EDUCATION

In order to reverse this untoward spiral which might lead ultimately to complete organizational debilitation, new patterns of individual and organizational behavior must be learned and implemented. We suggest that the needs are greatest for teaching people (1) to be more analytical in gathering data about other people and about problem situations; (2) to be less self-centered, less defensive, and more aware of the effects of their own behavior on others; (3) to be more accepting of the necessity for facing up to conflict—in fact, to develop strategies for bringing conflict into the open—in order to be able to work out constructive resolutions; and, (4) to develop both the skills and the motivation to work interpersonally with others for the purpose of learning more about behavior in the work setting and the problems they face in relation to their meeting organizational goals.

Undoubtedly, these areas of needed behavior re-education are far from unique to the three organizational units we described. In fact, we concur with Argyris that patterns of behavior in these units illustrate what may be expected in *most* organizations in response to such crises as runaway expansion, extreme competitive pressures, excessive losses of key people, or any other internally or externally induced state of organizational threat.[6] There is a widespread

need in today's organizations for teaching business managers to be more analytical, more aware of how they effect others, develop better interpersonal skills, and use constructive approaches for resolving conflict.

Does laboratory education accomplish these goals? Certainly, most of the advocates of the method would argue that it does. For example, the following list—drawn from many sources—is a distillation of the desirable outcomes sought by and advocated, either implicitly or explicitly, by most T-group and/or laboratory education practitioners:

1. Increased self-insight or self-awareness concerning one's own behavior and its meaning in a social context—this refers to the process of learning how others see and interpret one's behavior, as well as insight about one's reasons for behaving in various ways in different interpersonal situations.

2. Increased sensitivity to the behavior of others—this outcome is closely linked to the first. It refers, first, to the development of an increased awareness of the full range of communicative stimuli emitted by other persons (voice inflections, facial expressions, body positions, and other contextual factors, in addition to the actual choice of words); and, second, to developing the ability to infer accurately the emotional or noncognitive bases for interpersonal communications. This goal is very similar to the concept of empathy as it is used by clinical and counseling psychologists; that is, the ability to infer correctly what another person is feeling.

---

6. Based on his theories of human and organizational behavior, Argyris argues that most individuals in industry tend to have their needs for growth and maturity frustrated by the demands for dependency made by most organizations. The initial result is employee apathy, but when the employee is faced with organizational stress, the apathy may become aggession or withdrawal, which is countered by the organization with further controls and constraints, followed in turn by further employee counteractions. Thus, the vicious cycle of organizational constraints, employee counteractions, further constraints, and so on, is set off. For Argyris's account of his theories and a case study of onset of "sickness" in one organizational unit, see C. Argyris, *Understanding organizational behavior* (Homewood, Ill.: Dorsey, 1960), and *Integrating the individual and the organization* (New York: Wiley, 1964).

3. Increased awareness and understanding of the types of processes that facilitate or inhibit group functioning and the interactions between different groups—specifically, why do some members participate actively, while others retire to the background? Why do subgroups form and wage war against each other? How and why are pecking orders established? Why do different groups, who may actually share the same goals, sometimes create seemingly insoluble conflict situations?

4. Heightened diagnostic skill in social, interpersonal, and intergroup situations—achievement of the first three objectives should provide an individual with a set of concepts to be used in his analysis of conflict situations. Moreover, he should be equipped to work constructively with others to resolve interpersonal and/or intergroup conflict.

5. Increased action skill—the ability to intervene successfully in inter- or intragroup situations in order to increase member satisfactions, effectiveness, or productivity.[7] The major thrust of increased action skill is toward intervention at the *interpersonal* instead of merely the technological level, thereby enhancing the likelihood that coordinated, instead of alienated and disputative, efforts will be brought to bear in solving technological problems.

6. Learning how to learn—this refers not simply to an individual's cognitive approach to the world, but instead, and far more importantly, to his ability to analyze continually his own interpersonal behavior in order to help himself and others achieve more effective and satisfying interpersonal relationships.[8]

7. Although very similar to point 4, this is mentioned separately in M. B. Miles, Research notes from here and there—Human relations training: Process and outcomes, *Journal of Counseling Psychology*, 1960, 7, 301-6.
8. The sources for the above listing of T-group goals include: C. Argyris, T-Groups for organizational effectiveness, *Harvard Business Review*, 1964, 42, 60-74; P. C. Buchanan, Evaluating the effectiveness of laboratory training in industry, in *Explorations in human relations training and research*, No. 1 (Washington, D.C.: National Training Laboratories, National Education Association, 1965); L. P. Bradford, J. R. Gibb, and K. D. Benne, *T-group theory and laboratory method*

Obviously, these outcomes fulfill the organizational needs for behavioral re-education we listed earlier. It should now be asked: Are these behavioral outcomes really accomplished? If they are, by whom—everyone undergoing such training or just a few? And, if a few, who, and under what conditions? Can sick organizations be "cured" through T-group training and laboratory education? In short, what research evidence can be offered either to support or to question whether this relatively new training strategy accomplishes the aims claimed for it?[9]

ANSWERS ARE HARD TO COME BY

The above questions—easy to pose—are difficult to answer. This is because learning what training accomplishes behaviorally is probably the most difficult and least well-handled area of behavioral-science research in industry. Evaluation is poor because training, education, and learning are believed by most people in our society to be inherently good—almost everyone believes that this fundamental truth needs no proof. Moreover, faced with the kinds of organizational needs we have been talking about, what trainer, personnel development expert, or consulting psychologist could afford, or would want, to "fiddle around" designing an elegant experiment to show the world whether or not he actually accomplishes what he set out to? A good physician doesn't withhold his educated guesses during diagnosis, nor does he ignore therapeutic opportunities, simply because all the evidence is not in. Similarly, a "company doctor" must accept responsibility for doing something, and the something will nearly always need to be a promising, but not yet

(New York: Wiley, 1964); E. H. Schein and W. G. Bennis, *Personal and organizational changes through group methods: The laboratory approach* (New York: Wiley, 1965); R. Tannenbaum and others, *op. cit.;* Miles, *op. cit.*
9. See Appendix A for a generalized description of T-group procedure.

entirely proven, method of individual or organizational behavior modification.

We are not condoning this state of affairs. We are just calling attention to it and stating that we understand the reason for it. In doing so, we have been wearing the mantle of the professional—the individual who seeks to deduce from his repertoire of behavioral science knowledge a plan of action for alleviating an organization's ills. Now, however, it is time to slip into the mantle of the scientist and to become more demanding about the research evidence offered in support of claims made, and hopes possessed, by the professionals. For, without a tough-minded scientist's view, little impetus for better answers will ever be provided and the practices of the professionals will show little or no improvement over the years—eventuating possibly in charlatanism rather than informed or truly expert professionalism.

WHAT NEEDS TO BE DONE?

The *scientific* standards necessary for properly evaluating training experiences are few in number and disarmingly simple, but (for the reasons mentioned above) they are almost never put into practice. First, measures of trainees' status should be obtained *before* and *after* the training experience. Ideally, the measures should sample, as broadly as possible, trainee *behaviors* relevant to the organization's problems and/or to the aims of the training procedures; but attitudinal, perceptual, and other self-report measures may also prove useful. Second, measured changes shown by the trainees between pre- and post-training periods should be compared with changes, if any, occurring in a so-called control group of similar, but untrained persons. Using control groups is the only way to assure that changes observed in the experimental (or trainee) groups are actually the result of training procedures instead of possible artifactual effects—such as the mere passage of time, poor reliability of measures, Hawthorne Effects, or other spurious components.

Finally, a third standard necessary for most training evaluation studies stems from the possibility of interaction between the evaluation measures and the behavior of the trainees during the program. For example, if trainees are asked beforehand to answer questions about their supervisory "styles," they may be alerted to look for the "correct answers" during training in order to answer the same questions "more appropriately" (i.e., more in line with the desires of the trainer) when they are asked again after training. One way of estimating the degree of interaction between such measures and the training content is to provide a quasi-control group which takes part in the training program *without* first completing the measures. Then, comparisons between the two trained groups (experimental and quasi-control) on the after-measures may give estimates of the relative amounts of change actually due to training or due simply to having been alerted by prior exposure to the measures.

Unfortunately, these three rather simple standards for learning what training accomplishes are actually very difficult to meet, and they have been applied only rarely in studies to evaluate the effects of laboratory education.

THE EVIDENCE

We turn now to a review and evaluation of published research studies done to assess the effects of laboratory education. We have classified the investigations into five groups roughly located at various points along a continuum extending from private (not publicly verifiable), individual perceptions to very broad organizational outcomes. The primary changes measured by studies in each of the groups are:

1. self-reports of changes in the work setting;

2. changes in attitudes, outlooks, perceptions of others, or orientations toward others;

3. changes in self-awareness or interpersonal sensitivity;

4. observed changes in behavior on the job; and

5. changes in organizational outcomes. The major results shown by studies in each of these areas are summarized below.

Self-Perceptions and Self-Reports

There is an overwhelming amount of anecdotal evidence on the presumed effects of laboratory education. Most, however, involves introspection, free association, or testimonies collected in an uncontrolled and nonsystematic way. Here is a greatly abbreviated excerpt from one such report:

The leadership laboratory was a marvelous experience. I was in it a month ago, and I am still awestruck. I might be able to give you a glimmer or two about what happened in relaxed conversation, oiled by a martini or two, but a letter is bound to miss, but I'll give it a try anyway. The process is like the dropping of Salome's seven veils. Eventually the group comes to a condition of complete trust, and communications become so acute that they seem metaphysical. Not that the group gets this way without strain. It was fascinating to see how the group came to respect the need for time for an idea to sink in. When an important point was made to a member, the group often fell silent while the point perked, even if it took 30 seconds. The silence wasn't oppressive or embarrassing; it served a purpose. After the last day's session, each group ate at a long table by itself. You never saw such uninhibited, free people. The next morning, my group had a final session and then we walked around the place like a bunch of bananas, we felt so close.[10]

The above account is highly favorable about what happened in the group, but it also is highly subjective, introspective, and nonbehavioral. Because of this, we chose *not*

to attempt a review of such reports. As a consequence, we found only two studies using structured or systematic measures for assessing self-report of behavior changes. Neither of the studies used pretraining measures. In both studies, supervisors who had been in intraorganizational laboratory training groups reported (after three to seven months back on the job) changes in the effectiveness of their units or critical job incidents they believed were due to the laboratory training. Buchanan and Brunstetter found that the 224 managers reported relatively more examples of effective changes than a comparison (control) group of 133 untrained managers. Morton and Bass used no control group, but 359 incidents were reported by 97 trainees, and nearly all of them were judged by the authors to be favorable influences relating to improved working relationships.[11]

Obviously, self-reports of the type obtained in these two studies—even though elicited in a systematic way and focused on job behaviors—are subject to a wide variety of biases. The trainees knew that their training was intended to produce certain behavioral effects; thus, they probably tended to note and report many occurrences which would otherwise go unnoticed and unreported. In a sense, one might argue that the trainees had been committed by their company to enumerate instances of the worth or return on the training investment. Thus, self-imposed internalized organizational expectations and response-set biases seem to us an equally viable explanation for the results obtained.

Attitudes, Outlooks, and Orientations

Several studies have examined possible effects of laboratory education on trainees'

---

10. Drawn from a letter from one of the first author's close friends, who prefers to remain anonymous.

11. R. B. Morton and B. M. Bass, The organizational training laboratory, *Journal of American Society of Training Directors*, 1964, 18, 2-15; P. C. Buchanan and P. H. Brunstetter, A research approach to management development: Part II, *Journal of the American Society of Training Directors*, 1959, 13, 18-27.

attitudes and outlooks. Discovering attitudinal effects of laboratory education is important because several of the goals of such training (e.g., better understanding of intergroup processes, improved interpersonal diagnostic skills, increased interest and skill in interpersonal intervention, and stronger drive toward personal learning or improvement) strongly imply the necessity of marked attitudinal changes. Table 41-1 lists the nine studies we found in this area along with relevant details about measures used, subjects, experimental designs, and results obtained.

We conclude from these studies that there is little firm evidence of any significant change in attitude, outlook, orientation, or view of others as a result of T-group training. This statement is based on the following three observations.

1. Control groups were not included in five of the nine studies. Because of this, interpretation of the results in terms of T-group training per se is strained, at best. The changes occurring in the trained groups could easily be attributable to the passage of time or to the mere act of taking the same test a second time. Two of the four studies using control groups report no significant differences between the trained and untrained individuals; in the two where differences were obtained (Smith; Schutz and Allen), the nature of the changes is only sketchily described, offering little basis for speculation or further hypothesis formulation.

2. Eight of the nine studies failed to collect data about possible interaction effects between the evaluation questionnaires or tests and the training program. This is serious when the effort is directed toward evaluating changes via such self-report measures as attitude or orientation inventories because the results from such instruments very often are made available to trainees and actually become a part of the feedback process during training. The result is that trainees, in effect, are either explicitly or implicitly "coached" on the instruments to be used later in evaluating the presumed

effects of training. None of the studies we reviewed mention whether or not such strategies were used as part of the training "package," but even if they were not, merely taking the instruments in the pretest session often serves as kind of an alerting mechanism for trainees to alter their responses to the questionnaires when they take them again later.

At least two quasicontrol approaches can be suggested for learning more about the possibility and nature of such instrument-interaction effects. First, a group might take the questionnaires, get feedback on their results, and then retake them after an intervening period of no training. Results would provide an estimate of the possible magnitude of response changes (independent of training content) due to learning more about what the questionnaires are "getting at." Second, an additional trained group might take the evaluation instruments only after training. This is the approach used by Bass in the first study listed in Table 41-1. If the "after-only" trained group scores like the trained group with both "before" and "after" measures, the possibility of interpreting changes as due only to artifactual interaction effects is greatly lessened.

3. Finally, the actual magnitudes of changes obtained in these studies (even when control groups weren't used and interaction effects weren't checked) are small, and it would be unwise to argue that these minor attitudinal changes indicate, in any substantial way, the accomplishment of the broad behavioral goals and objectives of laboratory education.

Thus, it seems clear that research has not yet demonstrated that T-group training and/or laboratory education has any marked effect on one's "scores" on objective measures of attitude, orientation, outlook, or style.

Self-Awareness and Interpersonal Sensitivity

Our listing of the goals of laboratory education placed self-insight or self-awareness (i.e., the ability to perceive one's self as

Table 41-1

	Nature of measures	Use of measures	Description of subjects	Experimental design	Results
Bass	Subjects finished series of incomplete sentences after seeing film *Twelve Angry Men*	Before and after two-week T-group training	34 Executives	No control group; two other groups saw film *only* after training to check interaction effects	Subjects became more oriented toward interpersonal relations depicted in the film
Blake and Mouton	Attitudes toward five distinct managerial styles described and "taught" in managerial grid training	Before and after phase I of Managerial Grid training	33 Manager and 23 union representatives	No control group; no check on interaction effects	Managers increased on style depicting maximum concern for both production and people (9, 9). Union men increased emphasis on production (9, 1) and decreased emphasis on people (1, 9)
Baumgartel and Goldstein	Estimates of needs for *affection, inclusion,* and *control* and desires for others to behave with *affection, inclusion,* and *control* (FIRO-B); also estimates of one's major values (Allport-Vernon-Lindzey)	Before and after a 15-week college course in Human Relations (including T-groups)	100 Kansas University students; 59 male, 41 female	No control group; no check on interaction effects	Females changed more than males; valued religion less, increased in desire for *control* and decreased in desire for *affection;* definite evidence showing effect of individual differences in nature of changes
Harrison	Descriptions of self and others—scorable in categories of *concreteness* and *tendency toward inference*	Before, three weeks after, and three months after NTL laboratory training	115 Persons from many occupations and institutions	No control group; no check on interaction effects	No effects found for short-term (three-week) follow-up. Modest increase in use of *inferential* concepts for three-month follow-up
Kassarjian	Tendencies toward "Inner" versus "Other" directedness	Before and after college course focused on T-group participation	125 Day school and night school students	Control group of 55 persons similar to those in T-groups; no check on interaction effects	No significant changes or differences between experimental and control groups
Kernan	Questionnaire describing one's orientation toward *consideration* and *initiating structure* (Leadership Opinion Questionnaire)	Before and after three-day laboratory training program	40 Engineering supervisors employed in the same company	Control group of 20 engineering supervisors; no check on interaction effects	No significant changes on either measure for either of the groups

Table 41-1—Continued

	Nature of measures	Use of measures	Description of subjects	Experimental design	Results
Oshry and Harrison	Checklist of causes of unresolved work problems and how to deal with them	Before and after two weeks of NTL laboratory training	16 Middle-level managers from various companies	No control group; no check on interaction effects	After training managers viewed their work problems less impersonally and believed they were more directly involved in the problems, but showed no change in the nature of what they would do about problems
Schutz and Allen	Estimates of needs for *affection*, *inclusion*, and *control* and desires for others to behave with *affection*, *inclusion*, and *control* (FIRO-B)	Before, after, and six months after a two-week laboratory program of the Western Training Laboratory	71 Persons with widely varying backgrounds	Control group of 30 education students at University of California (Berkeley); no check on interaction effects	Correlations between *before* and *after* scores were lower for trainees than for control group; lowest correlations between *before* scores and six-month follow-up; no information given on the nature of the changes
Smith	Estimates of needs for *affection* and *control* and desires for others to behave with *affection* and *control* (4 scales of the FIRO-B)	Before and after T-group training	108 English managers and students (11 T-groups)	Control groups of 44 students in six discussion groups; no check on interaction effects	Disparity between needs and desires from others decreased for trainees, but not for control group members; changes were in direction of less need for *control* and greater need for *affection*

Sources: B. M. Bass, Reactions to *Twelve Angry Men* as a measure of sensitivity training, *Journal of Applied Psychology*, XLVI (1962), 361-64; R. R. Blake and Jane S. Mouton, Some effects of managerial grid seminar training on union and management attitudes toward supervision, *Journal of Applied Behavioral Science*, II (1966), 387-400; H. Baumgartel and J. W. Goldstein, Need and value shifts in college training groups, *Journal of Applied Behavioral Science*, III (1967), 87-101; R. Harrison, Cognitive change and participation in a sensitivity training laboratory, *Journal of Consulting Psychology*, XXX (1966), 517-20; H. H. Kassarjian, Social character and sensitivity training, *Journal of Applied Behavioral Science*, I (1965), 433-40; J. P. Kernan, Laboratory human relations training: Its effect on the personality of supervisory engineers, *Dissertation Abstracts*, XXV (1964), 665-66; B. I. Oshry and R. Harrison, Transfer from here-and-now to there-and-then: Changes in organizational problem diagnosis stemming from T-group training, *Journal of Applied Behavioral Science*, II (1966), 185-98; W. C. Schutz and V. L. Allen, The effects of a T-group laboratory on interpersonal behavior, *Journal of Applied Behavioral Science*, II (1966), 265-86; and P. B. Smith, Attitude changes associated with training in human relations, *British Journal of Social and Clinical Psychology*, III (1964), 104-13.

others see one) and interpersonal sensitivity (i.e., broader awareness of interpersonal stimuli and increased accuracy in inferring others' feelings) in a position central to accomplishing the other goals. In a way, it is unfortunate that the practitioners of T-group or sensitivity training have claimed improved self-awareness and interpersonal sensitivity as goals, for measurement problems in the area of interpersonal perception are among the most difficult the behavioral scientist has ever faced.[12] Still, we agree that methodological difficulties, no matter how great, should not deter investigators from considering the area, for we believe that T-group advocates rightly emphasize the crucial role of interpersonal perception in getting to know, and learning to work constructively with, other people.

We located a total of only seven studies related to the effects of laboratory education on self-awareness or interpersonal sensitivity. Of these, only one (Dunnette's) utilized a measurement methodology designed to control the various interpersonal prediction strategies discussed in Appendix B. Table 41-2 lists the seven studies along with relevant details about measures used, subjects, experimental designs, and results obtained.

Casual examination of this table reveals that most studies failed to use control groups, possible interaction effects between the questionnaires and the training programs were not examined, and (with the exception of the Dunnette study) no precautions were taken to assess the nature of possible

differences in the prediction strategies used by subjects in the studies designed to get at possible changes in "interpersonal sensitivity." In terms of self-awareness, the studies by Burke and Bennis and by Gassner, Gold, and Snadowsky deserve special mention. With no control group, Burke and Bennis apparently showed that T-group training has the effect of reducing discrepancies in subjects' descriptions of real and ideal selves. But Bassner, Gold, and Snadowsky obtained the same results for *both* T-group trained and control-group subjects, thereby substantially weakening the tenability of any assertions about the *unique* effects of T-group training on the nature of one's self-perception or its relative accuracy.

The study by Dunnette is the only one in this group showing any evidence that T-groups may result in increased interpersonal sensitivity. The methodology was designed to reduce substantially the likelihood of accurate predictions due to stereotypy or assumed similarity strategies. Therefore, accuracy, when it occurred, was much more likely to be the result of truly individualized patterns of interpersonal perception. Moreover, the T-group and control group meetings were recorded and rated according to the quality of interpersonal interaction.[13] Members of the more interactive groups were more accurate in their designations of whom they knew best (as measured by the empathy inventories) than members of the less interactive groups. This is the only direct evidence we know of that the interpersonal interaction of a "good" T-group has the effect of developing greater and more accurate social differentiation among the group's members.

Thus, from this group of studies we must conclude that evidence in favor of any claims that laboratory education can increase or change interpersonal awareness,

12. See Appendix B for a brief discussion of the problem. Recent articles summarizing the difficulties are: M. D. Dunnette, People feeling: Joy, more joy and the slough of despond, *Journal of Applied Behavioral Science*, 1969, 5, 25-44, and J. P. Campbell and M. D. Dunnette, The effectiveness of T-group experience in managerial training and development," *Psychological Bulletin*, 1968, 70, 73-104. Earlier, more technical statements, include L. J. Cronbach, Processes affecting scores on "Understanding of Others" and "Assumed Similarity," *Psychological Bulletin*, 1955, 52, 177-93, and N. L. Gage and L. J. Cronbach, Conceptual and methodological problems in interpersonal perception, *Psychological Review*, 1955, 62, 411-22.

13. A system of rating interpersonal interaction called the Hill Interaction Matrix was used to rate the quality of group interchanges. See W. F. Hill, *A guide to understanding the structure and function of the hill Interaction matrix* (Los Angeles: University of Southern California, 1967).

Table 41-2

	Nature of measures	Use of measures	Description of subjects	Experimental design	Results
Bass (self-description)	27 Adjectives descriptive of nine different mood factors	Administered five times during 10-day T-group laboratory	30 Supervisors, engineers, and administrators	No control group; check on interaction effects is purpose of the study	Skepticism decreased throughout training; concentration and depression increased and then declined; no significant amount of anxiety expressed at any time
Bennis et al. (self-awareness)	34 Item inventory of various role behaviors	Before and after semester-long T-group meetings to describe "real" and "ideal" self	12 Business administration students	No control group; no check on interaction effects	No significant changes in discrepancies between real and ideal self-descriptions
Bennis et al. (sensitivity)	34 Item inventory of various role behaviors	Members "predicted" how other members filled in inventory and discrepancy scores were computed	12 Business administration students	No control group; no check on interaction effects; no control on different strategies	No significant relationships
Burke and Bennis (self-awareness)	19 Bipolar adjectival rating scales	Described (1) each other group member; (2) "How I really am"; (3) "How I would like to be" during first week and during last week	84 Participants in six different NTL groups	No control group; no check on interaction effects	Subjects changed in direction of closer agreement between real self and ideal self-ratings and saw themselves more as others saw them
Gassner, Gold, and Snadowsky (self-awareness)	Hill's Index of Adjustment and Values (40-item adjectival checklist)	Before and after training for descriptions of (1) This is characteristic of me; (2) I would like this to be characteristic of me; and (3) Most students would like this to be characteristic of them	3 Experiments; CCNY students; 45-50 in trained groups; 25-30 in control groups	Control groups were used; no check on interaction effects	Subjects changed in direction of less discrepancy between real and ideal selves. However, trained subjects changed no more than control group subjects.

Table 41-2—Continued

	Nature of measures	Use of measures	Description of subjects	Experimental design	Results
Lohman, Zenger, and Weschler (sensitivity)	Gordon Personal Profile (measuring ascendancy, emotional stability, etc.)	*Before* and *after* semester-long T-groups; completed for themselves and for how they felt; trainer filled it in	65 UCLA students	No control group; no check on interaction effects; no control for different strategies	*Slight* increase in accuracy of students' predictions of trainer's responses, but finding is useless because of confounding of different strategies
Gage and Exline (sensitivity)	50-item questionnaire involving opinions about group processes, leadership styles, etc.	Before and after three-week NTL laboratory training. Subjects gave own opinions and also predicted for group as a whole	2 Groups of 15 and 18 persons	No control group; equivalent forms used to control effects of taking inventory twice	No changes in various accuracy and similarity indexes between before and after administrations
Dunnette (sensitivity)	Computer developed "empathy inventories" based on subjects' answers to preference inventory, adjective checklist, and manifest-need statements	*Before* and *after* six weekly two-hour discussion or T-group sessions	65 University of Minnesota students and trainers; 10 T-groups comprised of 1 trainer and 4 members each; 3 control "discussion" groups of 1 leader and 4 members	Control groups discussed innocuous subjects; no interpersonal discussion; different inventories used before and after training; new methodology employed to control for different prediction strategies	Groups showing highest incidence of interpersonal interaction showed greatest ability to differentiate between persons "best known" and those "least known" at the end of experiment. Control groups and less interactive T-groups showed least ability to differentiate

Sources: B. M. Bass, Mood changes during a management training laboratory, *Journal of Applied Psychology*, XLVI (1962), 361-64; W. Bennis, R. Burke, H. Cutter, H. Harrington, and Joyce Hoffman, A note on some problems of measurement and prediction in a training group, *Group Psychotherapy*, X (1957), 328-41; R. L. Burke and W. G. Bennis, Changes in perception of self and others during human relations training, *Human Relations*, XIV (1961), 165-82; Suzanne Gassner, J. Gold, and A. M. Snadowsky, Changes in the phenomenal field as a result of human relations training, *Journal of Psychology*, LVIII (1964), 33-41; K. Lohman, J. H. Zenger, and I. R. Weschler, Some perceptual changes during sensitivity training, *Journal of Educational Research*, LIII (1959), 28-31; N. L. Gage and R. V. Extine, Social perception and effectiveness in discussion groups, *Human Relations*, VI (1953), 381-69; M. D. Dunnette, People feeling: Joy, more joy and the slough of despond, *Journal of Applied Behavioral Science*, 1969, 5, 25-44.

"self-insight," or interpersonal sensitivity is very nearly nonexistent. Dunnette's is the only study offering much hope to the practitioners of T-group training, and the conclusions from it must be carefully qualified because the subjects were not industrial employees, and no measures of interpersonal sensitivity outside the immediate confines of the T-groups were obtained. As in the other two areas already discussed, we must conclude that much additional research needs to be done; the final answers are still far in the future.

OBSERVED CHANGES IN JOB BEHAVIOR

So far, we have reviewed studies bearing quite directly on whether or not T-groups actually accomplish their stated goals. Now, we move to those studies using more global (and, perhaps, more meaningful) measures of training outcomes. Earlier, we described three "sick" organizational units and characterized the managerial behavior patterns that seemed to be common to them. We also argued that individual behavior change was desirable in at least four broad areas for these organizations to overcome their "sickness" and regain operating effectiveness.[14] Now, we are able to ask about possible evidence in favor of laboratory education's bringing about behavior changes in any or all of these areas.

We located five studies bearing directly on this question.[15] Although carefully

designed and conducted, they all suffer from the possibility of bias in the behavior change reports. This is because control groups and job behavior observers were chosen by the trained subjects. Thus, reports of behavior change for trained and nontrained subjects are subject to the contaminating effects of the observers' prior knowledge of the training histories of the persons being described and to whatever selective bias may have affected the trainees' designations of people for inclusion in the control groups. Even so, since these studies did actually focus on independent observations of job behaviors and behavioral changes rather than merely subjects' self-reports or questionnaire responses, they come much closer than other investigations to giving us direct information about possible behavioral effects of laboratory education. Their results constitute the backbone of favorable evidence usually offered by T-group practitioners and advocates.

The central approach used in each of the five investigations was to ask associates of trained and untrained subjects to describe changes they may have observed in the subjects' job behaviors during the previous year (which included the training experience). Efforts were made to match the control group with experimental subjects on such dimensions as type of job, organization (or department), and age. Details on each study and the results obtained are described below.

1. Miles collected information from and about 34 high-school principals who had been through NTL T-group training. Two control groups were used, one a group of 29 principals matched with the trainees, the other a group of 148 principals chosen randomly from a national roster. Observations on job behavior were obtained from an average of five associates for each of the 211 subjects. Pretraining and post-training descriptions were obtained from associates of the trainees and the matched control

---

14. The four areas were to teach managers (1) to be more analytical in their study of people and problems; (2) to be less self-centered and more aware of how they effect others; (3) to face up to and to encourage conflict as an important basis for problem-solving; and (4) to develop both the skill and desire to work interpersonally with others.
15. J. B. Boyd and J. D. Elliss, *Findings of research into senior management seminars* (Toronto: Hydro-Electric Power Commission of Ontario, 1962); D. R. Bunker, Individual applications of laboratory training, *Journal of Applied Behavioral Science*, 1965, 1, 131-48); M. B. Miles, Changes during and following laboratory training: A clinical-experimental study, *Journal of Applied Behavioral Science*, 1965, 215-42; I. M. Valiquet, *Contribution to the evaluation of a management development program* (Boston: M.I.T. Press,

1965); W. J. Underwood, Evaluation of laboratory method training, *Training Directors Journal*, 1965, 19, 34-40.

subjects on the Leader Behavior Description Questionnaire (LBDQ)[16] and the Group Participation Scale (GPS).[17] A check was made on the possibility of interaction between these measures and T-group training content by obtaining only post-training descriptions from half the subjects. Many additional measures were obtained, including ratings of behavior during training, a series of personality descriptions (such as ego strength and flexibility), and various "organizational" measures (such as job tenure, number of teachers supervised, etc.).

More behavior changes were observed for trainees (job behavior changes were reported for 30 per cent of them) than for either of the two control groups (10 per cent for the matched control group and 12 per cent for the random control group). The nature of the changes were derived from a crude content analysis of the descriptions; they included increased sensitivity to others, increased communication and leadership skill, increased consideration toward others and more relaxed job behavior styles. Surprisingly, however, no significant differences were obtained on any of the structured questionnaires such as the LBDQ or the GPS. The most interesting finding was that job behavior changes were reported most often for those principals who had been perceived by their trainers to profit most from the T-group experience ($r=.55$ between job-behavior change and trainer ratings of amount of change during training).

2. Boyd and Elliss collected information from and about 42 managers selected after taking part in one of three different in-plant T-groups. Two control groups were used: one, 12 managers who had had no training; the other, 10 managers who had been in a standard human relations program. Boyd and Elliss personally interviewed each subject's superior, two of his peers, and two of his subordinates. These observer-associates also sorted a set of 80 statements describing different job behavior changes.

Relatively more observers reported job behavior changes for the T-group trainees (65 per cent) than for the conventionally trained control subjects (51 per cent) or the untrained control subjects (34 per cent). Here again, however, no significant differences were obtained between the three groups when the more structured behavior change descriptions (the set of 80 statements) were examined.

3. Bunker, in a much larger study, collected information from and about 229 persons (mostly managers or other administrators) who had been in one of six NTL sessions held during 1960 and 1961. One control group was used, consisting of 112 matched subjects whose names were obtained from the trainees in response to a request to "choose a person in a similar organizational position." Questionnaires about observed behavior changes were sent and returned by mail. From five to seven observer-associates completed questionnaires for each subject. Unfortunately, Bunker used no structured questionnaires in his study.

More behavior changes were reported for the trained subjects (at least two observers agreed on changes for 67 per cent of the trainees) than for control group subjects (two observers agreed on changes for only 33 per cent of the controls). In additional analyses, Bunker developed 15 content categories (on which independent judges showed 90 per cent agreement in their classifications) for investigating the nature of the reported behavior changes. Greatest differences between trained and untrained subjects were reported in areas related to more openness, increased interpersonal skills, and better understanding of self and others. Differences in behavior reports for the two groups were small for such things as initiating action, assertiveness, and confidence.

16. See R. M. Stogdill and A. E. Coons, *Leader behavior: Its description and measurement,* Business Research Monograph, No. 88 (Columbus: Bureau of Business Research, Ohio State University, 1957), for details of the development and use of the LBDQ. The questionnaire measures two major dimensions of leadership behavior: "consideration" and "initiating structure."

17. See H. B. Pepinsky, L. Siegel, and E. L. Van Alta, The criterion in counseling: A group participation scale, *Journal of Abnormal and Social Psychology,* 1952, 47, 415-419, for details of the development and use of GPS. It is a peer nomination device designed as an aid in evaluating the effects of, or describing the outcomes associated with, counseling.

4. Valiquet's study is similar, on a much smaller scale, to Bunker's. He collected information from and about 34 participants who had taken part in in-plant laboratory training. One control group of 15 untrained subjects was used. Questionnaires were mailed to an average of five observers nominated by the subjects. The content categories developed by Bunker were used in analyzing the results. Results were essentially the same as those reported by Bunker. More changes were reported for trained than for untrained subjects, and the major changes occurred in categories related to openness, interpersonal understanding, and skill in social interaction. Unfortunately, like Bunker, Valiquet relied exclusively on free or open-end responses; no structured questionnaires were used.

5. Underwood added an interesting twist in collecting information from and about 15 supervisors who had taken 30 hours of in-plant T-group training. He asked observer-associates of the 15 and of a matched control group of 15 untrained subjects to describe not only job behavior changes but also their effects on the subjects' over-all job effectiveness. Only one observer was recruited for each subject, and each was asked to keep track of observed changes over a 15-week period rather than relying merely on memory of what may have occurred over the past year. Some change was reported for nine trained subjects and seven untrained subjects; over two-thirds of the total of 36 changes were reported for the nine trained supervisors. Nearly all the changes occurred in areas bearing on personal and interpersonal behavior. Most surprising is the finding that although a large majority (about 70 per cent) of the changes in *both* groups were seen as enhancing job effectiveness, the effect was more marked among the *untrained* subjects (80 per cent) than among the *trained* subjects (67 per cent).

What may be concluded from results of these five investigations? Primarily, we can say that associates of most persons who have received T-group training report observable changes in their (the trainees') behavior back on the job. Whether or not these reported changes are based on actual changes in job behavior is difficult to know because of many possible sources of contamination and bias common to the studies. For example:

1. Asking the trained subjects to name persons for control group subjects very likely tipped the hand of the investigators. Trained subjects, knowing they were to be compared in some way with their control mates, might alter their behavior accordingly. Moreover, their selection of possible control persons might be biased in the direction of naming persons who had a history of less effective interpersonal behavior, who had shown fewer recent changes in their job behavior, or both. It is impossible to estimate whether or not these biases occurred or what their relative magnitude may have been. Only Miles, by choosing a random control group in addition to a nominated control group, guarded against such biasing components. It is encouraging, therefore, that his results were similar to those reported by the other researchers.

2. Many sources of potential bias are related to the subjects' nomination of observers. First, the original designation would be more likely to include friendly coworkers, who would tend to say "good" rather than unfriendly things. Second, subjects—particularly the trained ones—would have the opportunity to "brief" the observers before they responded to the questionnaires. Third, most observers—especially those from the intraorganizational studies—would be aware of which subjects had been through the T-groups and which had not, and such knowledge could easily result in either conscious or unconscious perceptual distortions of "changes" in subjects' behavior. Finally, since several observers were usually chosen for each subject, they would probably have ample opportunity to talk with one another and compare notes before completing and returning their questionnaires. Only Boyd and Elliss, by personally designating the observers ahead of time and by interviewing them instead of depending on questionnaire responses, probably avoided most of these biases.

3. Judgments about the extent and nature of the behavior changes reported

were undoubtedly subject to biases of interpretation, based as they were on analyses of anecdotal responses to open-ended questions. Miles and Boyd and Elliss asked observers to supplement their subjective descriptions with more objective behavior descriptions (such as the LBDQ, the 80-item checklist used by Boyd and Elliss, etc.). Since no differences between trained and untrained subjects were obtained on the objective instruments, it is difficult to know just what factors contributed most to the differences obtained on the subjective material. The probability is great that a major determinant of the differences may be the various biasing sources we have outlined here.

4. The studies are rendered even more difficult to interpret because all but Underwood relied on retrospective accounts. No observations of job behavior were made before training. Even Underwood used no before measures, but he did ask observers to be alert to and to record instances of behavior change as they occurred rather than relying on their memories and faulty perceptions of possible changes.

5. Finally, even if it is granted that the reported changes do indeed reflect actual changes in trainees' job behavior, we must note that the changes are restricted almost entirely to the domain of greater openness, better understanding, more consideration, and interpersonal warmth. Few, if any, of the reported changes were in the equally important areas of analytical problem-solving attitudes and skills, encouragement of and increased skill in resolving conflict, or decreased self-centeredness and greater self-awareness. Moreover, none of the studies except Underwood's attempted to estimate the possible effects of any observed changes on over-all job effectiveness. Unfortunately, his study yielded results opposite to those we should expect.

Based on these observations, we conclude that the evidence of training-produced changes in job behavior, though present, is severely limited by the two major considerations we have mentioned. First, the many sources of bias constitute competing explanations for the results obtained. Second, none of the studies yields any evidence that the changes in job behavior have any favorable effect on actual performance effectivenss. Thus, there is little to support a claim that T-group or laboratory education effects any substantial behavioral change back on the job for any large proportion of trainees. Whatever change does occur seems quite limited in scope and may not contribute in any important way to changes in over-all job effectiveness.

CHANGES IN ORGANIZATIONAL OUTCOMES

When a "company doctor" undertakes diagnosis and therapy on a "sick" organization, his ultimate aim must certainly be to turn the functioning of that organization around, to do whatever is necessary to get it on the move again, to restore it to efficient operation. Thus, the ultimate practical payoff for any training or personnel development program is not apt to be changes in trainee attitudes, levels of self-awareness, or even job behavior, but instead, the possibility of a "turnaround" in the over-all functioning of the organizational unit. Obviously, this is the broadest, most global level that one may use in undertaking a training evaluation study, and it is rare to find such studies reported. Nonetheless, we have located five (varying *greatly* in quality) which seem to qualify at this level.[18]

The studies by Blansfield and Buchanan are reported so sketchily that they deserve

18. See M. G. Bansfield, Depth analysis of organizational life, *California Management Review*, 1962, 5, 29-42; P. D. Buchanan, *Organizational development following major retrenchment* (mimeographed report, 1964); R. R. Blake, Jane Mouton, L. B. Barnes, L. E. Greiner, Breakthrough in organizational development, *Harvard Business Review*, 1964, 42, 133-155; B. M. Bass, The anarchist movement and the T-group," *Journal of Applied Behavioral Science*, 1967, 3, 211-26; and S. T. White, *Evaluation of an analytic trouble shooting program: A preliminary report* (research memorandum, Kepner-Tregoe and Associates, July 28, 1967), 14 pp.

only brief mention. Both involved lengthy laboratory programs within large organizational units. Blansfield's report is devoted exclusively to an anecdotal account of organizational changes presumably due to and reflecting favorably upon the program. Buchanan's report is centered on descriptive material showing changes toward decentralization in decision-making, greater cooperation among work units, and a substantial increase in organizational profits after the organization experienced widespread personnel retrenchment following the 1957 recession.

Blake, Mouton, Barnes, and Greiner presented the first phases of the Management Grid program to all 800 supervisors and managers of a large organization unit (4,000 employees) of a petroleum corporation.[19] A number of measures were made before and after training, and others only after the program had been completed. The former included organizational outcome indicators such as net profit, controllable operating costs, unit production per employee, and relative success in solving such problems as high maintenance and utility costs, plant safety, and management communication. The information about solving problems was, of course, mostly anecdotal and largely subjective. No comparable organizational unit was used as a control group. During the training program, profits increased substantially and costs decreased. Although a substantial portion of the profit

increase was due to economic and other noncontrollable factors and to manpower reduction, the authors estimate that 13 per cent (amounting to several million dollars) was due to improved operating procedures and higher productivity per man-hour.

What were these improved operating procedures? According to other indexes, they apparently included such things as more meetings, more efficient use of manpower skills as shown by more job transfers and a higher rate of promotion for young line managers (as opposed to highly tenured staff men), greater success in solving cost, safety, and communication problems, and increased use of the 9, 9 management style (as indicated by post-training responses to attitude measures).

It seems apparent from the report that this organizational unit did indeed accomplish a "turnaround" during the time the supervisors were exposed to the Management Grid program. What is far less apparent is the exact cause of the turnaround. Would *any* total push emphasis pointing up organizational problems, emphasizing the need for more cost consciousness, and calling for greater team effort among the 800 supervisors and managers have worked as well? Or was the specific technology of the T-group-like early phases of the grid program specifically responsible for the changes in organizational outcomes? Might the changes in profits not have occurred without any training at all—merely as a consequence of widespread cost emphasis and extensive manpower reductions? Unfortunately, it is impossible to answer these important questions from the data of this particular investigation.

Both Bass and White used control groups to assess effects of training on organizational outcomes. White's study involved training nonmanagerial employees in a real work setting, whereas Bass's study involved training business students and observing how they did in "running" computer-simulated organizations. Unfortunately, White's re-

19. For a thorough description of the Management Grid program, see R. R. Blake and Jane Mouton, *The Management Grid* (Houston: Gulf, 1964). The program involves several stages. Initially a series of T-group-like (but more heavily instrumented) sessions are used to explore peer relationships and the managerial styles of the participants. An important aim is to change individuals' styles in the direction of so-called 9, 9 management, a style giving heavy emphasis to *both* people and production. Over a year's time, other phases explore authority relationships among management levels, provide practice in resolving intergroup conflict, and offer aids to developing more collaborative problem-solving methods.

search was an evaluation of a variant of the Kepner-Tregoe decision-making program and does not, therefore, relate to T-grouping or laboratory education. Still, the study serves as a model of careful research and deserves mention for that reason, if for no other.

The study was conducted on two widely separated production lines—both producing doors—in a large automobile assembly plant. Production measures (readily translatable into dollar costs) were gathered for one month for both lines.[20] During the ensuing three weeks, 31 of the 44 troubleshooters on the experimental line received training in the Kepner-Tregoe Analytic Trouble Shooting program.[21] The 39 troubleshooters on the control line received no training; in fact, they were unaware of the training received by the men on the experimental line. Production measures were gathered again during the month immediately following the training program. Production measures gathered after training were lower (reflecting poorer efficiency) than those gathered before training for *both* lines because preparations were begun during the month for the model change-over. However, the loss in efficiency was negligible for the trained line and substantial for the untrained line.

Bass used the Carnegie Institute of Technology Management Game in an experimental setting to study transfer effects from the T-group setting to a new group.[22] The

Carnegie Tech game is extremely complex, simulating the activities of several firms in a multiproduct industry. Several students make up each firm, and they must interact effectively if the company is to prosper. Nine student T-groups (without trainers) met for 15 weeks. At the end of the 15 weeks, three of the groups were divided into thirds and reformed into three new groups, three were split in half and reassembled, and three remained intact. The nine teams then competed with one another in the game. The splintered groups broke even or made a profit, but the intact groups lost an average of 5.37 million dollars over the 15-week trial period, even though the intact groups gave the most positive descriptions of their openness, communication, and cooperation. On the basis of his observations, Bass attributed the lower performance of the intact groups to a general neglect of the control function. Apparently, the members of the intact groups never bothered to check on each other to see if assignments were being completed.

What may we conclude from these studies about the effect of laboratory education on organizational outcomes? Not much, actually. Of the five studies, three were purely descriptive, offering no experimental evidence about possible organizational effects due to the training technology specific to T-groups or laboratory education. It seems safe to say that concurrent T-group training is at least not incompatible with organizational "turnarounds" in profits and over-all operating efficiency, but this is a far cry from stating that laboratory education is *the* prescription for an organization's ills. Of the two experimental studies, only one utilized T-group training methodology and that in a simulated rather than real organization setting. The best of the lot (White's study) does yield solid, experimental evidence that a particular training approach, tailor-made to accomplish specific behavioral and organizational outcomes, apparently did so successfully. As such, the study may serve the important function of alerting T-group

20. Three measures were used: (1) manned downtime, (2) scrap, and (3) off-standard per cent (an index of production efficiency).
21. The program has two main objectives: to develop ability to anticipate and prevent trouble from occurring and to find and fix trouble more efficiently when it does occur. The program presents no technical knowledge, but teaches a method of production problem analysis. The program used in this experiment was five days long. Half of each day was spent in the classroom with the instructor, and the other half day was spent practicing the analytic method on actual production problems. The emphasis was entirely on increasing analytical skills and *not* on interpersonal or human relations skills.
22. See K. J. Cohen and E. Rhenman, The role of management games in education and research, *Management Science*, 1961, 7, 131-66, for a description of the Carnegie Tech game.

advocates to the old training dictum that the first step in training program development should be a checklist of training needs. Training and development programs might be tailored to accomplish changes in line with such needs, rather than being directed toward the broad and rather amorphous goals (such as increased sensitivity, interpersonal awareness, and social diagnostic skills) usually claimed for their programs by the advocates of laboratory education.

REPRISE, APPRAISAL, AND FORECAST

We have recounted many problems wrought by organizational malaise and reviewed research evidence about individual organizational effects of laboratory education. What may we conclude?

Laboratory education has not been shown to bring about any marked change in one's standing on objective measures of attitudes, values, outlooks, interpersonal perceptions, self-awareness, or interpersonal sensitivity. In spite of these essentially negative results on objective measures, individuals who have been trained by laboratory education methods are more likely to be seen as changing their job behavior than are individuals in similar job settings who have not been trained. These reported changes are in the direction of more openness, better self- and interpersonal understanding, and improved communications and leadership skills.

Unfortunately, these behavior reports suffer from many possible sources of bias and must, therefore, be taken with a grain of salt. Moreover, we have practically no evidence about possible effects of laboratory education on individuals' skills in analyzing problem situations, synthesizing information, facing up to and resolving interpersonal conflict, and deriving and implementing solutions to organizational problems. Most research has been restricted to "demonstrating" the so-called human relations effects of T-groups and has given little attention to other equally important areas in the total process of recognizing, diagnosing, and solving problems in an organizational setting. Finally, we do know (from the large-scale study by Blake, Mouton, Barnes, and Greiner) that laboratory education conducted extensively among supervisors can occur concomitantly with a "turnaround" in an organization's over-all functioning.

Over-all, then we must recognize that certain "truths" of medical diagnosis and treatment apply equally to the diagnosis and treatment of organizational ills. It is easier to describe symptoms than to identify causal agents. It is easier to prescribe broad spectrum treatments than to specify the exact therapeutic effects of any one. And, cures often occur without any clear indication of which therapeutic agent may have been most effective.

We sincerely hope that this review of research evidence will not be viewed as irrevocably damaging to laboratory education. It is true, unfortunately, that few if any individual or organizational behavior outcomes can be specified as due strictly to laboratory education. But this is not unusual. The same can be said for most present training procedures in industry.

Primarily then, our review has brought out weaknesses and gaps in the research related to the effects of laboratory education. We believe that research in the area of interpersonal behavior is too important to suffer a demise based on results from the studies done so far. We hope, therefore, that we have provided impetus for an expanded rather than a diminished emphasis on the behavioral effects of laboratory education.

We need to know the behavioral prescription—according to different individuals and different organizational situations—that may be attached to laboratory education and T-group training. We need to know the causal agents underlying the symptoms of organizational ill health described earlier. We need, in particular, to know not only the effects on interpersonal skills but also the cognitive, analytical, and information-processing effects of laboratory education.

All this must be studied with more sophisticated measures of interpersonal perception and problem-solving procedures, more frequent use of control groups, greater attention to possible interaction effects between measures and training content, application of behavioral observations and reports before as well as after training, and increased care to assure the absence of biasing factors in behavioral observations.

We predict that industrial practice is about to witness a revolution in training and training evaluation research. Excellent research investigations will become the rule rather than the exception. Fifteen years from now, we expect that a review article should be able to outline specific behavioral outcomes to be expected from different learners after exposure to particular training programs in response to carefully diagnosed organizational needs. Manpower development in the firm of the future will be centered on no single method or technique. Instead, industrial education will make flexible use of many approaches—carefully researched, programmed, and sequenced to instill in *all* learners the desired repertoire of knowledges, attitudes, and job and interpersonal skills.

APPENDIX A

Group Training Approaches

Procedures used in laboratory education differ, and no "typical" pattern can accurately describe what goes on in all settings. (For first-hand accounts of actual T-group experiences, see sources listed in footnote 3.) To describe a T-group in very general terms: The focal point is usually a small (10-15 people), unstructured group. There is no agenda, and no activities or topics are planned ahead of time. A professional (called a trainer or educator) is nearly always present, but he rejects a leadership role. Members are to discuss what goes on in the group—behavior, impressions formed, feelings elicited, reasons for these,

and so on. In the language of T-group practitioners, the focus is on the "here-and-now," a focus designed to avoid fruitless discussions of past history and behavioral self-reports not subject to direct examination by the group members. Emphasis on the "here-and-now" is intended to reduce the significance of any status symbols (e.g., company position, level of education, family background, etc.) possessed by the members.

Often, the trainer begins by merely stating that the purpose of the group is to improve each member's understanding of his own and others' behavior. He then falls silent and refuses further guidance. The vacuum is very often filled by feelings of frustration, expressions of hostility, and eventual attempts by some members to impose an organized, usually hierarchical (leaders, committees, etc.), structure on the group. Such attempts to assume leadership roles are usually resented by other members, and they may begin to consider why the self-appointed leader tried to force his will on the group. Such behavior soon generalizes and other members and other behaviors become a basis for discussion so that every participant soon has an opportunity to learn more about his own and others' behavior and its implications for his ability to handle different types of personal interactions successfully.

Two conditions are generally believed to be crucial for behavioral re-education to occur in the group situation. First, an atmosphere of interpersonal support or "psychological safety" must be generated. That is, each member must believe that the group's purpose is productive and good rather than destructive or bad. No matter what a member does or what he reveals about himself, the group must act in a supportive and nonevaluative manner. This atmosphere of support is obviously crucial; otherwise, members will not feel safe in exposing their feelings, dropping their defenses, or trying out new ways of interacting.

Second, for behavioral re-education to occur, articulate and meaningful feedback must take place. Each member must receive information about his impact on others in the group and feedback about the accuracy of the impressions and feelings he derives from the behavior of the others. The role of the trainer is of great importance, for it is up to him more than anyone else to assure that the members develop "here-and-now" behavior patterns of *both* openness and trust. The trainer thus serves mostly as a behavior model. He absorbs initial feelings of hostility and personal attacks without becoming defensive, provides behaviorally oriented rather than personally oriented feedback, expresses his own feelings openly and honestly, and is strongly supportive of similar expressions from other group members.

The T-group focus is used in varying degrees by different managerial laboratory education approaches. For example, in "instrumented" group training, the behavior model for group members is provided by a series of questionnaires requiring them to rate themselves and each other on how supportive they are, how freely they express feelings, and how skillfully they give feedback. These ratings, along with reading assignments, examinations, and other instruments form grist for the mill during the early phases of the widely used Management Grid program (see R. R. Blake and Jane S. Mouton, "The Instrumented Training Laboratory," in I. R. Weschler and E. H. Schein, editors, *Issues in human relations training* [Washington, D.C.: National Training Laboratories, National Education Association, 1962], or Blake and Mouton, *The management grid* [Houston: Gulf, 1964]).

In contrast to these approaches is the widely known and utilized approach advocated by C. H. Kepner and B. B. Tregoe (see their "Developing Decision Makers," *Harvard Business Review*, 1960, 38, 115-24). Their problem-solving training program makes no intended use of T-group methodol-

ogy, but it places heavy emphasis on improving the analytical and information synthesis phases of the problem-solving process. Here, the group members become deeply involved in solving a series of simulated problems involving many aspects of manufacturing, pricing, inventory control, and marketing. The problem-solving sessions (essentially, sophisticated role-playing exercises) are intertwined with reading assignments and lectures emphasizing the importance of problem analysis and hypothetical testing *before* taking action in meeting organizational problems.

APPENDIX B

Measuring Interpersonal Sensitivity

The difficulties involved in measuring the elusive phenomenon called "interpersonal sensitivity" will become apparent to the reader if he considers some of the possible strategies an individual might use to discern accurately what others are feeling. First, a person may have an accurate awareness of the modal feelings of various subgroups in our society (e.g., all women, all college graduates, all engineers, etc.). In other words, he may know what the typical response may be for the majority of persons in a subgroup. His strategy then becomes one of predicting that each member of a subgroup is like the majority of persons in the group; to discern a given person's feelings, he must know what "category" he belongs in and what the feelings of "people-in-general" in that category are. To the extent that he does actually possess accurate subgroup stereotypes, he will, of course, be right more often than he will be wrong. But, he will also be wrong a substantial portion of the time. It is a sad commentary, but it nonetheless is true that interpersonal sensitivity might be greatly enhanced if T-groups did nothing more than help the trainees learn to form *accurate* stereotypes; however, we believe that most

T-group practitioners would be greatly distressed if we charged them with doing only this.

A second strategy, which also yields accurate predictions of others' feelings, is the "assumed similarity" strategy. Here, an effective and accurate interpersonal perceiver might be "sensitive" in the sense that he can accurately identify the subset of persons whose reactions and feelings are similar to his own. Then, simply by studying his own feelings and attributing them to others, he can accomplish the desirable goal of "knowing others" in his environment.

Of course, he also runs grave risks of guessing wrong as he seeks to identify those who are like him. In this case, of course, the successful T-group will be one that manages to make people more similar to one another in their feelings or which successfully teaches people to be able to recognize more accurately those persons who really are similar to them. Here, the T-group would be training people to be more alike and presumably more conforming, a charge which also should engender some degree of distress among T-group practitioners. Most T-groups, we believe, hope that they are training people to overcome stereotyped expectations, tendencies toward projection, and the like; their meta-goal is to train people to get to know each new individual as an individual and to be able to make accurate predictions *for him*.

The major point of this discussion of interpersonal prediction strategies is to emphasize the elusive and complex nature of interpersonal sensitivity. There is no *one* strategy, no *one* "sensitivity"; instead, there seem to be many, varying greatly in the levels of interpersonal sophistication necessary for applying them. The nature of the sensitivities developed may differ greatly from person to person and from program to program. Unless the various components and strategies involved in interpersonal sensitivity are taken into account during the design of measuring instruments and during the design and implementation of research investigations, little new knowledge concerning T-group training effects or the likelihood of transferring skills back to the work setting will accrue. So far (as can be seen from our discussion in the text of this article), most investigators have been ignorant of the serious measurement and design problems inherent in this area.

42

Progressive Levels in the Evaluation of Training Programs

A. C. MAC KINNEY

It is an indication of the scientific orientation of personnel management today that the problem of evaluation is receiving increasing attention. This is evident in many areas of personnel practice but nowhere more conspicuously than in management training, where the evaluation of methods and results is a matter of urgent concern.

But evaluation is only the first step toward· applying the scientific method to personnel problems. In appraising management training, for example, the question is not merely whether training is effective, but *how* we determine whether it is or not: Is the method of evaluation itself valid?

This question has been discussed in a number of recent articles.[1] It is my purpose here to carry the discussion further and to suggest criteria for judging the validity of training evaluations. The point at issue is not the actual content or results of training programs but the validity of the measures used to evaluate them. Once it is recognized that training can be evaluated at different levels, it should be possible to improve our evaluative procedures and to get more accurate information about the effectiveness of training programs.

In speaking of "levels" of evaluation, it is implied that different procedures can be used to evaluate training, that these procedures are variable in quality, and that they can be arranged in a hierarchy from best to worst. It is this hierarchical arrangement that yields the various levels to be referred to here. The justification for making such a distinction is that the quality of the information provided at each level is different, the so-called higher levels giving better evaluative information. I shall advocate in this paper that we raise the level at which training activities are evaluated.

To begin with, let us consider various systems of levels worked out in previous studies.

LEVELS OF EVALUATION

In the Lindbom and Osterberg system,[2] for

1. See for example, T. R. Lindbom and W. Osterberg, Evaluating the results of supervisory training, *Personnel*, November 1954; D. M. Goodacre, The experimental evaluation of management training: Principles and practices, *Personnel*, May 1957; and P. C. Buchanan, Testing the validity of an evaluation program, November/December, 1957.

2. Lindbom and Osterberg, *op. cit.*

example, levels are classified according to the kinds of behavior being evaluated: (1) the trainee's classroom behavior, (2) the trainee's on-the-job behavior, and (3) his subordinates on-the-job behavior. This classification seems to be a hierarchy of levels, though it is not explicitly called such by its authors. No. 1 is low, for example, and No. 3 is high; that is, the on-the-job behavior of the trainee's subordinates gives much better information than the trainee's classroom behavior. I think that most people who are involved in personnel research would have little quarrel with this opinion.

It is important to note, however, that this method is merely one way of classifying levels of training evaluation. Another possibility is the use of the two-point scale of objective *versus* subjective, the objective evaluation being regarded as separate from the interpretations, biases, and feelings of the person doing the evaluation, and the subjective as reflecting these various elements.

Or we can talk about formal *versus* informal evaluation as another major classification. In formal evaluation, there is a specific plan by which the training is evaluated; informal evaluation is casual, based perhaps on comment or conversation. It is evident that the objective and formal levels are very much alike, as are the subjective and informal levels.

These two simplified classifications of levels of evaluation may be meaningfully contrasted with the classification system discussed by Goodacre.[3] This is based upon a three-unit scale. At the lowest level, training is evaluated in terms of the attitudes of trainees as measured by an attitude scale. The assumption is that effective training should be reflected in more favorable trainee attitudes. At the second level, evaluation is made in terms of the knowledge acquired by the trainees. Effective training should impart skills or knowledge, and these can be

3. Goodacre, *op. cit.*

measured by achievement tests. The highest level, according to Goodacre, is actual job performance. Effective training should increase the trainee's job proficiency. This level can best be reached, he suggests, through the rating of job performance by the trainee's immediate superior. Here, then, is a considerably more complex system of levels of evaluation.

At this point, let me introduce an alternative classification which is related primarily to the design of the evaluation used. In brief, this means that there are various ways of designing the evaluation procedure and that these determine the quality of the information we get.

At the top of our hypothetical scale is the *controlled* experimental study. This is a design in which two groups are used, the one to receive training, and the other to act as a control group. The procedure is as follows: (1) A "before" proficiency measure is taken for both groups; (2) one group is trained while the other is left on the job; (3) an "after" proficiency measure is taken for both groups; (4) the "before" is subtracted from the "after" for both groups to measure the gain in proficiency. If the training did any good, the trained group should have gained significantly more in job proficiency than the untrained group.

THE CONTROLLED EXPERIMENTAL STUDY

It may be asked why a control group is necessary. This can be answered by pointing out that certain changes may take place in an employee's job proficiency simply as a result of remaining on the job and that such changes have to be taken into account in any experimental evaluation of a training program. If it should turn out that the group remaining on the job gained as much in job proficiency or more than the group that was trained, there would be no justification for the additional expense of the training program. Odd as it may seem, it is not all uncommon for the control group to gain as much as the trained group in job proficiency.

The controlled experimental study uses acceptable criteria of performance. A criterion is a measure of proficiency on the job. An *acceptable* criterion is one that meets the various standards set up for the evaluation of criterion measures.[4] Most people in personnel research would agree, I believe, that the most difficult problem in this field is that of finding acceptable criteria. We shall return to this question later in this article.

In addition, the controlled experimental study utilizes acceptable statistical methods to aid in the interpretation of the results of the evaluation. Since certain changes can take place in job performance as a result of chance alone, statistical procedures are necessary to determine whether or not the changes observed after training might reasonably be considered as other than chance effects.

There is a further consideration in this experimental design. We need some sort of assurance that the changes taking place in the trained group are not merely a result of the amount of attention the trainees receive. As the studies at Western Electric showed, changes in productivity may occur not only as a result of changed working conditions but also in consequence of the amount of attention given to the workers. To eliminate this factor, the control group should receive, so far as is possible, as much attention (exclusive of training) as the trained group.

It is important to note that there is a sizable range within the level of the controlled experimental study because the criteria used for evaluation can actually vary in quality and still be acceptable. This point will be discussed later in considering levels of training evaluation as related to the relevance of the criterion.

LOWER LEVELS OF EVALUATION

At the second level in this classification system is the evaluation of training by means of the trained group only. This is not an acceptable experimental design. It must be admitted, however, that this type of evaluation is widely used and is perhaps better than no evaluation at all, assuming that adequate criterion measures and analysis procedures are employed. The evaluation design is a simple one. "Before" and "after" measures are compared and any gain is attributed to the training.[5] Statistics are used to test the significance of the gain from zero.

At the lowest level, we have the evaluation of the trained group only, as above, with the criterion measure taken *after* training, but not before. In this procedure, no statistical analysis is possible and the interpretation of the end result is simply a matter of intuitive judgment. All that can be done is to look at the information gathered after training and make some sort of guess as to whether it is "good enough." Obviously, this is an extremely weak method.

Of these two latter evaluation procedures, neither can be recommended. *In terms of experimental design considerations, the only way to evaluate training properly is by the controlled experimental study.* It is my urgent recommendation that training people should not waste their time and the company's money on anything short of a controlled study utilizing acceptable criteria. Even if such a study requires outside assistance, it is the only way of doing the kind of job that needs to be done.[6]

5. This may not be valid, as noted earlier.
6. Selecting a consultant to provide the help needed is not so simple as it sounds. Many of them, though thoroughly honest and reputable, operate with a single theoretical bias that renders them helpless when faced with a problem requiring some experimental work. There is no single pat answer to all personnel problems. Each problem is unique and requires a unique answer that is ground out experimentally. Beware of the consultant who has *the* system!

4. See, for example, R. L. Thorndike, *Personnel selection* (New York: Wiley, 1949). The whole of chapter 5 is excellent, especially pages 124-32.

THE RELEVANCE OF CRITERIA

We noted earlier that the criterion is a measure of proficiency on the job, a measure that tells us whether the performance of an individual or group is effective. In this section, we shall discuss levels of evaluation as they are influenced by the relevance of the criteria used in evaluating training.[7] "Relevance" is roughly equivalent to quality. A relevant criterion is a good criterion, one that accurately reflects the contribution of the group or individual to the organization and does not contain any extraneous factors.

The system of levels based on criteria, like that based on experimental design, represents a hierarchy. The criteria system can be thought of as being superimposed on the design system. In other words, a highly relevant criterion may appear in a good experimental design or in a poor experimental design. A good design usually has good criteria, but a less relevant criterion may accompany a good design simply because there is no other criterion that might reasonably serve. Hence both extremes of the experimental design system can be used at any level of the criterion system.

The highest level in this system comes about with the use of *objective performance scores* as criteria. Such measures are generally the most relevant ones we can use. The best objective performance score would be a measure of output automatically recorded by machine. Also acceptable are measures of scrap, defects, material or tool usage, manpower cost, etc. It is obvious that there is considerable variability within this level inasmuch as a direct measure of output is better than a less direct measure such as tool control.

Objective performance scores may be determined either for the trainee himself or for his subordinates. It is generally considered to be stronger evidence of the effectiveness of a training program if it is followed by improved performance not only on the part of the trainee but of his subordinates as well. In addition, if the trainee is in a supervisory capacity, evaluation may have to be based upon the performance of his subordinates for the simple reason that no objective criteria are available for supervisory personnel.

There are several dangers in the use of objective performance scores, however. Perhaps the most important of these is bias in the measure, that is, the influence to some unknown degree of factors other than the trainee's contribution to the organization.[8] Some bias in the measure is probably inevitable. Consider, for example, the interdependence of defects, particularly in an integrated assembly-line operation. What one man does early in the process may affect what another man does later on down the line. If defects are used as the criterion, the second man is being evaluated in part by the first man's performance. This is only one of many examples of bias in objective performance scores.

SUBJECTIVE ESTIMATES OF PERFORMANCE

The second level in this system is provided by subjective judgments or estimates of job performance. Here we are not talking about trait rating[9] but about the trainee's actual on-the-job behavior.[10] Trait ratings would

---

7. For a full discussion of this question, see Thorndike, *op. cit.*, pp. 125-27.

8. For a full discussion of this point, see Thorndike, *op. cit.*, pp. 130-31.
9. Traits are inferred personal characteristics presumably existing within the individual and hence very well hidden. They have no objective reality of their own but are inferred from certain observable behaviors. "Motivation," "morale," and "maturity" are three common examples. As a general rule, it is wise to avoid rating such abstractions.
10. Performance estimates may be made by anyone familiar with the trainee's job performance—subordinates, peers, or, most commonly, the supervisor.

be on some other level in this system and will not be treated here.

With subjective performance estimates, as with objective performance scores, there is considerable variability. The effectiveness of a man's performance can be judged by a formalized procedure or by casual comment. The latter extreme is characterized by "Joe's a good man." The former is represented by a well-constructed appraisal program.[11] Subjective performance estimates, like objective scores, may refer either to the trainee or to his subordinates.

The third level comprises evaluations of the trainee's knowledge and understanding of the content of the training course. Obviously such evaluation can be made only of trainees themselves, not of their subordinates, for example. The procedure is to use some kind of achievement measure similar to those in college courses to find out how much the trainee has learned as a result of his exposure to training. As most of us know from our own academic experience, achievement measures are variable in quality. A good test is not easy to construct; certainly it cannot be thrown together as an after-thought but requires considerable study and revision.

At the final level in our system, the criteria are opinions and attitudes. Here again there is a hierarchy within the level: opinions of the training course may come from the trainee's subordinates, from the supervisor, from the trainee, or from the trainer himself. The last source is the least dependable, of course, since it is only natural for the trainer to be favorably impressed with his own work.

Though opinions and attitudes may appear to be similar to performance judgments as criteria for evaluating training, they are in fact quite different. Performance estimates refer to actual changes in job performance that come about as a result of exposure to a training program, whereas opinions refer to the quality of the training program.

Attitudes and opinions may represent sound and thoughtful evaluations or casual snap judgments. In fact, they can be very effective criteria if used together with a well-constructed attitude scale and a controlled experimental study. Certainly this combination would rate a higher place in our hierarchy of levels.

COMPROMISE MAY BE NECESSARY

The purpose of this paper is to point out that training may be evaluated on different levels and that the quality of the evaluation is better at the higher of these levels. It recognizes, however, that, as those familiar with applied research in industry know, compromise procedures are often necessary and in such instances, all that can be expected is the closest possible approximation to the best study design.

---

11. A great deal of the confusion about appraisal would not exist if we were more careful to differentiate between *program, method,* and *form.* The *program* is the total appraisal effort including method, form, control, development, follow-up, and so on. The *method* is the system used to make the judgments such as forced choice, rank order, and so on. The *form* is just a piece of paper to write the judgments on. Too many people, I fear, think the piece of paper is the whole program. It isn't.

43

At Emery Air Freight:
Positive Reinforcement Boosts Performance

At Emery these days, P.R. stands for *positive reinforcement,* not public relations, and the payoffs from applying Skinner's ideas to the motivation of employees exceed the wildest claims ever made by public relations practitioners for the results of their art. One example: Small shipments intended for the same destination fly at lower rates when shipped together in containers rather than separately. By encouraging employees to increase their use of containers (from 45 per cent to 95 per cent of all possible shipments), Emery has realized an annual saving of $650,000.

"With savings this large we can't afford to worry about charges that we're manipulating our employees," says Edward J. Feeney, Vice-President—System Performance, the man primarily responsible for introducing P.R. at Emery. Continues Feeney:

Actually, the charge that you're manipulating people when you use positive reinforcement—I prefer myself to say that you're shaping their behavior—is a hollow one to start with. People in business manipulate their employees all the time—otherwise they would go bankrupt. The only

questions are, How effective are you as a manipulator and what ends do you further with your manipulation? Our end is improved performance, and we've been damned effective in getting it.

Feeney emphasizes that his approach and that of Emery's management generally is pragmatic, not doctrinaire. They're sold on the merits of Skinner's ideas, not because of their internal logic or the eloquence with which they are frequently proposed, but because so far at least they have paid off handsomely in each area Emery has seen fit to apply them.

IMPORTANCE OF PERFORMANCE AUDIT

Emery has been selective in its application of P.R.; it's a powerful tool that should be employed where it's most needed and where the potential for improvement is the greatest. These are things that Feeney feels strongly can't be left to intuition or guess-work—hence the necessity for a performance audit before you institute P.R. in a given area. Emery doesn't want to be in the

Reprinted by permission of the publisher from *Organizational Dynamics,* Winter 1973. © 1973 by AMACOM, a division of American Management Association.

position of the corporation that targeted tardiness reduction as the object of a major effort. Before the drive, tardiness averaged 1/2 of 1 per cent; after the drive, 1/4 of 1 per cent. Big deal! Emery has a different magnitude of payoff in mind.

Take the example of container utilization that we mentioned. Executives at Emery were convinced that containers were being used about 90 per cent of the times they could be used. Measurement of the actual usage—a measurement made by the same managers whose guesses had averaged 90 per cent—showed that the actual figure was 45 per cent, or half the estimate. Feeney saw no reason, given the proper motivational climate, why employees couldn't consistently meet a standard of 95 per cent and save Emery $650,000 annually—which, of course, subsequently happened.

The performance audit fulfills two primary purposes. First, it indicates the areas in which the biggest potential profit payoffs exist—the areas in which Emery should focus its attention; second, it convinces previously skeptical managers on quantitative grounds that no words can contravene that there is need for substantial improvement.

The performance audit would be justified for the second effect alone—convincing managers that improvement is needed and persuading them to cooperate with a program designed to bring about the improvement. "Most managers genuinely think that operations in their bailiwick are doing well; a performance audit that proves they're not comes as a real and unpleasant surprise," says Feeney.

We also suspect that an unpleasant surprise of some magnitude is necessary to secure the cooperation of a goodly number of managers in implementing a program that, with its concentration on praise and recognition as motivators and the elimination of censure, runs contrary to the beliefs and practices of a working lifetime.

On the other hand, Feeney emphasizes the importance of cushioning the blow if you want to enlist their cooperation. "We structure the performance audit so that the managers are heroes for making the audits, and we reassure them that irrespective of the current level, they will look good if they can improve."

What about the performance standards set as a part of each performance audit? How are they set? What do they signify? Sometimes, as in the case of the customer service department with its goal of customer call-backs within 90 minutes of the initial telephone query, the department had set the goal in advance of the audit study. On study, it appeared reasonable and it was left unchanged. Sometimes there is no standard, and one has to be set on the basis of observation and common sense.

The latter usually indicates the impracticality of setting perfection or 100 per cent performance as your standard. For example, the ideal in answering phone calls from customers would be for the customer never to get a busy signal that might lead him to call one of Emery's competitors. The problem is that studies have shown that in any given hour, five minutes, although not the same five minutes, is always going to account for 35 per cent of the calls during the hour. Hence, it's much too costly to staff a switchboard with the number of operators necessary to prevent busy signals during those peak five minutes.

Emery has experimented, with a measure of success, with having employees set the standards for their own jobs. It was done in the customer service office in Chicago. The employees set a higher standard: not just giving customers a progress report within 90 minutes, but having *all* the requested answers to customer queries within that time— and they have presently reached this standard, although they fall short of the 90 to 95 per cent achieved on progress reports. The problem, as Feeney sees it, is in giving the employees all the data they need to hit on a reasonable standard—a very time-consuming process. Otherwise, employee-set standards either will be unrealistically high or unacceptably low. Either way, both the company and the employee lose out.

The standard that is too low deprives the employee of self-satisfaction, and the company of work that it is paying for; the standard that is too high, achievable only once in a while by virtue of extraordinary effort or luck, will leave the employee frustrated and embittered. Sooner or later—and it's usually sooner—his performance will revert to a lower level than before he participated in setting the unattainable standard.

PROVIDING PRAISE AND RECOGNITION—AVOIDING CENSURE

In those areas in which Emery uses P.R. as a motivational tool, nothing is left to chance. Each manager receives two elaborate programmed instruction workbooks prepared in-house and geared to the specific work situation at Emery. One deals with recognition and rewards, the other with feedback. Under recognition and rewards, the workbook enumerates no less than 150 kinds, ranging from a smile and a nod of encouragement, to "Let me buy you a coffee," to detailed praise for a job well done.

Of all forms of praise, the most effective, according to Feeney, is praise for the job well done—expressed in quantitative terms. Not "Keep up the fair work, Murray," as shown on TV, or even "Great going, Joe—keep it up," but "Joe, I liked the ingenuity you showed just now getting those crates into that container. You're running pretty consistently at 98 per cent of standard. And after watching you, I can understand why."

In bestowing praise and recognition, Emery follows Skinner pretty closely. There is the same emphasis on reinforcing specific behavior; the same insistence that the behavior be reinforced as soon as possible after it has taken place; the same assertion that you reinforce frequently in the beginning to shape the desired behavior, but that as time

goes on, maintaining the desired behavior requires progressively less frequent and unpredictable reinforcement. As Skinner wrote, in reference to Emery's application of his ideas, "You don't need to maintain a system of contrived reinforcers indefinitely. People get the impression that I believe we should all get gumdrops whenever we do anything of value. There are many ways of attenuating a system of reinforcement. . . . But the main thing is to let non-contrived reinforcers take over."

At the gumdrop stage of P.R., Feeney urges supervisors to supply praise and recognition at least twice a week during the early weeks or months of behavior shaping. It's impractical to require them to provide P.R. more frequently—they are too busy, they would forget, etc. Once the desired behavior has been established, managers have more discretion—the key point being the unpredictability of the reinforcement, not the frequency. Keep P.R. coming on a descending scale of frequency—but keep the employee guessing as to when or whether he's going to be praised or recognized.

At least in the early days of shaping behavior, it's difficult to determine which deserves the most credit for the improvement in performance—providing praise and recognition or withholding censure and criticism. Particularly in these cases where the manager seldom praised before—even when he had good reason—the switchover from censure to praise produces instant, almost miraculous results. Performance improves dramatically, and along with it, employee morale and superior-subordinate relations.

What do you do with the employee when praise, recognition, and feedback don't work? Do you contrive to refrain from criticizing his or her work? At what point do you throw in the sponge?

Feeney's general answer was that P.R. worked with nine employees out of ten. On those occasions where it appeared not to be working, investigation usually revealed that below-standard performance was not the employee's fault—factors such as the wrong tools or work overload were responsible. And once they were corrected, the employee responded as positively to praise and recognition as anyone else. He cited several instances, not among the rank-and-file, where a custom-tailored program of P.R. salvaged men who were 30 days short of being fired.

Even with the below-par employee, the manager takes the positive note. He would probably ignore a day or a week in which no improvement took place, preferring to wait for a period of even slight improvement—say, from 70 to 75 per cent. Then he might follow-up his praise of the improvement by asking the man what he thought could be done to improve further. Everything he said from there on would be an attempt to solve the problem and provide the manager with additional opportunities for reinforcement.

All in all, we got the impression of a program that failed, on the few occasions when it did, not because of employee resistance, but because of supervisory intransigence—the boss was unable or unwilling to apply it, especially with the so-called problem employee—and a few supervisors have left Emery in consequence.

Feedback is easier to institutionalize than praise and rewards. A written report is a tangible artifact that you can see. But even with feedback you have occasional lapses, Feeney cautions, in any areas where it isn't mandatory. Some managers loathe paperwork; others are too busy to extend the measure of praise and recognition indicated by the feedback or they don't recognize behavior that deserves positive reinforcement. "The biggest problem with the program occurs," adds Feeney "when managers stop asking for feedback and stop offering recognition and rewards because there's been no recognition of their efforts from above—their boss hasn't asked, 'Why didn't I see your performance report?' or extended any reward or recognition himself.

In other words, the program breaks down whenever there are no consequences and no positive reinforcement for the manager who is supposed to implement it."

BEYOND GUMDROPS—CONTINUOUS FEEDBACK

Skinner talks about the necessity of letting the noncontrived reinforcers take over in any program of P.R.—which, in our view, explains the crucial importance at Emery, and probably in any industrial setting, of continuous feedback. Emery, in each area where it has utilized P.R., has required each employee to keep a record himself of what he or she has accomplished each and every day. In customer service, for example, each representative ticked off daily on a sheet how long it had taken to reply to each call. It took no special skill to compare this with the standard of 90 minutes. Similar sheets, all relatively simple and all recorded by the employees themselves, were instituted in all departments covered by P.R.

Noncontrived reinforcers they were not. Emery provided the sheets, gave no option on filling them out, and defined the terms and frequency. But we think this is an example of a contrived reinforcer laying the essential groundwork—providing the time framework for noncontrived reinforcers to mature and take over. Let's postulate three basic stages of development: (1) A period in which frequent P.R. by the supervisor plus continuous feedback leads to rapid progress towards the desired behavior; (2) a period in which infrequent P.R. by the boss is accompanied by continuous feedback—itself, of course, a species of P.R.; (3) a period in which the supervisor is only a very occasional source of P.R., and feedback is overwhelmingly the principal source of contrived reinforcement.

Feeney emphasizes the effect of feedback on improved performance. "We found that when we provided daily feedback only one week out of four or one out of five, performance in the periods without feed-back reverted to the previous level or was almost as bad." There's no question that feedback is the critical variable in explaining the success of the program, he adds.

What is continuous feedback, and what is its relation to Skinner's requirement that, in any program of P.R., "The main thing is to let noncontrived reinforcers take over"? The noncontrived reinforcer clearly is the con-viction on the employee's part that they are doing a good job, a fair day's work. But how are they to know? Part of the answer is observable—they've been busy, the cus-tomers have seemed satisfied, maybe the boss has extended P.R. More conclusive, if they're in doubt, they can look at the sheets and see at a glance exactly how they stand in reference to the standard. In other words, the internal or natural reinforcer—the con-viction and satisfaction of a job well done—is corroborated and itself powerfully rein-forced by the evidence of a sheet on which the work accomplished is compared daily with the standard for the job.

Feeney tells a story that illustrates both the necessity for continuous feedback and the way in which previous consequences determine present behavior. Emery requires any employee who receives a package dam-aged during shipment from an airline to fill out a fairly time-consuming form. At a certain installation, he pointed out to the boss that without feedback and P.R. the employees wouldn't bother—the rein-forcements they got from filling out the form were all negative. The paperwork was time-consuming and boring, they were likely to get some flack from airline representatives who would in their own good time find ways of hitting back, they were taking time from their number one priority—getting the ship-ment delivered on time.

A check revealed that no damage forms were turned in. However, a physical check of cartons received showed several damaged, one with a hole punched in the side, another that looked as if a hand had reached into the top and taken something out, etc. Feeney feels that his colleague, at this point, got the message. The only way around the problem of getting the damage slips filled out was to (1) specify the desired behavior—i.e., set the standard; (2) require the employee to pro-vide continuous feedback—keep daily re-cords on how many cartons were damaged and submit them to his supervisor; and (3) whenever feasible, positively reinforce the behavior—when the feedback showed that it was justified.

MONEY AND POSITIVE REINFORCEMENT

Skinner includes money in his list of positive reinforcers, as long as it is linked to specific behavior. The weekly paycheck doesn't posi-tively reinforce; it's a negative reinforcer. You work to avoid the loss of the standard of living supported by the paycheck. On the other hand, piece-rate payments geared to specific on-the-job behavior are positive rein-forcers; so are commissions paid to salesmen. Just as effective, Skinner argues, would be to take a leaf from gambling and introduce a lottery into industry, with each employee getting a weekly lottery ticket that might pay off in a weekly drawing. Here it's paying off unpredictably but in the long run on a determined schedule that provides the posi-tive reinforcement.

Emery does not use money as a positive reinforcer. Several reasons seem to underly the choice. First, Emery has no employees on incentive payments, not even salesmen; there is therefore no built-in necessity to link dollar payments to improved perfor-mance. Second, management holds the be-lief that performing up to standard is what it has a right to expect from each employee in return for his paycheck. The savings achieved through the program have helped to make it possible for Emery to pay as much as or more than its competitors, and offer equal or bigger benefits—facts not lost on its employees. Finally, Emery's experience suggests that praise and recognition, especially self-recognition through feedback, are enough. In some areas, employees have consistently performed up to standard for more than three years. The savings for Emery in consequence have been substantial, despite the omission of money as a positive reinforcer.

At first blush this seems surprising. Interestingly, AT&T had a similar experience with a job-enrichment program that also substantially increased employee productivity and performance. In an AT&T experiment with 120 women answering stockholder inquiries, various measures were taken to give employees more responsibility and control over their jobs. The response was uniformly positive, with one exception—a girl who quit because she wasn't getting more money for a more responsible job. She felt that she was worth more to the company and should be paid more. That only one employee out of 120 expected to get paid more as the consequence of a program that improved the value of their services calls for a little explaining. So does the continuing success of P.R. at Emery.

There are several possible explanations. People know a good thing when they see it. The programs at both AT&T and Emery have improved the intrinsic nature of the job as seen by the employees themselves—that's sufficient reward.

Also, many studies have shown that employees have a crude but keen sense of distributive justice on the job. They may do less than what they themselves consider a fair day's work for a large number of reasons, even though they frequently feel guilty about it. On the other hand, they resent and resist any attempt to exact more than their perception of a fair day's work in return for what they are paid. Improve the job—in Emery's case, provide via praise, recognition, and continuous feedback the evidence of a job well done—and eventually you will develop what Skinner would call the natural reinforcer of job satisfaction.

This, in turn, guarantees that the employee will want to live up to his own standard of a fair day's work.

In other words, part of the success of P.R. at Emery is that the standards set for employees were seen by them as reasonable to begin with. The missing element was any positive incentive to reach them. The weekly paycheck was ineffective—Skinner is correct—it took praise, recognition, and feedback to do the job. Similarly, at AT&T, job enlargement and job enrichment provided the incentives to improved performance that hitherto were lacking.

A story that Feeney tells illuminates the problem. A Harvard Business School student on a summer assignment with Emery was helping with a performance audit on one of the loading docks. In the process he managed to gain the confidence of a union steward, who told him in so many words that any problems Emery had with the workers were not due to money—they were well paid. The one thing they weren't getting paid was attention. Many of them worked at night with a minimum of supervision and recognition. A situation in which employees feel fairly paid in relation to the work expected of them but in which money is almost the sole recognition received is ripe for improvement via positive reinforcement.

PROOF OF THE PUDDING

At present, P.R. is fully operative in three areas at Emery—in sales and sales training, operations, and containerized shipments. The benefits in all three are impressive, and they have been sustained for periods of from three to four years. We can forget about the Hawthorne effect in explaining the success of P.R. at Emery.

In sales training, each salesman completes a programmed instruction course on his own, with plenty of feedback structured into the course to let him know how he is doing. In addition, sales managers apply P.R. in their day-to-day relations with salesmen, and sales reports provide the indispensable feedback. Sales have gained at a more rapid rate since P.R. entered the sales picture, and Feeney feels that it deserves some of the credit for the increased rate.

The relationship between P.R. and improved customer service, part of operations, is undeniable. Before P.R., standards were met only 30 to 40 per cent of the time; after P.R., the figure was 90 to 95 per cent. Most impressive is the rapidity of the improvement and its staying power. In the first test office, for example, performance skyrocketed from 30 per cent of standard to 95 per cent in a single day. Staying power? After almost four years, performance in the vast majority of Emery customer service offices still averages 90 to 95 per cent.

In containerized shipping operations the story is the same. With P.R., container use jumped from 45 per cent to 95 per cent —with the increase in 70 per cent of the offices coming in a single day.

There were a few cases in which feedback was temporarily interrupted because of managerial changes and other reasons. Whenever this occurred, performance slumped quickly by more than 50 per cent, only to return rapidly to the 95 per cent level once the feedback was resumed.

All in all, Emery has saved over $3 million in the past three years. No doubt about it: positive reinforcement pays.

On the basis of this kind of success, Emery has big plans to expand the use of P.R. It's already been extended to over-all dock operations. Emery's route drivers are covered and measured on items such as stops per hour and sometimes on shipments brought back versus shipments dispatched. Eventually P.R. will be introduced wherever it's possible to measure work and set quantifiable standards. Feeney and his group will set their priorities, of course, on the basis of what performance audits tell them about the potential for improvement and savings.

When you have scored the kind of success that Emery has you're not quick to in-

novate. However, thought is being given to the introduction in certain areas of different rewards and schedules, including having the computer acknowledge behavior and even using some kind of financial reward as a positive reinforcer.

WHAT DOES EMERY PROVE?

More precisely, what does Emery prove about the feasibility of behavior modification through positive reinforcement? The question must be asked and answered at several levels. At the first and most apparent level, the answer is easy: In those areas in which Emery has used P.R., behavior modification has been instant, dramatic, sustained, and uniformly in the desired direction. There also seems little doubt that P.R. deserves most of the credit for the dramatic improvement in performance.

A few qualifiers are in order. Positive reinforcement so far has been used selectively at Emery in areas where work could be measured and quantifiable standards set if they didn't already exist, and areas where observation showed that the existing level of performance was far below the standard. This last point applies equally to the customer-service representatives and the dock loaders, but is less true for the salesmen—their performance was lower than Emery felt it should be, but not in the same category as the other two employee groups.

Also Emery has yet to arrive at the point where the natural reinforcers—in this case an internally generated sense of job satisfaction—have taken over. After three to four years of P.R., praise and recognition from the boss is applied infrequently and unpredictably, but the other contrived reinforcer, continuous feedback, is still administered daily. In fact, Emery's past experience has been that whenever it stopped providing continuous feedback, performance rapidly reverted to the previous low levels. On the other hand, this experience occurred during the early days of supplying positive reinforcement. Perhaps now Emery could stop providing continuous feedback and maintain the current high levels of performance. We can only guess.

At another level we have to take into account the context in which P.R. has been used at Emery. We have to consider whether or not special conditions exist at Emery that favor the successful application of positive reinforcement. How far are we justified in claiming that what has worked at Emery will work equally well in a different organization with a different product, a different climate, and different problems?

On the basis of the available evidence, we can't go overboard in generalizing from Emery's undeniable success in applying positive reinforcement to solve its performance problems. That Emery has no incentive programs and is therefore spared the complexity and the conflict habitually generated in manufacturing situations where standards, performance, and earning are inextricably linked; that Emery has so far restricted P.R. to areas in which it has been possible to positively reinforce one employee without producing adverse consequences for any other employee; and that Emery, during the period it has applied P.R., has been a rapid growth organization, able to offer far more than the usual opportunities for growth and promotion, are factors that provide a partial measure of the conditions, by no means common in organizations, that have fostered an atmosphere conducive to the application of positive reinforcement.

The second condition we mentioned is something Emery has worked at. Feeney emphasized that Emery was careful not to set individuals or groups competing against each other to see which came closest to meeting the standard. Instead, managers were coached to urge employees to think in terms of what they were doing now compared to what they had done in the past. Comments Feeney, "If you set individuals or teams competing against each other, there's only room for one first—but lots of losers. If

you want to know the effect of this kind of competition on performance, all you need is to look at what happens at the end of the baseball season to the performance of the team that's 32 games behind."

Whether the conditions we have described are indispensable to the successful application of P.R. or merely helpful we have no way of determining. The problem is lack of evidence. Emery is the only company to date to have applied P.R. on a fairly broad scale over a fairly long period of time. Even with Emery, neither this report nor a previous article in *Business Week* (December 28, 1971) can claim to be the kind of objective in-depth study that's called for. A few other organizations—among them Cole National in Cleveland, Michigan Bell Telephone, and Ford Motor Co.—are in the early stages of experimenting with positive reinforcement, and more organizations are giving serious thought to using positive reinforcement. More than two hundred have contacted Feeney since Emery's work with P.R. received public recognition.

Will positive reinforcement work? Feeney believes that the question has already been answered with a resounding affirmative. He cites upwards of a thousand case studies involving mental patients, deliquent children, and problem pupils in which P.R. resulted in dramatic improvement in behavior. The only questions remaining, as he sees it, are questions of methodology and application.

Of course, none of these episodes took place in an industrial setting. Until we have a lot more evidence—both from Emery and from other sources—any conclusions about the use of P.R. in industry have to be tentative.

One last level of consideration. Positive reinforcement as the answer to organizational problems of productivity and performance has a plethora of rivals. A generation of theorists and practitioners has systematically overturned stones in the search for a formula or method for converting low-producing groups or individuals into high-producing ones. A partial enumeration would include job enrichment and job enlargement, organization development in all its varied guises, Theory Y, participative management, team development, the Scanlon Plan, autonomous leadership. We could go on—but we won't. How does P.R. stack up against these other—and—we think—competing approaches to improving productivity and performance?

At this point it's impossible to give a conclusive answer. We have seen the problems with the evidence on the results of positive reinforcement. Similar problems exist with the results of every other technique for improving productivity and performance. There's little objective evidence available, and what evidence there is abounds in caveats—the technique will work under the proper circumstances, the parameters of which are usually not easily apparent.

Take the entire field of organization development. An exhaustive search of the literature on the subject by Professor George Strauss of the University of California Business School at Berkeley turned up exactly three research studies worthy of the name. What did they prove? That under the proper circumstances OD can increase productivity, though perhaps not as much as conventional techniques such as purchasing new equipment, job simplication, and "weeding out" inefficient operators. So far, the search for a sure-fire all-purpose formula for turning low-producing groups into high-producing ones appears to be almost as elusive as the search for the philosopher's stone that would turn everything it touched into gold.

Which leads us to what conclusion as to the merits of positive reinforcement relative to its rivals? With the customary caveats, we feel that P.R. has much to recommend it. As an approach, it deserves more recognition and application than it has hitherto received. It suffers from its sponsorship: positive reinforcement has a bad name with businessmen and with the general public because of its association with Skinner, his alleged totalitarian leanings, his denial of free will, and the inescapable fact that his theory of human behavior is rooted in his experiments with pigeons. People instinctively resent a theory that seems to suggest that they're not much brighter than pigeons and can be controlled in similar ways.

We understand the problem, but it's unfortunate that it has prevented the more extensive application of positive reinforcement. On the basis of what little we can observe, P.R. is easier, less complex, and less expensive to introduce than most of its rivals, while the results are at least as impressive as those achieved by any of them.

Feeney is probably correct: a lot of managers practice positive reinforcement without knowing it. He cites, for example, Vince Lombardi, who provided endless feedback on performance to his players and who after a really bad defeat never uttered a word of criticism in the locker room. True, but until more organizations consciously and systematically apply positive reinforcement, it will never get the recognition that it appears to deserve.

44

Improving Attendance Through Rewards

WALTER NORD

The operation of all organizations and other social systems depends on the fact that a wide range of human behavior occurs more frequently if it is rewarded and less frequently if it is not rewarded. For example, a major problem in a "welfare state" is that people are rewarded even if they do not perform socially desired behavior. In such a "state," the undesired but rewarded behaviors occur more often than if they were not rewarded. Furthermore, the desired behaviors are apt to occur less often since there is now a competing path to rewards.

REWARDING GOAL-ORIENTED BEHAVIOR

Managers are quick to recognize the problems created by rewarding the undesired behaviors in the context of society, but fail to see the same problems in their organization's compensation and benefit programs. The problem with many current compensation and fringe benefit programs in organizations is clear. Rewards are often given for behaviors which do not lead to the realization of organization goals. Furthermore, behavior which leads to these goals is often left without reward. This paper attempts to show how reward systems may be modified to increase the rate of one type of behavior, work attendance, which is necessary to realize organizational goals.

The work of B. F. Skinner[1] and his followers is the basis for the "teaching machine" and programmed learning. However, the basic ideas of the Skinnerian approach emphasize that people will be most likely to engage in desired behavior if they are rewarded for doing so. The rewards are more effective if they immediately follow the desired response. Behavior which is not rewarded or is punished is less likely to be repeated. However, punishment is known to have many undesired effects and is often a less efficient means to develop desired behavior.

One further point about behavioral engineering must be made. It is possible to reward a person every time he behaves in a certain way. It is also possible to give the rewards only after some of the responses, much like a slot machine does. The evidence

1. Skinner, B. F. *Science and human behavior.* New York: Macmillan, 1953.

Reprinted from *Personnel Administration*, 1970 (November-December), 37-41, by permission of the International Personnel Management Association.

demonstrates that the latter method will achieve a more rapid rate of desired behavior.

POLICY INFLUENCES BEHAVIOR

Much of the behavior of people in organizations is subject to the same laws of behavior. Personnel policies need to reward desired behavior.

However, many of our personnel policies are inconsistent with this idea. Many current personnel policies reward people for not coming to work. "Sick" pay and paid holidays are obvious examples. Often money spent on personnel relations rewards employees for leaving their place of work. Recreation rooms and programs and employee lounges are common examples. Clearly the current practices are now expected by the employees and cannot be reversed without substantial discontent. However, additional benefits can be distributed in a more appropriate manner. Future rewards can be given in exchange for desired behavior.

TWO CASE HISTORIES

The two organizations discussed below are very different in their goals and in the educational background of most of their employees. The first organization, Leading Hardware, is a large retail hardware operation having six retail stores in a large metropolitan area. The second organization, Metropolitan School, is the public school system for a large city. Both organizations sought to reduce absenteeism. The hardware company also sought to reduce tardiness. Both developed systems for rewarding the desired behavior.

In discussing the two cases, it is important to recognize the exploratory nature of this report and the limits which must be placed on the findings. The data were obtained primarily through interviews with the personnel director in each organization after both programs had been in operation for some time. Neither organization had records of attendance before introduction of the new programs which could be used to make meaningful "before" and "after" comparisons.

A "Lottery" Method to Improve Attendance[2]

Late in 1966, the managers of Leading Hardware decided on a plan to reduce tardiness and absenteeism of its secretaries, sales and stock personnel, and porters in its stores, warehouses, and offices. The personnel director described the existing tardiness and absenteeism records as "lousy." Although the managers were not familiar with Skinnerian psychology, they devised a reward system which employed its basic principles.

The plan was described in the organization's newspaper as a six-month experimental plan to recognize punctual attendance. For each calendar month there would be a drawing for an appliance at each store location. Eligible for the drawings would be those who had perfect attendance and punctuality records for the preceding month. There would be one prize for every 25 employees. At the end of six months a drawing would be held for a major award, such as a color TV. To be eligible for the major award, perfect attendance and punctuality was required for the entire six months. Vacation time was the only absence which did not end one's eligibilty. The program was an experiment, and the employees were told it might be dropped after the first six months.

In actual practice, the program operates almost exactly as stated. The monthly prize has been an appliance worth about $25. The major prize has been color TV. The only major revision was that a person was not

2. The author is indebted to Mr. C., personnel director of Leading Hardware, for his help in making the information presented available, and to Richard Weis, one of the author's students, who first introduced the author to the operation of this plan.

disqualified by an absence at a funeral. In addition, the names of winners and those eligible for prizes were printed in the company newspaper as members of the Perfect Attendance Club.

The results of this program have been highly successful. It is now in its third six-month cycle. The personnel department estimates that sick leave payments have been reduced 62 per cent. The first year of the program reduced absenteeism and tardiness to about one-fourth its prior level. Although the program is still rated as highly successful, recently the improvement has not been maintained at quite as high a level as earlier in the program.

The personnel director suggested two particular areas where he thinks the program has some of its more powerful consequences.

First, female employees who used to feel sick in the morning and miss the day now are more likely to come in. Also, employees with slight colds are now less apt to stay home.

A second demonstration of the power of this approach came during a snow storm. That day employees left home very early to be sure to be at work on time. Many, despite the conditions, were at work a half-hour before their normal starting time.

In a business such as the Leading Hardware operates, where punctuality and attendance are crucial for organizational performance, personnel programs can be devised to increase the desired behavior. The principle employed in the Leading Hardware case is the same as a lottery system. The power of such systems to produce motivated behavior is great, as observation of Las Vegas casinos and church bingo games demonstrates. Personnel policies based on the same principles to reward desired behavior have been of great value to Leading Hardware.

An Interval Reward Program[3]

A second method of distributing rewards for

3. The author is indebted to Mr. N., personnel director of Metropolitan Schools, for his help in making the information presented available.

attendance is to reward everyone who has met the specified criterion with a fixed reward after a certain time interval. This is the method used by Metropolitan School. Under this program only teachers are included. Metropolitan felt that some teachers had viewed their ten-day annual sick leave as part of their pay. Rising costs and difficulty in obtaining high-quality substitute teachers pointed to a need to reduce absentees of the regular faculty. Further, it was felt that the demanding job of teaching merited some additional reward for regular attendance.

The system developed provided for a $50 award for every teacher who had not been absent for an entire semester. An absence was defined as missing a quarter of a day. Attendance at funerals or at court is not defined as an absence. After taxes, the net reward is about $31.50 per semester.

The program has been in operation for five years. The results are summarized in Table 44-1.

Two facts are apparent from Table 44-1. First the program's second and third years of operation were its most effective. The last two years have shown a trend toward the first-year level. Second, despite an increase in the number of teachers employed during this period, the costs of substitute teachers have been below those in the first year. It thus appears that this type of reward system is more potent in the short-run than in the long-run. Again, in the absence of any precise "before" figures, the estimates of the personnel director are the only available measure of success. The director believes that the current attendance rate is about the same as it was ten years ago. However, he believes that the record would have been worse had it not been for the program, because of a general tendency for such employees to be absent more. At any rate, the recent success has been small by comparison to the earlier benefit.

While the program has been successful at least to some degree over a five-year period, certain problems have been noted in administering it. Most of these were met early and

Table 44-1. Metropolitan School's Percentage of Perfect Attendance and Substitute Teacher Costs for First Semester of Five Consecutive Years[1] [2]

	Year of Program's Operation				
	1	2	3	4	5
Percentage of eligible teachers having perfect attendance	41	60	54	45	43
Adjusted cost of substitute teachers	$335,208	$219,984	$293,352	$326,424	$316,161

1. Substitute teacher costs per day rose $1 during each year the program has been in operation. The figures in this table were adjusted to constant dollar costs by assuming that the rate for all the years was the same as it was the final year.
2. During this period, the number of eligible teachers employed rose approximately 400, from about 3,700 to 4,100.

handled successfully. The union has called it a "bribe" and some union members complained about the system at first. The major problems, however, did not occur until the awards were first given out. Many people who had expected a reward were in fact not eligible for it, and a number of complaints had to be resolved. After these initial problems, the program has become routinely handled by the payroll department and only a handful of exceptional cases occur.

There are two other problems with the operation of this program. Both of these problems, however, attest to the value of the approach. First, custodians, counselors, and library personnel have sought to be included in the same or similar program. These requests suggest that employees are interested in a system of rewards. A second problem stems from the program's working "too well." It has been suggested by the union that teachers who have colds now come to school. The personnel director mentioned that sometimes this may be true, but that generally teachers had the good sense to stay home when they are ill.

COMPARISON OF THE RESULTS

Both programs are viewed as successful by the respective personnel directors. Both systems seem to have been more successful initially than later in their history. Both

organizations use relatively small rewards which are dependent on desired behavior. Together they suggest the power of the Skinnerian method to maintain desired behavior in an organization, at least in the short run.

Several important qualifications and suggestions for those wishing to experiment with this method are necessary.

First, these cases cannot be compared in any rigorous manner. The programs have operated for different lengths of time, in sharply contrasting organizations. The lottery plan may not be any more effective in the long run. Also, the available records permit only highly tentative conclusions.

Second, the lottery method is more consistent with knowledge about the control of human behavior. In this method, the rewards are more immediate (every month as opposed to every four months) and are distributed on a schedule similar to gambling devices. It is widely known that such schedules will lead to more of the desired behavior.

Third, the particular rewards, the type of program and the behavior rewarded will vary widely between organizations. This paper has just dealt with work attendance, but the same ideas can be applied to all aspects of the behavior of personnel.

Fourth, the behavior rewarded in the

cases described was attendance. Nothing has been said about productivity on the job or other desired behavior. Such behavior may or may not be improved by attendance; generally it also will depend on the rewards which follow.[4]

Finally, the data do not permit any knowledge about the distribution of absences among those who were not eligible for the rewards. It is possible that the high substitute costs in the school case were at least partially due to the fact that teachers who were once absent were thereafter absent very frequently. The reward program could thus be very effective for some teachers but still not reduce costs. The data do not permit an answer to this possibility. However, the decreasing percentage of teachers receiving the reward suggests that the decrease in the power of the reward has been marked and appears to be the more important explanation for the declining success. Still, once one is absent, the reward system has no effect on him for the rest of the semester and as a result no incentive is present. If the relevant time period for each reward were shorter, then the period over which an individual was given no additional incentive would also be shorter. Under the lottery method, it would be quite feasible to give larger rewards, more frequently. Hence, the lottery method with rewards given at short-time intervals would appear to be a more fruitful program to begin testing to reduce absenteeism.

In attempting to install such a program, several observations may be helpful.

1. The program should be presented to the personnel involved as experimental. In the development of the program, the use of employee ideas about the type of program and the rewards is apt to be beneficial.

2. *Before* and *after* records must be kept to evaluate the program.

3. The rewards and the manner of their distribution may need revision from time to time.

CONCLUSION

People behave in a certain way because they have been rewarded for it in the recent past. Many personnel practices reward people for behavior which leads away from organizational goals. By defining what behavior is desired and rewarding it, future personnel policies can contribute to an organization's ends more than they do now. The possibilities for applying rewards to reduce absenteeism can be beneficial, at least in the short-run. While longer-run benefits are possible, the results are highly tentative, and all applications must be strictly experimental at this stage.

One final issues remains. Many people say, "You mean I should reward people for doing what they ought to do anyway, like being on time for work?" The answer is, it depends on how badly you want the behavior. If it is not important, forget about it. If it is important and it is not being performed, you have three choices.

First, live with the problem.

Second, punish those who do wrong. However, a rather persuasive body of knowledge has been accumulated showing that punishment has many undesirable side effects.

Third, reward the desired behavior.

The principles outlined here give support and guidance to the development of the third alternative.

4. I have discussed some of these considerations elsewhere. See Nord, W. R. Beyond the teaching machine: The neglected area of operant conditioning in the theory and practice of management, *Organizational Behavior and Human Performance.*

45
Hiring, Training, and Retaining the Hard - Core Unemployed:
A Selected Review

PAUL S. GOODMAN, PAUL SALIPANTE, and HAROLD PARANSKY[1]

Many organizations are involved in programs to hire, train, and retain the so-called hard-core unemployed (HCU),[2] and recent years have seen an increasing amount of research on this problem. The purpose of this paper is (a) to provide a conceptual framework which serves to organize these research studies, and (b) to evaluate what has been learned and what directions for future research are needed.

One hundred and ninety-two articles on training or employing the HCU (private sector only) were examined; 28 per cent (54) of these related to firms' experiences in HCU programs. From this group 44 per cent (24) were selected on the basis of an empirical criterion, that is, they presented some systematic analysis between independent variables (e.g., type of training, individual differences) and criterion variables (e.g., turnover).

Conceptual Framework

The HCU worker operates in a complex social system. The focal organization providing the training and job, community organizations, government agencies, informal peer groups, and the HCU worker's family are all components of this social system that bear on the HCU worker's behavior. Within each organization there are role relationships and other structural properties (e.g., type of job available, promotion opportunities, pay level) that directly affect the HCU worker's behavior. Recognition of these multiple factors seems necessary in order to understand the HCU worker. Too often, researchers have defined a very limited social system composed primarily of the HCU worker, trainer, and supervisor (cf. Goodman, 1969a).

A social system implies not only multiple variables but the interdependence of

1. Work on this paper was supported by a grant to the first author from the General Electric Foundation. The review of the literature and initial write-up were conducted while the three authors were at the Graduate School of Business, University of Chicago.

2. It is difficult to define precisely the term "HCU" as used in these studies because of lack of information. However, a general characterization would be: the HCU is a member of a minority group, not a regular member of the work force, has less than a high-school education, is often under 22 and of a poverty level specified by the Department of Labor.

these variables. Change in one variable has a complex effect on the other dimensions. A major theme in most HCU studies is that change should be focused primarily on the HCU worker—that is, how to change him to fit (i.e., be retained by) the organization. A social-system model focuses on a broader perspective—what changes at the individual, organizational, or societal level are necessary to provide employment opportunities for the HCU worker.

An expectancy-performance model may also be used in viewing the HCU literature. Basically, this model holds that behavior is a product of the expectancies about behavior-reward contingencies and the attractiveness of these rewards. High retention rates would occur, then, when workers believe that remaining on the job leads to desired rewards, whereas leaving the job does not. Recent studies (cf. Heneman and Schwab, 1972) on the relationship between expectancies and rewards seem to indicate that these concepts are useful predictors of work behavior and that, therefore, they should be applicable to HCU worker behavior.

The basic thesis of this framework is that the HCU worker operates in a complex social system. The multiple factors in this social system affect his expectancies about behavior-reward contingencies and the relative attractiveness of these rewards. These expectancies and rewards, in turn, combine to determine the propensity of the HCU worker to remain on the job and to produce.

This review is organized around different dimensions of the social system that are arranged in terms of levels of social analysis. First, data relevant to individual factors are examined, and then other levels of analysis, such as role and structural characteristics of the organization, are examined. The expectancy-performance component is then employed to explain the findings on the relationships between the individual or structural factors and the behavior of the HCU worker.

INDIVIDUAL CHARACTERISTICS

Age

In a study of 347 HCUs in a large manufacturing company's program for hiring and retaining the disadvantaged, Quinn, Fine, and Levitin (1970) report that termination after job placement was greater for HCUs under 21 (50 per cent) than for those over 21 (37 per cent); age was not related to turnover during the prejob training. In a study of a similar HCU program, Hinrichs (1970) reports a greater turnover for trainees under 21 during training, after training, and 2 years after the training program. Greenberg (1968), Gurin (1968), Rosen (1969), Shlensky (1970), Lipsky, Drotning, and Fottler (1971), Davis, Doyle, Joseph, Niles, and Perry (1973), and Kirchner and Lucas (1972) report a similar relationship between age and dropouts during a training program. In terms of our model, younger HCU workers probably experience greater feelings of distrust toward the focal organization (Clark, 1968). Accordingly, they would perceive lower expectancies about the likelihood of receiving rewards and would be more likely to leave. Older workers probably have higher expectancies and a greater desire for the rewards (i.e., regular salary) that are contingent on attendance. Only Allerhand, Friedlander, Malone, Medow, and Rosenberg (1969) report no relationship between age and any of the criterion variables. There is not enough information on the comparability of this study with other studies we reviewed to determine why the results of Allerhand *et al.* differ from the other findings on age.

Sex

The evidence indicates that female job retention is significantly higher than the retention of males (Davis *et al.*, 1973; Greenberg, 1968; Gurin, 1968; Shlensky, 1970). Females are also more likely to have a job at the completion of training (Lipsky *et al.*, 1971). Only Allerhand *et al.* (1969) does not support these relationships.

Marital Status, Family Responsibilities, the Family Environment

Unmarried HCU workers exhibit higher turnover rates than married HCU workers (Hinrichs, 1970; Lipsky *et al.*, 1971; Quinn *et al.*, 1970). The degree of family responsibilities also seems to affect the HCU's behavior. Quinn *et al.* (1970) and Gurin (1968) report that male HCUs who are the main breadwinners are less likely to drop out. If HCU workers own or rent their own home or apartment, they are more likely to remain on their job (Hinrichs, 1970) and to earn higher wages (Gurin, 1968). (Gurin's study supported this relationship for males but not for females.) The impact of number of dependents—another measure of family responsibility—is more ambiguous. Gurin (1968), Rosen (1969), and Shlensky (1970) did not find number of dependents to be a significant predictor of HCU behavior. One study (Hinrichs, 1970) reports that number of dependents was positively related to retention, but since that study did not control other individual characteristic variables (e.g., age), its conclusions must be tentatively accepted.

The findings supporting relationship between family responsibilities (e.g., marital status, owning a home) and retention reflect the greater need for job-related rewards (e.g., money); that is, greater responsibilities demand greater resources which can be attained by job attendance. Following the expectancy model, the greater the attraction of rewards related to holding a job, the higher the retention rates.

Birthplace

The birthplace or the geographical area where the trainee spent his formative years seems related to turnover of HCU workers. Higher retention rates were reported for those born in the rural South (Quinn *et al.*, 1970; Purcell and Cavanagh, 1969) and the West Indies or Latin America (Shlensky, 1970), as opposed to those from the urban North. This relationship seems to parallel findings on rural-urban differences (cf. Hulin and Blood, 1968) which suggest that the value premises of rural-born individuals might be more congruent with organizational requirements.

Education

Evidence on the relationship between education and the criterion variables is mixed. Greenberg (1968) and Shlensky (1970) report significant positive relationships between education and job retention; in the latter study, the finding holds only for the black HCU. Gurin (1968), Quinn *et al.* (1970), Lipsky *et al.* (1971), and Davis *et al.* (1973) report no relationships for education. Unfortunately, there is little information in these studies on the distribution of education or the relationships between educational attainment and job requirements to permit a reconciliation of these findings.

Previous Job History

Present job behavior should reflect, to some extent, the patterns of past job behavior and earnings. Quinn *et al.* (1970) report that terminations were greater (54 per cent) for those with more than two jobs in the last 2 years, as compared with those (25 per cent) who held less than two jobs in the same time period. Many of the other studies (cf. Greenberg, 1968; Hinrichs, 1970) report similar relationships. It seems that the inability to stay on past jobs leads to lower expectancies that rewards will follow from job attendance and to lower expectancies by the individual that he is capable of remaining on jobs. Following our model, these lower expectancies should lead to lower job retention.

Personality and Description of Self

Researchers interested in explaining HCU

trainee behavior have examined the role of personality. Some studies have used traditional measures of personality characteristics, while other have employed single-item scales to tap specific attitudes and values. In general, the results are not encouraging. Quinn *et al.* (1970) introduced some 21 indexes in their study; only two exhibited significant differences in the criterion variables, of which one was in the direction opposite from the prediction. Frank (1969) used a more extensive battery of tests and also obtained few significant results. Gurin's (1968) analysis of five scales dealing with orientation toward work, personal efficacy, and attitudes about the Protestant Ethic also did not reveal any strong consistent relationships to the criterion.

Research by Allerhand *et al.* (1969), Hinrichs (1970), and Teahan (1969) indicates that there may be some relationship between personality factors and the criterion variables for HCU trainees. Hinrichs (1970) reports that trainees who rated their own ability as high were more likely to be considered highest in performance during a training program. Allerhand *et al.* (1969) report that individuals who indicated a strong need to be perceived as smart by their boss and who perceived themselves as having a high level of energy and activity were less likely to drop out of a prejob orientation program. Teahan's (1969) study focused on the time span concept. He indicates that terminators from an HCU training program possessed shorter time spans and were less optimistic about their future than were those who remained in training. Data from each of these studies seem to indicate that a favorable self-image and orientation toward producing positive results are related to successful outcomes in an HCU program.

It is interesting to note two differences between the sets of studies presented above. The first set examined more generalized personality traits, while the second set examined attitudes and beliefs about more specific objects. The first set also relied on more traditional personality batteries, while the second set used single items that are designed for the specific research. Since there seemed to be some relationship between personality type variables and the criterion variables in the second set of studies, it may be that the methodology of this set is more appropriate to an HCU population. That is, given a population with low education and potentially negative attitudes toward test taking, it may be preferable to use a smaller set of specific items instead of the traditional personality batteries. However, before one can weigh the relative importance of personality differences, future research must examine the implications of these different strategies. (See Friedlander, 1970, for a discussion of methodological issues relevant to research in HCU populations.) Also, there is need for a theoretical perspective to aid in identifying relevant personality variables.

ROLE CHARACTERISTICS

Within the organization the trainee interacts with supervisors, peers, counselors, trainers, and other organizational participants. The characteristics of these role relationships have a bearing on the likelihood that the HCU workers will remain in the company. For example, the supervisor can affect the amount of rewards the HCU worker receives. Or he can affect the expectation that certain behaviors are rewarded. The modification of rewards, or of expectations that certain behaviors and rewards are connected, should affect the HCU worker's behavior.

Supervisor Role

A number of studies indicate that the supportiveness of the supervisor affects HCU behavior. Beatty (1971) reports that consideration (measured by the Leadership Behavior Description Questionnaire) was positively correlated with performance ($r = .38$). A further analysis, however, indicated that for those trainees in the extremes of the distribution of performance scores, the relationship with consideration was negative.

Another important finding is that only first-level supervisory behavior, and not second-level supervisory behavior, was related to HCU trainees' performances. Friedlander and Greenberg (1971) report a similar positive relationship between supervisory supportiveness and performance.

Another interesting finding in their analysis is that significant discrepancies existed between the HCU worker and the supervisor in their perception of the supportiveness of the organization; that is, HCU trainees defined the work climate as much less supportive. Friedlander and Greenberg suggest that this differential perception of work climate increases the chances that some reliable (low-absenteeism) HCU workers will find this work situation intolerable and leave, while others will exhibit withdrawal behaviors such as tardiness or absenteeism. Quinn et al. (1970), using different measures of supervisory style, found that being treated fairly reduced the HCU worker's propensity to terminate.

Also, HCU workers with more than one supervisor experience greater turnover (57 per cent) than those with one supervisor (31 per cent). Davis et al. (1973) find no consistent positive relationships between supervisory behavior and the criterion variables. However, their measures of supervisory behavior (e.g., time spent with the worker) are not very specific in terms of how the supervisor deals with the HCU trainee.

In general, the studies seem to indicate that supervisory style does affect HCU worker behavior. Supportiveness from the supervisor probably allays some of the HCU worker's fears about the new work situation and provides feelings of positive reinforcement about the work setting. Having a single supervisor increases the predictability of the job and probably clarifies the expectations about rewards and expected performance. Following our model, these conditions seem to lead to higher retention and performance.

Counselor and Trainer Roles

Unfortunately there are few studies meeting our criteria which deal with the effect of the counselor-trainee role on HCU trainee behavior. Quinn et al. (1970) report findings similar to their analyses of the first-line supervisor—the fairness of treatment by the counselor during training is positively related to job retention.

Gurin (1968) provides a provocative analysis of the sources of attractiveness of counselors and trainers for the HCU trainees. Counselors (versus vocational and basic education teachers) were defined as the most attractive staff members by the HCU trainees. Black counselors, however, were perceived as more attractive than white counselors for male trainees, while race differences did not differentiate the attractiveness of the occupants of the training roles. This difference in preference for black versus white counselors may be attributed to the fact that black counselors expressed values and beliefs more congruent with those of the trainees. However, an analysis of trainees' perceptions indicated that they felt black counselors stressed middle-class values more than white counselors did.

This finding would seem to indicate that HCU trainees were more willing to accept middle-class socialization attempts from a black than a white counselor. Gurin confirms this point by indicating that there was a positive association (+.27) between stressing middle-class values and the attractiveness of the counselor for black male counselors but no association (−.04) for white male counselors. These findings and other reported by Gurin are important because they indicate that certain combinations of race and sex with specific roles have a more powerful effect on the socialization of the HCU worker. In terms of the model, it suggests that these combination effects will have a greater impact in changing expectancies and the attractiveness of rewards and, thus, on retention and job performance.

Peers in the Work Organization

Friedlander and Greenberg (1971) report that HCU workers' perceptions of the supportiveness of their peers and others in the organization to new workers was related to supervisory ratings of performance. In general, the more supportive the trainee viewed his peers and others in the organization, the more likely he was to be evaluated by his supervisor as competent, congenial, friendly, and conscientious, but not necessarily as more reliable. Case studies by Campbell (1969) and Kirchner and Lucas (1971), as well as an experiment by Baron and Bass (1969), also point to the importance of peer-group relationships.

Morgan, Blonsky, and Rosen (1970) examined the reactions at different levels of the existing work force in the firm to a program for the HCU. They found a shift from positive to neutral feelings at the end of the 12-week program. Differences in attitudes toward the HCU and the program varied in terms of the role distance between the trainee and the respondent. For example, individuals at the vice presidential level showed an increase in positive attitudes. For foremen and the rank-and-file group, there was a tendency for positive attitudes to decrease and for negative attitudes to increase ($p > .01$ for change in over-all attitudes).

The modification in perceived positive and negative consequences at different levels probably reflects greater realization of problems in dealing with HCU workers. The closer one is to the day-to-day problems, the more likely it is that one's perceptions and attitudes should reflect these problems. There are no data in this study to indicate the consequences of this attitude change on the criterion variables. On one hand, the changes might merely reflect reality testing—actual experiences and expectations are more congruent. On the other hand, especially at the foreman and rank-and-file

level, it might lead to less positive relationships with the HCU worker.

Roles Outside the Work Organization

Some researchers have looked at the social context of the HCU's family and peer group. Gurin (1968), for example, found that male HCU trainees in the lowest earning quartile more often came from families (reference is to the household of the trainees' mothers) where a greater percentage of adult males were unemployed. Friends of these HCU trainees also were more likely to be unemployed. Other findings (cf. Quinn et al., 1970) on the characteristics of the HCU worker's family, however, have not supported the relationships between indexes of family disorganization and the criterion variables. Therefore, although there is some indication that external role relationships affect HCU behavior, the process by which they affect expectancies, perceived attractiveness of rewards, retention, and performance is not clearly defined.

ORGANIZATION PROGRAM CHARACTERISTICS

Organizations involved in hiring and retraining the hard core have adopted a variety of training and counseling programs, as well as other supportive services.

Training

The selection of no training versus some, vestibule versus on-the-job training, and attitudinal versus skill training (general or specific) represent some of the choices in designing the training program portion of a program for the HCU. The Quinn et al. (1970) study permits analysis of a group that was trained and a matched control group of direct hires who received no training. The training program in question was prejob and primarily company oriented in nature.

An analysis of individuals on the job who had been trained versus those not trained indicated that there were no significant differences in the perceived levels of competence in job-related skills. Trained individuals were more likely to value work, to exhibit positive attitudes toward time schedules, and to show increased feelings of personal efficacy concerning achievement. Since data for this analysis were collected after the trainee was on the job, it is difficult to separate the effects of training from the effects of successfully completing training on these responses. In either case, the trained individual's sense of personal efficacy about accomplishment did increase.

Training, of course, may have dysfunctional consequences by raising expectations beyond the realities of the work situation. Quinn *et al.* (1970) indicate that trained individuals preferred more autonomy than they experienced on an entry-level job, and they perceived the quality of supervision as lower than did direct hires. That is, training leads to greater expectations than the job situation can fulfill. Hinrichs' (1970) study of 300 trainees in a 17-week vestibule training program also indicates some possible dysfunctional consequences of training. Not only did training not change attitudes in the intended direction, but in some cases it seems to have facilitated a change toward feelings of powerlessness. Unfortunately, there are no other data presented on the effects of training that could put this result in a broader perspective.

In Allerhand *et al.'s* (1969) and Frank's (1969) analyses of the effects of training on certain attitudinal and motivational dimensions, there do not seem to be any significant changes as a result of the training experiences. Similarly, Goodale (1971) found that changes in work values of HCU trainees over eight weeks of training were not significantly different from those of nonequivalent controls (insurance agents and college students).

The impact of training on job retention or performance seems negligible (Friedlander and Greenberg, 1971; Quinn *et al.*, 1970). A study by Rosen (1969) indicates that company orientation training led to lower termination among HCU workers than did quasi-therapeutic training. However, the retention rate of the company-trained HCU workers did not differ substantially from that of regular new hires. Farr (1969) reports that among HCUs placed under sensitivity-trained supervisors, trained HCUs had lower retention (20 per cent) than did untrained HCUs (55 per cent).

There are many case studies concerned with the effects of turnover and performance training. Some (cf. Gudyer, 1970; Habbe, 1968; Janger, 1969) indicate training affects the HCU's behavior (e.g., turnover): other studies (cf. Saltzman, 1969) do not.

In general, reviewing all the studies and their respective methodologies, it seems unlikely that training itself affects job retention or performance. This conclusion is quite congruent with our model of HCU behavior. Job retention is related to the expectancy that job attendance will lead to desired rewards. Although the training might initially affect these expectations, it is the actual work experiences which determine the HCU behavior; that is, the types and amount of rewards available and the frequency of and criteria for their allocation determine the expectancies and the perceived attractiveness of rewards. These factors are quite independent of the training experience.

Counseling

There are no experimental data on the relative effects of different counseling strategies. The earlier discussion of the counselor role sheds some light on how the demographic characteristics of the counselor may influence his effectiveness. Several studies (cf. Allerhand *et al.*, 1969; Hearns, 1968; Purcell and Webster, 1969; Rutledge and Gass, 1968) indicate that counseling may contribute to lower HCU termination rates. However, it is difficult to evaluate the impact of counseling on retention, since these studies do not separate its effect from other structural dimensions.

Although there is no evidence supporting any significant effects of a particular program characteristic (e.g., training), several studies (Davis *et al.*, 1973; Janger, 1972; Sedgwicks and Bodell, 1972) indicate that the combined effects of many program dimensions (e.g., counseling, training, providing transportation) increase job retention. The problem with this conclusion is that we do not know whether other uncontrolled variables might explain this relationship, nor do we know the nature of the interaction effects. Also, Davis *et al.* (1973) provide a contrasting finding for those considering formal, elaborate programs–the more visible the program, the higher the absenteeism and turnover.

ORGANIZATION STRUCTURAL CHARACTERISTICS

Job Structure

The nature of the job on which the trainee is placed affects his work attitudes and propensity to remain on the job. Quinn *et al.* (1970) identified four job characteristics which seem related to negative job attitudes and turnover. The inability to change one's job assignment now or in the future was related to higher termination rates for the HCU worker. Assignment to multiple work stations, or not having an idea what their work routine would be like, was also positively related to turnover. Trainees who did not understand some aspects of their job, or how it fit into the larger picture, were more likely to terminate than those who had a better understanding. When job activities were perceived as boring, turnover was more likely (63 per cent) than when HCU workers did not find their job boring (18 per cent); similarly, involuntary terminations were negatively related to skill level (Davis *et al.*, 1973). In addition, a number of case studies (Bonney, 1971; Campbell, 1969; Goodman, 1969b) indicate that job status and job mobility are positively related to retention rates.

Pay

Another organizational characteristic which bears on HCU workers' behavior is the pay system. Although none of the studies we reviewed examined the effects of different pay systems, a number of studies did examine the effect of pay levels. In Shlensky's (1970) analysis, pay was a major predictor among groups (e.g., blacks, young people, and males) that were more likely to terminate and thus served to reduce the propensity to terminate in these groups. Pay did not seem to relate to turnover for whites and older workers. Other studies (cf. Allerhand, 1969; Davis *et at.*, 1973; Purcell and Cavanagh, 1969) also indicate a positive relationship between pay and job retention and between pay and completion of training (cf. Lipsky *et al.*, 1971).

Organizational Commitment and Change

In a few multifirm studies that were reviewed, there is some indication that higher commitment (Allerhand *et al.*, 1969; Hearns, 1968; Janger, 1972), company willingness to change policies and procedures (Allerhand *et al.*, 1969; Goodman, 1969b; Hearns, 1968; Janger, 1972), and more realistic company expectations of the HCU (Allerhand *et al.*, 1969) are associated with higher retention rates.

Employment Stability, Size, Industry

Companies with lower turnover rates in entry-level jobs seemed to have higher retention rates with HCU workers than did other firms (Allerhand *et al.*, 1969). Medium-sized companies (100-500 employees) seemed to retain more HCU workers than did larger or smaller firms (Allerhand *et al.*, 1969). Using multivariate analysis, Lipsky *et al.* (1971) found that white-collar versus blue-collar jobs, and jobs in manufacturing versus nonmanufacturing industries, were two significant predictors of training program completions.

DISCUSSION

The evidence indicates that many factors—individual, role, and structural—affect the behavior of the HCU worker. Age, sex, family responsibilities, and place of birth are associated with termination and subsequent earnings of HCU workers. These variables probably relate to the expectancies that job attendance will lead to certain rewards and to the relative attractiveness of these rewards. The product of expectancies and rewards leads to job retention.

The relationships between these individual differences and the criterion variables are by no means simple. First, the individual-level variables may be interrelated. For example, Shlensky (1970) finds age related to turnover among males, but not among females; further, he finds sex related to turnover among HCU aged 16-20, but not among those over 20. It appears, then, that age, sex, and other individual differences do not have simple effects on the criteria; rather, there is evidence of some fairly strong interactions.

A second problem is the relative independence of the individual-level variables and the organizational-level variables. For example, it may be that HCU workers with certain characteristics (e.g., being older) might be placed in more desirable and higher paying jobs. If such were the case, it would be difficult to assess whether a relationship among the HCU between age and turnover were due to age differences or to the more desirable nature of the jobs in which older workers were placed. The evidence concerning this issue is that the relationships between individual variables and the criteria are reduced, but not eliminated, when organizational variables are entered into a regression analysis (cf. Greenberg, 1968; Shlensky, 1970).

Although the relationships are complex, both between individual and organizational variables and among the individual level variables, a number of observations can be drawn from these studies. First, there are clearly no simple selection rules. Also, selecting out HCU workers based on the individual-difference information would be inappropriate given the purpose of HCU programs. Second, the design of a program should reflect the differences among the HCU work force. If a firm must select HCU workers with heterogeneous characteristics, it would seem important to design the program to reflect differences in their expectations and preferences for rewards. That is, a young unmarried male would receive different program inputs than a married female with two children.

The HCU trainee operates in a large social system with many interconnected role relationships. The degree of conflict between the HCU trainee and his counselor, trainer, supervisor, and peers clearly can affect his behavior. In one study there was some indication of an interaction effect between the counselor-trainer role and the similarity of the background characteristics of the role occupant and the HCU trainee. This finding would seem to have implications for selection of individuals as counselor-trainers in an HCU program.

In the area of supervision, the perceived supportiveness of one's supervisor is related to job retention. However, there may be large perceptual discrepancies between supervisors and HCU workers on the degree of supportiveness existing in the organization (cf. Friedlander and Greenberg, 1971). Bridging the gap between the supervisor's and HCU worker's perception of the work climate and increasing the level of supportiveness in the organization may be one strategy to increase performance and job retention. At the same time, it is important to remember that other roles (e.g., peers) bear on HCU worker behavior; attention to only one role is not a useful strategy.

Much of the literature on the HCU

worker focuses on the effectiveness of the different training strategies to reorient this individual to the world of work. Unfortunately, in the studies reviewed, there is no clear indication that training significantly affects the turnover or performance of the HCU worker. These results seem consistent with our model; that is, it is unlikely that training would have a major impact on job expectancies and the availability and attractiveness of rewards. Our conclusion is not that training of HCU workers should be discontinued. On the other hand, large investments in intensive training programs may not be warranted. Future studies that examine the effects of different training combinations such as short prejob orientation combined with on-the-job training versus extended vestibule training will provide more definitive answers to this question.

Dimensions of the organization such as the type of job and pay system affect the HCU worker's behavior. The HCU workers were more likely to terminate from jobs that they did not understand or that afforded little opportunity for movement, etc. The implication of these findings is that the trainee's behavior must be understood within the technological system in which he operates and that job redesign may represent a useful strategy in affecting the HCU worker's behavior. The level of pay also affects the HCU worker's behavior. The data seem to indicate that firms with relatively lower wage rates for entry-level jobs should avoid HCU programs. Higher paying firms, on the other hand, are in a position to hire HCU workers who would otherwise be most likely to leave; that is, there is some evidence that higher pay reduces the propensity to terminate for those most likely to leave.

Our analysis of structural characteristics has been primarily at the intraorganizational level. Little attention has been paid to the larger institutional forces which bear on the expectations and values of the HCU worker. For example, limited housing opportunities affect the HCU worker's cost of going to work. Often employers are some distance from ghetto areas. Similarly, limitations in educational systems and in health and child care systems bear on the HCU worker's propensity to come to work. Changes in these larger institutional forces must be considered when analyzing HCU behavior and HCU programs.

The over-all theme of this review is that multiple variables affect the HCU worker as he operates in a complex social system. Changes in the behavior of the HCU worker are related to changes in the role-, organizational-, and societal-level variables. In many studies on the HCU worker, there has been an unfortunate assumption that the worker must be changed to fit the organization. Our concept of the complex social system suggest changes must occur at all the main levels of analysis—that is, individual, role, organizational, and societal.

Two other issues, until now implicit in this review, need to be specified. First, designing a program to hire and to retain the HCU worker is an exercise in decision making. It requires a judgment about the allocation of resources to a variety of options (e.g., type of training, counseling, pay). Basically the manager is interested in the effect of this allocation on the retention (or performance) of HCU workers in relationship to the costs of this decision. What is surprising is that given the large investment of resources by many firms in programs for the HCU worker, there has been little attempt to collect and develop data systems that would provide guidance in the design or re-evaluation of such a program.

There are studies cited in this review that may serve as models for developing data systems to aid in decision making about HCU programs. Quinn et al. (1970) demonstrate how an experimental design may be successfully used in evaluating an organization's HCU program. Although their study is more elaborate than a firm would undertake, their general design could be utilized to evaluate the contribution of different factors (e.g., training) to the retention of the HCU worker.

A different data collection strategy, which includes a number of firms in a cross-sectional design, is suggested by the Shlensky (1970) study. This type of study is valuable since it permits the assessment of variables such as pay level, type of job, and size of the firm, which are more amenable to multifirm investigations. The critical issue, however, is that designing programs for the HCU worker requires data which indicate the relative importance of the multiple variables identified in this review.

The second issue concerns the role of the industrial psychologist and research on the HCU worker. Research in this area provides a number of opportunities. One can test theories about work attitudes, motivation, and performance. Empirical results from other studies can be cross-validated in this population. Psychologists interested in organizational change and action research have a "ready-made" laboratory. The research opportunity is also unique, since the data bear on an immediate social issue in our country. What is interesting in reviewing the studies in this area is that relatively few psychologists have become actively involved in research in what would seem to be a fertile area. The question is, Given an area with good theoretical research opportunities, one in which managers need data that could be gathered by psychologists, and one which concerns a relevant social problem, why is there not greater utilization of the skills of industrial psychologists?

REFERENCES

Allerhand, M. E., Friedlander, F., Malone, J. E., Medow, H., and Rosenberg, M. *A study of the impact and effectiveness of the comprehensive manpower project of Cleveland (AIM-JOBS)*. (Office of Policy, Evaluation and Research, U.S. Department of Labor, Contract No. 41-7-002-37) Cleveland: Case Western Reserve University, Cleveland College, AIM Research Project, December 1969.

Baron, R. M., and Bass, A. R. *The role of social reinforcement parameters in improving trainee task performance and self-image*. (Final Report, U.S. Department of Labor, Office of Manpower Administration, Contract No. 81-24-66-04) Detroit: Wayne State University, September 1969.

Beatty, R. W. First and second level supervision and the job performance of the hard-core unemployed. Paper presented at the meeting of the American Psychological Association, Washington, D.C., September 1971.

Bonney, N. L. Unwelcome strangers: A study of manpower training programs in the steel industry. Unpublished doctoral dissertation, University of Chicago, 1971.

Campbell, R. Employing the disadvantaged: Inland Steel's experience. *Issues in Industrial Society,* 1969, 1, 30-42.

Clark, K. No gimmicks please whitey. *Training in Business and Industry,* 1968, 5, 27-30.

Davis, O., Doyle, P., Joseph, M., Nyles, J., and Perry, W. An empirical study of the NAB-JOBS program. *Public Policy,* 1973, 2 (Spring), 235-62.

Farr, J. L. Industrial training programs for hardcore unemployed. Paper presented at Seventeenth Annual Workshop in Industrial Psychology (Division 14, American Psychological Association), Washington, D.C., August 1969.

Frank, H. H. On the job training for minorities: An internal study. Unpublished doctoral dissertation, University of California, Los Angeles, 1969.

Friedlander, F. Emerging blackness in a white research world. *Human Organization,* 1970, 29, 239-50.

Friedlander, F., and Greenberg, S. Effect of job attitudes, training, and organization climate on performance of the hard-core unemployed. *Journal of Applied Psychology,* 1971, 55, 287-95.

Goodale, J. G. Background characteristics, orientation, work experience, and work values of employees hired from human resources development applicants by companies affiliated with the National Alliance of Businessmen. Unpublished doctoral dissertation, Bowling Green State University, 1971.

Goodman, P. S. Hiring and training the hard-core unemployed: A problem in system definition. *Human Organization,* 1969, 28, 259-69. (a)

Goodman, P. S. Hiring, training and retaining the hard core. *Industrial Relations,* 1969, 9, 54-66. (b)

Goodman, P. S. Methodological issues in conducting research on the disadvantaged. In W. Button (Ed.), *Proceedings of Conference on Rehabilitation, Sheltered Workshops, and the Disadvantaged.* Binghamton, N.Y.: Vail-Ballou Press, 1970.

Greenberg, D. H. *Employers and manpower training programs: Data collection and analysis.* (U.S. Office of Economic Opportunity Memorandum RM-5740-OEO) Santa Monica, Calif.: Rand Corporation, October 1968.

Gudyer, R. H. A. corporate experience: American Airlines. In W. D. Drennan (Ed.), *The fourth strike: Hiring and training the disadvantaged.* New York: American Management Association, 1970.

Gurin, G. *Inner city youth in a job training project.* Ann Arbor: University of Michigan, Institute for Social Research, 1968.

Habbe, S. Hiring the hard-core unemployed: Pontiac's operation opportunity. *The Conference Board Record,* 1968, 5, 18-21.

Hearns, J. P. New approaches to meet post-hiring difficulties of disadvantaged workers. In *Proceedings of the Twenty-First Annual Winter Meeting. Industrial Relations Research Association.* Madison, Wis.: Industrial Relations Research Association, 1968.

Heneman, H. G., III, and Schwab, D. P. Evaluation of research on expectancy theory predictions of employee performance. *Psychological Bulletin,* 1972, 78, 1-9.

Hinrichs, J. R. *Implementation of manpower training: The private firm experience.* Unpublished paper, IBM Corporation, White Plains, N.Y., 1970.

Hulin, C., and Blood, M. Job enlargement, individual differences and worker responses. *Psychological Bulletin,* 1968, 69, 41-56.

Janger, A. New start for the harder hard core. *The Conference Board Record,* 1969, 6, 10-20.

Janger, A. *Employing the disadvantaged: A company perspective.* New York: The Conference Board, 1972.

Kirchner, W., and Lucas, J. Some research on motivating the hard-core. *Training in Business and Industry,* 1971, 8, 30-31.

Kirchner, W., and Lucas, J. The hard-core in training–who makes it? *Training and Development Journal,* 1972, 26, 34-38.

Lipsky, D., Drotning, J., and Fottler, M. Some correlates of trainee success in a coupled on-the-job training program. *The Quarterly Review of Economics and Business,* 1971, 11, 42-60.

Morgan, B. S., Blonsky, M. R., and Rosen, H. Employee attitudes toward a hard-core hiring program, *Journal of Applied Psychology,* 1970, 54, 473-78.

Purcell, T. V., and Cavanagh, G. F. Alternative routes to employing the disadvantaged within the enterprise. In *Proceedings of the Twenty-Second Annual Winter Meeting, Industrial Relations Research Association.* Madison.: Industrial Relations Research Association, 1969.

Purcell, T. V., and Webster, R. Window on the hard-core world. *Harvard Business Review,* 1969, 47, 118-29.

Quinn, R., Fine, B., and Levitin, T. *Turnover and training: A social-psychological study of disadvantaged workers.* Unpublished paper, Survey Research Center, University of Michigan, 1970.

Rosen, H. *A group orientation approach for facilitating the work adjustment of the hard-core unemployed.* (Final Report, U.S. Department of Labor) Washington, D.C.: U.S. Government Printing Office, 1969.

Rutledge, A. L., and Gass, G. Z. *Nineteen Negro men: Personality and manpower retraining.* San Francisco, Calif.: Jossey-Bass, 1968.

Saltzman, A. W. Manpower planning in private industry. In A. Weber, F. H. Cassell, W. L. Ginsberg (Eds.), *Public-private manpower policies.* (IRRA publication No. 35) Madison: Industrial Relations Research Association, 1969.

Sedgwicks, R., and Bodell, D. The hard-core employee–key to high retention. *Personnel Journal,* 1972, 50, 948-53.

Shlensky, B. Determinants of turnover in NAB-JOBS programs to employ the disadvantaged. Unpublished doctoral disseration, Massachusetts Institute of Technology, 1970.

Teahan, J. E. Future time perspective and job success. In *Supplement to H. Rosen, A group orientation approach for facilitating the work adjustment of the hard-core unemployed.* (Final Report, U.S. Department of Labor) Washington, D.C.: U.S. Government Printing Office, 1969.

8

HUMAN FACTORS ENGINEERING, WORKING CONDITIONS, SAFETY, AND FATIGUE

Prior to World War II the design of machines and other physical equipment was primarily the responsibility of industrial engineers. For the most part these engineers designed equipment with little thought about the capabilities and limitations of the workers using it. Their approach to equipment design consisted mainly of applying their technical knowledge of engineering principles. Efforts to increase worker productivity during these prewar years were based upon "time and motion study" rather than upon design of equipment in terms of human considerations. Briefly, time and motion study entailed analyzing the movements comprising a job in order to determine the one set of motions that resulted in maximum productivity. Readers interested in knowing more about time and motion study are referred to such sources as Barnes (1963) and Taylor (1947).

The importance of designing equipment so that humans can use it more effectively was clearly recognized during World War II. At this time a wide variety of complicated military equipment was developed. These devices were more elaborate than man had ever encountered before. Unfortunately, it was soon learned that much of this equipment (e.g., radar systems, airplanes, submarines) was designed in such a way that it could not be handled adequately by human operators. Consequently there were many human errors that resulted in equipment damage and serious accidents. This situation pointed out the necessity of taking human factors into consideration while designing equipment. This was the beginning of the subarea of industrial-organizational psychology referred to as *human-factors engineering, human engineering, engineering psychology, ergonomics, or biomechanics.*

Today, human factors engineering is concerned primarily with designing effective "man-machine systems." Basically a man-machine system is a combination of one or more items of physical equipment and one or more men working together in order to accomplish some desired outcome (McCormick, 1970). A taxicab driver and his automobile is an example of a simple man-machine system. More complex illustrations of man-machine systems include a crew of workers and the large machine they are operating, several astronauts and their manned spacecraft, and airport control tower operators and their radar equipment.

Every man-machine system can be designed in a variety of ways. For instance, it can vary depending upon what functions of the system the engineering psychologist decides to allocate to men and to machines. This problem is considered by many to be the most crucial one in designing man-machine systems that are maximally effective. The first article in this section, by Chapanis, discusses why some of the past solutions to this problem have been practically useless. He explains the current state of the problem and presents his own strategy for solving it.

Human factors engineers design equipment, tools, machines, and factory facilities to be compatible with the workers who use them. They are involved in improving the design of the immediate employee work-space and in determining the job methods that are best in terms of speed of work, safety, quality, etc. The article by Teel was chosen because it gives examples of human factors engineering research dealing with methods design, work-space design, and equipment design. Teel discusses the research results in terms of both statistical and practical significance.

A great many organizations today follow a 24-hour, 7-day-week work schedule. This pattern can be observed in police and fire departments, hospitals, airline terminals, and utility companies. This round-the-clock cycle is common also in industrial organizations that find it uneconomical to keep expensive equipment idle at any time, especially if stopping and starting may increase the likelihood of breakdowns and maintenance costs. The 24-hour work day is typically divided into three shifts: day (8 A.M. to 4 P.M.); evening (4 P.M. to 12 A.M.); midnight or "graveyard" (12 A.M. to 8 A.M.). In an effort to be fair to employees, many companies use what is called a rotating shift.

Although there are many types of rotating shifts, the most common pattern, according to Bass and Barrett (1972), is that in which the worker spends a week on each of the three shifts. Each worker shares equally the inconveniences of being on the evening and graveyard shifts, which may involve loss of sleep and interference with family responsibilities. The article by Bloom focuses on some of the problems experienced by shift workers who are required to change frequently from one shift to another. These workers experience disruption in their normal biological rhythms, and this results in physiological fatigue and loss of efficiency. The reader who has experienced jet-lag has a good notion of how some employees feel for several days after changing work shifts. Bloom offers several useful suggestions for handling the difficulties of shift work.

A recent trend in some organizations has been to experiment with modifying the length of the conventional 5-day, 40-hour workweek. One of the most popular and interesting trends is the four-day pattern, which entails 10-hour workdays. If the four-day workweek becomes widespread, it will be important to find out what effect it will have on worker productivity, satisfaction, boredom, fatigue, absenteeism, "moonlighting," and recreational activities. Unfortunately, at the present time we know relatively little about the effects of the four-day week, for the reason that so little rigorous research has been conducted in this area. Companies that have tried the shortened workweek report that employees seem to like it, unions react favorably, and rescheduling of work causes no great difficulties (Poor, 1970). The article by Nord and Costigan is the only empirical study that provides longitudinal data on the reactions of employees to the shortened workweek. Nord and Costigan found that employees generally had positive attitudes toward the four-day week and that absenteeism declined 10 per cent after 12-16 months. They report also that reactions to the four-day week may depend on employee age and sex. Although this study is rigorous exploratory research, it does not investigate the effects of the shortened workweek on productivity. Future research is needed to test the effects of the four-day week on productivity over a period of time, using controlled conditions in order to minimize confounding from extraneous variables. Readers interested in a further treatment of this topic are referred to Poor (1970), Swados (1958), and Northrup (1965).

Many other environmental factors affect worker efficiency besides shift-changing and length of the workweek. Numerous studies have appeared in the literature concerning the effects of temperature, music, noise, illumination, and ventilation on productivity. These more conventional conditions of the work environment are adequately covered in most textbooks on industrial-organizational psychology.

On April 28, 1971, the William-Steiger Occupational Safety and Health Act of 1970 (OSHA) became effective. The purpose of this legislation was to assure safe and healthful working conditions throughout the country. The U.S. Department of Labor has major responsibility for administering the Act by issuing job-safety and job-health standards. To secure compliance by employers and employees with these safety and health requirements, the Department conducts periodic on-site inspections by trained compliance officers. According to the Act, employees have the right to bring unsafe conditions to the attention of the officer making the investigation. Moreover, without fear of being discharged or discriminated against by his employer, any worker can notify the Department of Labor and request an investigation if he feels that unsafe and unhealthful working conditions exist in his job situation.

If during the inspection the investigator feels the Act has been violated, a citation of violation and proposed penalty is given to the employer together with a reasonable time for elimination of the hazard. When the employer fails to comply within the time limit, the Secretary of Labor notifies the employer about the violation and the penalty. This notice and assessment become final unless the employer contests the citation within fifteen days. The size of the penalty generally depends upon the severity of the violation and the amount of time it takes the employer to remedy the situation. For example, a willful or repeated violation could incur penalties of up to $10,000 for each violation. The article by Simonds discusses what organizations can do now to prepare themselves for possible future Federal and/or State compliance reviews. Simonds also describes some of OSHA's past practices in dealing with organizations, and presents a study that emphasizes the importance of top management interests and involvement in the reduction of industrial injuries.

In addition to reducing accidents in industry, psychologists have been conducting research aimed at reducing motor vehicle accidents. The importance of this research can be illustrated by the fact that of the 112,000 accident deaths in the United States during 1967, 53,100 of these fatalities were the results of motor-vehicle accidents, as compared to 14,200 accident deaths at work (National Safety Council, 1968). The article by Barrett reviews the history of the various methods used to reduce motor vehicle accidents. Barrett points out some deficiencies of the early research and presents a new approach using a perceptual information-processing model. Barrett describes the results of research investigating the relation between measures of perceptual style and driver reactions in an automobile simulator. He discusses the implications of his findings for public policy regarding the reduction of motor vehicle accidents.

Because of its obvious importance to both the worker and his employer, the study of fatigue has been one of the most intensive areas of research for the industrial-organizational psychologist. Unfortunately, the study of fatigue has been frustrating, because fatigue is a complex concept that can be defined in various ways. It can be used to refer to a worker's reported feelings of tiredness (i.e., subjective fatigue), to reductions in his productivity, to changes in his physiological state (i.e., acute or physiological fatigue), and to his psychological state (i.e., the result of prolonged emotional stress, mental effort, and loss of job interest). To complicate matters further, it has been shown that these different types of fatigue do not necessarily occur at the same time in a given employee. That is, any combination of one or more types of fatigue can occur. All forms of fatigue, however, can cause performance decrements and increases in accidents, absences, and waste.

Psychologists have used a wide variety of approaches in attempting to alleviate fatigue. These approaches link the topic of fatigue with other topics in this section as well as topics in other sections. Effective selection and placement procedures often help to reduce fatigue by assigning employees to jobs which they like and can perform well. Careful design of work methods, physical equipment, and working conditions can also help in reducing fatigue. It has been shown that decreases in fatigue accrue as a result of careful training of workers. Reducing the length of the working day, shortening the workweek, and introducing rest pauses are additional approaches for minimizing fatigue. The final article by McFarland discusses the problems that exist in defining the concept of fatigue, the many forms of fatigue, and several recommendations for controlling or preventing it.

REFERENCES AND SELECTED READINGS

Barnes, R. M. *Motion and time study.* New York: Wiley, 1963.

Barrett, G. V., and Thornton, C. L. Relationship between perceptual style and driver reaction to an emergency situation. *Journal of Applied Psychology,* 1968, 52, 169-76.

Bass, B. M., and Barrett, G. V. *Man, work, and organizations.* Boston: Allyn and Bacon, 1972.

McCormick, E. J. *Human factors engineering.* New York: McGraw-Hill, 1970.

National Safety Council, *Accident facts.* Chicago: National Safety Council, 1968.

Northrup, H. R. The reduction in hours. In C. E. Dankert, F. C. Mann, and H. R. Northrup, *Hours of work.* New York: Harper & Row, 1965, pp. 1-16.

Poor, R. (Ed.), *Four days, forty hours: Reporting a revolution in work and lei-* sure. Cambridge, Mass.: Burk & Poor, 1970.

Swados, H. Less work—less leisure. In E. Larrabee and R. Meyersohn (Eds.), *Mass leisure.* New York: Free Press, 1958, pp. 353-63.

Taylor, F. W. *Principles of scientific management.* New York: Harper & Row, 1947.

46

On the Allocation of Functions Between
Men and Machines*

ALPHONSE CHAPANIS

Numerous writers agree that one of the first and most important problems in man-machine system design has to do with the allocation of functions between men and machines (see, for example, Bamford, 1959; Chapanis, 1960a, 1960b, and 1961; Gagné, 1962; Lomov, 1963; Morgan, Cook, Chapanis, and Lund, 1963; Sinaiko and Buckley, 1961). This problem can be viewed from several points of view and there is a considerable amount of uncertainty about how allocation decisions can best be approached (see, for example, Fitts, 1962; Jordan, 1963). In my paper this morning I shall try to do four things:

1. describe the nature of the allocation problem;

2. say something about the approaches that have been taken to this problem in the past;

*This is substantially the text of a paper read at a symposium on "The Design of Man-Machine Systems" held at the 15th International Congress of Applied Psychology, Ljubljana, Yugoslavia, 5 August 1964. The paper was prepared under Contract Nonr-4010(03) between the Office of Naval Research and the Johns Hopkins University. It is Report No. 8 under that contract.

3. give you a few of my views on the contemporary status of the problem;

4. suggest a strategy for dealing with it.

THE NATURE OF THE PROBLEM

Industrial engineers and operations researchers use the words "allocation model," "allocation problem," or "assignment problem" to refer to those situations in which they want to combine activities and resources so as to maximize the effectiveness of a system (see, for example, Churchman, Ackoff, and Arnoff, 1957). The kind of allocation problem with which we are concerned is a special case of this more general one. However, you will not find our problem discussed in textbooks of industrial engineering or operations research because our problem has no neat mathematical model and no elegant mathematical solution.

The nature of our allocation problem can be described very simply. In planning any man-machine system, an engineer can usually think of many alternative ways of designing it (see Chapanis, 1961, for a specific example). These alternative designs may vary in a number of respects. For

From *Occupational Psychology*, 1965, 39, 1-11, by permission of the author and the National Institute of Industrial Psychology.

example, the designer may use different numbers and size of machine units: he may design one very large machine or several smaller ones to do exactly the same thing. Or he may use different kinds of linkages— mechanical, hydraulic, or electrical—between various parts of the system. Also among the things which a designer may also vary is the number of people in a system and the functions which these people perform.

Let's take a specific example. Think of an industrial engineer who is designing a system to handle checking accounts in a bank. He could, conceivably, design the system in such a way that virtually all of the functions were performed by people. Tellers would receive the checks, sort them into their proper accounts, enter the amount of each check into the appropriate ledgers by hand, compute the bank balances by mental arithmetic or with the help of a simple device like an abacus, prepare monthly statements by hand, and mail off monthly statements to account holders. There are, in fact, some banks in the world which still operate in essentially this way.

A somewhat more complex type of system might provide the clerk with machines (for example, adding machines) to assist him in his computations, although he might still make entries and do all other operations by hand. Still more complex would be a system in which machines not only assisted the clerk in making his computations but printed out the bank balances on the appropriate forms. Next we might consider a system in which all of the accounts and all of the checks carry an identifying number such that the numbers are read and sorted by machine into the appropriate accounts. Further we might consider a system in which the checks are not only sorted into accounts automatically, but in which balances are computed automatically by machine, the amounts of the checks and balances are printed out on the appropriate statements, and the statements are addressed and mailed out to the account holder, all by machine.

Each of these alternatives is realistic and workable. Further, I have discussed them in an order which represents increasing amounts of machine participation and decreasing amounts of human participation in the system as a whole. Incidentally, although I have mentioned only five different systems here, some engineers (see, for example, Amber and Amber, 1957) distinguish as many as ten different levels of automaticity in man-machine systems. The important thing to notice, however, is that the functions which human operators perform in each of these systems is different.

When we ask about the allocation of functions between men and machines we are asking essentially: What functions of the system should be assigned to men and what to machines? Or, what kinds of things can and should human operators be doing in a man-machine system? These are fundamental questions about man-machine system design. They are important because decisions about the allocation of functions influence all of the later design-thinking about the system. In fact some decisions about the allocation of functions should ideally be made before the first blueprints are drawn and before the first components are built.

EARLIER CONCEPTIONS OF THE MAN-MACHINE ALLOCATION PROBLEM

If we look at what various writers have said about the way in which functions should be allocated to men and machines we find little of direct and immediate help. Usually one finds a general discussion of the kinds of things that people do in man-machine systems and statements about some general characteristics of man as a component in man-machine systems. Often, too, one finds some general statements about the kinds of things people can do better than machines and vice versa (see Table 46-1 for an example).

Comparisons such as these serve a useful function, but only in the most elementary kind of way. I think they are useful primar-

Table 46-1. A Highly Abbreviated List of Some of the Relative Advantages and Disadvantages of Men and Machines (from Chapanis, 1960b)

Men	Machines
Able to handle low probability alternatives, i.e., unexpected events.	Difficult to program. Difficult to anticipate all possible events and so virtually impossible to program for all such contingencies.
Able to perceive, i.e., to make use of spatial and temporal redundancies and so to organize many small bits of information into meaningful and related "wholes."	Zero, or very limited, ability to perceive. "Organization" has to be elaborately programmed, which is difficult to do because of the many alternative ways organization can be formed from elements.
Possess alternative modes of operation. Can accomplish same or similar results by alternative means if primary means fail, or are damaged.	Alternative modes of operation limited. May break down completely when partial injury or damage occurs. Not able to regenerate or heal.
Limited channel capacity, i.e., there is a maximum amount of information that can be handled per unit time, and this is small.	Channel capacity can be made almost as large as desired.
Performance subject to decrement over fairly short time periods because of fatigue, boredom, and distraction.	Behavior decrements only over relatively long periods of time.
Comparatively slow and poor computers.	Excellent and very rapid computers.
Flexible; can change programming easily and frequently. Very large number of programs possible.	Relatively inflexible. Flexibility in kind and number of programs can be achieved only at a great price.

ily in directing our thinking toward man-machine problems and in reminding us, in general terms, of some of the characteristics that men and machines have as systems components. But when we come face-to-face with the practical realities of assigning functions in a genuine man-machine system, we find such general statements of almost no help at all. Why is this the case? The answer, I think, lies in the following:

1. General man-made comparisons are frequently wrong.

Like most general statements, the ones that compare men and machines are wrong, or at least misleading, in particular instances. Consider, for example, the statement that machines surpass people in computational ability. In general, I think most of us would probably agree with this. The giant digital computers with which we are all familiar clearly do fantastic computational feats at

speeds which are incredibly fast by mortal standards. Yet does this mean that we should always use a digital computer, or any kind of a machine, when there are computations to be done in a system? Not at all. Many kinds of computations in man-machine systems are still most logically and sensibly done "in one's head." For still other kinds of computations, the most sensible implements to provide are a pencil and a pad of paper. I think it also correct to say that digital computers are not likely to supplant an engineer and his slide rule for many kinds of tasks.

Numerous exceptions of this same character can be found to all of the general statements contained in Table 46-1. To sum up, then, when we come to apply general rules about human or machine characteristics to particular functions in real man-machine systems, we often find that the rules are wrong or misleading.

2. It is not always important to decide on a component which can do a particular job better.

The second reason why general statements such as those in Table 46-1 are often not useful in practical situations is that the systems engineer is not necessarily concerned with which component is the better of the two for a particular function. He may often be interested only in the question: Is the component good enough to do the job? Let me illustrate this point with the following example.

There are in the United States a large number of super-highways—highways which have from four to twelve lanes engineered with carefully designed curves, grades, and crossings so that they may carry a large volume of traffic (up to 10,000 vehicles per hour) at average speeds of 60 or more miles per hour (97 or more kilometers per hour). Some of these highways are toll roads—that is, the motorist must pay a fee or charge every time he travels on them.

There are two principal methods used to collect these tolls. One method makes use of human toll collectors who accept money from the motorist, make change if necessary, deposit the money into a collection box or register, and signal the motorist that he may proceed. The other method makes use of a machine. The motorist drives up to a collection bin and drops his money into the machine. The coins may be in any combination whatsoever that adds up to the required toll. The machine counts the money, and if the correct amount has been received, it switches a signal from red to green to tell the motorist that he may proceed. After the motorist has passed over a treadle, the machine resets its own cycle for the next automobile.

If you compare the two components—the human versus the machine toll collector—you find that the human can do the job much better in certain respects. Not only can he make change (which the machine

does not do), but he can take care of more automobiles per hour than the machine can. But does this mean that for the system as a whole we should use only human toll collectors? Not at all. Even though human toll collectors are better, the machines do the job well enough. In fact, from the standpoint of the operation of the system as a whole, the machines have enough other advantages to make up for their deficiencies.

3. General comparisons between men and machines give no consideration to trade-offs.

The last sentence above suggests the third reason why general statements about men and machines are often of little help. In the practical business of designing systems, the engineer always has to consider trade-offs— the values of using a particular kind of component versus the costs of using that component. Incidentally, I use the word "costs" here in its most general sense to refer to all the disadvantages that come with a particular component.

The cost-value problem is perhaps illustrated most easily in the field of space exploration. Suppose that we are considering a vehicle to do scientific studies on the surface of the moon. I think most of you would agree that we can plan to do many more kinds of experiments with our space vehicle if we have a well-trained astronaut on board than if we do not. A human is generally much more flexible, that is, he can do many more different kinds of things, than a machine. This advantage, however, carries with it a terrific penalty, and that penalty is weight. To enable the astronaut to live we have to provide him with a carefully controlled artifical environment, food, water, and all other things necessary for his survival. This means that much of the weight of the space vehicle is taken up with materials which serve no purpose other than to keep the astronaut alive.

In such a situation, one question the systems engineer wants to know is this: Is it better to design a vehicle which contains a human operator and less equipment, or is it better to design a vehicle which has no human operator and more equipment aboard? Comparisons such as those given in Table 46-1 unfortunately never help us to solve these trade-off problems.

SOME CURRENT VIEWS
ON THE DIVISION OF FUNCTIONS
BETWEEN MEN AND MACHINES

I should like now to turn to the third part of my paper and summarize for you a few of my thoughts about the problem of assigning functions to men and machines. In particular I want to make three generalizations which do not seem to have been expressed before.

1. The allocation of functions in man-machine systems is determined in part by social, economic, and political values.

The first general statement I should like to propose is that decisions about the assignment of functions in man-machine systems are always influenced to some extent by social, economic, and political values. These are usually unstated and implicit. Unfortunately, we in the United States often forget about these hidden assumptions because we know, or think we know, what our own social and economic values are. Let me see if I can illustrate what I mean by a simple example.

Imagine that we are considering the design of a mail-handling system for a new post office. The question arises whether the mail should be sorted and cancelled by people or automatically by machine. The proper answer to this question depends on a great many things, among them the cost of human labor, the attitudes and stereotypes which labor has toward monotonous and repetitive work, the value to the national economy of having these operations done by people instead of by machines, the availability of the machines and spare parts, the availablity of skilled maintenance techni-

cians to service the machines and keep them operating, the volume of mail that is normally handled by the post office, the attitudes of the citizens towards postal services and government work, and so on.

Given certain conditions I think it is quite possible that we might decide to have these jobs done by people; given other conditions we would undoubtedly conclude that these jobs should be done automatically. In any event, it is fairly clear that postal and communications systems which work well in some countries are not at all appropriate for other countries at the present time (see, for example, The International Bank for Reconstruction and Development, 1961 and 1962).

In its broadest terms, then, I am suggesting that man-machine systems are not entirely culture-free. Failure to recognize this fact can lead a systems designer into making some serious errors.

2. Assignment functions must be continually re-evaluated.

The second generalization I want to make is that assignment decisions are not fixed and immutable. These decisions are always made at some point in time, and relative to a particular state of development of engineering art. Not so many years ago it would have been completely meaningless to consider the possibility that we should use a machine to "read" numbers on checks and sort the checks automatically into their proper accounts. Today this question is not meaningless, because we do, in fact, have machines which can do precisely that.

On the other hand, it is trivial to ask today whether we could use a machine to read the addresses on letters and sort the letters automatically according to their destinations. There simply aren't machines available to read all of the kinds of handwriting that people use. Twenty years from now, however, this might no longer be a meaningless question. There is much work in progress on machines to read handwriting, and I am confident that these efforts will eventually be successful enough to merit serious consideration.

Designing a system is something like writing a book. Unless you draw a line in time and work against that deadline, you will never complete either job. This continual re-evaluation means, to paraphrase a common adage, that a human engineer's work is never done.

3. Many of the difficulties experienced in making allocation decisions arise from engineering uncertainties.

Those of us who are in the human sciences often feel insecure and apologetic about our own science and subject matter. We often feel that it is our ignorance about human behavior which is responsible for the difficulties we have in making decisions about man-machine system design. If you have ever worked closely with systems engineers, however, you soon come to realize that there is much uncertainty on the machine side of the equation as well. In the first place, there is no such thing as a system-design process, precise and specifiable (see Kossiakoff, 1960, and Salzer, 1961, for example). Instead, systems designers often proceed with much trial-and-error just as anyone else does. In addition, although I realize it is dangerous to make a generalization about this point, I have the feeling that engineers are sometimes overly optimistic in their predictions about what they can do with their machines. As a result, the final products frequently fall short of what had been anticipated for them.

For these and other reasons, one usually finds that allocation decisions are not fixed even for a single system. Instead, we find the engineers making a series of approximations, modifications, and changes during the development of the system as they discover that certain things can or cannot be done with the machine components. These, in

turn, require a continual re-examination of the roles which the men and machines are to play in the system.

A STRATEGY FOR MAKING ALLOCATION DECISIONS

Finally, I want to say a few words about what I consider to be the best strategy for making decisions about the division of labor between men and machines in systems. Let me say at the outset that I shall not give you any simple method for making these decisions infallibly because I do not believe that any such method exists. Rather I think that the best I can do is to give you a general approach to the problem.

1. Prepare a complete and detailed system specification.

The first step consists of preparing a complete and detailed specification of the system (see Chapanis, 1960b). We need to know precisely what the system is supposed to do, the environment in which it will operate, the inputs it will receive, the operations it will perform on these inputs, and the outputs it is supposed to produce. We also need to know in detail all of the constraints—engineering, environmental, economic, and social—under which it must be constructed and operated.

2. Analyze and list system functions.

The second step is to prepare a detailed list of the functions which the system is to perform. Perhaps the greatest error committed in this area is that psychologists are too fond of vague and general descriptive names which are of little use in practical work. Take the term "decision-making," for example. Psychologists use this term to refer to a broad spectrum of human behaviors. What a subject does in a choice-reaction experiment is referred to as decision-making. Similarly, what an industrialist does when he tries to decide manufacturing strategies is also called decision-making. Yet these are vastly different orders of complexity. A machine can often do the former, but seldom the latter. Other vague terms that are often used in this work are: sensing, perceiving, monitoring, shunting, short-term memory, scanning, coding, and so on.

The key to success here is that our list of systems functions must be highly specific and operational in character. It must describe the particular things that need to be done. As an example, take a mail-handling system for a post office. What are the functions that need to be performed? They are such things as:

a. Letters and cards must be sorted into certain size ranges.

b. Letters and cards within a size category must be stacked with the postage stamps oriented in a particular direction.

c. Mail must be checked to insure that it is carrying sufficient postage.

d. Stamps must be canceled.

And so on.

3. Make tentative assignments for each function.

The next step consists of assigning each of the jobs to be done to a man or machine, or, what is much more common, to some combination of a man and a machine. These decisions are made in terms of assignments that will be best for the operation of the system as a whole, given all of the constraints under which it must be constructed and operated.

With a detailed list of functions before us, assignment problems become much easier. Sometimes, in fact, they are immediately obvious. Consider, for example, the function of checking the mail to see that it has the correct postage. This has to be a human function in part. No one knows how to build a machine to read the values of postage attached to an envelope.

Sometimes, of course, assignment deci-

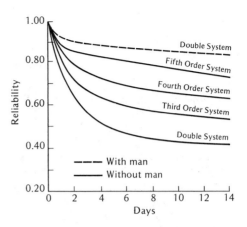

Fig. 46-1. The reliability of a double redundant navigation system in which one of the redundant components is a man (dashed line) as compared with the reliability of systems with various orders of redundancy in which all components are machines (solid lines). (After Grodsky, 1962.)

sions have to be made simply on the basis of our best judgment of what a man or a machine can, or cannot, do, or on the basis of our experience with similar systems which have been constructed in the past.

Finally, some decisions may have to wait for experimental evidence or the results of other types of studies to assist us in our decisions. It is unfortunate that the kind of information the human engineer, or the systems engineer, needs for these decisions is seldom to be found in textbooks of psychology. An example of the kinds of data the engineer needs is shown in Figure 46-1. This comes again from the field of space exploration. It compares the reliability of completely automatic systems of different levels of redundancy, against a single redundant system in which one of the components is a well-trained man. Notice how much more reliable the system is when we have a man provide the redundancy in the system. This is due, of course, to the flexibility which man brings to the system, but the important thing to notice is that the vague word *flexibility* has been translated here into a highly meaningful, systems-relevant criterion.

4. Evaluate the sum total of functions which have been assigned to man.

After individual tasks have been allocated to men and machines or to some combination of them, the sum total of the human functions must be carefully assessed to see that they make up a job which is interesting, motivating, and challenging to the human operator. Men, unlike machines, work best at some medium level of difficulty. If the job is too difficult, a man may give up in despair or break down under the strain of trying to do it.

On the other hand, it is not good to design a system in such a way that the human operator does nothing more than push a button occasionally. Under these circumstances, the operator soon realizes that he is being used inefficiently and he may become indifferent or inattentive, go to sleep, or even actively rebel against the system. This means that individual functions which might be done better by machine should sometimes be assigned to human operators solely for the purpose of making the job complex enough to match the human operator's psychological needs.

CONCLUSION

Let me conclude now with one more observation: The reason this is both such a difficult and such a challenging problem is that we are dealing here with integrated human behavior, with all its nuances, richness, variety, and complexity. In the final analysis, these are not problems of man versus machine, but rather of man versus man—man, the user and operator of machines, versus man, the designer of them

REFERENCES

Amber, G. H., and Amber, P. S., A yardstick for automation. *Instruments and automation,* 1957, 30, 677.

Bamford, H. E., Jr., Human factors in man-machine systems. Human Factors, 1959 1 (4), 55-59.

Chapanis, A. Le facteur humain dans la construction des systèmes. In *L'Automation: Aspects psychologiques et sociaux. Studia Psychologica.* Ed. by A. Chapanis, A. Lucas, E. H. Jacobson, N. H. Mackworth, L. Ancona, and G. Iacono. Louvain: Publications Universitaires, 1960a, pp. 7-38.

Chapanis, A. (1960b). Human engineering. In *Operations research and systems engineering* (ed. C. D. Flagle, W. H. Huggins, and R. H. Roy), 1960b. Baltimore: Johns Hopkins Press, pp. 534-82.

Chapanis, A. On some relations between human engineering, operations research, and systems engineering. In *Systems: Research and design* (Ed. by D. P. Eckman). New York: Wiley, 1961, pp. 124-66.

Churchman, C. W., Ackoff, R. L., and Arnoff, E. L. *Introduction to operations research.* New York: Wiley, 1957.

Fitts, P. M. Functions of man in complex systems. Aerospace Engineering, 1962, 21 (1), 34-39.

Gagné, R. M. (Ed.). *Psychological principles in system development.* New York: Holt, Rinehart and Winston, 1962.

Grodsky, M. A. Risk and reliability. *Aerospace Engineering,* 1962, 21 (1), 28-33.

International Bank for Reconstruction and Development. *The economic development of Tanganyika.* Baltimore: Johns Hopkins Press, 1961.

International Bank for Reconstruction and Development. *The economic development of Uganda.* Baltimore: Johns Hopkins Press, 1962.

Jordan, N. Allocation of functions between man and machines in automated systems, *Journal of Applied Psychology,* 1963, 47, 161-65.

Kossiakoff, A. The systems engineering process. In *Operations research and systems engineering* (Ed. C. D. Flagle, W. H. Huggins, and R. H. Roy). Baltimore: Johns Hopkins Press, 1960, pp. 82-118.

(Lomov, B. F. *Man and technology.* Leningrad: Leningrad University Press, 1963).

Morgan, C. T., Cook, J. S., III., Chapanis, A., and Lund, M. W. (Eds.) *Human engineering guide to equipment design.* New York: McGraw-Hill, 1963.

Salzer, J. M. Evolutionary design of complex systems. In *Systems: Research and design* (Ed. by D. P. Eckman). New York: Wiley, 1961, pp. 197-215.

Sinaiko, H. W., and Buckley, E. P. Human factors in the design of systems. In *Selected papers on human factors in the design and use of control systems* (Ed. by H. W. Sinaiko). New York: Dover Publications, 1961, pp. 1-41.

47

Is Human Factors Engineering Worth the Investment ?

KENNETH S. TEEL

The purpose of this paper is to demonstrate that human-factors engineering can be highly cost effective and yield high returns on investment. Three studies conducted at Autonetics during the past several years are reviewed: one in inspection, one in manufacturing, and one in missile silo safety. In each case, the study, its cost, and the savings resulting therefrom are described. These studies were chosen because (1) they represent work in three somewhat different areas, and (2) their findings appear to be applicable to many situations other than the specific ones studied. They were not chosen because they yielded unusually high returns on investment.

IMPROVING INSPECTOR PERFORMANCE

The first study (Chaney and Teel, 1967) was conducted to evaluate the effectiveness of specially prepared visual aids in improving the performance of machined-parts inspectors. Machined-parts inspectors examine precision parts for defects which might make them unsuitable for use. These inspectors were selected for study because previous investigations had indicated that they were

identifying less than 40 per cent of the defects in the items reviewed.

Fourteen inspectors with median inspection experience of eight years served as subjects. It was assumed that their performance was stable and would not improve as a result of incidental learning during the course of the study. The fourteen subjects were randomly divided into two groups of seven each, one group to serve as a control group, one to serve as the experimental group.

Four machined parts were fabricated for use in the study: two were brackets; the other two were motor supports. All four were fabricated to contain a representative sample of known defects. Each had approximately 100 characteristics to be inspected and 34 defects.

Initial (before) performance measures were obtained by having each subject independently inspect one bracket and one support. Final (after) performance measures were obtained by having each subject inspect the bracket and support he had not previously inspected. All subjects carried out their normal duties during the six months between testings.

Reprinted from *Human Factors*, 1971, 13 (1), 17-20, by permission of the author and the Human Factors Society.

Table 47-1. Defect Detection

Group	% Defects Detected Before	Detected After	% Change
Control	35.7	33.4	−6
Experimental	37.7	53.4	+42

The only difference between the control and experimental groups was in the type of inspection aids provided. The control group was given the standard inspection documents—a master blueprint and a set of written instructions for each of the two different parts. The experimental group was given a series of simple drawings of the sample parts—six for the bracket and eight for the support. The dimensions and tolerances for each characteristic were placed on the drawing; furthermore, similar items were grouped on a single page to encourage the inspector to examine the part fully for one class of defects before reviewing it for others. No training was given in the interpretation or use of the visual aids. Subjects in the experimental group were simply given the drawings immediately before their final inspections of the two parts and asked to use them in carrying out the inspection.

The results summarized in Table 47-1 indicate that use of the simplified visual aids resulted in significant improvements in defect detection ($p < .001$).

The estimated value of this improved inspection performance and the cost of the study are shown in Table 48-2. It is apparent from the table that the benefits gained by the company far exceeded the cost of the human factors engineering study. The total cost of the study was only $7,200, including the time of the inspectors who served as subjects, while the savings the first year were over $11,000. Since this particular production run was to continue for three years, the total savings over that time period were more than four times the cost of the study.

Furthermore, the figures cited are underestimates of the potential value of simplified visual aids, because the figures are based upon the use of such aids in the inspection of only two specific machined parts. Since the value of the aids has now been clearly demonstrated, it would be relatively easy and inexpensive to develop similar ones for use in inspecting other items of equipment, without incurring the expense of additional human factors engineering studies. If this were done, the return on investment from this particular study would obviously be much higher.

IMPROVING ASSEMBLER PERFORMANCE

The second study (Harris, 1968) was conducted to determine whether the performance of electronic assemblers could be improved through use of a specially designed, "human-engineered" work station.

The assemblers' task was to place 87 discrete components in the proper locations on a 3-x-3-in. ceramic printed-circuit module board. The assemblers normally determined

Table 47-2. Value of Visual Aids

Number of brackets and supports produced/year	500
Mean defects/500 parts	300
Number of defects (37%) detected without visual aids	111
Number of defects (53%) detected with visual aids	159
Number additional defects detected/year	48
Mean cost of correcting defect after machined part inspection	$ 45
Mean cost of correcting defect after next assembly	$ 275
Mean saving/defect detected at machined-part inspection	$ 230
Cost saving/year (48 defects × $230)	$11,040
Cost savings/three-year production run	$33,120
Cost of study	
Human factors engineering time	$ 3,600
Inspector time	$ 3,200
Preparation of visual aids	$ 400
Total	$ 7,200

where and in which direction a particular component was to be placed by consulting the narrative instructions and drawings contained in an operator instruction document. The inadequacy of the operator instruction document was evidenced by the fact that approximately 20 per cent of the completed boards contained at least one misplaced component.

In an attempt to reduce both assembly errors and assembly time, a human factors staff member, along with an industrial engineer, developed an experimental work station which features the projection of assembly instructions directly onto the module board. The station, consists of a film-strip projector, a film strip of instructions, numerically sequenced kits of parts, and a structure to tie these elements together. The circuit board is held on the work surface in a jig, and assembly instructions are projected on it. The instructions consist of a number, indicating which correspondingly numbered kit of components is to be used, and a series of light arrows indicating where and in which direction the components in the kit are to be inserted. When all components in one kit have been inserted, the operator advances the film strip to the next frame to obtain instructions for placement of the parts contained in the next kit.

An experimental comparison was made of performance following standard assembly methods with that using the projection work station. Six assemblers, with no previous experience with this type of module, served as subjects. All assembled the same module four times. They used the standard method on the first and fourth trials, and the experimental method on the second and third. In this way, the possible effects of learning were counterbalanced. Time and error measures were obtained on each trial.

The results, summarized in Table 47-3, indicate that performance was significantly faster and more accurate with the projection work station. Use of the projection station required 64 per cent less time and resulted in 75 per cent fewer errors.

Table 47-3. Module Assembly

Method	Mean Time/Module (Min.)	Total Errors
Standard	76	20
Experimental	28	5
	$p < .01$	$p < .05$

The value of the time savings and the cost of the study are shown in Table 47-4. Again, it is apparent that the savings to the company were approximately seven times as great as the cost of the study, even without attributing any value to the error reduction; that figure is not included because of the difficulties encountered in obtaining reliable estimates of the cost of identifying and correcting misplaced components. Furthermore, the cited return on investment is an underestimate of the true value because savings will accrue as long as the projection work station is used, while continuing costs will be limited largely to the preparation of new film strips.

VERIFYING WARNING SYSTEM AUDIBILITY

The third study (Plath, 1968) was conducted

Table 47-4. Value of Projection Work Station

Number of systems produced/year	190
Number of modules/system	44
Number of modules assembled/year	8,360
Assembly time/module with standard method	76 min.
Assembly time/module with projection station	28 min.
Time savings/module with projection station	48 min.
Cost saving/module (8/10 hour × $4.20) $4.20	$ 3.36
Cost saving/year ($3.36 × 8,360)	$28,090
Cost of study	
Human factors engineering time	$ 2,000
Subject time	$ 450
Design of work station	$ 750
Implementation (three stations)	$ 1,000
Total	$ 4,200

to test the audibility of a warning system used within a missile launch facility to indicate the leakage of toxic propellants.

The ballistic missile of interest contains limited quantities of monomethyl hydrazine, a liquid fuel, and nitrogen tetroxide, a liquid oxidizer, both of which are toxic. If a leak occurs in the propulsion system, toxic vapors are discharged into the launch facility. To safeguard personnel working in that facility, a portable vapor detector was developed which provides both visual and auditory alarms whenever vapor concentrations exceed safe levels.

Recently, concern was expressed that the auditory alarm might not be heard in the noisy environment of the launch facility and that, therefore, it might be necessary to install a more elaborate auditory warning system in all launch facilities. This study was undertaken to determine whether the portable vapor detector alarm could be heard under normal launch facility operating conditions.

The study was carried out in an operational missile silo at Vandenberg Air Force Base, California. The first step was to take noise-level readings at eight different locations chosen to represent the noisiest locations and those at which personnel most frequently work. Results indicated that ambient noise ranged from a low of 73 db. to a high of 89 db., with a median of 81 db. These findings confirmed the fact that the silo was a very noisy place in which to work, and supported the assumption that personnel working therein might have difficulty in hearing the portable vapor detector alarm signal.

The second step was to test the ability of the human operator to hear the alarm under normal operating conditions. Four contractor field representatives, from four different companies, served as subjects. The test was conducted as follows. The portable vapor detector was placed at its prescribed location in the silo. Three two-minute tests trials were conducted while the subjects were at each of their assigned stations. The alarm was sounded during some, but not all, of the two-minute trials. After each trial, subjects recorded whether or not they heard the alarm. They then moved to their next assigned stations for the next three trials. This procedure was repeated until all subjects had completed three trials at each of the eight locations at which noise levels had been measured, for a total of 96 trials in all.

Results indicated that subjects heard the alarm every time it was sounded, regardless of their location, and that they made no false reports that the alarm had sounded when it had not. This "perfect score" demonstrates clearly that the existing portable vapor detector auditory alarm system is adequate to insure the safety of personnel working in the silo.

The results also demonstrate that there is no need to retrofit approximately 500 silos with auditory amplification systems, Klaxon horns, or other more elaborate warning systems, to guard against personnel injury resulting from propellant leakage. Cost estimates for the installation of such systems ranged from $250,000 to over $1,000,000. These potential expenditures were avoided, in this case, by a human factors engineering study which cost slightly under $1,000.

DISCUSSION AND CONCLUSIONS

The above data indicate clearly that human factors engineering is worth the investment and has yielded returns far in excess of the cost of the studies conducted. The data cited, of course, are limited largely to the factory environment in which "before-after" cost figures are more readily available than in the engineering environment. The difficulty of obtaining comparable cost figures in the preliminary engineering area, in which human factors engineers do most of their work and perhaps make their most significant contributions, is well known to all workers in the field. Despite this fact, it seems reasonable to assume that human factors engineering work during the early stages of design and development would also yield high returns on investment because it prevents many design errors and eliminates much of the need for costly retrofit programs. As a matter of fact, work during the preliminary engineering phase might, when measured in dollar terms, prove even more cost-effective than the studies cited above.

In conclusion, human factors engineering has proven of significant value in reducing costs and improving effectiveness in inspection, manufacturing, and field maintenance activities. The data presented in this paper hopefully will represent initial entries in a data bank which in the future can be used to demonstrate further the cost-effectiveness of human factors engineering, not only in those areas but also in the design engineering field.

REFERENCES

Chaney, F. B., and Teel, K. S. Improving inspector performance through training and visual aids. *Journal of Applied Psychology*, 1967, 51, 311-15.

Harris, D. H. Projection work station for module assembly. IL 68-544-42-86. Autonetics, Anaheim, Calif.: December 1968.

Plath, D. W. Acoustical noise tests of portable vapor detector alarm—Vandenberg Air Force Base. T8-3048/501. Autonetics, Anaheim, Calif.: December 1968.

48

Shift Work and the
Sleep - Wakefulness Cycle

WALLACE BLOOM

Since the end of World War II, the need for shift workers has been rapidly expanding, both in the services and in industry. Our national defense now requires constant operational manning of missile bases, air-warning nets, communication facilities, base-security systems, and the like. And in industry, and particularly the chemical, metallurgical, and atomic industries, modern technology poses the same necessity for round-the-clock, seven-day-a-week operations.

Finding the most effective way of scheduling and assigning shift work is a problem with a direct bearing, therefore, on both our national security and our continued economic progress. Thus far, however, the attempts to solve it seem to have given insufficient attention to one of its most important aspects—the effects of shift work upon the biological rhythm of workers.

By habitually observing socially determined schedules specifying the hours for work, play, meals, and sleep, man has developed a diurnal rhythm—that is, a regularly recurring day-night variation in the chemical constituents of the blood and in the activity of the liver, kidneys, and endo-crine glands. It should be emphasized that this is not something with which we are born—it is induced by our observance of a particular pattern of sleep and activity. As our rhythm attains a degree of autonomy, it makes it easier for us to stay awake during certain hours of the day and harder for us to do so at other times.

Our diurnal rhythm also imposes a corresponding periodic character on our efficiency. This was shown as far back as 1906 in the tests of sensory activity, motor activity, and simple mental activity carried out by Marsh.[1] More recently, on the basis of a 20-year study of Munich industries, Lehman established a positive relation between efficiency and the amount of adrena-line in the blood.[2] And Kleitman, the recognized authority on sleep and wake-fulness, has demonstrated that there is a marked inverse relation between reaction

1. H.D. Marsh, *The diurnal course of efficiency* (Archives of Philosophy, Psychology, and Scientific Methods, No. 7). Columbia University Press, New York, 1906, p. 95.
2. G. Lehman, Diurnal rhythm in relation to working capacity, *Acta Medica Scandanavica* (Suppl. 278), CXLV, 108-9.

Reprinted by permission of the publisher and author from *Personnel*, March/April 1961. © 1961 by the American Management Association, Inc.

time and body temperature.[3] Reaction time is a good measure of alertness, while body temperature, which fluctuates through a range of about 2° F. each day, provides an accurate reflection of the rhythmic metabolic changes, for it reaches its low point between 2 and 5 A.M. and its high point in mid-afternoon. According to Kleitman's findings, we are most alert at the high point of our daily temperature curve and least alert at the low point.

But a particular temperature curve, like the rhythm of which it is an index, will eventually be altered if the day-night schedule that originally established it is replaced by a new one. As Kleitman points out:

If [man] remains awake during the entire night, both temperature and performance fall below their drowsiness levels, reaching minima between 2:00 A.M. and 4:00 A.M., when it is hardest to keep awake. Then there begins an upswing which crosses the drowsiness level at the usual getting-up time . . . . The curve can be shifted, inverted, distorted, shortened, or lengthened, by following a new schedule of activities for a certain number of weeks.[4]

The fixity of any individual's temperature curve is thus a simple measure of the degree to which he has adapted to a particular time cycle. When he is suddenly subjected to a new 24-hour schedule—as happens when a worker is assigned to a new shift—we can expect that his temperature curve will change, with the high point moving toward his activity period. This assumption has been confirmed by studies of the physiological effects of long-distance flights. The results are of course the same whether the new time schedule is imposed by shift rotation or by geographical change.

3. N. Kleitman, *Sleep and wakefulness*. University of Chicago Press, Chicago, 1939, p. 220.
4. Kleitman, The sleep-wakefulness cycle of submarine personnel, in *Human factors in undersea warfare*. Navy Department, Washington, D. C., 1949, pp. 329-30.

WHEN THE RHYTHM IS DISRUPTED

Until the adjustment has been completed, the individual will suffer a discrepancy between his accustomed sleep-wakefulness cycle and the one required by his new environment. Strughold has called this discrepancy "incomplete time or cycle adaptation."[5]

The effect of this discrepancy on shift workers, and particularly on rotating-shift workers, should perhaps be spelled out here. As we have seen, efficiency is directly related to diurnal rhythm. The worker suffering incomplete time adaptation therefore undergoes not only some physical discomfort but a loss in efficiency, for his body and mind are most ready to perform well at hours when he is off duty, or at only a few of his on-duty hours. Thus shift rotation, which at first glance seems so eminently fair because it provides for the equal sharing of the inconvenience of night work, imposes a physiological hardship on all the workers every time the shifts are changed and may lead to a general decrease in efficiency.

How long incomplete time adaptation persists has not yet been determined, but it is known that a flight across the Atlantic, which occasions a gain or loss of five hours, generally requires an adjustment period of a week or more. A change to a work shift six hours earlier or later than one's previous shift, even if it is preceded by a 24-hour rest period, must therefore impose an incomplete-adaptation period of at least several days. At all events, it seems certain that rotating the shifts at whatever time interval is most convenient administratively does not result in optimal performance and that many companies rotate their shifts too frequently for the adaptive powers of the employees concerned.

Besides the length of the adaptation period, several questions about the adapta-

5. H. Strughold, *The physiological day-night cycle in global flights*. U.S.A.F. School of Aviation Medicine, Randolph Field, Tex., 1952, p. 2.

tion process itself are worthy of further study. Does the adaptation proceed at a constant, gradual rate—say, one hour or two hours each day? Or is it irregular or even spasmodic—with no change occurring for the first several days and an abrupt change thereafter? Are there setbacks in the course of the adaptation—that is, reversions toward the original cycle? Research must provide the answers to these questions if management is to improve its shift scheduling to secure the highest possible degree of alertness on the part of the workers.

What we already know about the sleep-wakefulness cycle, however, affords a basis for several improvements upon current practice. The following suggestions will illustrate how the findings of physiological research might be applied by industry:

1. Selection of individuals for rotating shifts. It has been established that people vary in their ability to modify their diurnal rhythms. Some can adjust to a six-hour change in about a week; others find the adaptation very difficult. Kleitman and a companion once experimented with living an artificial six-day week. After six weeks, Kleitman was still experiencing seven temperature cycles a week, while his partner had changed to six.

"Since an individual's curve of performance follows his body-temperature curve," he recommended, "considerations of efficiency in doing work, in addition to purely humanitarian reasons, demand that the services concerned employ for night duty, or other abnormal shifts, only individuals who are capable of shifting or inverting their body temperatures on short notice."[6]

The problem of adaptation is doubly severe under shift rotation, for the workers involved must adapt both to the rotation itself and to night work. Companies that use this system should therefore carry out tests of the candidates' adaptability to these changes. The tests could take the form of

6. Kleitman, *Sleep and wakefulness*, p. 267.

measuring their temperatures after an experimental six- or eight-hour change in shifts or a change to night hours. When the men have spent a week or ten days on the new shift, the adaptability of their temperature curves can then be determined.

2. Special training and conditioning for shift work. Training programs for shift workers should include sessions at which physicians explain the diurnal rhythm and what happens in shift changes and during night work. The workers should also be told how they can best arrange their time-off activities for easing the adjustment to the new hours and getting to sleep during daylight hours. During the training period, the company should institute a gradual transition to the time schedule on which they will be working—by shifting their schedule one hour each day, for instance.

3. Fixed shifts instead of rotating shifts. Companies now using rotating shifts should review their scheduling problem to determine whether fixed shifts can be substituted. If they do decide to switch, they should explain all the reasons for their decision to the men involved.

The advantages of such a change were demonstrated in 1956 by an overseas military communications center. Partly on the advice of this writer but primarily because of a personnel shortage, the center abandoned its rotating four-shift schedule in favor of a fixed schedule of three shifts—from midnight to 7:30 A.M., from 7:30 to 4:30 P.M. (including time for a noon meal), and from 4:30 to midnight. The results proved beneficial in a number of ways. Performance improved as the men became familiar with the variations in work load peculiar to their shift. They grew accustomed to eating at the same time every day, and they no longer had to look at a calendar to ascertain which hours and days they were scheduled to work.

When some men were transferred and had to be replaced, the senior workers were given the option of changing their shifts. Most of them turned it down. The new men, though they did not like the system at first, soon adjusted to the schedule and fitted in well. Even those who had been accustomed to rotating shifts at their previous stations and were greatly upset by the new arrangement when they first arrived liked it better after a while.

The use of fixed shifts at this center also eased the manpower shortage: whereas 39 men had formerly been assigned to each shift to allow for rotation, the fixed shifts managed with from 33 to 39 men, according to the work load. The responsibility for setting the days-off schedule was given to the shift supervisors, and most men got two successive days off each week.

4. Fewer shift rotations. If rotating shifts prove unavoidable, the changes should be made infrequently. Rotating the assignments once a month rather than once a week (as many companies now do) would reduce the number of drastic physiological adjustments required of the workers from 52 to 12 a year. Since it takes air travelers at least a week to adjust to a six-hour change, we can expect that workers whose hours have been similarly altered are still suffering incomplete time adjustment on the third day of their new shift, when, in many companies, they once again have to change their working hours. The crews of transoceanic planes, Strughold recommended, should not be subjected to this change too often; and if they are regularly flying back and forth, they should be allowed to maintain the diurnal cycle of their home continent.

5. Longer rest periods between shift changes. Shift schedules should also be arranged to allow a maximum of time off between changes. With a reduction in the number of shift changes, it might be possible to allow workers as many as three days off.

6. Shorter time for the graveyard shift. Since the early-morning shift (from midnight onwards, say) is the period when it is most difficult to keep alert, shortening it would probably improve efficiency, as well as reduce the stress on the workers. A company with a four-shift cycle could cut the graveyard shift down to five hours by simply adding 20 minutes to each of the other three shifts.

7. More attention to personnel problems. Even with the aid of selection tests, no company can expect that it will assign to shift work only those employees who can make a healthy adjustment to it. Diagnostic interviews should therefore be held with shift workers who have accidents or show an above-average number of sick reports so that those with psychological difficulties can be weeded out.

These recommendations, derived as they are from the findings of physiological research, may perhaps seem somewhat unrelated to the practical requirements of a company that cannot confine its operations to a one-shift, five-day week. They are supported, however, by the findings of numerous studies of the effects of shift work, and particularly of shift rotation and night work, on the workers involved. Some of the more pertinent of these findings may be summarized.

In a survey of shift-work patterns among fifty large American companies in 1951, the National Industrial Conference Board found that fixed shifts were more usual than rotating shifts on a five-day operation with two or three shifts and that among companies with a rotating-shift system the rotation was generally on a weekly or fortnightly basis.[7] Some companies, the study found, added an extra (and versatile) man to each crew, so that it could work throughout the week while individual members still had regular days off. With seven men for every six jobs, say, there could be one man off each day, the extra man filling in for him; the latter, of course, would also get one day off a week.

7. See H. P. Northrup, *Shift problems and practices* (Studies in Personnel Policy, No. 118). National Industrial Conference Board, New York.

RESEARCH ON SHIFT WORK

The effects of various shift-work patterns have been studied in a number of countries, and from several points of view. Among American studies, two should be mentioned here. The first was concerned with the effects on a group of women workers of a change from a single nine-hour shift to two alternating six-hour shifts. Under the new system, some of the women, who worked in the morning for one week and in the afternoon for the next, reported difficulty in adjusting their habits of eating and sleeping. The second study found that workers whose shifts were changed found it even harder to adjust to the change in mealtimes than to get enough sleep. Of the workers questioned, 62 per cent complained of this difficulty, and 35 per cent said the adjustment took them more than four days.

In Sweden, researchers found many instances of failure to adjust to changing shifts. The shift workers, they pointed out, were being forced to live in a different time sequence from that of their community and of the many people to whom they were intimately related. In a study of errors made in entering figures in the ledgers of a large Swedish gas works under a rotating three-shift system, it was found that a very high number of errors occurred around 3 A.M. (The night shift ran from 10 P.M. to 6 A.M.) The number of errors did not vary significantly either by season or by day of the week. Moreover, the same variation in errors appeared on the last night of the week as on the first, indicating that the plant's weekly rotation system was not allowing the workers enough time to change the general pattern of their diurnal rhythm.[8]

Reviewing the findings of German research, Pierach reported one study that found ulcers eight times more common among shift workers than among day workers, and another that found them four times more common.[9] Of the 170 shift workers covered by still another study he mentioned, half gave up shift work because of ulcers. Only about 50 per cent of night workers can change to day work in one week, Pierach maintained, also noting that the loss of man-days through illness was greater in a three-shift than in a two-shift activity. During World War II some industries in Bavaria instituted a rotation system called the flying shift change, under which the crews worked for 12 hours and then had 24 hours off. This practice, however, had adverse effects on the workers' health.

A negative report on another scheduling system, the split shift, comes from a paper on the experience of the British munitions industries during the First World War. This system, under which a crew might work from 6 to 10 A.M. and then from 2 to 6 P.M., was very unpopular with workers, says the bulletin.

Finally, Japanese researchers have reported that officers engaged in coastal navigation lost sleep under a shift system and suffered chronic fatigue.

RESEARCH ON NIGHT WORK

Having to be awake during the usual hours for sleep poses a number of special problems, whether the workers involved are on a fixed night shift or are serving night duty on a rotating shift.

Perhaps the most obvious of these is the difficulty of getting enough sleep during the daytime. Of the workers questioned in a study by Maier, 42 per cent said that when they were on the night shift they did not sleep enough by day, and 75 per cent said

---

8. B. Bjerner et al., Diurnal variation in mental performance, *British Journal of Industrial Medicine,* April 1955, pp. 103-10. (Also reviewed in *National Safety News,* September 1955, pp. 55-56.)

9. See A. Pierach, Biological rhythm-effects of night work and shift changes on the health of workers, *Acta Medica Scandanavica* (Suppl. 307), CLII.

they got less than eight hours' sleep a day.[10]

Of the night workers covered in a German study reviewed by Pierach, slightly less than half reported getting more than five hours' sleep a day. The workers also complained of sleepiness, headaches, and a loss of ability to concentrate. Errors and accidents were more frequent during night work than during day work, the same study found. Some other effects of night work have also been reported by Pierach. A study of nurses on a night shift found that they suffered loss of appetite (as demonstrated by weight) and digestive interruptions, and that there was too much acid in their small intestines. Doctors have recommended that an ulcer patient be removed from night shifts. And, of the night workers studied in one investigation, 25 per cent eventually gave up night work.

Similiar data have been supplied by two studies of British industry. One cites as the main objection to night work the inability of workers to obtain adequate sleep by day. This problem may be attributable to the disruption of the workers' ordinary habits, the paper suggests, or its causes may be social—noises and disturbances, or the responsibility of caring for one's children. The workers studied said they were often tempted to curtail their period of sleep in order to join the family midday meal or to obtain some recreation. The study of munitions industries mentioned above found that it was difficult for night workers to consume substantial food at an unfamiliar meal hour and that their digestion was likely to be upset.

Further word on the sleep problem has come from some investigators in the United States who point out that the night worker's sleep is likely to be disturbed by the presence of daylight and the extra noise and heat of the daytime. Their studies have

convinced them that work should never be scheduled for the nighttime.

Since loss of sleep has been found to be so prevalent among night workers, its physiological effects deserve further mention.

In 1951, research psychologists at Tufts College conducted an experimental study of the effects of loss of sleep on subjective feelings.[11] As might be expected, of the 415 college undergraduates who participated, those who slept between eight and nine hours each day felt much better than those who slept only six hours. Subjects who went without sleep for long periods of time reported that feelings of sleepiness came in waves, reaching their peak between 3 and 6 A.M. The subjects also felt irritable and noted that their ability to carry out tasks requiring attention and effort had decreased. The 17 subjects who remained awake for 100 hours were restless as well, and complained of headaches. They did not recover until they had lived and slept normally for one week.

In a study of the effects of loss of sleep and rest on air crews, McFarland found that loss of sleep had marked effects on performance on mental tests requiring prolonged effort and continuous attention.[12] The most striking changes were loss of memory, hallucinations, heightened irritability, and wide fluctuations in emotional state.

The correlation between loss of sleep and loss of efficiency at tasks requiring continuous attention has been confirmed by other studies, though it is also known that short tasks may be performed with little diminution of efficiency over a considerable time.

10. N. R. F. Maier, *Psychology in industry.* 2nd ed.; Houghton Mifflin, Boston, 1955, p. 450.

11. Tufts College: Institute for Applied Experimental Psychology, *Handbook of human engineering data.* Special Devices Center, Office of Naval Research, Port Washington, N.Y., Part 7, chap. 2, Sec. I, Data T. 1-6.

12. R. A. McFarland, *Human factors in air transportation.* McGraw-Hill New York, 1953, p. 343.

In general, the quality of work suffers more than the quantity.

THE NEED TO RESPECT RHYTHM

To sum up, then, most shift workers experience serious inconveniences of two kinds: disruption of their normal diurnal body rhythms and, largely as a result of this disruption, loss of sleep resulting in fatigue. The effects of fatigue are cumulative and, to make matters worse, frequently show no obvious sign, so that a man's performance may be severely impaired without his being aware of it.

The need to respect the normal diurnal rhythm has been forcefully expressed by Pierach: "No organ or organ system is exempt from the 24-hour rhythm in its function. . . . Rhythm heals; continued activities contrary to rhythm make one weak and sick."[13]

For centuries now, men have studied the ebb and flow of the oceans and have used the knowledge thus gained to schedule the comings and goings of ships with a high degree of exactitude. By comparison, we still have much to learn about the tides within the human body—and what little we do know is still not being used to schedule the activities of men to best advantage. It is to be hoped that with further research and experimentation we shall ultimately be able to design shift-work schedules that will insure maximum efficiency and a minimum of personal hardship.

13. Pierach, *op. cit.*, p. 159.

49

Worker Adjustment to the Four-Day Week:

A Longitudinal Study

WALTER R. NORD and ROBERT COSTIGAN[1]

The four-day work week has been and most probably will continue to be introduced in many organizations. This change may have profound effects on the lives of many individuals. While considerable speculation and anecdotal information has been published, to date there is little reliable empirical evidence about the effects of the four-day week on workers.

The only major empirical study that could be found was reported by Steele and Poor (1970). Their data showed that workers overwhelmingly saw the change as beneficial for their lives at work and at home. However, because Steele and Poor's study was primarily descriptive and cross-sectional and the authors did not state how long various parts of their population had been on the four-day week, inferences concerning individual adjustment over time were not possible.

The present exploratory research was designed to provide longitudinal data on the responses of people to the four-day work week. Since it was expected that reactions to

the four-day week would change over time, the design called for repeated measurements in the same plant.

METHOD

Subjects

The data were collected from employees of a nonunionized medium-sized St. Louis-based pharmaceutical company that had recently changed from a work week of five 8-hour days to four 9½-hour days.[2] The plant employed approximately a hundred members of each sex for whom the average age was in the late 40s. The employees were described by management as a closely knit group; many of the workers were related to each other. Only foremen, group leaders, and lower-level employees who were working in the plant for at least ten of the twelve months covered by the survey and were employed there at the time of both the first

2. While initially the change was on a trial basis, there was every indication that it would be permanent if it was successful. Approximately three months after the beginning of the trial period, it was formally announced that the change would be permanent.

1. The authors wish to thank Francis Connelly for his help with parts of the data analysis.

Reprinted from *Journal of Applied Psychology*, 1973, 58, 60-66, by permission of the authors and the publisher. © 1973 by the American Psychological Association.

and the third administrations of the questionnaire were included in the analysis. From this pool, 131, 126, and 111 usable questionnaires were received for Surveys 1, 2, and 3, respectively. For most analyses all the subjects were included; however, for several analyses only those 59 subjects who responded to all measurements were included.

The plant itself was highly automated. Many jobs were heavily machine-paced; for the most part work on these jobs consisted primarily of monitoring machinery.

Procedure

A questionnaire was designed to elicit information on demographic factors, attitudes toward the four-day week, and changes in work and home life resulting from the new work schedule. The questions were mainly open ended, although some closed and scaled items were used. The questionnaire was distributed with each persons's paycheck at three different times. The first administration was July 7, 1971, 6 weeks after the initial trial period had begun; the second administration was August 24, 1971, 13 weeks after the initial trial period had begun; and the final administration was May 25, 1972, approximately 1 year after the initial trial period had begun. The same questionnaire was used each time, except for changes in time references and the addition of a question after each survey.

Interviews with the personnel and other managers were used to supplement the questionnaire data but, except in interpreting the absenteeism data, are given little attention in this report.

Analysis

Responses to the closed-end items were simply recorded. The open-ended responses were coded into the categories listed in Table 49-1. The coded and closed-end items for each survey were cross tabulated. Only the cross tabulations that were relevant to the effects of the four-day week were run; such relationships as age versus sex or age versus number of children were not considered.

To measure over-all attitudes, subjects were asked to check one of five statements that best described their feelings about the old and new work weeks. Two statements favored the four-day week, one was neutral, and two favored the five-day week. For purposes of analysis, the two favorable statements were interpreted as showing favorable over-all attitudes to the four-day week; the other three were interpreted as showing less favorable attitudes.

Information was also collected about the subjects themselves. The demographic variables of sex, age, marital status, and children living at home were dichotomized into age groups of 40 and under versus 41 and over, married versus not married, and one or more children living at home versus none living at home. In addition, data on the average number of hours of sleep and data on weight were included for analysis.

Finally, the jobs were classified as high or low paced. High-paced jobs were ones where the worker's pace was determined primarily by an assembly line or a machine; these jobs were mainly in shipping and receiving, processing, and packaging. Low-paced jobs included office, janitorial, maintenance, and cafeteria personnel.

Statistical analysis. Due to the small number of responses for each coding element shown in Table 49-1, the dichotomous categories were used as the unit for analysis. The NUCROS and CROSTAB programs were used to cross-tabulate the results of pairs of variables.

Several types of statistical tests were appropriate for various comparisons, depending on the type of data, number of subjects, and the purpose of the comparison. To test the differences between time periods, either analysis of variance or tests of differences between proportions were used. To test relationships within time periods, either the chi-square or the Fisher exact probabilities test was used.

RESULTS

Over-all Attitudes toward the Four-Day Week

For all three surveys, over-all attitudes toward the four-day week were very favorable:

Table 49-1. Open-Ended Questions and Major Categories and Elements for Coding

Dichotomous Coding Category	Element
1. What plans (if any) have you made for the three-day weekend?	
a. Plans versus no plans. b. Type of plan—task or recreational.	a. Plans listed or not. b. *Task*—shopping, doctor's appointments, work around house, moonlighting, special work projects. *Recreational*—sports, rest and relaxation, visit relatives and socialize, travel.
2. In the last —— weeks, have you noticed anything different about your job? If yes, please describe.	
Job changes—favorable versus unfavorable to company goals.	*Favorable to company goals*—more work done, higher employee morale, more relaxed at work, employees busier, better continuity of projects, less absenteeism, better adjusted. *Unfavorable to company goals*—less work done, greater fatigue, lower employee morale.
3. In the last —— weeks, have you noticed anything different about the plant (or office)? If yes, please describe.	
Changes in plant—favorable versus unfavorable to company goals.	*Favorable to company goals*—more work done, higher employee morale, more relaxed at work, employees busier, better continuity of projects, less absenteeism, better adjusted. *Unfavorable to company goals*—less work done, greater fatigue, lower employee morale.
4. In the last—— weeks, have you noticed anything different about your home life? If yes, please describe.	
Changes in personal life—favorable versus unfavorable to self.	*Favorable to self*—more time with family and friends, more rest and relaxation, get more done at home, other happiness feelings, moonlighting, better adjusted. *Unfavorable to self*—less time with family and friends, problems—e.g., meals, housekeeping, more tired after work, emotional problems, spend more money.

81 per cent highly favorable to 19 per cent less favorable. The percentages remained nearly constant for all three surveys.

Attitude and pace. Table 49-2 shows the frequency of responses for attitude toward the four-day week for individuals under high- and low-paced jobs. It can be seen that in all three periods, workers favored the four-day week for both types of jobs. While no significant association between job pace and attitudes was found 6 or 13 weeks after

initiation, after 1 year attitudes of workers on low-paced jobs tended to be less favorable toward the four-day week than those of workers on high-paced jobs ($\chi^2 = 4.21$, $p < .05$). To further explore the correlates of attitudes and job pace, chi-square and/or Fisher exact probabilities were calculated for the relationship of pace with perceived changes in home life, in the job, and in the plant for each survey. None of these tests reached statistical significance.

Table 49-2. Cross Tabulations of Attitude toward Four-Day Week and Job Pace Over Time

Job	Time since Initiation					
	6 weeks		13 weeks		1 year[a]	
	Favorableness of Attitude					
	Low	High	Low	High	Low	High
Low-paced	12	46	13	51	14	39
High-paced	10	54	8	45	6	49

[a]$\chi^2 = 4.21, p < .05.$

Over-all attitude and selected demographic variables. The results of cross tabulations of attitude with age, sex, marital status, and children living at home were subjected to chi-square analysis for each of the three surveys. No significant associations between attitudes and these demographic factors appeared for any of the three periods.

Over-all attitudes and specific attitudinal dimensions. To determine what specific attitudes might account for differences in over-all attitudes, all of the variables in Table 49-1 were tested for their association with over-all attitudes. Chi-square analysis was used to test the association between worker's over-all attitudes and the number of specific plans. These data, summarized in Table 49-3, indicated that people without plans held less unfavorable over-all attitudes toward the new work week than people with plans both 6 weeks and 1 year after the change ($\chi^2 = 18.74$, $p < .001$ and $\chi^2 = 6.12$, $p = < .01$, respectively). While many people without plans were still favorable to the four-day week, a large majority of those who held less favorable attitudes did not mention any plans for the three-day weekend. The mention of plans was also positively associated with favorableness of the reported changes in home life 6 weeks after initiation of the four-day week ($\chi^2 = 5.28$, $p < .05$).

Further analysis revealed that the type of plans people had (recreational vs. task oriented) were not related to their attitudes after 6 and 13 weeks. However, 1 year after initiation people with recreationally oriented plans were apt to show less favorable attitudes toward the four-day week (Fisher's exact test, $p < .001$).

The association of over-all attitudes with changes in job and plant were tested for each period using Fisher's exact test. No significant associations were found between attitudes and perceived changes at any time period. However, after both 13 weeks and 1 year, workers who perceived the changes as favorable to company goals held more favorable attitudes toward the four-day week ($p = .0006$ and $p = .0036$, respectively).

Specific Attitudes over Time

In order to see what specific changes occurred over time, the proportions of the number of reports of perceived changes in job, plant, home life, and the number of plans to the total number of subjects in each survey were calculated. The results presented in Table 49-4 showed a significant tendency for people to perceive more changes in their home life after 6 weeks than after 13 weeks ($Z = 2.22$, $p < .05$) and 1 year ($Z = 2.66$, $p < .01$). Moreover, they reported fewer plans

Table 49-3. Frequency of Attitudes toward the Four-Day Week versus the Presence or Absence of Plans for the Three-day Weekend by Time Period

Attitude	Time since Initiation					
	6 weeks[a]		13 weeks		1 year[b]	
	Plans					
	Yes	No	No	Yes	Yes	No
Favorable	62	44	51	50	43	42
Unfavorable	2	21	8	14	4	16

[a]$\chi^2 = 6.12, p = .01.$
[b]$\chi^2 = 18.74, p < .001.$

Table 49-4. Proportions of Reports of Changes to Total Number of Respondents by Time Period

	Time since Initiation of Four-Day Week		
Type of Change	6 weeks (N = 131)	13 weeks (N = 126)	1 year (N = 111)
Plant	.13	.13	.16
Job	.20	.24	.32
Home life	.48	.37*	.35***
Plans	.79	.68	.83**

   * Different from p1, p<.05.
  ** Different from p2, p<.05.
*** Different from p1, p<.01.

after 13 weeks than after 1 year ($Z = 2.55$, $p<.05$). Similarly, they reported making fewer plans after 13 weeks than after 6 weeks ($Z = 1.82$, $p<.07$). Also, they perceived more job changes over time: after 1 year more job changes resulting from the new work week were reported than after 6 weeks ($Z = 1.93$, $p<.06$). Thus, over the period of 1 year, subjects tended to report proportionately fewer changes in home life but slightly more changes in job life.

The data were tested for qualitative changes over time. Tests of proportions compared the three periods on changes in plant, changes in job, changes in home life, plans versus no plans, and type of plans. No significant differences in proportions between time periods were found for changes in plant, changes in job, plans versus no plans, and types of plans. However, as shown in Table 49-5, 6 weeks and 13 weeks after initiation 63 per cent and 64 per cent of the effects on home life were seen as favorable, whereas after 1 year only 45 per cent were seen as favorable. The differences between the first two and the third periods were both statistically significant ($Z = 2.13; 2.12; p<.05$, respectively). For the most part these differences were due to workers reporting few favorable effects after one year.

Personal Factors and the Four-Day Week

Data on the personal variables (a) hours of sleep and (b) weight were collected after all three periods. For each dependent variable, an analysis of variance for repeated measures was performed on the 59 subjects who answered these questions in all three surveys. No statistically significant weight changes were found. However, after one year on the four-day week, workers averaged 6.72 hours of sleep per night as compared to 7.05 hours per night on the five-day week and 6.98 and 7.02 hours per night after 6 and 13 weeks on the four-day week. This main effect was statistically significant ($F = 2.95$, $df = 3/171$). Most of this effect was due to a decline in the hours of sleep reported after 1 year on the four-day week.

Demographic factors. The appropriate test of association was run for age versus changes in home life, types of plans, changes in job, and changes in plant on the data from each time period. Of the 12 tests, only the relationship between worker's age and the type of plans they made reached an

Table 49-5. Frequency and Proportions of Responses Indicating Effects on Home Life over Time

Effect on Home Life	Time since Initiation					
	6 weeks		13 weeks		1 year[a]	
	Responses					
	No.	%	No.	%	No.	%
Favorable to personal life	63	63	47	66	29	45
Unfavorable to personal life	36	37	24	34	35	55
Total	99	100	71	100	64	100

[a]Proportions differed significantly from 6 and 13 weeks. $p<.05$.

Table 49-6. Frequencies of Type of Plans for Three-Day Weekend versus Age by Time Period

Plans	Time since Initiation of Four-Day Week					
	6 weeks		13 weeks[a]		1 year[b]	
	Age					
	40 and under	41+	40 and under	41+	40 and under	41+
Recreational	30	29	35	25	30	22
Task oriented	19	26	9	17	12	28

[a] $\chi^2 = 4.08, p < .05.$
[b] $\chi^2 = 6.99, p < .01.$

acceptable level of significance. As shown in Table 49-6, 13 weeks and 1 year after initiation, older workers tended to make more task plans and younger workers made more recreationally oriented ones ($\chi^2 = 4.08, p < .05; \chi^2 = 6.99, p < .01$).

The appropriate tests of association of sex of worker versus changes perceived in plant, home life, plans, and job were run for each survey. Of the 12 tests, 3 reached acceptable levels of significance; all 3 of these relationships appeared in the third survey. As shown in Table 49-7, after 1 year females (more than males) saw the change to the four-day week as resulting in changes on their job which were more favorable to the

company and changes in their home life which were more favorable to them. Moreover, females made more task-oriented plans and males made more recreationally oriented plans. Again, these relationships reached statistical significance only after 1 year.

The appropriate test of association was run for marital status versus home life and plans for all three surveys. None of these relationships was statistically significant.

In the surveys conducted 13 weeks and 1 year after the change, information on the number of children living at home was collected. The appropriate test for association was run on children living at home (none, one, or more) versus plans and home life. Of the four tests, only one relationship reached significance. One year after the change, people with one or more children living at home more frequently felt the four-day week had unfavorable consequences on their personal life ($\chi^2 = 4.66$, $df = 1$, $p < .05$) than did people with no children living at home.

Absenteeism

The average hours of absenteeism per day for the 5 months prior to and the 16 months following the introduction of the four-day week are reported in Table 49-8. In order to control for the partial confounding of the

Table 49-7. Frequencies of Responses after One Year for Sex versus Changes in Job, Plans, and Changes in Home Life

Sex	Changes in Job[a]		Plans[b]		Changes in Home Life[c]	
	Favorable to company goals	Unfavorable to company goals	Recreation	Task oriented	Favorable to personal life	Unfavorable to personal life
Male	14	10	29	23	13	16
Female	10	1	14	25	13	10

[a] $p = .05$ (Fisher's exact probability test).
[b] $\chi^2 = 3.83, p = .05.$
[c] $\chi^2 = 4.65, p < .05.$

change in the length of the work week with normal seasonal variation, two sets of comparisons were made.

1. The January-May 1971 period (prior to the four-day week) was compared with both the June-September 1971 period (the first 4 months following the new work week) and the January-May 1972 period.

2. The June-September 1971 period was compared with the October-December 1971 and June-September 1972 periods.

As the footnote to Table 49-8 implies, the periods were not directly comparable due to a 10 per cent reduction in the work force. However, even if a full 10 per cent was subtracted from the figures for the earlier periods, absenteeism after initiation would still be less than it was before. The January-May 1971 figure minus 10 per cent is about 42.7 compared to 37.7 for the comparable 1972 period and 40.5 for the June-September period of 1971. Similarly, the June-September 1971 figures minus 10 per cent is about 34.6 compared to 30.2 for the comparable 1972 period, although the October-December 1971 period would appear to be the same or slightly higher than that of the pre-introduction period. Thus, when seasonal factors and changes in the number of employees are controlled for, the four-day week was associated with a decrease in absenteeism of over 10 per cent. Moreover, a

Table 49-8. Hours of Absenteeism per Work Day

Year	Period		
	January-May	June-September	October-December
1971	47.4	40.5	44.5
1972	37.7	30.2	Not available

Note. During the 21-month period, employment declined approximately 10%. Thus, the early 1971 figures are based on slightly more people than the later 1971 and the 1972 figures.

comparison of the 4-month period immediately following the introduction of the four-day week was compared with the comparable period 1 year later, the level of absenteeism was approximately 10 per cent lower for the latter period.

DISCUSSION

The results of this study must be interpreted cautiously for several reasons. First, the data were collected from only one plant for one year. Second, the differences between some of the periods were confounded with seasonal variations and other uncontrolled forces. Finally, the effect of repeated questioning is unknown. Given these limitations, this exploratory study still revealed several trends to direct future research. In particular, employees had consistently positive attitudes toward the four-day week. They saw the change as favorable to company goals and as having little effect on their individual work environment throughout the research period. The perceived favorableness of the effects on home life varied over time. One year after the change, the effects of the four-day week on home life were perceived as significantly less positive than at first.

In addition to these findings, several possibly significant patterns emerged.

1. Most reports of unfavorable changes were home- rather than work-related. For all three surveys, only 37 responses indicating unfavorable changes in job and changes unfavorable to company goals were reported. By contrast, the corresponding number of unfavorable changes in home life was 95. Moreover, the proportion of negative changes on home life increased significantly over time; no similar changes occurred on work-related responses.

2. Although the data on absenteeism were confounded with decreases in employment and seasonal factors, absenteeism 12 to 16 months after the introduction of the four-day week was approximately 10 per cent less than the 4-month period immediately following the change.

3. Perhaps the most important implication of the present study for future research concerns the observed tendency for few significant patterns of response to occur soon after the change but for a larger number of patterns to become apparent over the period of one year. While a certain number of statistically significant results were to be expected as a function of the number of tests run, the tendency for significant results to appear after 1 year but not after 6 or 13 weeks suggests that many of the effects of the four-day week may be stronger over time. Thus, studies of the four-day week may yield sharply different results depending on how long after the change they are conducted. Individual adjustments to changes which effect established daily routines may take some time to develop into new stable patterns.

The specific content of some of the relationships that emerged over time also merit further investigation. The fact that after both 6 weeks and 1 year workers who reported making plans to use the three-day weekend were significantly more likely to perceive the new work week favorably draws attention to social psychological problems of leisure. While the findings in this study could be due to such factors as personality characteristics, if they are replicated in other research, organizations may find counseling in use of leisure to be a useful step. Further support for this argument came from the tendency for the reported effects on home life to become more negative over time. Perhaps when the novelty of the change subsided, some individuals, particularly the roughly 20 per cent who had not made any plans, found the larger block of leisure time less attractive than at first.

The data also suggested that age and sex may be related to plans to use leisure time. Since younger and male workers were more apt to make recreationally oriented plans than older and female workers, and females were more apt to see the influence on home life as being more favorable, perhaps females experienced interrole conflict between their job outside the home and their role of "homemaker." Their new full day of "leisure" permitted them to catch up on the "housework" that the social norms of our society still require of women. Their new leisure time was more "structured" and they felt better about their performance of one of their major social roles. Males, by contrast, may have had fewer tasks required by their nonwork roles. They made more recreational plans but did not feel the increment in satisfaction from a reduction in interrole conflict that females might have experienced. If future research replicates these findings, and our sex roles do not change radically, it may well be that the four-day week will be of greater benefit for females than for males.

REFERENCE

Steele, J. L., and Poor, R. Work and leisure: The reactions of people at 4-day firms. In R. Poor (Ed.), *4 days 40 hours.* Cambridge, Mass.: Burk & Poor, 1970.

50

OSHA Compliance:
"Safety Is Good Business"

ROLLIN H. SIMONDS

The Occupational Safety and Health Act (OSHA) is beginning to force tens of thousands of businesses to do what many of the larger companies have been doing for years—that is, carry on effective accident control programs. While larger companies are not necessarily better managed than smaller ones, their size makes it practical to employ many staff specialists that smaller firms cannot afford. These staff specialists have the knowledge, time, and facilities to prepare reports that help make higher levels of management cognizant of the impact of many facets of operation on their cost and profit structure. Thus, a former vice-president of General Motors could make an often-quoted comment that "safety is good business."

One can have some sympathy for the managers now almost frantically concerned to find out what OSHA or a state safety inspection force is requiring. It is true that in the tremendous task of determining a myriad of standards for many different industries in a short time, OSHA has established some that appear to need added flexibility to meet certain situations. The worried managements might take some comfort, however, from three facts:

First, even though the highest purpose of safety is the minimizing of human injuries and deaths, records show that accident reduction is generally accompanied by cost savings greater than the safety expenditures, including, of course, workmen's compensation insurance and statistically measurable uninsured costs, as well as many intangibles.

Second, the basic purpose of both OSHA and state safety bureaus is the prevention of injuries. Inspectors do not normally try to levy maximum fines for the least infraction of standards. When inspectors find management cooperative in correcting unsafe physical conditions and unsafe acts, they are inclined to try to give the company time to put things in order, even though violations except those of a "de minimus" character must be prominently cited. It is the imminently dangerous situation that they cannot allow to continue even temporarily, and it is failure to make corrections in such a situation that is likely to draw significant penalties.

Third, it is highly unlikely that a particular company will be inspected by OSHA for a long time. For the fiscal year ending June 30, 1973, 110,000 compliance inspections were proposed and funded, but the number actually made is far short of that—probably 55,000 or less. For this fiscal year, 80,000 inspections are budgeted. When one recognizes that more than 5,000,000 workplaces are covered by the Act, it is apparent that less than one in 60 is scheduled for an OSHA inspection this year.

As for the last two points, a system of priorities has been established for inspections, which will be made first where fatalities have occurred, in industries that are known to have bad injury records, and where employees have requested inspection. This means that most companies have considerable time to put their houses in order, particularly very small firms and those in industries where the severity of injuries is low. Furthermore, the fines for violations discovered by inspectors and then corrected are quite small—fines of $25 to $1,000 are not really great enough to have very serious effects. On the other hand, however, failure to correct violations for which citations have been issued can, after administrative review, result in penalties of up to $1,000 a day.

COMPLYING WITH FEDERAL AND STATE STANDARDS

What should a company do to keep out of trouble with OSHA or a state inspection and enforcement agency? First, depending on the size and nature of the company, someone should be assigned full-time or part-time to develop or carry on a safety program. This person should obtain from the *Federal Register* statements of standards applicable to the industry in question. He should then be sure to include compliance with these in his over-all program and should also set up procedures for reporting work injury data as required by OSHA. The U.S. Government Printing Office has a series of self-inspection guides and a kind of index or subject locator that facilitates use of the *Federal Register*. Still another source of information is the OSHA monthly publication, *Job Safety and Health*.

Generally, the OSHA requirements will be approximately paralleled by state standards if the state has been authorized to carry out inspections and enforcement

within its borders. But meeting these standards is only a part of a total activity for accident control; indeed, a well-conceived and well-run program for injury control would include a great part of what have become OSHA standards even if there were no such federal law.

The *Federal Register* does not provide full instructions for the operation of a safety program; it is only a source for current legal standards; so the person who has been assigned general safety responsibility will need a basic textbook and might benefit from other materials, such as those that can be obtained from the National Safety Council. Another source of guidance is the advisory service of the insurance company carrying a company's workmen's compensation insurance. Since the amount insurance companies spend on this service is likely to be in the neighborhood of one or two per cent of premiums, however, it is clear that unlimited help cannot be expected here.

Some state safety bureaus also provide assistance. One of the most useful of these is the safety education and training division of the Michigan Department of Labor Bureau of Safety. This unit makes available a consultant who will show the economics of accident control through cost estimates, work with management to establish an over-all program, and point out some of the correctable conditions or practices. While most of these activities are in greatest demand by small companies, the division also provides training courses used by some industrial giants.

MAIN CONCERN: PHYSICAL CONDITIONS, HUMAN CONDUCT

No outside assistance can substitute for an interested management and an effective safety manager inside. Basically, two activities are necessary to control work accidents—correcting accident-producing physical conditions, and minimizing unsafe acts. Avoiding the establishment of unsafe physical conditions or correcting any already in existence is the preferable procedure for several reasons:

Frequently, sound engineering or construction will completely preclude the possibility of a particular kind of accident. For example, if the hazard involves a point of operation where hands could be mangled, the equipment may be designed or guarded in such a way that it is impossible for a worker's hands to get into the space where they could be cut or pinched. If the hazard is an open fly-wheel or belt, it can be enclosed so that a break will not send parts flying free. If it is a process releasing toxic vapors, a change in chemicals or an operational design that removes the vapors and then renders them harmless is better than requiring personal protective equipment for workers. Masks, gloves, safety glasses, ear muffs, and so forth are essential in some situations, but elimination of the danger is not only more comfortable for the worker but a more certain control. The control of human behavior is never absolute.

To take a less humanitarian view and consider legal risks, unsafe physical conditions are likely to be more easily spotted by government inspectors and more specifically detailed in federal or state standards than unsafe acts. The construction of new facilities always affords opportunity either to build in safety or to create long-run, costly problems for accident control, but the present legislation largely cancels the option of taking a calculated risk in erecting structures with accident-producing features. To illustrate, a new power plant now being constructed in Michigan is expected to cost something in the neighborhood of $2 million more to meet the federal safety standards than it would have cost otherwise. Still, the total construction cost of that plant will probably be around $200 million; so, although OSHA is adding significantly to the construction cost, if the safety features do avoid accidents, 1 per cent of building cost will not add exorbitantly to power costs.

WHAT FACTORS DETERMINE INJURY FREQUENCY?

Obviously, the primary goal of all the safety efforts is the minimizing of occupational deaths and injuries. Since 1912, accidental work deaths per 100,000 population in the United States have been reduced more than 65 per cent, but the annual toll of occupational accidents still includes around 14,000 deaths and 2,000,000 injuries.

The average injury frequency (number of disabling injuries per million man-hours worked) for all industry is usually in the neighborhood of six for National Safety Council members and 13 as estimated by the Bureau of Labor Statistics; however, there are thousands of business organizations with frequencies of 50, 100, 150, and even higher. What are the factors that make one company much more effective than another in controlling injuries when inherent industrial hazards are the same?

First, the writer's studies have indicated that the company with a full-time safety director has a big edge in safety. When companywide safety supervision is a part-time duty of a person, it often becomes secondary to other matters for which he is being pressured. Making safety the one responsibility of one person ensures that he will be constantly alert to hazards and will continually remind, persuade, and prod others about them. Of course, as has been said, it is not practical in many small companies to have a full-time safety specialist; concerns with fewer than two or three hundred employees typically do not even have a full-time personnel manager. Perhaps this failure to have one person with safety as his full assignment is a major reason the worst accident records are most often found in small firms.

Foremost among the others with safety responsibilities are the first-line supervisors. They are really the key people in accident control: They are on the spot when most accidents occur; the actual operations are under their direction; and they know the workers, the equipment, and the materials. It is neither fair nor very efficient, however, to delegate accident control solely to the foreman and blame him when things go wrong. For one thing, local union practice can help or hamper the foreman.

Generally, officials of the big unions are safety-conscious, because they can see the "big picture" of thousands of members and can pretty accurately predict about how many will be killed or injured in the coming year. Locals, on the other hand, in their desire aggressively to support all close-to-home grievances and in their zeal to get high wages and comfort for workers (whom they sometimes know personally), can make it very difficult for foremen to enforce safety rules. For example, at a training program for forty foremen from scattered plants of a large company, the writer was urgently requested by the participants to use whatever influence he might have to push legislation that would mandate union, as well as management, support for accident control.

PINPOINTING INJURY FREQUENCY IN SMALL COMPANIES

In an effort to identify other characteristics that lead to better or worse accident records, Iranian Colonel Yaghoub Shafai-Sahrai made an intensive study of 22 American firms of small or relatively small size.[1] The study covered eleven pairs of companies in eleven different industries in Michigan, with each pair of approximately the same size carrying out similar work, but with a major difference in work-injury experience. In size they ranged from 80 to 650 employees. The

1. This study was carried out with the assistance and direction of the writer, in fulfillment of the doctoral dissertation requirement at Michigan State University. The Bureau of Business Research of the Graduate School of Business of Michigan State University plans to publish this dissertation in book form in the near future.

eleven industries were meat products, dairy products, canning and preserving, household furniture, containers and boxes, iron and steel foundries, nonferrous metal-rolling, other primary metal products, metal stampings, metal-working machinery, and motor vehicles and equipment.

Originally, 26 firms were selected on an essentially random basis (except for getting two of similar size in each industry). The Michigan Bureau of Safety could not release injury records for companies by name until authorized by the company in question, but it was inferred from the variety of injury experience reported to the bureau that wide variation could be expected from the sample. The fact that 22 of the 26 companies readily authorized full disclosure of their injury records not only argued against bias in selection, but also indicated widespread interest in the problem of accident control. (In fact, four of the companies tried to hire Dr. Shafai-Sahrai.)

Injury frequencies of the companies ranged from 12 to 173. The average difference in frequency rate between each two pair members was 50, the median 43, the lowest 11, and the highest 129. The ratio of frequency rates between pair members averaged 3.05 to 1, with a median of 3.1 to 1, a low of 1.3 to 1, and a high of 4.6 to 1. Thus, the "twin" companies varied tremendously in accident experience. The rates as a whole were very high compared with national averages; but, as was mentioned earlier, this experience is common among firms in this size range.

The investigative procedure used was plant visits and inspection; analysis of company injury records, both on the site and, after authorization, at the Michigan Bureau of Safety; and executive interviews, which included both a structured part alike for all and an unstructured part. Methods were developed for assigning numbers to indicate relative degrees of elements such as management support, width of span of control, safety devices, and so on. Then the Wilcoxon

Fig. 50-1. Differences Between Top Management's Involvement in Safety
in Firms with Low and High Injury Rates

Top Management's Activity with Regard to Safety	Firms with Low Accident Frequency Rates (N=11)		Firms with High Accident Frequency Rates (N=11)	
	Yes	No	Yes	No
Does he attend any safety meetings in the company?	8	3	6	5
Does he chair any of these meetings?	3	8	2	9
Does he regularly receive safety reports?	11	0	11	0
Does he personally conduct any safety audit or inspection?	9	2	4	7
Is he a member of any safety organization?	0	11	0	11
Does he regularly attend any safety meetings or conferences outside the company?	2	9	0	11
Does he emphasize plans for achieving certain safety objectives?	10	1	8	3
Does he actively participate in execution of safety plans?	10	1	7	4
Does he hold review and analysis sessions to compare the results of carrying out safety plans with projected objectives?	9	2	3	8
Are safety figures, reports, and achievements included on the agenda of company board meetings?	8	3	3	8
Total scores	70	40	44	66

matched-pairs signed rank test was used to test significance; for other factors, such as percentage of workers who were married and whether accident costs were included in the records, only the sign test was used.

The findings indicate that no one factor is the sole key to fewer or more injuries. Eight factors correlated highly with the better injury record within the pairs—in only one instance was there a negative correlation among these. Thus, it is not possible to determine which were the more controlling variables or if certain variables caused the other variables.

The one variable that perhaps had a double effect—a direct one and also indirect by its influence on other conditions favorable to accident control—was top-manage-

ment interest and involvement in safety. One hypothesis checked was that "in the firms with lower work injury frequency and severity rates, top management is highly interested and involved in the company's over-all safety programs and actively participates in and supports safety activity." Statistically, this was strongly supported to a significance level of .05.

Figure 50-1 shows the kinds of top-management activities evaluated and how many were found in the high versus the low injury frequency company in each pair.

It is evident that in the firms with the better safety records, the chief executives put more emphasis on personal audit and inspection than did those in firms with the poorer records. Top management in the former firms also showed more interest in plans to achieve specific safety objectives and held review and analysis meetings to evaluate progress. In eight out of eleven of the better-record companies, safety figures, reports, and achievements were included on the agenda of company board meetings, whereas this was true of only three out of eleven of the firms with poorer experience. Probably the most important reason for the effectiveness of these top-management activities is that they show other members of management, and ultimately all employees, that the boss is genuinely concerned about controlling accidents.

In all instances where accident cost analysis was included in the records in one company of a pair and not in the other, the accident experience of the organization with cost analysis was significantly better. In fact, the frequency rates of the "cost conscious" companies in the five pairs that differed in this regard averaged only about one-third as high as the rates of their "twins."

To turn to another aspect of the study, findings supported to the high significance level of .01 attested to the fact that the percentage of employees who were married was higher in the firms with better accident records. Although in most pairs the percentage of employees married was not greatly different between the two companies, in the three where the difference was marked, the difference in injury experience was also great, as is shown in Figure 50-2. This study corroborated many others that have found a negative correlation between employee age and accident experience, but the striking difference in percentage of employees married and in injury records in two of the above companies cannot be accounted for on the basis of average employee age.

Space does not permit reporting here the full findings of the study, but another relevant factor over which management has control is the span of control at the level of first-line supervision, usually the foreman. The hypothesis that relative span of control for first-line supervisors is wider in the firms with the higher injury rates within the pairs was strongly supported, to a significance level of .05. Span of control is, of course, dictated in considerable measure by the nature of the work to be done and the layout of a plant or other facility. Some of these differences were offset, however, by the use of the matched pairs in this study. The average span of control among the companies with better records was 16, while the average among the others was 21.

Probably more meaningful is the fact that in only two of the eleven pairs did the larger span of control go with the lower injury frequency. In all four pairs where the high frequency was four or more times as high as the low one, the span of control was greater in the company with more injuries. The average span for the four better-record concerns was 18.5, compared with 26.5 for their counterparts. That this is not an overriding factor is apparent, however, in the fact that in one pair the company with a frequency of 18.8 had a control span of 18, while the other, with a frequency of 61.9, had a span

Fig. 50-2. Marital Status and Age as Factors in Injury Frequency

	% of Married Employees	Accident Frequency Rate	Average Age
Pair 1 Co. A	85	25	37
Co. B	32	89.4	20
Pair 2 Co. A	90	14.5	37
Co. B	65	45.1	32
Pair 3 Co. A	90	4.17	43
Co. B	35	71.1	37

of only 13. In the other pair that was completely contrary to the general result in this respect, a frequency of 34.1 went with a span of 23, while a frequency of 45 accompanied a control span of 18.

An unfortunate difficulty of research in the social science area, including business, is, of course, that "all other things being equal" is generally impossible—one can seldom find situations where only one element is the variable. Therefore, this use of matched pairs only reduces the variability of other factors of possibly important influence. Still, the study adds strong support to the premise that there are factors subject to managerial control that can have a strong impact on the incidence of employee injuries.

5

Public Policy and the Prediction
of Accident Involvement

GERALD V. BARRETT[1]

The central problem of the driver-vehicle-highway system is the reduction of accidents. Over the years a number of approaches have been attempted to reduce the number of highway accidents. Each approach has involved public policy decisions and countermeasures. Six previous approaches can be identified and classified as follows: prediction of "accident prone" individuals, removal of accident repeaters from the highways; driver licensing; driver education; improvement of highways; and reduction of secondary collisions.

Prediction of "accident prone" individuals

Hugo Musterberg, one of the pioneers of industrial psychology, investigated individual differences and driver accident involvement as early as 1913. His tradition of attempting to predict the "accident prone" individual was continued into the 1930s by Viteles and other researchers.

Over the last sixty years there have been repeated attempts to relate individual attributes to accident involvement. In an often-cited extensive review of the literature, Goldstein (1962) found nonsignificant or very low relationships between a number of variables and accident involvement. For

1. This paper was prepared especially for use in this volume.

example, the correlations between accident criteria measures and visual functioning as measured by visual acuity were seldom above .20 in 45 separate studies. Correlations were no higher between reaction time and accident criteria in four studies using very large samples of drivers. Psychomotor tests, paper-and-pencil tests, perceptual tests, personality inventories, and cognitive measures all showed correspondingly low correlations with accident criteria. A more recent review by A. D. Little, Inc. (1966), of approximately 1800 reports published primarily during the 1954–64 period also concluded that there was little evidence relating individual psychological characteristics to involvement in traffic accidents.

Removal of accident repeaters from highways

Another approach to the accident problem was to eliminate drivers from the road on the basis of their prior accident records. This was based on the assumption that the best predictor of future behavior is past behavior. As early as 1938, Forbes had shown that selecting drivers out of the system based on prior accident involvement was ineffective in reducing accidents. This was due to the fact that only a small proportion of the drivers who were involved in accidents in a one year period also had an accident in the second or succeeding years.

Driver licensing

A third approach involved the establishment of driver licensing by all of the states. It was assumed that the written tests of driver knowledge of highway laws and actual driving tests would in some manner improve the quality of the drivers in the system. In an extensive review of the literature, Miller and Dimling (1969) concluded that the present concept of driver licensing has not made a significant contribution in reducing accidents. This was based upon the reality that eventually almost all applicants passed the driving tests. In addition there was little evidence that driver-licensing test scores were related to accident involvement.

Driver education

A fourth approach that has developed over the years was to implement various programs of driver education and training to reduce the accident toll on the nation's highways. A review by McGuire and Kersh (1969) concluded that driver-education programs, in their present form, have not been effective in significantly reducing the accident involvement of drivers.

Improvement of highways

A fifth approach has involved the physical change of highways and roads. This program has concentrated on building limited-access highways and eliminating dangerous curves and road hazards. This program has shown some success in reducing the highways traffic death toll.

Reduction of secondary collisions.

A sixth approach was strongly advocated in the 1960s by Ralph Nader. In his popular book, Unsafe at Any Speed, Nader emphasized that since we were unable to identify the characteristics of a good or a poor driver we should concentrate upon making the vehicle itself more crash worthy. The assumption was that since accidents cannot be prevented, the best public-health policy decisions would be to reduce the "secondary collision" between the driver and the interior of the car. This policy has evolved into the present program of regulations involving the installation of seat belts and other passive driver restraints. This approach has reduced the severity of injury to drivers and passengers involved in accidents.

NEW APPROACHES TO THE PREDICTION OF DRIVER PERFORMANCE

Past research studies attempting to relate individual attributes to driver performance contain a number of major faults and methodological problems that have limited the usefulness of the results. One of the major difficulties was the failure to develop a theoretical model of driver behavior that could be a guide for the selection and study of the appropriate predictors or individual attributes. The past studies have also had a problem with measurement of the accident or driving criterion. Accidents are rare and infrequent events that are extremely difficult to predict and quantify. The number of accidents that an individual may have is certainly a function not only of his own individual attributes but also of other diverse factors such as the number of miles he drives, the conditions under which he drives, and the behavior of other drivers.

In a controlled psychological experiment you are required to have individuals subjected to exactly the same conditions in order to arrive at a determination of the most effective predictors of behavior. This type of experimental control cannot be easily achieved in the "real" world of drivers and accidents. Experimental control can be obtained by using a driving simulator that reproduces the essential aspects of the driver's environment. The value of this approach was demonstrated by Barrett and Thornton (1968) when they found that very accurate predictions could be made of a driver's ability to respond to an emergency situation using a driving simulator. The simulator consisted of a real car with a projected visual depiction of a highway environment in front of the driver. The emergency situation involved a simulated

Table 51-1. Correlation of Perceptual Style with Emergency Behavior

Perceptual style	Reaction Time to Pedestrian	Deceleration Rate	Hit-Miss
	.67	.69	.45

pedestrian moving in front of the car at a controlled rate. Table 51-1 shows the correlation of a measure of individual perceptual style (the ability of an individual to extract salient information from a complex background) with behavior in an emergency driving situation. These correlations indicate that it is possible to predict driver response to an emergency.

This research had certain deficiencies that limited its usefulness. First, it was performed in a simulated driving situation, and there is always the question as to how the results might hold up in the "real world" driving situation. Second, the research was not based on an extensive theoretical framework that took into account other aspects of driver behavior. Third, only one test was selected and used to predict the driving behavior. The study indicated that a more fully developed model should include a number of individual predictors arranged into some form of a test battery.

USE OF PERCEPTUAL INFORMATION-PROCESSING MODEL AS A HEURISTIC DEVICE TO PREDICT DRIVER BEHAVIOR IN THE REAL WORLD

Broadbent's (1971) information processing model can be used to categorize driving

behavior into three elements: *detection, diagnosis,* and *decision.* This model allows investigators a framework for the choice of tests that will predict actual accident involvement. Mihal and Barrett (1974) selected a sample of sixty commercial drivers who had worked for an urban Utility Company for at least five years. The company maintained detailed records on accident involvement. This sample insured the investigators that they would have reasonably accurate accident records.

The selected tests could then be correlated with the prior accident involvement over the five-year period. Table 51-2 shows the mean scores on the selected tests for the accident and non-accident groups, and Table 51-3, the related correlation coefficients between the predictors and the measure of accident involvement.

It is important to note that this study employed a "*post*dictive" design. This is a common design in accident research in which the predictors are taken on the individuals a number of years *after* the criterion measure. This is in contrast to the usual *predictive* design, in which the test is administered, and at some future time the performance or criterion measure is obtained.

Tables 51-2 and 51-3 illustrate a number of important points that are relevant to the

Table 51-2. Mean Score on Each Test for Accident and Non-Accident Commercial Drivers

Test	Accident (N=31) (mean score)	Non-Accident (N=29) (mean score)	Difference Between Means
Simple reaction time	.41	.40	N.S.
Choice reaction time	.52	.51	N.S.
Complex reaction time	.85	.77	$p < .05$
Perceptual style	5.21	2.85	$p < .001$
Selective perception	47.60	25.0	$p < .01$

Table 51-3. Correlation of Tests with Accident Group Membership

Test	Correlation Coefficient	Significance Level
Simple reaction time	.10	N.S.
Choice reaction time	.09	N.S.
Complex reaction time	.25	$p < .05$
Perceptual style	.35	$p < .01$
Selective perception	.36	$p < .01$
	R	
Perceptual style and selective perception	.41	$p < .01$

prediction of accident involvement and behavior in general. Much of the early research that attempted to predict accident involvement relied upon "face validity," which means that a test or predictor seems to be related on the surface to the behavior or the criterion. In Tables 51-2 and 51-3 it can be seen that tests of simple reaction and choice reaction time have no value in terms of differentiating the accident- and non-accident involved commercial drivers.

These reaction-time measures were obtained while the driver was seated at a simulated driver's station and responded to brake signals. The early researchers had assumed that reaction time should be an important measure of accident involvement. The past research was unsuccessful, and these measures were specifically included in this investigation to show that they would not be predictive of accident involvement and to point out some of the fallacies in relying upon "face validity" in the selection of tests and predictors. In contrast, it should be noted that the measure of perceptual style very clearly differentiates between the accident- and non-accident involved drivers.

Conceptually, from a psychological point of view the relationship makes very good sense. From a "face validity" point of view the layman may wonder how this sort of relation can be obtained when the actual task involved in measuring perceptual style is taken into consideration. The individual is asked to adjust a luminescent rod surrounded by a frame to a true vertical position. The room is dark, and the only cue available to the individual is the tilted rod and frame (Witkin et al., 1954). Some people use internal body cues to adjust the rod to the "true" vertical, ignoring the misleading cues provided by the frame. Others are influenced by the tilted frame and adjust the rod to the frame and not to the true upright. This measure on the surface appears to have nothing to do with driving behavior.

In the same manner, the selective perception test, which is also very effective in differentiating accident involvement, has very little "face validity." In the selective perception test, the individual is presented with 24 dichotic messages through earphones. A dichotic message involves presenting one sound to one ear simultaneously with a different sound to the other ear (Gopher and Kahneman, 1971). It should be noted that this task is an auditory one and does not involve visual processes, which are assumed by many to be more important in driving. Conceptually, the task makes very good theoretical sense for predicting accident involvement based upon an information-processing model.

Only the complex reaction-time measure, which involves responding to complex scenes at a simulated driver station, has any degree of relationship with accident involvement. While this test has more "face validity," it can be seen that it does not predict accident involvement as well as measures of perceptual style and selective perception. The important point here is that reliance on "face validity" is *not* the optimum way to predict behavior. Unfortunately, such reliance on "face validity" is not always limited to laymen, as is evidenced by the following assertion: "If you want to know how well a person can drive a car (the criterion), sample his ability to do so by giving him a driver's test." (McClelland, 1973). It has been well documented that driving tests are not valid predictors of accident involvement, and that psychological measures that do not have "face validity" are much more effective predictors of this behavior. The study by Mihal and Barrett (1974) demonstrated that psychological variables could be utilized to determine the effectiveness of drivers in the "real world." We now return to the basic question in terms of the appropriate public policy decisions and countermeasures for accident reduction.

PUBLIC POLICY AND ACCIDENT REDUCTION

In our prior discussion we indicated that the various approaches which have been attempted in the past have had limited value, except for the highway and vehicle improvement programs. The other four approaches were based on either attempting to predict behavior, set a minimum standard of driving performance by licensing, or training the driver.

The prediction of the "accident prone" individual from psychological and psychomotor tests failed because the individual attributes important for accident avoidance had not been identified or conceptualized. The individual attributes measured in much of the previous research had only "face validity." Investigators would test a driver's response to a light, and measure his reaction time—assuming that this was an important variable in determining accident avoidance. Reaction time might have "face validity," but it has not been demonstrated to be empirically valid for the prediction of accident involvement.

The previous research also failed to realize that many of the individual attributes being measured were important as setting minimum driving performance levels only, and that there was no particular reason that these same attributes would predict subsequent accident involvement. For example, visual acuity measures have often been correlated with accident involvement—with little success. By the process of consensual validation a judgment has been made that a driver needs at least 20/30 vision to operate a motor vehicle. It does not necessarily follow that a driver with better visual acuity will be involved in fewer accidents. In the same manner, the usual driver-licensing examinations establish only minimum competence levels.

The ineffectiveness of present driver-training programs in reducing accidents is based on a different set of problems. To train a driver to be effective in accident avoidance, the relevant individual attributes must be identified, and training techniques developed to improve these attributes. Recent research has indicated that perceptual information-processing skills are important. Present driver-education programs do not involve training or materials involved with the change or improvement of perceptual informational-processing rates. They concentrate instead on information and appeals for caution and safety.

A basic problem in any potential public-policy issue is the analysis of the potential benefit of alternative approaches for the solution of the problem. An example of this is a study undertaken for the U.S. Department of Transportation to identify the potential value of an alternative approach based upon a testing and training model (Barrett, Alexander, and Forbes, 1973). The basic concept of the study was the proposition that an effective countermeasure for accident reduction was to identify those individuals with the highest probability of subsequent accident involvement and to train these individuals on those attributes in which they were deficient. The analysis involved a modification of the Cronbach and Gleser model (1965) combined with a Bayesian approach (Raiffa, 1964) to formulate a cost-benefit framework. The potential value of this approach is best exemplified by a few examples. In the study of commercial drivers the validity of the test battery to identify drivers with a high probability of accident involvement was .41. If all new drivers between the ages 18 and 25 were trained on the identified attributes, the cost of training and testing could be recovered in 4.6 years from the savings resulting from accident reduction.

Another approach would involve training only that proportion of the population which had the greatest accident liability, and the costs to society would be recovered in a relatively shorter period of time. This approach is based upon the assumption that all individuals who apply for a driver's license eventually receive it. This technique does not involve eliminating individuals from the driving system but training in areas of deficiency based upon test results.

The proposed test-training approach appears to be a viable alternative to traditional countermeasures that have had limited success in reducing accident involvement. Future research in this area should concentrate on the identification of other individual attributes related to accident involvement, and the development of training techniques to modify these attributes.

REFERENCES

Barrett, G. V., Alexander, R. A., and Forbes, B. J. Analysis of performance measures and training requirements for decision making in emergency situations. Management Research Center, University of Rochester, Technical Report No. 73-55, January 1973.

Barrett, G. V., and Thornton, C. L. Relation between perceptual style and driver reaction in an emergency situation. *Journal of Applied Psychology,* 1968, 52, 169-76.

Broadbent, D. E. *Decision and stress.* New York: Academic Press, 1971.

Cronbach, L. J., and Gleser, G. *Psychological tests and personnel decisions.* Urbana: University of Illinois Press, 1965.

Forbes, T. W. Age performance relationships among accident-repeater automobile drivers. *Journal of Consulting Psychology,* 1938, 2, 143-48.

Goldstein, L. G. Human variables in traffic accidents. Highway Research Board Bibliography. National Research Council Publication 1054, 1962.

Gopher, D., and Kahneman, D. Individual differences in attention and the prediction of flight criteria. *Perceptual and Motor Skills,* 1971, 33, 1335-42.

Little, A. D. *The state of the art of traffic safety.* Cambridge, Mass.: A. D. Little, 1966.

McClelland, D. C. Testing for competence rather than for "intelligence." *American Psychologist,* 1973, 28, 1-14.

McGuire, F. L., and Kersh, R. C. *An evaluation of driver education.* Berkeley: University of California Press, 1969.

Mihal, W. L., and Barrett, G. V. Prediction of accident involvement from individual differences in perceptual-information processing. Unpublished paper, 1974.

Miller, L., and Dimling, J. A. *Driver licensing and performance.* Vol. 1. *Research review and recommendations.* Springfield, Va.: National Technical Information Service Report, PB 183527, 1969.

Raiffa, H. *Decision analysis.* Reading, Mass.: Addison-Wesley, 1970.

Witkin, H. A., Dyk, R. D., Faterson, H. F., Goodenough, D. R., and Karp, S. A. *Psychological differentiation: Studies of development.* New York: Wiley, 1962.

Understanding Fatigue in Modern Life

R. A. McFARLAND

One of the most perplexing problems in modern life concerns our lack of understanding and control of what is called "fatigue." There is probably no single word in our vocabulary which has been less adequately described or understood, yet few people would deny personal acquaintance with it. Definitions of the nature of fatigue are almost as numerous as the articles that have been written about it, since each depends largely upon the interests or technical background of the author.

The many different interpretations of fatigue have been caused by the fact that the word does not have a specific scientific meaning. In medical terms it is not a distinct clinical entity. It refers, generally speaking, to a group of phenomena associated with impairment, or loss, of efficiency and skill, and the development of anxiety, frustration, or boredom. In common usage, it is not unlike the word "unconscious," which has become a convenient category used to classify certain phenomena that are not clearly understood, yet are none the less real.

Earlier workers were primarily concerned with muscular work on fatigue of nervous fibres. Their points of view can be classified according to whether they emphasized a reduced work output; physiological changes in body functions and the production of chemical products of fatigue; or a feeling of tiredness. These early studies of muscular fatigue are not directly related to many of the highly skilled tasks encountered in our modern life, which require complex, co-ordinated, and accurately timed activities. Deterioration of a skill in such workers is therefore very different from loss in ability to lift a weight repeatedly.

The kind of fatigue caused by hard muscular work is best called acute. It results in a loss of efficiency, which is temporary, and is relieved by rest. Chronic fatigue, on the other hand, with which we will be primarily concerned, is not relieved by rest or sleep, and is cumulative in its effects. It is largely a psychological or psychiatric problem characterized by boredom, loss of initiative, and progressive anxiety, but it is nevertheless very real to those who suffer from it. It is often puzzling to the physician because there is usually no physical cause. In a few cases there may be an organic basis ranging from simple anaemia to the onset of a neuromuscular disease. In the medical treat-

Reprinted from *Ergonomics*, 1971, 14 (1), 1-10, by permission of the author and the publisher.

ment of chronic fatigue, the results have generally been poor. There is now some evidence, however, both subjective and objective, that certain salts of potassium and magnesium are beneficial in their effects on this condition.

One of the most widely accepted current explanations is that fatigue is an outcome of conflict and frustration within the individual. It is manifested in its extreme or chronic forms as a well-developed anxiety neurosis. To limit fatigue to any single cause, however, may be misleading, as will be brought out below.

PHYSIOLOGICAL FACTORS IN FATIGUE

For many years, physiologists, in various laboratory experiments, have attempted to localize fatigue in certain parts of the body, such as the muscles or the nervous system. The muscular fatigue found in treadmill studies, however, does not resemble the fatigue of modern life, because the muscles are used in very different ways. Similarly, laboratory studies of isolated nerve fibres are equally inconclusive, except for special circumstances such as the important role of oxidation in the efficient functioning of the nervous tissue.

Other physiologists have attempted to associate fatigue with the accumulation of toxic substances, such as lactic acid, in the blood. As an explanation of fatigue, however, lactic acid is much more restricted than at first believed. That it is not the only factor is demonstrated by the fact that many track records are broken by athletes even after running several heats and accumulating large amounts of lactate in their blood. Furthermore, many industrial workers doing heavy work, as well as miners at high altitudes, have normal values of blood lactate.

Another physiological approach to fatigue relates to the exhaustion of energy reserves. Experiments indicate that in very exhausting work, as in a marathon race,

ingesting glucose definitely helps to maintain efficiency. In severe exercise on a bicycle ergometer, very low blood sugar levels resulted in complete exhaustion and sensory impairment in human subjects. However, these effects were rapidly counteracted by ingesting glucose, and the subjects could then continue their severe exercise for an hour or more. Those who are in poor physical condition have low energy reserves and a reduced capacity for transforming energy, and they, as well as the athlete, may also benefit from glucose or some other readily utilizable fuel taken between meals.

However, it is hard to explain how sugar might counteract the effects of fatigue in mental performance, since it is known that the metabolic cost of mental work is very slight indeed. In carefully controlled experiments years ago, Benedict and Benedict (1933) found that sustained mental effort for several hours required only the number of calories in half a peanut! Other experiments have shown that in mental work it is not the nervous system that increases oxygen consumption, but rather it is owing largely to the increased muscular tension associated with sustained attention.

In general, fatigue cannot be considered a simple physiological condition resulting from sustained activity. Furthermore, if one thinks of the body as a whole, fatigue cannot be defined solely in terms of biochemical changes in the muscles or nerves, or by the exhaustion of energy reserves. If one is placed under stress, however, various forms of exhaustion and fatigue may result. Emotion or prolonged effort may influence adversely. Also a person's adaptation, and mental performance, and skill may deteriorate. It appears to be more relevant therefore to consider the role of psychological variables.

PSYCHOLOGICAL ASPECTS OF FATIGUE

Quite possibly those psychologists who have

stressed the role of higher nervous functions as opposed to neuro-muscular ones may be on the right track. They have shown experimentally that "mental" functions show a loss of efficiency through simple and prolonged repetition of arithmetical or color-naming tests. This loss appears as a mental lapse or "blocking" during which the individual finds it impossible to carry on the activity without frequent errors. As he tires, the lapses are longer and the errors more frequent.

Fatigue also has an emotional component which, though not easily measured, must be taken into consideration. Although a person can readily adjust to temporary conflicts, there seems to be a cumulative ill effect from prolonged emotional stress and mental effort which is often designated as fatigue.

The interesting concept of skill fatigue developed by Bartlett (1951) has helped to explain the deterioration of performance in pilots. In the Cambridge "Cockpit Studies" a large group of R.A.F. pilots were studied under simulated flying conditions in a standard spitfire cockpit with full controls and instruments. The pilots "flew" for at least two hours, some continuing until exhaustion after six to seven hours. Although piloting errors due to the misuse of the controls decreased steadily throughout the experiments, this improvement was more than offset by a deterioration in accuracy of timing and skill.

As the subjects became more fatigued, they were willing to accept lower and lower standards of accuracy and performance. Furthermore, they failed to interpret the various instrument readings as being part of a single integrated system, but paid attention to one or the other of them as individual, isolated instruments. As fatigue increased, the pilots' range of attention decreased, and forgetting or ignoring the more distant instruments was common. Possibly the most significant finding was the general tendency for a sudden increase in errors at the end of a flight. A tired airman, it seems, has an almost irresistible tendency to relax when he nears the airport.

In skill fatigue, then, the "standards" accepted and followed by the central nervous system unwittingly deteriorate. Although a person may think he is doing better work, actually his performance is getting poorer and poorer. At first, it is more likely that he will do the right things at the wrong time; but if accurate timing is important, gross errors will finally begin to appear.

FATIGUE RESULTING FROM STRESS

In understanding the relation of the stresses of our modern environment to fatigue, the contributions of physiologists such as Cannon and Selye are very helpful. Cannon (1932) has described the ways in which the body maintains a physiologic constancy or steadiness under conditions which might be expected to prove profoundly disturbing, frustrating, and fatiguing. Selye (1956), as an example of the modern trend, has worked out detailed observations concerning specific nervous and humoral alterations reflecting the general adaptation of the organism to stress.

The working hypothesis that has resulted from these kinds of studies is that measurable substances in the blood and urine indicate glandular activities of the body in response to stress. Thus, chronic fatigue resulting from stress, can, in fact, have an underlying physical basis. Interestingly enough, chronic fatigue can also apparently contribute to some of the other ailments so characteristic of our modern life, such as mental illness, peptic ulcers, and certain aspects of heart disease such as high blood pressure.

We also know that anxiety and fatigue are related. Whether they are causally related is not necessarily important, since the existence of either state may react on and intensify the other. Even the normal person has latent anxieties which may be accentuated if he becomes fatigued. The neurotic individual, on the other hand, is fatigued in proportion to the extent of his anxieties.

PSYCHOPHYSIOLOGICAL CONCEPTS OF FATIGUE

In recent years there have been many advances in our understanding of what happens in the central nervous system when we are tired. One relates to the electrical rhythms or patterns from the brain that can be observed on electroencephalograms. Some years ago a physiologist (Hess 1927) implanted electrodes in the brain of a cat. He observed that the electrical stimulation of certain parts of the brain, specifically the *medial thalmus,* seemed to make the animal lethargic and sleepy. Later workers using similar techniques showed that this suppressive action can also take place in the cerebral cortex, the seat of all our conscious processes.

This inhibitory system in the brain, however, is matched by what one might call an activating system based in the reticular formation. As Grandjean (1968) has stated, a person's ability to perform "is dependent on the degree of activity of the two systems: if the inhibitory system dominates, the organism is in a stage of fatigue; while if the activating system has the upper hand, the organism is ready to step up performance." This tends to explain situations that are familiar to all of us, such as the fatigue or tiredness that occurs in monotonous or boring situations, and the sudden change, or awakening, that takes place when something new and interesting or unexpected happens.

FATIGUE AND POOR PERFORMANCE

In the past, most of the studies relating to the effects of environmental stresses such as loud noise, hot and cold temperatures, and changes in work cycles on fatigue, have shown but little impairment. In laboratory studies the subjects tend to compensate for the subtle effects of noise and temperature on performance by trying harder. Also, the

measures of fatigue in industry are often difficult to appraise except by an increase in accidents. Recently, experimental psychologists have devised new techniques of measurement. By progressively increasing the complexity of the tests, or by superimposing one task upon another, a percentage decrement in performance (known to be present, but hard to measure) is finally revealed. What is needed to prevent the masking of fatigue is a combined measure of both speed and accuracy. With the development of information theory, a non-arbitrary way of combining measures of speed and accuracy in a simple "rate-of-information-transmission" measure is available (McFarland 1969).

Two avenues of approach have been developed to detect and scale increased effort in performance tests. One is concerned with the spare mental capacity for a central task in relation to a peripheral task at the same time. The other area relates to physiological measures such as arousal and tenseness. A number of techniques for measuring not only muscular tenseness, but also central nervous system activity, and even specific components of neural reaction to signals, have been developed. Some of these measures appear promising for the study of the deleterious effects of fatigue.

INDUSTRIAL FATIGUE, PRODUCTIVITY, AND WORK SCHEDULES

Fatigue appears to be the chief factor limiting a person's output. Various studies have shown that when the working day is lengthened, hourly productivity goes down, and when the number of hours worked is reduced, hourly performance increases. Thus long working days and overtime are relatively inefficient, since production does not appear to be maintained at the earlier high rate. It should be pointed out, however, that these findings can only be verified where the individual has some control over his work rate. On an assembly line a worker cannot make voluntary adjustments, and must maintain the scheduled pace. Nevertheless, extended working hours in these situations will result in "fatigue" with a consequentially greater likelihood of accidental errors, and illness.

There is some evidence that eight hours of work a day in the United States, where the work is fairly intensive, is the maximum that should be permitted for optimum productivity. For easier work or where it is possible to schedule several relaxing breaks over the course of the work day, longer hours may well be permissible.

On the Continent, in the transition to a five- from a six-day week, Grandjean (1968) notes that a drop in the number of hours worked is not matched by a proportionate drop in worker productivity, since most personnel slightly increased their hourly output. However, when the same number of hours are worked in a five-day week as in the former six-day week, i.e., a 9- to 9¾-hour working day, the results are much less desirable, and many European industrial physicians believe that a five-day week is advantageous only when the daily working hours do not exceed 8½ hours.

Similar trends were noted also during the Battle of Britain, when factories began working 24 hours a day, 7 days a week. At first there was an increase in output, but, after a few months, absenteeism and sickness increased, and employees often arrived late for work. Sunday work was discontinued without reducing production. One factory, after reducing the hours, set a new record for one week's production. It was concluded that increased hours of work above an optimum number, which varies slightly with different industries, do not increase production proportionately and may even result in a decrease. From these and many other similar observations, it may be inferred that fatigue and recovery are normal cyclical phenomena to be accepted as a part of life. Only when recovery from physical effort is not completed in 24 hours do we need to be concerned.

The time of day at which work is carried out is also related to fatigue. In most studies dealing with this topic one of the commonly used criteria is work output, and where this has been related to work shift, consistently slightly higher outputs have been recorded for the day shifts. Similarly, in an exhaustive industrial study of 62,000 errors made in hourly readings of different measuring instruments, the greatest incidence of error was found during the night shift, with the peak at about 3 A.M. The general explanations advanced for these differences in industrial performance are: the human circadian, or day-night system; the incompatibility of the socio-temporal environment of the night shift worker; and from the interaction of these, impairment of health.

Preliminary studies have been conducted of the physiological and psychological reactions of subjects who were flown on long west-east, east-west and north-south jet flights. These assessments were made before the flight, after arrival at the distant destination, and after return. Significant physiological changes were found after both the east-west and west-east flights which involved primary shifts in circadian periodicity, but not after the north-south flight. An impairment of psychological performance was noted on the east-west, but not the west-east or north-south flights. The only finding in common to all three flights was an increase in subjective "fatigue."

It is interesting to note that this subjective fatigue, or feelings of tiredness, persisted as long as the body temperatures remained elevated, in most cases for a day or two following the flights. One practical result of these studies relates to the fact that several large international companies now give their personnel an extra day off to recuperate after crossing several time zones in jet flights. This policy is also followed for some U.S. Government officials.

OPERATIONAL FATIGUE IN AIRCREWS

Since fear and apprehension, as well as

boredom, can give rise to fatigue, we might expect to find fatigue present to some extent in commercial aviation. The author served as medical adviser to PAA in the opening of air routes in the Pacific in 1936-37, and in the Atlantic in 1939, as well as in South America and Africa. It had been anticipated that flying fatigue would be pronounced, and the government regulatory bodies therefore required frequent layovers of the air crews.

Contrary to expectations, however, few cases of operational fatigue were observed. This was due to the fact that the operating and engineering departments did everything possible to train the men for their duties, and to provide equipment that was as reliable as possible. In this way fear and apprehension were apparently allayed and, in addition, comfortable living facilities, including athletics, were provided for the pilots on the ground. In fact, the only evidence of fatigue that the author was able to identify was in Hawaii, where an excess of "relaxation" occurred on some occasions! (McFarland 1953).

FATIGUE RESULTING FROM EXCESSIVE LEISURE AND BOREDOM

In modern life the way in which we adjust to leisure time is an excellent example of the kinds of problems our modern technology is creating as well as solving. In the days of Socrates and Plato the "end-aim" of life was leisure for the exercise of man's highest faculties. They had slaves to do their chores, and we have machines. Yet ours is a work-centered, and for some a "work compulsive" society, and it is probably unrealistic to expect that "free time" resulting from reduced working hours will be used creatively or productively in the sense of the Greeks. The minds of men must be exercised, and if there are no problems we usually create them, even artificial ones. For us idleness often brings uneasiness, a feeling of lack of purpose and, eventually, fatigue.

CONCLUSION

Since fatigue in its many forms can result from a variety of causes acting singly or in combination, it is difficult to give clear-cut rules or principles for its control or prevention. Each case must be evaluated according to its own peculiar characteristics. Nevertheless, a few rather general remarks can be made.

For the individual suffering from chronic fatigue, the most logical first step would be an examination by a physician to determine whether or not any organic basis for the condition exists. Where it does not, attention must be directed towards finding the most likely cause, or causes, among the major ones outlined in this article, and making the necessary changes in one's life and schedule of living. Easier said than done, admittedly; but then, there is no sure cure, or cures, for chronic fatigue which will work equally well for different people.

A few recommendations of general applicability would include: adequate, though not excessive, sleep; the establishment of a daily work-rest cycle acceptable to the individual; the elimination, in so far as possible, of conditions resulting in excessive stress, anxiety, or boredom; the institution of a definite, adhered-to schedule of physical exercise or sports, compatible with the individual's capabilities; the possible use of stimulants or medications—but only under a physician's direction.

For the organizational control of fatigue, as in industry, the coordinated efforts of the medical and administrative departments are needed. The medical department should be concerned with the maintenance of fitness through adequate physical and mental hygiene programmes, and, in industries where it is appropriate, with the selection of emotionally stable and fatigue-resistant personnel. They should also, in conjunction with the engineering or industrial safety departments, see that harmful excesses of environmental variables such as noise, vibration, temperature, etc., are removed or controlled. In addition, all equipment used by the worker, and his work task, should be designed with optimum efficiency, safety, and comfort in mind. Finally, those in charge of administration can contribute most by seeing that work schedules, working conditions and personnel relations are all maintained at levels consistent with the interests and well-being of the employee as well as of the company.

REFERENCES

Bartlett, F. C., The bearing of experimental psychology upon human skilled performance. *British Journal of Industrial Psychology*, 1951, 8, 209-17.

Benedict, F.G., and Benedict, Cornelia G., *Mental effort in relation to gaseous exchange, heart rate, and mechanics of respiration.* Publication 446. Washington, D.C.: Carnegie Institution of Washington, 1933, p. 83.

Cannon, W. B., *The wisdom of the body,* New York: W. W. Norton, 1932.

Grandjean, E., Fatigue: its physiological and psychological significance. *Ergonomics,* 1968, 11, 427-36.

Hess, W. R., Stammganglien-Reizversuche. *Ber. ges. Physiol.,* 1927, 42, 554-55.

McFarland, R. A., *Human factors in air transportation; Occupational health and safety.* New York: McGraw-Hill, 1953.

McFarland, R. A., 1969, The effects of altitude on pilot performance. In *Proceedings of XVII International Congress on Aviation and Space Medicine, Oslo.* Ed. by B. Hannisdahl and C. W. Sem-Jacobsen. Oslo: *Universitetsforlaget,* 1968, pp. 96-108.